Reader's Digest

GREAT
BIOGRAPHIES

Reader's
Digest

GREAT
BIOGRAPHIES

selected
and
condensed by
the editors
of
Reader's
Digest

The Reader's Digest Association, Inc.

Pleasantville, New York

Cape Town, Hong Kong, London, Montreal, Sydney

The credits and acknowledgments that appear on pages 575–576
are hereby made part of this copyright page.
Copyright © 1989 by The Reader's Digest Association, Inc.
Copyright © 1989 by The Reader's Digest Association (Canada) Ltd.
Copyright © 1989 by Reader's Digest Services Pty. Ltd., Sydney, Australia
Copyright © 1989 by The Reader's Digest Association South Africa (Pty.) Limited
Copyright © 1989 by Reader's Digest Association Far East Limited
Philippines copyright 1989 by Reader's Digest Association Far East Limited
Reader's Digest, The Digest and the Pegasus logo
are registered trademarks of The Reader's Digest Association, Inc.

FIRST EDITION

Printed in the United States of America

Contents

A CONDENSATION OF

CHRISTOPHER COLUMBUS, MARINER

by
SAMUEL ELIOT MORISON

On October 12, 1492, Christopher Columbus
landed on the beach at Fernandez Bay, San Salvador,
the Bahamas, and took possession of a New World for
Spain. Having been sent out by King Ferdinand and
Queen Isabella to find a highly coveted trade route
to the treasures of the East, he believed that he
had indeed reached an island of the East Indies, and
that the gentle native inhabitants who offered
him their possessions were in fact "Indians."

Columbus was a self-made man with little
schooling, and he led his little fleet into the unknown
Atlantic wastes knowing less about celestial navigation
than a modern sailor in boot camp. How he managed it,
what kind of a man he was and what happened to him
afterward are related with incomparable vividness by
Admiral Morison, a distinguished historian and sailor,
who himself retraced every mile of Columbus's four
voyages in the New World.

Christopher Columbus, Mariner, is a shorter version,
rewritten by the author himself, of Admiral Morison's
definitive biography *Admiral of the Ocean Sea,*
which was awarded the Pulitzer Prize. In collaboration
with Mauricio Obregón he has also published
The Caribbean as Columbus Saw It.

1. Christopher Columbus Goes to Sea

CHRISTOPHER COLUMBUS, Discoverer of the New World, was first and foremost a sailor. Born in Genoa, one of the oldest European seafaring communities, as a youth he made several voyages in the Mediterranean, where the greatest mariners of antiquity were bred. Living between the Middle Ages and the Renaissance, he showed the qualities of both eras: he had a firm religious faith and he also had scientific curiosity, zest for life, and the desire for novelty.

At the age of twenty-four, by a lucky chance, he arrived in Lisbon, center of European oceanic activity; and there he conceived the great enterprise that few but a sailor would have planned, and none but a sailor could have executed. That enterprise was to reach "The Indies"—eastern Asia—by sailing west. . . .

THE STORY STARTS in Genoa with the Discoverer's parents: Domenico Colombo, a wool weaver, and his wife Susanna. Domenico belonged to the middle class of Genoa. He owned his own looms and employed journeymen. Popular in his community, he was elected to small offices in the local wool-weavers' guild, the medieval equivalent of a trade union. Between August and October 1451, the exact day is unknown, Susanna Colombo gave birth to a son who was named Cristoforo.

The Colombo family were respectable, but rather happy-go-lucky. Domenico was always on the move, always taking on new "lines" besides weaving, and losing money on them. He was the kind of father whom boys love, who would shut up shop on a fine day and take them fishing. After Christopher, he had a boy who died young; a girl who married a neighboring cheesemonger; Bartholomew, who became the Discoverer's partner and shipmate; and Giacomo, Christopher's junior by seventeen years, who also accompanied him to the New World and is known by the Spanish equivalent, Diego, of his first name. Domenico's brother Antonio also had a large family, and one of his sons, Giannetto (Johnny), commanded a caravel on the Third Voyage. Family feeling was very strong among the Genoese, so Christopher Columbus, a stranger in Spain, felt he could best trust his brothers and kindred.

The little we know about the Discoverer's childhood and early youth can be quickly told. He had very little formal schooling, spoke the Genoese dialect, which was almost unintelligible to other Italians, and didn't learn to read and write until he was twenty-five. He had a long face, an aquiline nose, ruddy complexion and red hair, and we can picture him as a little, freckle-faced redhead with blue eyes. One imagines he must have disliked working in his father's loom shed, as he took every opportunity to go to sea.

And there were plenty of opportunities in that seafaring community. Almost all the traffic along the Ligurian coast was seaborne. And everyone who had no other job, besides many who did, went fishing. Big carracks and galleons were built in the harbor—there were boatyards in every cove along the shore—and the ships of the republic traded with all parts of the Mediterranean and with northern Europe.

Exactly when Christopher decided to quit the weaving trade and make the sea his profession we do not know. Facts about his early life are few, but it is probable that, between fifteen and twenty-three, Christopher made several long voyages in the Mediterranean. When he was nineteen, he served in a Genoese warship and also made at least one voyage to Chios in the Aegean, in a ship owned by Genoese merchants.

In May 1476, in his twenty-fifth year, came the adventure that changed the course of Christopher's life. Genoa organized  an armed convoy to carry valuable cargo to northern Europe, and in this convoy Christopher sailed as seaman in a vessel named *Bechalla*. On August 13, when it had passed the Strait of Gibraltar and was off the southern coast of Portugal, the fleet was attacked by a French force. The battle raged all day, and by nightfall three Genoese ships had gone down. *Bechalla* was one of the casualties. Christopher, though wounded, managed to grasp a floating sweep and reached the Portuguese shore six miles distant. The people of Lagos, near which he landed, treated him kindly, and on learning that his brother Bartholomew was living at Lisbon, sent him thither as soon as he could travel. That was one of the best things that could have happened to Christopher Columbus.

Fifteenth-century view of Genoa.

PORTUGAL WAS THEN the liveliest and most progressive country in Europe, and Lisbon the center for exploration and discovery. Almost half a century earlier Dom Henrique, the Portuguese prince whom we call Henry the Navigator, had set up a sort of marine intelligence office at Cape Saint Vincent, which attracted ambitious seamen from all over the Mediterranean. He subsidized voyages into the Atlantic to discover new islands, and a way to India around Africa. The Portuguese colonized the Azores, the Madeira Islands and the Cape Verde Islands off Africa. That "dark continent" was Prince Henry's particular interest. Every few years his captains reached a new point farther south along the west coast, and by the time Columbus reached Lisbon, they had crossed the Gulf of Guinea. Fleets of caravels set forth from Lisbon every spring carrying cloth, glass beads, hawkbells and horses, and every fall returned with rich cargoes of ivory, gold dust, Malagueta pepper and Negro slaves. Enterprising merchants and seamen of all countries flocked to Lisbon to share the wealth.

Lisbon was a learned city where it was easy for a newcomer like Columbus to learn Latin and modern languages, and to acquire books that increased his knowledge of the world. Bartholomew, who had already joined the Genoese community there, was employed in a chart-making establishment, where he got a job for Christopher. Before long the Columbus brothers had a thriving chart business of their own, which put them in close touch with mariners, charts at that time being based on information and rough sketches that seamen brought home. The two brothers would be on hand whenever a ship returned from Africa or the Western Islands to invite the pilot to dine with them, and would extract from him all the data they could for correcting their charts of known countries or extending those of the African coast. It may well be that in one of these conferences a captain remarked, "I'm sick of sailing along the fever-stricken Guinea coast; why can't we sail due west beyond the Azores, till we hit the Golden East, and make a real killing?"

Why not, indeed? People had been talking of that since the days of the Roman Empire. That it was possible to reach the Orient by sailing west every educated man would admit, since every educated man knew the earth to be a sphere, but nobody had done anything to test the theory. The ocean was reputed too broad, winds too uncertain; ships could not carry enough cargo to feed their crews for several months, and sailors had acquired deep respect for the North Atlantic, and would not engage in such an enterprise. In 1476, when Columbus reached Lisbon, the proposition of sailing west to reach the Orient was at about the same stage as aviation in 1900—theoretically possible but full of practical difficulties.

We do not know when and how Columbus came by the idea of sailing west to reach the East, but once he had it, he began pestering people to finance his project. His combination of creative imagination with obstinate assurance, his impatience with all who were slow to be convinced, made him a fool in the eyes of some men and a bore to most. Like the pioneers of aviation, he was considered a little touched in the head.

More maritime experience than that of a foremast hand and apprentice chart maker was needed before he could hope to convince anyone. In the fall of the year he arrived in Lisbon, and then shipped on one of the Portuguese vessels that exchanged wool, dried fish and wine between Iceland, Ireland, the Azores and Lisbon. His vessel called at Galway, where, in later years, he recalled having seen two dead people in a drifting boat, of such extraordinary appearance that the Irish said they must be Chinese. The vessel in which Columbus sailed went exploring north of Iceland for a hundred leagues before returning to Portugal, so Columbus could boast that he had sailed to the edge of the Arctic Circle.

The following year, the Genoese firm under which Columbus had earlier sailed to Chios employed him to purchase a quantity of sugar at Madeira and carry it to Genoa. They neglected, however, to supply him with money to pay for it, and the merchants of Funchal refused to deliver on credit, so Columbus reached Genoa without the sugar. There was a lawsuit, and Christopher made a deposition about the case at Genoa in the summer of 1479. That was probably his last visit to his native place. But "that noble and powerful city by the sea," as he called it in his will, was ever close to his heart.

Upon his return from Genoa, Christopher married Dona Felipa Perestrello e Moniz, scion of one of the first families of Portugal, daughter of Bartholomew Perestrello, hereditary captain of Porto Santo in the Madeira group. The young couple lived for a time in Lisbon with Dona Felipa's mother, who broke out her late husband's logbooks and charts for the benefit of her son-in-law. Later they settled in Porto Santo, where their only child, Diego, was born. About the year 1482 they moved to Funchal in Madeira, and while there Columbus probably made two voyages to São Jorge da Mina, the fortified trading post which the Portuguese crown had established on the Gold Coast. On at least one of these voyages he was in command.

Christopher Columbus, now aged thirty-one or -two, had "arrived," according to the standards of his day. He was a master mariner in the Portuguese merchant service, then the finest and most far-ranging merchant marine in the world. He had sailed from the Arctic Circle to the equator, and from the eastern Aegean to the outer Azores. He had learned all that he could of practical navigation. He could make charts and figure latitude from the North Star. Besides, he was an avid reader of books on geography and cosmography. Columbus had only to continue in this career, persevere in the African trade, and retire after a few years, a rich man.

But Christopher had a vaster ambition. His mind was seething with the notion of sailing west to the Orient, acquiring wealth beyond the dreams of avarice, and glory exceeding that of any earlier mariner.

2. A Great Enterprise is Born

THE INDIES, MEANING India, Burma, China, Japan, the Moluccas and Indonesia, cast a spell over European imagination in the fifteenth century. These were lands of vast wealth in gold, silver and precious stones, in silk and fine cotton, in spices, drugs and perfumes, which were taken by caravans across Asia to Constantinople or to Levantine ports, thence distributed through Europe by ship, wagon and packtrain. The cost of handling by so many middlemen and over such long and complicated routes made the prices of Oriental goods to the European consumer exorbitant; yet the increase of wealth and luxury in European cities kept the demand far ahead of the supply. That is why the kings of Portugal made repeated attempts to get around Africa to India, where Oriental products could be purchased cheap. Columbus decided that the African route was the hard way to the Indies; he proposed to find a bold but easy way, due west by sea.

European knowledge of China at that time was slight and inaccurate. Most of it came from *The Book of Ser Marco Polo*, the

Venetian who spent three years in China around the turn of the fourteenth century. In this account of his experiences Marco Polo not only confirmed the rumors that Chinese emperors were rolling in wealth, but he wrote a highly embellished account of an even wealthier island kingdom named Cipangu (Japan) which, he said, lay 1500 miles off the coast of China.

Nobody in Europe had any suspicion of the existence of the continent that we call America. The voyages of the Northmen in the eleventh century to Newfoundland, which they called Vinland, were either unknown or forgotten in southern Europe. Everyone regarded the Ocean Sea as one and indivisible, flowing around Europe, Asia and Africa, which formed one big island in one big ocean. The great questions were, How far west *is* the Far East? How many miles lie between Spain and China or Japan? How long would the voyage take? And is such a voyage practicable?

Everyone admitted that the earth was a sphere, and the convention of dividing a circle into 360 degrees had been arrived at by the Greeks. But how long was a degree? Your answer to that depended on your estimate of the size of the earth. Ptolemy of Alexandria said that a degree was 50 nautical miles* long— the correct measure is 60. Alfragan, a Moslem geographer of the ninth century, said a degree measured 66 nautical miles. Columbus decided that Alfragan was right, but he misread him and concluded that Alfragan's degree was 45 miles long. In other words, he underestimated the size of the world by 25 percent.

Famed Venetian traveler, Marco Polo.

Besides this mistake, Columbus made another colossal error

---

*I use in this book the standard nautical mile of 2000 yards, which is equivalent to one minute of latitude or to one minute of longitude on the equator. The old authorities I quote from used different units, but I have reduced them all to nautical miles.

in reckoning how far eastward Asia stretched. The combined length of Europe and Asia is roughly 130 degrees from Cape Saint Vincent in Portugal to Peiping, China, or 150 degrees to Tokyo. Ptolemy guessed that it was 180 degrees. Marinus of Tyre, an earlier authority, stretched out this land mass to 225 degrees. Marco Polo made some rough calculations and tacked on 28 degrees more for China and 30 degrees additional for Japan; this would place Tokyo on the meridian that runs through western Cuba, Chattanooga, Grand Rapids and western Ontario! Moreover, as Columbus proposed to start from the western Canary Islands, which lie 9 degrees west of Cape Saint Vincent, he figured he would have only 68 degrees of westing to make before hitting Japan. Combining that gross miscalculation with his underestimate of the length of a degree, he figured that the length of the ocean voyage from the Canaries to Japan would be 2400 nautical miles. The actual air-line distance is 10,600 miles!

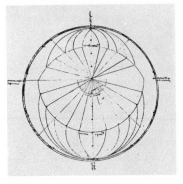

Planisphere drawn by Columbus.

Columbus did not, however, come to this conclusion all by himself. He had the support of a learned physician of Florence, Paolo Toscanelli, who dabbled in astronomy and mathematics. Toscanelli, believing Marco Polo's estimate of the length of Asia to be correct, had written to a Portuguese friend in 1474, urging him to persuade the King to organize a voyage west to Japan and the Chinese province of Mangi. He envisioned a voyage of 3000 miles from Lisbon to Cipangu (Japan) and 5000 miles from Lisbon to Quinsay (Hangchow), and sent a chart to demonstrate his theory. Columbus, when he heard about this, wrote to the Florentine sage asking for more details, and received an encouraging letter and another chart, which he carried with him on his great Voyage of Discovery. This correspondence took place shortly after Columbus's return from the Gold Coast, in 1481 or early 1482. The Toscanelli letter and chart were always his Exhibits "A" and "B."

Of course he had other exhibits as well: some literary, others practical. Aristotle was said to have written that one could cross the ocean from Spain to the Indies in a few days. Pierre d'Ailly's *Imago Mundi*, Columbus's bedside book for years, insisted that the ocean was "of no great width."

The statement in the aprocryphal Second Book of Esdras (6: 42), "Six parts hast thou dried up," was frequently used by Columbus to prove that six-sevenths of the globe is land; *ergo*, the ocean covers only one-seventh of the globe and cannot be very broad.

On the practical side, in the course of his voyages he observed evidence such as exotic tree trunks and "horse-beans," which are the fruit of an American mimosa, washed ashore in the Azores; the flat-faced corpses seen at Galway, who, if Chinese, could not have floated many thousands of miles without decomposing.

In 1484 he made his first effort to interest a prince in his project. This was John II, King of Portugal, a nephew of Henry the Navigator. "The King," says one of the contemporary Portuguese historians, "as he observed this *Christovão Colom* to be a big talker and boastful . . . and full of fancy and imagination with his Isle *Cypango* . . . gave him small credit." Nevertheless, the King submitted the project to two physicians of reputed skill in celestial navigation. They turned it down, flat. We may assume that they had a more accurate idea of the distance to be covered than did Columbus. It may be, however, that Columbus simply asked too much, since the kings of Portugal were accustomed to having their discoveries made free.

In 1485, the same year that the Portuguese committee turned Columbus down, his wife Dona Felipa died at Lisbon. That broke his strongest tie with Portugal, so Columbus decided to try his luck in Spain. He knew no one there except a sister of his late wife who was married to a Spaniard in Huelva, so to that part of Spain Columbus took ship with his five-year-old son.

It must have been with sinking heart that Columbus entered the Rio Saltés and sighted the sleepy little ports of Huelva and Palos, a sad contrast to bright bustling Lisbon. As his ship rounded into the Rio Tinto, he observed the Franciscan friary of

La Rábida. That suggested a solution to his problem of what to do with Diego, as the Franciscans were known to take boarders. So, after landing at Palos, he walked with his little son four miles to the friary, knocked at the gate and asked the porter for a drink of water and some bread for the boy. Fortunately, Antonio de Marchena, a highly intelligent Franciscan who had studied astronomy, got into conversation with Columbus. He invited both father and son to stay, accepted Diego as a pupil and introduced Columbus to the Count of Medina Celi, who was an important shipowner of Cadiz and also a grandee of Spain.

Queen Isabella

Medina Celi, of whom Columbus asked "three or four well-equipped caravels, and no more," had almost decided to underwrite the enterprise when it occurred to him to ask permission of the Queen. He did so, and Isabella refused, believing that so important an enterprise as that of Columbus should be conducted by the crown.

ABOUT NINE MONTHS elapsed before Columbus could obtain an audience with the Queen. The court was traveling from city to city and he had no funds to follow. From Seville, where his negotiations with Medina Celi had taken place, he went to the nearby city of Cordova to await the Queen's good pleasure.

At Cordova, Columbus became acquainted with Diego de Harana. Diego invited him to his house, where he met a twenty-year-old cousin of the Haranas, Beatriz Enríquez. She became Columbus's mistress and in 1488 bore him his second son, Ferdinand. The fact that Columbus never married Beatriz has troubled his more pious biographers, but nobody at the time seems to have held this lapse of morals against him. His wife had been a lady of rank who helped him to establish a position in Portugal, and according to the standards of the day, a second marriage with a peasant's daughter would have been unsuitable for one who intended to be a nobleman and admiral. The Harana family were pleased with the connection, and the friendship between them and the legitimate Colóns continued for two or three generations.

On May Day, 1486, almost a year from the day he had first set foot in Spain, Columbus was received by the Queen at Cordova. Isabella the Catholic was one of the ablest European sovereigns in an age of strong kings. Blue-eyed and auburn-haired, she had an intuitive faculty for choosing the right man for a job, and for doing the right thing at the right time. Her marriage

King Ferdinand

with Ferdinand of Aragon had united all "the Spains," excepting Portugal, to which she was allied, and the remnant of the Moorish Caliphate of Cordova, which she had resolved to conquer. Some spark of understanding evidently passed between Christopher and Isabella at their first meeting, and although she turned down his request for support more than once, he found that he could count on her in the end. On this occasion she appointed a special commission under Hernando de Talavera, her confessor, to examine the Great Project and recommend whether she should accept or reject it.

Then began a period of almost six years, the most unhappy in Columbus's entire life. He had to sustain a continual battle against prejudice, contumely and sheer indifference. A proud, sensitive man who *knew* that his project was feasible, he had to endure clownish witticisms and crackpot jests by ignorant courtiers, to be treated worse than a beggar, and at times actually to suffer want.

In the Talavera commission, meeting in 1486, at least one member, Diego de Deza, was in favor of the Great Enterprise, and it was doubtless due to his influence, or Talavera's, that early in 1487 Columbus was given a retaining fee of 12,000 maravedis a year. That was the pay of an able seaman, enough to support a man of Columbus's simple tastes—had it been paid regularly.

Month followed month, another Christmas passed, but nothing issued from the Talavera commission. So, early in 1488, Columbus wrote to John II of Portugal, requesting another hearing. The King replied promptly and most cordially, urging Columbus to come immediately. There were probably two reasons for this sudden and flattering change of attitude: two Portuguese mariners who had set forth to discover Antilia—an island believed to have been settled by refugees from the Moorish wars in the eighth century—had not located the mythical island; and Bartholomeu Dias, who had embarked on perhaps the twentieth Portuguese attempt to reach the Indies by rounding Africa, had been gone seven months and nothing had been heard from him.

For want of funds, Christopher was delayed in leaving for Lisbon, and before he and his brother Bartholomew could "do business" with John II, Dias returned. The Columbus brothers were present in December 1488 when Dias sailed proudly up the Tagus River. He had rounded the south cape of Africa—the Cape of Good Hope, the King named it—and was well on his way up the east coast when his men mutinied and forced him to turn back. That ended King John's interest in Columbus. His man had found a sea route to the Indies, so why invest money in the doubtful West-to-the-Orient project?

Around New Year's, 1489, the Columbus brothers decided on a plan of action. Christopher returned to Spain, where he still had hopes from the slow-moving Talavera commission, while Bartholomew embarked on a long journey to try to sell their venture to some other prince. Unable to make any impression on Henry VII of England, Bartholomew proceeded to France, where Anne de Beaujeu, the sister of King Charles VIII, befriended him. Through her, Bartholomew became friendly with the French King but never obtained any certain prospect of his support.

Success to Christopher always seemed to be just around the corner, but in 1489 he still had three years to wait before obtaining anything definite. We know very little of how he passed the time. According to one contemporary, he started a branch of "Columbus Brothers, Chartmakers and Booksellers" at Seville. There is some indication that he joined the Spanish army as a volunteer.

Late in 1490 the Talavera commission issued an unfavorable report. The experts advised the Queen that the West-to-the-Orient project "rested on weak foundations"; that the voyage would require three years even if the ship could return, which they judged doubtful; that the ocean was infinitely larger than Columbus supposed, and much of it unnavigable. And finally, it was not likely that God would have allowed any uninhabited land of real value to be concealed from His people for so many centuries. Rejection could not have been more flat, and we must admit that all the arguments, save the last, were sound.

For the present, all the Queen would do was to give Columbus fresh hope. He could apply again, said she, when the war with the Moors was over. He waited almost another year and then decided to join his brother in France. Calling at La Rábida friary to pick up his son Diego, now about ten years old, he was persuaded by the prior to give the Queen another chance, and wrote to her to that effect. She replied by summoning Columbus to court.

Columbus always found more friends and supporters among priests than among laymen. They seemed to understand him better, since his thoughts were permeated with religious emotion. He was far more particular than most laymen in saying the daily offices of the church, he seldom missed an opportunity to attend Mass, and in an age of picturesque and elaborate profanity, he was never heard to utter any other oath than "By San Fernando!"

At Christmastime, 1491, Columbus again appeared at court, then being held in the fortified camp of Santa Fe during the siege of Granada. A new commission was appointed, and a royal council reviewed its findings. It seems probable that the commission recommended that Columbus be allowed to try his project, and that the council rejected it because of the price he asked. For this extraordinary man, despite poverty, delays and discouragement, had actually raised his demands. In 1485 he had been willing to sail for Medina Celi on an expense-account basis, without any particular honors or emoluments. Now he demanded not only ennoblement and the title of Admiral, but also that he be made Governor and Viceroy of any new lands he might discover, that both titles be hereditary in his family, and that he and his heirs be given a 10 percent cut on trade. He had suffered so many outrages and insults during his long residence in Spain he would not glorify Spain for nothing. No more bargaining! Take it, Your Majesties, or leave it.

Leave it they did, in January 1492. Ferdinand and Isabella told him this at an audience which the King, at least, intended to be final. Columbus saddled his mule, packed the saddlebags with his charts and other exhibits, and started for Seville, intending to take ship for France and join Bartholomew in a fresh appeal to Charles VIII.

Just as in Oriental bargaining a storekeeper will often run after a departing customer to accept his last offer, so it happened here. Luis de Santangel, keeper of King Ferdinand's privy purse, called on the Queen the very day that Columbus left Santa Fe and urged her to meet Columbus's terms. The expedition, he pointed out, would not cost as much as a week's entertainment of a fellow sovereign, and he would undertake to raise the money himself. As for the honors, Columbus asked for them only if he succeeded, and they would be a small price to pay for the discovery of a western route to the Indies. Isabella, who had probably felt that way all along, jumped at this, her really last chance. She sent a messenger who overtook Columbus four miles from Santa Fe and brought him back.

Although everything was now decided in principle, it was not until April 1492 that the contracts between Columbus and the Sovereigns, the Capitulations, as they are generally called, were signed and sealed. Therein the Sovereigns, in consideration that Cristóbal Colón (as henceforth Columbus called himself) is setting forth "to discover and acquire certain islands and mainlands in the Ocean Sea," promise him to be Admiral of the Ocean Sea, Viceroy and Governor of lands that he may discover. He shall have 10 percent of all gold, gems, spices or other merchandise produced or obtained by trade within those domains, tax free; he shall have the right to invest in one-eighth of any ship going thither; and these offices and emoluments will be enjoyed by his heirs and successors forever. The Sovereigns also issued to him a brief passport in Latin, stating that they were sending him with three caravels "toward the regions of India," and three identical letters of introduction, one to the "Grand Khan" (the Chinese Emperor) and the other two with a blank space so that the proper titles of other princes could be inserted.

THE SUCCESS of the Enterprise depended on an infinite number of practical details. First, for several reasons, it was decided to fit out the fleet and recruit the men at Palos. Columbus had made friends there of the Pinzón family, leading shipowners and master mariners; both ships and sailors were available. And Palos had committed some municipal misdemeanor for which the Queen conveniently fined the city two well-equipped caravels. Columbus had been promised three caravels, not two, but it so happened that a ship from Galicia, owned and captured by Juan de la Cosa, was then in port, and Columbus chartered her as his flagship.

Santa María, as this ship was called, is the most famous of Columbus's ships. Although no picture or model of her has survived, her cargo capacity was probably 100 "tuns" or double hogsheads of wine. Her rig was the conventional one of the period: a mainmast higher than she was long, a main yard as long as the keel, carrying an immense square sail, which was counted on to do most of the driving. Above this was spread a small main topsail. The foremast, a little more than half the height of the mainmast, carried a square foresail. The mizzenmast on the high poop carried a small lateen-rigged (triangular) sail, and under the bowsprit was spread a small square sail called the spritsail, which performed rather inefficiently the function of the modern jib.

A Spanish ship in those days had an official name and a nick-

Columbus taking leave of the King and Queen in Palos.

name which the sailors used; *Santa María* was *La Gallega* (The Galician). One of the two caravels provided by the town of Palos was named *Santa Clara*, but she is universally known by her nickname *Niña*, so given because she belonged to the Niño family of Palos. *Niña* was Columbus's favorite. She carried him safely home from his First Voyage, took him to western Cuba and back to Spain on the Second, and made another voyage to Hispaniola. She measured about 60 tons, her length was not over 70 feet, and at the start she was rigged with three lateen sails, but in the Canaries Columbus had her rerigged square, because square sails are much handier when running before the wind.

Pinta, also a locally built caravel, was probably a little larger than *Niña*, and square-rigged from the first. Her real name we do not know; *Pinta* probably was derived from a former owner named Pinto. She was a smart sailer; the New World was first sighted from her deck and she was first home to Spain.

All vessels carried inside stone ballast; their sides were painted gay colors above the waterline and, below it, payed with pitch to discourage barnacles and shipworms. Crosses and heraldic devices were emblazoned on the sails, and the ships carried a variety of large, brightly colored flags which were flown on entering and leaving port. Queen Isabella's royal ensign was hoisted on the top of the mainmast, and on the foremast was displayed the special banner of the expedition: a green cross on a white field, with a crown on each arm. All three vessels carried a little crude artillery, to repel possible pirates or other unwelcome boarders, but they were not combatant ships, and carried neither soldiers nor gunners.

Columbus could never have recruited officers and men without the enthusiastic support of three leading shipping families of Palos—the Pinzóns, Niños and Quinteros. Martín Alonso Pinzón commanded *Pinta*. A brother of his, Vicente Yáñez Pinzón, commanded *Niña*, whose master-owner was Juan Niño; and a brother of Juan, Peralonso Niño, served as pilot of *Santa María*. Columbus himself commanded the flagship, but her owner, Juan de la Cosa, remained on board as master. Each vessel had a pilot, an officer who shared the duties of the modern first officer and had charge of navigation, and a surgeon. In the fleet were several specialists—Luis de Torres, who knew Arabic, which, it was thought, would enable him to converse with the Chinese and Japanese; Rodrigo de Escobedo, secretary of the fleet, who would make an official record of discoveries; Rodrigo Sánchez, the royal comptroller, whose main duty it was to see that the crown got its share of the gold; Pedro Gutiérrez, butler of the King's dais, who apparently was tired of court life, since he shipped as chief steward; and Diego de Harana, the marshal of the fleet. The total number of officers and men of *Santa María*, *Pinta* and *Niña* was about ninety.

Almost all the enlisted men—stewards, boatswains, calkers, able seamen and gromets, or ship's boys—were from the Niebla or nearby towns of Andalusia. There is some foundation for the tradition that the crews included jailbirds. Three lads who had been given life imprisonment for helping a condemned murderer to break jail were set free in order to ship with Columbus; they turned out to be trustworthy men and went with the Admiral on later voyages, as did a large number of the others. These men and boys overcame the natural conservatism of a mariner in the hope of glory, gold and adventure. Those who survived won plenty of the first two, and all shared in one of the greatest adventures of history—Columbus's First Voyage.

3. First Crossing of the Atlantic

BY THE SECOND DAY of August, 1492, everything at last was ready. That night every man of the fleet confessed his sins, received absolution and made his communion. Columbus went on board his flagship in the small hours of Friday the third and gave the signal to get under way. Before the sun rose, all three vessels were floating down the Rio Tinto on the morning ebb, using their long sweeps to maintain steerageway.

Columbus's plan for the voyage was simple, and its simplicity ensured his success. Not for him the boisterous head winds, the monstrous seas and the dark, unbridled waters of the North Atlantic, which had already baffled so many Portuguese. He would run south before the prevailing northerlies to the Canary Islands, and there make, as it were, a right-angle turn; for he had observed on his African voyages that the winter winds in the latitude of the Canaries blew from the east, and that the ocean around them, more often than not, was calm as a millpond. An even better reason to take his departure from the Canaries was their latitude, 28 degrees north, which he believed cut through Japan, passing en route the mythical Isle of Antilia, which would make a good break in the westward passage.

The first leg of the voyage was made in less than a week. Then, within sight of the Grand Canary, the fleet ran into a calm that lasted two or three days. Columbus decided to send the *Pinta* into Las Palmas for needed repairs while *Santa María* and *Niña* sailed to Gomera, westernmost of the Canaries which the Spaniards had wrested from their native inhabitants. At Gomera the Captain General (as we should call Columbus on this voyage before he made Admiral) sent men ashore to fill extra water casks, buy breadstuffs and cheese, and to put a supply of native beef in pickle. He then sailed to Las Palmas to superintend *Pinta*'s repairs and returned with her to Gomera.

On September 2 all three ships were anchored off San Sebastián, the port of that island. Columbus then met Doña Beatriz de Bobadilla, widow of the former captain of the island. Beatriz was a beautiful lady still under thirty, and Columbus is said to have fallen in love with her; but if that is true, he did not love her warmly enough to tarry to the next full moon, and on September 6, 1492, the fleet weighed anchor for the last time in the Old World. By nightfall on the ninth the three vessels were alone on an uncharted ocean. Columbus gave out the course: "West; nothing to the north, nothing to the south."

CELESTIAL NAVIGATION was in its infancy. Rough estimates of latitude could be made from the height of either the North Star or the sun above the horizon, but the motion of a ship threw off the instruments of observation—a wood or brass quadrant and the astrolabe—to such an extent that most navigators took their latitude sights ashore. Columbus relied almost completely on dead reckoning, which means plotting your course and position on a chart from direction, time and distance.

He had his direction from a compass similar to those used until recently—a circular card graduated to the 32 points (N, N by E, NNE, NE by N, NE, and so on), with a lodestone under the north point, and so mounted that it could swing freely with the motion of the ship. Columbus's compass was on the poop deck, where the officer of the watch could see it. The helmsman, who steered with a heavy tiller attached directly to the rudder, was belowdecks and could see very little.

Time was measured by a half-hour glass. As soon as the sand was all down, a ship's boy turned the glass and the officer of the deck recorded it by making a stroke on a slate. Eight glasses made a watch. The time could be corrected daily in fair weather by noting the moment when the sun lay due south, which was local noon. Distance was the most variable of these three elements. Columbus had no method of measuring the speed of his vessels. He and the watch officers merely estimated it and noted it down. Our careful checking of Columbus's Journal of his First Voyage proves that he made an average 9 percent overestimate of his distance covered per day. On September 9, the day he dropped the last land below the horizon, Columbus decided to keep a true reckoning of his course for his own use and a false one to give out to the crew, so that they would not be frightened at sailing so far from land. But, owing to his overestimate of speed, the "false" reckoning was more accurate than the "true"!

Sixteenth-century Spanish astrolabe.

Even after making the proper reduction for his overestimation, the speed of his vessels is surprising. Ships of that day were expected to make 3 to 5 knots in a light breeze, up to $9\frac{1}{2}$ in a strong, fair gale, and at times to be capable of 12 knots. In October 1492, on the outward passage, the Columbus fleet made an average of 142 miles per day for five consecutive days, and the best day's run, 182 miles, averaged 8 knots.

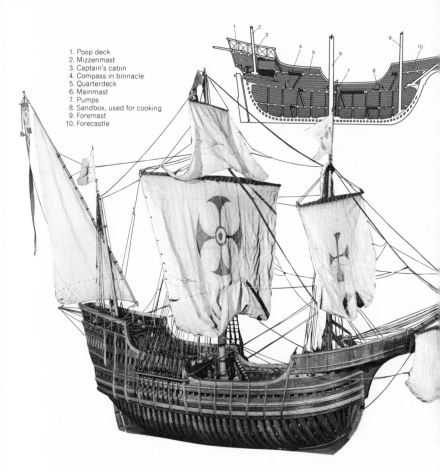

1. Poop deck
2. Mizzenmast
3. Captain's cabin
4. Compass in binnacle
5. Quarterdeck
6. Mainmast
7. Pumps
8. Sandbox, used for cooking
9. Foremast
10. Forecastle

Comforts and conveniences were almost totally lacking. Cooking was done on deck over a bed of sand in a wooden firebox protected from the wind by a hood. The diet was monotonous: salt meat, hardtack and dried peas. For drink they had wine, while it lasted, and water in casks, which often went bad. Only the Captain General and the ships' captains had cabins with bunks; the others slept where they could, in their clothes.

In those days, sailors were the most religious of men. On each vessel a boy recited the Lord's Prayer and the *Ave Maria* at daybreak. After sunset, all hands were called to evening prayers.

28

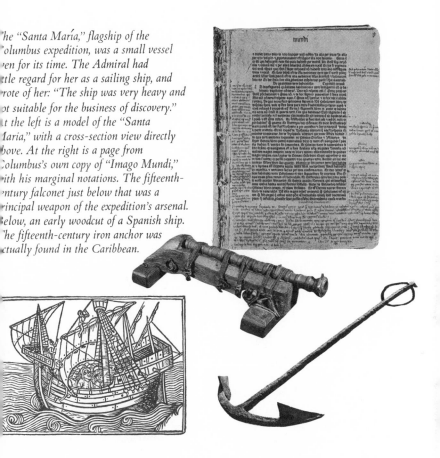

The "Santa María," flagship of the Columbus expedition, was a small vessel even for its time. The Admiral had little regard for her as a sailing ship, and wrote of her: "The ship was very heavy and not suitable for the business of discovery." At the left is a model of the "Santa María," with a cross-section view directly above. At the right is a page from Columbus's own copy of "Imago Mundi," with his marginal notations. The fifteenth-century falconet just below that was a principal weapon of the expedition's arsenal. Below, an early woodcut of a Spanish ship. The fifteenth-century iron anchor was actually found in the Caribbean.

The service began with the boy whose duty it was to light the binnacle lamp singing:

> "God give us a good night and good sailing;
> May our ship make a good passage,
> Sir Captain and Master and good company."

All hands then said the Lord's Prayer, the Creed and the *Ave Maria*, and concluded by singing the *Salve Regina*. Columbus said, "Seamen sing or say it after their own fashion," bawling it out in several keys at once. But was it the less acceptable to the Virgin, under whose protection all sailors felt secure?

DURING THE FIRST TEN DAYS (September 9 to 18), the easterly trade wind blew steadily, and the fleet made 1163 nautical miles westward. This was the honeymoon of the voyage. "What a delight was the savor of the mornings!" wrote Columbus in his Journal. That entry speaks to the heart of anyone who has sailed in the trades; it recalls the beauty of the dawn, kindling clouds and sails rose-color, and the smell of dew drying on a wooden deck. The sea was smooth, and the air, remarked the Captain General in his Journal, was "like April in Andalusia; the only thing wanting was to hear the song of the nightingale." During this period the fleet encountered its first field of sargassum (gulfweed) and found that it was no hindrance to navigation.

On September 19, only ten days out from land, the fleet temporarily ran into variable winds and rain near where the fabled island of Antilia should have been; all hands expected to sight land. The Captain General even had the deep-sea lead hove, and found no bottom at 200 fathoms; no wonder, since the ocean is about 2300 fathoms deep at that point.

For the next five days only 234 miles were made. During a spell of moderate weather a seaman of *Pinta* gave the "Land ho!" and everyone thought he saw an island against the setting sun. Columbus fell on his knees to thank God, ordered *Gloria in excelsis Deo* to be sung by all hands, and set a course for the island. But at dawn no island was visible. It was simply a cloud bank above the western horizon resembling land, a common phenomenon at sea. Martín Alonso Pinzón wished to search further for this island, but Columbus refused, since his object was to reach the Indies, as his Journal recorded.

The trade wind now returned, but moderately, and during the six days from September 26 to October 1, the fleet made only 382 miles. The crew began to mutter and grumble. Three weeks was probably more than they had ever been out of sight of land before. They were all getting on each other's nerves. There was nothing for them to do in the light wind except follow the ship's routine, and troll for fish. Aggrieved cliques formed. Spain was farther away every minute, and what lay ahead? Probably nothing, except in the eye of that cursed Genoese. Let's make him turn back, or throw him overboard!

On the first day of October the wind increased, and in five days the fleet made 710 miles. On the sixth, when they actually lay directly north of Puerto Rico, Columbus knew that the fleet had sailed more than the 2400 miles which, according to his calculations, lay between the Canaries and Japan. Although uneasy, he held to the course.

On October 7 great flocks of birds passed over the ships, flying west-southwest; this was the autumn migration from eastern North America to the West Indies. Columbus decided that he had better follow the birds rather than his chart, and changed course that evening. That was "good joss"; it was his shortest course to the nearest land. Now, every night, the men were heartened by seeing against the moon flocks of birds flying their way. But by the tenth, mutiny flared up again. No land for thirty-one days. Even by the phony reckoning which Columbus gave out they had sailed much farther west than anyone had expected. Columbus, says the record, "cheered them as best he could, holding out good hope of the advantages they might gain; and, he added, it was useless to complain, *since he had come to go to the Indies, and so had to continue until he found them, with Our Lord's help.*"

That was typical of Columbus's determination. Yet even he, conscious of divine guidance, could not have kept on indefinitely without the support of his captains and officers. On October 9 Columbus persuaded the Pinzóns and La Cosa to sail on, with the promise that if land were not found within three days, he would turn back. Next day the trade wind blew fresher; it continued on the eleventh, with a heavy following sea. Signs of land, such as branches of trees with green leaves and flowers, became so frequent that the crew were content with their Captain General's decision, and the mutinous mutterings died out in the keen anticipation of making a landfall.

As the sun set under a clear horizon on October 11, the northeast trade breezed up to gale force. Columbus's promised time was running out. He signaled everyone to keep a particularly sharp watch, and offered extra rewards for first landfall in addition to the year's pay promised by the Sovereigns. That night of destiny was clear and beautiful with a late rising moon, but the sea was the roughest of the entire passage. The men were tense and expectant, the officers testy and anxious, the Captain General serene in the confidence that presently God would reveal to him the Indies.

On rush the ships, pitching, rolling, throwing spray—white waves at their bows and white wakes reflecting the moon. *Pinta* is perhaps half a mile in the lead, *Santa María* on her port quarter, *Niña* on the other side. They are all making the greatest speed

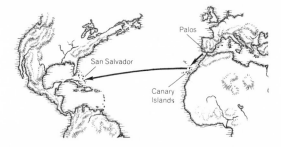

of which they are capable. With the sixth glass of the night watch, the last sands are running out of an era that began with the dawn of history. A few minutes now and destiny will turn up a glass the flow of whose sands we are still watching. Not since the birth of Christ has there been a night so full of meaning for the human race.

At 2 a.m., October 12, Rodrigo de Triana, lookout on *Pinta*, sees something like a white cliff shining in the moonlight, and sings out, *"Tierra! Tierra!"* (Land! Land!) Captain Pinzón verifies the landfall, fires a gun as agreed, and shortens sail to allow the flagship to catch up. As *Santa María* approaches, the Captain General shouts across the rushing waters, "Señor Martín Alonso, you *did* find land! Five thousand maravedis for you as a bonus!"

Yes, land it was, a little island of the Bahamas group. The fleet was headed for gray coral cliffs on its windward side and would have been wrecked had it held course. But these seamen were too expert to allow that. The Captain General ordered sail to be shortened and the fleet steered clear of the island. At dawn they passed the southern point of the island and sought an opening on the west coast, through the barrier reef. Before noon they found it, sailed into the shallow bay now called Long or Fernandez, and anchored in five fathoms.

Here on a gleaming beach of white coral now marked by a cross occurred the famous first landing of Columbus. The Captain General (now by general consent called Admiral) went ashore in the flagship's boat with the royal standard of Castile displayed, the two Captains Pinzón in their boats, flying the banner of the Expedition—the green-crowned cross on a white field. "And, all having rendered thanks to Our Lord, kneeling on the ground, embracing it with tears of joy for the immeasurable mercy of having reached it, the Admiral rose and gave this island the name San Salvador"—Holy Saviour.

THE NATIVES OF GUANAHANÍ, the original name of this island, fled to the jungle when they saw three marine monsters approaching, but curiosity was too much for them, and when they peered out and saw strangely dressed human beings coming ashore, they approached timidly, with propitiatory gifts. Columbus, firmly believing that he had discovered the Indies, called these people "Indians," and Indians the native inhabitants of the Americas have become.

Those first encountered were of the Taino branch of the Arawak language group. Coming from the mainland in dugout canoes, and with no better weapons than wooden spears, they had wrested the Bahamas and most of Cuba from the more primitive Siboney. The Tainos knew how to make cassava bread, to spin, and to make pottery. The Spaniards observed with wonder their handsome bodies almost completely naked, and noted with keen interest that some of them wore, suspended from the nose, little pendants of pure gold. The guilelessness and generosity of these children of nature, their ignorance of money and of iron, and their nudity, suggested that they were holdovers from the Golden Age. Columbus would much rather have encountered sophisticated Orientals than "noble savages," but as usual he made the best of the situation. He observed "how easy it would be to convert these people—and to make them work for us." In other words, enslave them but save their souls.

For two days Columbus explored San Salvador. It was a pretty island then, with a heavy covering of tropical hardwood.

Columbus saw the first maize ever observed by a European, the first hammocks, woven from native cotton, and the first yams; also a tree that he guessed, correctly, would be good dyewood. But the Admiral knew full well that, interesting as these discoveries might be, he had to bring home evidence of Japan or China, or plenty of gold and spices, to prove his voyage a success. The natives of San Salvador indicated by sign language that scores of islands lay to the west and south; it seemed to Columbus that these must be the ones shown on his chart, lying south of Cipangu, and that if they did not lead him to golden Japan, they would be stepping-stones to China.

Indian sleeping arrangement

So, detaining six Indians as guides, Columbus shoved off on October 14. That day he discovered another island which he named Santa María de la Concepción. The natives proved to be similar to those on San Salvador and were equally pleased with the gifts of red caps, glass beads and hawkbells. These were little spherical bells about the diameter of a quarter dollar or shilling, which were attached to the birds used in falconry; they had a pleasant little tinkle and the natives loved them. Lace points, the metal tips to the laces then used to fasten men's clothing, and brass tambourine jingles were additional favorites.

The Admiral's native guides, eager to please, kept assuring him that in the next island there would be plenty of gold, but each one—Long Island, Crooked Island, Fortune Island—was just a flat, jungle-covered bit of land inhabited by friendly natives who had no gold except for a few ornaments. Where they got them Columbus could never make out, because of the language barrier.

34

As the Admiral and his Indian guides came to understand each other better, he heard about a big island called Colba (Cuba) and made up his mind that it must be either Japan or part of China. So to Colba he must go. On the morning of October 28 they entered Bahía Bariay, in the Cuban province of Oriente. Columbus observed in his Journal that he had never seen so beautiful a harbor—trees all fair and green, some with bright flowers and some heavy with fruit, and the air full of birdsong. But where were the golden-roofed temples of Japan, the dragon-mouthed bronze cannon, the lords and ladies in gold-stiffened brocade? Poor Columbus! He tried hard to find compensation in these strange new things for the Oriental objects he so much wanted to see, but it was difficult to describe Cuba in such a way as to interest important people in Spain. Nor could he accept the teasing thought that this was not the Orient after all, but a New World.

Next day the three ships sailed westward and anchored in Puerto Gibara. There they remained for twelve days.

As the San Salvador interpreters assured the local Indians that the strangers in the white-winged monsters were fine people, with piles of good trading truck, business for a time was brisk. Eager to please, they told Columbus that there was gold in the interior, at a place they called Cubanacan, which meant mid-Cuba. The Admiral, eager to present his letter of introduction to the Chinese Emperor, mistook this for El Gran Can, the Great Khan. So nothing would do but to send an embassy to Cubanacan. Luis de Torres, the Arabic scholar, was in charge, and second in command was Rodrigo de Xeres, an able seaman who had once met a black king in Guinea and so was supposed to know the proper way to approach pagan royalty. Indians carried the diplomatic portfolio, a gift considered suitable for royalty, and strings of glass beads to buy food from the natives. The embassy tramped up the valley to what they hoped would be Cambaluk, the imperial city where the Great Khan resided. Alas, it was a village of about fifty palm-thatched

At sunrise, December 20, Columbus sailed into a bay of surpassing beauty. To the right, Acul Bay, in the Dominican Republic. Below this at the far right, an engraving portraying Columbus's landing in Hispaniola, welcomed by Indians bearing gifts. The woodcut beside that shows an Indian habitation of the time. Below, a West Indian village as it might have looked to Columbus. Below right, what must have been a strange sight to the Spaniards—an Indian smoking tobacco. The object at right is a hawkbell—a popular trading item.

huts. The two Spaniards, regarded as having come from the sky, were feasted by the local cacique, while the populace swarmed up to kiss their feet and present simple gifts. Rodrigo loved it— he had never had it so good in Africa—but Torres was mortified that his Arabic was not understood, and, expecting a reception by mandarins in a stone-built capital of ten thousand houses, he felt very much let down.

Yet, on their way back to the harbor, the embassy made a discovery which (had they only known it) would have more far-reaching results than any treaty with China. As Columbus records it, they met "many people who were going to their vil-

lages, with a firebrand in the hand, and herbs to drink the smoke thereof." This was the first European contact with tobacco. The Tainos used a form of cigars which they called *tobacos;* a walking party such as the embassy encountered would carry a large cigar and at every halt light it from a firebrand; everyone then took three or four "drags" from it; after all were refreshed, the march was resumed, small boys keeping the firebrand alight until the next stop. Not long after Spaniards settled in the New World, they tried smoking tobacco and liked it, and through them its use spread rapidly through Europe, Asia and Africa.

While the embassy was absent, the Admiral began a collection of botanical specimens which he hoped would convince people at home that he was at least on the fringe of Asia. There was a shrub which smelled something like cinnamon; the gumbo-limbo, which he supposed to be a form of gum mastic; and a small inedible nut which he took to be the coconut mentioned by Marco Polo. But no gold. When the Spaniards asked for gold, the Indians always waved them on to some other place. According to them, there was an island called Babeque where the people gathered gold on the beach by candlelight and hammered it into bars. This choice piece of misinformation brought about the first rift in the Spanish high command. Without asking the Admiral's permission, Martín Alonso Pinzón took off in *Pinta*, hoping to be the first to reach Babeque. He called at Great Inagua Island, which lay in the general direction indicated by the Indians, and, needless to say, found no gold by candle or any other light.

The Admiral in *Santa María*, with *Niña* (whose captain, Vicente Yáñez Pinzón, always remained loyal), sailed eastward along the superb coast of the Oriente province of Cuba. They called at Bahía Tánamo and at the beautiful Puerto Cayo Moa, "a lagoon in which all the ships of Spain could lie and be safe," as Columbus said. The charm of this placid harbor, so calm between lofty mountains and a barrier of foaming reefs, was noted by Columbus in words that are not in the least exaggerated. On he sailed, with a breeze from the west. At sunrise December 5 the fleet was off Cape Maisí, easternmost point of Cuba. In the hope that this was the extremity of Asia, Columbus named it Cape Alpha and Omega, where East ends and West begins.

Now the fleet crossed the Windward Passage, and at nightfall arrived off the Haitian harbor of San Nicolas Môle, so named by Columbus because he entered it on the feast day of that saint. His Indian guides had indicated that gold was to be found on this great island, and this time they were right. It may be that this island—Hispaniola—saved Columbus's reputation, for if he had returned home with no more "evidence" than he had yet obtained, people would have said, "This Genoese has found some interesting islands inhabited by gentle natives, but as for their being the Indies—pooh!"

At daylight a fair breeze took the two vessels to Moustique Bay, where they were detained five days by easterly winds and rain. It was here that the Admiral, "seeing the grandeur and beauty of this island, and its resemblance to . . . Spain," named it La Isla Española (The Spanish Isle). Three of his seamen captured a young girl clad only in a golden nose plug, and brought her on board. The Admiral "sent her ashore very honorably," decently clad and bedecked with jingles and hawkbells. This move proved to be good public relations, as the damsel was a cacique's daughter. Next day nine Spaniards were conducted to a big village and given everything they wanted—food, drink, parrots and girls.

On December 15 the two ships beat up the Tortuga Channel to the mouth of Trois Rivières, a clear mountain stream. Next day, when the fleet lay off a beach, some five hundred people came down, accompanied by their youthful cacique, who made the Admiral a state visit. He had dinner with Columbus in his cabin, and behaved himself with royal poise and dignity. He and his suite were bedecked with solid-gold jewelry!

At sunrise December 20 the ships were off Acul Bay, the beauty of which was so striking that the Admiral ran out of adjectives describing it. Acul certainly is one of the fairest places in the world. The high mountains part to reveal a conical peak at the head of the valley. Here the natives lived in an even more pristine state of innocence than elsewhere; the women did not even wear a scanty cotton clout, and the men did not mind exhibiting their wives and daughters to strangers. Also, they seemed to have plenty of gold. About a thousand people came out in canoes to visit *Santa María*, and some five hundred more swam out, although she was anchored over three miles from shore. A messenger arrived at Acul from Guacanagarí, the cacique of Marien, an even more important potentate than the one entertained a few days earlier. Guacanagarí sent the Admiral a magnificent belt with a solid-gold mask for buckle, and invited him to call. So, before sunrise on December 24, *Santa María* and *Niña* departed Acul Bay, all hands planning to spend a merry Christmas at the court of Guacanagarí.

Fate decreed otherwise. With a contrary wind, the two vessels were unable to cover the few miles between Acul and Guacanagarí's capital on Caracol Bay in a day. By 11 p.m., when the watch was changed, *Niña* and *Santa María* were becalmed. Everyone was exhausted from the previous all-night entertainment of natives, and with only a slight ground swell and no wind, a feeling of complete security—the most dangerous delusion a seaman can entertain—stole over the flagship. Even the Admiral retired to get his first sleep in forty-eight hours; the helmsman gave the tiller to a small boy and joined the rest of the watch in slumber.

Just as midnight ushered in Christmas Day, *Santa María* settled on a coral reef, so gently that nobody was awakened by the shock. The boy helmsman, feeling the rudder ground, sang out. The Admiral came first on deck, followed by Captain La Cosa and all hands. As the bow only had grounded, Columbus saw a good chance to get her off and ordered La Cosa and a boat's crew to run an anchor out astern. Instead of obeying orders, they rowed to *Niña*. Captain Vicente Pinzón refused to receive them and sent a boat of his own to help. *Niña*, more vigilant than the flagship or not on the same bearing, had passed the reef safely.

Owing to La Cosa's insubordination, an hour was wasted, and that doomed *Santa María*. The ground swell had been driving her higher and higher on the reef, and coral heads were punching holes in her bottom. As the hull was filling with water, Columbus ordered abandon ship.

Guacanagarí and his subjects worked hard with the Spaniards to get her off after daybreak, when the tide might help, but it was too late. All they could salvage were the equipment, stores and trading truck.

Columbus, with his strong sense of divine guidance, tried to figure out what this disastrous accident meant. Presently he had it: God intended him to start a colony with *Santa María*'s crew. Guacanagarí begged him to do so, as he wanted firepower to help him against enemies elsewhere on the island. The Spaniards fell over each other to volunteer, because signs of gold were now plentiful. So Columbus gave orders to erect a fortified camp and named it Villa de la Navidad (Christmas Town) in honor of the day of disaster, which he fondly thought had been turned to his advantage.

Navidad, the first attempt by Europeans since that of the Northmen to establish themselves in the New World, was soon built, largely out of *Santa María*'s timbers. Thirty-nine men were left under command of Columbus's Cordovan friend Diego de Harana. The Admiral gave them provisions, most of the trading truck and the flagship's boat. They were instructed to explore the country with a view to finding a permanent settlement, to trade for gold and to treat the natives kindly.

Columbus was now certain that he had found the Indies. Hispaniola might not be Japan, but it was a great and rich island off the coast of China. He now had enough gold artifacts to convince the most skeptical that a land of wealth and plenty had been discovered.

On the day after New Year's, 1493, Guacanagarí and Columbus held a farewell party. After final expressions of mutual love and esteem, the new allies parted and the Admiral went on board *Niña*. He would return home in her, with *Pinta* if he could find her; otherwise, alone. She set sail at sunrise January 4.

4. Homeward Passage

WHEN HE departed Navidad, Columbus intended to shape a course directly for Spain, lest Pinzón get there first with the good news. But two days later he sighted *Pinta*. That evening Martín Alonso came on board and gave an account of his doings during the last three weeks. He had sailed along the coast of Hispaniola and anchored in Puerto Blanco. There a shore party found plenty of gold. Pinzón had heard of the flagship's wreck by Indian "grapevine" and had decided to sail back and lend the Admiral a hand. Columbus was inclined to let bygones be bygones in view of the good news of gold, and he was pleased to have company on the voyage home. Nobody in that era sailed on a long voyage unescorted if he could help it. One reason was to have someone to rescue survivors in case of sinking. Columbus made an unusual record by never losing a ship at sea, unless we count the *Santa María*'s grounding.

While waiting for a fair wind, Columbus explored the lower course of the Rio Yaque del Norte and found gold nuggets as

Map of northwest Hispaniola drawn by Columbus.
It is the only extant one known to have come from his hand.

large as lentils. Even today there is gold in that river valley; the countrywomen pan it out laboriously, and when they have enough to fill a turkey quill, they take it to town for their shopping.

At midnight January 8 *Niña* and *Pinta*, passing along the coast of Hispaniola, looked in at Puerto Plata (so named by Columbus on account of silver clouds over the mountains) and anchored near the mouth of Samaná Bay. There, at a place still called the Point of the Arrows, the Spaniards encountered the first natives who were not pleased to meet them. These, the Ciguayos, were armed with bows and arrows. By catching one Ciguayo, treating him well and sending him ashore with an assortment of cloth and trinkets, the rest were appeased, and a brisk if cautious trade was conducted. One or two were persuaded to join the native contingent returning to Spain.

On Wednesday, January 16, three hours before daybreak, the caravels sailed from Samaná Bay. A rough voyage lay ahead, and a very difficult problem in navigation. This homeward passage was a far greater test of Columbus's courage, seamanship and ability to handle men than anything he had yet experienced. With the greatest geographical discovery of all time locked in his breast, knowing that it would be of no use to anybody unless delivered, the Admiral had to fight the elements and human weakness as no one before or since.

Throughout January *Niña* and *Pinta* constantly edged farther north and closer to Spain. As they were near the northern limit of the trades, the sea was smooth and, providentially, the wind held and blew them across the horse latitudes, as seamen used to call the calms between latitudes 30 and 33 degrees north. They successfully crossed the Sargasso Sea, having the rare experience of sailing with a fresh wind over an undulating meadow of weed, under a full moon. That is indeed beautiful to the eye, and the ear, too, as the sound of parting waters is replaced by a soft "hush-hush" as the weed brushes by.

Without knowing it, Columbus had employed the best sailing strategy for getting home quickly. If he had tried to sail straight for Spain (as on his return passage in 1496), he would have had to beat to windward most of the way, but this long northerly leg took him up to the latitude of Bermuda into the zone of rough, strong westerlies.

On the last day of January the wind swung into the west, and four days later, when the Admiral figured that he had reached the latitude of Cape Saint Vincent, he set the course due east. The weather now turned cold and a fresh gale blew up. For four days the caravels made an average of 150 miles, at times attaining a speed of 11 knots.

Niña and *Pinta* were having the finest kind of sailing. They were running before a fresh gale over deep blue, white-crested water. On they sped through bright, sunny days and nights brilliant with familiar constellations that seemed to be beckoning them home. It is hard for any sailor to be sorry for Columbus, in spite of his later misfortunes; he enjoyed glorious sailing weather on almost every voyage. But one of his worst experiences was about to come.

The two caravels were sailing into an area of very dirty weather in one of the coldest and most blustery winters on record—a winter in which hundreds of vessels were wrecked, the harbor of Genoa froze over, and ships lay windbound at Lisbon for months. The center of an area of very low pressure was passing north of the Azores with winds of full gale strength, and the caravels had to pass through three weather fronts.

On February 12 *Niña* stripped down to bare poles and scudded before the wind, laboring heavily. Opposing winds increased next morning, resulting in frightful cross seas which formed dangerous pyramidical waves that broke over the caravels from stem to stern. *Niña* was underballasted owing to the depletion of her stores. The Admiral and Captain Vicente Pinzón took turns as officer of the deck and watched each wave to warn the helmsman below. One mistake by either and she would have broached-to, rolled over and sunk, and *Pinta* could never have rescued survivors in such a sea.

The following night the two caravels lost sight of each other and never met again until they reached Spain. And they almost did not get there. We have no record of how *Pinta* fared, but *Niña*'s crew almost gave up hope on Saint Valentine's Day. Officers and men all made a vow to go on a pilgrimage to the first shrine of the Virgin they might encounter if they were saved. The wind then began to abate. Columbus afterward admitted that he was as frightened as anyone. Desperate lest both ships and all hands perish, at the height of the gale he wrote an abstract of his journal of the voyage, wrapped it in waxed cloth, headed it up in a cask and hove it overboard in the hope that someone might pick up the true story of his discovery. The cask never was recovered, but sundry faked versions of the Admiral's "Secrete Log Boke" are still being offered to credulous collectors.

Shortly after sunrise February 15 land was sighted dead ahead. Columbus correctly guessed that it was one of the Azores. As the wind then whipped into the east, three days elapsed before *Niña* was able to come up with this island and anchor. The Admiral sent his boat ashore and ascertained that it was Santa Maria, southernmost of the Azores. He anchored near a village called Nossa Senhora dos Anjos (Our Lady of the Angels), where a little church was dedicated to the Virgin. Anjos was an answer to a prayer, and the proper place for the crew to fulfill their vows made at the height of the storm.

There then took place what seems the most comic incident of the entire First Voyage. Here were men bursting with the greatest piece of news since the fall of the Roman Empire, a discovery that would confer untold benefits on Europe; yet, what was their first reception? While saying their prayers in the little chapel, clad only in their shirts (as a sign of penitence), half the crew were set upon by "the whole town" and thrown into jail. The Portuguese captain of the island suspected that they had been on an illicit voyage to West Africa! He even rowed out to capture Columbus and the few members of *Niña*'s crew who had stayed on board. The Admiral refused to receive him and threatened to shoot up the town and carry off hostages if his people were not released. Before the captain could make up his mind, another storm blew up, *Niña*'s cables parted, and she was blown almost to the biggest of the Azores, São Miguel, and back. And she did well to get back, because only three seamen and the Indians were left on board to help the Admiral and the skipper. By the time *Niña* returned, the Portuguese captain, having grilled the captured sailors and discovered no evidence of poaching on his King's preserves, surrendered them and furnished the entire crew with much-needed fresh provisions.

So on February 24 Columbus resumed his homeward voyage. The distance to Cape Saint Vincent was 800 miles, which should have required only a week in the prevailing north wind. But in this piece of ocean in winter low-pressure areas linger, and the winter of 1493 was unusually foul. Two cyclones were moving slowly eastward, taking six days to pass *Niña* and giving her an even worse beating than the storm west of the Azores.

Trouble began on February 26. The wind shifted to southeast, and for three days *Niña* was blown off course. "It was painful," wrote Columbus, "to have such a tempest when we were already at the doors of home." On the night of March 2 the circular storm overtook *Niña* with a violent squall which split the mainsail and blew the furled foresail and mizzen out of their wrappings, whipping them to ragged ribbons in a few minutes.

Columbus did the only thing he could; he drove on under bare poles, *Niña* pitching and rolling frightfully. The wind made another shift, to northwest, on March 3. This was the "backlash" of the cyclone, worse than the forelash. As the dark winter afternoon waned, anxiety became intense. Columbus knew by dead reckoning that they were driving right onto the ironbound coast of Portugal, and that only a miracle could prevent a smashup against the cliffs.

Shortly after six o'clock, when the sun set, the crisis came. Lightning flashed overhead, great seas broke aboard from both sides, the wind blew so strong it "seemed to raise the caravel into the air." Fortunately a full moon sent enough light through the clouds so that at seven o'clock land was sighted dead ahead, distant perhaps five miles. Columbus then performed the difficult maneuver of "clawing off" a lee shore. The coast ran north and south, the wind was northwest, so they set one little square foresail that had been saved in the locker and shaped a course parallel to the coast, with wind on the starboard quarter. No wonder *Niña* became the Admiral's favorite vessel, to respond to this difficult maneuver without broaching.

When day broke on March 4 Columbus recognized the prominent Cabo da Roca, which juts into the ocean just north of the entrance to the Tagus River on which Lisbon is situated. With only one square sail between him and utter destruction, the Admiral naturally elected to call at Lisbon rather than attempt to continue around Cape Saint Vincent to Spain. He knew perfectly well that he was taking a big risk in placing himself in the power of ruthless King John II, who had turned him down twice, but his considerations were to get the word of his discovery to Spain and to save his ship and crew. So, after sunrise, *Niña* whipped around the cape, and by nine o'clock anchored off the outer port of Lisbon.

To be safe in a snug harbor after long tossing at sea gives the sailor a wonderful feeling of relief and relaxation. But the Admiral and his battered crew still had plenty to worry about. *Niña* would have to be refitted before she could proceed to Spain. Would King John allow it? And what had happened to *Pinta?*

The first Portuguese gesture was not assuring. Moored near *Niña* was a large warship whose master was Bartholomeu Dias, discoverer of the Cape of Good Hope. Dias came over in an armed boat and ordered Captain Colom (as he knew Columbus) to report on board the warship and give an account of himself. Columbus stood on his dignity as Admiral of the Ocean Sea, and refused. But he showed his credentials, which satisfied Dias. Columbus had already sent a letter to King John, asking permission to enter the port of Lisbon. On March 8 a nobleman brought the answer, not only granting his request, and ordering that *Niña* be supplied with all she needed, gratis, but inviting the Admiral to visit the King at his country residence.

Columbus decided he had better accept, although it meant another week's delay, and he feared that visiting the King of Portugal before reporting to Queen Isabella would offend her, as indeed it did. So, selecting two or three followers and the healthiest of his Indians, Columbus landed at Lisbon and chartered a train of mules to take himself and suite up-country. Pity the poor Indians who, after their terrible buffeting at sea, must now suffer the rigors of a two-day muleback transport along the narrow, muddy roads of Portugal!

John II received Columbus with graciousness, but his court chronicler tells us that the King was inwardly furious with the Admiral, for he suspected that the new discoveries had been made in a region where Portugal had prior rights. The courtiers urged the King to have this boastful upstart discreetly assassinated, but, fortunately, he refused. The King had to admit that his Indian guests looked very different from any Africans he had ever seen. And these Indians were remarkable geographers. Two of them impressed him deeply by making a rough chart of the Antilles with beans, at which the King was convinced, and cried out, "Why did I let slip such a wonderful chance?"

On March 11 Columbus and suite departed. During the Admiral's absence, *Niña* had been fitted with new sails and rigging, and had taken on fresh provisions and wine. She was now ready for the last leg of the voyage, all her crew were on board, and on March 13 the gallant little caravel weighed anchor from Lisbon.

Strange to relate, *Pinta* was following her, out of sight but not far astern. She had missed the worst of the tempests that swept over *Niña*, and she made port in northern Spain about the end of February. Martín Alonso Pinzón, whom Columbus had suspected of wanting to beat him home with the news, attempted to do just that. He sent a message to Ferdinand and Isabella at Barcelona, begging permission to come and tell them about the voyage. The Sovereigns replied that they preferred to hear the news from Columbus himself. *Pinta* then sailed for Palos.

At midday, March 15, *Niña* crossed the bar of Rio Saltés just as the tide was turning fair and dropped anchor off Palos. *Pinta* entered on the same tide. The sight of *Niña* already there, snugged down as if she had been at home a month, finished Martín Alonso Pinzón. Older than Columbus, ill from the hardships of the voyage, mortified by his snub from the King and Queen, he could bear no more. He went directly to his country house near Palos, took to his bed and died within the month.

So ended, 224 days after it began, one of the greatest voyages in history. Columbus's final words to his Journal have been preserved:

> Of this voyage I observe that the will of God hath miraculously been set forth by the many signal miracles that He hath shown on the voyage and for myself, who for so great a time was in the court of Your Highnesses, with the opposition and against the opinion of so many high personages of your household, who were all against me, alleging this undertaking to be folly, which I hope in Our Lord will be to the greater glory of Christianity, which to some slight extent has already occurred.

Even in triumph, Columbus could not resist lashing back at the skeptics who had derided or doubted him. Almost every pioneer in science has oppositions to endure, and if he has no money he must expect ridicule and rudeness. When he finally succeeds he does well to keep quiet about this, and even to congratulate those who doubted him for the help they failed to give. But Columbus never learned to do so. He could hardly write one letter without derogatory comments on his detractors, which naturally made them despise and hate him rather than love and esteem him.

48

COLUMBUS HAD ALREADY sent his official report on the voyage (generally called the Columbus Letter) overland from Lisbon to Barcelona. Fearing lest it miscarry, or be impounded by King John II, he sent one copy to the Sovereigns by official courier, and a third to Cordova, where his mistress Beatriz was awaiting him with five-year-old Ferdinand and thirteen-year-old Diego.

On or shortly after Easter Sunday, April 7, his cup of happiness overflowed upon receipt of a letter from Ferdinand and Isabella, addressed to "Don Cristóbal Colón, their Admiral of the Ocean Sea, Viceroy and Governor of the Islands that he hath discovered in the Indies." These were the exact titles that they had promised him if he did reach the Indies, and the use of them indicated their belief that he had. They commanded him to attend court, and ordered preparations for a second voyage to be started immediately.

Columbus promptly drafted a report for the Sovereigns on how Hispaniola should be colonized. He proposed to recruit a maximum of two thousand settlers who would be required to build houses in a designated town in return for a license to trade with the natives for gold. Each one must return to his town at stated intervals and hand over his gold for smelting to an official who would deduct the Sovereign's fifth, the Admiral's tenth, and another tax to support the church. There should be a closed season on gold hunting in order to insure that the settlers would grow crops. Foreigners, Jews, infidels and heretics must be kept out of the Indies, but plenty of priests should be sent there to convert the natives.

Columbus realized that the Tainos's wants were few and easily supplied, so they could not be expected to flock to the beach to sell gold, as the natives of Africa did. Spaniards would have to work the interior of Hispaniola, and perhaps visit other islands to do business. But everyone must check in at a trading factory on the coast, and all transatlantic traffic must go to and from Cadiz, in the interest of fiscal control.

After sending this report ahead by courier, the Admiral purchased clothes suitable for his rank and formed a procession with some of his officers, servants and six of the long-suffering Indians. These wore their full native dress (largely feathers and fishbone-and-gold ornaments) and carried parrots in cages. Everyone flocked to marvel at these strange-looking men, so unlike any in European experience. Traversing Andalusia, they entered Cordova, where Columbus was given a great reception, and he could visit his family. Around April 20 the cavalcade arrived at Barcelona, where "all the court and the city" came out to meet the great man.

Now the fortunes of Columbus reached apogee. As he entered the hall where the Sovereigns held court, his dignified stature, his gray hair, and his noble countenance, tanned by eight months on the sea, made the learned men present compare him with a Roman senator. As he advanced to make obeisance, Ferdinand and Isabella rose from their thrones, and when he knelt to kiss their hands, they bade him rise and be seated on the Queen's right. The Indians were brought forward and presented, the gold artifacts and samples of alleged rare spices were examined, a multitude of questions asked and answered, then all adjourned to the chapel of the Alcazar, where a *Te Deum* was chanted. It was observed that at the final verse, *"O Lord, in Thee have I trusted, let me never be confounded,"* tears were streaming down the Admiral's face.

It is probable that Columbus at this point could have had anything he wanted—a title, a castle, a pension for life. It would have been well for him had he taken them and retired with honor, leaving to others the responsibility of colonizing. But he was not that kind of man, and if he had been, he would not have discovered America. He must see that the islands he discovered were settled, the gold trade put on a proper footing and the natives converted; he must make contact with the Grand Khan, or some Oriental potentate. He was in good health, full of energy, in the prime of life (age forty-one), and he believed that God had appointed him to do this work. His sense of a divine mission appears in the curious signature he now adopted, and of which no contemporary explanation exists. He wrote it as follows:

. S .

S . A . S .

X M Υ .

: X͠ρο FERENS

Many attempts have been made to solve the riddle. My own belief is that the letters on the first two lines stand for *Servus Sum Altissimi Salvatoris;* and the third for *Christou Mariae Viou*, meaning Servant am I of the Most High Saviour, Christ the Son of Mary. The last line is a Greco-Latin form, Christoferens, of his Christian name, emphasizing his role as the bearer of Christianity to lands that never knew of Christ.

Columbus was at court for Whitsuntide, Trinity Sunday and Corpus Christi, but probably the ceremony that interested him most was the baptism of the six Indians. The King and Queen and Infante Don Juan graciously consented to act as godparents. The first in rank, kinsman to Guacanagarí, they christened Ferdinand of Aragon; another, Don Juan of Castile; while the clever interpreter was named Diego Colón. Don Juan remained attached to the royal household and died within two years; the other five returned with the Admiral to the New World.

While these baptisms expressed the good intentions of the Sovereigns and Columbus toward the Indians, it is notorious that in the Indies conversion and Christian treatment of them never came about until human greed was satisfied. Almost the entire native population of the Bahamas, Puerto Rico and Hispaniola was exterminated within half a century, by forced labor and Spanish cruelty.

Columbus stayed for several weeks at Barcelona, entertained by the nobility and higher clergy and looking after his own interests. The rights and privileges granted him conditionally were confirmed. As Viceroy and Governor of the islands he discovered that he and his heirs could appoint and remove all officials in the Indies and have civil and criminal jurisdiction over them; as Admiral of the Ocean Sea he would have jurisdiction over all who sailed the ocean west and south of a line from the Azores to the Cape Verdes.

Nobody had the faintest notion what enormous wealth would pour in on the Columbus family if all these privileges were respected. Sovereigns and Discoverer alike only presupposed a trading factory on a cluster of islands not far from China. Yet, Columbus within twenty years would have become one of the richest men in Europe. As it happened, Ferdinand and Isabella,

with little respect for vested rights, began to revoke his privileges before he had gained much profit.

During the three months that Columbus resided at Barcelona, news of his discovery spread by means of the printed version of his Letter, the Latin translation of which was printed in Rome, Paris, Basle and Antwerp. But the news traveled very slowly. Columbus's brother Bartholomew, living near Paris, did not hear it in time to join the Admiral on his Second Voyage.

Judging from letters and chronicles, the items that aroused most public attention were gold, the opportunity for conversion, and the nakedness of the natives. Columbus had stressed conver-

April 1493, fresh from discoveries
...e New World, Columbus stood
... again before the King and Queen.
...eft, a lithograph of his triumphal
...otion at court. Below that, the
... of arms conferred upon him by
Sovereigns, and to the far left,
...ld disk of a crocodile god from
...ama. The Spaniards were the
... Europeans to see such wondrous
...ts as flying fish, plantain, and
...apple, shown above and at right.
... letter is one from Columbus
...e Sovereigns setting forth
...deas on colonization. The
...pbacked idol is from Dominica.

sion in his Letter, as well as opening of a new trade route to China. But nobody paid much attention to that. There was not one hint of the real significance of this, the most spectacular and far-reaching geographical discovery in recorded history: the discovery of a New World. For America was discovered by Columbus by accident, and although he later called the continent a "New" and "Other World," he never knew a hundredth part of what he had opened up. But that does not diminish the magnitude of his achievement. No other man had the persistence, knowledge and sheer courage to sail thousands of miles into the unknown ocean until he found land.

53

5. Second Voyage to America

ALTHOUGH NO VOYAGE, unless it be Magellan's, can ever equal Columbus's First for interest and importance, we must not forget that the Discoverer made three more voyages to America, each of which was sufficient to place him in the first rank of the world's navigators.

The Second Voyage, the biggest overseas colonizing expedition ever sent out by a European nation, was organized at Cadiz. The Sovereigns gave Columbus carte blanche and on May 29, 1493, issued their instructions. Prime object of the Second Voyage was the conversion of natives, for which purpose six priests, headed by Fray Buil, were assigned to the fleet. It is strange that more and abler priests were not appointed, since the six took three years to win their first convert. The second objective was the establishment of a permanent trading colony in the New World. Third, the Admiral was to explore Cuba and ascertain whether it was the Asiatic mainland.

Although Columbus was "Captain General of the Armada," Don Juan de Fonseca, Archdeacon of Seville, was appointed to organize the fleet while the Admiral completed his diplomatic business at court. In June, accompanied by his younger brother Diego, Columbus took the pilgrims' road to Guadalupe in the Estremadura, passing through Trujillo, where a thirteen-year-old boy named Francisco Pizarro, the future conqueror of Peru, was caring for his father's swine. Columbus prayed long and fervently before the famous shrine of the Virgin of Guadalupe.

Early in July they arrived at Cadiz. Fonseca had done an excellent job. He had bought or chartered seventeen vessels, victualed them for a round voyage of six months, recruited twelve hundred sailors, soldiers and colonists, and collected the necessary plants, domestic animals and implements for the colony. One curious element in the expedition was a cavalry troop of twenty lancers, who sold their fine Arab chargers in Cadiz, purchased some sorry hacks and lived high on the difference; but the substitute nags proved to be good enough to terrorize the natives of Hispaniola.

Of the seventeen vessels we know the names of very few. One was gallant *Niña*. The biggest, named *Santa María* like the flagship on the First Voyage, was a big, brave ship nicknamed *Maríagalante*. Of the personnel, the Pinzón family were conspicuously absent, but most of the sailors were from around Huelva, as on the First Voyage. In 1492 it had required the utmost persuasiveness to induce any but the very young and adventurous to ship with Columbus; now the Admiral was embarrassed by thousands of men and boys eager to go with him. No women were taken. Everyone was on the royal payroll except about two hundred gentlemen volunteers.

Unfortunately, no official log of this Voyage has survived, but we have detailed accounts from three participants—Dr. Diego Chanca, the fleet surgeon; Michele de Cuneo, a childhood friend of Columbus; and Melchior Maldonado, a former Spanish diplomat. Columbus, moreover, told Andrés Bernáldez, a Spanish chronicler with whom he stayed at the conclusion of the voyage, many details which Bernáldez set down in his History.

On September 25, 1493, a bright autumn day with a light offshore breeze, "this fleet so united and handsome," as Columbus called it, departed Cadiz. Every vessel flew the royal standard of Castile, and every skipper dressed ship with big, brightly colored banners and waistcloths emblazoned with the arms of the gentlemen volunteers. A fleet of row galleys from Venice, which happened to be in the harbor, escorted the ships and caravels to the open sea, with music of trumpets and harps and the firing of cannon.

On October 2 the fleet called at the Grand Canary, and on the fifth at Gomera. It ran into the usual Canary calms and took its final departure either on the first anniversary of the discovery of America or on October 13. Although his destination was Navidad, the Admiral did not wish to repeat the route of the First Voyage, but to make discoveries in the Lesser Antilles.

The Indians had told him that an island named Matinino (Martinique) lay to the eastward, and so was the nearest island in the Caribbean to Spain; and that the second in order was Charis (Dominica). So the Admiral set a direct course for that strategic corner of the Lesser Antilles.

The ocean passage was uneventful except for a thundersquall which split a number of sails and lighted those ghostly flares called corposants on the tips of the masts and yards. The rest of the way the ships enjoyed fair wind and made the 2600 nautical miles to Dominica in twenty-one or twenty-two days.

This outward passage must have been very close to a sailor's dream of the good life at sea. Sailing before the trades in a square-rigger is as near heaven as any seaman expects to be on the ocean. There is a constant play of light and color on the bellying square sails (silver in the moonlight, gold at sunset, white as clouds at noon), the gorgeous deep blue of the sea, flecked with whitecaps. From the high-pooped flagship one could see the white sails of the fleet all around the horizon. Every day the faster vessels romped ahead, racing one another, but toward sundown, as the hour of singing the *Salve Regina* approached, all closed *Maríagalante*. Imagine the beautiful spectacle, and what good ship handling it required! As night fell, every ship lit her stern lantern, and throughout the hours of darkness, kept assigned stations.

On All Saints' Day the Admiral was so confident of making land within seventy-two hours that he issued an extra allowance of water. At sundown November 2 he knew land was near by the gathering clouds over the horizon and the flight of birds. He ordered sail to be shortened that night, lest they overrun the land in the darkness—there was to be no moonrise until shortly before dawn. On Sunday, November 3, as the first faint gray of dawn appeared in the east, a lookout in *Maríagalante* noted a dark cone blotting out a section of the star-studded horizon. He sang out, *"Albricias! Que tenemos tierra!"* (The reward! For we have land!) The cry of *"Tierra! Tierra!"* passed from ship to ship; all was bustle and excitement, and the Admiral summoned all hands to prayer on the quarterdeck, where they sang the *Salve Regina*.

IT WAS THE ISLAND of Dominica that they saw, so named by the Admiral from his Sunday landfall. The most amazing thing about this voyage is that Columbus hit the Lesser Antilles at the exact spot recommended by sailing directions for the next four centuries! At that point there is a clear passage between the islands, without dangerous reefs, and once inside the island chain you are almost certain to have a fair wind, wheresoever you are bound.

As the light increased on November 3 and the fleet sped westward, they picked up next a round, flat island which Columbus named Santa María Galante (now Mariegalante) as a tribute to his flagship, and a group of islands which he called Todos los Santos for the day of All Saints just passed. Columbus settled on an anchorage on the lee side of Mariegalante, where he went ashore and took possession for Spain, while the secretary of the fleet recorded everything in proper legal form.

During the day a high island was sighted a few leagues to the west. Columbus ordered anchors aweigh and course set thither. This big, kidney-shaped island he named Santa María de Guadalupe after the shrine in Estremadura. Guadeloupe, as the French called it, became their oldest colony and a valuable sugar island.

As Columbus's fleet approached Guadeloupe, they saw a beautiful high waterfall, slender as a silver thread, that appeared to plunge right out of the clouds hanging over the mountains. The vessels anchored in a sheltered bay under the island's five-thousand-foot volcano, and there remained five or six days.

Columbus did not intend to stay more than one night, but his shore party under Diego Márquez got lost in the dense tropical rain forest, the first that Spaniards had ever encountered. The Admiral did not dare to leave them behind to be picked up later, since there would have been nothing but bones to pick. In the course of their wanderings, four search parties had learned a good deal about the customs of the natives called Caribs, from which the word cannibal is derived. In huts deserted by the natives they found human limbs and partly consumed flesh, as well as boys who were being fattened for a feast, and twelve Taino girls who had been captured in a raid on Hispaniola.

Diego's men were finally located by one of the search parties.

From Guadeloupe on, the fleet enjoyed a spectacular passage along the coasts of the Lesser Antilles. Those waters afford the finest winter sailing in the world. Each island is a mountain peak rising four or five thousand feet from the Caribbean, whose depths a few hundred yards from shore are sapphire blue, while the shoals vary from brilliant emerald to golden yellow.

Columbus, even more than most sailors, was devoted to the Virgin Mary, protectress of mariners, and for several days he named almost every island after one or another of her shrines.

After Guadeloupe the fleet passed an island that Columbus named Santa María de Monserrate from a famous monastery near Barcelona. Next came a little round island that he called

Sixteenth-century woodcut of man-eating Indians.

Santa María la Redonda, and Santa María la Antigua, named after an ancient painting of the Virgin in Seville.

The night of November 12–13 the Admiral set a course almost due west, to an island whose direction his Indian guides pointed out. This island, which the Admiral called Santa Cruz, and for which we now use the French form Saint Croix, is the first future United States territory discovered by Columbus. Unlike the heavily forested islands that they had passed, Saint Croix was intensively cultivated by its Carib inhabitants, and resembled one great garden. They anchored off a small estuary now called Salt River Bay, and here had their first fight with the natives of America.

At noon November 14 Columbus sent an armed boat with twenty-five men to the head of this harbor, where he saw a small village. The inhabitants fled, but as the boat was returning to the flagship, a Carib dugout suddenly came around the point. The Indians at first were stupefied by the sight of the great ships, but presently recovered their courage, and though they numbered only four men and two women, took up their bows and arrows and let fly, wounding two Spaniards, one mortally. The boat rammed and upset the canoe, but the Caribs swam to a rock where they fought like demons until overcome and taken. One of the men had been shot up so that his intestines hung out, and the Spaniards threw him overboard, but he struck out toward shore. Recaptured, bound hand and foot and again thrown into the sea, "this resolute barbarian" managed to cast off his bonds and swim. He was then shot through with crossbow arrows until he died. A horde of Caribs, so painted as to terrify the Spaniards, ran down to the shore, eager for revenge, but they had no weapons that could reach the ships.

This skirmish at Salt River Bay gave the Spaniards a healthy respect for the Caribs, whom they left alone, visiting their islands only with strong armed parties and attempting no settlement for many years.

Columbus did not tarry at Saint Croix, lest the Caribs bring up reinforcements and give real battle. Having already noted a number of islands over the northern horizon, he decided to investigate them. As the ships approached, more and more islands appeared. The Admiral appropriately named them Las Once Mil Virgines after the eleven thousand seagoing Virgins from Cornwall who, according to legend, were martyred by the Huns at Cologne. To explore these Virgin Islands the Admiral used the smaller ships. He sent them through the easterly passage to look at Anegada, after which they squared away down the passage now named after Sir Francis Drake. The sailors marveled at the dazzling colors of some of the rocks and at the pink coral beaches. In the meantime *Maríagalante* and the larger vessels sailed in deep water south of the two larger islands, now Saint John and Saint Thomas.

After another night hove to, the fleet made the south coast of a big island which the natives called Boriquen; the Admiral named it for Saint John the Baptist. One of his shipmates on this voyage, Ponce de León, early in the next century founded the city of San Juan de Puerto Rico. From that city this island has derived its modern name. All day November 19 Columbus's fleet sailed along the steep southern coast of Puerto Rico and on the morning of the twentieth beat into spacious Añasco Bay at the southwest end. There the men went fishing, took on fresh water and visited a big Carib village from which all the natives had fled.

At eventide November 22 the fleet made landfall on Cape Engaño, Hispaniola, the great island discovered on the First Voyage. An Indian whom Columbus had picked up at Samaná Bay in January recognized it and directed the fleet to his home village. He was set ashore, well provided with trading truck, in the hope that he would mitigate the fears of the suspicious Indians there. Apparently that worked, and a number of Ciguayos visited the ships and traded.

The fort at Navidad, in the illustrated edition of the Columbus letter, 1493.

From now on Columbus ranged a coast that he had already discovered. Although eager to contact his men at Navidad, he anchored off Monte Cristi to investigate a site for settlement. There a shore party got the first hint of what had happened to the Navidad garrison. On the banks of the Rio Yaque del Norte they found two dead, naked bodies; they were unrecognizable but bearded, and Indians do not grow beards.

On the evening of November 27 the fleet anchored outside Cape Haitien harbor; the Admiral, in view of what had happened to the *Santa María* on the previous voyage, refused to enter in the dark. Flares were lighted and cannon fired, but there was no answer from shore. Late at night a canoe approached, full of Indians calling for "Almirante." When they recognized Columbus, they presented him with gifts from Guacanagarí and assured him that the Spaniards at Navidad were all right—except that a few had died. A gross understatement! Diego Colón, the Indian interpreter, got the truth out of them: so horrible a tale that Columbus at first refused to believe it.

The Spaniards at Navidad had acted without reason or restraint. Two of the leaders, including Gutiérrez, the crown official, formed a gang and roamed the island looking for more gold and women. They fell afoul of Caonabó, cacique of Mayguana in the center of Hispaniola, who was made of stouter stuff than the feeble Guacanagarí. He seized and killed the Gutiérrez gang and then attacked Navidad. In the meantime, most of the other Spaniards had gone a-roving; only ten were left to guard the fort, and they had posted no guards. Caonabó disposed of them easily, and then hunted down and slaughtered all the Spaniards who had taken to the bush.

This ended the honeymoon period between Christians and natives. And it reduced the Spaniards' respect for Columbus, who had always dwelt on the timidity of the Tainos and their lack of weapons. Fray Buil, head of the priestly contingent, recommended that Guacanagarí be put to death as an example to the rest; the Admiral refused, and that cacique remained a faithful ally to the Spaniards.

The immediate problem before Columbus was to choose a site

for his trading-post colony. Dr. Chanca ruled out the swampy shores of Caracol Bay. So the Admiral decided to sail eastward in search of a good harbor. Going against the trades and the current meant a long, tedious beat to windward; it took the fleet twenty-five days to make good about 32 miles. Frequent shifting of sail and constant wetting with spray wore the sailors down, and killed a large portion of the livestock. Thus it was that on January 2, 1494, when the fleet anchored in the lee of a peninsula that afforded shelter from the east wind, Columbus decided to pitch his settlement then and there. It was founded under an evil star, although named Isabela after the Queen.

Despite the fate of Navidad, Columbus must have derived great satisfaction from this voyage to Hispaniola. He had conducted across the Atlantic seventeen vessels, made a perfect landfall, and continued through a chain of uncharted islands with no accident serious enough to be recorded. He had discovered twenty large islands and over twoscore small ones. Over the biggest fleet that had yet crossed deep water, bearing twelve hundred seamen, colonists and men-at-arms, he had kept discipline during a voyage that lasted fourteen weeks. In a region inhabited by fierce man-eating Caribs he had avoided conflict save for one brief skirmish, and lost but a single man.

Plenty of trouble was awaiting the Admiral when he exchanged the function of Captain General for that of Viceroy. The turn in his fortune was sharp and quick. In the years to come, when suffering in body from arthritis and in mind from the ingratitude of princes, Columbus must have sought consolation in the memory of those bright November days of 1493, the fleet gaily coasting along the lofty, verdure-clad Antilles with clouds piling up over the summits and rainbows bridging their deep-cleft valleys, of nights spent hove to with his gallant ships all about, stars of incredible brightness overhead, and hearty voices joining in the evening hymn to the Blessed Virgin.

6. The First Colony

COLUMBUS PLANNED a colony in Hispaniola where he believed that he would deal with a wealthy Oriental race who had vast stores of precious metals, gems and spices which they would be glad to sell. The concept would have been sound if the premise had been correct, but unfortunately for Columbus, it was not. He had noted with some discomfiture on his First Voyage that the Indians had little to sell and even fewer wants, but they kept baiting him with tales of abundant gold in the Cibao, the interior valley of Hispaniola.

So Isabela was founded as a trading post. As such it was ill chosen. There was no fresh water handy and no proper harbor. The place was swarming with malaria-carrying mosquitoes. But Columbus was in a hurry to get his men ashore and send the ships home. He had wasted a month looking for a site which the Navidad garrison should have found, and the gold which they should have collected was not there. He must start trading quickly and produce something to please his Sovereigns.

So all the colonists and some of the seamen were landed at Isabela. A town was laid out with church and governor's palace fronting on a plaza. Men were set to work felling trees and digging a canal to bring water from the nearest river. About two hundred wattled huts were built as temporary housing. But insufficient provisions had been brought. Workers fell ill of malaria or from drinking well water and eating strange fish. Columbus, impatient to get things done, drafted some of the gentlemen volunteers for the hard labor, which caused great indignation. Many, however, were appeased by an early opportunity to gather gold. Isabela had been founded only four days when the Admiral organized an armed party to explore the Cibao and find the alleged mine. It was commanded by Alonso de Hojeda, an agile, wiry and handsome Andalusian who had attracted the Queen's notice and obtained command of a caravel by the singular feat of pirouetting on a beam that projected from a tower two hundred feet above a street in Seville.

Hojeda's party penetrated the great central valley of Hispaniola and reached the foothills of the Cordillera Central in the Cibao. There he found plenty of gold, including one nugget with metal enough for a fifty-dollar gold piece. Within two weeks, he was at Isabela, bringing the first good news for many weeks. "All of us made merry," wrote Cuneo, "not caring any longer about spicery, but only for this blessed gold."

But the crew of seventeen ships were accumulating pay and using up food, several hundred men were sick, Dr. Chanca was out of drugs, and there were barely enough provisions left to get the fleet home. So, retaining only five ships, the Admiral dispatched the other twelve vessels under command of his flag captain, Antonio de Torres. The cargo they carried was topped off with gold to the value of 30,000 ducats—about $70,000 in pre-1934 gold dollars. A pretty sample, indeed!

Torres made a quick homeward passage, arriving at Cadiz on March 7. He was entrusted by Columbus with giving the Sovereigns a report of the voyage so far. Through Torres he excuses himself for not sending more gold because many of his men have fallen sick, a strong garrison has to be kept at Isabela, and with no beasts of burden to carry the heavy metal the accumulation of a shipload would require too much time.

Next, the Admiral enjoins Torres to tell Their Highnesses that the cause of the prevalent sickness "is the change of water and air; . . . the preservation of health depends upon this people being provided with the food to which they are accustomed in Spain." As it will take time for the wheat and barley that he had planted to make a crop, and for the vines and ratoons that he has set out to bear grapes and sugarcane, food must be supplied from Spain, particularly wine, ship biscuit, bacon and pickled beef. He also needs cattle and sheep, and asses and mares to breed mules. He would also appreciate a few luxuries for the sick, such as sugar, raisins, rice, almonds and honey. Clothing was another problem. The Spaniards were rapidly wearing out clothes and shoes; Columbus wants quantities of each, and he needs more firearms, crossbows, and cuirasses for protection against poisoned arrows, and plenty of powder and lead.

Ferdinand and Isabella felt that their Viceroy's requests were reasonable. They ordered Archdeacon Fonseca to make arrangements to send out all the items that the Admiral wanted. The Admiral concluded his memorandum by a generous tribute to Dr. Chanca and other subordinates, asked to have their salaries raised, and recommended that the two hundred gentlemen volunteers be placed on the royal payroll so that they could be controlled.

This report shows good sense on the part of the Discoverer, and a flexibility that was unusual for him. His trading-post idea had gone down the drain because the Indians of Hispaniola were not traders and cared little for European goods. He no longer wants a trading factory, but a beachhead—a springboard to conquest. To obtain gold the Spaniards must go and get it, a procedure which turned out to be very unfortunate for the Indians.

About a month after sending the fleet home, Columbus organized a reconnaissance of the interior. In military formation with drums beating, trumpets sounding and banners displayed, several hundred men started south from Isabela, crossed the Cordillera Setentrional and came to a spacious valley that the Admiral named Vega Real (the Royal Plain). The hidalgos marched between maize fields, under mahogany, ebony and silk-cotton trees, and past villages where they were offered little packets of gold dust. Crossing the Rio Yaque del Norte, they pushed up the northern slope of the Cordillera Central to a mesa where Columbus left fifty men to construct a rough earthen fort. One of his ablest lieutenants, Pedro Margarit, was left in command of this fort, which was named Santo Tomás as a joke on one of the hidalgos who doubted the existence of gold in Hispaniola.

Those left behind at Isabela had found no gold to compensate for living in that unhealthy spot, and almost the last of the provisions were spent. Discontent was rife, mutiny was seething, several troublemakers were in irons, and as a precaution Columbus placed all arms and munitions on board his flagship.

To raise morale and get rid of the troublemakers, he now planned a second reconnaissance under Hojeda, consisting of four hundred men with orders to march to Santo Tomás, relieve Margarit's garrison, and then explore the country and live off the natives. This was one of Columbus's worst decisions. He instructed Hojeda to do the Indians no harm, but the first thing that Hojeda did was to cut off the ears of an Indian who stole some old clothes. Next, he manacled the cacique whom he considered responsible and sent him in chains to Isabela. Hojeda then relieved Margarit, whose garrison roamed the Vega Real extorting gold from the natives, exhausting their food supplies, carrying off boys as slaves and young girls as concubines.

Before Columbus could learn of these doings, he had departed to explore Cuba, leaving his younger brother in charge at Isabela. Diego was a virtuous person, peaceable and simple, whose real ambition was to be a bishop. He was incapable of

65

raising the morale of the colonists, much less of controlling egoists like Hojeda and Margarit. But Columbus felt that there was no one else whom he could trust.

ONCE COLUMBUS adopted a geographical theory, it was almost impossible for him to give it up. He had explored enough of Hispaniola to decide that it bore no resemblance to the Japan described by Marco Polo. So he decided that Cuba was the Chinese province of Mangi, the name which Marco Polo gave to all south China.

Three caravels, *Niña*, *San Juan* and *Cardera*, sailed from Isabela April 24, 1494. It was the best season for navi-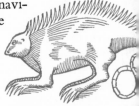gating the Greater Antilles, when the trades can be depended on; the air is still cool, and there is no danger of hurricanes. On the twenty-ninth Columbus landed at Cape Alpha and Omega, set up a cross and again took formal possession of Cuba for Spain.

A sixteenth-century representation of an

On the advice of his officers, he decided to range the south rather than the north coast, "because anything good would be to the southward." This was Aristotle's ancient theory, supported by Portuguese experience in Africa, that the farther south one sailed, the more gold and precious wares would be encountered.

As evening fell on the last day of April, they entered a great sickle-shaped harbor which Columbus named Puerto Grande. This was Guantánamo Bay. A shore party found that the natives had fled in the midst of cooking a gigantic dinner of fish, roast iguana (the favorite native delicacy) and hutía (the small Cuban quadruped) for a visiting cacique. The cooks were persuaded to return and share the feast with the Spaniards and were well paid with hawkbells and other trifles for their trouble.

On May Day morning the fleet departed with the land breeze. The Guantánamo Indians having passed the word by "grapevine," as the ships sailed close to the shore, multitudes flocked to the water's edge or paddled out in canoes, offering cassava bread and sweet water and begging the "men from the sky" to call. It will be remembered that there had been no unfortunate incidents between Spaniards and natives in Cuba, and Columbus, to his credit, so kept it to the end of this voyage.

West of Guantánamo, Columbus landed at a cape which he named Cabo de Cruz, because it was the accepted date of discovery of the True Cross. Here, instead of turning into the Gulf of Guacanayabo, the Admiral decided to take off for Jamaica, the existence of which he had been told by the Indians. He hoped here to find gold.

The fleet had a rough passage of two days. Since it had been "all hands on deck" for many hours, Columbus sent all hands below for a much needed rest as soon as *Niña* was hove to. Later the Admiral, noting that the weather was moderating, came on deck and set about making sail himself in order not to disturb the weary watch. This consideration that Columbus showed to his crew helps to explain the loyalty of his sailors, despite the many hardships he led them into and the few rewards that his voyages brought them.

On May 5 the fleet anchored in Saint Ann's Bay, Jamaica, which Columbus named Santa Gloria. He declared that this island was "the fairest that eyes have beheld" and the most heavily populated of the Greater Antilles. Sixty or seventy Indian warriors in big dugout canoes came out to meet the fleet and showed every intention to fight, but a cannon shot sent them paddling fast to shore. They promptly appeased the Spaniards with provisions, but were unable to produce gold. So the fleet resumed its exploration of the south Cuban coast, alert for evidences of Chinese culture. At sunrise May 15 they sighted an archipelago of small islands which Columbus named El Jardín de la Reina (The Queen's Garden). According to his description, these cays were then very beautiful. The Spaniards admired "great birds like cranes, but bright red"—flamingos—and watched the natives hunting turtle with tame fish. An Indian would catch a pilot fish with suckers on his head and let it out on a leash when turtles were about. The fish would attach itself to a turtle, and the Indian only had to haul it in. Cubans still practice the same method.

As the three caravels sailed along the bold coast of Sierra de Trinidad, natives again flocked to the shore bearing gifts and welcoming the Spaniards. But not one Chinese junk or sampan or temple or bridge! Could it be that the culture of Cathay had not reached this outlying part of the Grand Khan's dominions? Or was this only one more big island?

Columbus investigated the Gulf of Cochinos, noting the subterranean streams that break out under the sea and enable sailors to fill their water casks without going ashore.

The fleet then entered the Gulf of Batabanó, where the Admiral saw a phenomenon that has intrigued many later navigators —water turning as white as milk, and then black as ink. The white is caused by fine marl becoming roiled by waves in the shallow sea, and the inky color by black sand similarly stirred up. The shores of this gulf, said the Admiral in very vivid language, were of mangrove, "so thick a cat couldn't get ashore." By May 27 he anchored near the present town of Batabanó.

And no sign of China! The natives near Trinidad, either to please the Admiral or because they knew no better, said that the coast continued westward indefinitely, and that the western region was called Magón, which Columbus interpreted to mean the Chinese province of Mangi.

Sailing westward along the southern shore of the province of Pinar del Río, the caravels became involved in the worst shoals yet experienced. They could get through some channels only by the laborious process of kedging—rowing an anchor ahead, dropping it and hauling the vessel up to it by the windlass while her keel scraped the mud.

Captain Lecky remarks in his famous *Wrinkles in Practical Navigation*, "comparatively few sailors are good mathematicians, and . . . it is fortunate that such is the case; for Nature rarely combines mathematical talent . . . with that practical tact, observation . . . and readiness in an emergency, so essential to a successful sea Captain . . ." How well that description fits Columbus! He now figured that he was at least halfway around the world, when he was actually less than one quarter. Assuming the Bahía Cortés to be the Gulf of Siam, he believed that he need only round the Malay Peninsula to enter the Strait of Malacca. Why not return to Spain around the world, following the tracks of Bartholomeu Dias and Vasco de Gama?

Fortunately the common sense of a good seaman came to the rescue. The caravels were leaky because of frequent groundings; their sails and rigging were fast becoming reduced to shreds and tatters; provisions were low, and the seamen were grumbling. So the Admiral decided to reverse course. They were then about fifty miles from the western promontory of Cuba. He had everyone on board sign a paper to the effect that they judged Cuba to be a promontory of China, and that it was no use sailing farther west.

The return to Isabela began on June 13, 1494. For the most part it was a very tiresome beat to windward among the same cays as on the outward passage, because Columbus could make no progress in deep water against the trade winds and the westward-flowing current.

Columbus learned that the only way to make progress windward was to stay in smooth water, avoiding the current, and to work the land breeze at night. It took him twenty-five days to make good about 200 miles. By the time he reached The Queen's Garden he could stand no more mud navigation and steered into blue water. And it then took him ten days to make 180 miles to windward. Provisions had to be rationed, and the sailors pumped water constantly. Finally, on July 18, they reached Cape Cruz and were well entertained by friendly Indians. Rather than endure another long beat to windward to Guantánamo, the Admiral decided to learn more about Jamaica.

Montego Bay was entered on July 21. From there he hauled around the south coast and edged along, anchoring every night. The Indians were friendly, one cacique embarrassingly so. He came out to the flagship with a fleet of canoes, his family and suite dressed in magnificent feather headdresses and little else. The cacique wore a coronet of small polished stones and some large disks of gold and copper alloy that he must have obtained from Central America. In the bow of his canoe stood a herald wearing a cloak of red feathers and carrying a white banner. His wife was similarly adorned with native jewelry, although she wore nothing that could be called clothing except "a little cotton thing no bigger than an orange peel"; their daughters, aged about fifteen and eighteen, were completely naked and very beautiful. When this array of savage magnificence drew along-side, the Admiral was praying in his cabin and did not know what was up until they were all on board. The cacique then proposed that he and his family sail to Spain with the Admiral to visit the Catholic Sovereigns. Here was a golden opportunity for Columbus to make a hit at court, but humanity prevailed. He thought of the cold weather on the voyage home, of the indignities that the pretty daughters might suffer from the sailors, and of the effect of civilization on these innocent souls. So he sent them ashore with gifts, after receiving the cacique's homage and fealty to Ferdinand and Isabella.

By the end of August the fleet reached Alta Vela, the rock which marks the southernmost point of Hispaniola. Swarms of Indians paddled out and told Columbus that all was well at Isabela—which was far from correct. He landed a party of nine men and sent them across the island to announce his coming.

The Admiral intended to make a side trip to Puerto Rico, but crossing Mona Passage he became very ill. His symptoms suggest a nervous breakdown as the result of lack of sleep and inadequate food. His officers decided to scud before the wind to Isabela, where the three caravels anchored on September 29, 1494. The Admiral was carried ashore in the arms of his seamen.

Although Columbus had not found the empire of the Grand Khan, he had accomplished a great deal on this five months' voyage from Isabela. He had opened up what proved to be the most valuable of Spain's insular possessions, having explored the south coast of Cuba, and discovered Jamaica. He had demon-strated that he was no less apt at coastal piloting than at conduct-ing a fleet across an ocean. Shipmates of that voyage never tired of extolling his feats of navigation.

THE FIRST NEWS that the Admiral received upon landing at Isabela was good. His brother Bartholomew, whom he had not seen for six years, had arrived. Bartholomew had reached Spain too late to catch the start of the Second Voyage. But Ferdinand and Isabella were highly impressed by "Don Bartolomé," and gave him command of three caravels to take provisions to Hispaniola, as Columbus had requested.

Christopher was overjoyed to see his brother. Bartholomew was a man of action, a perfect executive to carry out the ideas of his brilliant brother. He was a good linguist and had an innate sense of leadership. Tough with subordinates, he lacked Christopher's sweetness and benignity, but he was dependable. He never lost courage, and he met unexpected situations with promptness and resolution.

It is most regrettable that Bartholomew "missed the boat" on the Second Voyage because he, if anyone, could have averted the appalling situation in Hispaniola which the weak Diego had allowed to develop. It must be said, however, that the Columbus brothers had two strikes against them from the start, because they were Italians and the colonists were Spaniards. Spain was fiercely nationalistic, and the Spaniards who went to America to seek their fortunes were not only rugged individualists, but greedy and unreasonable. Christopher made two bad mistakes—appointing Diego his deputy, and turning Hojeda and Margarit loose in the interior.

During the Admiral's absence, Diego heard about the rapacity of Margarit and sent him an order to mend his ways, which so enraged the Spaniard that he roared into Isabela demanding retraction. When he didn't get it, he joined other malcontents, who seized the caravels that Bartholomew had brought from Spain, and sailed home. One of those rebel leaders was Fray Buil, the ecclesiastic in charge of conversion. He had not won a single convert among the docile Tainos, but had consistently opposed all that the Columbus brothers did. When the stolen caravels arrived in Spain late in 1494, Fray Buil went directly to court to circulate slanders against the Admiral and his brothers, while a Sevillian goldsmith of the party declared that none of the gold in Hispaniola was genuine. That probably was a "cover story" for the rebels, who secretly sold their loot without paying the Crown's 20 percent or the Admiral's 10.

Within a month or two of Columbus's return to Isabela, Antonio de Torres sailed into the roadstead in command of four caravels bringing more provisions and supplies. He delivered a friendly letter to the Admiral from the King and Queen, who urged him to leave Hispaniola in charge of his brother and come

Thick, steamy jungles presented a major obstacle to the Spaniards. On the right-hand page is a typical mangrove swamp of the sort that often confronted the expedition. Below that, an early woodcut showing Indians manning a canoe. The gold eagle ornament is from Panama. A strange, beautiful bird often sighted by the Spaniards in the New World was the flamingo, portrayed on this page by the sixteenth-century watercolorist, John White. Below left, a woodcut showing New World natives. The cedar Indian paddle below was in use during the time of Columbus.

home to help them in negotiations with Portugal. Here was an opportunity for Columbus to refute the slanders of Buil and Margarit. But he stayed on, either because he was too ill to face the ocean voyage, or because he wished to get the local situation well in hand. Moreover, in order to provide a profitable export to Spain, since the amount of gold was still short of expectations, he adopted the questionable policy of rounding up and enslaving Indians who had resisted Margarit's men.

By the close of February 1495, when Torres was ready to sail to Spain, the Columbus brothers had collected fifteen hundred Indian captives at Isabela. Torres loaded five hundred of

72

them, all his four ships could take. The Admiral then allowed every Spaniard at Isabela to help himself to as many of the remainder as he chose, and the rest were told to get out. Cuneo records how these wretched captives, when released, fled as far as they could from the Spaniards; women even abandoned infants in their fear and desperation to escape further cruelty. At least they were free; the lot of the slaves shipped home was worse. About two hundred died on the voyage, and half the survivors were sick when they arrived. At Seville they were put up for sale. Almost all died, since the climate did not agree with them.

Among the captives taken to Isabela was a cacique named Guatiguaná, who escaped by gnawing through his bonds. He tried to unite the Indians of Hispaniola, estimated to be at least 250,000 in number, against the Spaniards. But the natives were incapable of united action. Caonabó joined him, but Guacanagarí remained loyal to Columbus, and the caciques of Xaragua and Higuey remained neutral. Nevertheless, Guatiguaná managed to collect a formidable army to march on Isabela. The Spaniards wisely did not wait to be surrounded, but took the offensive. The Admiral, Bartholomew and Hojeda marched to the Puerto de los Hidalgos with 20 horses, 20 hounds and 200 foot, half of them armed with arquebusses. The fire from these primitive muskets alarmed the Tainos more than it harmed them, but when the cavalry dashed into the closely huddled mass of Indians, and at the same time big savage dogs were unleashed, the rout became complete.

Hojeda followed up his victory by capturing Caonabó, who had been responsible for exterminating the Navidad garrison. He was invited to make a state visit to Isabela, and Hojeda persuaded him to wear handcuffs and shackles by telling him that they were fashionable jewelry in Spain. Then the wretched Indian was thrown into the Isabela calaboose, where he fretted and grated his teeth "like a lion."

The original Isabela beachhead was now expanded to cover the entire island. Hispaniola, by 1496, was so thoroughly subdued that a Spaniard could safely go wherever he pleased and help himself to the Indians' food, women and gold.

This conquest of Hispaniola was typical of the manner in which several European nations took possession of the Americas. Their conquest of native empires was not merely by superior weapons, horses and dogs; in every instance the Europeans had native allies. The inability of Indians to unite, and their lack of sea power, doomed them to eventual defeat. Europeans were always able to set one tribe against another. Occasionally the natives would overwhelm a European garrison by sheer numbers, or even rush one ship with a fleet of canoes, but the white men always came back.

For almost a year the Columbus brothers were occupied with

subjugating Hispaniola. Several forts were built in the interior, and armed men were sent to force the natives to deliver a tribute of gold, the alternative to being killed. Every Indian fourteen years old or over had to pay four hawkbells full of gold dust annually; caciques had to pay the equivalent of $225 in gold every month. The system was irrational and abominable. After the Indians had handed over the gold ornaments which they had accumulated through several generations, the only way they could get enough to pay the tribute was by continual, unremitting labor, washing grains of gold out of the gravel of streams or clearing the land of trees and sluicing it. Even after the tribute was cut down 50 percent it was impossible to fulfill. Indians took to the mountains; many died of starvation; others took poison. By 1508 a census showed 60,000 of the estimated 1492 population of 250,000 still alive. Fifty years later, not 500 remained. The cruel policy initiated by Columbus and pursued by his successors resulted in complete genocide.

Calumnies against Columbus made their mark on the Sovereigns, who sent Juan Aguado, a colonist who had returned to Spain with Torres, to investigate the charges. Columbus realized he had better return home to mend his political fences. The Spanish population of the island had now fallen to 630, partly because many had died from diseases, or gone home. A large number of those left behind were sick, and all were discontented. In this rich, fertile land with a beautiful climate, they were still dependent on imported provisions. Nobody unless under compulsion would trouble to sow grain, said Cuneo, because "nobody wants to live in these countries."

Columbus named Bartholomew the commander in his absence. Ordering him to abandon Isabela and found a new capital on the south coast, he sailed home in *Niña* on March 10, 1496.

On June 11 Columbus's Second Voyage to America ended in the Bay of Cadiz. This return was a sad contrast to the pomp and pride of the outward passage in 1493. Every available banner was run up to make as brave an appearance as possible, but it was a sad show at best, with the miserable Indians and Spanish passengers whom an onlooker described as wasted in their bodies and with "faces the color of saffron."

When the Admiral's great fleet had departed Cadiz, he had had grand expectations of starting a valuable colony and locating the Emperor of China. Now Columbus appeared to many to be an importunate and impractical dreamer. Cuba was no limb of China. Isabela was a miasmic dump which even the Columbus brothers were abandoning. Instead of the promised gold mine, gold was diffused in small quantities and could only be produced by slave labor. Instead of peaceful simplicity, the natives were showing fight. And so loud and angry were the cries of returned Spaniards against the Columbus brothers that possibly the Sovereigns would have been tempted to forget about the Indies had they not heard that the King of Portugal was about to fit out a new expedition to India, and that even England was interested in finding an ocean route to Cathay.

Hispaniola must be held, if only to keep rivals out.

7. The Third Voyage to America

IT WAS ALWAYS a puzzle to Columbus why things turned out so badly for him. He performed his religious duties regularly; why, then, did Providence frown on his undertakings? He had served the Sovereigns faithfully and had won for them a new domain. Why, then, did they listen to Fray Buil and send Aguado to insult him? Perhaps it was because after his First Voyage he had worn excessive apparel and had taken too much pleasure in high company. Pride, to be sure, is a deadly sin. So, upon arrival at Cadiz, and ever after, Columbus assumed the coarse brown habit of a Franciscan as evidence of repentance and humility; instead of accepting invitations to palaces, he put up in religious houses with rough quarters and coarse fare.

But although Columbus might be simple in his habits, he knew very well the value of publicity to impress Spaniards. So, when a gracious invitation came from the Sovereigns to visit them, he organized an impressive cavalcade. A brother of

Caonabó, who had been christened Don Diego, and another member of the cacique's family accompanied the Admiral on muleback. Servants went ahead with cages of brightly colored parrots whose screams gave advance publicity worthy of Barnum. Whenever they approached a town, feather headdresses and golden objects were unpacked from saddlebags to adorn the Indians. Don Diego wore a gold collar around his neck and on his head the elaborate crown of Caonabó.

Columbus found the King and Queen at Valladolid, and his two sons, Diego and Ferdinand, now pages to the Queen, were there to greet him. He was courteously received, especially after presenting the Sovereigns with a big basketful of gold nuggets as big as pigeons' eggs. Promptly he put in a plea to be outfitted for a Third Voyage to seek out a continent which the King of Portugal believed to be the "fourth part of the world" south of the equator.

John II of Portugal was dead, but the fact that he believed in the existence of such a continent was an incentive to Ferdinand and Isabella to get there first, and they knew that John's successor was fitting out a big overseas expedition for Vasco da Gama. His destination was secret: he might well be looking for the "fourth part of the world."

Between the end of April and the middle of June 1497, Ferdinand and Isabella confirmed Columbus's titles and privileges, and ordered him to recruit three hundred colonists, and thirty women, for Hispaniola at royal expense. These ladies got neither pay nor keep, but were expected to marry upon arrival. They were the first Christian women to go to the New World. The Sovereigns offered a pardon to all malefactors confined in jail, except those guilty of major crimes, if they would accompany the Admiral to the Indies and stay a year or two. Hispaniola had been so discredited that this was supposed to be the only way to get emigrants to the future "Land of Promise." Columbus sent these fellows ahead of him to Hispaniola, which he later had reason to regret. *Niña* and *India* sailed in January 1498. Three more caravels, whose names we do not know, were to sail directly to Hispaniola with supplies, under the command of Alonso de Carvajal, who had left his job as mayor of Baeza to command a ship on the Second Voyage, and who became one of Columbus's most faithful captains. The Admiral reserved two caravals, *La Vaqueños* and *El Correo*, and the flagship, *La Nao*, for his own Voyage of Discovery.

Columbus's vessels and the three under Carvajal departed Seville during the last week of May 1498. This time, Columbus decided to sail a more southerly course than before, both to discover King John's continent and to seek more gold. The Admiral knew very well that he must accomplish something spectacular on this voyage or the whole Enterprise of the Indies might be abandoned.

At Gomera, in the Canary Islands, Carvajal parted company with the exploring squadron. Columbus gave them their course, west by south to Dominica.

From the Canaries, Columbus set a course for the Cape Verde Islands. On July 1 he called at São Tiago in the hope of obtaining cattle to breed in Hispaniola. After staying a week there in heat so intense that many of his people fell ill, he departed without cattle. The vessels were becalmed for three days within sight of Fogo, but on July 7 the trades sprang up. Columbus shaped a course southwest. But the wind grew more and more soft, and finally died completely on July 13.

Columbus was in the doldrums, and for the next eight days his vessels drifted with the equatorial current, while their crews, who would have thought it suicidal to strip down and get tanned, sweltered in their thick woolen clothes.

On July 22 a fresh trade wind sprang up, slack lines became taut, limp sails bellied out, the ships quickly got under way, the temperature dropped, and the sailors, who had half expected to rot and die in mid-ocean (for none had before experienced whole days of calm), began talking about the gold they were going to find. The Admiral set the course due west, and for nine days, with a prosperous blast from the trade winds, his fleet made an average speed of 6 knots or better.

This leg of the voyage must have been almost pure delight to the Admiral and his men. Day and night the fleet made wonderful speed. The fair and steady wind singing in the rigging, the sapphire, white-capped sea, the rush of great waters alongside, and the endless succession of puffy trade-wind clouds lift a seaman's spirits and make him want to shout and sing.

On July 31 the Admiral announced that he was on the meridian of the Lesser Antilles, which was correct, and since the supply of fresh water was low, he decided to make a detour to water up in Dominica or some other Caribbee isle.

At noon the Admiral's servant Alonso Pérez, having gone aloft, sang out that he saw land to the westward in the form of

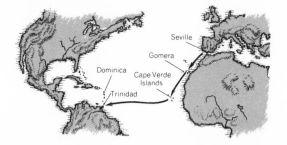

three hills. This seemed to Columbus a happy omen. He had placed this voyage under the protection of the Holy Trinity, so he named the island Trinidad. It was the last day of July 1498.

Next day, the first of August, the Admiral continued along the south coast of Trinidad, searching for a bay with a river emptying into it. With his usual good judgment, he chose the best watering place on that coast, now called Erin Bay, where a stream of cool, sweet water crosses the beach. The men went ashore, washed their clothes and wallowed in the fresh water to sluice the caked salt and sweat from their bodies.

Just before hauling into Erin Bay, Columbus had his first sight of the South American continent, but he thought it was just another island. As Erin Bay affords slight protection from the trades, Columbus weighed on August 2 and sailed into the great Gulf of Paria that lies between Trinidad and the mainland of Venezuela. He anchored in the lee of Icacos Point, Trinidad, and ordered all hands ashore for a few days' relaxation.

The only contact with the natives at this point was both comic and pathetic. Columbus had been hoping that this time he would encounter either Chinese mandarins or black potentates like those on the Gold Coast. But when a canoe approached, he observed with disgust that it contained only Indians, looking much the same as Caribs, but, fortunately, with better manners. The Admiral, hoping to start trade, caused some brass chamber pots and other shining objects to be displayed over the bulwarks, but the Trinidadians were not impressed. Next, the Admiral tried putting on a show: he ordered a pipe-and-tabor player to sound off, tambourines to be jingled, and the ships' boys to dance. The Indians evidently took this as a warming-up for a fight and let fly a shower of arrows, none of which hit. And that was all that the Spaniards saw of the natives of Trinidad.

ON AUGUST 4, as the caravels were about to square away to explore the gulf, the Spaniards had probably the greatest fright in their lives. An enormous bore or tidal wave, evidently caused by a volcanic disturbance, roared through the strait leading to the Gulf of Paria, snapped the anchor rode of *Vaqueños*, raised the flagship to what seemed an immense height, and dropped her so low that one could see bottom. The Admiral decided that this was no place to stay and named the strait La Boca de la Sierpe (The Serpent's Mouth).

Attracted by the sight of mountains of the Paria Peninsula across the gulf, Columbus now steered due north. As he approached the end of the peninsula, he enjoyed the same gorgeous view that greets a sailor today. Astern lay the placid gulf, its far shores below the horizon; westward under the setting sun stretched a succession of mountains and rugged headlands; eastward were the high, broken islands that divide the famous Bocas del Dragón, and behind them rose the mountains of Trinidad.

Columbus anchored for the night at Bahía Celeste and next day started to explore its southern shore along the gulf. Here are many harbors, and the most attractive, Ensenada Yacua, is probably the one that Columbus chose for a landing. He found a large thatched house and a fire burning, but the natives had fled, their places taken by swarms of monkeys who chattered indignantly at the Spaniards. This was the first place where Columbus set foot on the mainland of America; the first time, indeed, that any European had done so since the Vinland voyages, John

Cabot the previous summer having got no farther than Newfoundland. As usual, the Admiral did not know what he had discovered; he believed that Paria Peninsula was an island. The date was Sunday, August 5, 1498.

Since it would have been undignified to take formal possession for Spain with no other audience than monkeys, Columbus postponed the ceremony until two days later when a horde of friendly natives appeared at the mouth of the Rio Guiria. The Admiral himself was suffering severely from sore eyes, so he stayed on board and sent his senior captain, Pedro de Terreros, to take possession of this "Province."

After a preliminary distribution of beads, sugar and hawkbells, the Indians came out in a fleet of canoes bringing fruits of the country and a beer called *chicha*, fermented from maize. This is still brewed in Venezuela. They wore as ornaments great polished disks made of an alloy of copper and gold. As they had to import copper from Central America, it was more valuable to them than gold. So, greatly to the Spaniards' delight, these natives of Paria were willing to swap objects of which the greater part was gold for their weight in brass or copper.

On August 8 the fleet resumed the exploration of the gulf, and found a rich lowland with gardens and groves of big, glossy-leaved mahogany and fustic trees. Columbus named the place Los Jardínes (The Gardens). The women of one village came on board wearing necklaces of fine pearls, which caused great excitement among the Spaniards because pearls meant the Orient. The Indians were willing to sell what pearls they had for the usual trading truck, but unfortunately they had no spares; so the Admiral begged them by sign language to accumulate a few bushels of them against his return; but return he never did.

The Admiral turned west in search of an outlet to the sea. The water became fresh and turbid. Caravel *Correo*, sent ahead to reconnoiter, reported four river channels to the westward. These were the mouths of the Rio Grande, and a mouth of the Orinoco emptied a few miles away. Columbus, stubborn as usual in his geographical ideas, was not yet convinced that this was a river or that he was exploring the mainland. He turned east again at the rising of the moon on August 11.

In the small hours of the thirteenth, the fleet weighed and stood into a large strait. There they found the usual turmoil between fresh water flowing out and the salt tide roaring in, and "thought to perish" when the wind dropped and the caravels drifted toward rocks; but the fresh water prevailed over the salt, and they were slowly carried out to sea and safety. Columbus named this strait Boca del Dragón because they had escaped, as it were, the dragon's mouth, and the name is still used for all four channels that connect the Gulf of Paria with the Caribbean. Dangerous they still are for small craft.

At dawn August 15 Columbus sighted an island that he named Margarita, but he did not tarry to look for pearls as he was in a hurry to get to Santo Domingo. That decision, as it turned out, was a mistake. Discovery of the pearls that were there in abundance would have helped his prestige at home; conditions in Hispaniola would have been no worse if he had stayed another month. Again, each of his roles of Discoverer and Colonial Administrator hurt the other.

It was on this very day that it suddenly dawned on the Admiral what Paria was. For two weeks he had been sailing along the coast of the continent he sought, yet refused to believe that it was one because it did not match his idea of a continent! The vast volume of fresh water was the evidence that changed his mind. In his Journal he recorded, "I believe that this is a very great continent, until today unknown. And reason aids me greatly because of that so great river and fresh-water sea . . . and further I am supported by . . . many Carib Indians . . . who said that to the south of them was mainland . . . and they said that in it there was much gold. . . . And if this be a continent, it is a marvelous thing, and will be so among all the wise, since so great a river flows that it makes a fresh-water sea of 48 leagues."

From Margarita on August 15 he set a course for Santo Domingo, the new island capital. Due to his very proper fear of running on reefs in the dark of the moon, his navigation was cautious. He ordered the caravels to heave the lead frequently, and to make sail only by day, when dangerous reefs could be detected by changes in the color of the water. The result was that Columbus made landfall on Alta Vela, 120 miles southwest of Santo Domingo. It weighed on him to have fallen off so much, but he decided correctly that his miscalculation was caused by a strong current—the westward-running equatorial current which he had no means of gauging.

On August 21 Columbus saw a caravel approaching from the direction of Santo Domingo. The stranger luffed up alongside the flagship, and to the Admiral's delight he was hailed by his brother Bartholomew. He was pursuing the provision squadron under Carvajal, which had been sighted from shore, but had missed Santo Domingo. After this happy reunion the four caravels beat up to the new capital in eight days.

To all intents and purposes, Columbus's Third Voyage ended August 31, 1498. The Admiral had found the gateway to a vast territory extending from the Rocky Mountains to the Straits of Magellan. He wrote in his Journal: "It would be the greatest thing for Spain to have a revenue from this undertaking. . . . Your Highnesses will gain these vast lands, which are an Other World, and where Christianity will have so . . . great an in-crease. . . ."

Marvelous prophecy! At a time when Spain's first overseas colony was languishing, and settlers had to be recruited from jails; when few people believed in Columbus or thought his discoveries worth the smallest of the Canary Islands, he foretold the vast revenue that Spain would obtain from these conquests, making her the first power in Europe, and predicted that Christianity would advance triumphantly into this New and Other World.

THE CONTRAST between the terrestrial paradise of Paria and the hell that Hispaniola had become was profound and distressing. The only good news for Columbus from Bartholomew was the abandonment of hateful and unhealthy Isabela and the founding of Santo Domingo, a town of palm thatch and wattle, well sited at the mouth of a river with a well-protected harbor. Renamed Ciudad Trujillo, Santo Domingo is now the capital of the Dominican Republic.

The worst news was the rebellion led by Francisco Roldán, whom the Admiral had appointed chief justice of Hispaniola.

Roldán promised the Spaniards more gold, more slaves, a passage home for all who wished it and freedom from the rule of the Genoese. To the Indians he promised less work and no more tribute or slave raids. Guarionex, the cacique of Magua, and the Ciguayos of the Samaná peninsula joined Roldán. Bartholomew subdued them first. When he was ready to deal with Roldán, the rebel leader with seventy men retreated to Xaragua, the southwest peninsula of the island. There then occurred a most unfortunate break for the administration. Carvajal's three caravels, which had missed Santo Domingo, fetched up at Roldán's headquarters. Carvajal was steadfastly loyal to Columbus, but the former jailbirds among his passengers swarmed ashore and flocked to the rebel standard. Roldán, thus reinforced, marched on the fortress of La Vega in the center of the island. As many of the loyal Spaniards at Santo Domingo were down with various forms of disease, the Columbus brothers were unable to muster an army of equal size and dared not risk a battle. They tried appeasement.

After almost a year of parleying, in which Roldán constantly raised his terms, Columbus restored the rebel to his office of chief justice, proclaimed that all charges against him were baseless, promised free passage home with gold and slaves to those of his followers who wished to leave and land grants in Xaragua to those who wished to stay.

As part of this settlement with Roldán, and in favor both of rebels and loyalists, Columbus abandoned the last vestiges of his trading-factory colonial policy and adopted the system of *repartimientos*. This meant that a Spanish settler was allotted a plot of land to cultivate, together with, as his personal slaves, the Indians who were living on it. The caciques consented to this blow to their authority as the means of getting rid of the intolerable gold tribute, and the Spaniards liked it since it provided them with free labor and guaranteed them all the gold they could find on their own land, less the Crown's and the Admiral's percentages. *Repartimientos* did not at once make the colony pay, or save Columbus from disgrace, but they did abolish the cruel gold tribute and induce colonists to settle down.

Other problems were crowding upon the Admiral. Nothing

was more clear in his original contract than his complete authority as Viceroy and Governor over the lands he might discover, as well as his complete control over trade with or exploration of them. But when his flagship and *Correo* returned to Spain in the fall of 1498, Alonso de Hojeda got possession of the Journal and chart that Columbus sent to the Sovereigns and obtained a license to make an independent voyage to Paria to search for pearls. He took with him a map maker and a Florentine named Amerigo Vespucci, whose amusing account of this voyage led a European geographer to name the continent America. Hojeda picked up the route of Columbus's Third Voyage from the point near Margarita where he had broken off, collected a large number of pearls, discovered Aruba and Curaçao and the Gulf of Maracaibo (which he named Venezuela, Little Venice, from the native villages on piles), and finally returned to Spain. All this in the year 1499 and early 1500.

In the latter year, Peralonso Niño, former pilot of *Santa María*, made a rich haul of pearls, and Vicente Yañez Pinzón, former captain of *Niña*, discovered the northernmost mouth of the Amazon. Pretty soon every ambitious conquistador would be fitting out a voyage to America without Columbus's knowledge or consent.

At court, in the meantime, the Admiral's stock was falling. Complaints against the rule of the Columbus family accumulated. Spaniards who returned from the Indies were making nuisances of themselves. Ferdinand Columbus recorded how he and his brother Diego were mortified by these wretches shouting at them, "There go the sons of the Admiral of the Mosquitos who discovered lands of vanity and delusion, the ruin and the grave of Castilian gentlemen!"

Yet it must be admitted that as administrators the three brothers had been failures. They had been weak when they should have been firm, and ruthless at the wrong time; they had not saved the Indians from exploitation, but had offended most of the colonists.

Before receiving news that Roldán had made peace and that the repartimiento reform had been adopted, the Spanish Sovereigns appointed Francisco de Bobadilla royal commissioner in

Hispaniola, with unlimited powers over persons and property. If Bobadilla had sailed immediately, he would have arrived when matters were peaceful and the Columbus brothers were doing fairly well. Unfortunately for them, his departure was delayed for over a year, and he arrived at Santo Domingo on August 23, 1500, when the Admiral was at La Vega, Bartholomew at Xaragua, and the weak Diego in charge of the city. Upon landing, the first thing that Bobadilla saw was a gallows from which were hanging seven Spanish corpses. These men had rebelled and had been defeated and captured with Roldán's assistance. Bobadilla was shocked; without waiting to hear Columbus's side of the affair, he took over the fort, tossed Diego into the brig of his flagship, and won over the populace by proclaiming a general freedom to gather gold anywhere; when the Admiral appeared in obedience to his summons, he too was chained and confined in the town calaboose. Bartholomew, then in the interior with a loyal army, might have marched on the capital and released his brothers, but the Admiral did not wish to defy the authority that Bobadilla represented. On his advice, Bartholomew submitted, and received his share of the fetters.

Bobadilla, after compiling a file of anti-Columbus depositions from the discontented Spaniards, decided to send the three brothers home for trial. In early October the Admiral and Diego, both chained and without any of their gold or other property, were placed on board caravel *La Gorda*, bound for Spain; Bartholomew was sent in another vessel. The captain of *La Gorda* "would have knocked off the Admiral's irons," says son Ferdinand, "but he would not permit it, saying that they had been put on him by regal authority, and only the Sovereigns could order them struck off."

FAIR WINDS ATTENDED the voyage home of *La Gorda*. Before the end of October Columbus was set ashore at Cadiz, and, accompanied by his jailer, went to stay at the monastery of Las Cuevas in Seville. Six weeks elapsed before the Sovereigns ordered him released and summoned him to court. The three brothers presented themselves at the Alhambra in Granada shortly before Christmas, 1500. Son Diego, now in his twenty-first year, was there, too, and son Ferdinand, a boy of twelve. As courtiers they must have been mortified to see their aged, ailing father with marks of iron fetters on his ankles and wrists. Thereafter the Admiral kept the chains in his chamber, as a gloomy souvenir of his humiliation, and ordered that they be buried with him.

The Sovereigns spoke to Columbus in a kindly and consoling manner, and promised that justice would be done and his privileges restored. Weeks stretched into months, but nothing happened. There was always more urgent business than the affairs of distant Hispaniola to occupy the Sovereigns' attention. In the meantime, Peralonso Niño, Hojeda and others were making voyages on their own along the coast of the "Other World."

Columbus by Ridolfo Ghirlandaio

Columbus wanted complete restoration of his rights, properties, title and offices. But it was hopeless for him to expect to get everything back. He and his brothers had made too many mistakes in Hispaniola to be given the government again, and, now that the coast of South America was being opened up, it was idle to suppose that the Sovereigns would confirm privileges over an entire continent. Again, Columbus would have been well advised to settle for reasonable security, such as a castle, a pension and a title; there was no objection to his continuing to style himself Viceroy and Admiral, only to his exercising those functions. But he was not the man to give anything up.

In September 1501, after waiting eight months, Columbus learned the worst. Instead of his being sent back in triumph to Hispaniola, Bobadilla was recalled and Don Nicolás de Ovando was appointed Governor of the Islands and Mainlands of the Indies. Columbus did obtain permission to retain his titles of Viceroy and Admiral and to send out an agent in Ovando's fleet to make Bobadilla disgorge the moneys due him. Perhaps it was some consolation that the Sovereigns decided that the Enterprise of the Indies must go on. Ovando departed in February 1502 with a magnificent fleet of thirty sail, carrying 2500 sailors, soldiers and colonists.

Impatient to embark once more, Columbus asked for money and ships to make a fourth voyage to the Indies. The Sovereigns so ordered, only a month after Ovando sailed for Hispaniola.

8. The High Voyage

COLUMBUS'S FOURTH and last voyage to America is in many respects the most interesting, and he evidently thought so, too, as he always referred to it as El Alto Viaje (The High Voyage). Although at fifty-one the Admiral was already an old man by the standards of the day, he showed the highest quality of seamanship, superb courage and fitness to command.

The celerity with which Columbus got away and the ample provision made for his fleet strongly suggest a desire to get rid of him on the part of Ferdinand, and an uneasy conscience over his treatment on the part of Isabella. He actually organized an expedition in a little more than two weeks.

The Admiral's main object in this voyage was to find a strait between Cuba (which he still assumed to be China) and the continent that he had discovered in 1498. Since that time Hojeda had pushed along the Spanish Main as far as the Gulf of Darien, but the shores and waters of the Caribbean west of a line drawn from Darien to Bahía Cortés, Cuba, including the entire Gulf of Mexico, were still unknown to Europeans. Here, Columbus believed, was the key to the great geographical riddle, the relation of his recent discoveries to Asia. Here he expected to find the strait through which Marco Polo had sailed from China into the Indian Ocean. The Sovereigns gave him a letter of introduction to Vasco da Gama, again outward bound around the Cape of Good Hope, in the hope that the two would meet somewhere in India! Nobody yet suspected the existence of the Pacific

Ocean. There was only one Ocean, of which the Indian Ocean was merely another big bay, like the Mediterranean, readily accessible through the expected strait in the western Caribbean.

The Admiral had four caravels, each about the size of *Niña*, square-rigged with small main topsails. The largest, the name of which we do not know, was called *La Capitana* (The Flagship). Her captain was Diego Tristán, who had been with the Admiral on his Second Voyage, and she carried two trumpeters, presumably to provide a dignified entry for the Admiral to Oriental courts. One of her passengers was an Irish wolfhound which the Admiral brought along for anti-Indian warfare. Pedro de Terreros, the only man known to have sailed on all four of Columbus's Voyages, commanded *La Gallega* (The Galician), and Juan Quintero, her owner, shipped as master. *Santiago de Palos*, nicknamed *Bermuda* after her owner Francisco Bermúdez, was captained by Francisco Porras, whose brother Diego sailed with him as chief clerk and comptroller. Bartholomew Columbus sailed in *Bermuda* without office or pay but always took command in time of stress. Smallest of the fleet was *Vizcaína*, commanded by Bartolomeo Fieschi, scion of a leading Genoese family which had befriended the humble Colombos in times past.

Comparing the crew list with that of the First Voyage, the only other complete one we have, the principal difference was the large number of boys between twelve and eighteen on the Fourth Voyage. The Admiral had evidently discovered that on a voyage of discovery and high adventure young fellows make better seamen and obey orders more briskly than old shellbacks who grouse and grumble.

The fleet sailed from Seville April 3, 1502. At Cadiz, Columbus joined with his fourteen-year-old son Ferdinand. We are indebted to Ferdinand for a detailed account of this High Voyage, in his biography of his father. He wrote it many years later, but his youthful impressions were still vivid, and although the Admiral said that Ferdinand qualified as able seaman in the course of it, he never cared to go to sea again.

The fleet was delayed by foul winds until May 11, when it sailed with a favoring northerly. After calling at Arzila on the coast of Morocco, it reached Las Palmas and sailed from the

Grand Canary on the twenty-fifth. "West and by South," the same course as the Second Voyage, was set by the Admiral. On June 15 they made landing on Martinique for three days' rest and refreshment, and then ranged the entire chain of Antilles discovered on the Second Voyage.

On June 29, the Admiral hove to off Santo Domingo. The Sovereigns had expressly forbidden him to visit his former viceroyalty on the outward passage, lest he and Ovando run afoul each other, but the Admiral had several good excuses to look at his capital. He knew that Ovando was about to dispatch a grand fleet home and wished to send letters by it, and he hoped to persuade some shipmaster to swap a small, handy vessel for *Bermuda*, which had proved a dull sailer but would be good to carry cargo. Most important, he knew that a hurricane was making up and wished to take refuge. He had experienced hurricanes, and recognized the portents only too well.

So the Admiral sent ashore his senior captain, Pedro de Terreros, with a note to Governor Ovando, predicting a hurricane within two days, requesting permission to take refuge in Santo Domingo harbor, and begging the governor to keep all his ships in port and double their mooring lines. Ovando had the folly not only to disregard both request and warning, but to read the Admiral's note aloud with sarcastic comments to his heelers, who roared with laughter over this "soothsayer" who pretended to be able to predict the winds.

The great fleet proceeded to sea that very day, as the governor had planned. It had just rounded into the Mona Passage when the hurricane burst upon it from the northeast. Some ships foundered at sea, others were driven to shore and destroyed; among those that went down with all hands was the flagship commanded by Antonio de Torres, carrying Bobadilla and a cargo estimated at over half a million dollars in gold. Nineteen ships sank with all hands, six others were lost but left a few survivors, and four scudded safely back to Santo Domingo, arriving in a sinking condition. The only one that got through to Spain was the smallest, *Aguja*, bearing Columbus's agent Carvajal with the Admiral's own gold, which he had forced Bobadilla to disgorge.

Denied shelter for his fleet, Columbus sought it off the mouth of the Rio Jaina, a short distance west of Santo Domingo. When night fell the north wind reached the height of its fury. The three smaller caravels parted their cables and were driven out to sea, but they were well handled and escaped with only superficial damage. The Admiral had every bit of ironmongery on board frapped to *Capitana*'s cables, and she rode it out. As he remarked in a letter home, "What man ever born, not excepting Job, would not have died of despair when in such weather, seeking safety for son, brother, shipmates and myself, we were forbidden the land and the harbor that I, by God's will and sweating blood, won for Spain!"

All four ships came through, and, as agreed before the hurricane struck, all made rendezvous in Puerto Viejo de Azua. Each feared that the others were lost, but, as if by a miracle, all caught the southeast breeze that followed the hurricane and scudded into that little landlocked harbor within a few hours of each other on July 3.

After resting a week or ten days at Azua, Columbus put to sea again, steering west. They sailed along the south shore of Jamaica, then northwest. On July 27 the wind turned and the fleet crossed the Caribbean, 360 miles wide at this point, in three days. When the wind moderated, a lookout sighted the Bay Islands off the coast of Honduras. They were now in undiscovered territory.

At Bonacca, first of the Bay Islands where the fleet anchored, the Spaniards encountered the biggest native canoe any of them had seen: "long as a galley" and beamy, with a big cabin for passengers. Its interesting cargo included native cotton cloth, copper implements, crucibles for smelting ore, gourds full of beer made from the hobo fruit, and cacao beans which the Jicaque Indians of Honduras used as currency. The canoe had come from the mainland and was trading with the islands.

From the Bay Islands it was only thirty miles to Cape Honduras, off which the fleet anchored. Here began in earnest the Admiral's search for a strait. He figured he was halfway down the Malay Peninsula and that the Strait of Malacca lay east and south. So he turned eastward.

For twenty-eight days the fleet had a long and distressing beat to windward. "It was one continual rain, thunder and lightning," wrote Columbus. "The ships lay exposed to the weather, with sails torn, and anchors, rigging, cables, boats and many of the stores lost. Other tempests I have seen, but none that lasted so long or so grim as this. Many old hands whom we looked on as stout fellows lost their courage. What griped me most were the sufferings of my son; but Our Lord lent him such courage that he even heartened the rest, and he worked as though he had been to sea all of a long life. I was sick and many times lay at death's door, but gave orders from a doghouse that the people clapped together for me on the poop deck. My brother was in the worst of the ships, and I felt terribly having persuaded him to come against his will."

Nobody without Columbus's perseverance would have kept it up. The wind blew steadily from the east and the current ran counter to the course. Some days they gained a few miles; on others they fetched up opposite the same grove of mangroves off which they had spent the previous night pitching and tossing and fighting mosquitoes. The average distance made good was only six miles a day. But the Admiral dared not stand out to sea lest he miss the expected strait.

At last, on September 14, the fleet rounded a cape that the Admiral named Gracias a Dios (Thanks be to God). It marked the end of his long beat because the land now trended southward, and although the wind still blew from the east, they were able to jog along on the port tack a safe distance from shore. They anchored off Rio Grande, Nicaragua, to obtain wood and water, and then passed San Juan del Norte and entered a region that the Indians called Cariai, the present Costa Rica.

Ten days were passed at anchor behind Uva Island, off the present Puerto Limón. Here they had friendly though somewhat aloof relations with the local Talamanca Indians. The usual roles were reversed, the natives eager to do business and the Spaniards somewhat coy. First, the Indians swam out to the caravels with cotton jumpers and ornaments of *guanin*, the gold and copper alloy that Columbus had found in Paria on the Third Voyage. Evidently *guanin* was regarded in Spain as a poor substitute for pure gold, and Columbus would have none of it, but gave the would-be traders some presents to take ashore. Next, to break down "sales resistance," the Indians sent on board two virgins, one about eight and the other about fourteen years old; "they showed great courage," recorded Ferdinand (who was then about the same age as the elder), "exhibited neither grief nor sorrow but always looked pleasant and modest; hence they were well treated by the Admiral, who caused them to be fed and clothed and sent them ashore." The Spaniards' continence astonished the natives. Next day when Bartholomew went ashore, attended by clerk Torres with paper, pen and inkhorn, to take formal possession, the Indians took this to be magical apparatus and tossed brown powder into the air as "good joss" to counteract these apparently sexless sorcerers from Spain.

On October 5 the search for the strait was renewed, and toward evening Columbus believed that he had found it in a channel, the Boca del Dragón, that leads into a great bay now named Almirante after him. Once inside, he found Indians wearing disks of fine gold on their breasts.

When Columbus asked for a strait to a wide ocean in sign language—extending his arms, pointing to salt water and describing a circle—the Indians waved him on by similar gestures to a narrow strait (now called Split Hill Channel). The caravels sailed through, although the channel was so narrow that their yards brushed the trees, and were rewarded by the sight of a great expanse of water. But, alas, there were mountains on every side; this was not the Indian Ocean but Chiriqui Lagoon.

For ten days the fleet idled about its shores, the Guaymi Indians plying a brisk trade in gold disks and bird-shaped amulets that they wore about their necks. From them Columbus learned that he was on an isthmus between two seas, but that a high mountain range barred his way. He understood them to say that their neighbors on the other side of the cordillera had warships complete with cannon, and that the Ganges River was only ten days' sail away! Apparently he also satisfied himself that no strait existed, since from now on he concentrated on gathering gold and establishing a trading post.

On October 17, 1502, the fleet passed out of Chiriqui Lagoon by the eastward channel and sailed along Mosquito Gulf. These shores are superficially attractive but fundamentally inhospitable. From Chiriqui Lagoon to Limón Bay (the Caribbean entrance to the Panama Canal), a distance of over 125 miles, there are no harbors except where a river mouth has built up a bar over which only a canoe can enter if the bar is not breaking. Because of this,

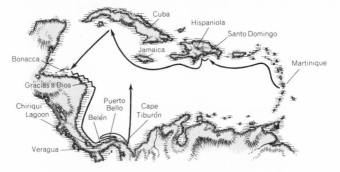

and because the Indians made menacing gestures at the few road-steads where he sent a boat ashore, Columbus merely planted a mental buoy off the gold-bearing coast and pressed forward, hoping to find a more hospitable spot for a trading post.

An unusually boisterous rainy season set in before the end of October. On November 2 the four caravels entered a fine harbor which the Admiral named Puerto Bello. If Columbus had decided to locate there, his garrison would certainly have heard of the Isthmus of Panama and obtained a glimpse of the Pacific Ocean ten years before Balboa did. But the Indians there, though friendly, had no gold, so the Admiral stayed a week, obtained provisions and cotton, and continued his voyage.

On November 9 the fleet made a little easting, but next day the wind forced them back several miles and they entered a harbor which Columbus named Puerto de Bastimentos (Harbor of Provisions). There the Columbus fleet remained twelve days, making minor repairs while the wind stayed in the east.

Their next stop was at a tiny harbor which they called El Puerto del Retrete, now called Escribanos. It was so small that the four caravels had to tie up alongside the banks as to a wharf. This gave the men a chance to sneak off to Indian villages and do some private trading with a gun, and that made trouble. A swarm of Indians gathered on the beach and made threatening gestures, and the Admiral had to mow down a few with gunfire before the rest would disperse.

Tired of sitting out the east wind, Columbus now decided to turn back to obtain more of that gold. On December 5 the fleet returned to Puerto Bello. Next day the wind whipped around into the west again. For a month the caravels were batted back and forth between Puerto Bello and the mouth of the Chagres River. The current always changed with the wind; it was no use trying to buck it. The weather was unusually foul. Recorded Columbus: ". . . it was like another deluge." Once the fleet was threatened by a tremendous waterspout, but it passed harmlessly by after the Admiral had exorcised it by reading aloud from the Gospel according to Saint John the account of that famous tempest on the Sea of Galilee concluding, *"Fear not, it is I."* Then, clasping the Bible in his left hand, with drawn sword he traced a cross in the sky and a circle around the fleet. That night *Vizcaína* lost sight of her consorts but found them again after three very dark and tempestuous days. The people were so worn out, said the Admiral, that they longed for death to end their sufferings. Then came two days of calm, during which great schools of shark lashed around the caravels; many were taken and some eaten, as provisions were running low, and the hardtack was now filled with weevils.

Indians attacking Spanish ships; detail from a seventeenth-century engraving.

On December 23 the fleet put in at the present harbor of Cristóbal, Panama Canal Zone, and there kept Christmas and New Year's, 1503, very miserably. Here Columbus was within a few miles of solving the riddle of the strait. He might have sent his boats up the Chagres, where from the head of the river he would have been only 12 miles by land from the Pacific Ocean. But he and his men were so beaten down by their long buffeting that they had no energy left for exploration. So Columbus missed by a few miles the most important geographical discovery that he could have made on the High Voyage.

RETURNING WESTWARD along the inhospitable coast of Veragua, Columbus searched for a likely place to found a trading post which would draw in the abundant gold of that region, and on January 6 anchored off the mouth of a river that he named Belén (Bethlehem), because it was the Feast of the Three Kings.

The coastal plain here is very narrow, and behind it rises rugged country covered by impenetrable rain forest, and behind that, verdure-clad mountains whose summits are usually covered with clouds. The trade wind beats in on this coast, which consists of long sand beaches separated by rocky bluffs. It is dangerous to try to anchor and in most places impossible to land in small boats. Rainfall is so excessive that agriculture on any large scale is unprofitable. The few people who live along that shore today have no means of communication with the outside world except by dugout canoe; boats can be launched only when the sea is exceptionally calm.

A few days after the Epiphany, Bartholomew Columbus took the ships' boats westward along the coast and rowed up the next river, the Veragua, toward the seat of a cacique named Quibián. Dignified but friendly, Quibián came downstream with a fleet of canoes to greet the visitors, and next day was entertained by the Admiral on board *Capitana*.

Veragua has one of the heaviest rainfalls in the world, and the ground is so thoroughly soaked that every storm starts a freshet. Columbus experienced this on January 24, 1503. Following a rainstorm in the mountains, a torrent roared down on the caravels in the Belén mooring basin. *Capitana* dragged, fouled *Gallega* and carried away her mizzenmast, and only by quick work were both vessels kept from broaching on the bar. Two weeks of rain and flood followed; it was not until February 6 that the sea was calm enough for the boats to get out. Bartholomew then made a return visit to Quibián and marched upcountry. His men, in one day, with no other implements but heir knives, collected about ten dollars' worth of gold apiece. The discovery of this auriferous region so pleased the Admiral hat he decided to build a fortified trading post at Belén, leave his brother in charge, and return to Spain for reinforcements. A little hill near the mouth of the river was chosen for the site, and the men began to construct the post, which Columbus named Santa María de Belén. He had chosen just about the worst spot on the coast of Central America to establish a beachhead.

By the time that Santa María de Belén had become an incipient trading factory of a dozen palm-thatched houses, the river fell so low that the caravels could not cross the bar. And at this juncture, when the fleet was caught, there came the inevitable change of attitude on the part of the Guaymi Indians. Sailors had been sneaking off by twos and threes to trade with gun and get women. Quibián could put up with a good deal of that if he believed that his importunate visitors would shortly depart, but now that it was evident they intended to settle, he decided it was time to give them "the treatment." He sent reconnoitering parties in canoes to Belén, who acted so suspiciously that Diego Méndez, a gentleman volunteer in the fleet, offered to row along the coast to learn what was going on. After a few miles he came upon a camp of a thousand howling warriors. Méndez, with amazing nerve, stepped ashore alone to confront them; then, returning to his boat, kept just out of arrow range ll night, observing the Indians' movements. They, realizing that surprise had been lost, retreated to Quibián's village. Méndez, after reporting to the Admiral, followed them thither, and in the midst of an ungodly uproar, coolly pulled out a barber's kit and had his hair cut by his companion, Rodrigo de Escobar. This not only stopped the shouting but so interested Quibián that he had his hair trimmed, too, and was then presented with the shears, mirror and comb; and Méndez returned in peace.

Columbus should have taken Quibián's hint and realized that his trading post would be untenable in the face of the hostility of thousands of Indians. Instead, he made a very bad decision—to seize Quibián and hold him as hostage for the Guaymis' good behavior. The cacique and about thirty members of his household were ambushed by an armed party of Spaniards and carried downriver, together with a big haul of gold objects. But Quibián escaped and promptly raised the country against the intruders.

In the meantime seamen were towing three caravels over Belén bar, intending to leave *Gallega* behind as a floating fortress for Bartholomew and the garrison. On April 6, while farewells were being said and only twenty men and an Irish wolfhound were guarding the fort, it was attacked by four hundred whooping, yelling Indians armed with bows and arrows and spears.

The Admiral, ill with malaria, remained alone on board *Capitana* anchored outside the bar while his men rowed ashore to help the garrison. The Indians were beaten off, largely through the rough work of the hound, but they promptly got their revenge by killing Captain Diego Tristán of *Capitana*, who with a boat party was filling the flagship's water casks upstream. Only one Spaniard escaped from the boat and ten were killed.

For eight days matters remained at an impasse. No boat could get over the bar, and *Capitana* had to be given a skeleton crew from *Vizcaína* and *Bermuda*. In the meantime some of the Indian hostages on board *Bermuda* escaped, and those who did not managed to hang themselves from the deck beams while confined in the hold.

The Admiral now made a hard but wise decision. Reflecting that without hostages Bartholomew's situation ashore would be desperate, he asked for a volunteer to swim across the bar and get to his brother. Pedro de Ledesma volunteered. He returned with an urgent request from Bartholomew that he and the garrison be allowed to abandon the fort. Columbus consented. Diego Méndez built a raft upon which all the Spaniards ashore, with most of their stores and gear, were lightered across the bar. *Gallega* was abandoned, along with Santa María de Belén.

No subsequent attempt to found a European settlement there ever succeeded. The descendants of the Guaymís have retreated to the interior, and, except for a few clearings where a handful of half-breeds live in poverty, the coast of Veragua is as wild, wet and forbiddingly beautiful as when Columbus landed there on the Feast of the Three Kings in 1503.

ON EASTER SUNDAY, April 16, 1503, *Capitana*, *Bermuda* and *Vizcaína* departed Belén, hoping to make Santo Domingo by Whitsuntide for repairs and provisions before returning home. Estimating that he was many leagues west of Hispaniola, and knowing by experience that it was almost impossible to beat against the easterly trades and the equatorial current, he planned to edge along the coast of Panama, working the land breeze and anchoring in bad weather, until he reached a point due south of Hispaniola, then to head north across the Caribbean to Santo Domingo.

Unfortunately the bottoms of all three caravels were riddled with shipworms. As the voyage progressed, all hands were kept at the pumps or bailing with kettles. Nevertheless, *Vizcaína* had to be abandoned in a hopelessly leaky condition at Puerto Bello, and her crew divided between *Capitana* and *Bermuda*. They crawled along into the Gulf of San Blas. All hands were too busy trying to keep afloat to admire the scenery of this coast, the jagged cordillera rising from behind gleaming white beaches, and the magnificent tropical rain forest of mahogany, ebony and other valuable woods, above whose glossy-leaved canopy an occasional giant of the forest thrusts a top bursting with pink or orange blossoms, as though a torch were being held up from the dark jungle.

On May 1, at Cape Tiburón, where the coast begins to trend southeastward into the Gulf of Darien, the pilots and captains, wildly figuring that they were east of the meridian of Guadeloupe, ganged up on Columbus and forced him to leave the coast and strike northward. Actually they were about on the meridian of Kingston, Jamaica—900 miles *west* of Guadeloupe—but the Admiral was so beaten down by arthritis, malaria and the failure of his plans that he gave in.

So worm-eaten *Capitana* and riddled *Bermuda* stood northward, constantly set to leeward by the current. On the twelfth of May they made a most unwelcome landfall on the Cuban archipelago which Columbus had named The Queen's Garden on his Second Voyage. "Full of hunger and trouble," as Ferdinand records, the caravels dropped anchor in a little harbor with poor holding ground at Cay Breton. The crew had "nothing to eat but hardtack and a little oil and vinegar, exhausted by working three pumps day and night because the vessels were ready to sink from the multitude of worms that had bored into them." On top of that, a thunderstorm for which this coast is notorious burst upon them, causing *Bermuda* to part her cable and foul *Capitana*. The flagship passed her a line; *Capitana*'s one remaining anchor fortunately held them both.

After six days the wind moderated and the caravels, with

Route taken by rescue party

planking "like a honeycomb," as Ferdinand said, and the sailors "spiritless and desperate," continued to struggle east along the Cuban coast. When the water gained on *Bermuda* at an alarming rate the Admiral ordered both caravels to square away for Jamaica.

On June 25 the wretched vessels, their decks almost awash, entered Saint Ann's Bay, Jamaica, which Columbus had named Santa Gloria on the Second Voyage. He ran them aground side by side on a sand beach and shored them up to keep on an even keel. High tides rose almost to their decks, upon which palm-thatched cabins had to be built for the people. And there they stayed for a year.

These 116 Spaniards marooned on Jamaica were fairly well situated for defense; the ships' hulks made a dry home and no mean fortress. A large and friendly Indian village lay nearby. Columbus, who knew by bitter experience that the natives would not long remain friendly if his people were allowed to make contact with them, allowed nobody to go ashore without his permission.

The first thing that needed attention was the food supply.

Columbus sent Diego Méndez and three men on a foraging expedition. They traveled almost to the east end of the island, purchased a dugout canoe, loaded it with native provisions, and returned to Santa Gloria in triumph; and, to insure a continuing supply, Méndez drew up a tariff agreement with the neighboring Indians to sell a cake of cassava bread for two glass beads, two of the big rodents called hutia for a lace point, and a great quantity of anything, such as fish or maize, for a hawkbell. Why they could not fish for themselves or plant their own cornfields has never been explained; it is clear that if the Indians had not fed them they would have starved to death.

But how to get home? The final resting-place of the two caravels commanded a wide sea view, but the chance of any Spanish or other vessel coming within sight was infinitesimal, since Columbus had let it be known that there was no gold in Jamaica. *Capitana* and *Bermuda* were beyond repair, and their crews appear to have been incapable of building a small vessel to escape. The only way to avoid spending the rest of their lives in Jamaica was to send a messenger to Hispaniola to procure a rescue ship.

As usual, everyone said, "Let Diego Méndez do it!" That faithful and indefatigable Spaniard hauled out the big dugout canoe he had purchased, and fitted a mast and sail. On his first attempt he was captured by Indians somewhere near Northeast Point, escaped, and returned to Santa Gloria. On the next he had plenty of assistance. Bartolomeo Fieschi, the Genoese captain, undertook to pilot another

New World Indians making bread.

canoe with him to Hispaniola, and in Jamaican waters Bartholomew Columbus provided an armed escort in a fleet of dugouts. At or near Northeast Point farewells were exchanged, and the two canoes pushed out into the Windward Passage.

More to-do was made about this canoe trip than about anything else on the High Voyage. Neither the Spaniards nor these Indians were used to small-boat journeys, and they certainly took this one hard. Each captain had a crew of six Christians, and ten Indians to do the work. They started in a flat calm and on the first day out were troubled only by the heat. The night was cool, but next morning it was discovered that the Indians had drunk all their water rations. By the second sunset everyone was discouraged; one Indian died of thirst and others were too weak to paddle.

A third night fell with no sight of land. But when the moon rose, Diego Méndez observed the outline of Navassa Island. They reached it in about seventy-two hours from Jamaica, having made a little better than a mile an hour. On Navassa everyone drank his fill of fresh water (some of the Indians dying of it), and they kindled a fire and cooked shellfish. Now they could see the lofty mountains of Hispaniola, and the following evening they made the coast.

Fieschi wished to return to Jamaica to tell the Admiral that they had made it, but his crew refused. Diego Méndez obtained some fresh Indian paddlers, continued along the coast to Azua and then marched inland to meet Ovando and request that the Admiral be succored. It was now August 1503. The governor, who was enjoying his own rule in Hispaniola and feared lest Columbus be restored to office, was perfectly willing to let him spend the rest of his life in Jamaica. He kept Méndez in the interior for seven months, putting him off with promises. Finally, in March 1504, he was allowed to go on foot to Santo Domingo and try to charter a vessel. Ovando had refused to send one to rescue the Admiral.

Meanwhile Columbus and his men had no means of knowing whether their messengers had arrived or perished. After six months had elapsed, and the winter northers made their position on the grounded ships very uncomfortable, a mutiny formed around the Porras brothers.

Forty-eight men began the mutiny on the day after New Year's, 1504. Crying the watchword "To Castile! To Castile!" the mutineers piled into ten dugout canoes and started eastward along the coast, robbing the Indians wherever they stopped. They had made only about 15 miles from Northeast Point when a freshening breeze from the east forced them to put back. All their plunder had to be thrown overboard, and most of the

Indian paddlers, too. Two more attempts were made to cross, but both failed. So the Porras party abandoned their canoes and trudged back to Santa Gloria.

Columbus's loyal men, in the meantime, were becoming very hungry. The Indians had few surplus stocks of food, and their demand for beads, lace points and hawkbells had been exhausted. Moreover, said Ferdinand, the food consumption of one Spaniard was equal to that of 20 Indians. At this critical juncture, the Admiral pulled his famous eclipse trick. He had an almanac which predicted a total eclipse of the moon on the last night of February 1504. That day he summoned the caciques on board stranded *Capitana*, told them that God desired the Indians to supply the Christians with food and would presently give them a clear token from Heaven of His displeasure at their failure to do so. They had better watch the moon that night. The eclipse began at moonrise, and, as the blackout area increased, the Indians flocked to the ships, howling and lamenting, praying the Admiral to call it off! Columbus retired to his cabin while the eclipse lasted, emerged when he was certain from the almanac that the total phase was about over, and announced that he had interceded with the Almighty and promised in their name that they would provide the food the Christians wanted, in return for which God had consented to take the shadow away. It worked perfectly, and there was no more food shortage.

At the end of March 1504, over eight months had elapsed since the messengers had left for Hispaniola, and nothing had been heard of them. Suddenly a small caravel sailed in to Santa Gloria and anchored near the Spanish camp. It had been sent by Ovando to ascertain whether Columbus was still alive and to report what he was doing. The Governor was mean enough to order the captain not to take anyone home. But the caravel did bring a welcome message from Méndez that he was doing his best to charter a rescue ship.

When this caravel disappeared over the horizon, the morale of the Spaniards reached an all-time low. At the same time Columbus made advances to the Porras party. The Porrases rejected his offers, in the hope of suborning the Admiral's men and seizing the houseboats. They marched on Santa Gloria.

The Columbus brothers mustered loyal men to meet them. A pitched battle, fought largely with swords for want of gunpowder, took place on May 29, and the loyalists won. The mutineers surrendered, and all were pardoned except the Porras brothers, who were allowed to stay on shore under guard.

Rescue was not long coming. Diego Méndez finally managed to charter a caravel in Santo Domingo and sent her to Jamaica under command of Diego de Salcedo, a loyal servant of the Admiral. He made Santa Gloria in the latter part of June 1504, took everyone on board, and on the twenty-ninth departed for Hispaniola. The survivors of the Fourth Voyage, about a hundred strong, had been in Jamaica a year and five days. The caravel was in poor condition; she leaked so badly that they feared she would founder, and it took her six and a half weeks to reach Santo Domingo. There Columbus chartered another vessel and embarked for Spain on September 12 with his brother, Ferdinand, and 22 others. A majority of the Fourth Voyage survivors elected to remain in Santo Domingo rather than risk another ocean passage. They had had enough work at the pumps to last ten lives!

The Admiral's homeward passage in the chartered ship was long and tempestuous; the foremast was sprung and the mainmast broke, but the Columbus brothers contrived a jury mast out of a spare yard. They did not reach Sanlúcar de Barrameda, north of Cadiz, until November 7, 1504, a passage of 56 days.

So the High Voyage was over, after two and a half years at sea, including the year marooned in Jamaica. The most adventurous of the Admiral's four voyages, it was also the most disappointing. He had not discovered the strait, since none there was; the isthmus that he reported was of no interest to the Sovereigns, and the gold-bearing Veragua that he discovered was unexploitable. But he had done his best. As he wrote to son Diego shortly after his arrival:

> I have served their Highnesses with as great diligence and love as I might have employed to win paradise and more; and if in somewhat I have been wanting, that was impossible, or much beyond my knowledge and strength. Our Lord God in such cases asketh nothing more of men than good will.

9. Home to Die

UPON HIS ARRIVAL in Spain after this long and distressing voyage, Columbus expected to be summoned to court to tell his story. But the report he had sent home by Diego Méndez did not make a good impression. By the time the Admiral reached Seville, about November 9, 1504, the Queen was confined to her bed at Segovia with an illness that turned out to be her last. That was the excuse for not inviting the Admiral to court. She died on November 26, 1504, at Medina del Campo, greatly to Columbus's grief and loss. Isabella had never sneered at him; she had understood what he was trying to do, and protected him from envious detractors. But the King had always considered the Admiral a bore, and he was not interested in the New World, only in European wars and diplomacy.

Columbus was now living in a hired house in the parish of Santa María, Seville. He was not badly off. His share of the gold obtained on the Fourth Voyage was considerable, and Carvajal had brought home a substantial sum for him in the *Aguja*, which survived the hurricane of 1502. But Columbus felt that he had been defrauded, and besought his son Don Diego, now about twenty-four years old and a member of the royal bodyguard, to obtain confirmation of what he called his "tithes," "eighths" and "thirds." The "tithe" was the ten percent of the net exports from all lands that he discovered, guaranteed by the original contract of 1492. Columbus complained that the government allowed him only a tenth of their fifth of the gold; that is, two instead of ten percent. The "eighth," similarly guaranteed, meant the profits on the Admiral's investments in one-eighth of the cargo of any vessel trading with "The Indies." He had exercised this option in certain cargoes, but claimed that Bobadilla or Ovando had impounded his share and failed to pay up. The "third" was really a preposterous claim. Columbus's grant of the new office of Admiral of the Ocean Sea stated that it carried "pre-eminences and prerogatives . . . in the same manner as . . . the Grand Admiral of Castile." Having ascertained that the Grand Admiral collected a thirty-three and one-third percent tax on overseas trade within his jurisdiction—between Spain and the Canary Islands—Columbus claimed it as his due for the entire inward and outward trade of the Indies. Obviously, if that had been admitted, there would have been little profit left in American trade for anyone else, and he and his descendants would have become wealthier than the King of Spain or any other prince. As it was, even by collecting a mere two percent of the gold, he was a rich man according to the standards of the day, and left substantial amounts to his sons.

It should be said that Columbus never intended to keep all this money. Even on his deathbed he was planning to accumulate a fund to finance a new crusade, and so provided in his last will and testament. It was always on his mind that the profits of his "Other World" might be used to recover the Holy Sepulcher from the Turks.

Even more was the Admiral concerned over collecting pay for the seamen and officers who had returned with him. They now had two full years' wages due, and most of them were poor men. Thrice the Admiral begged the treasurer of Castile to pay them off, without result. Years elapsed before they received anything.

By the first of 1505 Columbus came to the conclusion that it was useless to expect King Ferdinand to send him back to Hispaniola as Viceroy and Governor. In fact, the state of his health would have made another transatlantic voyage too risky. So he concentrated on trying to persuade the King to confer the viceroyalty on his son. Diego was then only twenty-five, but he was a clever courtier and made himself solid with the King by marrying a lady of royal blood. Three years after Columbus's death, he was appointed governor of Hispaniola and succeeded to his father's hereditary titles.

By the spring Columbus felt well enough to travel. So, in May 1505, the Admiral started on his long journey to court, then at Segovia, north of Madrid.

King Ferdinand received him graciously and proposed that an arbitrator be appointed to settle his claims against the crown. Columbus refused, because the King insisted that his viceroyalty and admiralty be adjudicated as well as the pecuniary claims, and he was too proud to arbitrate anything to which he had a clear legal title. The King then hinted that if Columbus would renounce all titles and offices, with the revenues pertaining to them, he would be granted a handsome estate with a fat rent toll. Columbus rejected that, absolutely. He considered it a dishonorable proposal. He would have all or nothing, and it was nothing that he got.

As the court moved to Salamanca and then to Valladolid, Columbus painfully followed. A year passed, nothing was accomplished, and in the meantime his arthritis grew worse. A large part of the time he was confined to bed in a hired house. But he felt so certain of justice being done that he made a will providing all sorts of legacies out of his rightful revenues, such as a fund for the crusade, a house in Genoa to be kept open perpetually for his descendants, a chapel in Hispaniola endowed so that daily Masses might be said for his soul forever.

Almost at the last moment of his life, Columbus had his hopes raised by the arrival of the Infanta Juana in Spain to claim her mother's throne of Castile. She had been at court when Columbus first returned from the Indies, and he hoped that she might confirm the favors granted by her sainted mother. He was too ill to move, so he sent brother Bartholomew to bespeak the young Sovereign's favor.

While Bartholomew was absent on this mission, the Admiral began to sink. On May 19, 1506, he ratified his final will, creating son Diego his principal heir and commending all other relatives, including his former mistress Beatriz, to his son's benevolence. Next day he suddenly grew worse. Both sons, brother Diego and a few faithful followers gathered around his bedside. A priest was summoned, Mass was said, and everyone received the Sacrament. After the concluding prayer, the Admiral, remembering the last words of his Lord and Saviour, murmured as his own, *"In manus tuas, Domine, commendo spiritum meum."* (Into Thy hands, O Lord, I commit my spirit.)

It was a poor deathbed for the Admiral of the Ocean Sea, Viceroy and Governor of the Islands and Mainlands in the Indies; and a poor funeral followed. No bishops, no dignitaries attended. Columbus had the ill fortune to die at a moment when his discoveries were little valued, and his fortunes were at their lowest ebb.

Little by little, as his life receded into history and the claims of others to be the "real" discoverers of America faded into the background, his great achievements began to be appreciated. Yet it is one of the ironies of history that the Admiral himself died ignorant of what he had really accomplished, still insisting that he had discovered a province of China and an "Other World"; but of the vast extent of that Other World, or of the ocean that lay between it and Asia, he had no knowledge.

Now, more than five hundred years after his birth, when the day that Columbus first sighted an island in the New World is celebrated throughout the length and breadth of the Americas, his fame and reputation may be considered secure for all time. He had his faults, but they were largely the defects of the qualities that made him great—his indomitable will, his superb faith in God and in his own mission as the Christ-bearer to lands beyond the seas, his stubborn persistence despite neglect, poverty and discouragement. There was no flaw in the most outstanding and essential of all his qualities—his seamanship. As a master mariner and navigator, Columbus was supreme in his generation. Never was a title more justly bestowed than the one which he most jealously guarded—*Almirante del Mar Océano*, Admiral of the Ocean Sea.

MARIE
ANTOINETTE

A CONDENSATION OF

MARIE
ANTOINETTE

by
STEFAN ZWEIG

TRANSLATED FROM THE GERMAN
BY EDEN AND CEDAR PAUL

ILLUSTRATED BY
JEAN LEON HUENS

Fate, they say, makes heroes of the most improbable people. Marie Antoinette was born the daughter of the Emperor Francis I of Austria, with an empire for her playground. She was an adored and charming child whose every girlish whim was indulged without limit. Brought up by her mother, the Empress Maria Theresa, to become Queen of France, at the age of fifteen she was indeed married to the young Dauphin of France, later to become King Louis XVI.

Having raised her to such dizzy heights, Fate now saw fit to cast this pampered darling into the vortex of the French Revolution. Yet this same Marie Antoinette, hunted down and abused by the Terror, summoned to her defense a brave spirit and a dignity no one knew she possessed.

Behind the familiar frivolous façade Stefan Zweig shows us the truth of a woman in the toils of a tragic destiny, which somehow she finds the courage to defy.

A CHILD MARRIAGE

Marie Antoinette's
Coat of Arms as the Dauphine

UPON DOZENS of German, Italian, and Flemish battlefields, the Habsburgs and the Bourbons had engaged in deadly strife, each party hoping to make itself predominant in Europe. Now, extenuated with fatigue, the longtime rivals perceived that their insatiable jealousies had served only to give free scope to the ambition of other ruling houses. In view of this the monarchs of France and Austria, and their servants the diplomats, entered into an alliance; and they decided that the friendship between the dynasties should be cemented by marriage.

The most natural possibility was to betroth the young Dauphin, the grandson of Louis XV, to a daughter of Maria Theresa of Austria and a provisional proposal was made in 1766 concerning Marie Antoinette, then eleven years old. On May 24, the Austrian ambassador in Paris wrote to the Empress: "The King has spoken in such a way that Your Majesty can regard the matter as settled." But a year, two years, three years passed without any definitive arrangements having been concluded. Maria Theresa became alarmed lest her troublesome neighbor, Frederick of Prussia, frustrate the scheme. Bringing all her cunning to bear, she saw to it that her daughter's virtues should become the talk of the French court. Empress rather than mother, concerned about the power of the Habsburgs and the peace of Europe, she turned a deaf ear to warnings that nature had not been kind to the Dauphin.

Meanwhile, in the rooms and the gardens of Schönbrunn Palace, the innocent pawn in these games of diplomatic chess, the eleven-year-, twelve-year-, thirteen-year-old Toinette, was romping with her sisters, her brothers, and her friends, but troubling little about books and lessons. Maria Theresa, busied in affairs of state, discovered one day to her great distress that the future Queen of France, though now thirteen, could write neither French nor German correctly, and was lacking in the most elementary knowledge of history or the other requisites of a sound education. In respect to music, the girl was little better off, though the composer Christoph Gluck had been her teacher. There was no time to lose. With the utmost speed the self-willed and idle Toinette must be transformed into a cultured lady. Fresh diplomatic negotiations followed upon the recognition that her education was a matter of prime concern to the French court, and a certain Abbé Vermond was sent to Vienna as tutor.

It is to Vermond that we are indebted for the first detailed accounts of the young archduchess. He was charmed. "She has a most graceful figure; holds herself well, and if (as may be hoped) she grows a little taller, she will have all the good qualities one could wish for in a great princess. Her disposition, her heart, are excellent." But the worthy abbé showed far more restraint in what he had to say about his pupil's accomplishments. Spoiled, inattentive, high-spirited, vivacious to a fault, Marie Antoinette, though quick of apprehension, showed not the slightest inclination to busy herself with serious matters. "She is more intelligent than has been generally supposed. Unfortunately up to the age of twelve she has not been trained to concentrate in any way. Since she is rather lazy and extremely frivolous, she is hard to teach . . . I came in the end to recognize that she would only learn so long as she was being amused."

Already, when she was but thirteen, the dangers implicit in Marie Antoinette's character had become obvious. At the

French court, however, during the epoch when the King's mistresses held sway, much more was thought of a woman's deportment than of her intrinsic worth. Marie Antoinette was pretty, of suitable standing, and of good disposition. These qualifications sufficed; so at length, in 1769, Louis XV sent a missive to the delighted Maria Theresa, formally demanding the young princess's hand for his grandson and proposing Easter 1770 as the date for the marriage.

Although the financial position alike in France and in Austria made strict economy essential, both the monarchy and the empire were resolved to celebrate the wedding with the utmost pomp and circumstance. The respective chamberlains worked like galley slaves over problems of precedence and the right to be present at the ceremonies. The French embassy in Vienna was too small to house the fifteen hundred guests. At top speed annexes were run up. In Paris new court dresses, trimmed with costly jewels, were provided for the Dauphin. Maria Theresa, not to be outshone, was determined that her daughter's trousseau should be no less sumptuous.

At length the Marquis de Durfort made his appearance in Vienna as special envoy to fetch the bride, and his coming provided an attractive spectacle for the Viennese. Eight-and-forty six-in-hands were driven slowly through the flower-bestrewn streets to the Hofburg, among them two traveling carriages of unprecedented splendor for the archduchess. These were constructed of rare woods, coated with glass, lined with satin, and lavishly adorned outside with paintings and crowns.

Thereafter, festival followed upon festival: the official wooing; Marie Antoinette's formal renunciation of her Austrian rights before the Holy Bible; a full-dress military review; a ball for three thousand persons; and at length, on April 19, marriage by proxy in the Augustinian church, Marie Antoinette's brother, the Archduke Ferdinand, representing the Dauphin. The day was concluded by an affectionate family supper; and on April 21 came a formal farewell, with last embraces. At length, the reverential populace lining both sides of the road, Marie Antoinette drove away, in the chariot sent by the King of France, to fulfill her destiny.

TO SAY FAREWELL TO HER DAUGHTER had been hard for Maria Theresa. For years this weary and aging woman (she was now well over fifty) had longed for this marriage; and yet, at the last moment, she became filled with anxiety regarding the fate she had meted out to her daughter. Being a keen judge of character, she was under no illusion concerning the youngest of her brood, the spoiled darling Marie Antoinette. She knew the girl's spirit, good nature and cordiality; but she also knew Toinette's immaturity and frivolousness. Hoping to make a queen out of this temperamental hoyden, Maria Theresa had had Marie Antoinette sleep in her own bedroom during the last two months before the departure. In lengthy conversations, the mother tried to prepare the daughter for the great position that awaited her.

As the hour of departure approached, the Empress became more and more troubled in spirit. She gave Marie Antoinette a written list of regulations for the conduct of life, and, before the girl could have reached Versailles, she sent her an additional exhortation to follow the guidance of this document. "Let me recommend you, beloved daughter, to reread it on the twenty-first of every month. . . . The only thing I am afraid of is that you may sometimes be backward in saying your prayers, and in your reading; and may consequently grow negligent and sloth-ful. Fight these faults. . . . Do not forget your mother who, though far away, will continue to watch over you until her last breath." While the world was rejoicing over the daughter's triumph, the mother went to church and besought the Almighty to avert a disaster which she alone foresaw.

MARIE ANTOINETTE's huge cavalcade made its way slowly through Upper Austria and across Bavaria to the imperial frontier, de-layed by innumerable festivals and receptions. Meanwhile, carpenters and upholsterers were at work upon a singular edifice. After endless deliberations as to whether the formal reception of the bride was to take place on Austrian or on French territory, the court chamberlains hit upon the choice of an uninhabited sandbank in the Rhine, between France and Germany, and therefore in no-man's-land. Here was erected a pavilion for the ceremonial transference—a miracle of neutrality.

The handing over of Marie Antoinette was to signify her farewell to all which linked her with the House of Habsburg. In the Austrian antechamber, therefore, in the presence of her Austrian followers, this girl of fourteen had to strip to the buff. Naked as on the day she was born, she was quickly re-dressed in a chemise of French silk, petticoats from Paris, stockings from Lyon, shoes made by the shoemaker to the French court, French lace. And from this same moment she was to part company with all the familiar Austrian faces. Can we be surprised to learn that the poor child burst into tears?

Yet what could she do but pull herself together? Count Starhemberg, the best man, took her by the hand, and, followed for the last time by her Austrian companions, she entered the hall of transition where, in great state, the Bourbon delegation awaited her. The matchmaker who represented his master Louis XV delivered a solemn address, the marriage contract was read aloud, and thereupon ensued the great ceremony. It had been rehearsed as carefully as a minuet. The table in the center of the hall symbolized the frontier. Before it stood the Austrians; behind it, the French. The best man relinquished Marie Antoinette's hand, which was taken by the French matchmaker, and he, with stately steps, led the trembling girl around the end of the table. Then, keeping time with the advance of the French suite to welcome its future Queen, the Austrian nobles retired.

Soundlessly, with ghostly magnificence, was this chill ceremonial fulfilled; but at the last moment the terrified girl found it unendurable. Instead of giving a cool and dignified response to the profound curtsy of the Comtesse de Noailles, she flung herself, sobbing, and with a gesture of appeal, into the arms of her new lady-in-waiting. The horses harnessed to the glass chariot were pawing the ground, the bells of Strasbourg cathedral were pealing, salvos of artillery were being fired; and, amid jubilations, Marie Antoinette quitted forever the carefree realm of childhood.

Her arrival was a memorable occasion for the French people, which had not been overindulged with public spectacles. Strasbourg acclaimed the gorgeous procession. With blue and

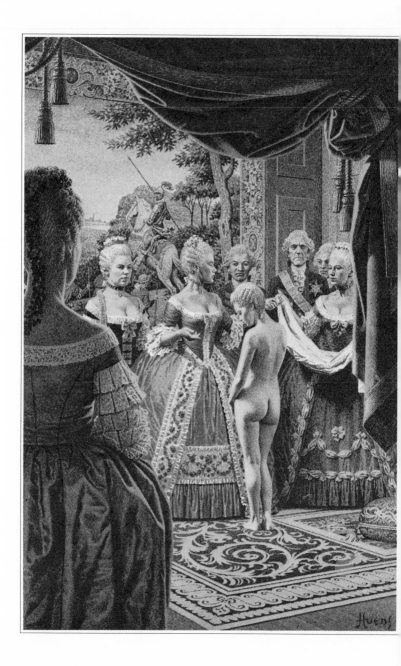

sparkling eyes, the girl smiled from the glass chariot at the huge crowd of persons who had assembled from all the towns and villages of Alsace. Hundreds of children clad in white strewed flowers in its path; a triumphal arch had been erected; garlands decorated the gates; wine flowed from the city fountains; oxen were roasted whole; free bread was provided for the poor. Till far on into the night the populace thronged the streets and the banks of the river; bands played; lads and lasses danced; there was a general feeling that the arrival of the blonde girl from Austria heralded a return of the golden age; and hope surged up in the embittered hearts of the French people.

But Marie Antoinette could not linger in homelike Alsace. The King of France must not be kept waiting! Through many more triumphal arches, the bridal train wound its way toward the forest of Compiègne, where, with a great park of carriages, the royal family was assembled to welcome this new member. Under the May sunshine, the woods were bright with the play of color. As soon as fanfares had announced the approach of the procession, Louis XV got out of his chariot to receive his grandson's bride. But Marie Antoinette was beforehand with him. Light of foot, she hastened up to him, and curtsied. The King, who was a connoisseur of girlish charms, leaned with tenderness over this appetizing creature, helped her to rise, and kissed her on both cheeks. Not until after this did he introduce her future spouse, a gawky, shortsighted fellow, five feet ten inches tall, who was looking on with clumsy embarrassment. Now, without showing any particular zest, he kissed the new arrival on the cheeks formally, as etiquette demanded. A moment later, Marie Antoinette was seated in the chariot between grandfather and grandson, the old man chattering in sprightly fashion, while the husband-to-be leaned back, bored and tongue-tied. When the pair retired for the night in separate rooms, this sorry lover had not yet spoken a single affectionate word to the fascinating girl. In his diary, he penned the curt entry: *"Entrevue avec Madame la Dauphine!"*

The second wedding festival, the real one, in succession to the proxy affair in Vienna, took place on May 16, 1770, at Versailles in the Chapel of Louis XIV. Only nobles of high descent could be granted access to the consecrated building, where the Archbishop of Rheims consecrated the marriage. When the ceremony was over, however, the people were graciously allowed to participate in the festival, and crowds thronged the gardens at Versailles. The tidbit of the show, a great display of fireworks, had been reserved for the evening. But in the afternoon rain fell in torrents; tens of thousands of the *canaille*, drenched to the skin and robbed of their spectacle, hurried homeward to Paris, while behind the windows of the newly built *salle de spectacle*, blazing with thousands of candles, the magnificent wedding feast began.

When the festival was over, His Majesty conducted the wedded children, whose joint ages barely exceeded thirty years—to their sleeping apartment. The Archbishop of Rheims blessed and sprinkled the nuptial couch with holy water, and the court left the youthful husband and wife to their privacy. Louis and Marie Antoinette were alone together, and the rustling curtains of the great four-poster closed around an unseen tragedy.

II

SECRET OF THE ALCOVE

The Dauphin
(later Louis XVI)

The Dauphine
(Marie Antoinette)

WHAT FIRST HAPPENED in the great four-poster was—nothing! *Matrimonium non consummatum est;* as far as its essential physical purpose was concerned, the marriage remained unfulfilled, today, tomorrow, for several years. And in the eighteenth century a king's competence or impotence, and a queen's fertility or barrenness, were frankly regarded as matters of state. Upon them depended the succession, and therewith the fate of the whole country. At first the belief was that only timidity or inexperience had made the youth of sixteen impotent.

Toinette must not be in too great a hurry, thought the mother, for that, by increasing her husband's uneasiness, will only make matters worse. But when this distressing state of affairs had lasted a year, two years, the Empress grew anxious about the *conduite si étrange* of the young man, and wrote letter after letter to Paris. Finally King Louis XV, whose experience in this domain had been vast, took his grandson to task. Lassone, physician to the French court, was summoned; and it became plain that the Dauphin's impotence was due to a trifling organic defect—phimosis. Consultation followed upon consultation, as to whether the surgeons should intervene with the knife. But in 1775, when five years had elapsed since his marriage, Louis XVI—as he had now become—was not yet an effective husband, and, being a young man of vacillating character, he found it impossible to make up his mind to so energetic a course. Thus matters dragged on for another two years, making in all seven years of humiliating frustration.

The reports of foreign envoys at the court of France were full of the problem. All over Europe princes and kings were making fun of their maladroit colleague. Not only in Versailles, but in the streets of Paris and the whole land of France, the King's conjugal inefficiency was an open secret. At length Emperor Joseph II, Maria Theresa's heir and co-regent, undertook the journey to Paris that he might inspire his rather pusillanimous brother-in-law with sufficient courage for the operation. The needful was done, and our pitiful Caesar was enabled to cross his Rubicon. Unfortunately, however, during these seven years, the characters of the King and the Queen had been warped, each in its own fashion—and the fate of this one marriage was intertwined with the fate of the world. Seldom has the logical sequence between an extremely private cause and a political effect been so plain.

Louis XVI's character displays the clinical traits of an inferiority complex determined by a sense of defective virility. He was neither stupid nor narrow-minded; his face was not devoid of a certain nobility. Having read widely, he was well informed.

But because he had been unable to play the man in his sleeping apartment, he could not play the monarch in public. A good enough fellow, fundamentally eager to do the right thing, he occasionally tried to assume airs of authority. Invariably, he overacted his part, becoming unconvincingly rough.

Many of his personal tastes were typically ultravirile. By riding for hours, hunting boar and wearying one horse after another, by wielding a hammer in his smithy, he found momentary compensation for his defect in proofs of bodily strength. No sooner was he among his courtiers, however, than his embarrassment returned. Rarely did he laugh or look happy.

The most disastrous consequence of his sense of weakness became apparent in his mental attitude toward his wife. He disliked her unceasing round of social amusements, her perpetual noisy pleasure-seeking, her extravagance in money matters, her levity. A man able to play a man's part would speedily have made his young wife conduct herself as he wished. But how could he, who night after night was shamed by his inefficiency as a spouse, assert himself as master in the daytime? He gave her whatever she wanted, thus ransoming himself from his sense of culpability. Even when Louis XVI had become a husband in the full sense of the word, he remained the thrall of Marie Antoinette, simply because to begin with he had been ineffective.

The impotence of Louis XVI had results that were no less sinister as regards the mental development of Marie Antoinette. By nature, she was normal enough: a tender, womanly woman, foreordained to motherhood. But because she was unceasingly stimulated, and never satisfied, the high spirits of a spoiled child inevitably degenerated into a compulsive mania for pleasure, regarded on the whole as scandalous.

Moments of frantic melancholy showed, however, that this frivolity was an escape from a gnawing sense of disappointment. When her relative, the Duchess of Chartres, gave birth to a stillborn child, Marie Antoinette wrote to her mother: "However distressing, I only wish the same thing could happen to me!" Only a sympathetic comprehension of the despair that underlay her craze for pleasure can explain to us the extraordinary change which took place when, finally, Marie Antoinette became wife and mother. Another, a second, Marie Antoinette appeared upon the scene, the self-controlled, strong-willed, intrepid woman she showed herself to be during the latter half of her life. But this transformation came too late.

It was inevitable that the wits of the court should continually be asking each other how Marie Antoinette, young, spirited and coquettish, had sought relief for her husband's incompetence. Just because there were no solid grounds for suspicion, suspicion ran riot. If the Queen rode with a good-looking cavalier, he must be her lover; if she took a morning stroll in the park, there were incredible orgies. Songs, lampoons, pamphlets, and pornographic poems concerning the Queen's love life were rife. When revolutionary propaganda began, the Jacobin journalists had not far to look for arguments enabling them to represent Marie Antoinette as a prodigy of dissipation.

For the time being, however, the storm was invisible. These consequences of conjugal failure were still distant from the merry child of fifteen who cheerfully looked forward to ascending a throne.

III

DEBUT AT VERSAILLES

View of Versailles

VERSAILLES is a challenging gesture of autocracy. In a flat piece of country a few miles west of the capital, a huge palace stands on an artificial mound, looking down through hundreds of windows upon artificial waterways and artificially designed gardens—and then forth into vacancy.

That was what Louis XIV wanted! By removing his court

from the capital, establishing the most sumptuous palace in the world amid vacancy, he emphasized the fact that a king of France had no need of the great city, of its citizens, of the masses, as supports for his power. Versailles was built to give France a tangible demonstration that the people were nothing and the king everything.

The crown passes from head to head, but power and majesty are not necessarily inherited. Those who succeeded to the huge palace, to the firmly established realm, were narrow of outlook, infirm of purpose. Versailles declined under Louis XV to become no more than a stage for private theatricals, where the leading roles were played by titled amateurs—the most artificial and the most expensive theater the world had ever known.

On these splendidly decorated boards there now appeared a debutante of fifteen summers who became the cynosure of all eyes. The spectators' first impressions were extremely favorable. With her bewitchingly slender form this fair-haired little archduchess of Austria recalled a Sèvres figurine; her tint was that of colored porcelain; she had soft and extremely beautiful blue eyes, which at one moment would brim with tears and at the next sparkle with amusement; a mobile, well-formed arrogant mouth, and an ingratiating smile. She walked as if on wings, danced divinely, and yet, born to the purple, she held herself confidently as she made her dignified progress along the Gallery of Mirrors, and dispensed greetings to right and to left without a trace of embarrassment.

There was only one complaint as to her deportment. The child showed a puzzling inclination to throw off all restraint even in these sacred halls. She was, in fact, a romp and at times a regular tomboy, when, with flying skirts, she larked with her young brothers-in-law. At Schönbrunn formal behavior was kept for appropriate occasions, and she could not readily adapt herself to the chill reserve, the tedious ceremony which were expected of a crown princess at the French court. Self-willed and uncontrolled, Marie Antoinette would everlastingly be in revolt against rules. Now she seized every opportunity of evading the admonitions of her strict lady-in-waiting, Madame de Noailles, whom she mockingly nicknamed Madame Etiquette.

Good-natured Marie Antoinette had no dislike for the elderly people around her. But she wanted friends and playmates of her own age, and her clumsy husband, who was only a year older than herself, avoided any real intimacy with her. With Louis's younger brothers, the Comte de Provence and the Comte d'Artois, lads of fourteen and thirteen respectively, she sometimes had a gay enough time. Getting hold of various costumes, they dressed up and played at private theatricals; but all the properties and the clothes had to be hustled out of sight as soon as Madame Etiquette drew near, for a Dauphine must not be caught playacting.

Marie Antoinette's craving for amusement, and for a little tender affection, had curious results at times. On one occasion she begged Count Mercy, the Austrian ambassador, to arrange for a dog to be sent to her from Vienna, *un chien mops*—a pug. Another time, Madame de Noailles discovered to her horror that the future Queen of France had called the two little children of one of her waiting maids into her room and was romping with them on the floor regardless of her fine clothing. The unconscious longing of this poor child, who had too early been made a pawn in the political game, was to get what was sedulously withheld from her amid all the luxuries of her station, namely, a few years of unalloyed childhood.

Those mainly responsible for her education, for her "breaking in," over and above the chief lady-in-waiting, were her husband's three aunts, the daughters of Louis XV, bigoted and ill-natured old maids, Madame Adelaide, Madame Victoire, Madame Sophie. In Marie Antoinette's daily routine, there was little place left for amusements, though it was for these, above all, that her impatient heart yearned. Here is her own description of one of her days:

I get up at half past nine or ten o'clock, dress, and say my morning prayers. Then I have breakfast, and go to see my aunts, where I generally find the King. . . . Thereafter, at eleven, I go to have my hair dressed. Next comes the *levée*. . . . I rouge my cheeks and wash my hands before the assembled company; then the gentlemen withdraw, the ladies remain, and I dress myself in their presence. Now it is time for church. . . . If the King is away, I go alone with the Dauphin. After Mass we have our dinner in public, but this is over by half past one, for we both eat very quickly. Then I am with the Dauphin for a time, and when he has business to do I retire to my own room, where I read, write, or work. Needlework, for I am embroidering the King a coat . . . I hope that, with God's grace, it will be finished in a few years. . . . At four, the abbé comes to me, and at five my piano teacher or singing master, till six. At half past six I almost always go to my aunts, unless I go out. I should tell you that my husband almost always goes with me to my aunts. From seven till nine we play cards. . . . At nine o'clock we have supper, and when the King is not there the aunts have supper with us. But when the King is there, we go to the aunts after supper. . . . I lie down on a big sofa, and go to sleep until the King comes. When he is away, we go to bed at eleven. That is how I spend my day.

Abbé Vermond, who had been her tutor in Vienna, and was now her confessor and reader rolled into one, had a hard time of it with Marie Antoinette. At fifteen, while she had forgotten a good deal of her German, she had not yet gained an adequate mastery of French; her handwriting was extremely bad and there were faults in her spelling. The worthy abbé read aloud to her every day, and also made her read to herself—for Maria Theresa was continually asking about her daughter's reading. Her little Toinette, with mingled simplicity and shrewdness, was well able to twist Abbé Vermond around her finger. What should have been the reading hour often degenerated into an hour of idle chatter. Toinette learned nothing or next to nothing.

Maria Theresa was fully informed concerning her daughter's position at the foreign court. She had sent to Paris, not only as ambassador, but also as Marie Antoinette's trusty counselor, the ablest among her diplomats. Writing to Count Mercy with singular frankness, she said: "I dread my daughter's youth, the effect which undue flattery may have upon her, her idleness, and her lack of any inclination for serious activity. Let me urge you to keep a watchful eye upon these matters, and to see to it that she does not fall into bad hands. . . ."

Count Mercy, a wealthy and unambitious bachelor, fulfilled his position of trust with pitiless sincerity. Thanks to his detailed reports, the anxious mother in far-off Schönbrunn knew every word that Toinette spoke, every book that the young woman read—or failed to read. She knew what dresses were worn, how the days were spent, with whom the girl had conversation, what mistakes were being made. Mercy had cast a fine-meshed net of informers around his protégée.

"There is really not an hour of the day," he wrote to the Empress, "as to which I am not instructed concerning what the Archduchess may have said or done or heard."

Marie Antoinette, who was not of a suspicious nature, seems often to have wondered how it was that Schönbrunn could be so well posted concerning every detail of her life; but she never imagined that the fatherly ambassador was her mother's private spy, or that Maria Theresa's affectionate but admonitory letters had many of them been sent at his insistence. For it was only through an appeal to the maternal authority that the ambassador could exert any control over the giddy girl! Although subservient to no one else in the world, she reverently bowed her head before even the harshest criticism from her mother. And it was thanks to Maria Theresa's unceasing supervision that Marie Antoinette was saved, during her first years at Versailles, from the greatest of all the dangers to which she was exposed, that of her own unruliness.

AT THE TIME of Marie Antoinette's arrival, there were two main factions at Versailles. The Queen had died two years before, and her precedence and authority should have accrued to the King's three daughters. But these tedious old maids could exert no influence over their royal father, who was absorbed in his pleasures. All the glory of court life had accrued to Madame Du Barry, the King's latest mistress.

Sprung from the dregs of the populace, with a past which would not bear investigation, she had got her complaisant protector to buy her a titled husband, Comte Du Barry, a most accommodating person who disappeared forever after the paper marriage. Her position thus legitimized, the King's inamorata lived at Versailles, her apartments separated by only three rooms from those of the scandalized daughters, and connected with the King's quarters by a specially built staircase. Since the only way to the King's favor lay through her salon, the hangers-on at court crowded around her; foreign envoys danced attendance in her anteroom; kings and princes showered gifts upon her; she could have ministers dismissed, could allot lucrative posts, and could squander the royal treasure.

Naturally the King's daughters loathed the impudent strumpet who sat in the first rank and had virtually replaced their deceased mother. Their only thought was to do her an ill turn. And now, by the favor of fortune, there appeared at Versailles this foreign child, only fifteen, but by right the first lady in the land. From the moment of Marie Antoinette's arrival, it was the chief aim of the three spiteful old maids to make the unsuspecting girl a pawn in their game. Accordingly, with every semblance of affection, they drew the little princess into their circle.

The court of Maria Theresa was a strictly moral one, and Marie Antoinette had known nothing of such women as the Du Barry. But her worthy aunts were not slow to enlighten her, for a few weeks after her arrival we find Marie Antoinette writing to her mother concerning the *"sotte et impertinente créature."* Frankly, unreservedly, she passed on to Maria Theresa all her dear aunts' backbiting about the Du Barry, and was openmouthed in talk with her daily associates—to the great amusement of the bored court which relished such sensations. The fact was that Marie Antoinette had taken it into her little head (or rather her aunts had put it into her little head) to rid Versailles of this audacious intruder. According to the rigid etiquette that prevailed at court, no lady of lesser rank could address a lady of higher rank uninvited, but must reverentially wait until the superior began the conversation. Coolly, smilingly, and challengingly, the Dauphine let the Du Barry wait and wait and wait for a word. Week after week, month after month, she chattered like a magpie to everyone else and looked through the bejeweled countess as if she had been a windowpane.

Now the Du Barry was by no means ill-natured. But, playing in the tragicomedy of illegitimate power, her supreme ambition was to be recognized by the legitimate powers of this world. Though princes fawned upon her and though she was the spoiled darling of the courtiers, she still had an overwhelming desire: to be "recognized" by the young woman who was indubitably the chief lady of the realm. In this contest the Du Barry controlled the King. He would have preferred to have nothing to do with the affair. But his mistress was incessantly dinning in his ears that she could not allow herself to be humiliated before the whole court by a young minx from Austria, that King Louis must safeguard her dignity, and therewith his own. At length the King sent for Madame de Noailles. The Dauphine, he said, was talking somewhat too freely and it would be well to let her know that this could not fail to have a bad effect in family life. Madame de Noailles hastened to transmit the warning to Marie Antoinette, who retailed it to her aunts and to Vermond. The latter, needless to say, passed it on to Mercy, who, thinking above all of the alliance between Austria and France, sent an express messenger to Vienna.

Here was a painful situation for pious Maria Theresa! In Vienna she was accustomed to give short shrift to ladies of easy virtue by having them confined in reformatories. Was she now to tell her own daughter to be civil to a creature of that sort? The mother, a rigid Catholic, but also a stateswoman, was in conflict. Ultimately, she managed to evade the issue. She did not write in person to her daughter, but instructed Count von Kaunitz, her first minister, to send Mercy a reply urging Marie Antoinette to remember her political duties.

Kaunitz's letter, though plain to a fault, left Marie Antoinette cold, for she was being perpetually spurred on by her aunts. The civil words which Du Barry, the King, Kaunitz, Mercy, and even Maria Theresa wanted remained unspoken. War had now been declared. Wagers as to the winner were freely laid. It was years since Versailles had witnessed so amusing a spectacle.

When matters had reached this pass, the King grew seriously annoyed. To Mercy's surprise he was summoned to an audience with the King in the apartment of Comtesse Du Barry. Louis XV took charge of the ticklish conversation, and Mercy was not slow to grasp that the affair had become a matter of state; the King

was insisting upon unqualified surrender. The ambassador sent an express to Vienna, and made strong representations to Marie Antoinette. He made her understand that if the alliance between the Habsburgs and the Bourbons, her mother's lifework, were now to be broken, the blame would lie at her door.

The heavy artillery had its due effect. With tears of anger in her eyes, Marie Antoinette promised the ambassador that, on a certain day when there was to be a card party, she would say the required word to the Du Barry. The stage was carefully set. At the end of the card party, Mercy was to enter into conversation with the Du Barry. Then, as if by chance, the Dauphine was to come that way, catch sight of the ambassador, say good-evening to him, and seize the opportunity of uttering a word or two to the King's favorite as well.

Marie Antoinette had the best intentions in the world when she went to the card party. As previously arranged, she began her circuit of the hall, conversing now with this lady, now with that—until only one lady remained between her and Mercy. In two minutes, in a minute, she would reach him and the favorite. At this decisive moment Madame Adelaide, the most venomous of the three old maids, played her great coup. Stepping up briskly to Marie Antoinette, she said in a commanding tone: "It is time for us to leave. We will go and await the King in my sister Victoire's room." Marie Antoinette, taken by surprise, utterly lost courage. Flushed, confused, she turned upon her heel and fled; and the word—the long-desired, commanded, diplomatically wrestled for, and faithfully promised word—still remained unspoken. The comtesse was in a fine rage; and so was Louis XV. "Well, Monsieur de Mercy," said he acidly to the ambassador, "apparently I must come to your aid!"

The King of France had uttered threats in his anger. The ambassador promptly reported to the Empress, who was greatly distressed, nay alarmed, all the more since unsavory political intrigues had been going on in Vienna. Months before, Frederick the Great, whom she regarded as Lucifer's emissary on earth, and Catherine of Russia, whom she mistrusted no less, had approached Austria with a proposal for the partition of Poland. The idea, which the Empress had first rejected as essentially unjust, had secured enthusiastic support from Kaunitz and Joseph II. At length, with a sore conscience and a sad heart, Maria Theresa had given way, and now she awaited in trembling the day when the secret treaty would become known to the world. Would France protest this robbery of Poland? Everything turned upon the mood of Louis XV, and here was the alarming news that he was extremely angry with Marie Antoinette. Because the inconsiderate child would not speak the necessary word to Comtesse Du Barry, the partition of Poland might very well lead to war! The Empress wrote to her daughter as follows:

> What a pother about saying "Good day" to someone, a kindly word concerning a dress or some such trumpery.... I cannot keep silent about the matter any longer.... You are His Majesty's first subject, and you owe him obedience and submission. It behooves you to set a good example.... All that is expected is that you say an indifferent word, look at her beseemingly—not for the lady's own sake, but for the sake of your grandfather, your master, your benefactor!

This cannonade broke down Marie Antoinette's defenses. On New Year's Day, 1772, the stage was once more set in due form. New Year greetings were being given, and the ladies of the court filed past the Dauphine, among them the Duchesse d'Aiguillon, wife of the minister of state, with Madame Du Barry. Marie Antoinette, having said a few words to the duchess, while the onlookers held their breath lest a syllable be lost, uttered the momentous words for which so strenuous a combat had been waged. *"Il y a bien du monde aujourd'hui à Versailles"*— "There are quite a lot of people here today."

That was all that Marie Antoinette could bring herself to say. In truth it was a memorable utterance, for it was the price paid for King Louis XV's tacit acceptance of a great political crime, the partition of Poland. General harmony had been restored. The King embraced the Dauphine tenderly as if she were a long-lost child; Mercy thanked her in moving tones; the victorious Du Barry strutted through the hall like a peacock but cherished no animosity.

As for Marie Antoinette, her youthful pride had suffered defeat. For the first time she had bowed her neck, but she was not to do so again until it bowed beneath the guillotine. Moreover, being fundamentally straightforward, she soon cast off the tutelage of the aunts who sought to teach her the art of slander and underground intrigue. She never learned to assume a false front, never learned to conceal her likes or dislikes.

IV

CONQUEST OF PARIS

Entrance of Marie Antoinette into Paris

ON DARK EVENINGS the skies to the eastward of Versailles glowed with the lights of Paris. What could be more natural than that, soon after the wedding, the Dauphine should propose a visit to the metropolis of her future realm? But the heir to the throne of France, accompanied by his spouse, could not visit the capital until His Majesty's consent had been accorded. And this was something which the great ones at court wished to postpone as long as possible. No matter how deep the grudge they might bear one another, they all joined hands to prevent Marie Antoinette's enjoying a triumph which would make too obvious her coming rank. Three years passed before, on the eighth of June, 1773, the Dauphine made her formal entry into Paris. The summer day was brilliant and the progress from Versailles took place through double lines of onlookers, shouting acclamations and waving their hats frantically. Within the gates of Paris salutes were fired from the Invalides, from the Hôtel de Ville and the Bastille, while the state carriage wound its way across the city, along the Quai des Tuileries to Notre-Dame. Everywhere, at the cathedral, at the university, the couple was received with speeches, and they drove through triumphal arches built for the occasion; but their heartiest welcome came from the common people. When, at length, from the balcony of the Tuileries, Marie Antoinette looked forth over the vast assembly, she cried out, almost in alarm: "*Mon Dieu*, how many of them there are!" Maréchal de Brissac, the governor of Paris, who was standing beside her, answered with typical French gallantry: "Madame, I hope His Highness the Dauphin will not take it amiss, but you have before you two hundred thousand persons who have all fallen in love with you."

Marie Antoinette was awestruck by her first encounter with the French people. She wrote to her mother:

> We were received with all imaginable honor. Though this was pleasant enough, what touched me much more was the affection and the zeal of the poor people, which, though crushed by taxation, was overflowing with joy at the sight of us. When we were driving to the Tuileries, the press was so great that we were blocked for three-quarters of an hour without being able to move forward or backward. . . . We kissed our hands to the people, at which they were greatly pleased. How fortunate to be in a position in which one can gain widespread affection at so little cost. Though the cost be small, such love is infinitely precious. The fact was borne home to me, and I shall never forget it.

But she who would "never forget" was in truth forgetful. During her early visits, curiosity led her to seek out the museums, great houses of business and manufacture, a popular festival or two, and once even an exhibition of pictures. Therewith, however, and for the next twenty years, she devoted herself indefatigably to amusements, appearing regularly in the royal box at the opera, the Comédie Francaise, the Italian Theater, going to routs and gaming houses—in a word, enjoying "the night side of Paris." How delightful it was after the constrained life of the court! Especially was she fascinated by masked balls at the Opera House, for, a prisoner of her position, nothing but a mask could set her free to laugh and dance to her heart's content. But not once did she visit a hospital or a market; not once did she attend a sitting of the Parlement of Paris; not once did she try to learn something of the daily life of the French people.

The sweet poison of flattery was circulating in Marie Antoinette's veins. Her reception by Paris had worked a transformation in her. Self-confidence is always promoted by admiration, and now an uprush of pride swept away uncertainty and timidity. The ardent girl was ripening to live the life of a woman. And since Marie Antoinette, her heart still untouched, knew no other man than Louis to love, at eighteen she fell in love with herself. The more she was admired, the more did she crave for admiration; and before she was legally queen, she wanted to rule the court, the capital, the whole realm, thanks to her charms.

V

THE KING IS DEAD, LONG LIVE THE KING!

Madame Du Barry   Louis XV, 1773

ON APRIL 27, 1774, King Louis XV, when out hunting, suddenly declared himself suffering from severe headache, and returned to his favorite palace of the Trianon. Next morning, alarmed about his condition, his doctors ordered his removal to the adjoining great palace of Versailles; a king of France could not be allowed to die elsewhere than in the royal bed of state. *"C'est à Versailles, Sire, qu'il faut être malade."*

In the evening the news ran like wildfire through the building that His Majesty had smallpox. A gust of terror traversed the huge palace. King Louis's daughters showed the courage of piety, keeping watch over him throughout the day, while at nighttime Madame Du Barry sat by his bedside. The heirs to the

135

throne, the Dauphin and the Dauphine, were forbidden by court regulations to run any risk of infection.

It was speedily recognized that the King's case was hopeless; so now began the struggle for his sinful soul. The priests refused to administer the last rites unless the King, who had been a slave to his lusts, gave plain signs of repentance. First of all the main cause of the offense must be swept away, and in stifled tones, obsessed by the specter of hellfire, King Louis bade farewell to Madame Du Barry, the one human being he was really fond of. She drove forthwith to the Château of Rueil.

At length confession and communion were possible. But the Church demanded from a monarch who had lived in open sin a public avowal of his faults. Drums sounded as the high clergy marched in solemn procession from the chapel to the sickroom, bearing the Host. In the breathless silence of the anteroom, the assembled court could hear the cardinal's low tones; through the open doors they saw him administer Holy Communion to the King. Then, turning to the doorway, he uplifted his voice: "Gentlemen, the King instructs me to tell you that he asks God's pardon for the scandalous example he has set his people; that if God vouchsafes the restoration of his health, he will devote himself to repentance, to the support of religion, and to relieving the lot of his people." Thereupon a murmur, heard only by those near him, came from the dying man. "I wish I had been strong enough to say that myself."

Now the court waited impatiently for the fall of the curtain. Horses stood harnessed to remove the new Louis from further risk of infection the instant the old King had expired. At one of the sickroom windows a candle was burning; its extinction would be the signal. At length, on May 10, 1774, it was given. The murmur of the onlookers rose and swelled; shouts passed from room to room: "The King is dead, long live the King!"

Marie Antoinette was sitting apart with her husband in a small room. Suddenly they heard a strange clamor, drawing ever nearer. Then the door burst open. As if blown by a storm, Madame de Noailles entered, knelt, and was the first to kiss the new Queen's hand. Behind her came the others, more and more, the whole court, for everyone was eager to pay homage.

The royal chariot bore a new king and a proud and carefree new queen through the gilded park gates of Versailles. The people in the streets shouted joyously as they drove by, inspired with an old delusive hope. Neither Marie Antoinette nor Louis had done anything or promised anything, and yet both the young rulers were greeted with enthusiasm. Surely a new golden age will begin, thought the credulous people, now that the courtesan who was so spendthrift has fallen from power, now that the old voluptuary Louis XV has died; now that we have a king who is simple in his tastes, modest, and pious; now that we have a queen who is so charming, so young, and so kindly.

Only one person in Europe, the Empress Maria Theresa, was deeply moved at the death of Louis XV. Thirty laborious years had taught her how burdensome is a crown. To her daughter's proud letter announcing the promotion, Maria Theresa replied:

> I do not compliment you on your new dignity, which is dearly bought, but which will become even more costly unless you can go on leading the quiet and innocent life you have led during these three years. . . . You must learn to interest yourself in serious matters, for this may be most useful if the King should ask your counsel.

At the very time when the whole world was making much of Marie Antoinette and envying her good luck, the mother wrote to Mercy with a sigh: "I fancy her good days are past."

And in truth, to be Queen meant nothing more for Marie Antionette, who had forgotten her people, than increased scope for personal freedom.

WHEN THE DAUGHTER of his old adversary Maria Theresa mounted the French throne, the King of Prussia, Frederick the Great, became uneasy. He had good reason to scent danger. Louis XVI, though of sound enough intelligence, was timid and had lead in his veins. Marie Antoinette had merely to exert her will and all the threads of French diplomacy would have been in her hands. But, fortunately for Prussia and disastrously for herself, Marie Antoinette was not in the least attracted by the great historical possibilities that loomed before her. She had no thought of trying to understand the time in which she lived; no political ideas to stamp upon the wall.

From the outset, the Queen's mistake was that she wished to conquer as woman instead of as queen. Her utmost ambition, for fifteen years or so, was to be admired as the smartest, the most coquettish, the best dressed, and above all the best amused woman at court; to set the tone for an artificial society which regarded itself as the world. Throughout this period she played her role as Queen of the Rococo with unrivaled grace and charm, acting in her private theater at Versailles, which was built over an abyss. A glance would have told Marie Antoinette that outside her narrow circle millions of the French people toiled and hungered, hoped and despaired. But she would not look. She wanted to go on living in her sanctuary, youthful, heedless, and unmolested.

Such was her fault. And yet it is understandable by the strength of the temptation. Marie Antoinette's eighteenth-century court knew from the start how to bewitch an immature, nineteen-year-old girl, still curious about herself, not yet ready for power. Whatever she said was acclaimed as wonderfully clever; whatever she wanted was done; did she commit a folly, the whole court imitated her; for this vainglorious and ambitious crowd her glance was a gift; her laugh entranced them; her coming was a festival. If she passed a mirror, she saw a very pretty young woman, gorgeously attired, beaming with delight at her own triumph.

How could one with the heart of a child defend herself against such intoxication? Her frivolous outlook was not peculiar to Marie Antoinette. "Let me enjoy myself! Why should I bother to think things over, to calculate and economize?" Such was the dominant feeling of a whole generation of persons of station— of the Rococo generation to which, symbolically, she was assigned as Queen.

Marie Antoinette became the embodiment of the manners and artificialities of the eighteenth century. The writer Madame de Staël commented on her: "It is difficult to put more grace and more kindliness into civility than she does. She . . . does not allow us to forget that she is queen, and yet always produces in us the impression that she herself has forgotten it."

It was her delicate charm which everyone admired in Marie Antoinette. But her real witchery lay in the inimitable grace of her movements. When she impetuously ran as if on wings up the stairs, when she stretched forward her white hand to be kissed, every movement seemed the result of feminine intuition. And movement was the Queen's true element. She liked to buzz hither and thither. To be always beginning some new task which she would never finish; to sleep only a short time, never to think long, to be perpetually on the go, frittering away her days. During her years on the throne, Marie Antoinette moved increasingly in an orbit around her own ego.

What is the first thought of the Queen of the Rococo when she wakes of a morning in her palace at Versailles? To read the reports from the capital or from the provinces? Nothing of the sort. The day begins with an imposing ceremony. The mistress of the robes appears with the chemises and other articles of apparel essential to the morning toilette. By her side, the first lady's maid holds out to the Queen a folio volume into which patterns of all the dresses in the wardrobe have been pinned. Marie Antoinette has to decide which gowns she would like to don today. How difficult, how responsible is the choice, seeing that for each season of the year twelve dresses for state occasions, twelve for private entertainments, and twelve robes of ceremony are available. The selection usually takes a considerable time.

Need we be surprised that the chief dressmaker, the divine Mademoiselle Bertin, exerted more influence over Marie Antoinette than the ministers of state? For her sake there was a palace revolution nearly eighteen years before the real revolution began. Mademoiselle Bertin had made short work of the rule of etiquette which forbade any bourgeois or bourgeoise the entry into the *petits cabinets* of the Queen. This artist of scissors and needle achieved what proved beyond the power of Voltaire or of any of the great writers or painters of the day. When she appeared twice a week with her schemes for new creations, Marie Antoinette left the court ladies to their own devices and held a private council with the venerated modiste.

To be queen in the world of fashion above all, seemed to

Marie Antoinette her unequivocal duty. After three months on the throne, she had become the talk in this respect of every drawing room and every court in Europe. Maria Theresa, who could have wished Toinette to be better occupied, sent back to Mercy in Paris a picture showing her daughter decked out in the most preposterous way, with an angry request to be informed whether this was the presentment of an actress or that of the Queen of France.

The second great task of the morning was the dressing of the Queen's hair. Happily in this matter too she had the assistance of a great artist, Monsieur Leonard, the Figaro of the Rococo, who constructed above the forehead of every lady of rank a towering edifice of hair decked with symbolical ornamentations. Not only were landscapes and panoramas, with fruit, gardens, houses, ships, modeled on the summit of this *pouf*, but current events were taken note of to produce frequent changes in fashion. If the King was inoculated for smallpox, due notice of this remarkable occurrence was taken by the appearance of *poufs de l'inoculation*. When the American rebellion was the center of fashionable interest, the *coiffure de la liberté* made its appearance. When the populace was on the verge of famine, and the baker shops in Paris were being plundered, the frivolous society of the court could find nothing better to do than to record the incident in ladies' headdresses as *bonnets de la révolte*. These artificial structures surmounting empty heads attained such altitude that ladies could no longer sit in their carriages, but had to kneel down. The very doorways in the palace had to be made higher and the ceilings of the boxes in the theaters were reconstructed into arches.

As for the third great concern of Marie Antoinette's toilette, it related to this question: Could a woman dress in a new creation without having an appropriate change of ornaments? Of course not! Obviously, moreover, a queen needed larger diamonds and thicker strings of pearls than any other woman. Marie Antoinette, as everyone at Versailles knew, had gone mad about ornaments. She simply could not resist when her shrewd and subtle jewelers, Boehmer and Bassenge, showed her their latest ear pendants, rings, and diamond-headed pins. Marie Antoinette incurred debts all over the place, confident that in case of need her thrifty spouse would come to her rescue.

Another growl from Vienna: "I have news from Paris to the effect that you have been buying bracelets at a cost of two hundred and fifty thousand livres, with the result that you have thrown your finances into disorder. . . ." Again: "I know too well how extravagant are your tastes, and I cannot keep silent about the matter, for I love you too heartily. . . . Everyone knows that the King is extremely modest in his expenditure, so the whole blame will rest on your shoulders. I hope I shall not live to see the disaster that is likely to ensue."

Diamonds are expensive, fine gowns are expensive, and although on coming to the throne the kind Louis had doubled his wife's allowance, there must have been a hole in her purse, for it was almost always empty.

How was she to keep herself in funds? Luckily the devil had provided her with the gaming table. Louis XIV had stopped gambling at court. But Marie Antoinette rediscovered for herself the notorious faro which, as we learn from Casanova, was the favorite hunting ground of eighteenth-century cardsharpers. When the passion for high play possessed her, nothing could restrain her, and courtiers and court ladies alike recked little that Louis XVI had forbidden gambling under severe penalties. The police had no access to the Queen's salons, and the doorkeepers had been instructed to give the alarm when the King was coming. In order to liven up the play and increase the turnover of coin, the Queen admitted to her gaming table anyone who had money in his purse. Touts and nighthawks were quick to avail themselves of their opportunities; and it was not long before rumor was rife in Paris that cheating at cards was the order of the day in the Queen's drawing room. Besides King Louis, there was only one person who failed to be aware of the fact—Marie Antoinette who did not want to know, because she was blinded by her craving for amusement.

Nothing but perpetual change in the round of pleasures appeased her nervous unrest. "If what you did were always done in the King's company," her mother wrote, "I should hold my peace, but what distresses me is that almost invariably you gad about apart from him, and in the company of all that is worst and youngest in Paris. . . . The newspapers, the leaflets which used to delight me because they had so much to say about my daughter's magnanimity and kindness, have suddenly changed their tone. I read in them nothing except accounts of horse races, gambling, the turning of night into day, so that I can no longer bear to look at them. . . ."

Concerning such maternal reproof, Marie Antoinette unbosomed herself to Mercy with alarming frankness: "What does she want? I am terrified of being bored."

No novelist could have invented a more glaring contrast than that which existed between the King and Queen. He was dull, she was sparkling; he was irresolute, she was quick to make up her mind; he was strictly religious, she was worldly; he was pedantic, she was frivolous; his world was the day, hers the night. Toward eleven at night, when Louis XVI went to bed, Marie Antoinette began to wake up thoroughly—one day at the card table or in the gaming room, another day at a ball. She did not turn over in bed until he had been up for many hours at the chase. Their habits, their tastes were utterly disharmonious.

Am I describing a marriage in which the partners were perpetually at odds? By no means! Both Marie Antoinette and Louis XVI did their utmost to avoid tension, he from bodily and she from mental indolence. Though she smiled at him a little for being so complaisant a husband, she had no malice in her smile; for in a careless way she was fond of him, looking upon him much as if he had been a huge, rough St. Bernard whom it was amusing to pat now and then. She would never be unkind to this prematurely obese and awkward spouse who accorded her every freedom and, in his frigid way, was devoted to her. Marie Antoinette came to esteem the character of one who deserved respect notwithstanding his weakness. By degrees they became good comrades, so that in this regard the marriage compared favorably with most royal marriages of the time.

But as for love, Marie Antoinette's liking for her husband was tinged too much with compassion and even condescension to be worthy of the word. Joseph II, returning to Vienna after his visit to Paris, said bluntly: "She has absolutely no love for him."

TRIANON

Marie Antoinette's dairy at the Little Trianon

MARIE ANTOINETTE wanted to combine two things which are, in actual human experience, incompatible; she wanted to reign and at the same time to enjoy. But freedom for every caprice was not possible at Versailles, where every step the ruler took was open to public gaze. Marie Antoinette detested control of any kind, and, almost immediately after she became Queen, she asked her obliging husband to provide her with some corner where she need not be Queen. Whereupon Louis XVI bestowed on her the summer palace, the Little Trianon.

This retired nook in Versailles park was one of the most graceful creations of French taste, delicate in design, perfect in execution. It was a dollhouse, a villa in the neoclassical style, well out of sight of Versailles and yet conveniently near. Having excellent taste, the Queen introduced nothing pompous or ostentatious into its seven or eight rooms. All was done lightly in that new and intimate style which is wrongly termed "Louis Seize," for it is Marie Antoinette whom its charming characteristics recall. Everything of the Little Trianon reminds us of her frivolous and bewitching feminine figure.

To Marie Antoinette this Lilliputian palace was more important than the whole of France where dwelt her twenty million subjects. Here she felt emancipated; in this petty realm she and no one else was supreme. Even her husband, the Most Christian King of France, appeared at the Little Trianon as a guest. Tactful and complaisant as ever, he was careful not to turn up uninvited or at inconvenient times.

Marie Antoinette soon was so fascinated by the informal life at her "country house" that she found it hard to go back to Versailles in the evening. Her court duties became more irksome to her and, as was her wont, she followed her preferences. For practical purposes, the summer palace became her residence.

At Trianon her idle spirit had at length found occupation. Superadded to dressmaker and jeweler were the architect, the landscape gardener, the decorator; new ministers of her petty kingdom, helping her to while away the hours and to empty the treasury of the state. Spurred on by the Queen's impatience, hundreds of workmen, guided by plans and drawings, began to conjure up an artificially natural landscape. First of all, as an indispensable requisite of a pastoral scene, there must be a gently murmuring brook. Since there was no local spring to tap, the water had to be brought in pipes all the way from Marly, and much gold as well as water ran through the conduit!

Further expensive trifles were continually being added to the garden. A tiny temple, consecrated to the god of love, crowned a hillock, winding paths led through the little wood, and the lawns were planted with exotic flowers. Various extras were engaged to intensify the genuineness of this pastoral comedy: real peasants; real cows, real calves, pigs, rabbits, and sheep. Hard by Trianon, Marie Antoinette had the famous *Hameau* built. Mique, the distinguished architect, and Hubert Robert, the famous painter, designed and superintended the building of eight little peasant farms with thatched roofs, farmyards, hay-ricks, barns and dungheaps, all complete, imitating the romantic decay of the actual dwellings of the countryfolk.

In this outdoor theater, at a time when throughout France the unhappy peasants were growing riotous, sheep were led to pasture by ribbons of blue silk. Sometimes the Queen, with a parasol held over her head by one of her ladies, came to look on while the washerwomen did their work in the rippling brook. Marie Antoinette wore dresses of thin muslin, rural in their simplicity, and had herself painted in them for a few thousand livres. She enjoyed the most innocent pleasures: she fished; she culled flowers; she played catch ball. She and intimates hung swings between the trees; they played hide-and-seek among the cottages and in the shady paths; they staged little dramas, being audience and actors by turns.

Private theatricals were the most recent of Queen Marie Antoinette's discoveries. She had begun by the building of a tiny private theater for performances by Italian and French companies. This caprice cost her 141,000 livres. Then she was bitten by the idea of appearing herself on the boards, and her light-hearted companions were delighted to join in the frolic. After this it was carnival time at Trianon all through the year.

The final account for the Trianon was not cast up until August 31, 1791. The total amount was more than two million livres. When on trial before the Revolutionary Tribunal, the "Widow Capet" had to admit: "It is likely enough that the Little Trianon cost huge sums of money, and perhaps more than I intended. . . ."

In the political field, as well, the Queen had to pay dearly for her caprices. By leaving Versailles to its own devices, she robbed court life of vital significance. The lady whose function it was to hand her her gloves, the maids of honor, the knights of honor, the thousand underlings—what was left for them to do when the Queen spent all her time at Trianon? Ere long, good society began to keep away from Versailles. The French nobility, as ancient as the Habsburgs, had too high an opinion of itself to be satisfied with occasional bowing and scraping at a formal reception. More and more conspicuous, and more and more envenomed, became the Fronde party that was formed by the neglected blue bloods of France against the Queen.

Had Marie Antoinette continued to hold her court at Versailles, amid the customary pomps and ceremonies, in the hour of peril she would have had the support of her royal relatives and of all the distinguished and powerful persons in France. But scarcely had she settled into her bright and cheerful abode than she began to ply a new broom. She wanted only young people around her, merry folk, who would not spoil sport by the foolishness of taking life too seriously.

This cheerful company of idlers had a sort of contemptuous liking for the King, who was ready to sign "Louis" on the decrees with which Marie Antoinette assigned them their well-paid posts. But the excellent and tedious creature was out of his element in the new society. It was his youngest brother, the Comte d'Artois, who represented the royal family at Trianon. A libertine, a shallow-pated and amusing spendthrift, he was the leader of the company in any new pleasure, and a gay companion for Marie Antoinette. In truth, however, she neither liked him nor loved him, although there was much gossip at court about their relations.

More dangerous to the Queen than her untrustworthy cavaliers (the Duc de Coigny, the Duc de Guines, the young hothead Duc de Lauzun) were her women friends, for here strangely mingled energies played a sinister part. Taken early from her mother, wedded to a man who was neither physically competent nor spiritually affectionate, she had, as a matter of course, the inclination to find relief in a passion for somebody. Since, for propriety's sake, she would not (or would not yet) seek it in a man, it was only natural that her first relationships with women friends should be strongly tinged by affection. It was also natural that at the French court, where the French attitude toward matters sexual was dominant, such unconventional behavior on the part of a queen should be grossly misinterpreted. Whispers began to circulate concerning the Queen's Sapphic inclinations. "There have very generally been ascribed to me two tastes, that for women and that for lovers," writes Marie Antoinette serenely to her mother.

The Queen's first favorite, Madame de Lamballe, was a comparatively fortunate choice. Belonging to one of the best families of France, and therefore with no greed either for money or for power, and quite free from ambition, she responded to Marie Antoinette's affection with sincere friendship. One evening, however, at a court ball during the year 1775 the Queen noticed a young woman with a face pure as an angel's and was informed that it was the wife of Jules de Polignac. Going up to the young lady, the Queen asked her why she so seldom appeared at court. "I am not well enough off to figure on state occasions," replied the Comtesse de Polignac artlessly. The Queen was charmed by such sincerity. Instantly she invited the Comtesse de Polignac to become a regular attendant at court, showing so marked a preference for her as to arouse envy. Within a few months the impoverished noblewoman had become supreme over Marie Antoinette and her circle.

Unfortunately, however, this tender and innocent angel had not come down from heaven, but sprang from a family up to the eyes in debt and eager to turn such unexpected favor to pecuniary account. To begin with, the debts were paid, and in due time the whole worthless clan wallowed in money and in honors, and was able, over and above this, to empty a cornucopia filled with privileges into the greedy hands of their friends. Marie Antoinette had become utterly enslaved by this cold and designing band of worthless creatures who constituted her daily entourage. Need we be surprised that there was increasing bitterness among those excluded from position and sinecure, that from the desolate windows of Versailles hatred with a hundred eyes glowered at the lightsome and unsuspecting play world of the Queen?

VII

A HAPPY TURN IN EVENTS

Count Mercy   Emperor Joseph II

IN THE YEAR 1777 Marie Antoinette's pleasure hunt attained its climax. Never had her restlessness been more crazy. Mercy sent dispatch after dispatch to Vienna: "Her Majesty has utterly forgotten her dignity. . . . The different varieties of pleasure follow each other with such rapidity that it is difficult to find a moment in which to speak to her of serious matters."

Now a new danger threatened. In 1777 Marie Antoinette was no longer the simple girl of fifteen who had arrived in France.

She was two-and-twenty, voluptuously beautiful, and it would have been unnatural if she had remained cold amid the sensual atmosphere of the Versailles court. She had tried to gratify her longing for the tender passion by intimate friendships. But since she was a thoroughly natural and normal woman, this did not suffice her.

More and more, in her association with the young gentlemen of her circle, Marie Antoinette began to lose the untroubled confidence of her early poise, to play with fire. She grew pale and red by turns; she trembled in the proximity of these youths. She was confused at times, her eyes brimming over with tears, and she continually craved gallant compliments. We read in Lauzun's memoirs of a remarkable scene in which, after she had just lost her temper with him, Marie Antoinette suddenly flung her arms around him, and then, frightened and ashamed, fled from the spot.

Presumably Mercy, the watchdog, knew that the moth was fluttering nearer and nearer to the flame, and realized what a catastrophe it would be if the Queen were to give herself to the embraces of an illicit lover before she had presented her husband with a lawful heir. He therefore sent still another dispatch to Vienna begging Emperor Joseph to come to Versailles and see if he could set right the matter of the King's nonfulfillment of his marital duties.

As we know, the Emperor complied, and found little difficulty in persuading his brother-in-law to submit to the needed operation. Within a few weeks of Joseph's visit, his sister could report to Vienna: "I have attained the happiness which is of the utmost importance to my whole life. More than a week ago my marriage was thoroughly consummated."

This happy turn in events did not long remain a secret. The Spanish ambassador, best informed of the diplomatic corps, was actually in a position to acquaint his royal master with the precise date (August 25). But it was not until the following April that the impatient wife had good reason to believe herself with child. On July 31 she was unmistakably certain of it, and she announced his fatherhood to her husband in a way which was extremely original. Entering his presence, she pulled a long face, as if she had been ill-used, saying: "I have come, Sire, to complain of one of your subjects who has been so audacious as to kick me in the belly." The worthy Louis was puzzled for a moment, then laughed with a comfortable pride, and clasped his wife in his arms.

The public announcement of the pregnancy was followed by innumerable ceremonies. *"Te Deums"* were sung in the churches; the Parlement of Paris sent congratulations, a hundred thousand livres were held in readiness for distribution among the poor. All the world was agog waiting for the Queen to be brought to bed, and not least the members of the court. For in accordance with a custom hallowed by centuries, the delivery of a queen of France was anything but a private affair. It must be witnessed by all the princes and princesses and by the court grandees.

On December 18 the ringing of bells announced that the labor pains had begun. A few minutes later, more than fifty spectators forced their way into the Queen's bedroom. Some seated themselves in order of precedence in the armchairs around the bed. Others climbed on benches ranged beside the walls. No one thought of opening a window, and the scene of public torture lasted for seven hours. At length, Marie Antoinette gave birth to the child—alas, a daughter.

The royal infant had been reverently carried into the dressing room to be washed, when suddenly there came a shout from the *accoucheur:* "Air and hot water! Her Majesty must be bled." The Queen had lost consciousness, half suffocated by the pestilential atmosphere. The alarm was general; the King opened a window with his own hand, and the room was cleared. The surgeon ventured to open a vein in the foot. Blood flowed freely; the Queen opened her eyes; she was saved.

Now there was an outburst of rejoicing and public festival in the wide land of France. The disastrous spell on the royal marriage had been broken. Yet there was one person, not in France, who was but partially satisfied—Maria Theresa. As Empress, as stateswoman, she had dynastic considerations at heart. "We absolutely need a dauphin, an heir to the throne," she admonished her daughter.

But this last joy of knowing that a king of France with Habsburg blood in his veins had been born was not to be granted her. Not until 1781, a year after Maria Theresa's death, did Marie Antoinette give birth to a son. In view of the menace of disaster during the first childbed, only the Queen's closest relatives had access on this occasion. When the newborn child was taken away, however, the Queen was still too weak to ask whether it was a boy or a girl. The King came to her bedside, tears flowing down his cheeks, as he said in his sonorous voice: *"Monsieur le Dauphin demande à entrer."*

All the ceremonies proper to the birth of a crown prince were now carried out. The guilds, one and all, sent delegations to Versailles, each attended by musicians, and the ceremony of their reception occupied nine days. The members of the chimney sweeps' guild carried a chimney on the top of which were seated little chimney sweeps singing merrily; the sedan-chair men had a gilded chair in which fancy-dress figures of a wet nurse and a little dauphin were seated; the shoemakers bore babies' shoes. As for the locksmiths, who knew the King had a special taste for their craft, they brought a huge, artfully contrived lock out of which, when Louis XVI unlocked it, there sprang a tiny dauphin marvelously fashioned in steel. The marketwomen, many of them the same women who a few years later were to hail the Queen with the vilest invectives and obscenities, had decked themselves out in black silk dresses and recited an address penned by the poet de Laharpe.

The populace was still one with its rulers; the Dauphin had been born, not only to his royal parents, but also to the country at large, and his arrival was an occasion for universal delight. Everyone loved, everyone praised the King and Queen who had at length so valiantly performed their duty.

Twice more did Marie Antoinette become a mother. In 1785 she gave birth to a second son, the future Louis XVII, a vigorous and healthy boy, "a typical peasant youngster." In 1786 was born Sophie Béatrix, who died just before reaching the age of one. With motherhood began the first transformation in Marie Antoinette, not yet a decisive metamorphosis, but the beginning of one. She soon began to find it more agreeable to play with her children than to stake money at the gaming table; the

tender emotion which, for want of a better object, had been squandered upon carousals, had at length found a normal outlet. Could she have had a few tranquil and happy years, she would herself have grown tranquil, this lovely woman with the gentle eyes. But this respite was never to be accorded her by fate.

VIII

THE QUEEN BECOMES UNPOPULAR

Duc d'Orléans   Comte de Provence

WITH THE BIRTH of the Dauphin, Marie Antoinette had become, as it were, queen for a second time. What was now needed was that she should take a decisive step—from Trianon back to Versailles, to Paris, out of the Rococo world into the real one, out of her giddy entourage back to the old nobility and to the people. Then all would be well. But as soon as the popular festivals were over, she resumed the costly and disastrous amusements at the Little Trianon. Thenceforward her course led downward toward the abyss.

To begin with, all that could be noticed was that the ladies and gentlemen of the court grew increasingly aloof. People served the Queen with due attention, but they preserved a chilly silence—the malicious and ominous silence of a conspiracy.

This conspiracy had its headquarters in various royal palaces. Evil-tongued gossip against Marie Antoinette was led by the three maiden aunts whom she had thrust into the background and who had retired to the Château of Bellevue. The numerous ladies who were not invited to Trianon, the disregarded Madame Etiquette, the dismissed ministers of state, the unsuccessful place hunters, gathered around them in this arsenal of scandal.

Here were composed spiteful couplets, winged words which flew from Bellevue to Versailles, and thence farther afield.

More dangerous than this toothless yesterday, which could no longer bite, was the intelligent and cultured middle class that had come into being and was weary of being kept in the background. The new bourgeois had been taught by Jean Jacques Rousseau that they possessed rights. Those of their order who returned to France after taking part in the American War of Independence brought tidings of a remarkable country where differences of caste had been abolished by the notions of equality and liberty. In France, however, they found nothing but rigidity and decay. With growing bitterness the enlightened bourgeoisie saw how the nation's position of power in the world was being forfeited, how the army and the navy were shrinking, how the colonies were being lost.

There were good reasons why this patriotic discontent should make Marie Antoinette its target. The whole country knew that the King was incapable of effective decision and that her influence was all-powerful. Prompted by the Polignac clique, she was continually interfering when there was question of filling an important post, amateurishly thrusting her finger into every pie, meddling in matters of the utmost moment. And since the various generals and ambassadors and ministers she appointed were for the most part incompetent, since France was drifting swiftly toward bankruptcy, the blame for these disasters was placed upon the Queen's shoulders, although, from her own outlook, she had done nothing more than provide a few delightful persons with good positions.

Those who wanted a better ordering of public affairs had long been in need of a rallying point. At length it was discovered in one man, the Duc d'Orléans in the Palais Royal. The duc was vain, and Marie Antoinette had mortified his vanity, for, with a quip about her cousin's achievements as a warrior, she had prevented the bestowal on him of the office of lord high admiral of France. The Duc d'Orléans had not been slow to take up the gauntlet. Sprung from a branch of the royal house as old as that to which Louis belonged, wealthy and independent, he did not hesitate to run counter to the King's will in the Parlement of Paris and to treat the Queen as a declared enemy. It was natural, therefore, that he should become the leader of the malcontents, and that the Palais Royal should be the first of the revolutionary clubs.

Between these two groups of the Queen's enemies, the revolutionists and the reactionaries, there stood the man who was perhaps the most dangerous of all to Marie Antoinette, her brother-in-law, the inscrutable Comte de Provence. A cautious intriguer, moving like a shadow, he later mounted the throne as Louis XVIII, fulfilling what had been since early childhood a supreme ambition. His expectations of succession had risen high during the seven unfruitful years of Louis XVI's marriage; they had been dashed when his sister-in-law was at length with child; and the birth of the Dauphin seemed to all a final blow to his hopes. It was not until the Revolution loomed that this secret pretender to the crown began his suspicious machinations in the Luxembourg Palace.

The animosities directed against Marie Antoinette from all sides, after her ten wasted years on the throne, had become virulent. Malicious printed or written leaflets were passed from hand to hand beneath the table. Distinguished noblemen would visit the bookshops of the Palais Royal and purchase the latest lampoon directed against the Queen. Ostensibly printed in London or Amsterdam, it would really be damp from the press, probably machined in the Duc d'Orléans's palace or in the Luxembourg. Secretly distributed, these derogatory writings fluttered like bats through the park gates of Versailles and into the châteaux of the provinces; but when the lieutenant of police tried to run the offenders to earth, he found himself checked by invisible powers. The Queen would find a versicle at table when she unfolded her napkin; the King would come across one among his official documents. When Marie Antoinette went to the theater, one would be pinned to the balustrade in front of her seat.

The lampoons of the early years were outrageous, but it was after the birth of the Dauphin, incontestably the rightful heir to the throne, that they assumed their worst form. Marie Antoinette was described as a nymphomaniac with perverse inclinations; Louis was a poor weakling on whom his wife had put the horns; the Dauphin was a bastard (which was in the interest of the Comte de Provence).

The concert of calumny was in full swing. Marie Antoinette was prejudged before ever she was indicted at the Revolutionary Tribunal. It was the court which really drafted the indictment.

A THUNDERCLAP IN THE ROCOCO THEATER

Louis, Cardinal de Rohan

IN THE BEGINNING of August 1785 the Queen was busier than usual. Beaumarchais's *Le Barbier de Séville* was to be produced in the little gold-and-white palace theater, with a distinguished cast. The Comte d'Artois was to appear as Figaro; Vaudreuil, Madame de Polignac's lover, was to play the Count; the Queen was to represent the merry girl Rosine. She was all unaware that the curtain was about to rise upon another comedy in which, unwittingly, she had been chosen to play the chief part.

On a day when the rehearsals of *Le Barbier de Séville* were drawing to a close, Marie Antoinette was having misgivings. Would she really look young enough and pretty enough as Rosine; and why was Madame Campan, with whom she was to go through her part once more, so late? Ah, here she was at last, but in a great state of excitement.

At length Madame Campan recovered her composure, and was able to explain stammeringly that Boehmer, the court jeweler, had come to her much perturbed, asking her to procure for him an audience of the Queen. A few months ago, he said, the Queen had secretly purchased from him the famous and costly diamond necklace which he and his partner had made, and had arranged to pay for it by installments. But the first installment was long overdue, and he needed money forthwith.

All of this was incomprehensible to Marie Antoinette. Of course she knew about the necklace which had been offered her for 1,600,000 livres. Of course she would have liked to buy it, but she could not get the money out of the ministers of state. There must be some preposterous misunderstanding. She had an appointment made with Boehmer, and, on August 9, he told her a story that made her think the man must have gone mad. He spoke of a Comtesse de Valois, who was unknown to the Queen, as "an intimate friend of Your Majesty." This comtesse had declared that the Queen wished to buy the necklace secretly. "Then," Boehmer went on, "His Eminence the Cardinal de Rohan took possession of the necklace, stating that he had been commissioned to do so by Your Majesty."

Outraged, the Queen commanded the jeweler to write a full account of the whole affair. By the twelfth of August this strange document, which is still to be seen in the archives, was in her hands. When she read it, her wrath concentrated upon one name, that of Louis Cardinal de Rohan whom for years she had loathed with all the uncontrol of her impulsive character.

The Queen's detestation of the Cardinal was inherited from her mother. Louis de Rohan, a worldly-minded nobleman in Holy Orders, had formerly been ambassador in Vienna and had aroused the fierce anger of Maria Theresa. It was intolerable to her that a man of God should wear a brown shooting jacket, and, surrounded by fawning ladies, bring down one hundred thirty head of game in a single day. Maria Theresa could not bear that her strictly religious Vienna should become a frivolous Versailles. Letter after letter went to her daughter, demanding that this "contemptible creature" be recalled. And in fact, very soon after Marie Antoinette became Queen, she obediently saw to it that Louis Rohan was dismissed from his ambassadorship.

But when a Rohan falls, he falls upward. He was made a bishop, and shortly afterward grand almoner of France, thus becoming the highest ecclesiastical dignitary at the court. Spendthrift and frivolous, Rohan squandered his considerable income with both hands, and soon it was an open secret that his finances were embarrassed. From the first, therefore, the Queen was convinced that this Brother Lightfoot had organized the swindle of the necklace in order to raise funds, believing, as she wrote to Joseph II, that "he would be able to repay the jeweler at the appointed time without anything being discovered."

During the last eight years Marie Antoinette had not addressed to Rohan a single word, but had flouted him in the face of the whole court. It seemed to her, therefore, an act of revenge that he should have dragged her name into a conspiracy of cheats; of all the attacks on her honor by the French nobility, she regarded this as the basest. Passionately, with tears in her eyes, she told the King about the business on August 14, and implored him to defend her honor by making a public example of this deceiver.

The King, being completely subservient to his wife, did not trouble to scrutinize the details of the charge. On August 15 he astonished and alarmed the ministerial council by announcing his intention to have the Cardinal arrested immediately. Since it was not only the Feast of the Assumption but the Queen's name day, the Oeil de Boeuf and the galleries were thronged with courtiers, and among them was the unsuspecting Rohan, who was to fulfill his pontifical function on this august occasion.

But Louis XVI and his wife did not appear in state at Mass together as was expected. Instead Rohan was summoned into the King's private apartments. There stood the Queen with gaze averted. "My dear cousin, I want to know all about the diamond necklace which you bought in the Queen's name," the King said bluntly.

Rohan turned pale. "Sire," he said stammeringly, "I was myself deceived, but I have deceived no one." Words failed him, and the kindly Louis told him to write what he had to say about the matter.

His Eminence wrote and handed to the King about fifteen lines. A woman named Valois had commissioned him to get the necklace for the Queen. He realized now that she had cheated him.

"Where is this woman?" asked Louis.

"Sire, I do not know."

"Have you the necklace?"

"It is in this woman's hands."

Although the Cardinal offered to pay for the necklace, Marie Antoinette could not contain herself. She asked Rohan angrily how he could possibly have believed that she, who for years had addressed him never a word, would have employed him as a go-between in order to buy the necklace behind her husband's back. To this reproach the despairing Cardinal could find no answer. He was now unable to understand how he could ever have been fool enough to become involved in the imbroglio. Louis was sorry for him, but said: "I hope you will be able to justify yourself! Meanwhile I have no choice but to have the seals placed on your house and to put you under arrest. The Queen's name is precious to me." Rohan besought the monarch to spare him this disgrace, but the interview was over.

In the crowded anteroom the nobles were waiting impatiently. Mass ought to have begun long since. Suddenly the folding doors leading into the King's private apartments were thrown open. The first to appear was the Cardinal de Rohan in his scarlet cassock, pale of countenance and with pinched lips; behind him came Baron Breteuil, the minister of state, his eyes sparkling with excitement. He shouted to the captain of the bodyguard: "Arrest Monsieur le Cardinal!"

A cardinal to be arrested! A Rohan! And in the King's anteroom! Before he had been conveyed to the Bastille, the prisoner took advantage of the prevailing consternation to pencil a few lines instructing his private chaplain to burn with all possible speed the documents in a red portfolio. These, as subsequently transpired at the trial, were the forged letters purporting to have been written by the Queen. One of the Cardinal's mounted couriers galloped off with this message and reached his master's house before the police arrived to place the papers under seal. As for the Mass, no Mass was said at Versailles that Assumption Day.

Behind the closed door remained the Queen. No one, not even her closest friends, came to her. The nobles did not trouble to conceal their indignation that the Cardinal de Rohan should have been so dishonored. Marie Antoinette began to be uneasy. That evening her ladies-in-waiting found her in tears.

Soon, however, her habitual high spirits returned. Foolishly self-deceived, she wrote to her brother Joseph: "For my part, I am delighted that we shall no longer hear anything about this horrid affair." The trial before the Parlement of Paris could not possibly take place before December. No need to stop the performance of a delightful comedy. Instead of studying the police reports relating to the great trial, the Queen went on studying the part of the lively Rosine in *Le Barbier de Séville*.

X

THE DIAMOND NECKLACE

Comte
Nicolas de Lamotte

Comtesse
de Lamotte-Valois

THE FIGURE around whom the affair of the diamond necklace circled had been a neglected child, daughter of an impoverished nobleman and a dissolute serving maid. When her father died and her mother became a streetwalker, the girl took to begging, and at seven, by a stroke of luck, she approached the Marquise de Boulainvilliers with what seemed incredible patter: "Give alms to a poor orphan sprung from the blood of the Valois!" What! Was this dirty and affamished little creature in truth of royal blood? The marquise told her coachman to pull up, and she questioned the little beggar girl exhaustively.

The girl Jeanne was in very fact the legitimate daughter of Jacques-Rémy, who, though a poacher and a drunkard, was unquestionably an offspring of the House of Valois, which was just as old and just as distinguished as the House of Bourbon. The Marquise de Boulainvilliers, profoundly touched by the sad fate of such royal spawn, took Jeanne under her care, and when she was fourteen, the girl was admitted to a convent for daughters of the nobility. It became apparent, however, that little Jeanne was unfitted for a cloistered existence. Penniless, but high-spirited and adventurous, she ran away from the nunnery at twenty-two and turned up in Bar-sur-Aube. There a sprig of the lesser nobility, Nicolas de Lamotte, an officer in the gendarmerie, married her. From the first Jeanne had had but one thought—to climb, no matter how. She importuned her benefactress the Marquise de Boulainvilliers until the latter secured for her the entry to Cardinal de Rohan's palace at Zabern. Being clever as well as pretty, she was able to play upon the weaknesses of the Cardinal. Through her intermediation (presumably at the cost of wearing an invisible pair of horns) her husband was appointed captain in a regiment of dragoons and had his debts paid.

This was but one step in an ascending career. On his own responsibility, Jeanne's spouse dubbed himself comte, and to a pretty and unscrupulous woman, determined to plunder the vain and the foolish, so fine a name as Comtesse de Lamotte-Valois was worth a hundred thousand livres a year. In order to open their campaign, this precious pair rented a mansion in Paris, in the Rue Neuve-Saint-Gilles, prattled to moneylenders about the huge estate to which the comtesse was rightfully entitled as a descendant of the Valois, and kept open house with the funds thus obtained. There were many amusing (and lucrative) card parties for the pigeons who came to be plucked. Still, the earnings did not balance expenditures. When their creditors began to press for payment, the Comtesse de Lamotte-Valois fobbed them off by telling them she was going to Versailles to push her claim at court.

It need hardly be said that she did not know a soul in these circles. But, being a skilled adventuress, she had planned her great coup. While among other petitioners in the waiting room of Madame Elisabeth, the King's sister, she suddenly fell into a faint. Everyone crowded around her, her husband disclosed her exalted name, and, with tears in his eyes, explained that weakness resulting from years of semistarvation could alone account for the fainting fit. Amid general sympathy this thoroughly healthy invalid was carried home upon a stretcher; two hundred livres were sent to her forthwith; and the modest pension that the Marquise de Boulainvilliers had secured for her from the King was increased from eight hundred livres to fifteen hundred.

But this was no more than a beggarly allowance for a Valois! Creditors were ever more urgent, and, if our worthy couple were to save themselves from prison, they must widen the scope of their operations.

For a swindle in the grand style at least two things are needed, a great swindler and a great fool. The fool was not far to seek, being no other than that illustrious member of l'Académie Française, His Eminence the Bishop of Strasbourg, the grand almoner of France, Cardinal de Rohan. This charming prince of the Church suffered like so many of his contemporaries from the malady of his century: credulity. Since Voltaire had put religious belief out of fashion, superstition had taken its place in the salons of eighteenth-century society, and a golden age had dawned for alchemists, cabalists, charlatans. No lady or gentleman of rank or fashion could refrain from consulting them. And the most credulous of all was the Cardinal de Rohan, who was in the toils of the most skillful of humbugs, a pope among the swindlers of his day, the "divine" Cagliostro. Since augurs and cheats recognize one another at the first glance, Cagliostro and the Comtesse de Lamotte-Valois, having met at Zabern, were soon thick as thieves. Informed by Cagliostro, the Valois knew that Rohan's supreme ambition was to become first minister of France; and she knew likewise what he dreaded as the only serious obstacle in his path: Marie Antoinette's inexplicable dislike.

For some time the Comtesse de Lamotte-Valois had made a great to-do about the gracious way the Queen (who had never heard of her) had welcomed her dear relatives at court. Now, in April 1784, she began to drop casual remarks to the effect of how much confidence her "dear friend," the Queen, reposed in her; and more and more the unsuspicious Cardinal came to believe that this pretty little woman would be an ideal advocate with Marie Antoinette. If only someone could at length convince the Queen of his devotion and loyalty!

Appearing to be much moved, this "intimate friend" prom-

ised to plead his cause with Marie Antoinette; and by May, to
Rohan's astonishment, she convinced him that her influence wa
powerfully at work. The Queen, she said, was no longer ad
versely inclined, and, to show her change of mood, Mari
Antoinette would, at the next formal reception, nod to th
Cardinal in a particular way. We are all apt to believe what w
want to believe. Rohan actually imagined that at the receptio
he had noticed a certain nuance in the Queen's response to h
salutation, and paid hard cash to the go-between as a reward

But in order to get the Cardinal more firmly in her snare, th
Valois felt it necessary to show him a more tangible sign c
the royal favor. What about some letters? Was not forgery on
of the arts of her "secretary," a certain Rétaux de Villette, wh
shared not only her rogueries but her bed? Unhesitatingly Ré
taux drafted letters ostensibly from the Queen to her frien
Valois. Since their pigeon gulped these down as genuine, wh
not rig out an interchange of letters between Rohan and th
Queen? Acting on the Valois's advice, the besotted Cardina
spent days composing a detailed justification of his previous be
havior, and finally handed over the document to this woma
who was priceless in more senses of the term than one. Withi
a few days the Comtesse de Lamotte-Valois brought a little not
from the hitherto cold Queen to the Cardinal: "I am delighte
that I need no longer regard you as blameworthy. It is not ye
possible to grant you the audience you desire. I will let you kno
as soon as circumstances permit of this. Meanwhile be discreet.
The bamboozled victim could not contain himself for joy
and the more he was filled with pride at the thought of standin
high in Marie Antoinette's good graces, the more successful w
the Comtesse de Lamotte-Valois in emptying his pocket.

If the game were to continue, however, it was necessary fo
the conspirators to play a bolder move. Since it was certain tha
the Queen would never speak to Rohan, could not someone b
found to impersonate Marie Antoinette and make the foo
believe that he had had an interview with the Queen? Comt
de Lamotte set out in search of what was wanted in the ga
dens of the Palais Royal, the paradise of Parisian harlots, and h
soon put his hand upon the needed impersonator, an easily pe

suaded young lady named Nicole, ostensibly a modiste, known afterward as the Baronne d'Oliva. On August 11 Nicole was conveyed to lodgings at Versailles, and with her own hands the Comtesse de Lamotte-Valois dressed her in a white muslin gown, a skillful imitation of the one which the Queen is seen wearing in the portrait painted by Madame Vigée Lebrun. The most audacious piece of knavery in all history was under way.

Swiftly, silently, the pair of rogues with their pseudo-queen sped across the terrace at Versailles on this moonless night. They mounted to the grove of Venus, where, since it is so thickly shaded by pines and cedars, barely more than the outline of a face and figure could be discerned. But the poor little *cocotte* began to tremble as she held the rose and the letter which, as arranged, she was to hand to a distinguished gentleman who was coming to speak to her at the appointed spot. Then a man loomed in the darkness; Rétaux the secretary, who, in the livery of one of the royal servants, was conducting Rohan to the meeting place. Nicole felt herself vigorously thrust forward, and her companions vanished as if they had been swallowed up by the night. She stood alone. No, not alone, for, tall and slender, a stranger approached: the Cardinal.

How foolishly this stranger behaved. Making a profound obeisance, almost to the ground, he kissed the hem of the little modiste's garment. In her confusion Nicole dropped the rose and forgot the letter. The utmost she could do was, in stifled tones, to stammer out the few words she had learned by heart: "You may hope that the past will be forgotten." This brief utterance seemed to delight the unknown gentleman beyond measure. Again and again he bowed, and, in broken words, murmured his subservient thanks. At this juncture there sounded another footstep on the gravel, a hasty one this time, and an excited whisper: "Come away quickly, quickly, Madame and the Comtesse d'Artois are close at hand." The Cardinal took alarm, and departed swiftly with Madame de Lamotte, whose husband led away little Nicole. With palpitating heart the pseudo-queen of this comedy slunk past the palace where, behind the closed shutters, the real Queen was sound asleep.

The trick proved gloriously successful. The Cardinal, bereft of his senses, looked forward confidently to becoming first minister of France and the Queen's favorite. A few days later the Valois announced to him another signal proof of Marie Antoinette's favor. Her Majesty wanted to bestow fifty thousand livres upon a noble family that had fallen upon evil days, but at the moment she was short of cash. Would the Cardinal be good enough to undertake this gracious service on her behalf? Rohan, in his exuberance, never stopped to wonder that the Queen should be stinted in funds. Indeed, all Paris knew that she was heavily burdened with debt. Sending for a moneylender, he borrowed the requisite sum, and handed it over to the Valois. These were heavenly days for Comte and Comtesse de Lamotte. The Cardinal's money jingled in their pockets.

And now chance thrust the ace of trumps into the Valois's hand. At one of her parties a guest told her that the court jewelers Boehmer and Bassenge were in trouble. The poor fellows had sunk their capital and a good deal of their credit in a most wonderful diamond necklace which had not been purchased. Would it not be possible for the Comtesse de Lamotte-Valois, who was on such intimate terms with Marie Antoinette, to persuade her royal friend to buy this beautiful piece of workmanship? Glittering thoughts coursed through the Valois's shrewd and impudent brain, and very soon she had a new tale ready for the Cardinal. There was to be another sign of royal favor. The Queen wanted (of course without her husband's knowledge) to buy a costly trinket. A go-between whose discretion could be relied upon would be needed, and Her Majesty, to show her confidence in Rohan, had chosen him to fill this honorable position. A few days later the comtesse was able to tell the delighted Boehmer that a purchaser had been found for the diamond necklace—the Cardinal de Rohan. On January 29 in the Hôtel de Strasbourg, terms of purchase were arranged. The price was to be sixteen hundred thousand livres, payable within two years in four installments. The necklace was to be handed over on February 1, the first installment becoming payable on August 1, 1785. The Cardinal wrote the conditions with his own hand, and gave the agreement to the Valois who was to submit it to "her friend," the Queen. Two days

later the Comtesse de Lamotte-Valois brought back the contract. In the margin beside each clause was inscribed the words, *manu propria*, approved, while at the end of the document was the holograph signature, "Marie Antoinette de France."

The following morning the jeweler brought the necklace to the Cardinal, who himself took it to the Valois the same evening, wishing to convince himself that it would be conveyed to the Queen by trusty hands. He was not kept waiting long in the Rue Neuve-Saint-Gilles. In fact he was able to observe the entry into an adjoining room of a young man, dressed in black (of course it was once more Rétaux, the secretary), who presented himself with the words: "By order of the Queen." Thoroughly reassured by this magic phrase, Rohan handed over the casket to the Valois, who, in turn, gave it to the mysterious emissary. The latter disappeared as swiftly as he had come, and with him the necklace vanished until the last trump—for the comtesse promptly had it broken up into its component parts.

A few days later the Valois packed her husband off to London, his pockets stuffed with diamonds—greatly to the advantage of the jewelers of Bond Street and Piccadilly, who purchased the precious stones at far below their market value. Hurrah! Now there was plenty of money, far more money than even this accomplished female swindler had ever dreamed of making. Intoxicated by her success, she did not hesitate to flaunt her newly acquired wealth. Should the bubble burst, the Cardinal de Rohan would see to it that no harm came. It would not suit the grand almoner of France to become involved in a scandal, and still less in an affair that would make him intolerably ridiculous. Rather than that he would, without a grimace, pay for the necklace out of his own pocket. Why worry, then?

However, nearer and nearer drew the first of August, the day fixed for the payment of the opening installment of four hundred thousand livres. To secure a respite, the tricksters hit upon a new expedient. The Queen, said the Comtesse de Lamotte-Valois, had been thinking matters over, and had come to the conclusion that the price was excessive. Unless the jewelers would agree to a rebate of two hundred thousand livres, Her Majesty had decided to send the trinket back to them. The Valois had counter-on a lengthy period of chaffering, but the jewelers, who had asked a fancy price, agreed without parley to the proposed reduction in price. With Rohan's approval, Boehmer delivered a letter announcing the firm's consent to Marie Antoinette on July 12, when he was taking the Queen some other jewels which she had really ordered. The letter ran as follows:

> Your Majesty, it is with the utmost gratification we venture to think that the last arrangement proposed to us, to which we have agreed with zeal and respect, affords a new proof of our submission and devotion to Your Majesty's orders, and it gives us great satisfaction that the most beautiful diamond necklace in the world is at the disposal of the greatest and best of Queens.

If the Queen had read this involved epistle attentively and had given careful thought to its twisted phraseology, surely she would have asked herself in surprise: "What diamond necklace? What arrangement?" But on this occasion as upon a hundred others, Marie Antoinette failed to read the document attentively to the end. She glanced at the subservient letter and cast it into the fire. This destruction was characteristic. Afraid of her own heedlessness and dreading the espionage to which she was subjected at court, she had made it a practice never to keep any letters except those from her relatives.

Thus, by a chain of circumstances, the disclosure of the fraud was delayed. But the jewelers wanted their money, and they knew that the Cardinal was up to his ears in debt. The huge edifice of falsehood and misunderstanding fell with a crash when Boehmer came to Versailles on August 9 for his audience with the Queen.

From a study of the numerous official documents and other utterances concerning this affair of the diamond necklace, the irrefutable fact emerges that Marie Antoinette had absolutely no inkling of the scandalous way in which her name and her honor were being misused. All the same, she cannot be "discharged from court without a stain upon her character." The fraud was so successfully staged because the tarnish upon her reputation gave courage to the cheats, and because those that were gulled were predisposed toward unhesitating belief in the Queen's heedlessness. Had it not been for the follies of Trianon, continued year after year, this comedy of lies would have been inconceivable.

YEARS LATER, with his usual keenness of insight, Napoleon recognized that Marie Antoinette's crowning error lay in her demanding the diamond-necklace trial. "The Queen was innocent, and, to make sure that her innocence should be publicly recognized, she chose the Parlement of Paris for her judge. The upshot was that she was universally regarded as guilty." There lies the truth. Unfortunately for the Queen, no one else believed in Rohan's guilt; and murmurs soon became rife to the effect that she had had the Cardinal thus brutally arrested simply in order to disencumber herself of a confederate. In an almost hysterical fit of temper, Marie Antoinette had referred her cause to a tribunal which heretofore she had despised —the tribunal of public opinion. Her clumsy action served only to deprive her of the protective mantle of sovereignty.

Now, at length, it became possible for the Queen's secret adversaries to make common cause, and the higher clergy, like the nobility, were outraged. Complaints were lodged at Rome. Another powerful group whose interests were touched were the freemasons, for the gendarmes had hurried off to the Bastille not only their patron, the Cardinal, but the great Cagliostro, worshipful master of a lodge. The matter was also of supreme interest to the common folk, who as a rule were excluded not only from the festivals but from the scandals of the court. Nothing attracted so much attention as did this trial instituted by a Queen which by degrees became a trial of the Queen herself. Just before the proceedings began, the speeches for the defense were freely printed without censorship. Twenty thousand copies were torn from the hands of the hawkers.

The trial was attended by hundreds of persons, many of them from the provinces. In the courthouse, Pandora's box was gently opened. The contents had a disagreeable smell. One thing, at least, was advantageous to the defense, namely, that what remained of the necklace was in London. Each of the rogues and dupes could endeavor to shift the possession of the invisible object to another of the band, and thus leave open the implication that perhaps, after all, the necklace was still in the Queen's jewel case. The Valois, who stopped at nothing in the effort to clear herself, accused Cagliostro (perfectly innocent in this matter) of the theft, and dragged him into the trial. But at length the authorities were able to lay hands upon her accomplices, Rétaux the secretary and the "Baronne d'Oliva" the little modiste, and their evidence threw a much-needed light upon the situation. There was one name which was carefully kept out of the proceedings both by the prosecution and by the defense, that of the Queen. Yet this very fact worked adversely upon public opinion, so that the idea was more and more widely expressed that the word had been passed around to "shelter" Marie Antoinette. Soon a whisper became general that the Cardinal had magnanimously taken the blame upon himself. Those letters which, by his orders, had been committed to the flames—had they really been forgeries after all?

Judgment was given on May 31, 1786. From five in the morning huge crowds thronged the square in front of the Palace of Justice. Even the Pont-Neuf and the northern shore of the Seine were packed with persons waiting impatiently to hear the verdict. Before the judges began deliberating, they knew that the whole country was anticipating the Cardinal's acquittal. However, the deliberations lasted for sixteen hours.

All the judges were agreed that the Cardinal must be acquitted, for the evidence had made it clear that he was a dupe and no cheat. Where they differed was on the form of the acquittal. The royal party insisted that it must be accompanied by a reprimand for Rohan's "criminal presumption" in believing that a queen of France could give him a secret rendezvous. Censure of this sort would have compensated Marie Antoinette for the misuse of her name. The other faction, however, demanded an unqualified acquittal—and this would imply a moral condemnation of Her Majesty. It was a grave political issue that was under discussion—whether the Parlement of Paris still regarded the Queen's person as sacred, or as subject to the laws of the state just like any other French citizen. For the first time the red dawn of the coming

Revolution was reflected in the windows of the Palace of Justice.

By six-and-twenty votes against two-and-twenty, the Cardinal was acquitted "without a stain upon his character." So was his friend Cagliostro; and so was the little modiste of the Palais Royal. The minor confederates were banished. It was the Valois and her husband who had to pay for all. He was sent to the galleys. She was sentenced to be flogged, to be branded with a V (*voleuse*), and to be imprisoned for life in the Salpêtrière.

From the steps of the Palace of Justice, the news of the acquittal was enthusiastically shouted to the assembled crowd. "Long live the Parlement; long live the Cardinal," rose the cry, instead of the customary "Long live the King!" The judges were vigorously embraced; the marketwomen kissed them. As for the acquitted, they made a triumphal progress. Ten thousand, at least, followed the Cardinal to the Bastille, where he had still to spend a night. The whole nation extolled this man who had done nothing more for France than to inflict a deadly blow on the prestige of the Queen and the monarchy!

Vainly did Marie Antoinette try to hide her despair. Mercy reported to Vienna that her distress was "greater than seemed reasonably justified by the cause." It was instinct which made the Queen realize that she had sustained an irremediable defeat.

As for the Valois, she was dragged to the scaffold at five o'clock in the morning, by thirteen myrmidons of the law. Seized with a fit of hysterics, the woman began yelling at the top of her voice, shouting invectives against the King, the Cardinal, and the Parlement of Paris, so that all the sleepers in the neighborhood were awakened. She panted for breath, spat, kicked, and it was necessary, instead of baring her shoulder in a seemly manner, to tear the clothes from the upper part of her body in order to expose it to the branding iron. At the moment when the hideous deed was being done, the agonized creature struggled convulsively, so that the fiery V was imprinted upon her bosom instead of upon one of her shoulders. With a beastlike howl, she bit the torturer savagely through his jerkin, and then collapsed in a dead faint. Like a corpse she was carried off to the Salpêtrière where she was to be clad in sackcloth and nourished only on black bread and lentils.

Scarcely had the abominable details of this punishment become generally known than public sympathy veered toward Madame de Lamotte. Here was a new and perfectly safe way of forming a front against the Queen. The Duchesse d'Orléans initiated a public collection in the "victim's" behalf; day after day fine carriages were in waiting outside the Salpêtrière. With astonishment, the abbess in charge of the institution recognized among these kind visitors one of the Queen's best friends, the Princesse de Lamballe. Had this lady come on her own initiative, or (as was promptly whispered) under secret instructions from Marie Antoinette? Gossip upon these lines was rife. When, a few weeks later, the Comtesse de Lamotte-Valois was mysteriously enabled to escape to England, it was universally believed in Paris that the Queen had effected this gaol delivery of her "friend" because of gratitude to the Valois for having, in court, magnanimously kept a still tongue concerning Marie Antoinette's participation in the necklace affair.

In reality Madame de Lamotte's escape had been planned and effected by King Louis's affectionate relatives to enable them to stab the Queen in the back. Once safely across the Channel, the Valois could adopt the part of accuser, could have the most abominable calumnies printed. Her quickly published memoirs contained all that could gratify a scandal-loving public's lust for sensation. The trial before the Parlement of Paris was described as a sham. She declared, of course, that the Queen had ordered the necklace and had received it from Rohan, and that she herself, innocent of offending, had confessed to the alleged crime from friendship for Marie Antoinette and in order to restore the latter's tarnished honor. It mattered nothing that most of these falsehoods were obviously absurd. For instance, Madame de Lamotte declared that Marie Antoinette, while still an archduchess, had had a liaison with the Cardinal de Rohan, then French ambassador in Vienna. All persons of good will could satisfy themselves that Marie Antoinette was Dauphine in Versailles long before Rohan had become ambassador to Austria. But persons of good will had become rare as far as Marie Antoinette was concerned, and the public appetite grew by what it fed on.

One foul lampoon followed another, each outdoing the last in lasciviousness. Ere long there was published a "List of All the Persons with Whom the Queen Has Had Debauched Relations." This contains no fewer than four-and-thirty names of persons of both sexes. Louder and louder rose the chorus of hatred; ever more detestable grew the lies, which were believed because people wanted to believe them. Within two or three years after the necklace affair, Marie Antoinette's reputation had been damaged beyond recall. She was regarded as the most depraved, the most crafty, the most tyrannical woman in France.

XI

THE PEOPLE AND THE QUEEN AWAKEN

Necker

THE HISTORICAL significance of the necklace trial lies in this: it threw the searchlight of publicity upon the Queen's person and upon the windows of Versailles—in troublous times extreme visibility is always dangerous. There had already been a few flashes preluding the great storm: homesteads had been plundered and châteaux menaced. But now came two vivid outbursts of lightning: the diamond-necklace trial was one; the finance minister's revelation concerning the deficit was the other. Charles de Calonne was the first man in his position to make a clear budgetary statement. Thereby what had hitherto been carefully hushed up was made generally known. During the twelve years of Louis XVI's reign the sum of twelve hundred and fifty million livres had been borrowed. The announcement was fulminating in its effect. Who had spent this vast sum, and for what? The trial before the Parlement of Paris gave the answer. The general misfortune found a cause for itself, bankruptcy grew aware of its origin, and the spendthrift Queen, who bought jewels so lightly, acquired a new name: Madame Deficit.

The thundercloud had burst. A hailstorm of pamphlets and polemics, of sermonizing, a drenching rain of proposals and petitions was discharged: the people had begun to awaken. Once the King's divine right had been openly questioned, the widespread discontent had no further need of mask or of caution. When the Queen appeared in her box at the theater for the first time after the diamond-necklace trial, she was greeted with such loud hisses that henceforward she thought it best to keep away. Wherever she went, Marie Antoinette could not but be aware of the detestation with which she was regarded. The pent-up excitement of the whole country was being spurted as from a fire hose against one individual. Whipped at length into wakefulness, her ears opened, the Queen exclaimed in despair to those few who still remained faithful to her: "What do they want of me? . . . What harm have I done them?"

She began to realize her errors, and made a hasty endeavor to atone for the worst of them. Instantly she cut down her expenditures. Mademoiselle Bertin was dismissed. Economies amounting to more than one million livres a year were effected in the wardrobe, the housekeeping expenses, and the stables. The gaming tables disappeared from her drawing room; a number of sinecures were canceled. Such reforms were regarded with little sympathy by the Queen's bloodsucking favorites, but now she showed herself firm of purpose. Conspicuously she withdrew from the disastrous company of the Polignacs, to resume close ties with her former counselors, Mercy and Vermond (who had long ere this been dismissed).

"Too late!" was, however, the answer to all her endeavors. The court, greatly alarmed by the general tumult, had to recognize that mere retrenchments would no longer be of any avail. One minister after another was summoned to try his hand at balancing the finances, but none of them could suggest more than temporary palliatives. When bankruptcy was imminent, it was realized that the whole system must be changed, and that the desired saviour need not be a member of one of the best families,

but that he must be (and this was an entirely new idea) popular—
a man who would inspire confidence in the unknown and
dangerous entity termed "the people."

There was such a man, Necker, whose advice had already been
sought, though he was not only a bourgeois, but a foreigner, a
Swiss, and still worse, a heretic, a Calvinist. But Louis XVI had
found the peppery outsider offensive and had sworn that he
would never recall him. Never? Necker was the man of the
moment. Since her irresolute husband hung in the wind, the
Queen made up her mind, and grasped at the dangerous Necker
as a sick man will grasp at a remedial dose of poison. In August
1788 she summoned him to Versailles. "Long live Necker; long
live the King!" Both were shouted that evening in the galleries
of the palace and in the streets of Paris as soon as the appointment
of the Swiss financier was announced.

Yet the anxious Queen wrote that same day to Mercy:

> I tremble at the thought that Necker's recall has been my
> work. It seems to be my fate to bring misfortune, and if some
> devilish machination should make him fail like his predecessors,
> or if he should do anything to impair the King's authority, I shall
> be hated even more than I am hated now.

She had learned the burden of responsibility, had begun to feel
the weight of the crown which hitherto had pressed as lightly on
her brow as a hat made by Mademoiselle Bertin.

NECKER STEERED a resolute course in the teeth of the storm. He
knew that the nation no longer believed in the King's promises
or in his paper money, that if credit was to be consolidated and
anarchy averted, a new authority must be created, were it only
for a time. A severe winter had hardened the hearts of the starving people. At any moment they might begin to riot. Though he
hesitated too long, as usual, at the twelfth hour the King agreed
to summon the Estates General, and this, in the new times
that were dawning, meant an appeal to the whole population of
France. Acting on Necker's advice, Louis—in order from the
outset to counterbalance the concentrated power of the first
estate and the second, the nobility and the clergy—decided to
double the number of representatives of the third estate. As a

result (it was supposed) the forces would be equally balanced, and in the end the decisive authority would remain in the hands of the monarch.

It was the first time in France that "common folk" had thus been called in council. A flame of enthusiasm ran from town to town and from village to village; the elections became popular festivals. At length the actual work could begin when, on May 4, 1789, the Estates General, soon to become the National Assembly, met at Versailles, which thereby became not merely a king's palace but the capital of the whole realm of France.

Before the deliberations opened, God's blessing was invoked upon the deputies in their exalted task. The church bells pealed early in the morning, and half Paris flocked to Versailles to watch the great procession that inaugurated a new era. A wonderful sight, indeed, was this march. For the last time the court of Versailles was flaunting its manifold splendors.

At ten o'clock the royal train left the palace, headed by pages in bright liveries, and falconers with their birds on their wrists. Then, slowly and majestically, there followed the royal chariot, gleaming with gold, drawn by plumed and caparisoned horses. The King's elder brother sat on His Majesty's right, his younger brother on the box. Jubilant shouts of "Long live the King!" greeted this first equipage, in painful contrast to the silence which fell as the second vehicle, that containing the Queen and the princesses, drove by. The chariots pulled up in front of the Church of Notre-Dame de Versailles, where the three estates, each of the twelve hundred deputies holding a lighted candle, were awaiting the court, ready to form in line and follow the royal progress through the town.

At the head of the long train marched the last who would soon be first—the somberly clad deputies of the third estate, in two parallel files. They were followed by the estate of nobles, while the clergy brought up the rear. When the last representatives of the third estate were passing, there were loud outbursts of applause from the populace at the sight of the Duc d'Orléans, who was openly challenging autocracy by functioning as one of the elected of the third estate. Some of the spectators, wishing to underline their opposition to the court, chose the moment when Marie Antoinette drew near to raise shouts, not of "Long live the Queen!" but of "Long live the Duc d'Orléans!" Marie Antoinette turned pale. Next day, at the formal opening of the Estates General, further contumely awaited her. Whereas the entry of the King had been greeted with loud cheers, a frosty silence hailed her coming.

"Voilà la victime," whispered Mirabeau to his nearest neighbor. It was not until the close of Necker's almost interminable speech, when she stood up in order to leave the hall with the King, that a few of the deputies, sympathizing with her in this extremity, raised scattered cries of *"Vive la Reine!"* Touched by the demonstration, Marie Antoinette acknowledged it with a bow, and thereat the whole audience joined in the greeting. But, as she returned to her palace, the Queen was under no illusion of reconciliation. She realized that a life-or-death struggle had begun—and there was no fight in her.

All those who saw Marie Antoinette during these days were struck by her disquiet. While she was on parade, in his little bed at Meudon her eldest son, the eight-year-old Dauphin, was dying of rickets. Within a month he was dead and buried. Throughout this period Marie Antoinette's mind was wholly absorbed in her own sorrows. Not until later, fighting a lone and desperate campaign, could she rally her forces to a last resistance. For the nonce, she had no energy left, and the energies of a Titan were requisite.

For within a few days of the opening of the Estates General, the two privileged estates, the nobility and the clergy, were at daggers drawn with the third estate; and soon the latter, balked of its will by the higher orders, took the initiative into its hands and declared itself the National Assembly, and on June 20 defied the royal decree of dissolution and took the famous Tennis Court Oath not to dissolve until the will of the people had been fulfilled and a constitution granted. At this hour, when resolution was the primary need, the court vacillated hopelessly. Louis XVI would lock up the third estate in the meeting hall, and would then timidly retreat from this bold position as soon as Mirabeau declared "The National Assembly will give way only to the point of the bayonet."

The royal authority was crumbling and being washed away like a child's sand castle by the rising tide. On July 11, 1789, trying to convince himself of his own strength, the King threw down the gauntlet to the nation by dismissing the popular Necker, who had persistently favored yielding and conciliation.

The days that immediately followed were signalized by events that are graven in history, and yet they have left scarcely a trace in the diary penned by the simple and unsuspecting Louis. The entry of July 11 is only: "Nothing. Departure of Monsieur Necker." In Paris people took another view. On the morning of July 12 the tidings of Necker's dismissal had the effect there of a spark in a powder barrel. In the Palais Royal, where thousands of agitators assembled, Camille Desmoulins, a political intimate of the Duc d'Orléans, jumped onto a bench, brandished a pistol, shouted that the King was planning a new Saint Bartholomew's Day massacre, as in 1572, and called the people to arms. Arsenals were plundered, and on July 14 twenty thousand men marched against the Bastille, the detested stronghold of feudalism. Yet at Versailles, only ten miles from this world-shaking event, the court might have been in another hemisphere. Messenger after messenger came to the National Assembly to report disturbances in Paris. The King listened to the news, but there was little change in the routine of his daily life. The entry in his diary for July 14 is only the one word: *"Rien."* This signified that His Majesty had not gone out hunting, had not brought down a stag, so that nothing noteworthy had occurred. As usual, he went to bed at ten o'clock. He was sleeping the sleep of the just, when the Duc de Liancourt came galloping to Versailles, with fuller information about the uproar in Paris. The messenger insisted that His Majesty must be awakened, and was at length admitted into the royal bedchamber. He reported: "The Bastille has been taken by storm, the governor has been murdered! His head, on the point of a pike, is being carried in triumph through the streets!"

"You are bringing me news of a revolt," said the unhappy sovereign in alarm.

The bearer of evil tidings unhesitatingly amended his master's phrase: "No, Sire, it is a revolution."

FRIENDS DESERT—THE FRIEND APPEARS

Storming of the Bastille

THE PARADOX which was so disastrous to King Louis was not that he could not understand the Revolution, but that, a man of mediocre capacity, he earnestly endeavored to understand. When he was Dauphin, Louis XVI had been fond of reading history, and *The History of England*, by the famous David Hume, had been his favorite book. He had conned and reconned the chapter in which Hume described the revolutionary movement against Charles I, which culminated in the King's execution. Now it seemed to Louis XVI that he might learn to guide his footsteps by recognizing the mistakes of his unhappy predecessor a hundred and fifty years before. Where Charles had tried the strong hand, he would be gentle and pliable, and would thus (so he hoped) escape the crowning disaster. Yet this very attempt to read the riddle of the French Revolution by the light of the English analogies was doomed, seeing the circumstances were utterly different.

Therein lay the tragedy of Louis XVI. For by refraining from a single word of censure upon those who had murdered the governor of the Bastille, the King recognized the Reign of Terror as the legitimate power in France. His timidity was a justification of revolt. In gratitude for this abasement, Paris was ready enough to welcome him on July 17, and to give him (though only for a brief space) the title of "*Restaurateur de la liberté française.*" Subserviently Louis XVI pinned to his hat the tricolor cockade which the populace had adopted as a sign of rebellion against his authority. On the fourteenth of July Louis

178

XVI had lost the Bastille; on the seventeenth he cast aside his dignity, and made so profound an obeisance to his adversaries that the crown dropped from his head.

It was otherwise with Marie Antoinette. She'd not go to books for counsel. Her human strength rested entirely upon instinct. Now this instinct of hers rose in revolt against the Revolution. Her childish arrogance was transformed into pride, and the powers which had previously been frittered away were concentrated to endow her with a vigorous character. Born in a royal palace, brought up to believe in divine right, she remained convinced until she perished that her position as absolute ruler was not open to question. Like her brother Joseph she said: *"Mon métier est d'être royaliste."* Her place was above, that of the populace was below.

Marie Antoinette had not the remotest understanding of the historical justification or the constructive will of the Revolution. This could hardly have been expected of her, but the upshot was inevitable. Since Marie Antoinette was unjust to the Revolution, the Revolution was unjust to Marie Antoinette. The Revolution was the enemy—such was the Queen's standpoint. The Queen was the chief obstacle in its path—such was the fundamental conviction of the Revolution. Louis XVI, "the good King," counted for nothing. With their infallible instinct, the masses of the people knew that there was one person left in France to defend the throne, one vigorous will to stand firm against the Revolution. As Mirabeau put it, the Queen was "the only man at court." Anyone, therefore, who was on the side of the Revolution must necessarily be against the Queen.

And a silence of death now surrounds this Queen whose taste it has always been to live amid turmoil. The great flight has begun. Her former friends have vanished like the snows of yesteryear. Evening after evening another carriage drives through the gilded gateway never to return. Fewer and fewer footsteps sound in the wide halls. Versailles has been deserted by those whose first thought is for their own safety.

At this juncture, when the Queen had been forsaken, there emerged from the darkness the man who had in very truth been her friend all along, Count Axel Fersen. So long as it brought power and glory to be accounted a favorite of Marie Antoinette, he had remained in the background, mindful of her honor. Now, when to appear in public as a friend of the maligned woman brought no advantage, when it needed courage and self-sacrifice —now Marie Antoinette's only true lover and the only man she truly loved stepped boldly forward to her side, and therewith made his entry upon the stage of history.

This love drama opened in quite the rococo style of the day. At eighteen Axel Fersen was sent to Paris, so that he might complete his cosmopolitan education with a final courtly polish. He was a remarkably good-looking young man, upright, broad-shouldered and virile. In his portraits we cannot help being charmed by his frank expression, his regular features, his thoughtful eyes and warm lips. Here was a man to arouse both the love and the trust of a passionate woman.

One evening in 1774, at the opera ball, a slender girl who moved as if on wings accosted him without introduction, and, under cover of her mask, opened a lively conversation. Fersen responded gallantly, and at length the young woman who had been flirting with him thought best to remove her mask. It was Marie Antoinette!

Thenceforward the youthful Swede, though by no means of outstanding rank, was always a welcome guest at Versailles balls and receptions. But it was not very long before the death of Louis XV put an end to what can have been nothing more than an innocent flirtation, for it made the little princess Queen of France. Two days later Axel Fersen left for his native country.

The second act did not begin until Fersen returned to Paris four years later. His father had sent him to look for a rich wife. But Axel Fersen had no penchant for matrimony; and his reasons are obvious enough. Immediately after his arrival he presented himself at court. And the Queen, directly she caught sight of him, cried impetuously: *"Ah, c'est une vieille connaissance"*—Hullo, here's an old acquaintance. Her interest in him promptly revived; she invited Fersen to her parties and overwhelmed him with kindnesses, betraying—without herself being fully aware of it—that her heart had gone out to him. On one occasion, so the story ran, when she was sitting at the piano singing an aria from *Dido* before the assembled court, at the words, *"Ah, que je fus bien inspirée quand je vous reçus dans ma cour,"* her blue eyes turned enthusiastically toward the Swedish count.

Gossip was rife at court, and Fersen was quick to perceive that the situation was untenable. No one knew better than he that the Queen was in love with him, and he, in his turn, both loved and honored her. Being a fine fellow, he speedily put thousands of miles between himself and the lady to whom his presence was a danger, enrolling himself as Lafayette's aide-de-camp in the French contingent that was fighting on the side of the American insurgents.

"Young Count Fersen has behaved in the most exemplary way," writes the Swedish ambassador to his King, Gustavus III. "During the last days before he left, the Queen could not keep her eyes off him, and when she looked at him, they were filled with tears."

We come to the third act. After four years' voluntary exile, Fersen landed at Brest with the American auxiliary corps and hastened to Versailles. Obviously upon Marie Antoinette's instigation, and despite the protests of his puzzled father in Sweden, he promptly applied for the command of a French regiment so that he might stay near the Queen. It was at this time, in a private letter to his sister, that he laid his heart bare. "I have determined never to marry. It would be unnatural. . . . I cannot belong to the one woman to whom I should like to belong and who loves me, so I will not belong to anyone."

Now for two years, much against his will, the young man had to act as aide-de-camp to King Gustavus, but in 1785 he returned to France to take up his commission. During his absence there had been a decisive change in Marie Antoinette. The affair of the diamond necklace had almost created a solitude around her. He, who had shunned her favor when she was idolized by the world and surrounded by a thousand flatterers, ventured at length to love her when she was lonely and in urgent need of help. *"Elle pleure souvent avec moi, jugez si je dois l'aimer,"* he wrote to his sister. At the very moment when all had forsaken her, and when she had lost all, the Queen found what she had vainly sought throughout her life—a sincere and courageous friend ready to die with her and for her.

It was during these final years that the intimacy between Marie Antoinette and Fersen probably reached its climax. And now that a mere superficial attraction had become a union of two spirits, both did their utmost to conceal their love from the world.

XIII

THE LAST NIGHT IN VERSAILLES

Maillard   Marquis de Lafayette

NEVER IN THE ancient realm of France had seed ripened so swiftly as did the impatient seed of the Revolution in this summer of 1789. With a stroke of the pen, the Assembly put an end to the neglect of decades, to the injustice of centuries. On the fourth of August, amid universal jubilation, another Bastille, another ancient stronghold of feudalism fell. The nobles had to renounce *corvées* and tithes, the princes of the Church must forgo their rents and revenues. Serfdom was abolished. The third estate became supreme. The press was declared free. The Rights of Man were proclaimed. To Marie Antoinette and to Louis it seemed best to remain quietly in the background.

But the Revolution had to make headway. Stagnation would be its doom; it must demand more and ever more concessions in order to maintain itself. The drums for this unceasing march were beaten by the newspapers. Freedom had been given to the written word; and freedom, in its first exuberance, is always fierce. Thirty, fifty journals appeared in Paris, each of them louder, more savage than the others. The louder, the better;

make the court the target of universal hatred! The King was planning treason; the government was interfering with the supplies of grain; foreign regiments were being sent to dissolve the Assembly by force. Wake up, citizens! Wake up, patriots! There must be an end to this insufferable bargaining between King and people. There are muskets and cannons in the arsenals. Get them out ... fetch the King and Queen from Versailles!

Informed of a proposed attack, Versailles decided to take a strong line, but, since French soldiers were not to be trusted to act against their fellow citizens, a Flemish regiment was summoned on October 1 for the protection of the palace. The court had prepared a cordial reception for the troops, a banquet in the great opera hall, and the King and the Queen, the latter leading the Dauphin by the hand, visited the banqueteers. It was an unprecedented honor!

Officers and men rose from their seats, and raised a shout of welcome. It was long since the Queen had heard an enthusiastic "Vive la Reine!" The sound gladdened her heart, and she smiled bewitchingly. The sight of this gracious lady, accompanied by her children, aroused a rapture of loyalty in the soldiers. The Queen, too, was profoundly moved. Her confidence was restored; the throne was still secure.

On October 2 and 3, however, the drums of the newspapers were rattling once more. The Queen and the court had made the soldiers drunk with red wine that these armed men might shed the red blood of French citizens; servile officers had trampled upon the tricolor—and the mischief had been wrought by the challenging smiles of the Queen. Patriots, have a care! Paris is about to be attacked!

On October 5 there was a tumult in Paris, and, spontaneous though it may have seemed, it was in truth remarkably well organized. Its outstanding feature was that the King was to be brought from Versailles to Paris, not by an army of men, but by an army of women. Men who undertake such a deed can be shot down as rebels. But the sharpest bayonet finds the armor of a woman's soft breast invulnerable.

It was, in fact, a young woman who, on the morning of October 5, broke into a guardroom and seized a drum. Behind her, in a trice, there ranged themselves a vast number of women, clamoring for bread. The supply to Paris had somehow been held up for two days. The riot had begun, and speedily men dressed up as women mingled with the crowd. Within half an hour the Hôtel de Ville had been stormed, pistols and pikes and even two cannon had been seized, and then there suddenly appeared as if from nowhere a leader, Maillard by name. This young revolutionist organized the disorderly into an army, and incited it to march on Versailles; ostensibly to demand bread, though really in order to bring the King to Paris. Too late, as usual, Lafayette, commanding officer of the National Guard, appeared upon the scene, mounted on his white charger. His duty was to prevent the march on Versailles; his men, however, would not obey orders. There was nothing left for him but to lead the National Guard as rear column of the army of women, thus giving revolt a cloak of legality.

Not until noon did the court of Versailles hear a word about the approach of the thousand-headed danger. In accordance with his daily custom, the King had ridden off into the woods of Meudon; and the Queen had walked over to Trianon.

She was sitting upon a stone bench in the grotto when one of her pages came to her with a report that the mob was marching on Versailles. Snatching up her hat, wrapping her cloak around her, she hastened to the palace so swiftly, one may presume, that she never looked back. How could she foresee that she was bidding farewell forever to her Hameau, her Trianon?

At Versailles Marie Antoinette found the nobles and ministers of state in hopeless perplexity. Only vague rumors in advance of the march had arrived. Subsequent messengers had been intercepted by the mob. Now at length came a horseman, who sprang from the saddle and ran up the marble staircase: Fersen, who had circumvented the army of women, was determined to be at the Queen's side in the moment of danger. At length the King also appeared. That evening his diary would record that he had had a poor day's hunting, with the comment "interrupted by events."

A council was held. There were still two hours, still time for energetic action. But Louis could not make up his mind to act.

At length there came a confused murmur of many voices from the Avenue de Paris. The army of women was close at hand, their skirts drawn up over their heads as a protection against the heavy rain which had begun to fall. The vanguard of the Revolution was in Versailles. The opportunity for decisive action, whether by resistance or by flight, had been lost.

The women's first visit was to the National Assembly, which had been in session since early that morning, and their first demand was for bread. A deputation of six women was sent into the palace, accompanied by Mounier, the president of the Assembly, and some representatives of the third estate. At the entrance the lackeys politely opened the doors for these dressmakers, fishwives, and streetwalkers, and escorted them up the marble staircase. Among them was a tall, rather corpulent and genial-looking man whose name gives his first encounter with King Louis peculiar significance. It was Dr. Guillotin, professor of anatomy at the University of Paris, through whom an improved form of the instrument subsequently called by his name was adopted by the revolutionists as a "humane killer."

Good-natured Louis received the ladies in so friendly a fashion that their spokeswoman, a young person who sold flowers to the habitués of the Palais Royal, actually fainted from embarrassment. She was sedulously cared for. The worthy father of his country put his arm around the terrified girl, promised the gratified members of the deputation bread in plenty and everything else they wanted, and even placed his own carriages at their disposal to save them the trouble of the long walk back to Paris. But when the deputation went down the steps it was received with cries of rage by the general body of the women, who had, meanwhile, been worked upon by the secret agitators among them. Their representatives must have been bribed! "We have not tramped for six hours from Paris, through a cloudburst, in order to go home again with gnawing stomachs and empty pledges. We shall stay here until we can take back the King and the Queen and the whole band to Paris." The women crowded into the meeting hall of the National Assembly to sleep there.

Toward midnight drums were heard in the distance. Lafayette was coming. He, too, paid his first visit to the Assembly and his second to the King. Although, with honest devotion, and a profound obeisance, he said: "Sire, I have come to bring you my head in order to save Your Majesty's," no one gave the aspirant to popular favor any thanks, least of all Marie Antoinette. The King declared he did not desire to leave Versailles. Everything seemed settled. Louis had given his word; Lafayette and his forces were on hand to protect him, and so the members of the Assembly went home to bed, while the National Guard sought shelter in the barracks. Lafayette, after making a final round to inspect his sentries, likewise went to bed, at four in the morning, in the Hôtel de Noailles. Marie Antoinette and Louis retired to their separate chambers, never dreaming that this was the last night in which they would sleep at Versailles.

THE AUTHORITIES of the old regime, the monarchy and its guardians, had gone to bed. But the Revolution was young. It needed no rest. Secret instructions were conveyed from group to group, and at five in the morning, when the palace was still shrouded in darkness and in sleep, a considerable number of the insurgents, under cunning guidance, made their way through the chapel court and halted beneath the windows of the palace. What did they want? Who were the leaders? There can be little doubt that the main instigators were behind the scenes. However this may be, suddenly a shot was fired, one of those provocative shots that are always fired when a collision is intended. Instantly there rushed up from all sides hundreds upon hundreds of insurgents, armed with pikes and mattocks and muskets; the regiments of women and of men disguised as women. The assault had a definite and preconcerted aim. "To the Queen's apartments!" A few of the bodyguard tried to bar the staircase leading to the Queen's private suite. Two of them were cut down and barbarously murdered. But a third guardsman escaped, though wounded, and, hastening up the stairs, he shouted at the top of his voice: "Save the Queen!"

This cry did actually save her. One of her ladies-in-waiting burst into her room to warn her. The Queen slipped a petticoat over her nightdress and drew a shawl around her shoulders. Thus, barefooted, her stockings in her hand, she ran along the corridor leading to the Oeil de Boeuf and on through this wide chamber to the King's apartments. Alas, the door was barred! The Queen and her ladies beat upon it with their fists, but it remained inexorably closed. For five interminable minutes, while the hired assassins were breaking into one room after another, stripping the coverlets from the beds and searching the cupboards, the Queen had to wait until a servant within heard the knocking and opened the door. At length Marie Antoinette could take refuge in her husband's suite, and at this moment the governess brought the Dauphin and the little princess. The family's lives had been saved. But nothing more than their lives.

Also awakened was the sleeper who, above all, ought not, on this momentous night, to have surrendered to the embraces of Morpheus—Lafayette, thenceforward often spoken of contemptuously as General Morphée. With the utmost difficulty he cleared the invaders out of the palace. Now it was possible to hold a royal council. But what was there left to discuss? The multitude, ten thousand in number, held the palace grounds. As with one voice, the masses beneath the windows shouted the demand which yesterday and today had been secretly impressed upon them by the agents of the revolutionary clubs: *"Le Roi à Paris! Le Roi à Paris!"*

Hoping to keep the raging mob from proceeding to extremities, the King resolved to appear upon the balcony. Hardly had the worthy fellow presented himself and nodded in friendly fashion than the crowd below broke out into loud acclamations! The populace always acclaimed the King when he had been conquered. But the crowd was not yet satisfied with its triumph. The Queen, the arrogant, the immalleable Austrian woman, must also bow her neck beneath the invisible yoke. Louder and more savage grew the cries: "The Queen, the Queen to the balcony!"

Marie Antoinette, pale with wrath, biting her lips, did not stir. Lafayette advanced to her side, and said: "Madame, it is indeed necessary that you should do this in order to placate the people." "In that case I shall hesitate no longer," answered Marie Antoinette. Head erect, her mouth firmly set, she appeared on the balcony, but not as a petitioner. She looked like a soldier marching to the attack. So profound was the tension caused by her defiance that for a whole minute perfect silence prevailed in the courtyard. No one could foretell whether the silence would be broken by a howl of wrath or by a shot. At this juncture, Lafayette, who had kept his presence of mind, stepped up to her side, bowed profoundly, and kissed her hand. Thereupon a most surprising thing happened. Again there was a universal shout, but this time came the words: "Long live the Queen! Long live the Queen!" Without themselves knowing why, the very people who had, a few minutes before, been delighted by the King's weakness were now enchanted by the unyielding pride of this woman who would not woo their favor with a false smile.

Marie Antoinette was not deceived by this belated acclamation of the populace. When she reentered the room, there were tears in her eyes as she said: "They will compel us, the King and me, to go back with them to Paris, while they carry in front the heads of our bodyguards, on the tops of their pikes."

Not for nothing had the huge machine been set in motion. Within an hour or two, the mood of the rabble was once more threatening; within an hour or two the National Guard showed themselves more than half inclined to join in storming the palace. At length notes were thrown from the balcony to inform those below that the King had decided to remove to Paris. Marie Antoinette was right. At two o'clock in the afternoon the huge gilded gates of the palace grounds were opened. In a calash drawn by six horses, the King, the Queen, and their children drove forth to leave Versailles forever. A chapter of French history, a millennium of monarchical autocracy, had been closed.

The hearse of the monarchy, followed by the carriages of the court, and by carts filled with sacks of flour from the royal stores, took six hours to drive at a foot's pace from Versailles to Paris. From the houses that lined the way, people flocked out to see the show, every one of them wanting to contemplate the King and the Queen in their abasement. The women of Paris, leading the way, shouted triumphantly to such onlookers: "We are bringing back the baker, the bakeress, and the bakerling. We shall no longer go hungry now!"

At length the calash pulled up at the gates of Paris. By the

flickering light of torches, Bailly, the mayor, welcomed the King and the Queen, who were not yet to be allowed to repose. They must drive to the Hôtel de Ville, that the city might gloat over its prey. When they were led to the window, the people, intoxicated by their unexpected triumph, were in a generous mood. It was long since so hearty a shout of "Long live the King; long live the Queen!" had been uttered.

Thereafter, by the glimmer of borrowed candles, a sort of camp was improvised for the royal family in the palace of the Tuileries, forsaken since the building of Versailles. "How ugly everything is here, Mamma," said the little Dauphin. "My son," replied the Queen, "Louis XIV used to live here, and liked the place well enough. You must not be more exacting than he was."

XIV

THE TUILERIES

Comte de Mirabeau

THE NATIONAL ASSEMBLY, the Paris municipal council, the bourgeoisie in general, being fundamentally loyal to the monarchy, were outraged at the exploits of the amazons who had delivered the King into their hands. From shame they did everything possible to describe the rape of the royal family as a voluntary change of residence! Deputation followed deputation to make respectful obeisance to Their Majesties.

But Marie Antoinette, incapable of false pretenses, and Louis, ever ready to follow her lead, stubbornly resisted these efforts. The whole world should know how the divine right of a king had been challenged. Unceasingly both of them emphasized their defeat. The King abstained from hunting; the Queen refused to visit the theater; neither of them would appear in the streets; they sedulously refrained from doing anything that might have once more made them popular in Paris. The result of this segregation was to create a growing and dangerous prejudice against them. Because the court insisted that it was subjected to constraint, the people grew more convinced of their own power. It was the King and Queen who dug the invisible trenches around the Tuileries.

Still, while stressing its view that the Tuileries was a prison, the court was determined that the prison should be regally equipped. Furniture was brought from Versailles; carpenters and upholsterers were put to work; valets, lackeys, coachmen and cooks from the old staff soon crowded the servants' quarters. Even the ceremonial of Versailles was carried over to the new abode.

The part of the palace set in order for the royal family was that which gave upon the gardens (the part burned in 1871 during the days of the Commune and never rebuilt). Here, Marie Antoinette deliberately isolated herself from the rest of the family. She had her apartments on the ground floor, her boudoir being so placed that she could receive visitors without their having to use the main entrance and the public stairway.

This ancient palace, with its dark passages and above all with the ever present National Guards who had replaced the noble bodyguards, was by no means an agreeable residence; and yet the royal family, crowded together by fate, was able to lead a more tranquil, more intimate life than in Versailles. The Queen could, for the first time in her life, find opportunity for serious and lucid reflection. "Tribulation first makes one realize who one is." This touching phrase appears in one of her letters.

The woman, who for twenty years had never been able to read attentively, now discovered within herself unutilized reserves of intelligence. She changed her writing table into that of a chancellor's, her room into a diplomatic cabinet. Taking the place of her husband (whom everyone thrust contemptuously aside as an incurable weakling), she held counsel with the ministers and ambassadors, watching over their undertakings and revising their dispatches. Marie Antoinette had grasped in the very depths of her soul that she was destined to become a historical figure, and she felt it incumbent upon her to be *"digne de Marie Thérèse,"* to be worthy of her mother. "Courage" became the leitmotiv of her progress toward imminent destruction. Again and again we find such declarations as that "nothing can break my courage."

The thought of her children was the only one which she now ventured to associate with the word "happiness." For instance: "If I could be happy, I should be made happy by these two little beings. . . . I have them with me as much as possible." Her love had concentrated passionately on the two children that were left to her. Although she idolized her little boy, *"un chou d'amour"* as she fondly wrote of him, she was determined not to spoil him. "Our affection for him must not lack an element of severity," she wrote to the new governess, Madame de Tourzel, "we must not forget that we are bringing him up to be a king." The Queen, when appointing this lady to her position, gave her a description of the Dauphin which is inspired by a psychological insight and spiritual intuition hitherto lacking in Marie Antoinette.

> In two days my son will be four years and four months old. Like all children who are vigorous and in good health, he is very thoughtless, extremely scatterbrained, and subject to violent fits of anger; but he is a good boy, and most affectionate when his thoughtlessness does not get the better of him. His self-esteem passes all reasonable bounds, but still, if he is carefully guided, even this may be turned to good account. He is to be depended upon when he has given his word; but he is extremely indiscreet, being always ready to repeat whatever he has heard. Often enough, without any intention to tell a falsehood, he embroiders it with his imagination. This, indeed, is his chief fault, and the one which it is, above all, essential to correct. It has been my way with my children to make them confide in me, so that, when they have been naughty, they will come and tell me about it themselves. I was able to achieve this by assuming an air of being distressed rather than angry at what they had done. I have also taught them to understand that my yes or no is irrevocable; but I have never failed to give them reasons for my decision (reasons within the bounds of their understanding). . . .

It seems hard to believe that this epistle was penned by the mother who once looked at the world so lightheartedly. "When will you at length become your true self?" had been, again and again, the distressful question of Maria Theresa. Now, when the hair on her temples was beginning to turn gray, Marie Antoinette was developing into her true self.

HITHERTO, THE QUEEN had set her trust in only one ally—time. But week by week the Revolution marched onward, gaining thousands of new recruits. At length the King and the Queen began to realize the danger of their isolation, and looked hither and thither in search of assistance. Honoré Gabriel Riqueti, Comte de Mirabeau, sent as deputy to the National Assembly by the third estate of Aix-en-Provence, had been ready since September (at a price) to espouse the King's cause. But his questionable past—pamphlets, seductions of women, duels, scandals, sojourns in prison—aroused distrust, and Marie Antoinette, who detested renegades from the nobility, had still believed herself strong enough to dispense with the favors of this *monstre*.

But now five months had intervened and Mirabeau's help was indispensable. The Comte de La Marck was informed that the Queen was ready to negotiate with Mirabeau, or, in plain words, to buy his services. On May 10, 1790, he pledged himself to serve the King with "loyalty, zeal, energy and courage."

Both parties to the agreement knew well enough that the pledge was not an honorable one. In the public eye, Mirabeau had to remain an ardent revolutionist while working in the National Assembly on behalf of the King's cause. It was understood that he would never visit the Tuileries, but he wrote letter after letter of advice to Louis (though these letters were in truth addressed to Marie Antoinette). In his overweening self-confidence, Mirabeau persuaded himself that he alone could and would save the monarchy, the Revolution and the country; he foresaw himself as simultaneously president of the National Assembly and first minister of the King and the Queen. But not for a moment did Marie Antoinette dream of giving this *mauvais sujet* effective power. Her secret intention was to dismiss the incalculable creature as soon as she no longer had need of him as agitator and informant in the National Assembly.

It was not long before Mirabeau perceived that his letters only helped to fill the royal wastepaper basket instead of stimulating a spiritual fire. His experience in political life and in his countless love affairs had shown him that he was even more effective with the tongue than with the pen, for his personality radiated an electrifying influence. He therefore was perpetually urging his emissary, the Comte de La Marck, to procure him an opportunity for a conversation with the Queen.

For a long time Marie Antoinette was deaf to these proposals. At length, however, she gave way, and arranged to receive Mirabeau on July 3 in the park of the palace of Saint-Cloud, where at midsummer, 1790, there was a brief respite from detention at the Tuileries. We do not know what took place at this secret encounter between Mirabeau and Marie Antoinette since there were no witnesses. This much only has transpired, that it was not Mirabeau who bent the Queen to his will, but the Queen who bewitched Mirabeau. On leaving the park, he said with characteristic fervor: "She is great, noble, and unfortunate; but I shall save her." And he wrote to the Comte de La Marck: "Nothing shall stop me, I would rather die than fail to fulfill my promises." At length, to this scarcely credible being there had been allotted a task proportional to his genius: to stop the march of destiny, to reverse the rolling of that revolutionary stone which he himself had set in motion. His guiding principle at this juncture was that Satan should cast out Satan, that the Revolution by its excesses should annihilate itself. The populace was to be secretly incited to send the National Assembly to the devil. The flames of injustice and dissatisfaction were to be fanned throughout the country until there would arise a universal demand for order, for order of the old kind. "Four enemies are advancing on the double," he trumpeted, "taxation, bankruptcy, the army, winter. We must take the bull by the horns. . . ." Those who desired to reestablish the royal authority should shrink from nothing, not even from civil war.

The Queen trembled at the thought of such bold measures and would not listen to the clairvoyant amoralist. "His scheme is crazy from beginning to end," she wrote to Mercy. By degrees Mirabeau began to feel a contempt for the royal sheep who were submissively being driven to the slaughter. He realized that the court was incapable of effective action, and that he was fighting for its cause in vain. "I exposed myself to disaster in the hope of saving them. But they did not want to be saved."

Yet to his last hour Mirabeau went on fighting. With a body ravaged by his excesses, with a frame racked by fever, he went on serving both the King and the Revolution until death touched him on the shoulder. When Mirabeau finally died, in April 1791, there died the last man who was perhaps capable of mediating between the monarchy and the people. Thenceforward Marie Antoinette and the Revolution confronted one another with none between them to temper their mutual animosity.

XV
THE FLIGHT TO VARENNES

General Bouillé

ONCE MORE the court stood utterly alone. There were two plain possibilities, resistance or capitulation. As usual, the court wobbled, choosing the unlucky middle course of flight. Since the situation grew worse from day to day, the Queen wrote to Mercy in Brussels:

> Our position is horrible. . . . If we remain here, we have no alternative but to do blindly all that the *factieux* demand, or else to perish under the sword which is perpetually suspended over our heads. . . . if we must perish, let us do so gloriously, and having done our best to fulfill our duty. . . . I believe the provinces to be less infected with corruption than the capital. . . .

If only the King could show himself freely in a fortified city, the number of malcontents who would disclose themselves would be amazing.

Marie Antoinette entrusted the practical arrangements for the flight to the one friend left to her, Fersen. The difficulties were well-nigh insuperable. After escape from a palace around which the National Guards were posted as sentries, and where almost every servant was by now a spy, the refugees would have to traverse a hostile city. As for travel through the countryside, that would be rendered possible only by negotiation with General Bouillé, who had (in secret) remained loyal to the King. The plan was that squadrons of his cavalry regiment should be spread out along the road as far as Châlons, on the way to the frontier fortress of Montmédy, so that, should the royal carriage be recognized or pursued, the King and the royal family could instantly be protected. Since some sort of justification was needed for the conspicuous troop movements, an Austrian army corps had to be concentrated on the imperial side of the frontier. The requisite correspondence, a considerable amount, had to be conducted with the utmost caution. Another difficulty was that the flight demanded the expenditure of vast sums of money, and both the King and the Queen were almost penniless.

But Fersen's passion for his mistress quadrupled his energies. He corresponded with the foreign princes and with General Bouillé; he selected the most trustworthy among the nobles to carry the letters to the frontier and back, and to accompany the flight. He ordered the carriage in his own name; he procured forged passports; he supplied funds by mortgaging his estate, and, in the last resort, he actually borrowed three thousand livres from his own steward. Piece by piece, he brought the necessary disguises into the Tuileries, and smuggled the Queen's diamonds out of the palace.

Only one thing more was needed—a sort of moral justification for this flight. In one way or another the world must be convinced that the King and the Queen had not run away in a blue funk, but had actually been compelled to leave by the Terror. To furnish this pretext, the King announced to the National

Assembly that he wanted to spend Easter week at Saint-Cloud. Instantly the Jacobin press raised a clamor that the palace outside the fortifications of Paris would be the starting point for an escape. On April 18, 1791, when the King and his family were about to enter their carriage for the drive to Saint-Cloud, huge crowds assembled, and forcibly restrained them from leaving the Tuileries by not allowing the horses to be harnessed. The public exhibition of the fact that the King was a prisoner in his own palace was precisely what the Queen and her advisers had wanted, for it proved that anarchy was supreme in France, that the canaille could insult the royal family without punishment, and that the King was morally entitled to flee from Paris.

If, next evening, effect had speedily followed cause, then insult and indignation, thrust and counterthrust, would have occurred in natural sequence. And if two simple, light, inconspicuous carriages had driven away, the royal family would have made its way to the frontier without attracting remark.

But even when only a finger's breadth separated life from death, immortal etiquette must come as traveling companion. Here was the first vital error: it was decided that the whole royal family should occupy one of the carriages, the father, the mother, the sister, and the two children, the very group which was known even in the smallest of French villages thanks to a hundred copperplate engravings. But this was not enough. Madame de Tourzel, the governess, must form a sixth member of the company. In a carriage thus grossly overloaded, it was naturally impossible to drive fast. Then came a third mistake: there must be lackeys and outriders, all of noble birth, and, since it was inconceivable that a Queen should dress herself, there must be two ladies-in-waiting in a second carriage. What should have been a secret flight had become an expedition.

But the greatest of all the mistakes was this. If the King and the Queen had to drive for four-and-twenty hours, even to get out of hell, they must drive comfortably. A new carriage was ordered, exceptionally wide, exceptionally well sprung, a sort of little warship on four wheels, with all thinkable conveniences. A wine cellar was built into the framework, and to crown the absurdity, the vehicle was lined with a light-colored damask. So luxurious an equipage, which could not fail to arouse curiosity, needed at least eight horses. This signified that, whereas a light post chaise with two horses would be delayed only five minutes at a posting station, here the supply of a new relay occupied almost half an hour.

After interminable delays, June 19 was fixed upon for the flight. At the last moment, however, Marie Antoinette postponed matters by a day because one of her ladies-in-waiting, who was suddenly suspected of being a spy, was to have a day off on June 20. A sinister delay! The minutest details had already been prepared; and now fresh orders had to be sent to Bouillé, the cavalrymen must be instructed to unsaddle, and there was a superadded nervous tension for Fersen.

Yet, on the evening of June 20, 1791, not even the most suspicious onlooker could have detected that anything unusual was afoot in the Tuileries. As always, the National Guards were at their posts; as always, the servants, male and female, had been dismissed to their supper; and in the great salon, as was customary, sat the King with his brother the Comte de Provence and the other members of the royal family engaged in quiet conversation. Was there anything remarkable in this, that at about ten o'clock the Queen should leave the room for a moment or two? Hastening to her daughter's bedroom through the empty corridor, she knocked gently. The girl awoke with a start and, while she was being dressed, the Queen went to wake the Dauphin. Madame de Tourzel now dressed young Louis, heavy with sleep, in girl's clothes, explaining to him that they were going to a masked ball. The two children were noiselessly led down a private staircase into the Queen's room. They all now hastened to her private exit, where no sentry was posted.

Opening the door, the Queen looked forth, unaffrighted as ever at such moments. From one of the waiting carriages there emerged a man dressed as a coachman. Without a word he took the Dauphin by the hand. It was Fersen, risking his life by leading the Dauphin of France out of the King's palace.

Her children vanished into the darkness, while the Queen, as if she had merely gone away to write a letter, returned to the salon and resumed an indifferent conversation. At eleven came the most critical hour. The Comte de Provence and his wife, who were to make good their escape that same night (without ostentation), left the palace as usual. The Queen and Madame Elisabeth sought their apartments. To avoid arousing suspicion, Marie Antoinette had herself undressed by her lady's maids, and told them to order the carriages next morning for a drive.

The instant the door had closed behind the maids, the Queen jumped out of bed and dressed as quickly as she could, putting on a simple gown of gray silk, and a black hat with a violet veil thick enough to make her face unrecognizable. Going out of the private door, she crossed the dark Place du Carrousel. A few steps farther and she reached the *fiacre* which contained all that she loved most on earth—Fersen and her children.

It was not so easy for the King to get away. First of all he had to receive Lafayette, on the commandant's nightly visit, which lasted longer than usual. At length, toward half past eleven, the unwelcome guest departed, convinced that everything was in order. Thereupon Louis XVI retired to his bedroom, where he had to engage in a last desperate struggle with etiquette. Ancient custom decreed that His Majesty's valet must sleep in His Majesty's chamber, a string tied around his wrist, so that a pull upon the cord would instantly awaken him. If, therefore, Louis was to get away, the first thing the poor man had to do was to escape from his own valet! The King allowed himself to be undressed as usual, got into bed, and had the curtains drawn on both sides as if he were settling down for the night. Really what he was waiting for was the moment when the attendant retired into the neighboring closet to undress. Then, seizing his opportunity, Louis jumped out from behind the curtains, and fled barefooted in his nightgown through the door into his son's forsaken bedroom, where there had been laid out for him a simple suit of clothes, a roughly made wig, and (a further shame) a lackey's hat. Meanwhile the faithful valet had tiptoed back into the royal bedchamber lest he should awaken his master, whom he supposed to be asleep behind the curtains, and had carefully attached the end of the pull cord around his wrist. Having dressed as quickly as possible, the King, unrecognizable in the bottle-green coat and with the lackey's hat upon his exalted head, strode across the deserted courtyard of his palace. The National Guards, failing to recognize him, let him pass without protest. By midnight the family was assembled in the fiacre, and it seemed the worst difficulties had been overcome. Fersen, dressed as a coachman, mounted the box, and drove them across Paris.

But Fersen, a man of rank, was not used to driving himself through these labyrinthine streets. That task was ordinarily left to his coachman. It was not until two in the morning, instead of at midnight as previously arranged, that he conducted his precious cargo through the gates of Paris. Two hours, two irrecoverable hours had been lost. More time was wasted in finding the brand-new chariot, which was discovered with its lights veiled, and it was three o'clock when they at length reached Bondy. Now the Queen had to say farewell to her lover, and this was a painful duty. The King had expressly declared he did not wish Fersen to accompany them any further. Fersen rode once more around the chariot to see that all was well, and, in a loud voice, to deceive the postilions who were harnessing fresh horses, called out: "Adieu, Madame de Korff!"

The huge chariot now made good progress along the road. Its occupants were in a good mood. Jokes were exchanged about the false names under which the various travelers were passing. Madame de Tourzel was supposed to be Madame de Korff, the lady of the party; the Queen, Madame Rochet, was the governess of Madame de Korff's two girls; the King, in his lackey's hat, was Durand, the steward; Madame Elisabeth was the lady's maid. The family felt at ease in this roomy and comfortable carriage. The liberally stocked food baskets were opened, and a hearty breakfast was eaten off silver platters. The children were delighted by this strange adventure; the Queen responded to their chatter with a light heart; and the King, with a map upon his knees, followed the progress of the journey from village to village. Relays were obtained without difficulty, and, as the day wore on, the party approached Châlons-sur-Marne.

Neither malice nor suspicion animated the crowd of country folk which assembled around the posting station at Châlons. Their main impulse was curiosity and the desire to pass the time of day with strangers. They were quick to perceive that the vehicle was something quite out of the ordinary; the travelers must certainly be of high rank, and were probably refugees. Strange, however! Why on this hot midsummer afternoon, after so long a drive, did all six of them remain seated in their carriage as if glued there, instead of stretching their legs a little? Why did these liveried servants assume the airs of people of importance? No one knew how it came about, but within half an hour of the chariot's departure the town was buzzing with the report that the King and the royal family had just driven through on their way eastward.

The travelers, however, suspected nothing. They were glad at heart, since surely now they were safe. Less than half an hour's drive beyond Châlons the first squadron of cavalry would be waiting for them under the command of the young Duc de Choiseul. Madame Elisabeth was continually thrusting her head out of the window, hoping to be the first to see them. At length a horseman appeared in the road, but only one, a lone advance officer of the guard.

"Where is Choiseul? And the rest of the hussars?"

"Gone. Not one of them here."

The refugees' hearts fell. There must have been a hitch some-where and night was at hand. The Queen tried to console her companions. There would certainly be dragoons in Sainte-Menehould, only two hours' drive farther. But on arrival at· Sainte-Menehould, again there was no escort. The cavalrymen had spent the whole day in the little town, and, bored by the delay, had drunk freely in the inns and had let their tongues wag, so that the populace had grown suspicious. In the end their commanding officer, misled by a confused message, had thought it better to send his men out of the town and to stay unattended to receive the royal party.

Here was the chariot at last, an imposing vehicle. To the worthy provincials it was a startling apparition, after the strange events of the day. Drouet, the postmaster, a member of the Jacobin Club and an ardent republican, opened his eyes wide. These must be émigrés, he thought; blue bloods. He told his postboys to moderate the pace of the convoy as much as they could, and thereupon the chariot rolled sleepily onward.

Within ten minutes rumor had done its work. Perhaps some-one had brought the news from Châlons. Anyhow, the belief was rife that the royal family had passed through the town. A clamor was raised, the commanding officer of the dragoons realized the danger, and, having now summoned his men back to Sainte-Menehould, wanted to gallop after the royal carriage and provide it with an escort. His impulse came too late. The populace raised objections. The dragoons, plied with wine, refused to obey orders. Amid the tumult, Drouet had a horse saddled, and galloped away by a shortcut to reach Varennes in advance of the cumbrous chariot. As has happened a thousand times in history, the course of events was turned by the action of one energetic man.

Meanwhile the chariot was making its way along the winding road to Varennes. At the gate of the city, however, a couple of young fellows stopped the first outrider with a peremptory "Halt!" In a trice both the carriages were surrounded and accompanied into Varennes by a considerable number of youths. Drouet, who had arrived ten minutes earlier, had dragged the revolutionary youths out of beds and taverns.

"Your passports!" said someone.

"We are pressed for time, and you must not delay us," re-plied a woman's voice from the carriage.

It was the reputed Madame Rochet who spoke—the Queen, the only one to retain her presence of mind in this moment of deadly peril. But it was futile to resist. They had to drive to the nearest inn, which, by one of the ironies of history, bore the sign *Au Grand Monarque*. Waiting there was the mayor, a shopkeeper by trade, bearing the name of Sausse. He examined the passports hastily, afraid to mix himself up in so troublesome an affair, and said: "The papers are in order."

Young Drouet, however, thumped the table and shouted: "It is the King and his family, and if you let him escape to a foreign land you will be guilty of high treason." This was enough to in-timidate the worthy mayor. Besides, the revolutionists were already sounding the tocsin. To escape from his embarrassment, he informed the travelers that in any case it was too late for them to proceed on their journey. Madame la Baronne de Korff and her company could put up for the night in his house. By morning, thought the shrewd fellow, matters would be cleared up.

Hesitatingly, the King accepted the invitation. No fresh horses had been put to, and in an hour or so, surely Choiseul would be there. Wearing his inappropriate wig, Louis XVI went quietly into Monsieur Sausse's house, and his first royal action was to ask for a bottle of wine and some bread and cheese.

ON THIS JUNE 21, 1791, Marie Antoinette, in the six-and-thirtieth year of her life and in the seventeenth year of her reign, for the first time entered the house of a French bourgeois. She had first to pass through the shop, smelling of rancid oil, sausage, and spices. Then, by a sort of companion ladder, the royal party mounted to the first story, where there were two rooms, a bedroom and a parlor, low-ceilinged, poor-looking, and dirty. The children, tired out, were put to bed, and quickly fell asleep. The Queen dropped into an easy chair, the King cut himself a slice of cheese. No one uttered a word. After a while, however, there came the clattering of horses' hoofs in the streets, and loud shouts from the crowd that had gathered: "The hussars! The hussars!" Choiseul had at length found the trail, and now arrived on the spot. He made his way upstairs and unfolded a plan of escape. He could spare seven horses. Louis, Marie Antoinette, and the rest of their company were to mount and ride away with all speed, guarded by the troop of hussars, before the National Guard of the neighborhood had been mustered. Then he saluted. "Your Majesty, I await your orders."

But Louis XVI had never been the man for quick decisions. Could Choiseul be quite certain that the Queen, Madame Elisabeth, one of the children, might not be hit by a bullet? There sat the old regime, in a sordid little room, hesitating, hesitating. The Revolution, however, was in no mood to wait. Summoned from the neighboring villages by the tocsin, the National Guard, the citizen militia, had been quickly gathered together; barricades were erected in the streets. As for Choiseul's soldiers, they had been hours in the saddle, and were ready to drink and to fraternize with the people. The streets became more thronged. Then came a new exciting incident on this dramatic night. A carriage drove in by the road from Paris, and in it were seated two of the deputies dispatched that morning by the National Assembly along all the main roads to overtake the King. Their arrival as official representatives of the power of the people was greeted with yells of delight. Triumphantly, they were escorted to Sausse's house; they entered the shop and climbed the steep stairs in search of the King.

One of the two deputies, Romeuf, was pale of countenance, and embarrassed. As Lafayette's aide-de-camp he had often kept watch over the royal pair in the Tuileries, and both had often addressed him in friendly tones. At the bottom of his heart he had but one desire that morning—to help the fugitives to escape. As fate would have it, however, his companion on the expedition was a certain Bayon, an ambitious fellow and an ardent revolutionist, who had been like a hound on a hot scent. And now it was incumbent upon Romeuf to present to Their Majesties the National Assembly's decree commanding that the flight of the royal family should be stayed. Marie Antoinette could not conceal her surprise: "What, monsieur, you? I should not have expected it of you!" She turned away. But Louis took the decree and read it. It was to the effect that his rights had been suspended. For the first time it was made plain by the Assembly that the King was no longer a free agent.

Yet he made no protest, being content to say sleepily: "There is no longer a king in France." Thereupon, absentmindedly, he tossed the decree onto the bed in which the children were still sleeping. The action, however, roused Marie Antoinette. Snatching the missive, she crumpled it up and threw it contemptuously onto the floor, saying: "I will not have my children soiled by contact with this document."

All in the room were greatly perturbed; the King by his wife's rashness, and the two envoys by the painful situation into which that rashness had thrust them. There was a general sense of indecision. At this juncture Louis made a proposal which was outwardly one of compliance with the Assembly's order, but behind which craft lurked. After two such terrible nights, he said, he would like the deputies to allow them two or three hours' rest before starting on the return journey. Romeuf saw what was in the King's mind. Within two hours Bouillé's cavalry squadrons would be on hand, quickly followed up by infantry and artillery. Since he wanted to save the monarch, he raised no objection. But Bayon, the other deputy, was no less quick of apprehension, and made up his mind to answer cunning with cunning. Seeming to agree for the moment, he made his way into the street. When the crowd surrounded him, he sighed sanctimoniously: "They don't want to start yet . . . Bouillé will be here soon, and they will wait for him." The fat was in the fire! The revolutionists were not going to allow themselves to be humbugged! "To Paris!" shouted the crowd. The chariot was jubilantly turned around and horses harnessed so that there should be no excuse for further hesitation.

Now began a humiliating attempt to postpone departure. Louis and Marie Antoinette tried one unlikely expedient after another while time ran on and Bouillé's men failed to appear. At length, when everything was ready for the start, Louis XVI said he was hungry. Surely no one would refuse to give a king a reasonable meal? No one would refuse! But they were quick about the preparations. No further pretext for postponement could be thought of. With a sigh the King led the way to the carriage. Marie Antoinette followed, on the arm of the Duc de Choiseul. Despite her own troubles she had asked him: "Do you think that Fersen has escaped?"

The royal family got into the chariot. There were six thousand persons surrounding it, all of triumphant Varennes. Amid the strains of revolutionary songs, the great equipage started. Twenty minutes later squadrons of cavalry were galloping into town. At length they had come, Bouillé's men, so long and so vainly desired! If the King could have succeeded in putting off his departure for half an hour, he would have been in the midst of a loyal army, and the revolutionists would have had no option but to slink away to their homes. When Bouillé heard that His Majesty had yielded, he withdrew his troops.

THE CHARIOT had driven from Paris to Varennes in twenty hours; the return was to last three days. Drop by drop and to the dregs the King and Queen had to drink the bitter cup of humiliation.

In every town and in every village the populace assembled to gloat over the sad royal homecoming. Better, then, to shut the windows, and, in spite of the suffocating heat, to escape the coarse invectives, the continual molestation.

The night was passed at Châlons. Rest was what they needed above all, and a change of clothes was a refreshment. Next morning, however, another hot and seemingly interminable day of fierce animosity had to be endured. When, after leaving the carriage to stretch her legs, the Queen mounted the steps again, a woman hissed at her: "Take care, little one. You will soon look on other steps than those!" A nobleman who greeted her in passing was dragged from the saddle, stabbed and pistol-whipped. The King and Queen began to realize that it was not Paris alone which had succumbed to the "error" of the Revolution, for the new seed was sprouting everywhere. They had become almost indifferent to what fate might bring when mounted couriers arrived from the capital to tell them that three members of the National Assembly were on the way to safeguard the journey of the royal family.

The carriage was halted in the open road, for the three deputies, Maubourg the royalist, Barnave the bourgeois lawyer, and Pétion the Jacobin, were already at hand. The Queen herself opened the carriage door. "Messieurs," she said, extending her hand to the three of them, "I hope you will see to it that no disaster happens, that those who have accompanied us will not be sacrificed, that their lives will not be attempted." With the tact customary to her on great occasions, she sounded the right note. It was not becoming for a queen to ask protection for herself. Her energy and dignity disarmed the deputies and overcame their patronizing attitudes. Two of the delegates, Barnave and Pétion, took places in the carriage in order to safeguard the royal family against further peril. Thus there were now eight persons in the chariot, and it can be said beyond question that never were the royal family and the deputies of the National Assembly so close together as during these hours.

To begin with, of course, both parties were determined to keep their distance. Then a trifling incident brought about a relaxation. The little prince had jumped down from his mother's knee. Fingering a brass button on Barnave's official uniform, he laboriously spelled out the inscription: *"Vivre libre ou mourir."* Of course the two deputies were delighted that the future King of France should in this way become acquainted with one of the fundamental maxims of the Revolution. The ice had been broken, and by degrees a friendly conversation ensued. Each party found the other, on closer acquaintance, much less objectionable than had been supposed. The two revolutionists were astonished to find that the Queen called Madame Elisabeth "little sister," that Madame Elisabeth addressed the King as "my brother," that, among themselves, the members of the royal family were much like other human beings.

And the Queen, no less, had been shaken out of her preconceptions. After all, the scelerats, those monsters of the National Assembly, were good fellows with excellent manners. Before the strangely assorted party had been three hours on the road, the two sides had begun to woo one another's favor. The Queen introduced political topics, hoping to convince the revolutionists that the royal circle and the aristocracy were not so narrow-minded and spiteful as the people supposed. The deputies, on their side, wished to make it clear to the Queen that she was in error if she supposed the aims of the National Assembly to be identical with those vociferated by Marat in *L'Ami du Peuple*.

Barnave, a revolutionary idealist, was delighted that the Queen of France should modestly invite him to explain the fundamental principles of the Revolution. He spoke ardently, and was surprised that this reputedly thoughtless woman should listen attentively, understandingly. With her apparent readiness to be influenced by his discourse, Marie Antoinette worked a spell upon a simple and credulous nature. Barnave became convinced that she had been unjustly treated, scandalously maligned. When the Queen gave him to understand, during a stop at Meaux, that she was greatly in need of a counselor to keep her acquainted with the true wishes of the people, to convince the National Assembly of her democratic inclinations, she was able to enlist Barnave in her services. Thus by her blandishments did Marie Antoinette win a last victory for the royal cause.

The third day of the return from Varennes was the hottest and most uncomfortable of all. At length, however, the procession reached the gates of Paris. Neither acclamations nor abuse greeted its passing through the city, for bills had been posted forbidding both. At the Tuileries the lackeys were waiting, drawn up in line. The table was set as usual for the evening meal. All the rules of precedence were observed. The travelers who had returned might have fancied their journey had been no more than a dream. In reality, however, during these five days the King had fallen to a much lower plane, and the Revolution had risen much higher.

The tired man did not seem much perturbed by the matter. In his customary firm handwriting he noted in his diary no more than this: "Left Meaux at half past six. Reached Paris at eight without halting on the way."

XVI

RECIPROCAL DECEPTION

Barnave

THE FLIGHT to Varennes opened a new phase in the history of the Revolution, for its outcome was the birth of a republican party. Now, when elections for the National Assembly were at hand, there came treading on the heels of the third estate, of the bourgeoisie, the fourth estate, the proletariat, of which the bourgeoisie was no less terrified than the King had been terrified of the bourgeoisie. Full of belated anxiety, the propertied classes were eager to establish a constitution which would limit both the power of the King and the power of the people. Therefore, since forbearance must be shown Louis XVI if his consent to this were to be gained, he was not reproached for his flight to

Varennes, and it was bruited abroad that he had been kidnapped. The Queen was not deceived as to the value of these measures. There were now frequently heard beneath her windows shouts of "Long Live the Republic!" She knew full well that the proposed republic could only be established through the destruction of herself, her husband, and her children.

Moreover, it soon became plain to her that the most disastrous outcome of the Varennes affair was the fact that her brother-in-law the Comte de Provence had made good his escape. For some time the émigré French princes, the Comtes d'Artois and de Provence, had been inconsiderately rattling their sabers across the frontier. And now, having arrived safely in Brussels, the Comte de Provence had declared himself regent, the legitimate representative of the French monarchy so long as King Louis XVI was a prisoner in Paris. He incited the powers of royalist Europe to make war on a France infected with republicanism. If, thanks to his machinations, Louis XVI, Marie Antoinette, and the little Dauphin should perish—so much the better. At one stride he would be able to style himself Louis XVIII. Unfortunately for the French royal family, the other European sovereigns were only too ready to listen to him. It was of no moment to them which Louis might be seated on the throne; the essential thing was the maintenance of monarchical authority and the eradication of the revolutionary poison from Europe.

Marie Antoinette had to fight against the twofold danger from within and without, against republicanism in France and against the intrigues of her brothers-in-law beyond the frontier. In her utmost necessity, convinced that Barnave had considerable influence in the National Assembly, she resolved to take advantage of his weakness for flattery. "... Let me then work hand in hand with you," she wrote to him. "If you will discover a means of interchanging ideas, I shall reply with frankness, and shall shrink from no sacrifice where the public welfare is concerned."

Barnave showed this letter to his friends, who were simultaneously delighted and alarmed, and at length decided to hold secret parleyings with the Queen. Their first demand of Marie Antoinette was that she should induce her brothers-in-law to return to France, and should do her utmost to persuade her brother, the Emperor Leopold (Joseph had died), to recognize the coming French constitution. Appearing to comply, the Queen wrote to Leopold in terms suggested by these advisers—who believed themselves to have found an attentive and thankful pupil. In reality the Queen had not the slightest intention of being guided by their counsels and the letter to Leopold was secretly countermanded by a dispatch to Mercy. Her only object in the negotiations was to gain time until her brother should have summoned the "armed congress" for dealing with the Revolution which had long been desired.

It was a sinister double game that Marie Antoinette was playing. She saw clearly enough that her conduct was immoral; but unhesitatingly she thrust responsibility for this misbehavior upon the times, upon circumstances, which had forced her to play so deplorable a part. "Sometimes," she wrote in great distress of mind to Fersen, "I cannot understand myself, and have to ask myself again and again whether it is really I who am speaking. Still, what am I to do? These things have become necessary."

But it was not only the Queen who was cheating, for in this crisis the constitutionalists dissembled by making Marie Antoinette believe they still possessed a power which had long since slipped from their hands. Nor was Leopold playing a straight game with his sister, inasmuch as he had made up his mind not to risk a soldier, not to spend a taler, in her behalf.

Meanwhile the National Assembly finished its draft of a constitution and laid the document before Louis XVI. When the pen was already prepared for the signing of the capitulation, Marie Antoinette wrote to Mercy that in his innermost heart King Louis had no thought of keeping his pledge to the people:

> As regards the acceptance of the constitution, it is impossible that any thinking person can fail to see that, whatever we may do, we are not free. But it is essential that we should give the monsters who surround us no cause for suspicion. However things turn out, only the foreign powers can save us. . . .

By this pseudo-acceptance the royal family won breathing space, a fleeting moment of popular favor. As soon as, on September 13, 1791, the King had announced that he would solemnly pledge himself to observe the constitution, the National Guards who had been watching the Tuileries were withdrawn, and the gardens of the palace were thrown open to the public. The imprisonment was over, and (so most people were only too ready to believe) the Revolution likewise. For the first time after weeks and months, and also for the last time of all, Marie Antoinette heard enthusiastic shouts of "Long live the King; long live the Queen!"

Came a few days, a few weeks, of illusory well-being. Marie Antoinette, however, had long since lost credulity. When the new National Assembly was elected, she regarded it as a "thousand times worse than the other." One of its first decisions was that the King should no longer be spoken of as "His Majesty." Within a short time, the leadership had passed into the hands of the Girondists, who outspokenly favored the establishment of a republic. The struggle was renewed.

Yet it was not merely to the progress of the revolutionary movement that the rapid deterioration in the royal position had to be ascribed. It suited the Comte de Provence and the Comte d'Artois marvelously that the King, under constraint, had accepted the constitution; this gave a specious justification to the assertions of journalists in their pay that Marie Antoinette and Louis XVI were cowards who had sought safety by abandoning the cause of the monarchy, and that they themselves were the true defenders of that sublime institution. Vainly, through Mercy's instrumentality, did Marie Antoinette beg her brother the Emperor to keep within bounds her brothers-in-law and the other émigrés. The Comte de Provence represented that all of the Queen's commands were issued "under constraint," and everywhere the bellicose royalists took the same view.

But what were Marie Antoinette's true wishes and designs? The French revolutionary leaders believed that the Queen, that the *comité autrichien* in the Tuileries, was organizing a crusade against the French people, and many historians of later days have shared this view. In actual fact, Marie Antoinette, who had entered the paths of diplomacy only because of the promptings of despair, never had a clear idea or a consistent plan. She had some vague scheme for an armed congress of the powers, a half measure. As to the how and when of this congress, her mind was hazy. She did not think logically. She would write that "nothing but armed force can set things right again." A few days later, the opposite view was urged, and she wanted to arrest the movement against the republicans: "An attack from without would put our heads under the knife." In the end it was impossible for those with whom she was corresponding to gain a consistent idea of her wishes. Even Fersen was unable to ascertain what the Queen hoped for, war or peace. And he resolved, since he could not keep closely in touch by correspondence, to seek out the Queen in Paris, in that city where, if he were discovered, he would unquestionably be put to death. Fersen's announcement of this intention terrified Marie Antoinette. It was impossible, she said, for her to accept so heroic a sacrifice. But, "I live only to serve you," he wrote to her on February 11, just before beginning one of the most foolhardy enterprises in the history of the Revolution.

Provided with a false passport at the foot of which he had forged the signature of the King of Sweden, Fersen set forth ostensibly as part of a diplomatic mission to Lisbon—representing himself to be the servant of his own orderly. He reached Paris safely, and on quitting the post chaise made direct for the Tuileries. Night had fallen, and by an extraordinary piece of good luck he effected his entry to the palace unobserved. After eight months of cruel severance, Fersen and Marie Antoinette were together for the last time. In his private journal, Fersen wrote: "Went to see her; made very anxious because of the National Guards." But concerning the hours in which he and the Queen were alone together he said no word even in his private journal. Fersen had a fine capacity for silence.

The first night and the next day belonged to the lovers; and, so far as we know, it was not until evening came that politics had their turn. Then the discreet husband came to his wife's room in order to hold converse with the bold envoy. The upshot of their talk was that Louis XVI rejected the proposal to attempt escape once more, and this for two reasons: he held the difficulties to be insuperable, and he had pledged his word to the National Assembly to stay in Paris. "I know that people charge

Huens

me with weakness and irresolution," he said, "but who has ever found himself in so difficult a position? I missed my chance of escape on the fourteenth of July, and have never had so good an opportunity since. The whole world has left me in the lurch."

The Queen had no more hope than the King that they would be able to save themselves. She felt rescue would come only from the powers. Now came the farewell before Fersen slipped out into the night. The lovers tried to persuade themselves that it was not a last farewell, but in their secret hearts they knew the inevitable. They had seen one another for the last time.

XVII

FLIGHT INTO WAR

Emperor Francis II

WHEN GOVERNMENTS find that home conditions are critical they are wont to seek relief in some foreign imbroglio. For months the spokesmen of the Revolution in France, the Girondists, hoping to escape an almost inevitable civil war, had been clamoring for war against Austria. Moreover, this seemed to them the best method of bringing down the monarchy, for it could not fail to entangle the royal family, through its relatives, in a conflict with the nation.

Fortunately for Louis and Marie Antoinette, the cautious Emperor Leopold, who was temperamentally opposed to war, discountenanced the fire-breathing princes and scrupulously avoided challenging behavior. On March 1, 1792, however, Leopold died after a brief illness and the new Emperor, his son Francis, had no concern for the fate of his royal relatives in France. Thinking only of his own interests, he gave a chill reception to Marie Antoinette's imploring letters, caring not a jot that her life was endangered by his policy. All that he could see was a fine chance of enlarging his own power, and he therefore rejected the demands of the National Assembly.

This suited the Girondists' book, and gave them the upper hand. On April 20, 1792, after long resistance, Louis XVI was compelled to declare war upon the "King of Hungary." The armies were set in motion, and destiny took its course.

To which side did the Queen's heart turn in this war? Toward the land of her birth or the land of her adoption? Her attitude is unmistakable. She wholeheartedly desired the triumph of the foreign allies and the defeat of the French troops. She even did all in her power to hasten the defeat of France. A few days before war was declared, she acquainted the Austrian ambassador with the revolutionists' plan of campaign, insofar as it was known to her. To use plain terms, she betrayed France. It must not be forgotten, however, that a century and a half ago the concepts of "national" and "nation," as we understand them today, could hardly be said to have come into existence. A country belonged to its king; where the king stood, there stood the law; he who opposed the monarchy was a rebel, even though he were defending his own country.

The undeveloped condition of patriotism was strikingly shown in this particular war by the fact that many of the ablest and best among the Germans of that day—Schiller and Fichte, for instance—being enthusiasts for liberty, actually hoped for the defeat of the German troops, which were not popular armies, but professional soldiers fighting on behalf of despotism.

Although the French people had no proof, they were intuitively aware that Marie Antoinette had betrayed their army and their cause. If the war was to be won, the royal influence on it must be checkmated. Once more the newspapers led the way, demanding the deposition of Louis. In the Assembly, extremist proposals were brought forward, in the deliberate hope that the King would feel impelled to make use of his constitutional right of veto. The most notable of these schemes was one to which it seemed certain that Louis XVI, a devout Catholic, could never agree, namely, that priests who refused to swear loyalty to the constitution should be expelled from the country. In actual fact, the King asserted himself for the first time, and vetoed the measure. The unhappy man chose the most ill-omened of hours in which to display his vigor. The veto was to be the King's last word against and to his people.

In order to read the King and the arrogant Austrian woman, his wife, a convincing lesson, the Jacobins, the shock troops of the Revolution, prepared the storming of the Tuileries. On June 20, 1792, the third anniversary of the Tennis Court Oath, to the sound of the tocsin, five thousand men assembled under the command of one Santerre, a brewer. The march began as a mere festival performance in front of the hall of the National Assembly. The five thousand, parading to the strains of *"Ça ira,"* carried huge placards bearing legends of "Down with the veto!" and "Liberty or death!" At half past three this phase of the spectacle was over. But now came the real demonstration. For, instead of going peaceably to their homes, the huge crowd that had gathered, together with the five thousand organized demonstrators, made for the entrance to the Tuileries. The palace front was lined with National Guards; they offered no resistance, and the masses pushed in a steady stream through the gateway, then made their way into the palace and up to the first story. The doors were forced, and before anything could be done to safeguard the King, the foremost were in his presence, separated only by a small body of National Guards. Now within his own dwelling Louis XVI had to take orders from his rebellious subjects. Patiently he complied with the most outrageous demands, obediently donning the red Phrygian cap which one of the *sans-culottes* snatched from his own head.

Simultaneously another troop of the insurgents had stormed the Queen's apartment. Here, the officers on guard had speedily summoned a number of their men, had pushed Marie Antoinette into a corner of the room, and had drawn a large table in front of her with three ranks of National Guards on the other side. The furious men and the still more furious women of the mob could not get at her to do her bodily mischief, but they were close to their victim. Coldly, impassively, she endured the hostile glances and the rude utterances. Not until they tried to make her put the "cap of liberty" upon her little boy's head did she revolt, saying to the officers: "This is too much, and passes the limit of human patience." Otherwise, not for a moment did she lose composure. After a long time Pétion, now mayor of Paris, arrived on the scene and requested the crowd to disperse. "I am still alive, though by a miracle," the Queen wrote to Fersen. "However, do not be anxious about me. Have faith in my courage."

Marie Antoinette's one remaining wish was to hold her head high. Hatred had breathed its venom into her very face; she knew that the royal fate was sealed unless help came speedily. She ceased now to walk in the gardens of the palace, for even this exercise was impossible without her hearing the popular song:

> *"Madame Véto avait promis*
> *De faire égorger tout Paris."*

She slept little. Whenever a church clock struck, a shudder ran through the palace, for it might well be the first note of the tocsin that would sound for the assault on the Tuileries. Kept informed by its spies as to what was going on in the secret societies, the court knew full well that it was only a question of days until the Jacobins would have recourse to the strong hand.

The horror of the dread expectation is reflected in the Queen's letters to Fersen, passionate cries of alarm that were smuggled out of the Tuileries in chocolate boxes, rolled up beneath hat-brims, penned in secret ink or in cipher. In the last letter Fersen ever received from her, under date August 1, 1792, Marie Antoinette described the overwhelming risks of the situation with the clairvoyance of despair:

The King's life has obviously been threatened for a long time, and so has the Queen's. The arrival of about six hundred men from Marseille and of a number of deputies from the various Jacobin clubs has increased our anxiety, which, unfortunately, is only too well grounded. It is a long time since the factieux have taken the trouble to hide their plan of annihilating the royal family. At the two last nocturnal meetings, the only differences of opinion concerned the best means to employ for this purpose. Unless help arrives promptly, no one but Providence can save the King and his family.

217

Marie Antoinette's lover received these missives in Brussels, and we can imagine his despair. He wrote letter after letter, heaped visit upon visit, urging prompt military action, a rapid advance of the troops. But the Duke of Brunswick, the pigheaded commander in chief, declared that he would not be ready to cross the French line before the middle of August and refused to modify his plans.

Knowing that this would be too late, racked by the cries of anguish from the Tuileries, Fersen decided upon a fatal course, which was to accelerate the attack on the Tuileries instead of hindering it as he intended. For a long time Marie Antoinette had been asking the allies to issue a manifesto. But she urged that in this manifesto the foreign powers must sedulously avoid interfering with the internal concerns of France. "Be careful," she said, "not to say too much about the King, and not to arouse the impression that your main purpose is to give him support." She dreamed of a pronunciamento which would at one and the same time be a declaration of friendship for the French people and a menace to the terrorists.

The unhappy Fersen, however, with terror in his soul, insisted that the manifesto should be couched in the harshest terms. He wrote a draft, got a friend to convey it to headquarters —and, as ill luck would have it, this draft was accepted! It contained all the errors which the Queen had hoped to avoid. There were repeated references to the sacred person of the Most Christian King; the French soldiers were peremptorily told to come over to the side of Louis, their legitimate monarch. The town of Paris was threatened with complete destruction in the event of the Tuileries being stormed by the mob.

The result of these paper threats was alarming. Even those who up till now had been loyal to the King became ardent republicans as soon as they learned how dear their monarch was to the enemies of France. With his silly warnings, Fersen's hand threw a lighted candle into a powder magazine. In Paris, the allied threat to raze the city to the ground should the Tuileries be stormed was regarded by the populace as a good reason for attack. Preparations were instantly begun, and the only reason for delay was that it was thought better to wait until the six hundred republicans arrived from Marseille. On August 6 they marched into Paris, stepping bravely in time to a new marching song that would resound throughout the land—*"La Marseillaise."* Everything was now ready for the last thrust against the crumbling monarchy. *"Allons, enfants de la Patrie!"*

THE NIGHT of the ninth to the tenth of August heralded a sultry day. The streets were quiet. But the silence deceived no one. Revolution does not sleep. In the neighborhoods, in the clubs, the general staff of the rising, Danton, Robespierre, and the Girondists, were issuing orders to an illegal army, the people of Paris.

Nor was anyone asleep in the Tuileries. It was fully understood that the Marseillais were to attack. The windows were wide open upon this suffocating night; the Queen and Madame Elisabeth had their ears pricked for any sound. At a quarter to one in the morning came the faint knell of a tocsin, the call to arms in a distant suburb; then a second, a third, a fourth alarm.

All had been made ready in the palace. The most trustworthy force at the disposal of the crown, the Switzers, nine hundred strong, had been assembled for the defense. The passages were full of officers and armed noblemen. Since six on the previous evening, the stoutest battalions of the National Guards and the best squadrons of cavalry had been stationed around the Tuileries. To maintain discipline in the defensive force, the Marquis de Mandat was on hand, now commandant of the National Guards, a brave officer, not likely to be intimidated. But the revolutionists knew how valuable Mandat would be to their adversaries, so at four in the morning they ordered him to the Hôtel de Ville. Louis was fool enough to let him go, and Mandat obeyed. Within two hours he was foully murdered.

The defensive force had been deprived of its leader. The Switzers were firm, but the National Guards began asking one another, "Shall we put up a fight or not?" Quivering with outraged pride, the Queen went to them in person, hoping to inspire them with her own determination. She knew, however, that at such a moment a queen could not represent the King. She therefore urged Louis XVI to hold a last review of his forces when the struggle was about to begin, and to put heart into the defense.

The idea was a good one. A pledge from the King to fight to the death among his men would have buttressed the crumbling battalions. But who came to encourage the defenders? A cumbrous, unwarlike man, shortsighted, awkward, his hat under his arm. The National Guards watched him contemptuously as he drew near. Then instead of the expected "Long live the King!" came the cry, "Long live the nation!" Finally, when His Majesty advanced as far as the railings, it was to hear open cries of revolt: *"A bas le veto! A bas le gros cochon!"* Horrified at this insolence, his supporters and ministers formed a ring around the King and conducted him back into the palace. Marie Antoinette turned from this pitiful scene with her eyes filled with tears.

By now the disorderly vanguard of the rebels had arrived, some having already massed on the other side of the drawbridge. Roederer, the public prosecutor, urged the King to betake himself to the National Assembly at once and to put himself under the protection of the deputies. Louis was as if paralyzed, but Marie Antoinette promptly interposed: "Let me assure you, monsieur, that we have a considerable armed force ready to defend us. . . . It is time to decide which shall have the upper hand, the King and the constitution, or the rebels." Roederer shook his head. "Madame," he replied, "all Paris is marching to the attack; action on your part is useless; resistance is impossible." The Queen could no longer conceal her impatience; her cheeks flushed with anger. But in the presence of the King of France, no woman, not even his wife, could give orders for battle. She waited, therefore, for the ever irresolute Louis to decide. At length he sighed, and then said: "All right, we'll go!"

Thereupon Louis XVI and his family walked out of the palace, the palace which his forefathers had built and which he was never to reenter. They passed through the gardens, the King leading the way with Roederer; behind them the Queen, holding her little boy by the hand. With more haste than dignity they made their way to the covered Riding School, where in the old days the members of the court used to enjoy themselves on horseback, and where now the National Assembly could rejoice because the King, in terror for his life, had come to seek its protection. The distance was no more than two hundred paces, but by taking them Marie Antoinette and Louis XVI bade farewell to their power and their glory. The monarchy was over and done with in France.

In the magnanimity of his first surprise, Vergniaud, the president of the Assembly, declared: "You can count, Sire, upon the loyalty of the National Assembly. We have all pledged ourselves to give even our lives to maintain constituted authority." And amid the chaos which now prevailed, the National Assembly continued to act as if a legally established order was in being. It even pedantically insisted upon the observance of the paragraph in the constitution by which the King was forbidden to be present in the hall during its deliberations. Since the discussion had to continue, it was agreed that the royal family should be accommodated in an adjoining room, ordinarily occupied by the stenographers. The place was no more than a cubbyhole, so low that no full-grown person could stand upright; in front were two stools, and along the wall a bench. Marie Antoinette and King Louis had to spend eighteen hours in this superheated cage—they and their children—exposed to the glances of the deputies. But what made their humiliation even greater was the disdainful neglect of the National Assembly. No one troubled to come to say a word to them. Those who had sought asylum were as little regarded as if they had been doorkeepers.

Suddenly a wave of excitement passed through the Assembly. There was plainly audible in the adjoining Tuileries the sound of musket shots, soon followed by the boom of artillery fire. The rabble, on breaking into the palace, had found their way blocked by the Swiss guards. In the hurry of his flight the King had forgotten to give them fresh orders. True to the command to fire when the assailants opened fire and to stand to their guns, the Switzers defended the forsaken palace. Soon they had cleared the courtyard, had seized the cannon brought by the mob, and had thus shown that a resolute sovereign could, with their aid, have effectively defended himself. At this juncture the King sent orders to the Swiss guards to cease defending the palace. Such consideration came too late. His forgetfulness had already cost the lives of more than a thousand men. Unresisted now, the furious crowd swarmed into the Tuileries, and the heads of slaughtered royalists were brandished on pike points.

Huddled together in their cage, not daring to utter a word the members of the royal family saw their faithful Switzers, begrimed with powder and blood, rush into the Riding School, followed by the victorious rebels. The loot from the palace was heaped upon the president's table: silverware, ornaments, letters, cashboxes. Marie Antoinette had to listen with compressed lips while the leaders of revolt were praised. She had to listen defenseless, mute, while delegates from the sections mounted the tribune and, in violent terms, demanded the King's deposition. Vergniaud, the president, who, only two hours before, had declared that the Assembly would die in defense of constituted authority, now capitulated to the mob, proposing the immediate suspension of the King's executive powers, and demanding that the royal family should be transferred to the Luxembourg Palace "under the protection of the citizens and the law"—which, in plain words, signified imprisonment.

Eight hours, twelve hours, fourteen hours the session continued. The children, who understood nothing of these strange matters, had fallen asleep. The King and the Queen were dripping with perspiration. Gradually the King's eyelids drooped and, in the very midst of the struggle which cost him his throne, he slumbered for an hour or so. Marie Antoinette, not wishing to show her bitterness, turned her face to the wall. She alone felt to the full the abasement of their situation, and foretasted the horrors to come. Yet never for a moment did she lose her dignity. At length, after eighteen ghastly hours, the King and the Queen were allowed to withdraw to what in old days had been the Convent of the Feuillants where, in one of the deserted cells, a bedroom was hastily installed for their convenience.

Next morning and the day after, the royal family had again to attend the sittings of the National Assembly, being still cooped up in the same narrow pen. Hour after hour they watched and listened while the last vestiges of their power were consumed in this smelting oven. Yesterday the deputies had spoken of "the King"; today Danton referred to him and his wife as "the oppressors of the people." The Commune, the new revolutionary municipal government which had come into being on the night of the tenth of August, refused to allow the Luxembourg Palace to be used as the King's residence. Only in the Temple would it be possible to ensure the safety of the *détenus*—the notion of imprisonment growing plainer and plainer. The National Assembly, which was in truth glad to shift the responsibility, entrusted the King to the care of the Commune.

At length, on August 13, 1792, the Temple was ready for the royal family. So, under Pétion's charge, they were conveyed there—at six in the evening, an hour before sunset, for the populace was to enjoy the spectacle of its former sovereign and above all, the arrogant Queen, being driven off to jail.

On this same evening there was likewise a change of residence for the new master of Paris. The guillotine, which had hitherto done its fell work in the courtyard of the Conciergerie, was threateningly established in the Place du Carrousel. France was to be made fully aware that it was governed no longer by Louis XVI, but by the Terror.

XVIII

THE TEMPLE

Jacques René Hébert   Princesse de Lamballe

NIGHT HAD FALLEN when the royal family reached the Temple. The ancient fortress in former days had been the Parisian castle of the Knights Templar. It was a gloomy stronghold, standing foursquare and sinister like the Bastille, with round towers at the corners, narrow windows, and a sunless inner court. The next few weeks were devoted to making the place of incarcera-

223

tion secure. The trees in the courtyard were felled, that there might be no obstacle to perpetual supervision of the prisoners. An outer rampart was built, so that gates in three successive walls had to be transversed before the inner citadel was reached. Guardrooms were established at every exit. Each day, four deputies of the Commune visited every room of the fortress, and at nightfall took charge of the keys to all the doors. Besides these officials and the town councillors themselves, no one was allowed to enter the place without a special permit.

Still harder to bear was another precaution: persons other than members of the royal family were to be removed from the fortress. It was especially painful for the Queen to part from Madame de Lamballe who, after having gotten away safely to London, had returned in order to stand beside her friend in the hour of peril. Both women felt that they would never meet again. The governess, Madame de Tourzel, was likewise transferred to another prison, and so were the King's attendants, except for one valet. Therewith the last glamour of court life was destroyed. Louis XVI, Marie Antoinette, their two children, and Princess Elisabeth were left to their own devices.

During the first days after the removal to the Temple, the Commune did its best to make the prison comfortable. The great tower was refurnished and redecorated; one story with four rooms was assigned to the King, and another with four additional rooms was allotted to the Queen, Madame Elisabeth, and the children. Whenever they liked, in the daytime, they could walk in the garden; and, above all, the Commune was liberal in respect to matters upon which Louis's comfort greatly depended. At his midday meal there were at least three soups, two entrées, two roasts, four entremets, compotes, fruit, malmsey, claret, and champagne. No less than thirteen persons were appointed to minister to the pleasures of the table!

Louis XVI's request for books was also granted, and he received a library containing no less than 257 volumes, mostly classical Latin authors. In fact, during this opening epoch, which was brief, the detention of the royal family was not punitive in character, so that both the King and the Queen (apart from their sense of spiritual oppression) were able to lead a fairly comfort-ble life. But the sentries were always there. At the midday meal each slice of bread was cut by an enemy hand and carefully examined lest secret correspondence had been introduced into the loaf. Neither the King nor the Queen could move a step without being shadowed by an armed guard; they could not exchange their thoughts unless in the presence of witnesses; and whatever they read had passed the censorship. Only in their bedrooms at night could they know the happiness of solitude.

Jacques René Hébert, to whom the guardianship of the royal family had been entrusted, was a typical and repulsive specimen of the rising class of revolutionists, who were so from spite rather than from idealism. Openly accused of embezzlement, unscrupulous and unemployed, he leaped into the stream of the Revolution as a hunted beast will jump into a river. The more the Republic became bespattered with blood, the redder were Hébert's writings in *Le Père Duchesne*, his own newspaper, the basest "rag" of the Revolution. In the vulgarest of tones he flattered the worst instincts of the mob.

It need hardly be said that such a man, placed as watchdog over the royal family, took a malicious delight in inflicting every possible mortification upon an archduchess of Austria, a queen of France. Although civil in personal intercourse, in *Le Père Duchesne* he gave vent to his mean anger because Marie Antoinette declined to discuss matters with him. Naturally, fear of Hébert influenced the conduct of the sentries. Yet they did not find that their experience squared with what they read in his newspaper about the "bloody tyrants," and about the "dissolute, spendthrift Austrian woman." What did the sentries actually see? A portly *petit-bourgeois* taking his son by the hand for a walk in the garden, and amusing the little boy by measuring how many square feet there were in the courtyard. Soon they came to recognize that the excellent and rather dull-witted paterfamilias had no wish to hurt a fly. The Queen, of course, was determined to keep her distance! She never spoke to the man on guard, never complained to her jailers, nor asked for a kindness. Yet this very aloofness in misfortune impressed the watchers. Though outwardly rough, by degrees they conceived a liking for the royal family.

At length bad news for the Revolution came from the frontier. The Prussians and the Austrians had begun their advance, and, at the first clash, had routed the revolutionary troops. In the Vendée, the peasants had risen in revolt; a civil war had begun; food was growing scarce and the populace was restless. The most dangerous of words, "treason," was being shouted through the streets of Paris after every reverse, stirring up the whole city. At this juncture the leaders of the Revolution hoisted the banner of the Terror, resolving that, during three days and nights of September, any suspect prisoners should be butchered. Among the two thousand thus massacred was the Queen's friend, the Princesse de Lamballe.

The prisoners in the Temple heard the tocsin ringing, and knew only that a new disaster was at hand. "What can it mean?" they whispered to one another. The sentries at the gate of the fortress were better informed—and soon greatly excited. A vast crowd approached the Temple, one of their leaders carrying on a pike the head of the murdered Princesse de Lamballe, while two other ghouls dragged her nude, mutilated corpse along by the legs. The assassins, drunk with blood and wine, wanted to enjoy the hideous triumph of showing Marie Antoinette these ghastly remnants of her dead friend. Knowing that the guards could not resist the onslaught of a raging mob, hoping to keep its fury within bounds, the commandant decided to admit some of the rioters into the center court of the fortress. The crowd, like a foaming and dirty torrent, rushed through the gates.

Force could effect nothing against these maniacs, so one of the officials of the Commune tried cunning. Wearing the scarf of a deputy, he demanded silence and made a speech. He began by praising them for their splendid achievements, and then went on to say that it would be better to carry the head through the streets of Paris, so that the entire population might feast its eyes upon this "trophy" as "an everlasting monument of victory." Happily his flattering tongue served his purpose, and with savage yells the murderers lurched forth into the street.

Meanwhile the captives in the tower had heard the confused cries of an enraged multitude. Overcome by uneasiness, the King asked one of the National Guards what was the matter.

"Well, sir," replied the man, "if you want to know, it is the head of Madame de Lamballe which they have brought to show you."

At these words there was a faint cry from the Queen, who sank in a swoon. "This was the only time," we are told by her daughter, "in which she showed a lack of firmness."

Three weeks later, on September 21, crowds were again shouting in the streets. This time, however, the populace was not angry but delighted. The newly established National Convention had decided to abolish the monarchy. Next day came deputies to announce to the King, no longer a king, that he had been deposed. "Louis the Last," as he was called until the name of "Louis Capet" was contemptuously bestowed on him, received these tidings as indifferently as Shakespeare's King Richard II. Not even from Marie Antoinette was there a word of protest. Perhaps their dethronement came as a relief. Henceforth they had no more responsibility. Their best course was to find pleasure in the ordinary affairs of life; in teaching their daughter needlework or to play the piano; in helping their son to improve his penmanship, for he still wrote in large, stiff, childish letters—and they often had to destroy what in his innocence he had written. The child was still fond of writing the first words he had been taught, "Louis Charles Dauphin." Above all they tried to forget about the past and to refrain from thinking about the dread possibilities of the future.

Now, with the King deposed, it seemed the Revolution had reached its goal, But, for one who mounts it, a revolution is like a rolling ball; there can be no safety except in unceasing advance. At the present juncture of affairs in France, every party knew this full well, and each was in perpetual dread of being regarded as backward in the good cause. Even deposed and dethroned, the unhappy Louis, though no one could consider him personally dangerous, remained a symbol of monarchy. The leaders, therefore, decided that the political death of Louis XVI must be followed up by his bodily death, and the trial of Louis Capet was fixed for December.

In the Temple this alarming decision was announced by the removal of "all cutting instruments"—knives, scissors, and forks. Furthermore, Louis XVI was separated from his family, a senseless piece of barbarity. Throughout these fateful weeks the wife was not permitted to see her husband, nor even to learn how the trial was going on. All she knew about him was that his heavy tread could be heard as he paced up and down his room on the floor below. When, on January 20, 1793, an official of the Commune told Marie Antoinette, with a somewhat dolorous mien, that by an exceptional indulgence, she and the children were to be allowed to visit her husband, she was quick to grasp that it was for the last time, that Louis XVI had been sentenced to death.

There is no official or unofficial report of the interview. Who can doubt that the adieu to the father of her children must have been one of the most painful moments in Marie Antoinette's life? Though they had been united for reasons of state, their joint misfortunes had cemented their bond, and during the sad days in the Temple they had drawn closer and closer together.

In these last formidable hours the King's imperturbability gave him a certain moral grandeur. So much, at least, we have learned from the deputies who were looking on through a glass door, that there were no tears in his eyes and that he never raised his voice. When saying farewell to his wife and children this pitifully weak man showed more strength and more dignity than ever in his life before. Quietly, as on any other evening, he rose from his chair at ten o'clock, and thus gave his family the signal to depart.

Thereafter, throughout a long and sleepless night, the Queen was alone in the upper story of her tower. At length day dawned, and with it came the dreadful noises of preparation. Nearer, ever nearer drew the hour which was to deprive her children of their father and herself of the man who had been her kindly, honorable and considerate companion for more than two decades. Penned in her room, with inexorable sentries stationed at the door, the sorely tried woman was forbidden to go downstairs. Then, after stir and bustle, there was perfect stillness beneath. The King had left the building. Within an hour, the guillotine had given Marie Antoinette, sometime archduchess of Austria, then Dauphine, and at length Queen of France, a new name—"Widow Capet."

MARIE ANTOINETTE ALONE

Chevalier de Jarjayes Baron de Batz

FOR A WHILE not one of the deputies had any thought of bringing an accusation against Marie Antoinette. They felt that in this daughter of the Habsburgs they held a sort of hostage—something that would make it easier to bargain with Austria.

But the Convention greatly overestimated the strength of the Habsburg family feeling. Emperor Francis, cold and avaricious, had never a thought of ransoming his aunt and his little cousins. Mercy, now well up in years, acting upon a hint from Fersen, reminded the court of Vienna that Marie Antoinette, having been deprived of the title of Queen of France, had once more become an archduchess of Austria, so that it was the Emperor's duty to claim her. But one imprisoned woman is of little account in a world war, one life is a trifle in the cynical game of politics!

Danger is like *aqua fortis*. Courage and cowardice are sundered by this fiery test. The poltroons of the old regime had fled to foreign lands; none but the faithful had remained. One of the most notable among these stalwarts was a sometime general, the Chevalier de Jarjayes, whose wife had been lady-in-waiting at the court. To be near Marie Antoinette in this time of trouble, he left the safety of Koblenz, and, coming to Paris, managed to let the Queen know that he was prepared to make any sacrifice in her behalf. On February 2, 1793, a fortnight after the King's execution, a stranger came to Jarjayes and proposed that he help Marie Antoinette escape from the Temple. Jarjayes suspected the newcomer of being a secret agent, for the man's aspect was that of a thoroughgoing sans-culotte. However, the stranger handed him a note which he recognized as being beyond question in the Queen's handwriting, and which ran as follows: "You can trust the man who comes to you from me bringing this missive. His feelings are well known to me. . . ." The bearer of the note was Toulan, one of the regular guardians at the Temple, who had been among the first volunteers for the storming of the Tuileries, and was believed by the Commune to be an absolutely incorruptible republican. But touched by the misfortunes of the woman over whom he was keeping watch, he was now her devoted adherent, invariably referred to in Marie Antoinette's secret communications as *le fidèle*.

Within a few days Toulan had smuggled Jarjayes into the Temple for an interview with the Queen, in a way which reminds us of a modern detective story. Every evening a lamplighter came into the quadrangle of the tower, and Toulan had humbugged this man into believing that he had a friend who, just for the fun of the thing, wanted to see the inside of the prison. For a consideration, the lamplighter was to lend the friend his clothes and equipment for one evening. The story was amusing and plausible enough; the lamplighter pocketed his bribe, and handed over the requisites. Thus suitably disguised, Jarjayes gained admission to the Temple, and arranged with the Queen a bold scheme for escape. She and Madame Elisabeth, dressed as men in the uniforms of municipal councillors, and provided with stolen passes, were to quit the tower as if they had been officials of the Commune who had been holding an inspection. As for the children, luck had it that the genuine lamplighter was often accompanied on his rounds by his own children. Once more, therefore, his role was to be assumed by the resolute nobleman, who, after lighting the lamps in the courtyard, would lead out the two royal children, poorly dressed to fit their parts. Three light carriages were to be in waiting: one for the Queen, her son, and Jarjayes; another for Marie Antoinette's sister-in-law, Madame Elisabeth, and Toulan; the third for the little princess and the Queen's second conspirator, a member of the Commune called Lepitre, who was indispensable to the scheme.

A remarkable role was played in the plot by this Lepitre.

Neither human kindliness nor yet love of adventure brought him into the affair, but the promise of a large reward—which, unfortunately, Jarjayes, who undertook to get in touch with him, did not possess in hard cash. Thus valuable time was lost until, at length, the money was provided by the Queen's former banker. Meanwhile, however, Lepitre, who had already provided forged passports, had grown fainthearted. He refused further help, and this made it impossible to get the four captives out of the Temple simultaneously. The Queen would have to make good her escape alone. Jarjayes and Toulan did their best to persuade her, but nothing would induce her to forsake her children. "We have dreamed a pleasant dream, that is all . . ." she wrote to Jarjayes.

Yet there was still one service which this loyal adherent could perform for the Queen. On Jarjayes's departure from Paris, Marie Antoinette entrusted him with a farewell token for Fersen. She still had a signet ring she had had made, adorned with the Swedish nobleman's coat of arms. Now she took an impression of the arms in wax and sent it to Jarjayes. "I want you to transmit it to the person that you know to have come from Brussels to visit me last winter," she wrote, "and whom you will tell that the device has never been truer than it is now."

The motto inscribed beneath Fersen's arms consisted of five Italian words, "*Tutto a te mi guida*"—Everything leads me to you.

MARIE ANTOINETTE no longer makes any attempt to escape. Jarjayes has left the capital, and the faithful Toulan has been removed from his post as guardian, so there is no one at hand to help her. If hitherto an attempt at escape had been dangerous, now it would be foolish and suicidal.

Yet there are persons to whom danger is a lure. The wealthy Baron de Batz, who had stayed on in Paris under dozens of aliases, was a man of this type. Not until the other royalists had given up the King for lost did the Don Quixote of loyalty begin his heroic and foolhardy efforts to save poor Louis. The maddest, so far, had been that, when the King was being driven to execution under guard of eight thousand armed men, the Baron de Batz had drawn his sword with the cry: "Join me, friends who wish to save their King!" But no one joined him. Finding himself unsupported, he had vanished in the crowd before the guards had recovered from their surprise. This failure had not dispirited him in the least. He was now staging a preposterously venturesome plan for the rescue of the Queen.

Baron de Batz had been quick to recognize the weak point of the Revolution, the poison gnawing at its vitals—corruption. Government posts were paid for in money, which corrodes souls as rust corrodes steel. Cash passed through the hands of officials unaccustomed to great sums, and stuck to their fingers. Few could resist the temptation to feather their nests. Into this turbid pool of corruption Baron de Batz threw his well-baited hooks, whispering the magic word, "million." He did not, like Jarjayes, deal with subordinates, but resolutely devoted himself to bribing the chiefs. Above all he made advances to the sometime lemonade-seller Michonis, inspector of prisons, and therefore in charge of the Temple, and to Cortey, the military commander of the section.

A master conspirator, Batz calmly had himself enrolled as a private, under the name of Forguet, among the guards of the Temple. Musket in hand, dressed in the ragged uniform of the National Guards, the millionaire aristocrat took his turn with his fellow soldiers in doing sentry go in front of the Queen's door. There was no need for personal interviews with Marie Antoinette, for Michonis, who was to earn a big share of the million, was in touch with her. At the same time, thanks to Cortey's position, an even larger number of men in the baron's pay were introduced among the sentries. Thus there ensued one of the most improbable situations in history. A day came in the year 1793 when, in the center of revolutionary Paris, the stronghold of the Temple (which no one could enter without a permit from the Commune) was actually under guard of a battalion almost entirely composed of disguised royalists.

At length it seemed to Batz that the time was ripe for his coup. When darkness fell on the chosen night, everything was ready to the last detail. Cortey marched into the yard at the head of his detachment, accompanied by the Baron de Batz, and distributed his men so that the exits were in the hands of the royalists. Simultaneously Michonis was on duty upstairs in the Queen's room, and had already provided Marie Antoinette, Madame Elisabeth, and the Queen's daughter with uniform cloaks. At midnight these three, wearing military caps and shouldering muskets, were to march out of the Temple with bribed members of the National Guards, the Dauphin in their midst. As to what was to happen afterward, Batz had arranged everything. Under a false name he owned a country house not far from Paris. There the royal family was to remain in hiding until an opportunity arose to get them across the frontier.

It was nearly eleven o'clock. Michonis was only waiting for a sign from Baron de Batz. At this juncture, however, came an alarm. Someone knocked loudly at the prison gate—and was admitted lest suspicion be aroused. It was Simon the shoemaker, a steadfast and incorruptible revolutionist, a member of the Commune, who had come in haste to make sure that the Queen had not already been carried off. A gendarme had brought him a mysterious missive betraying Michonis's plans for the night, and Simon had instantly acquainted his fellow members of the town council with the news. The story had seemed to them wildly improbable. Still, they had finally decided, no harm would be done by entrusting Simon, instead of Michonis, with the charge of the interior of the Temple for this one night. The instant Cortey saw the newcomer, he realized that the game was up. Simon, however, never guessed that Cortey was one of the conspirators. He went on upstairs to Michonis.

Baron de Batz deliberated for a moment. Should he dog Simon and blow out the man's brains? The sound of the shot would instantly bring the rest of the guards upon the scene and they were not all in the plot. The Queen's escape had become impossible; an act of violence would needlessly endanger her life. The only thing that remained was to get safely out of the Temple. Cortey, who was sweating with alarm, quickly gathered the conspirators into a patrol. With Baron de Batz among them, they quietly marched out into the street.

Meanwhile Simon had been furiously taking Michonis to task, insisting that the latter must instantly come to the Commune and give an account of his doings. Strangely enough, the Commune gave Simon rather a chill reception. Though he was extolled for his zeal, he was given to understand that he must have been seeing spooks. As far as appearances went, the town councillors did not take the conspiracy seriously. In actual fact, however, they took it very seriously indeed, but, alarmed by the venality it had brought to light, they were chiefly concerned to avoid having any fuss made about the matter.

The Commune decided to deal harshly with the prisoner, with the bold woman who was fired with an invincible spirit of revolt. From this time onward Marie Antoinette was watched like a criminal. Several times Hébert paid her surprise night visits, during which her rooms and belongings were searched. But no excuse for a prosecution could be discovered. Convinced nonetheless that she must still be engaged in counter-revolutionary activities, the Commune of Paris assailed her where she was most sensitive—in her maternal affection. This time they hit the bull's-eye. On July 1, 1793, a few days after the conspiracy had been discovered, the Committee of Public Safety, acting upon a resolution passed by the Commune, decided that the ex-Dauphin, Louis Capet, should be separated from his mother. And since, in these circumstances, she could no longer carry on his education, the lad, now eight years old, was to have a tutor. Who was this tutor to be? The choice was left to the Commune, which, grateful to Simon the shoemaker for having prevented Marie Antoinette's escape, decided that he was the very man for the job. The deliberate aim of the Commune was that little Louis should be brought up, not to become a man of culture, but one of the uninstructed who constituted the lowest class of the population. He was to forget his high birth, for this would make it easier to ignore him.

Marie Antoinette had not had the slightest warning of this decision to remove her child from her care when, at half past nine one evening, six deputies from the Commune entered her sitting room. We have no reliable testimony as regards the scene that then took place between the despairing mother and the officials who carried off the lad. Of this, at least, there can be no doubt: the needlessly cruel separation from her little son was harsh almost beyond belief for Marie Antoinette.

Although the Dauphin was to stay on in the Temple in a room only a few yards from the tower occupied by his mother, she was never to be allowed to exchange a word with him, or visit him even when he was ailing. She was actually forbidden to converse with Simon, from whom she might have gleaned a little information about her son. His seclusion from her was to be unconditional and absolute.

After a while, however, Marie Antoinette discovered that from one of the window slits in the spiral staircase of her tower she could, from the third story, get a glimpse into the courtyard where the Dauphin often played. There she would stand hour after hour, waiting till fortune vouchsafed her a fleeting glance of the fair-haired little boy upon whom her affections were now centered. The child had quickly adapted himself to the changed circumstances. Loudly and energetically he would sing the *"Carmagnole"* and the *"Ça ira,"* which Simon and the other revolutionists had taught him. It seemed to him amusing to wear the red cap of the sans-culottes. He played games with the soldiers who were set to keep watch over his mother. During these weeks of uttermost distress, the light in Marie Antoinette's countenance was extinguished—the Queen had abdicated. She had ceased even to fear. No further happenings could either astonish or alarm her.

Marie Antoinette was not affrighted when, at two o'clock one morning, there came a knocking at her door. Rising from bed, she dressed, and opened her door to the commissaries. They read aloud to her the Convention's decree to the effect that the Widow Capet, since she was to be prosecuted, must be transferred from the Temple to the Conciergerie. Having listened quietly, she made no answer. She knew well enough that an accusation before the Revolutionary Tribunal was equivalent to a death sentence, and that imprisonment in the Conciergerie was the last stage on the way to the guillotine. She offered no protest, did not ask for a postponement. Indifferently she submitted to having her clothes searched. Then she had to make the last of many farewells, parting this time from her sister-in-law and her daughter. She had grown accustomed to such partings!

With a firm gait she walked to the door of the room and quickly down the stairs, rejecting offers of assistance. She had long since endured the worst that fate could bring; death, now close at hand, would be easier. She was ready, perhaps eager, to meet it. Swiftly, therefore, she sped forth from this tower of haunting memories, so swiftly that she forgot to stoop as she passed through the low portal of exit, and knocked her forehead against the hard stone archway. Her conductors, honestly distressed, asked her whether she had hurt herself. "No," she answered unmoved; "nothing can hurt me now."

XX

THE CONCIERGERIE

Michonis

ANOTHER WOMAN had been called out of her bed that night, Madame Richard, wife of the governor of the Conciergerie. Instructions had been brought to her to prepare a cell for Marie Antoinette. Madame Richard was alarmed. She was a woman of the people, brought up under the old regime, and the word "queen" produced its familiar reaction. A queen was a person to be revered. She searched her linen cupboard for the finest and whitest sheets.

At three in the morning the noise of wheels was heard. The carriages pulled up at the gate. Now there appeared in the dark passage some gendarmes carrying torches, followed by Michonis the lemonade-seller, who had been clever enough to escape arrest for his complicity in the Batz affair and had retained his office of inspector general of prisons. Behind him, in the flickering light, walked the Queen, attended by her little dog, the only creature dear to her she had been allowed to bring with her to this new prison. Madame Richard's kitchen maid, a country girl named Rosalie Lamorlière, timidly followed Marie Antoinette into her cell and offered to help her undress. "Thank you, child," answered the Queen, "I have become accustomed to looking after myself." She hung her watch upon a nail in the wall to record the brief and yet long-drawn-out time that remained to her. Then she undressed and got into bed. A gendarme with a loaded musket came in, and the door was shut. The last act of the great tragedy had begun.

The Convention had no thought of bringing the ex-Queen, a precious hostage, to a speedy trial. Her removal to the Conciergerie, greeted (as desired) with a cry of horror by the foreign newspapers, was meant to be like the crack of a whip which might frighten the House of Habsburg and quicken the tedious bartering now in progress with Austria. Although the prosecution of the prisoner had been trumpeted in the Convention as imminent, the sword was kept hanging over her head.

Unfortunately for Marie Antoinette, the news of her removal to the Conciergerie did not disturb the Austrian chiefs. A deposed queen, an ordinary woman fallen upon evil days, was held of no account by ministers of state, generals, kings, and emperors. Sentiment must not be allowed to interfere with diplomacy. There was but one person in Europe, and he a man without power, to whom the news came like a dagger thrust in the heart—Fersen. In despair he ran from anteroom to anteroom, begging the soldiers, the statesmen, the princes, the émigrés to bestir themselves. Old Count Mercy, reminded of his pledge to Maria Theresa to protect her daughter to the last, set energetically to work beside Fersen. But not one of the European rulers would put himself out in an attempt to save Marie Antoinette. "They would not have tried to save her even if they had with their own eyes seen her mounting the guillotine," Mercy scornfully declared.

Reduced to their own initiative, Fersen and Mercy tried bribery. Money was sent to Paris, and no one knows through whose fingers it trickled away. In any case the golden bullets had been fired too late. At the very time that her shrewdest friends were trying to save her, a well-intentioned but maladroit ally had given Marie Antoinette a final push into the abyss.

AMONG ALL THE PRISONS of the Revolution, the Conciergerie, "the anteroom of death," had the strictest rules. Yet, within a few days after she had been transferred there, Marie Antoinette had been able—thanks in part to the magic of her name and in part to her personal dignity—to transform her guardians into friends, helpers, faithful servants. The headwarder's wife cooked for her the most dainty food she could procure; she offered to dress Marie Antoinette's hair; every day she procured from another quarter of the town a bottle of drinking water which the Queen found preferable to that supplied in the prison. As for the gendarmes whose business it was to prevent such indulgences— what did they do? We have official records to show that day after day they brought Marie Antoinette flowers, purchased with their own money, to adorn her comfortless quarters. It was among the common people, better acquainted with misfortune than the bourgeoisie, that there was so keen a sympathy for the sovereign lady who had been so much detested in her happier days. In the very place where violent death seemed imminent, humane feelings blossomed as an unconscious defense.

It must also be said that the jack-o'-lantern of Baron de Batz's millions shone glitteringly even in the dark cells of the Conciergerie, and Michonis continued to play his bold double role. Every day he solemnly entered the Queen's room, rattled the bars on the window to make sure they had not been tampered with, tested the door fastenings. But as soon as the gendarmes had quitted the apartment, our worthy friend entered into conversation with the prisoner, giving her news of her children in the Temple. Moved by avarice, or perhaps by kindly feeling, he would occasionally, when making an inspection of the prison, smuggle in some inquisitive visitor. It was he who brought the priest who is supposed to have heard Marie Antoinette's last confession, one of those who refused to take the oath of loyalty to the Republic. He brought the painter who executed the portrait to be seen in the Carnavalet Museum. Finally, and most unfortunately, he introduced the bold fool owing to whose excess of zeal these liberties and favors were suddenly annulled.

This notorious *affaire de l'oeillet* is an obscure business. If we are to believe the Commune and the story told by Michonis, the episode was of trifling importance. Michonis's tale ran to the effect that one evening he was talking to some friends about the Queen. Then a stranger, whose name he never learned, thrust into the conversation and wanted to know whether it would not be possible sometime to accompany the inspector on his rounds. Michonis, being in a good mood, complied without further inquiry, having made the unknown pledge himself not to say a word to Marie Antoinette.

Now, are we to suppose that Michonis, the Baron de Batz's confidant, did not trouble to inquire as to the identity of the person whom he was to smuggle into the Queen's cell? Had he done so, he would have learned that the man was an old friend of hers, the Chevalier de Rougeville, one of the noblemen who on June 20, 1792, had defended the Queen at the risk of his own life. There is little doubt that the plot was more widespread than can now be proven. At any rate, on August 28, the bolts on the door of the Queen's cell were shot back and Michonis entered, accompanied this time by a strange gentleman to whom the prisoner paid no attention. Marie Antoinette began to chat with the inspector, and asked him how her children were, this being always her first and most pressing inquiry. Michonis answered kindly, and the Queen grew almost cheerful.

Then, suddenly, she turned deadly pale. She trembled. She had recognized Rougeville, whom she knew ready to run any risk. Had he some plan for her escape? Had he brought a message? She did not dare even look at him significantly; and yet she could not fail to see that he was making incomprehensible signs to her. But she dreaded lest she should betray herself. One may presume that Michonis became aware of her confusion. Saying that he had other cells to inspect, but would return before quitting the prison, he went out, accompanied by the stranger.

When Michonis and Rougeville came back Marie Antoinette was in full possession of her faculties. While she was conversing composedly with Michonis, she watched Rougeville and perceived from a sign he made that he had thrown something into the corner behind the stove. As soon as the visitors had departed, she made an excuse for sending the gendarme on duty after them "to ask something she had forgotten." She availed herself of this moment to pick up what had been thrown into the corner. What? Nothing but a carnation? Ah, but there was a tiny note crushed among the petals. Opening it, she read:

Patroness, I shall never forget you, and shall continually try to find some means of showing my zeal for your service. If you need three or four hundred louis for your guardians I will bring them to you next Friday.

It is not difficult to imagine Marie Antoinette's feelings at this miraculous revival of hope. The will to live flamed up again. She was quick to understand that the three or four hundred louis were intended as a bribe for the gendarme on duty in her room. With a surge of hopefulness she set to work. Having torn the dangerous note into tiny fragments, she proceeded to "write" an answer. She had no pen, only a scrap of paper. But necessity is the mother of invention, and, having a needle, she pricked her reply with its point. Promising a liberal reward, she gave the note to Gilbert the gendarme with instructions to hand it to the stranger should he again visit the Conciergerie.

Gilbert seems to have hesitated. Three or four hundred louis were a great temptation to the poor devil, shining in his imagination like so many stars, but the axe of the guillotine had a more sinister sheen. What was he to do? To carry out her commission would be treason to the Republic; to play the informer would be a breach of the trust which the prisoner, with whom he sympathized, had placed in him. The worthy fellow, therefore, took a middle course, asking the advice of Madame Richard. She shared his perplexity, and at length took the same course. She did not inform the authorities, but instead of shouldering the responsibility, she tried to pass it on, telling Michonis what was afoot. Michonis took fright. At this stage the affair becomes even more involved. We do not know whether Michonis had previously been aware that Rougeville was a plotter who wished to help the Queen to escape, or whether he only realized this when he heard Madame Richard's story. Anyhow, with two intermediaries apprised in addition to the principals, the matter seemed to him perilous. Assuming the airs of a strict official, he took the paper from Madame Richard, put it in his pocket, and told her to say not a word more about it to anyone.

Nothing further might have been heard of Rougeville's scheme had it not been for the misgivings of the gendarme. A handful of gold pieces might, perhaps, have induced him to hold his tongue, but the Queen had no money, and by degrees the risk to his own neck became his chief concern. On September 3, after he had been steadfast for five days, he made a report to his superiors. Two hours later the officials of the Commune raided the Conciergerie and held a strict inquiry.

To begin with, the Queen denied everything. Michonis, too, played the ignoramus, hoping that Madame Richard, who had been bribed, would hold her tongue. The latter, however, avowed having handed him the Queen's missive, so he had no choice but to produce it—having prudently made the text illegible by additional needle pricks. At a second inquiry held next day, Marie Antoinette ceased to feign ignorance. It was true, she said, that she was acquainted with the person who had visited her cell in Michonis's company, that he had conveyed to her a letter hidden in a carnation, and that she had replied to it. Determined, however, to protect the man who had wanted to help her, she did not mention the name of Rougeville, declaring that she had forgotten what he was called. She also magnanimously sheltered Michonis, thus saving his life.

For the Queen, however, this clumsy plot was disastrous, quickening the onset of doom. Severity was now the order of the day. Such personal possessions as had been left to her were taken away; the last of her rings, the gold watch which her mother had given her before she left Austria, and even a locket in which she kept little tresses of her children's hair. She was forbidden the use of candles when night fell and half the grated window of her cell was bricked up. Michonis was cashiered as too easygoing an inspector; Madame Richard was replaced by a new supervisor.

Marie Antoinette had reached the last extremity of loneliness. The new wardens and gendarmes, though kindly disposed, no longer dared take the risk of saying a word to the poor woman. Nothing had been left her but the little dog. Forsaken, in the valley of the shadow, Marie Antoinette at length began to seek the consolation which her mother had so often commended to her. For the first time in her life she asked to be supplied with books; and her jailers could not bring her a sufficiency. She did not want novels or plays, which might have reminded her too keenly of past joys, but only true tales of adventure: Captain Cook's voyages, stories of shipwreck and bold journeyings, books that would snatch her thoughts away from the desolate present. These heroes of real romance were the only companions of her solitude. No one came to visit her.

XXI
THE TRIAL

Fouquier-Tinville

THE END was at hand. Summer had passed, so that the gloomy cell became more and more coffinlike. No better than a damp cellar, it reeked of mold and corruption and death. Her health was giving way more and more in this unwholesome environment. It seemed to her a thousand years since she had been the lighthearted Queen of the merry land of France.

Thus entombed, Marie Antoinette, though in the heart of Paris, heard no murmur of the storm which that autumn was raging in western Europe. Never was the French Revolution in greater peril than during these days. Two of the strongest of the republican fortresses, Mainz and Valenciennes, had fallen; the British had occupied the chief ports; Lyon, the second capital of France, was in revolt. The government seemed tottering to its fall. The Republic could only overcome its own fear by spreading fear far and wide. "Let us put Terror on the agenda"—this dire word resounded through the meeting hall of the Convention. The slaughter of the Girondists and of the Duc d'Orléans was at hand. The guillotine was already busily at work when Billaud-Varenne addressed the Assembly as follows: "The Convention has been giving a signal example of severity to the traitors who were plotting the ruin of their country; but there is still an important duty undischarged. A woman, the shame of humanity and of her sex, Widow Capet, must at long last expiate her crimes upon the scaffold."

The proposal was unanimously adopted. Yet Fouquier-Tinville, the public prosecutor, now manifested a perplexing hesitation. Neither that week, nor the next, nor the next following, did he draft his indictment against the Queen. He wrote to the Committee of Public Safety asking for incriminating documents, and, strangely enough, the committee, in its turn, was slow to move. At length it got together a few unimportant papers, but Fouquier-Tinville still held his hand. However, at the eleventh hour, he received from Hébert (the embittered, the resolute enemy of the Queen) the most infamous document in the records of the French Revolution. It provided the necessary impetus, and in a trice the indictment was drafted.

What had happened? On September 30 a letter was sent from the Temple to Hébert, a letter signed by Simon the shoemaker, the Dauphin's tutor, asking him to come quickly to see him. What Hébert heard from the shoemaker seemed so sinister even to the tough-minded editor of *Le Père Duchesne* that he would not undertake the responsibility of dealing with it, but promptly summoned a committee of the whole Commune under the chairmanship of the mayor. Thereupon the councillors betook themselves in a body to the Temple for the three hearings which would provide materials for the indictment of the Queen.

We have reached that episode in the history of Marie Antoinette which seems incredible, inconceivable, and which can be explained only as due, in part to the heated feelings of the time, and in part to the systematic poisoning of public opinion concerning the Queen which had been going on for years and years.

One day Simon or his wife discovered the little Dauphin masturbating. Caught in the act, the child made no attempt to deny his bad habit. Sharply questioned by Simon as to who had initiated him into evil ways, the unhappy lad volunteered the information, or was hectored into declaring, that his mother and his aunt were the culprits. Simon, ready to believe anything wicked of the "Austrian tigress," pushed his questions home, until he ultimately induced little Louis to say that in the Temple the two women had frequently taken him into their beds, and that his mother had had incestuous relations with him.

In normal times any reasonable person would have been extremely skeptical as to the truth of such accusations made by a lad who was not yet nine years old. However, thanks to the scurrilous lampoons circulated by the revolutionists, neither Hébert nor his friend the tutor ever thought of doubting the youngster's accusation. All that remained was that the Queen's misconduct, her abominable lasciviousness, should be recorded in black and white so that France at large should be made acquainted with the corruptness of the Austrian woman. That was why there were three sittings of inquiry, the witnesses being a boy of eight, a girl of fifteen, and Madame Elisabeth—scenes so cruel, so shameful, that we should find it hard to believe they ever took place were it not that the yellowing documents are still preserved in the national archives.

During the inquiry, the talkative little Dauphin adhered to his statement. His sister, Madame Royale, intimidated by the reiterated and improper questions of severe-looking strangers, could only take refuge in the assertion that she knew nothing about the matter and had seen nothing of the kind. Madame Elisabeth, however, a vigorous and self-possessed young woman of nine-and-twenty, was not so easily browbeaten. When the minutes of the Dauphin's testimony were given her to read, she flushed angrily, thrust the paper contemptuously aside, and said that such scandalous accusations did not need an answer. Thereupon the boy was recalled to repeat his evidence, and Madame Elisabeth could no longer contain herself. *"Ah, le monstre!"* she exclaimed in her outrage. Nevertheless Hébert declared himself ready to sustain the charges against Marie Antoinette.

This base accusation brought by a boy against his own mother, being perhaps unprecedented in historical annals, has always been a tough nut for Marie Antoinette's biographers to crack. But there is no great difficulty in explaining it nowadays, when scientific study and experience in the law courts have taught us so much about the mendacity of children in sexual matters. For one thing, we have the testimony of the Dauphin's mother, dating from four years earlier, as to the youngster's tendency to give unduly free rein to his imagination, for (it will be remembered) she wrote to the governess as follows: "He is extremely indiscreet, being always ready to repeat whatever he has heard. Often enough, without any intention to tell a falsehood, he embroiders it with his imagination."

By this delineation of her little boy's character, Marie Antoinette gives us a clue to the enigma. We are assisted in our understanding by a statement of Madame Elisabeth's. She told the committee that her nephew had for a long time been addicted to indulgence in *plaisirs solitaires*, and that she recalled having taken him sharply to task about the matter. His mother, too, had often scolded him on this account. The boy had been caught by his mother and by his aunt, and had been punished more or less severely. Detected by Simon in the same offense, and asked who had taught him his bad habit, by a natural association his mind turned to the earlier transgressions. Subconsciously, he wanted vengeance on those who had chastised him, and, without considering the import of what he was saying, he mentioned their names. Everyone knows how children caught in a misdemeanor incline to pass the blame on to someone else. Once involved in a web of deceit, there was no way out. Feeling, moreover, that his questioners were glad to hear his slander, he cheerfully acceded to everything the deputies might suggest. His whole behavior at the inquiry implies a sort of playful and defiant impudence. "The young prince," writes an eyewitness, "was seated in an armchair, swinging his little legs, for his feet did not reach the floor."

The Queen's seclusion in the Conciergerie saved her, until the penultimate day of her life, from hearing of the charge brought against her. It was then that the indictment made her acquainted with this last indignity, this sorest of wounds inflicted by her own child's tongue. The terrible thought, the profound shock, went with her to the scaffold.

MARIE ANTOINETTE

ON OCTOBER 12, 1793, Marie Antoinette was summoned to the big council chamber for her preliminary examination. Opposite her sat the public prosecutor Fouquier-Tinville, Hermann his assessor, and a few clerks. The Queen sat alone. She had no defender, only the gendarme who kept watch over her.

But, during these many weeks of solitude, Marie Antoinette had rallied her forces. Danger had taught her to collect her thoughts, to speak eloquently, and, better still, to be silent when silence was preferable. Her answers were surprisingly vigorous, and at the same time cautious and shrewd. Not for a moment did she lose composure. At the close of her life, Marie Antoinette came to realize the responsibilities inherent in her position. In this darkened courtroom, she knew that she must show herself to be the true Queen she had failed to be in the glittering hall at Versailles. Her responses here and at the Revolutionary Tribunal were given not to the pettifogging lawyers but to the only genuine and sincere judge—history.

To the formal question, "What is your name?" she answered loudly and clearly: "Marie Antoinette of Lorraine and Austria, widow of Louis Capet, sometime King of the French, thirty-eight years of age." Then followed the accusations. She had, before the Revolution, had political relationships with the "King of Bohemia and Hungary," with the result that she had "in a terrible way" embarrassed the finances of France. She had "sent millions to the Emperor, funds to be used against the people which had nourished her." Since the Revolution began, she had conspired against France, had entered into negotiations with foreign agents, had induced her husband the King to exercise the veto. Marie Antoinette categorically denied these charges.

Realizing that he had failed to break down the ramparts of her caution, Hermann began to assail her vehemently. She had corrupted the Flemish regiment, had plied the soldiers with drink, had been in correspondence with foreign courts, was responsible for the outbreak of the war. The Queen corrected her accuser's facts. The declaration of war had been a decision of the National Assembly and not of her late husband. As for corrupting the Flemish regiment, she had only walked twice from end to end of the hall in which the soldiers were dining.

246

Hermann, however, had kept his most dangerous questions for the last, those which were designed to make Marie Antoinette repudiate her own sentiments if she wished to avoid expressing hostility to the Republic.

"Do you think that kings are necessary for the happiness of the people?"

"An individual cannot decide that matter."

"No doubt you are sorry that your son should have lost a throne which he might have mounted had not the people, awaking at length to their rights, destroyed the throne?"

"I shall never regret my son's loss of anything should his loss prove to be the gain of his country."

It will be seen that the examiner for the prosecution was not making much headway! Marie Antoinette, indeed, had shown a jesuitical skill in her answer to the last question. When speaking of her son she had said that France was "his" country. It was "his" country just as it was that of any other Frenchman, so that, in using the pronoun, she had said nothing derogatory to the Republic; and yet the word could be taken to imply that it was the Dauphin's country in another sense—she had not, even in her imminent peril, sacrificed what to her was the most sacred thing in the world, the boy's right to succeed to his father's throne.

Now that the semblance of legality had been given by this preliminary hearing, Fouquier-Tinville could proceed to draft the indictment. His pen moved swiftly over the paper, listing the accusations which have previously been cited, and including Hébert's infamous charge. On October 13 this forensic master-piece (when the ink was hardly dry) was delivered to Chauveau-Lagarde, who had been appointed counsel for the Queen. No time to prepare an adequate defense was granted him. The trial began next morning at eight, and everyone knew how it would end.

THE SEVENTY DAYS in the Conciergerie had made Marie Antoinette an elderly and sickly woman. She had been worn out by fatigue and hardship, and again and again the prison doctor had had to prescribe remedies for heart weakness. Today, however, when a memorable trial was to take place, she was determined that no one in court should have reasons for deriding the weakness of a queen and the daughter of an emperor. They must be made to realize that the woman who appeared in the dock was a scion of the House of Habsburg, and, notwithstanding the decree of deposition, a queen. More carefully than of late she arranged her white locks, then donned a freshly starched cap of white linen, from either side of which her mourning veil fell. It was as a widow of Louis XVI, the last King of France, that she was to present herself before the republican judges.

At eight o'clock Marie Antoinette entered the packed hall with an indifferent air and composedly sat down to await the formal opening of the court. When at length Fouquier-Tinville rose to his feet and read the indictment, she scarcely troubled to listen, for she had already discussed the items with her lawyers the day before. Her fingers played indifferently upon the arms of her wooden chair "as if she had been playing the piano."

Now came the turn of the forty-one witnesses. Most of their testimony was useless to the prosecution, and much of it was ludicrous. Consider, for instance, the deposition of a serving maid who bore witness to having heard, in 1788, how the Duc de Coigny told someone that the Queen had sent her brother Joseph two hundred million. Or the preposterous statement that Marie Antoinette had carried pistols with the intention of murdering the Duc d'Orléans. Not a single document in Marie Antoinette's handwriting was produced in court; again and again Fouquier-Tinville had to come back to unattested generalities.

"Was it not at the Little Trianon that you saw the woman Lamotte for the first time?"

"I never saw her."

"Was she not your victim in the notorious affair of the necklace?"

"She could not have been, for I did not know her."

Had there been any grounds for hope, Marie Antoinette might have entertained it at this stage, for her defense grew continually stronger. When really dangerous matters came up, she replied, "I do not know, I cannot remember." Not once was Hermann, now the president of the court, able to triumph over her by showing that she had spoken an untruth or by leading her into a contradiction; not once, during the long hours, did she give any occasion for the intent auditors to utter a cry of hatred, or to break forth in patriotic applause. The trial was dragging out its slow length ineffectively. It was time for the prosecution to bring a crushing charge. With this end in view, Hébert was at last called as a witness, for he was to bring the terrible accusation of incest.

Resolutely, convincingly, loudly, he uttered his charge. Speedily, however, he became aware that its very incredibility was undermining its force. No one was giving the expected cries of horror. His testimony was received in silence; the auditors were pallid and perplexed. Marie Antoinette said no word; she seemed contemptuously to ignore Hébert's existence. And Hermann, quick to realize how painful an impression had been produced, deliberately abstained from asking for the calumniated mother's reply to the accusation. As luck would have it, however, one of the jurors requested that he do so. Now the president had no option. He had to put the question to the accused. Marie Antoinette raised her head proudly, answering loudly, with unspeakable disdain: "If I have made no reply, it is because nature refuses to answer such a charge brought against a mother. I appeal in this matter to all the mothers present in the court."

At this passionate appeal, there was a sensation in the hall of the Revolutionary Tribunal. The women-of-the-people in the audience held their breath at the words, for they felt a strange kinship with this ex-Queen of France. In her, all their sex had been affronted. Without a word Hébert retired from the witness-box, by no means proud of his achievement. Even he could not but be aware that the accusation had brought the Queen a great moral triumph in the hour of her utmost difficulty. What had been designed to abase her had uplifted her.

Marie Antoinette knew that in this matter she had triumphed. Still, she had heard a voice from among the spectators, "See how proud she is," and she therefore asked her defending counsel whether she might not have assumed too much dignity in her reply. Chauveau-Lagarde consoled her, saying: "Madame, be your own self, and you will always do well."

The Queen had still another weary day of trial. The court had sat more than fifteen hours on the first day. On the second, more than twelve had passed before Fouquier-Tinville rose to summarize the case for the prosecution. When he had done so, the two defending counsels replied—somewhat tepidly, since they could not but remember that the defender of Louis XVI, who had been ardent in his endeavors, had been claimed for the scaffold. Now, before President Hermann put his questions to the jury, Marie Antoinette was removed from the hall. The judge brushed aside all vague and irrelevant charges, and formulated the main heads of the indictment in four questions which ran as follows:

1. Is it true that there have been machinations and communications with the foreign powers and with other foreign enemies of the Republic, maneuvers and communications tending to supply these enemies with monetary help, to assist them in their invasion of French territory, and to facilitate the advance of their armies?

2. Is it true that Marie Antoinette of Austria, widow of Louis Capet, participated in these machinations and was instrumental in maintaining these communications?

3. Is it true that there was a plot and a conspiracy to bring about civil war in the interior of the Republic?

4. Is it true that Marie Antoinette of Austria, widow of Louis Capet, participated in this plot and in this conspiracy?

In silence the jurors rose and withdrew into an adjoining room.

Marie Antoinette had not been proved guilty of the crime of treason in the legal sense of the word "guilty." Today we are acquainted with the documents which establish her treasonable practices against the Republic beyond a shadow of dispute. They are preserved in the state archives in Vienna and in Fersen's literary remains. But in mid-October 1793 not one of those documents was in the hands of the Revolutionary Tribunal. Throughout the two days of the trial, no valid proof of treason had been laid before the jurors. Their deliberations were no more than a semblance, and if they considered their verdict longer than a minute, it was only to keep up appearances. They

knew well enough that the Convention did not look to them for a legal decision.

At four o'clock in the morning the jurors filed back into the hall. Dead silence awaited their verdict. They unanimously declared Marie Antoinette guilty of the crime specified in the president's concluding address. Then the prisoner was brought in. The verdict was read to her. Fouquier-Tinville demanded a death sentence, and this, likewise, was unanimously agreed to

Marie Antoinette listened to the verdict and the sentence unmoved, giving no sign of fear or anger or weakness. When Hermann asked whether she still had objections, she merely shook her head. Looking straight in front of her and amid a universal stillness she walked through the hall and down the stairs. Then the poor, weary woman was taken back to prison Her life was now numbered only by hours.

In her narrow cell, as a special favor to one condemned, two candles were burning on the table. Her jailer likewise showed indulgence when she asked for pen, ink, and paper. From this gloomy solitude she wished to send a farewell to Madame Elisabeth, her husband's sister and henceforward to be the guardian of her children. Marie Antoinette wrote as follows:

> It is to you, Sister, that I am writing for the last time. I have just been sentenced to death, but not to a shameful one, since this death is shameful only to criminals, whereas I am going to rejoin your brother. Innocent like him, I hope to show the firmness which he showed during his last moments. I am calm, as one may well be when one's conscience is clear, though deeply grieved at having to forsake my poor children. . . . It was only during the trial that I learned my daughter had been separated from you. Alas, poor child, I do not dare to write to her. . . . However, through you I send them both my blessing, in the hope that some day, when they are older, they will be with you once more and will be able to enjoy your tender care. If only they will both continue to think the thoughts with which I have never ceased to inspire them, namely, that sound principles and the exact performance of duties are the prime foundation of life, and that mutual love and confidence will bring them happiness. . . . I hope my son will never forget his father's last words

which I here purposely repeat for him: Let him never try to avenge our death!

I have to speak to you of one matter which is extremely painful. I know how much my little boy must have made you suffer. Forgive him, my dear sister; remember how young he is, and how easy it is to make a child say whatever one wants, to put words he does not understand in his mouth. I hope a day will come when he will grasp the full value of your kindnesses and of the affection you have shown both my children.

It remains to entrust you with my last thoughts. . . . I die in the Catholic, Apostolic, and Roman religion, in that of my fathers. . . . Having no hope of any spiritual consolation . . . I sincerely ask God's forgiveness for all the faults I have committed since I was born. I trust that, in His goodness, He will hear my last prayers, as well as those which I have long been making that, in His pity and His goodness, He may receive my soul.

I ask the forgiveness of all those whom I have known, and, especially of you, my sister, for the sorrow which, unwittingly, I may have caused them. I forgive my enemies the evil they have done me. I here bid farewell to my aunts and to my brothers and sisters. I had friends. The thought of being separated from them forever and of their distress is among my greatest regrets in dying. Let them know, at least, that down to the last they were in my mind.

Adieu, my good and affectionate sister. I trust that this letter will reach you. Continue to think of me. I send you my most heartfelt love, and also to my poor, dear children. How heartbreaking it is to leave them forever! Adieu, adieu. . . .

Shortly before the executioner came to take her to the scaffold, Marie Antoinette gave this letter to the governor of the prison, asking him to transmit it to her sister-in-law; but the man lacked the courage to deliver it without authorization. He therefore handed the document to Fouquier-Tinville, who filed it away. Not for twenty-one years after the Queen had penned it did this remarkable good-by come to light. Too late, alas! Except for her daughter, who was sent to Austria in exchange for some captive commissaries, almost all those whom Marie Antoinette had wished to greet in her dying hour had followed her to the tomb. Madame Elisabeth was guillotined in May of the next year. The Dauphin either perished in the Temple or else lived out his life elsewhere, his identity unknown to himself and to others (the truth about the lad has never been cleared up). Fersen, too, had perished before the Restoration. Nor, indeed, was he mentioned in the letter, but to whom else can the words have been applied: "I had friends. . . . Let them know, at least, that down to the last they were in my mind"? As if he had been aware of Marie Antoinette's longing to be in touch with him in her final hours, Fersen wrote in his diary on receipt of tidings of her death: "The most terrible pang of all is that she had to be alone during those last moments. . . ."

XXII
DRIVE TO THE SCAFFOLD

Marie Antoinette in the tumbril—1793

At five in the morning, while Marie Antoinette was still writing her farewell letter, in the eight-and-forty sections of Paris the drums were beating. By seven the whole armed force of the capital was afoot; a vast display of soldiers against a lonely woman who herself wished for nothing but the end.

At seven Rosalie the kitchen maid stole into the Queen's cell and perceived that Marie Antoinette, fully dressed and wearing her black widow's gown, was lying on the bed. The country girl was full of passionate sympathy for this Queen who was about to be put to death. "Madame," she said, "you had nothing to eat yesterday evening. What can I bring you?"

"Child, I want nothing more, since for me everything is finished," answered the Queen, without sitting up.

When the girl urged her to take some soup which had been

specially prepared for her, she answered: "Very well, Rosalie, bring me the soup." She swallowed a few spoonfuls, and then the serving girl began to help her undress. Marie Antoinette had been forbidden to go to the scaffold in the mourning she had worn when on trial before the Revolutionary Tribunal, since the authorities were afraid that this widow's dress might be regarded by the people as provocative. Well, what did a dress matter now? She made no objection, and decided to don a simple white gown.

But a last humiliation had been kept in store. Wanting to put on fresh undergarments in which to go to her death, she begged the gendarme to withdraw for a few minutes. And he, having strict orders not to let her out of his sight, had no choice but to refuse. The Queen, therefore, crouched in the space between the bed and the wall, and, while she was changing her shift, the kitchen maid stood between her and the gendarme to hide her. Then she dressed herself with particular care. The desire that animated her to do so was no longer feminine vanity, but a sense of dignity for a historical hour. She carefully smoothed her white gown, wrapped her neck in a muslin cloth, and put on her best shoes. Her white hair she covered with a two-winged cap.

At eight o'clock there came a knock at the door. No, it was not yet the executioner, but only a herald of the executioner, a priest, one of those who had taken the oath of fealty to the Republic. The Queen recognized no priest but the nonjurors, and she refused, courteously, to confess her sins or seek absolution from a man whom she regarded as an apostate. When he asked her whether he should accompany her upon her last journey, she answered indifferently: "As you please."

This seeming indifference was the wall of defense behind which Marie Antoinette was preparing her fortitude for the drive to the scaffold. When, at ten o'clock, Samson the executioner, a gigantic young man, entered to cut her hair, she made no protest and offered no resistance, nor yet when he tied her hands behind her back. Life, she knew, could no longer be saved, but only honor.

At about eleven the gates of the Conciergerie were thrown open. Outside stood the tumbril in which, drawn by a heavily built horse, the victims of the Revolutionary Tribunal were driven to execution. Louis XVI, indeed, had made his royal progress to death in due state, seated in his closed court chariot, protected by the glass wall from the crudest exhibitions of popular hatred. Since then, however, the Republic had made advances. There must be equality even on the drive to the guillotine. A knacker's cart was good enough for Widow Capet! The seat was a bare board fixed to the uprights. Danton, Robespierre, Fouquier-Tinville, Hébert—all those who were now sending Marie Antoinette to her death—would take their last drive seated on the same hard piece of wood; and the condemned of today was only a few stages in front of her judges.

The first to emerge from the dark entry of the Conciergerie were some officers, who were followed by a company of soldiers with muskets at the ready. Then, composedly, and with a steady gait, came Marie Antoinette. Samson the executioner was holding her by a long cord, the end of the cord with which he had tied her hands behind her back. Some of the bystanders, despite themselves, were shocked at this unexpected and needless humiliation. Not a sound was uttered as the Queen walked to the tumbril. There Samson helped her to get in. Girard the priest, who did not wear a cassock but was dressed in civilian attire, seated himself beside her. The executioner, with an unmoved countenance, remained standing throughout the drive, still with the cord in his hand. However, during the journey he and his assistants held their three-cornered hats under their arms, as if, by this unwonted token of respect, they were asking pardon of the defenseless woman whom they were about to slay on the scaffold.

The tumbril rattled slowly over the stone pavement. On the hard seat the Queen was jolted by every movement of the roughly made cart, but she gave no sign of fear, no indication that she was aware of the inquisitive crowd that had gathered to see her going to her doom. Nothing could shake her equanimity; not even when the women gathered at the Church of Saint-Roch assailed her with cries of scorn; not even when Grammont the actor, in his uniform of a National Guard, rode a few paces beside the tumbril, swinging his saber and shouting: "There she

is, the infamous Antoinette! She's done for at last, my friends!"
She seemed neither to hear nor to see.

At the corner of the Rue Saint-Honoré, where the Café de la
Régence now stands, a man stood waiting, an artist's block in one
hand and a pencil in the other. It was Louis David, a despicable
bootlicker and turncoat, but one of the greatest painters of his
day. In a trice he had sketched the Queen as she was passing, a
cruelly magnificent drawing, made from life with sinister skill;
the picture of a woman prematurely old, no longer beautiful, to
whom nothing but pride remains. Her mouth is arrogantly
closed; her expression is one of profound indifference; with her
hands tied behind her back, she sits as upright on the wooden
seat of the tumbril as if she were seated upon a throne. Every
line of her stony countenance speaks disdain. Suffering transformed into defiance gives her tortured face a new and dreadful
majesty. Not even hatred, which made this picture, can deny the
awful dignity with which Marie Antoinette endured the shame
of her drive to the place of execution.

The huge Place de la Révolution, now known as the Place de
la Concorde, was thronged by a mighty crowd. Tens of thousands had been standing there since early morning, lest they
should miss the unique spectacle of a queen, as Hébert had
coarsely phrased it, "being shaved by the national razor." They
had been kept waiting there hour after hour. The great scene was
worth a little patience.

Towering above the heads of this inquisitive and lively throng
were to be seen the only motionless objects in the great square,
first of all the uprights of the guillotine, connected at the top by
two crossbars—a wooden bridge leading from this world to the
next. Below the summit, like a signpost on the way, the knife
gleamed sharp and clear in the chill October sunshine. Nearby,
much taller than the gateway of death, towered the huge statue
of liberty upon the pedestal which once had borne the monument of Louis XV. A seated figure, her head crowned by the
Phrygian cap and the sword of justice in her hand; she sat there,
petrified, the Goddess of Liberty, dreaming, dreaming. Her
white eyes stared across the restless crowd and across the "humane killer" into distances invisible to human eyes.

There was a stir in the crowd, and a sudden silence. This silence was broken by savage shouts from the Rue Saint-Honoré. A squadron of cavalry rode into the Place, followed by the tumbril in which was seated the bound woman who had once been Queen of France; behind her stood Samson the executioner. So still was it in the huge square that the stamping of the horses and the scraping of the wheels was plainly audible. The thousands upon thousands of spectators regarded with a sort of consternation the pale victim, who seemed to ignore their presence. She was but awaiting the final test. In a few minutes death would come, to be followed by immortality.

The tumbril drew up beside the scaffold. Unaided, "with an air even more composed than when leaving the prison," the Queen mounted the wooden steps, tripping up them as lightly in her high-heeled black satin shoes as if they had been the marble staircase at Versailles. One last glance skyward over the heads of onlookers! The end had come. The executioner and his assistants seized her by the back, thrust her into position, kneeling with her throat in the lower half of the round; the upper board was adjusted to the back of her neck; they pulled the string; a flash of the falling knife; a dull thud; and, by the hair, Samson picked up a bleeding head and lifted it on high for the multitude to gloat upon. Those who had been holding their breath for the last half minute now broke into a wild shout of "Long live the Republic!" Then the onlookers hastily scattered.

The executioner has wheeled away the body in a little hand cart, the head thrust betwixt the legs. A few gendarmes are left to guard the scaffold.

Except for the gendarmes the only spectator left in the Place de la Révolution is the Goddess of Liberty, looking out as before into the distance, toward her invisible goal. Of the happenings that morning in the square she has seen and heard nothing. Severe of aspect, disregarding the savageries and follies of mankind, she contemplates the eternal distance. She knows not, nor wishes to know, the deeds that are done in her name.

THE
HEAD AND
HEART OF
THOMAS
JEFFERSON

A CONDENSATION OF

THE
HEAD AND
HEART OF
THOMAS
JEFFERSON

by
JOHN DOS PASSOS

The man who drafted the Declaration of Independence and became the third President of the United States was one of the most remarkable human beings America has produced. Regarded by many as one of the great philosophers of the eighteenth century, he was in addition a fine architect, an innovator in agriculture, a gifted engineer and an eloquent writer. Yet underlying all this impressive talent was a serious, kindly man who believed passionately in the worth of ordinary people and in their right and ability to govern themselves.

What were the forces of heritage and history that could produce so extraordinary a man? This is the question that interested John Dos Passos, renowned author of the trilogy *U.S.A.* In *The Head and Heart of Thomas Jefferson* he has brilliantly re-created the first fifty years of Jefferson's life so that he stands alive, six-feet-two, warm and clear-eyed—a man of vision who in tumultuous times helped to realize the dream of a great, free country in the New World.

Chapter 1

IT WAS IN THE YEAR 1739 that Thomas Jefferson's father and mother were married. The marriage bond of Peter Jefferson and Isham Randolph's daughter Jane is on file at Goochland Courthouse, Virginia. In the plain bold signature which his son's was later to resemble he put his name down bluntly PET. JEFFERSON. Though he took his wife to live at his old house at Fine Creek, he was already clearing himself a plantation and planning a mansion on a hill in the gap where the red Rivanna River flowed out between the steeply forested foothill ranges towards the rolling cultivated lands along the James River. The newly patented tract lay in sight of the Blue Ridge Mountains. He named the place Shadwell after the parish in London where Jane Randolph had been born.

Marrying Jane, the adjutant general's daughter, was a step up in the world for Pete Jefferson. His eldest brother Thomas had died while on a trading voyage. The next brother Field had inherited the bulk of the family estate, leaving Peter with little more than an interest in the Fine Creek land on the south bank of the James a few miles below Isham Randolph's house.

Peter was a powerfully built man, ambitious, energetic, blunt, "of strong mind, sound judgment and eager after information," so his son wrote of him affectionately in his autobiography. He had his way to make in the world and very little except his skill as a surveyor to go on.

The energy and brains of the colony were on the move westward. Tobacco was the cash crop, but the tobacco planter didn't have the time or the hands needed to raise crops that would improve his soil and, as the best leaf was grown on virgin land, the Virginia landowners were continually crowding about the governor and council in Williamsburg, the colony's capital, to seek fresh grants. They would burn off the underbrush and girdle the big trees and raise a few good crops before the rains washed away the forest loam. By now the colony was outgrowing the tidewater lands, and a man who wanted to better himself began to look to the forest and to the valleys beyond the mountains for a livelihood and for a site for the homestead where he would found himself a family. It was particularly younger sons cut off by the strict rules of inheritance from the great estates who had to clear themselves fresh plantations in the forest. When a man went to work to patent a tract the first thing he had to do was survey it; so the rising young men tended to become surveyors by profession.

It was probably as a surveyor that Pete Jefferson first became associated with Jane Randolph's cousin William, who had inherited the Randolph estate of Tuckahoe, where stood the only great mansion yet built above the falls of the James. Two years before his marriage he and William Randolph and four others had taken up a patent on fifty thousand acres across the Blue Ridge. It was partly as a base for surveying trips behind the mountains that the partners picked the Rivanna gap for their future seats.

As time went on the affairs of the two men became more and more intertwined. There was a warm friendship between them. When they rode over the densely wooded hills of the adjoining parcels they had patented along both banks of the Rivanna, looking for a site for Jefferson's home—or manor plantation, as they called it in those days—the best location turned out to be on Randolph's land. He genially ceded Jefferson two hundred acres on which to build Shadwell "for and in consideration of Henry Wetherburn's biggest bowl of arrack punch to him delivered," and sold him another two hundred acres for fifty pounds to round out the farm.

Here, where in summer in the clearings the ranks of tobacco rustled a stately soft green between the stumps and the gray skeletons of girdled oaks or sycamores, in one of the small raw buildings the family lived in before the main dwelling was finished, amid the clang of axes felling trees and the sound of carpenters' hammers, his wife, who was already the mother of two little girls, Jane and Mary, in the spring of 1743 bore Pete Jefferson a son whom they named Thomas after his grandfather and great-grandfather and after his uncle who had died at sea.

AS THE LAND-HUNGRY GENTRY moved west with their oxcarts laden with plows and axes and their ladies riding with handkerchiefs tied over their faces against the dust, and their gangs of slaves and cattle and pigs herded by poor-white overseers, they set up new governments in the wilderness fringes of the original counties. When in 1744 the settlers between the North Anna and the James got a bill through the General Court carving out Albemarle County, Peter Jefferson became one of the first justices named in the new county.

In February of the following year Joshua Fry, Peter Jefferson, Allen Howard, William Cabell, the pioneer physician of Warminster on the James, and two others met to set up the Albemarle County court. Howard and Cabell brought with them a *dedimus potestatem* from the General Court at Williamsburg to administer the oaths of justice of the peace and judge of the Court of Chancery. They proceeded to swear in Peter Jefferson and Joshua Fry, who swore in the other two, and then everybody got on his horse and went home.

At a second meeting William Randolph produced his commission from Thomas Nelson, deputy secretary of the colony, to be county clerk. The minutes in the book for the rest of 1745 are various. Surveyors are appointed for clearing highways. Suits are argued by parties attempting to collect debts. A couple of assault and battery cases come up.

The first criminal case appears late in November, when Piers Reynolds is presented for petty larceny of a handkerchief worth elevenpence and is sentenced to twenty-one lashes and bound over for a year at twenty pounds.

At ensuing courts men are presented for profane swearing and several couples for living in adultery. Petitions are entered for new roads. Inspectors are appointed on pork, beef, tar and turpentine offered for sale in the county.

Much as it was in England at that time local government in Virginia was in the hands of the gentry. As justices of the peace they exercised functions judicial, legislative and executive. The landowner was the law.

MEN'S AND ESPECIALLY WOMEN'S LIVES were short in those days. The Virginia colony was notoriously unhealthy. That same year of 1745 William Randolph died. His wife had died a short time before, leaving two girls and an infant son. In his will he had appointed Peter Jefferson one of his executors, and added, "Whereas I have appointed by my Will that my Dear & only Son Thomas Mann Randolph should have a private education given him in my house at Tuckahoe my Will is that my Dear & Loving friend Mr. Peter Jefferson do move down with his family to my Tuckahoe house & remain there till my son comes of age with whom my Dear Son & his Sister shall live."

Probably the dwelling house at Shadwell was still far from finished so it was not too much of a hardship for the Jeffersons to move into Tuckahoe. Peter Jefferson packed up his wife and little Jane and Mary and two-year-old Thomas and Elizabeth the new baby and moved his headquarters back to the settled land above the falls of the James. There was a story among Thomas Jefferson's grandchildren that he used to say his first recollection was of being handed up and carried on a pillow by a mounted slave when the cavalcade set off for the seventy-mile ride down the rambling and rutted trail.

Little Thomas's first impressions of home must have been of Tuckahoe, of the great old frame house shaped like an H, with its Jacobean carved staircases and its stately parlors and its furnishings imported from England. Set on a steep knoll, the house overlooked the winding James River. As the colonies went, life at Tuckahoe was luxurious. There were many house servants. Amid the abundant hospitality and the backwoods pomp of the home of a Virginia magnate the Randolph and Jefferson children were brought up together.

Peter Jefferson had little education himself. Like many self-made men, he was determined that his children should have the learning he had missed. He brought in a tutor to teach the two little boys and the troop of girls their reading, writing and arithmetic. At Tuckahoe there is a square outbuilding with a coved plaster ceiling above a handsome walnut molding, which was the schoolhouse where the children learned their lessons, and, still preserved, a piece of plaster off the wall where young Thomas Jefferson is said to have scrawled his name.

Little is known about the boy's elementary education. From his letters we can deduce that he never learned too well to spell, but occasional remarks crop up in them that indicate his life-long gratitude to his father for having given him a good classical education.

In his autobiography he states tersely that his father "placed me in the English school at five years of age; and in the Latin at nine, where I continued until his death.

"My teacher, Mr. Douglas," he dryly added, "a clergyman from Scotland, with the rudiments of the Latin and Greek languages, taught me the French."

This William Douglas had been educated at the universities of Glasgow and Edinburgh. He had come to Virginia to act as a tutor for the Monroe family in Westmoreland County, and he had decided to settle in the colony; so he had returned home to take orders, and had brought back his wife, two adopted boys and a volume of the history of the house of Douglas. He lived on Dover Creek a few miles upriver from Tuckahoe and preached at the Dover Church.

Jefferson studied with him for four years, presumably boarding at the parsonage, because while he was in school there his family often went up in the forest to Albemarle, where the house at Shadwell was now nearly completed.

Young Jefferson was undoubtedly a sharp pupil. From

Douglas he must have picked up some inkling of the intellectual energy of Scottish ways of thinking. His education at Tuckahoe gave him the richest background in general culture the colony had to offer at the time. He was never to feel an outsider in whatever inner circle of power he encountered as he grew up. Neither would he feel a provincial in the republic of letters.

MEANWHILE HIS MOTHER, Jane Jefferson, was bearing children regularly, bringing more daughters than sons safe into the world. Thomas was still the only boy in a brood of girls. As his father was much away from home on surveying expeditions, it is likely that young Master Thomas, surrounded by petticoats and Negro mammies, was very much the lodestone of attention among the Jeffersons. All his father's ambition to found a great family equal in power and wealth to the Randolph clan must have centered in him.

Peter Jefferson could well boast that he never would ask any servant of his to do anything he couldn't do himself. Stories were handed down in the family of how, standing between them, he could head up two thousand-pound hogsheads of tobacco at a time; how he'd once pulled down an old barn with a rope when three Negro slaves couldn't budge it; how he'd lived on raw mule flesh while running a line through the wilderness. It was from his father that Jefferson picked up his "democratic" (using the word in its broad popular sense) notions and maxims.

A man of the forests, Peter Jefferson was a friend of the Indians. Visiting chiefs on their way through to Williamsburg often stopped at Shadwell. Very early he taught his boy to shoot and to sit a horse; and from the first the boy heard from him of action and of life in the woods. Most likely, too, evenings when he was home he let the boy play with the rules and compasses and pencils and paper he used to make the plats of his surveys.

Peter Jefferson led a punishing life. Even in the settled part of Virginia distances were great. Between plantations there was only wilderness. It was a hard four or five days' ride from Shadwell to Williamsburg. An immense amount of time was wasted on the road, tracking down strayed horses, waiting for a blacksmith, waiting to ferry across estuaries or waiting for the mud to dry in the rambling tracks they called roads.

It was a daily struggle with the forest to produce a crop. Then you had to sell it to advantage. The planter, once he had managed to get his tobacco cured and shipped to England, remained in the hands of the London or Glasgow merchants who sold it for him on commission. Money was so rare in the colony that most commercial transactions were reckoned in pounds of tobacco. The planter's debts across the ocean were a continual goad even when the price of tobacco was high. Slaves were expensive and they had to be clothed and fed. And there were no manufactures in the colony. The tools the slaves used to till the fields with, the clothes the planter and his family wore, the furnishings and window glass of his house, the saddles of his horses and his books and his pens and the ledger he kept his accounts in all had to be imported from England, and England was three precarious months of Atlantic weather away. In Virginia everything was scarce and dear except food and land.

The fresh forest loam lay to the westward. Down in the tidewater settlements the small farmer democracy that was still remembered from Peter Jefferson's father's time had come to an end. The great landowners whose families had achieved wealth a generation before had already bespoken all the seats on the governor's council at Williamsburg. There was little room for new men there. But beyond the Blue Ridge stretched the beneficent wilderness where a surveyor could stake out a fortune.

These westward hopes were the common bond between a number of men of great energy and of some intellectual brilliance who now formed the gentry of the new county of Albemarle. Joshua Fry, Jefferson's good friend and his partner in the surveying business, was one. Another was Dr. Thomas Walker, who had acquired eleven thousand acres on the eastern slope of the Southwest Mountains. While the Jeffersons were building Shadwell and Fry was building his place called Viewmont, Thomas Walker was at work on Castle Hill. In the summer of 1748 Walker went along as a surveyor on a trek westward into what is now Tennessee. He came home giddy with the immensity and fertility of the southwest country and promptly set to work to patent himself a tract. At the same time he and Peter Jefferson and two of the Meriwethers patented a tract of ten thousand acres on New River. But the business of settling the new Southwest was too big for scattered individuals. The land speculators of Albemarle decided to band together. Dr. Walker and Peter Jefferson and Joshua Fry, with John Harvie, a Scottish lawyer, and several of the Lewises and Meriwethers, chartered a company for the discovery and sale of western lands. They called it the Loyal Land Company.

On July 12, 1749, the governor and council granted "To John Lewis Esquire & Others eight hundred thousand acres in one or more Surveys, beginning on the Bounds between this Colony & North Carolina & running to the westward & the North so as to include the said Quantity." To set the limits of the grant the first thing needed was a definitive survey of the boundaries between Virginia and North Carolina. Jefferson and his partner Fry got themselves commissioned to run the line. The following year, after many months of adventure and hardship, they completed a map of greater Virginia. It was published in London, and laid the foundation for the accurate cartography of the region. All his life Thomas was proud of his father's map.

When Peter Jefferson was home he took young Thomas hunting, and taught him to look for birds and animals. If occasionally the boy was allowed to tag along with his father and Colonel Fry or Dr. Walker on some ride over the mountains, he must have kept his ears stretched for every word about elk and bear and buffalo in the new country beyond the next range.

The surveying office was busy. Outside of the surveys Jefferson and Fry made for others they kept patenting new lands on their own. Of course the fact that large acreages were patented did not mean that the land always came into effective possession, but patenting was the first step towards ownership.

During the summer of 1752 Peter Jefferson moved his family back to Shadwell for good. For some time his interests had centered more and more in Albemarle County. He had to build a worthy seat for the red-haired son who had now passed his ninth birthday, who could ride and shoot and was picking up avidly whatever Latin and Greek declensions and French irregular verbs the Reverend Douglas could teach him. Peter went to work with renewed energy on his farms on both banks of the Rivanna and on the plantation buildings. He was beginning to be a man of wealth and dignity in his own right.

When Thomas was ten the Albemarle County pioneers started to work up a plan of exploration on a scale so magnificent that it could not be put into effect until that young man had become President of the United States half a century later. In a book reputed to be the work of an early explorer, Joshua Fry had read that a passage by water was possible up the western tributaries of the Mississippi, with only short portages, to a river which flowed into the South Sea. If such a passage could be opened to the East Indies, he and his friends thought, what a fillip it would give the trade of the American colonies, which would then become "the general Mart of the European World."

Thomas Jefferson listened to the talk of his father's friends about Missisipia and the great plains beyond. The memory of small boys is retentive to a degree. He never went very far west, but all his life he responded to western questions as if he knew the country by heart. Years later when he was President he was to organize and sponsor the Lewis and Clark expedition. Often, out hunting in the woods alone as a boy, he must have imagined himself exploring beyond the blue mountains.

THE WAR THAT WAS TO BE CALLED the French and Indian War did not break out until 1754, but sporadic wars between England and France, aimed at dominating the eastern part of America, had been occurring in the New World since 1689. In 1748 a treaty signed at Aix-la-Chapelle had brought the last such war to an inconclusive end. This had given the French the breathing space they needed to strengthen the defense of their empire of fur traders and missionaries. Their government at Quebec went to work to build forts and to court the Indians. The plan was to pen in the English colonists, who were pouring over the Appalachians by every valley gap. French troops occupied the forks of the Ohio, where the Allegheny and Monongahela joined their waters, and built a substantial log fort which they named Fort Duquesne.

When the news came to Williamsburg, Governor Robert Dinwiddie looked about for a reliable man to do him a report on what the French were up to. He hit on a tall young militia officer with very large hands and feet who was doing some surveying for Lord Halifax. The young man had barely come of age. His name was George Washington.

After a tough wintry hike and adventures that taxed his wits and his physical strength young George Washington arrived back in Williamsburg early in February 1754. His firm conviction that Fort Duquesne was the key to the Ohio Valley impressed the authorities in London, and when the burgesses assembled at Williamsburg they agreed with him that forts had to be built and an expedition outfitted to push back the French. A force was assembled in the spring and Colonel Joshua Fry was placed in command with young Washington under him. But Colonel Fry, delayed by private business in joining the expedition, fell from his horse at Wills Creek (now Cumberland, Maryland), and died as the result of injuries sustained in the fall. So Washington found himself alone in his first command.

He was in tough straits. At the stockade which they had built at Great Meadows on the Monongahela and named Fort Necessity, closely besieged by the French and by large bands of Indians, the Virginians were forced at last to capitulate, marching out in a driving rain on the soggy trail back to Wills Creek. There on the thick trunk of an oak under which his superior officer lay buried, George Washington, whose first command had ended in disaster and disgrace, carved an epitaph famous in its day: *Here lies the good the wise the noble Fry*.

When Joshua Fry's will was read back in Albemarle it was found that Peter Jefferson was one of his executors. Fry's death also left a seat in the House of Burgesses vacant. In a special election Peter Jefferson was chosen to fill it. At twelve young Thomas was quite old enough to have been present at the courthouse when the electors brought in the returns. His father seems to have first attended the fifth session of that assembly, which was held at William and Mary College because the capitol building was being repaired.

As time went by matters worsened between the French and

the British. Even though His Excellency General Braddock and four regiments of British regulars were brought over from England, still the situation did not improve. In August the governor called an emergency meeting of the assembly. In Williamsburg Peter Jefferson listened to the stories of murder and pillage that came from the western burgesses as they dismounted from their sweaty horses around the inns and lodging houses. The governor's report to the assembly was disturbing.

"I am truly sorry," he said, "for the Occasion of calling you together so suddenly but the unexpected and total defeat of General Braddock at Monongahela made it absolutely necessary."

This defeat, he went on to explain, left Fort Cumberland, which was in Maryland, open to attack at any time. He told them that he had called out the Rangers and suggested that every able-bodied man in the colony be drafted into the militia. A bill was brought in to raise twenty thousand pounds. As soon as the supply bills passed, Dinwiddie prorogued the assembly. Peter Jefferson must have ridden home full of anxiety for his western lands and for the safety of his family at Shadwell. Shadwell was an easy day's ride across the gap from the valley where Indian bands were burning and killing and scalping.

The Albemarle settlers were in a state of agitation all that summer and fall of 1755. There was the drought and heavy taxes and Indian raids and news of defeats from all over. Peter Jefferson was particularly uneasy because his wife was again big with child. On October 1 she safely bore him twins, a boy they named Randolph and a little girl named Anna Scott.

Late that month he rode down to Williamsburg to attend a last session of the assembly. The burgesses were in a bitter mood. They felt that they were bearing more than their share of the burdens of the war, yet had no control over its management. The colonial officers were disgruntled by having regular army officers from England set over them regardless of rank.

Tobacco had gone up in value and money down. It had been the custom to pay the minister of a parish sixteen thousand pounds of tobacco a year. Now that the planters were feeling the pinch of rising tobacco prices, the burgesses passed an act to the effect that clergymen and other officials should be paid

their salaries in the depreciated currency of the colony at the rate of twopence a pound of tobacco. This act, which got to be known as the Two Penny Act, had set off a long wrangle between the planters and their clergymen. After a couple of weeks of fruitless argument, Dinwiddie dissolved the assembly and sent the burgesses home.

So Peter Jefferson finished his last term in public office. At home in Albemarle he went to work with a will to increase his holdings. In 1755 and 1756 he acquired around two thousand more acres of land in the vicinity of his home. He was getting to be one of the great landowners of Albemarle County. In the summer of 1757 he fell ill. His friend Dr. Walker visited him professionally late in June, three times in July and almost every day in August. On August 17 he died. He was just under fifty.

p, a steel engraving of
ieral Edward Braddock
h his British
ulars en route to Fort
quesne in 1755—a march
: was to end in disaster.
tom, the thriving
ıtation country of
ıteenth-century Virginia,
ed on maps that were
le during the lifetime
Thomas Jefferson.

Peter Jefferson had led a hard industrious life. A sturdy and practical young man, he had risen to a position of considerable wealth. As executors of his estate and guardians of his children he named a group of friends and relatives who were men not only of substance but of intelligence and education. The Honorable Peter Randolph Esquire led the list; Jane Jefferson's cousin, a grandson of the original Randolph, he had served as a burgess and as clerk of the House and as attorney general of the colony. Next were Peter's brother-in-law, Thomas Turpin the elder, a surveyor and justice of Goochland County; and Dr. Thomas Walker and John Harvie of the Loyal Land Company.

Peter Jefferson had cleared for his elder son a plantation in the forest and earned him a place among the small group of men who dominated the colony. The cast of his son's mind turned out to be aloof and scholarly and cogitative. His world began where his father's left off. From his father he had inherited energy and health. From his father's friends like Walker and Fry he had absorbed a knowledge of the empire that waited for settlement to the westward of the mountains. From his boyhood at Tuckahoe and his kinship with the Randolphs he had acquired the country gentleman's overweening assurance of the rightness of his own opinions. The wilderness which was a hunting ground, or the seedbed for new plantings of tobacco to the pioneer, was, to the son, landscape to be admired and molded to a gentleman's taste. Peter Jefferson had done the hard work of hewing out a fortune. To the son, starting out from the eminence of an established livelihood, would fall the task of designing a home for himself in the hilly acres in Rivanna gap; not only a home for himself, so it turned out, but a nation on the edge of the great new barely discovered continent.

WHEN HIS FATHER'S DEATH forced him to assume a man's estate Thomas Jefferson was only fourteen years old. His brother was an infant. He was the only grown male in a family of women. A Virginia plantation manned by irresponsible slaves kept at work by low-grade white overseers could not run a week without somebody to make the decisions and to insist on their being carried out. Women's training in the Virginia colony unfitted them for taking charge of anything more than the traditional household tasks. Nothing is known of Jane Jefferson's character that points to her having been in any way exceptional in these matters, so it followed that from the moment his father died every decision—where the slaves should work, when the cattle should be moved from one pasture to another, when to cut the hay, when to bring the tobacco into the barn—depended on young Thomas. With the daily exercise of free choice and the all too apparent bad results of the wrong choices, there began to grow in him that seasoned sense of responsibility for the conduct of his world that is the basic virtue of country gentlemen.

The business of the plantations was growing tobacco and drying it and rolling it to the warehouse. Thomas had the executors of his father's will to go to for advice. John Harvie who lived at Bellemont nearby seems to have taken over some of the estate. He had the counsel of the eminent Peter Randolph whose seat was at Chatsworth in Henrico County. At Castle

Hill, only a little farther than Bellemont, there was the versatile Dr. Walker, available whenever he was home from the war or from excursions to the west of the Blue Ridge.

One of the executors' first decisions was to put the young heir of Shadwell to school at the Reverend James Maury's. James Maury was a friend and near neighbor of Dr. Walker, as well as his associate in the Loyal Land Company. He had the reputation of being the ablest schoolmaster in the colony. Brought up in one of those lettered Huguenot families that had spread so much civilization through England and America after the Huguenots were driven out of France, Maury was a learned man with an original cast to his mind.

The Reverend Maury was a short stocky dark-haired man with a sarcastic tongue. Although he was, as Jefferson described him in his autobiography, "a correct classical scholar" he had his own ideas on education. His aim in teaching, he said, was to make each young gentleman a case by himself "to form his Morals & cultivate his Genius." He once wrote a long article advocating an American type of practical education for a boy who was going into the business of making money out of land and tobacco. For the planter's son, "unless he wished to make a Figure in Divinity, Medicine or Law," he counseled a thorough grounding in his own language first: "English Grammar, Reading, Writing, Arithmetic, History, Geography . . . so that he will be able to convey what he knows or thinks on any Subject, either on Paper or viva voce, in a neater, more elegant & better adjusted Dress."

All his life Jefferson looked back with a feeling of warm affection to the happy times at the Mountain, as he called it, and to the schoolboy friendships he formed there. Four boys in particular he always remembered. There was Dabney Carr from Bear Castle in Caroline County; there was the schoolmaster's eldest son James whom Jefferson liked to go hunting with after deer and wild turkeys and whom he used to take home to Shadwell with him weekends; there was Dr. Walker's lively boy Jack; and, youngest of the lot, there was James Madison, the son of John Madison of Port Republic, a cousin of the Montpelier Madisons, who grew up to be president of William and Mary College, an astronomer, mathematician and surveyor.

From Jefferson's correspondence with his lifelong friend, the younger James Maury, who became a merchant in the Atlantic trade and the first American consul in Liverpool, rise occasional echoes of high spirits, and holidays spent scrambling through the freshness of the forested hills, and swimming and fishing in the creek, and fiddling and horse racing. Thomas Jefferson at that time was a long-legged redheaded freckled youth with just a touch of the priggishness that comes from precocious ability, balanced in his case by his quick sympathy for other people's doings and thoughts which is the basis of a capacity for friendship. He had a very considerable aptitude for manipulating his fellows. George Tucker in his *Life of Thomas Jefferson* quotes the younger Maury's story about the sly way Jefferson used to get days off for hunting by putting other boys up to asking for a holiday.

Yet in scholarship he was more mature than his schoolmates. He had already formed habits of concentrated study. The early companionship of his father had filled him with the conviction that a man had work to do in the world. Being for so long the only boy in a family of girls had given him a feeling of quiet superiority. Although physically active he was beginning to feel that his real career lay in study. He didn't shine in conversation but with a book he was happy. He read everything he could lay his hands on, with the hunger for practical information and guidance that had been his father's, rather than with the collector's instinct of a pure scholar. In the midst of the leisurely backcountry life, he was already obsessed by the feeling that he had no time to waste. He was also restless and at times seemingly bored with the life at Shadwell after his father's death.

As often happens with people of more than ordinary capacities, Jefferson's growing up from boyhood to manhood was more than ordinarily painful. While the cogitative side of his intelligence was already highly mature, in his relations with people, particularly with people of the opposite sex, he was still an overgrown child and rather a spoiled child at that.

We know he deeply loved his sister Jane, but there is something strangely frigid about the scanty references to his mother that may well betoken real dislike. In all the vast hoard of Jefferson's correspondence and in the great variety of notebooks he assiduously kept there is hardly a mention of her. Except for a few entries about financial dealings with Mrs. Jefferson in connection with carrying out the terms of his father's will, Jane Randolph Jefferson remains a mere name. Her house burns, and her elder son thinks only of the books he has lost. When she dies of a sudden illness in March of 1776 he jots down a note. "My mother died about 8 o'clock this morning—in the 57th year of her age." In the deed book for that year at the courthouse at Charlottesville appears a meager entry under her name. It is the appraisal of Jane Jefferson's personal possessions at the time of her death:

One large halfworn portmanteau trunk	10/
One small trunk	3/
One smellingbottle seal and ring for keys	2/6

It will have to stand for her epitaph.

BY THE END OF 1759, when he was sixteen, Jefferson knew he had stood Shadwell as long as he could. Probably too he felt he had learned what there was to be learned from the Reverend James Maury. With a certain indirection which was to characterize his dealings with men all his life, and with a touch of that skill in putting his own ideas in other men's mouths and making them defend them as their own which was to be the basis of his extraordinary influence among his countrymen, he managed to put his own wishes into the mouth of the most influential of his guardians, the Honorable Peter Randolph, whom he'd ridden down to see at Chatsworth. From Shadwell on his return he wrote the letter to John Harvie which has been so often quoted because it is his first letter on record.

Sir,
I was at Colo. Peter Randolph's about a Fortnight ago & my Schooling falling into Discourse, he said he thought it would be to my advantage to go to the College, & was desirous I should go as indeed I am myself for several Reasons. In the first place as long as I stay at the Mountains the Loss of one

fourth of my Time is inevitable, by Company's coming here & detaining me from School. And likewise my Absence will in a great Measure put a stop to so much Company & by that means lessen the expenses of the Estate in House-Keeping. And on the other hand by going to the College I shall get more universal Acquaintance, which may hereafter be serviceable to me; and I suppose I can pursue my Studies in the Greek and Latin as well there as here, & likewise learn something of the Mathematics. I shall be glad of your opinion.

At sixteen Thomas Jefferson was already a man who knew what he wanted to do with his time, with every minute of it.

Chapter 2

WHEN JEFFERSON RODE towards Williamsburg to enroll at William and Mary College, splashing through the muddy ruts in the raw weather of the retarded spring of 1760, his seventeenth birthday was only a few days ahead. All the long ride down the valley of the James, through shaggy woodlands alternating with cultivated lands, his blood must have tingled with anticipation of city life; and the library full of books, and Hunter's printshop with new publications from England; and candlelit ballrooms rustling with pretty girls, and pleasant friends to gossip with round the punch bowl; and blooded horses to match on the racetrack. The first large building he saw most likely was the college. It was one of the largest buildings in the colony. The gold hands of the clock in the cupola gave it a metropolitan air.

Though Williamsburg boasted a mayor and aldermen and called itself a city, it was really a country village. Andrew Burnaby, an Oxford graduate with a taste for travel who had visited it the summer before, wrote of it without enthusiasm.

Williamsburg . . . consists of about two hundred houses, does not contain more than one thousand souls, whites and negroes; and is far from being a place of any consequence. It is regularly laid out in parallel streets, intersected by others at right angles; has a handsome square in the center, through which runs the principal street, one of the most spacious in North America, three quarters of a mile in length, and above a hundred feet wide. At the opposite ends of this street are two public buildings, the college and the capitol: and although the houses are wood, covered with shingles . . . and but indifferently built, the whole makes a handsome appearance. . . . The streets are not paved, and are consequently very dusty, the soil hereabouts consisting chiefly of sand. . . . There are ten or twelve gentlemen's families constantly residing in [Williamsburg], besides merchants and tradesmen: and at the time of the assemblies, and general courts, it is crowded with the gentry of the country; on these occasions there are balls and other amusements; but as soon as the business is finished, they return to their plantations; and the town is in a manner deserted.

Jefferson was arriving at one of the "public times" when the place was full of bustle. The burgesses met during early March and the session of the General Court was coming in April. Some of the members of the governor's council may well have already been lumbering about the rutted streets in their coaches. Families recently arrived from up-country might be seen at the doors of their friends' houses, men in silver lace and cocked hats, ladies in satins and silks, and servants in livery holding the heads of sleek horses. The Raleigh and the other inns and lodging houses swarmed with lawyers and delegates. In the common rooms, amid the smoke of clay pipes, the tables resounded with the banging of diceboxes. The merchants in their scattered stores had set out the latest goods arrived from England. In his shop the wigmaker and his apprentices were busy combing and curling gentlemen's wigs for official functions.

Williamsburg was one of those places where everybody knew everybody. The Randolph clan, to which Jefferson belonged through his mother, had intermarried so widely in the region that anyone who wore shoes was likely to be a cousin or a cousin by marriage through the Carter connection, or the Burwells, or the great tribe of Pages with their splendid house at Rosewell. A John Page, a likely lad of about Jefferson's age, was already established at the college, having been put to board at the president's own house. They became immediately fast friends and Page soon paddled him home across the York River to meet his father and uncle and the crowd of related Pages who inhabited the tall brick mansion with its vast carved stairway that led up to the lead-covered deck on the roof shadowed by great chimneys and a pair of cupolas. From there you could enjoy a mighty view of the green creek, and the box gardens and the fat lands of the Pages, and the broadening blue river and the anchored shipping beyond.

One of Jefferson's first duties upon arriving in Williamsburg would have been to pay his respects to the president of the college, the Reverend Thomas Dawson, and it is to be hoped he found him sober. Arrangements were made with the housekeeper for his laundry and for the mending of his stockings, and his name was entered for board and lodging in the bursar's book. His first sensations must have been of disappointment. He was entering the college in one of its least flourishing moments as an institution of learning. There were fewer than a hundred students and teaching was nearly at a standstill, the faculty having been torn apart by the wrangle over the Two Penny Act.

The professors had taken sides violently with the clergy in this controversy. They were opposing the House of Burgesses, which for two successive years had passed acts to the effect that clergymen and other officials should be paid in currency instead of tobacco. The burgesses were backed by the bulk of Virginia landowners. And Governor Francis Fauquier, Dinwiddie's successor, had transmitted the acts to London with his approval.

No other public servants complained, but the clergy roared to high heaven that the acts were illegal. They brought out pamphlets. They banded together to finance suits against their vestries in the courts. Three of the professors at the college became so vehement they were removed by the Board of Visitors. Two of them set sail for England to cry for relief in the lobbies of Parliament and in the anterooms of the Bishop of London, from whose diocese the Virginia church depended.

Eventually they returned with an annulment of the acts. More significantly, the right of the colonists to handle their own financial affairs had been challenged, and this was to have a lasting effect on men's minds in Virginia. The breach between the gentry and the clergy in Virginia was wide.

Meanwhile the college faculty was demoralized. Mr. Dawson, the president, who as commissary was representative of the Bishop of London, was so torn by conflicting sympathies that he took desperately to drink. When he was indicted for drunkenness before a grand jury, he humbly confessed his fault and promised to mend his ways. But he died not long afterwards, a confirmed drunkard.

The bottle was also making grave inroads on the teaching staff. Young Jefferson had hardly started on his courses when the Reverend Jacob Rowe, his professor of moral philosophy, was discharged for getting drunk and leading the students in a brawl against the boys of the town. His companion in this escapade was the master of the grammar school, the Welsh bard Goronwy Owen, who had married President Dawson's sister and was also addicted to too deep potations. This Owen was the author of an elegy on the death of a friend and of a poem on the Last Judgment, much admired by readers of Welsh, and is reported to have written the best classical Latin style of the period. He was allowed to resign and, with the help of Governor Fauquier, was settled in a parish in Brunswick County far from the temptations of Williamsburg.

Luckily for Jefferson one of the two men who remained to take over the teaching was neither a drunkard nor a clergyman. He was a competent young Scot named William Small.

"It was my great good fortune, and what probably fixed the destinies of my life," Jefferson wrote in his autobiography when he was an old man, "that Dr. William Small of Scotland was then Professor of Mathematics, a man profound in most of the useful branches of science, with a happy talent of communication, correct and gentlemanly manners, and an enlarged and liberal mind. He, most happily for me, became soon attached to me, and made me his daily companion when not engaged in the school; and from his conversation I got my first views of the expansion of science, and of the system of things in which we are placed. Fortunately, the philosophical chair became vacant soon after my arrival at college, and he was appointed to fill it per interim: and was the first who ever gave in that college, regular lectures on Ethics, Rhetoric and Belles Lettres."

The great Dr. Small had been born in Scotland in 1734, had attended Marischal College in Aberdeen, and seems to have been "laureated," as the Scots put it, Master of Arts somewhere between 1752 and 1755. He reached Williamsburg in 1758, and had just turned twenty-four when he took the oaths as professor of natural philosophy at the college. A keen air of intellectual enterprise was then freshening the universities of Scotland, and he arrived redolent with that air.

The young men who followed his teaching agreed that it was Small during the few years he spent at William and Mary who replaced the old recitation by rote with the lecture system which was becoming the vogue overseas. For a year or two after Dawson's death he virtually had charge of the college curriculum. Despite some grumbling among orthodox members of the faculty, he with the friendship of Governor Fauquier, who was a freethinker himself, let new light shine in the dilapidated halls of plastered brick.

Small eventually returned to England in 1764. All his life Jefferson remembered him with affection and gratitude. The only letter to his favorite teacher which has survived was written in 1775, the year Small died. As he became convinced that war against England was inevitable, Jefferson's mind evidently turned with affection towards old friends who might find themselves on the other side of the firing line. While as a Virginian he was a bitter partisan, he was looking for ways of assuring Englishmen, and even Tories like John Randolph among his friends, that as a gentleman and a philosopher he felt no personal bitterness towards them. To Small he wrote announcing the shipment of a present of six dozen bottles of Madeira: "I hope you will find it fine as it came to me genuine from the island and has been kept in my own cellar eight years." He gave him the news of Bunker Hill and explained with passion that he feared the breach between the colonies and the mother country had been made irreparable. In the first draft of the letter a number of passages were crossed out; evidently Jefferson, who by then had not seen Small for more than ten years, wasn't sure which side he was taking in the controversy, and was wary of saying anything that might hurt his feelings. He breaks off suddenly: "But I am getting into politics, tho' I sat down only to ask your acceptance of the wine, and express my constant wishes for your happiness . . . I shall still hope that amidst public dissension private friendship may be preserved inviolate, and among the warmest you can ever possess is that of Your obliged servt."

Jefferson had reason to feel obliged to Dr. Small. He had arrived in Williamsburg a lanky up-country lad whose experience had been limited to Shadwell and the raw plantations in the foothills. He had done a lot of reading, but it was Small who first opened his mind to the philosopher's world.

Young Jefferson had application. He had energy and vast curiosity, but it is not in the nature of the human brain to make something out of nothing. Small presented the materials his faculties needed to work on. The contagion of his intellectual enterprise started Jefferson's well-equipped mind to working. In his walks and talks with Small he established a connection with the main currents of the adventurous intellect of Europe which was not to be interrupted throughout his long life.

It was from his father, Peter, that Jefferson inherited his taste for mathematics. Mathematics was Small's passion; but he had the scientific mind in the nineteenth-century application of the term, as well as, what must have been highly attractive to Jefferson, a knack for the practical application of scientific principles. Animating this intense curiosity about the operations of natural laws, he had also a warm humanitarian bent.

It can be said of the inquiring thinkers of that day that they were members of a sect. Their common religion was enlightenment. From Small, Jefferson caught the feeling of kinship with men speaking other languages in other countries. He learned the duties and privileges, the manners and ethics and the profound faith in man's intellect implicit for that generation in the word "philosopher."

Small was one of those men who delight in cogitation and in sympathetic talk in the society of friends. Among the vinous and opinioniated clergymen who made up the William and Mary faculty he must have felt hopelessly out of place. When the lanky young man from Albemarle appeared in his courses, awkward, redheaded, freckled; but with the delicately cut nose and sharp-cut chin that indicated discrimination and breeding, who showed by his questions an irrepressible eagerness for information, it is no wonder that Small took him up for his companion and hurried to show him off to the only two real friends he had made in the colony.

"He returned to Europe in 1762," Jefferson wrote in his autobiography (writing when he was seventy-seven years old, small wonder that he was a couple of years off on the date), "having previously filled up the measure of his goodness to me, by procuring for me, from his most intimate friend, George Wythe, a reception as a student of law, under his direction, and introduced me to the acquaintance and familiar table of Governor Fauquier, the ablest man who had ever filled that office. With him and at his table, Dr. Small and Mr. Wythe . . . and myself, formed a partie quarrée [a party of four] and to the habitual conversations on these occasions I owed much instruction."

Jefferson had too much breeding to be abashed by the provincial splendors of the governor's palace. It was his good fortune that the governor, though not a man of rank, as rank was reckoned at the time, came from what was intellectually the best society in England. Of Huguenot extraction, Francis Fauquier was the son of a French physician who had fled to England, made himself a career and amassed wealth. Like his father, Francis moved in scientific circles in London. He was elected a Fellow of the Royal Society. In 1756 he published a pamphlet on taxation which brought him considerable fame. It is readable to this day.

When Jefferson arrived in Williamsburg, Fauquier was a man in his late fifties. He must have been a lonely man, for his wife, who couldn't stand the heat and the boredom of Williamsburg, had gone back to England. From all accounts he spent many evenings drinking and playing cards for high stakes with the local magnates and helped encourage a fever for gambling that ruined many an estate, but he had other sides to him. He was fond of music and kept up with a few friends a small amateur orchestra; Jefferson, who was passionately addicted to the violin, soon found himself playing second fiddle, and possibly the cello. To the young man the musical evenings were undoubtedly one of the great attractions the governor's palace offered.

Fauquier, as was the fashion among philosophers, also cultivated an interest in natural phenomena. He got his son to keep a record of the Williamsburg weather. Brought up in London on the repartee of the clubs and coffeehouses, and on the sober ratiocination of the meetings of the Royal Society, undoubtedly what he missed most in Williamsburg was conversation. The stimulus that he failed to find among the members of the governor's council, he found in his friendship for Small and for the lawyer, George Wythe, who at thirty-five was a showpiece in the colony for his classical learning.

Wythe was very much the learned provincial. He had been born and raised in Elizabeth City, in the most thickly settled part of the colony. His knowledge of the law and of Greek and Latin authors was so great that he had come to be known as "the walking library." His notes on the comparative etymology of Latin and Greek words must have interested Jefferson, whose mind had the same bent for grubbing down into roots and origins. When Jefferson first met him, Wythe was the familiar spirit of the capitol. He had been elected burgess for Williamsburg, and whenever the burgesses found themselves entangled in a particularly tough problem involving law or finance or procedure they put Mr. Wythe on the committee to deal with it.

Wythe had recently married Elizabeth Taliaferro and may well have been living with his father-in-law, Richard Taliaferro, in his charming new brick house (still standing and known as the Wythe House) a block from the governor's palace. This Richard Taliaferro was considered one of the colony's most skillful architects. He may have been the man from whom Jefferson learned the rudiments of draftsmanship, and he may even have worked with Taliaferro on several nearby mansions. Already the two parallel paths along which Jefferson's mind was to develop, statesmanship and architecture, were opening before him. Architecture, he said later in his matter-of-fact way, was for a new country the most important art "because it showed so much." Knowing George Wythe, the young Jefferson would have had a good chance to consult Wythe's father-in-law's architectural books.

Familiarity with the governor's palace as a member of Fauquier's unofficial family must in any case have stimulated his architectural eye. It was the first building he had frequented which was designed intentionally as a work of art. It has even been contended that the plans for the mansion came possibly from Christopher Wren himself at the Office of Works in London. The building as restored certainly has an air of distinction and originality. It evidently interested Jefferson and it is highly probable that he had a hand in the alterations made some years after his first introduction to it. It was Jefferson's own floor plans of the palace, found among his papers, that formed the basis for the reconstruction on its old foundations of the building as it now stands.

Walking today through the great mansion in a crowd of tourists shepherded by a good lady in fancy dress, it is hard to divine, under the timeless gloss of museum preservation, what the place smelled and felt like the afternoon some smiling doorkeeper ushered Small and Wythe, followed for the first time by skinny tall young Jefferson, across the black and white marble checkerboard of the hall where the armor hung, to some small private room where the men could sit with their host talking the afternoon out over a well-cooked meal. Fauquier was a man who liked to eat; he tenderly remembered his cook in his will. At his table Jefferson first encountered refinement rather than abundance in eating. Even better than well-cooked mutton flavored with thyme, or fresh vegetables from the kitchen garden, Fauquier liked philosophical inquiry about the vast realm of New World phenomena which as a city-bred man he had no way of seeing for himself. The only recorded instance of his leaving Williamsburg is when he and his lady traveled to Colonel John Dandridge's up the Pamunkey River to be present at George Washington's wedding to Martha Custis, the colonel's daughter. Fauquier's friend Wythe was a sedentary person who oscillated between his office in the back-yard of his home and the capitol down at the end of Duke of

Gloucester Street. Small, whose correspondence bears the stamp of physical indolence, was not an outdoor man. The plain-faced well-informed young Jefferson from up-country must have seemed to Fauquier a fertile source of information on the flora and fauna of the colony.

Jefferson was never a facile talker. The elaborate courtesies of the time must have demanded that he sit a silent fourth while his elders discoursed on such topics of the day as the progress of the industrial arts in the colony. Already men of information were worried about the one-crop system. The Board of Trade wanted to supplement tobacco with indigo and silk. The Royal Navy wanted a supply of resin and turpentine and timber. Wythe and Fauquier were both involved in a project to stimulate the growing of grapes. Then there were always the latest advices from London to talk about and the daily fodder of classical reading.

Although Jefferson was easier listening than talking, in response to some sharp questioning over the fruit and nuts, after the cloth had been taken away and the Madeira poured from the decanter, he could describe the marine shells his schoolmaster Maury had found high up on the Southwest Mountains; or the discovery of the bones of mammoths beyond the mountains and what the Indians told of them; or else he could describe the growth of the huge-leaved catalpa and the time of flowering of the tulip tree and the hunting of bison, or the habits of the wild turkey or the range of the Carolina parakeet.

This backwoods life, where the planter's proud intolerance of restraint stood out as white against black: this was the life young Jefferson took for granted. There must still have been a trace in his mind of the countryman's wonder and suspicion of city-bred men, as he sat slouched on one hip at the governor's table, listening to Small's and Fauquier's elaborate conversation, through which he peeped, as through a door ajar, out of his Albemarle hills into the metropolitan world of Great Britain.

The wilderness he described must have seemed awesomely uncomfortable to his lettered friends from overseas. In the back of their minds lurked a sense of solitude and hazard. Between them and home lay from six to ten weeks of danger and seasick-

ness. And Williamsburg was not a healthy place. Governor Dinwiddie had retired on account of illness. Fauquier and Baron de Botetourt, who succeeded him, were both to leave their bones in the colony. Explaining why he didn't want to go back to Virginia, Small, a few years later, told his friends in England he had never kept his health there. The "sickly season" was a season of dread. The sense of remoteness must have chilled their bones. Williamsburg was an outpost. Except for public times in spring and fall when there was bustle on the street and business to transact, and functions to attend, they must have suffered from the silence. In winter when freezing and thawing reduced the roads to muck, or in the dusty heat of summer, the little business of the day dragged on in a slow tantalizing round that could easily become an anguish of boredom, the faraway boredom of a little provincial capital.

Young Jefferson himself was at the age for boredom, although he was daily nourished by new impressions from books and conversation. He had to fill every minute of his time. He added hours to his periods of reading. He ran morning and evening for exercise. He rode hard, danced when he could. He was on hand for the horse races. At the college he argued with his friends. At meetings of the assembly he listened to the debates of his elders. He searched through every new shipment of books at Hunter's. But none of it was enough. Williamsburg was not London. Away overseas men were inventing an empire. On the stages of Parliament and court the great figures performed who were masters of a Virginian's destinies. There were times when the dead weight of provincial frustration hung heavy on him. It was not for nothing he dated some of his letters Devilsburg. Even dining at the governor's palace, entranced by Fauquier's worldly charm, Small's ingenuity and Wythe's parade of phrases out of the dead

nial Williamsburg, now
coration that attracts
rs from all over the
d, is a living lesson in
rican history. Near
of Gloucester Street,
George Wythe's
some brick mansion,
still stands. Bottom left
encil drawing of
son's beloved teacher,
William Small.

tongues, there must have been moments when conversation flagged, as the footsteps of the servant carrying off an empty decanter died in the halls, and he felt the soggy heat and listened to the flies buzzing on the panes, and outside among the palace gardens of trimmed box, rigid under a pall of dust, heard the black crows caw.

Chapter 3

ONE MORNING IN THE FALL of the year that Jefferson started college, King George of England woke early as was his custom and cheerfully drank his chocolate while he listened to the court gossip. When he got out of bed to go to the commode he fell on the floor and died. George III, his grandson, succeeded him.

The new king was a Tory, and the Whigs who had been dominating the scene in England now lost power. A period of Tory reaction set in.

Young Jefferson reading law during these years with George Wythe, or in some corner of the house full of women at Shadwell, must have been already deep enough in English constitutional history to follow with passion, through the reports in the gazettes, the course of the Tory reaction. While with eager curiosity he pursued the principles of English common law, a contest was preparing in Parliament which would dramatize the whole theory of constitutional government. At the same time in Virginia, the freeman's challenge to arbitrary authority— which was the root of the English constitution—began to take visible and audible form in his own experience.

Among Jefferson's friends there was now a young man whom he had met the winter before he started college at Williamsburg. That winter he had spent the Christmas holidays, which the Virginians celebrated in the old English style, at Colonel Dandridge's in Hanover County. There, "during the festivity of the season," he had seen a lot of a sallow-faced young man of Scottish descent. The young man was named Patrick Henry.

Although Henry was several years Jefferson's senior, a married man who had signalized himself largely by having already managed to fail at farming, at keeping store and even at tending bar, Jefferson was much taken by his gift of fluent speech. All his life he pleasantly remembered Patrick Henry at that early time as a good rough country fiddler and a great teller of stories round the campfire in the woods at night while the hunters sat waiting for the dogs to tree a coon or a possum.

Evidently Henry himself had cottoned to the spindly youth from Albemarle, who in spite of his bookishness loved fiddling and dancing and horseflesh. Jefferson was hardly settled in Williamsburg when the gaunt backwoodsman appeared at his rooms at the college with the tall tale that he had read law for six weeks and was ready to take the bar examination.

Peyton Randolph and his brother John were so carried away by Henry's gift of gab that upon his promising to do some more reading they signed his admission to practice before the General Court. According to Jefferson he never kept his promise; Henry, he used to say, was the laziest man for reading he had ever known. Finicky George Wythe refused to sign but Robert Carter Nicholas let himself be talked around. So Patrick Henry was admitted to the bar and promptly became the most successful jury lawyer in the colony.

When he moved up in the forest to a place called the Roundabout in Louisa, the settlers took him to their hearts and returned him to Williamsburg as a burgess. In the first session he attended he added to his popularity by putting a spoke in the wheel of the ruling clique of tidewater magnates.

The landowners controlled the governor's council, and the Speaker of the House at that time was a jovial well-connected planter named John Robinson. Also treasurer of the colony, Robinson for years had been making use of his office to loan money on flimsy security out of the public funds to members of his family and to other intimates. It seems not to have occurred to any of them that there was anything wrong about it. When he discovered one day that he had loaned out more than even his substantial fortune could repay and that the debtors had no cash in their tills to repay the treasury, his supporters, "the cyphers of the aristocracy," Jefferson called them, thought up a scheme. If they could establish a provincial loan office they could unload all the bad debts of the colony and nobody would be the wiser.

It was Patrick Henry's eloquence that stirred up the burgesses from the upper counties to put a stop to this proceeding. "What Sir," Jefferson reports his thundering, "is it then proposed to reclaim the spendthrift from his dissipation and extravagance by filling his pockets with money?" From that moment Jefferson, who was haunting the sessions of the assembly and the General Court for practical instruction in law and government, made of Henry his local parliamentary hero.

The next spring, when Patrick Henry rode into Williamsburg to find his colleagues smoldering with opposition to the stamp tax on transactions, which Parliament was considering, he was already the political leader of the upper counties. Immediately he found himself the spokesman of all the hotheads among the burgesses.

Most of the tidewater magnates, like Jefferson's relatives, the Randolphs, were ready to go along with the home government on the stamp tax. They were mostly interested in who would get the office of collector with its rake-off. George Wythe, always a moderate man, was for a moderate protest. Patrick Henry came out for uncompromising defiance.

When Jefferson stood, red-eyed from his punishing schedule of study, listening breathless in the door of the lobby to the "bloody" debate on the wording of the resolutions of protest, he must have felt that all his reading in English constitutional history was coming to life before him. He always referred to Patrick Henry's speech as one of the great moments. When Henry, standing up gaunt and shabby among the flushed burgesses with their wigs awry, soared to the legendary peroration: "Caesar had his Brutus, Charles I his Cromwell and"—in response to cries of treason—"George III may profit by their example!" and his resolution was carried, the law student saw in a flash that here, in dusty old Williamsburg, a man was hewing out the shape of history.

Latter-day historians have pointed out that, according to

another and less partisan account, Patrick Henry actually took fright at the cries of treason and apologized to the assembly for his vehemence. It is natural that an eager young man, who felt the orator was expressing his own profoundest feelings, should have forgotten the apology. Jefferson himself once remarked that people were often so moved by Patrick Henry's oratory they couldn't for the life of them remember what he'd been saying.

THE FOLLOWING YEAR, in 1766, after the passing of the hated Stamp Act had filled British North America with echoes of Patrick Henry's sacred rage, Jefferson set off on a trip to see something of the "sister colonies" from which Virginia was still isolated. He was now twenty-three. For years he had been hankering to travel. Shadwell had been made emptier than ever for him by the death of his favorite sister Jane. He'd always been of two minds about Williamsburg. He had a passion for study but he wasn't quite ready to get into harness yet. He needed to get married but he still had too much adolescent conceit to throw his whole being into courting a girl.

The young man hadn't learned to be at home with himself but he had learned to forget himself in study; reading, music, architecture had proved for him to be the escape from all the galling inadequacies of youth. His habit seems to have been to read through the day from dawn until late candlelight. The first year he started to read law he had an acute conjunctivitis. Already he suffered from sick headaches that were to plague him all his life. Now at last when, even according to George Wythe's and his own exigent standards, he was ready to take his bar examination, he set out alone, like a folklore hero, to try the adventures of the road on a drive to New York.

Characteristically, he had given the jaunt a practical and scientific pretext. There had recently been a good deal of smallpox in the colony. The most progressive medical authorities recommended inoculation. Of course, people in general considered inoculation a crazy business, but Jefferson had found there were doctors in Philadelphia who were willing to try it. He set off driving a sulky and carrying with him a letter from his friend

295

George Gilmer, who had recently returned from a medical course in Edinburgh, to a Philadelphian he'd known as a fellow student there, John Morgan.

Philadelphia, which had doubled in size in the last ten years, was now almost equal in importance to Edinburgh and Dublin. As a place to live it was pleasant and up-to-date. It was one of the chief ports of the colonies. Its ships sailed to the West Indies and some of its skippers had recently inaugurated a profitable run to Leghorn in Italy.

The city was also the terminus of the only passable wagon road to the West that rolled through rich farmlands to Lancaster and beyond. Lancaster was already a manufacturing town and produced the Pennsylvania rifles which were to play such a part in the coming war. There too were built the famous covered Conestoga wagons.

In Virginia everything a man needed had to be imported; but Pennsylvania already made many consumers' goods at home, pottery and farm tools and iron pots and kettles. On Philadelphia's Market Street there were tailors and hatters and shoemakers, and cabinetmakers who made fine furniture according to the latest Chippendale designs.

Even more interesting to a young man of Jefferson's tastes, a professional architect, Robert Smith of Glasgow, was at work there, building a house for Benjamin Franklin and getting ready to put up a new almshouse for the city. Several gentlemen had collections of paintings. One man owned what was reputed to be a genuine Vandyke taken by a privateer off a Spanish prize. One of the sights no one missed was John Bartram's botanical garden at Kingsessing. The greatest sight of all, of course, was Dr. Franklin, but he was in England as colonial agent at the moment.

Jefferson was in town in time to be present at the celebration of George III's birthday on June 4 which the inhabitants managed to transform into a celebration of the repeal of the Stamp Act. The newspapers reported that to honor the celebration on the banks of the Schuylkill "the *Franklin* smack and the new *White Oak Barge*" came up the river profusely decorated with bunting, with colors flying in the wind. The old white oak barge fixed in a cradle on four wheels was drawn by seven stately horses out through the main streets of the city, with musicians seated under a canopy, to a grove on the riverbank where four hundred and thirty persons dined at tables.

The letter to Dr. John Morgan was just what Jefferson needed to put him in touch with everything and everybody. The young physician was at that moment one of Philadelphia's best-known citizens. He was evidently a rather flashy young man. A few years older than Jefferson, he had arrived home two years before, after studies and travels abroad, with the express purpose of founding a medical school at the College of Philadelphia.

Almost as full of enthusiasm for painting and architecture as for medicine, during his travels he had collected paintings, drawings, and copies of old masters, and had jotted down many notes about architectural proportions. In Philadelphia he had settled in a fine house and had unpacked his collections. Already he had a flourishing practice, and he had married Molly Hopkinson, who was one of the best matches in town.

As Jefferson talked to John Morgan and visited his collections undoubtedly his "soul was struck and his ideas expanded" by this renewed glimpse into the European world of fashion and thought he had first seen through the eyes of the great Dr. Small in Williamsburg. There were plenty of better things to talk about than the repeal of the Stamp Tax and inoculation for smallpox. According to Henry S. Randall, whose biography of Jefferson was published in 1858, it was not Dr. Morgan but his rival, Dr. Shippen, who inoculated Jefferson. In any case, inoculated, and probably bled and purged to boot (the Philadelphia doctors were terrible bleeders and purgers), Jefferson recovered sufficiently to drive his sulky across the Jerseys, by the rough road that led through sand beds and pine barrens to the wharf where lay the sloop that ferried travelers to New York.

New York, then as now, was the American city nearest to Europe. The shops were full of novelties fresh off the packet. The latest sheet music could be bought, and bookstores carried the latest London publications. The city wasn't as large as Philadelphia, but it was livelier. There was a certain sportive elegance about it, with evening concerts at Ranelagh Gardens, yachting on the bay, horse racing on Long Island. The mixture of Dutch and English customs gave it a special air all its own. Many of the brick houses were built gable end to the street in the Dutch style. Travelers who visited Manhattan during these years speak of a pleasant custom people had of enjoying the summer evenings on balconies, or what we'd now call captain's walks, on the roofs of their houses. European visitors were amazed by the number of tree frogs that lived in the lindens and elms that shaded the streets; they found their singing so loud they sometimes couldn't hear themselves speak.

The port of entry for a vast half-discovered country beyond the upper Hudson, New York was also a rowdy seafaring and river-trafficking city. While Jefferson was there, Edward Bardin, advertising an evening concert in the newspapers, stated that "every possible Precaution will be taken to prevent Disorder and Irregularity."

There had been a great deal of disorder and irregularity in the city during the past year. The waterfront crowd that made up the rank and file of the local Sons of Liberty had taken the Stamp Act hard. The year before, the Vauxhall Gardens had been gutted by a mob protesting the use of stamps, and not too long before Jefferson's arrival the theater on Chapel Street had been pulled down, and its fittings burned, in another burst of political enthusiasm. In Boston too there had been rioting; and in a number of the *New York Mercury* that might well still have been on the tables when Jefferson visited the coffeehouses round Hanover Square there was an account of the burning of the stamps by the Sons of Liberty at New London, "amidst the acclamations of a numerous assembly."

So far as we know Jefferson had no friends in the city, so he must have spent his time strolling and shopping and reading the newspapers. It is easy to imagine him dressed perhaps in Mecklenburg silk in the style of the young exquisites of New York, who were soon to be dubbed macaronis, strolling round the city. Probably he frowned over last month's dispatches from London that carried the remonstrance of the peers against the Stamp Act's repeal.

But he didn't stay long in the city. Selling his horse, he sailed home down the coast. On July 23 he was already back in Williamsburg reporting to a friend that it had been an agreeable trip and that he was waiting for horses to be sent down from up-country to take him on a round of visits (he was obviously hungry for the conversation of his friends after the solitary journey) and eventually home to Shadwell.

The trip established the geography of the Atlantic seaboard in Jefferson's mind. He had been brought up to think of Virginia as extending west, ridge after ridge into the plains and to the mountains beyond and even to the scarcely conceivable South Sea. After this glimpse of the metropolitan life of Philadelphia and New York, Virginia, still the most populous colony, began to take its rightful place in his thinking as one of a string of not too dissimilar settlements stretching east and north along the seaboard. The settlers still spoke of England as home. They were Englishmen, but Englishmen with a difference. Already the people he met in Philadelphia and New York were beginning to speak of themselves as Americans.

THE WORD MONTICELLO appears for the first time in Jefferson's account book for 1767. Under the heading "Work to be done at Hermitage" he lists the planting of raspberries, strawberries, asparagus; wagoning wood and sand, and putting up a hen house. At some point Hermitage was crossed out and Monticello written in its place. In the first extant letter dated from Monticello in February 1771 he is writing a friend in Aberdeen, a young clergyman named Ogilvie. Shadwell had burned down. After reporting this fact, he explains: "I have lately removed to the mountain from whence this is dated, and with which you are not unacquainted. I have here but one room, which, like the cobbler's, serves me for parlor for kitchen and hall. I may add for bedchamber and study too. . . . I have hopes however of getting more elbow room this summer."

He was planning to marry. At last he had fallen in love. He needed a mansion for his bride, and he was speeding construction as fast as he could. By August the building had proceeded so far he was able to write Robert Skipwith who had just married his sweetheart's half sister: "Come to the new Rowanty,

©The R. W. Norton Art Gallery 1971

from which you may reach your hand to a library formed on a more extensive plan." (Skipwith had written him he had twenty-five to thirty pounds to spend on books for his library and asking for a list "suited to the capacity of a common reader.") "Separated from each other but a few paces, the possessions of each would be open to the other. A spring, centrically located might be the scene of every evening's joy. There we should talk over the lessons of the day or lose them in Musick, Chess, or the merriments of our family companions. The heart thus lightened our pillows would be soft, and health and long life would attend the happy scene. Come then and bring our dear Tibby with you: the first in your affections, the second in mine. Offer prayers for me too at that shrine to which, tho' absent, I pay continual devotion. In every scheme of happiness she is placed in the foreground of the picture, as the principal figure."

He is referring of course, in the high-flown formalities of courtship in this period, to Martha Skelton, John Wayles's daughter, the young widow with a taste for music whom he was to marry and to take up to Monticello as its mistress at the beginning of the following year.

His letters refer to obstacles to overcome. It is possible he was having difficulty persuading John Wayles that he was sufficiently well born to marry his daughter. About this time he wrote Thomas Adams, his tobacco agent, asking him to look up the Jefferson name at the College of Heralds in London to see if the family really had a right to their coat of arms. If Adams can't find one, he might buy one, Jefferson adds sardonically, "having Sterne's word for it, that a coat of arms may be purchased as cheap as any other coat." In another letter, on a subject closer to his heart, he asks Adams to ship him one of the newly invented fortepianos, "the workmanship of the whole very handsome, and worthy of the acceptance of a lady for whom I intend it."

Dimly through the haze of years there rises from the scanty record the figure of a small gentle high-spirited eager young woman. To Jefferson and her sisters she was known as Patty. "My sister Skelton," Skipwith wrote of her, "with the greatest fund of good nature has all that sprightliness and sensibility which promises to ensure you the greatest happiness mortals are capable of enjoying. May business and play, musick and the merriments of your family companions," he added, echoing Jefferson's words to him, "lighten your hearts, soften your pillows and procure you health long life and every human felicity."

It all came true. A pleasantly romantic tale came down in the Jefferson family about how the young couple were married at Patty's father's house, in Charles City County, on New Year's Day; and how they traveled by carriage through snowy roads as far as Blenheim, the empty seat of one of the Carters. They had to ride horseback the last eight miles, because the snow was so deep on the hills. They arrived at Monticello late at night and found the slaves all gone to bed and slept in the little building at the end of the south wing which Jefferson later used as his office and which is now known as the honeymoon cottage. There may be a spice of fable in the story but its essence rings true. Thomas Jefferson and Martha Skelton were well suited and loved each other dearly until she died.

Jefferson's only extant comment from that time is an entry in his garden book for 1772: "Jan. 26 the deepest snow we have ever seen."

THE SINGLE CHAMBER in which the pair slept and lived and ate must have been stacked with books. Shadwell had been destroyed by fire the previous year; and Jefferson wrote Skipwith that his library at Monticello, replacing the books he lost in the fire, was "formed on a more extensive plan." The air of the room must have been charged with the smell of fresh calf and morocco. It was a thoroughly up-to-date collection of everything that was newest from the London printshops.

We know Jefferson's sweet Patty loved music: we don't know how much she read books. The presence of all those handsome bindings when she woke up on that raw hilltop with three feet of snow outside must at least have given her a comforting feeling of civilization. That feeling was, you can imagine, tinged with amazement when, next day, or whenever the snow stopped falling, they walked out in their riding boots among the buried foundations and snow-covered stacks of lumber and piles of new-baked brick while Jefferson explained with fastidious exactness of detail his plan for a mansion as yet unimagined in Virginia.

There's no question that by the time he made his plan for the first version of Monticello he was steeped in the architectural style of Palladio. The first quarter of the century had been the period of the discovery of Palladio in England. Here was an architect who two centuries before had reinvented for the regal merchants of Italy the porches and colonnades of the age of Augustus. His designs were based on archaeological reconstruction of Roman ruins and on the laws of proportion laid down by Vitruvius. In England, Palladio was now beginning to be old-fashioned, but to the colonists he was all new. As a colonial, Jefferson was subject to a lagging afterglow of the fashions that had moved the English nobility a generation before. It was typical of his radical and personal approach to everything he handled that he immediately worked his way through the superficially fashionable elements of English Palladianism and came to grips with the basic problem.

What he wanted was a manor house with airy rooms, where he and his family could live their lives in rural elegance, and plenty of windows from which he could see the big Virginia hills and the blue plain that moved him as much as music; a manor house which, at the same time, would house the barns, storehouses, harness rooms, butteries, kitchens, tool sheds and stables essential to the functioning of a plantation.

Palladio's villas were a combination of dwelling house and barn. "There must be proper covers made for everything belonging to the *Villa* in proportion to the product of the Ground and the number of Cattle and contiguous to the main house," he wrote, "that the Master may easily go everywhere sheltered, without being hindered from minding his business by either Snow or Rain or the scorching heat of the Sun." It's highly typical of the quality of Jefferson's mind that in his design for Monticello he went back to Palladio's practical villa, and by skillful use of his hilltop he managed to go Palladio one better by establishing the working part of the buildings in wings built into the hill and lighted by loggias which could be used to shelter his equipment. Their roof he used as a terrace from which to enjoy his unobstructed view.

Thus Monticello embodied in its structure the basic plan of Jefferson's life, and of the lives he wanted for his friends and neighbors: a combination of practical American management of plantations large or small with the freedom enjoyed by the British noble.

THESE YEARS WERE THE HAPPIEST of his life. It was a time of warm friendships and affections. His sister Martha married Dabney Carr, the schoolmate from Maury's school who had become the intimate companion of his young manhood. Carr was a lawyer, with a mind addicted like Jefferson's to basic political principles. He left the reputation of being a brilliant speaker. He lived near enough so that they could meet constantly. "He speaks, thinks, and dreams nothing but of his young son," Jefferson wrote John Page of Carr. "This friend of ours, Page, in a very small house, with a table, a half a dozen chairs, and one or two servants, is the happiest man in the universe. He possesses truly the art of extracting comfort from things the most trivial. Every incident in life he so takes as to render it a source of pleasure."

The fire at Shadwell had been a disaster for Jefferson, but it had broken the last link with his childhood. It had forced him to set himself up as a man in the world, to carry through the plans for his marriage and for the building of his manor. Now his scholarship was becoming the wonder of the countryside. As a leading citizen of Albemarle his reputation was fast outrunning the memory of his father's. It was a time of high spirits.

His first essay in the public service had been as one of the trustees charged with opening the south branch of the James, his own Rivanna, to navigation by canoes and bateaux. Characteristically he'd climbed into a canoe and explored the river himself. In 1769 he'd been elected along with his father's friend, Dr. Walker, to the House of Burgesses. He had also been appointed to his father's post of county lieutenant, which carried with it the honorary rank of colonel. Like his father he became a licensed surveyor. His law practice grew with his reputation.

He was famous for his horsemanship. The practice of the law in those days entailed a great deal of hard riding. On the spring and autumn circuits judges and lawyers rode in a troop from courthouse to courthouse. When court was in session the ordinaries and law offices round the county courthouses were a hive of sociability. Settlers rode in from their lonely plantations to see their friends and hear the lawyers wrangle even if they had no stake in the cases on trial. In these years as a trial lawyer Jefferson got to know his Virginia and its people as intimately as his father had known them on his rough-and-tumble surveying trips. His practice took him particularly into the ruder northern and western counties, where present prosperity had not wiped out the memory of the scalpings and burnings and the war whoops of raiding parties during the French war.

The wild and picturesque scenery of the country beyond the Blue Ridge stirred him to the marrow. And as a philosopher he was learning to see nature as a process. Geology was the drama of the earth's formation. It must have been on the way to try a case at Staunton that he first saw Natural Bridge ("so beautiful an arch, so elevated, so light, and springing as if it were up to heaven!"), a freak of nature that so thrilled him that he acquired the land for his own.

A trail that led north from Fauquier Courthouse through Winchester, where he put in occasional appearances in court, may have led him through the mountains to the spot from which he first saw the upper valley of the Potomac. He described one of the great views many years later in *Notes on Virginia:* "The passage of the Potomac through the Blue Ridge is, perhaps, one of the most stupendous scenes in nature. You stand on a very high point of land. On your right comes up the Shenandoah having ranged along the foot of the mountain an hundred miles to seek a vent. On your left approaches the Potomac, in quest of a passage also. In the moment of their junction, they rush together against the mountain, rend it asunder and pass to the sea. . . . The mountain being cloven asunder, she presents to your eye, through the cleft, a small catch of smooth blue horizon, at an infinite distance in the plain country, inviting you as it were from the riot and tumult roaring around, to pass through the breach and participate of the calm below."

It was the exultation of that smooth blue horizon, when he looked out from the scaffolding and the fresh brick walls of Monticello, that made him call his mountain Rowanty in his letter to Skipwith. He had picked up the name somewhere in his reading as applied to the "mountain of the world," some dim peak in Kurdistan where according to legend the gods lived. The sky turned on Rowanty as on a pivot.

THE EXPRESSION IMPLIES that this young man in his twenties had already established in his mind a vantage point from which he could survey the kingdoms of the world that stretched away from under his feet into the horizon's blue.

The colonies were growing in every direction. In spite of restrictions, trade and manufactures were increasing. British North America now produced more pig iron in a year than England and Wales put together. Sure as the rivers would burst out into the foothills through the cloven rocks of the Blue Ridge, the colonies would make their way into the great world. A dissipated aristocracy and a stupid king could not forever be allowed to dam up the expanding energies of a new continent. It was not passive landscape Jefferson looked out on from Monticello, it was a world in the making.

Jefferson, with his taste for tracking ideas down to their roots, had taken up vigorously the study of the constitutional problems involved in this world. Under Wythe's guidance he had followed the common law back into the self-governing institutions of the ancient Anglo-Saxons.

"I took the ground . . ." he wrote in his autobiography, "that the relation between Great Britain & these colonies was exactly the same as that of England & Scotland, after the accession of James, and until this union, and the same as her present relations with Hanover, having the same political chief, but no other political connection: and that our emigration from England to this country gave her no more rights over us, than the emigrations of the Danes & the Saxons gave to the present authorities of the mother country, over England. In this doctrine, however," he added wryly, "I had never been able to get anyone to agree with me but Mr. Wythe."

Jefferson was seeking, in the Anglo-Saxon heritage, historical justification for his belief in self-government. He was coming to see the history of the English-speaking peoples as a conflict never quite resolved between authority and self-government. The purpose of self-government was to protect the freedom of action of each individual man. The conception of the law as a system of rules improvised by free men to deal with their equals without violence was what made the English-speaking society unique. In virtually every other society, authority had laid down the law.

Freedom meant choice. A man knew how to choose good rather than evil because he had the God-given faculty of reason. For the eighteenth-century theologians, deist and orthodox alike, reason had taken the place of revelation. Under religion, in his list of books recommended for Skipwith's library, Jefferson had listed works by John Locke and Viscount Bolingbroke, Lord Kames's *Essays on the Principles of Morality and Natural Religion* and Laurence Sterne's *Sermons of Mr. Yorick.* However much these authors differed in regard to their belief in miracles and in the divine origin of the Scriptures, they all agreed that reason was the faculty by which men could understand the universe God had created. Most of them believed that the exercise of reason was more important to salvation than the observance of ritual.

The philosophers whose doctrines he had absorbed in Small's lectures at college tended to hold a somewhat simplified view of the workings of the human mind, but their system of ethics was downright and practical. Under it Jefferson was able, when he sallied forth from the warm cloister of family life he had

307

now established for himself, to play his part in the founding of the republic without any basic hesitations. There was never a question in his mind that a man's freedom to exercise his reason was the highest good, or that by reason a man could reach enough understanding of the divinely invented machine of the universe to play his part as a citizen.

Chapter 4

JEFFERSON'S FIRST TERM as a burgess in 1769 had lasted only ten days. The assembly had expressed its solidarity with the rebellious sister colony of Massachusetts with so much vigor that one of the new governor's first official acts was to dissolve it. This was regrettable because the governor, Norborne Berkeley, Baron de Botetourt, had been sent as a conciliator. When Fauquier died it had been decided at Buckingham House that it would flatter and possibly somewhat overawe the Virginians if the royal governor should appear among them in person. Fauquier had been merely a deputy, actually a lieutenant governor.

Berkeley, a Tory who had sat in the House of Commons for Gloucestershire, was one of the more raffish members of George III's inner circle. The king had made him groom of the bedchamber and helped him, on somewhat doubtful title, revive the obsolete barony of Botetourt. He had poured out his money on wine, women and the gambling table. In spite of the king's support, his finances had reached a point where there was nothing for it but to put the ocean between him and his creditors.

A fashionable nobleman of the period couldn't imagine anything more horrible than exile to the wilds of Virginia. Yet Botetourt left the reputation among the Virginians of being a friendly and understanding man. Disembarking at Yorktown he had unloaded on the beach a hand-me-down royal chariot in cream and gold which had been thoughtfully furnished by King George's own uncle, the Duke of Cumberland. The Virginians were informed by the gazettes that the royal arms had been painted out and the arms of the colony painted in especially for the governor's progress down Duke of Gloucester Street from the palace to the capitol.

After the splendor of the equipage and the elegance of his lordship's court dress and the regal manner of his reading of the opening speech, it must have surprised nobody more than the baron that the first thing he had to do was to send the burgesses home. It must have shocked him indeed when instead of going home they merely adjourned to the Raleigh Tavern.

This first meeting in the long room of Mr. Anthony Hay's handsome hostelry in the spring of 1769 set a pattern for the colonial legislatures. Gradually the essence of sovereignty was transferred from the royal colony to the independent commonwealth. So long as Botetourt lived, his tact and friendliness helped keep the conflict in suspense, though that bland gentleman must have been shocked again to see at one of his balls a hundred ladies prancing in local homespuns instead of in imported silks. When he succumbed to the climate and perhaps to the result of youthful indiscretions, the burgesses commemorated his agreeable qualities by ordering a statue erected to him in front of William and Mary College.

The Earl of Dunmore, the Scottish nobleman who succeeded Botetourt, arrived determined to put the Virginians in their place. As it turned out he didn't do too badly at first. He brought his family to the palace and the members of the Council of State found them charming. The new daughter born there he named Virginia. That pleased the colonial ladies. He consulted young Mr. Jefferson, who already had some reputation as an architect, about improvements in the palace. When his assemblies showed fight he dissolved them promptly. His idea was that the less he saw of the burgesses the better. He didn't pay too much attention to the fact that the minute he dissolved the assembly they trooped up Duke of Gloucester Street to the Raleigh and there continued as a voluntary convention.

In March of 1773 Jefferson was one of a group of delegates who met at the tavern to discuss the need for establishing a committee of correspondence with the sister colonies. This sort of committee, an arrangement for obtaining continued action during the long gaps between sessions of the assembly, was no new invention in Virginia. In 1759 the burgesses had appointed an agent in London to lobby in the colony's interest and a committee of correspondence to keep in touch with him. When Jefferson's brother-in-law Dabney Carr introduced the resolutions drawn up at the Raleigh, several members of the original committee of correspondence were elected to serve on the new committee; they were Jefferson's cousin Peyton Randolph, Richard Bland, Robert Carter Nicholas, and Dudley Digges. At about the same time, in the raw New England spring, Samuel Adams was shepherding his resolution to establish similar committees through town meeting in Boston. These committees of correspondence were the first links in the structure of union on which the Confederation was built.

Under the lid of colonial government the Virginians were improvising institutions of their own. A network of county committees sprang up to enforce agreements. Their committee of correspondence kept track of events in the sister colonies. Dunmore put off the assemblies as often as he could. When they did meet he dissolved them before the burgesses had a chance to clear their throats. Adjourning to the Raleigh got to be a habit. There they would form themselves into a convention and go about the business of defending their rights. Eventually most of the members stopped taking the trouble of showing up at the capitol at all.

Local government in the counties was in the hands of the vestries and the justices of the peace sitting in the courthouses. It was not long before Dunmore was writing home to the Secretary of State for the colonies, "There's not a Justice of the Peace in Virginia that acts, except as a committee-man." The men were the same, the forms of procedure were the same. They proceeded in the name of the colony instead of in the name of the king. The habit of self-government was so ingrained that the transition was hardly noticed.

The committees of correspondence of the various colonies were responsible for the organization of the Continental Congress. Appeals forwarded from one county to another called for the appointment of delegates "by assemblies, conventions or by committees of correspondence" to a meeting planned at some convenient spot for early September of 1774.

Jefferson was absent, although he and Dr. Walker's son Jack had been duly elected for Albemarle, from the convention that sent the first batch of Virginia delegates to Philadelphia. It was August. He was taken with a fit of dysentery on the road and forced to turn back to Monticello. In his place he sent a paper, supplementing the resolutions urging solidarity with Massachusetts and the calling of a "general congress of deputies from the several American states" which the freeholders of his county had voted in their meeting in Charlottesville. This paper was printed in Williamsburg under the title of *A Summary View of the Rights of British America* and reprinted in London. Thomas Jefferson became widely known as the author.

The *Summary View* included, along with the list of the present grievances, a rapid sketch of British institutions from the point of view of the radical advocates of self-government throughout English history. Men of the radical wing of the American Whigs felt that he was expressing their inmost thoughts. He was baring the root of the struggle between central authority and local liberty which had kept alive the political institutions of the English-speaking peoples. When Virginia planters and Pennsylvania farmers and the mechanics and small traders who made up the Sons of Liberty read that "our ancestors, before their emigration to America were the free inhabitants of the British dominions in Europe and possessed a right which nature has given to all men . . . of establishing new societies under such laws and regulations as to them shall seem most likely to promote public happiness," and "that their Saxon ancestors had under this universal law, in like manner, left their native wilds and woods in the North of Europe, had possessed themselves of the island of Britain . . . and had established there that system of laws which has so long been the glory and protection of that country," they felt that their temporary difficulties and tribulations were part of the great sweep of history. The feeling that they carried with them the heritage of liberty made them bold to overcome obstacles.

Jefferson was still a minor figure in Virginia politics. He

was now just thirty-two years old. It was as a partisan of Patrick Henry and the radical up-country party that he sat in the convention which met in March of 1775 in St. John's Church in the little hamlet of Richmond. When he was appointed to the Continental Congress it was as Peyton Randolph's alternate.

At the Richmond convention it was Patrick Henry's voice that made the chandeliers ring with "Gentlemen may say peace, peace, but there is no peace . . . I know not what course others may take but as for me . . . Give me Liberty . . ."

"He stood like a Roman Senator defying Caesar . . ." wrote a delegate, "and then closed the grand appeal with the solemn words: 'Or give me death' . . . and he suited the action to the word by a blow upon the left breast with the right hand which seemed to drive the dagger to the patriot's heart."

Jefferson listened with breathless approbation. The church was so crowded that many delegates could hear only by clinging to the windows from the outside. A certain Colonel Carrington, dangling from a window frame to hear better, was so moved that he begged his friends, when he died, to see that he was buried in that spot. No wonder that, when the news of Lexington and Concord reached Virginia, although Washington was a member along with Jefferson of the committee of twelve to activate the militia, it was to Patrick Henry that the Virginians turned for leadership in the field.

Jefferson never was much of a speaker. All his life his influence was exercised through the give and take of committee meetings round a table or through letters and writings. It was merely as the author of the *Summary View* that he was known to his colleagues from the sister colonies when, the "good old speaker" having been called home to preside over the last stormy session of the colonial House of Burgesses, he drove his phaeton into Philadelphia in June of 1775 to take Peyton Randolph's place. Virginia's most seasoned frontier campaigner, whom John Adams, a delegate from Massachusetts, writing his wife Abigail, had called "the modest and virtuous, the amiable, modest, and brave George Washington Esq.," had just been elected generalissimo of the colonial forces now encamped behind Boston. The same day Washington wrote his brother John Augustin, "I am embarked on a wide ocean, boundless in its prospect and from whence perhaps no safe harbor is to be found." The sound of fife and drum, as many of the delegates and a troop of light horse in uniform accompanied their new general on the first stage of his road to Massachusetts, had hardly died out when post riders brought into Philadelphia news of the bloodshed on Bunker Hill. Jefferson wrote Francis Eppes, his wife's brother-in-law at The Forest, "War is now heartily entered into."

It was one of those periods when under the pressure of events months of hard work have to be compressed into days. In the heat of the white paneled hall in the Philadelphia statehouse, while the flies from a nearby livery stable buzzed in and out of the tall windows, a motley crew of sixty or so delegates: merchants, lawyers, doctors, clergymen, farmers, planters, from all the colonies from South Carolina north, were sweating and arguing and doing their best to arrive at unanimous decisions. Many of these men were rubbing up against people from other colonies for the first time in their lives. "It is like a large fleet," John Adams wrote Abigail, "sailing under convoy. The fleetest sailors must wait for the dullest and slowest." They were under continuous stress to raise money, to enroll troops, to find gunpowder, to organize colonial unity and to justify their actions before the reasoning world. They were discovering what it meant to be an American.

Immediately Jefferson found himself on a committee with Benjamin Franklin, John Dickinson, author of *The Letters from a Farmer of Pennsylvania*, and several others to draft a "Declaration of the Causes and Necessity of Taking up Arms." It was hoped this would convince at least the Whig sector of British opinion of the justice of their cause. Franklin was already an elderly man. Through the debates in Congress and in committee he sat with a drowsy smile on his lined face, now and then moderating the heat of his young friends' discussions with a shrewd and amusing remark. Jefferson the radical and Dickinson the conservative found themselves working out the phrasing of the declaration together.

Congress adjourned and Jefferson started south on August 1

to join the Virginia convention, sitting again in the clapboard
Richmond church which seemed at that time remote and
secluded from the guns of British men-of-war. There he was
reelected to Congress, this time in his own right. His reputation
had grown so that only Peyton Randolph and Richard Henry
Lee stood ahead of him in the voting. Since Congress was to
convene again in the fall, Jefferson got leave to go home to
Monticello where, apart from poignant domestic matters, he
had duties to perform as the leading member of the Albemarle
County Committee. Meanwhile the convention adjourned to
more comfortable quarters in Williamsburg. The capital had
been left vacant by Governor Dunmore's flight to a man-of-war
the *Fowey*. In Williamsburg in late August the delegates took
the last logical step in the transfer of sovereignty from the
Crown, vesting the executive power in a committee of safety
From then on Dunmore, cruising as an enemy off the coast of a
hostile commonwealth, was a governor without a government

DUNMORE CELEBRATED New Year's Day 1776 by burning
Norfolk. As a shipping point for tobacco, Norfolk was a sort
of distant suburb of Virginia Street in Glasgow, and was inhabited mostly by the factors and agents of Scottish tobacco
merchants. The Virginians considered it a nest of Tories and
had been debating that fall as to whether they oughtn't to
burn it themselves. Since the tobacco trade was totally interrupted the planters had nothing but unpaid bills to expect from
their British brokers. But nest of Tories or not, the burning of
the tobacco warehouses outraged them profoundly. Dunmore's
exploit, added to the news of the destruction of Falmouth down
east on Casco Bay, wrecked the last hopes of an accommodation
The minds of the colonists were ready for the Fourth of July.

The founding of a republic demanded a plan of government
The basic tradition was already there. The question was into
what form it should be molded. During the preceding fall
the representatives assembled in Philadelphia had in the privacy
of their lodgings done a good deal of talking about possible
forms of government. "We ought to consider," John Adams
of Massachusetts wrote George Wythe, "what is the end of gov-

rnment, before we determine which is the best form. Upon his point all speculative politicians will agree, that the happiness of society is the end of government as all divines and moral philosophers will agree that the happiness of the individual is he end of man. From this principle it will follow that the form of government which communicates ease, comfort, security, or in one word, happiness, to the greatest number of persons and in the greatest degree, is the best."

As the winter advanced plans multiplied for setting up this unique government which would ensure individual happiness to the greatest number of persons. Today when the need to take sides in the struggle for the freedom to seek individual happiness again confronts every man alive, we can understand, as the Americans of 1776 understood, what a bold enterprise it was. The American Whigs were maintaining that government was a makeshift construction which should serve the well-being of the citizen. That men were born to submit to authority had been, as it still is, the general opinion of mankind.

Tom Paine brought these discussions out in the open with the publication of *Common Sense* on January 10. To counteract what he considered dangerous errors in Paine's plan for a government John Adams rushed into print with a scheme he had been discussing with Richard Henry Lee and with George Wythe. Another plan, which perpetuated the life tenure of the Council of State, represented the opinion of the tidewater magnates of Virginia. Patrick Henry, the mouthpiece of the up-country party, told off the anonymous author as aristocratical in no uncertain terms. Meanwhile, George Mason was bringing his fine mind to bear on John Adams's scheme and molding it into the instrument which he forwarded to the convention in Williamsburg in May. It was in everybody's head that as Virginia was the most populous colony and as the feeling for independence was most universal there, Virginia's should be the first trial constitution.

Jefferson had hurried home from Congress over wintry trails at the end of 1775. Underlying his public anxieties over the slowness of the proceedings of Congress that fall had been his acute private anxiety about his wife's health. She never was well when she was childbearing; she never ceased childbearing until she died. At least he found her alive and cheerful. As soon as he was settled at Monticello, most characteristically, he plunged into his library to do a little historical research. In Congress and in the Virginia convention he had been insisting that a statement made recently by King George, that the colonies had been planted and nursed at the expense of the British nation, was a downright lie. He set out to prove his contention that the Crown had never invested a shilling in their establishment.

Meanwhile he knew that Williamsburg and Philadelphia were seething with argument over what form the new government should take, so the subject of a Virginia constitution must have been uppermost in his mind. In February his fat Yorktown friend Thomas Nelson, Jr., sent him what he described as two shillings' worth of *Common Sense*. The hearty phrasing in Paine's book stirred up Jefferson's thoughts about a scheme of government he had undoubtedly discussed with John Adams.

His friendship with the New Englander dates from those long fall sessions in Philadelphia, when the slowness with which the evolving will of the more laggard colonies was being made known to their delegates seemed unbearable to men, like Adams and himself, who had already made up their minds. In the fact that John Adams of Boston and Thomas Jefferson of Monticello were warm friends we can find a hint of why, despite all regional differences, this mixed bag of provincial lawyers, farmers, clergymen, merchants and doctors could find similarities in their thinking which were greater than the differences.

John Adams was one of the most indiscreet, impetuous and cantankerous little men who ever lived. He was full of petty vanity. A remark of Franklin's was going the rounds about him: "John Adams is always an honest man, often a wise one, but sometimes in some things, absolutely out of his senses." That fall he was still in hot water with the conservative wing of Congress on account of some letters, highly critical of his associates, which the British had intercepted and published during the summer. John Dickinson wouldn't speak to him. But Adams gloried in his unpopularity. Though the shape of his belief was not theirs he was as self-righteous as his Puritan

316

ncestors. He had the special intellectual snobbery of the pro-
incial townsman of New England where the fires of Cotton
Mather's hell still smoldered under the church pulpits.

When Adams wrote that happiness of the individual is the
nd of man he hastened to explain that the happiness and dignity
f man consisted in virtue. But by virtue, naturally, he meant
ehavior that a well-read New England townsman would
onsider virtuous. There was nothing orthodox about John
Adams's thinking. Virtue for him, instead of being a matter of
alvation in the next world, was a matter of civic duty in this.
While Adams took immediately to Jefferson, he was repelled
y Tom Paine whom he met that same winter. Paine offended
he New Englander's sensibilities; the old exciseman reeked of
he rum and radicalism of too many back rooms of taverns.
Adams's social fastidiousness, however, found an echo in Jeffer-
on's peculiar intellectual fastidiousness.

Physically there was the greatest contrast between the two.
ohn Adams was a stubby little man. Blue-eyed and red-faced,
ownright and explosive, he could have sat for a portrait of
ohn Bull. The reticent Jefferson was tall, rawboned and red-
aired. Under all the polish of his education there remained
good deal of the closemouthed frontiersman about him.
"Though a silent Member in Congress," Adams wrote retro-
pectively to Timothy Pickering years later, "he was so prompt,
rank, explicit, and decisive upon Committees and in Conver-
ation . . . that he soon seized upon my Heart."

Jefferson had met a mind that matched his own. He and
Adams were the two Americans most ardent in research into
onstitutional history. Reading in his library, attending to his
uties as county lieutenant and committeeman in Charlottes-
ille, making the daily decisions of plantation management, all
hat winter and early spring Jefferson must have felt the stimulus
f the burly vigor of John Adams's scholarship. Back in the
ear daily routine of the crowded family group at Monticello
where his frail Patty had to cater not only for her own little
aughter, but, since the death of his friend Dabney Carr, for
efferson's sister Martha and her orphaned children, he found
ime to think out his own plan of government.

Leisure was hardly the word for the life of a plantation owner. How much of a *familia* (in the Roman sense) Jefferson had around him we can learn from the census of that year. He listed thirty-four whites and eighty-three slaves on the plantation. Here indeed was a laboratory for the practical management of men.

He lingered four months on his hilltop. He made few entries that season in his garden or farm notebooks. War's paralysis hung over the countryside. "The crops of those who make tobacco still lie in their warehouses, the wheat of the farmer is rotting in their barns," he wrote to his uncle William Randolph, who had settled in England as a Bristol merchant.

Jefferson was back in Philadelphia May 14, 1776. Congress had already adopted John Adams's resolution urging each of the individual colonies to take over all the powers of government. May 15 the Virginia convention, acting on its own, recommended that Congress declare the colonies independent. A committee was set up in Williamsburg to draft a constitution for Virginia. While Thomas Nelson, Jr., was riding posthaste to bring the Virginia resolutions to Philadelphia, Jefferson was already in the thick of the debate on independence in Congress. Along with John Adams, Dr. Franklin and the New York lawyer Robert R. Livingston, he was appointed to the committee to draw up the declaration of independence.

The scholiasts have worn out the question of whose thinking was responsible for which line of the document, but there remains no doubt that most of the work fell on Jefferson. But while he sat at his traveling desk in the upstairs parlor of bricklayer Graff's new house, expounding in carefully cadenced phrases a set of principles already established as his belief, a large part of his mind was on the doings at Williamsburg. The declaration, though a magnificent state paper, was after all merely the elegant expression of the common denominator of the political belief of the American Whigs. There was never any doubt in Jefferson's mind that the work of the Virginia convention was more important. There the delegates were cutting out the pattern for a new society.

Sometime in May or early June Jefferson found time to write

ut his own outline for the constitution of the colony's new
overnment. When he found there was no way of getting a
:lease from Congress to go home himself, he sent copies of
is draft to George Wythe and to Edmund Pendleton who was
residing. One can't help entertaining the suspicion that the
onservative members of the convention, who were more or
ss under Pendleton's leadership, kept Jefferson in Philadelphia
n purpose. They probably feared that if he appeared at
Villiamsburg he would argue them into establishing principles
)o democratic for their tastes. When the Jefferson draft arrived
: Williamsburg, George Mason's constitution was on the point
f being reported in to the convention. The committee tacked
nto it Jefferson's statement of grievances, but they took no
:tion on the changes he proposed in the basic law of the colony.

HE FIRST OF THE PRINCIPLES he laid down in his draft of a
onstitution for Virginia was universal manhood suffrage.
:fferson's plan would establish as electors "all male persons
f full age and sane mind having a freehold estate in one fourth
f an acre of land in any town, or in 25 acres of land in the
)untry, and all persons resident in the colony who shall have
aid scot and lot to government the last two years shall have
ght to give their vote in the election of their respective rep-
:sentatives, and every person so qualified to elect shall be
apable of being elected."

To make sure that no man would be excluded from voting
y the property qualification, under the heading: "Rights
rivate & Public," he included a clause: "Every person of full
ge neither owning nor having owned 50 acres of land, shall be
ntitled to an appropriation of 50 acres, or to so much as shall
ake up what he owns or has owned: 50 acres in full & absolute
omination, and no other person shall be capable of taking an
)propriation." The acreage appears in brackets in each case.
Vhat he intended was that enough free land to make him a
oter should be distributed to every present adult male in-
abitant and to all future inhabitants.

The second principle wiped out the aristocratic custom of
anding down property and slaves to the eldest son. The

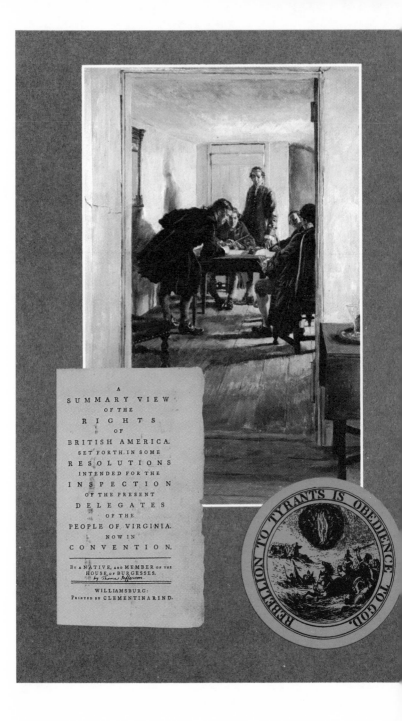

A
SUMMARY VIEW
OF THE
R I G H T S
OF
BRITISH AMERICA.
SET FORTH. IN SOME
RESOLUTIONS
INTENDED FOR THE
INSPECTION
OF THE PRESENT
DELEGATES
OF THE
PEOPLE OF VIRGINIA.
NOW IN
CONVENTION.

BY A NATIVE, AND MEMBER OF THE
HOUSE OF BURGESSES.
by Thomas Jefferson

WILLIAMSBURG:
PRINTED BY CLEMENTINA RIND.

REBELLION TO TYRANTS IS OBEDIENCE TO GOD.

wording of the first draft explains what he meant in layman's language. "Descents, instead of being to the eldest son, brother or other male cousin of the ancestor as directed by the laws heretofore, shall be to all the brothers & sisters of the said heir." "Females shall have equal rights with males," he wrote in his final draft. The intent was to abolish the machinery of entail and primogeniture by which the estates of the tidewater magnates had grown in size from generation to generation.

The third principle established freedom of religion and disestablished the Episcopal Church: "All persons shall have free and full liberty of religious opinion: nor shall any be compelled to frequent or maintain any religious institution."

In the Old Raleigh rn, a painting by ard Pyle. Jefferson is 'n leaning over the table R. H. Lee, Patrick y (standing), F. L. Lee Dabney Carr. Bottom :itle page of A Summary . Bottom right, Great of the United States, ned by Jefferson, us and Franklin.

The fourth laid the foundation for gradual elimination of slavery. "No person hereafter coming into this country shall be held within the same in slavery under any pretext whatever." On a number of Jefferson's principles, such as freedom of the press, and the division of governmental powers into legislative, judicial and executive, the radical and conservative Whigs were in agreement.

Although the tidewater magnates wanted to retain their hold on the governor and the Council of State, they were thoroughly outvoted by the up-country delegation with the result that, as both Patrick Henry and Jefferson discovered to their detriment when they assumed the office, the governorship was left with hardly any functions at all.

The constitution established for Virginia was substantially George Mason's. It was preceded by his famous declaration of rights, which laid down the political axioms that all men were created free and independent, that political power was vested in the people, that the majority had the right to reform any government, and that no man should be taxed without his consent.

MEANWHILE, AT THE SAME TIME as a republic was being established, the war had to be fought. Throughout the colonie
patriots were working as they had never worked in their lives
"Former labors in various public appointments now appear as
recreations compared with the present, which affords a scanty
allowance for food and sleep," Edmund Pendleton had written
to Jefferson from his home in Caroline County. Men's soul
were being tried.

It was another hot summer in Philadelphia. Congress wa
endlessly in session and committees dragged on into the night
Rules had to be improvised to regulate debate. A great seal for
the United States had to be designed. Plans had to be made to
clear up the confusion of the various colonial currencies. Dis
cussion of principles kept being interrupted by the compelling
need for salt, for gunpowder, for blankets for the troops. "We
suffer inexpressibly for want of Men of Business," John Adam
wrote to James Warren of Plymouth. "Men acquainted with
War by Sea or Land, Men who have no pleasure but in Busi
ness. If you have them send them along."

When Jefferson left for home again in early September o
1776, it is hardly likely that he was rating his declaration a
one of the great achievements of his life. Any thought of even
tual accomplishment was buried under a storm of presen
anxieties. Indeed at that time he was even teased by doubts a
to his own standing in Virginia. He feared that enemies were
undermining him. But his doubts as to his reputation, in
Congress at least, must have been set at rest by his appointmen
with Dr. Franklin and Silas Deane of Connecticut as commis
sioner to France. Jefferson refused the appointment on accoun
of his wife's ill health. He was glad to refuse it because hi
election to the House of Delegates which was to meet in
Williamsburg in October would give him a chance to take
part in the work his heart was set on. When the new constitu
tion was adopted by the Virginia convention, George Wythe
had written to Jefferson telling him that two or three parts o
Jefferson's draft had been included, but, wrote Wythe, "The
system agreed to in my opinion required reformation. In
October I hope you will effect it." The struggle to accomplish

his reformation was to take up most of Jefferson's political energies for the next five years.

When October came George Wythe, who was taking Mrs. Wythe along on his tour of duty in Congress, thoughtfully offered Jefferson his handsome house across from the palace in Williamsburg all equipped with orchard and servants. Patty was well enough to travel. At last Jefferson could set himself in full peace of mind, in the company of the woman he loved so tenderly, to a task he felt really suited him.

THE PUBLIC TIMES he saw in Williamsburg in the fall of 1776 were very different from any of the public times he had known in the past. Gone were the royal chariots and the provincial pomp and the splendor of gold lace and full wigs. Patrick Henry, who on his elevation had given up hunting shirts and homespun for a black suit and the scarlet cloak of the Glasgow merchant, was occupying the palace as governor, and Jefferson's personal friend and public opponent, Edmund Pendleton, was presiding as Speaker in the capitol.

Edmund Pendleton was a man of independent judgment who had the reputation of being the ablest lawyer in the Virginia colony. "Mr. Pendleton . . ." Jefferson wrote in his autobiography, "was the ablest man in debate I have ever met with. He had not indeed the poetical fancy of Mr. Henry, his sublime imagination, his lofty & overwhelming diction: but he was cool, smooth & persuasive: his language, flowing, chaste & embellished: his conception quick, acute and full of resource."

In the House of Delegates which Pendleton presided over, the tie wigs and the powdered hair and the frilled shirts and lace cuffs of the tidewater planters were still in evidence, but among them could be seen fur caps, homespun greatcoats and deerskin leggings. Lanky men from the Piedmont and from settlements west of the mountains predominated over the ceremonious tidewater magnates. There were a great many very young men. Their dress was as varied as their opinions. Some young bloods among the radical Whigs had taken up the fashion of wearing the conical felt hats affected by the Puritans of England.

One of the young men was James Madison, son and heir of the

Montpelier Madisons. He had appeared in Williamsburg for the first time as delegate from Orange at the May convention, and had made such a name for himself for modest diligence that as soon as he reported to the House of Delegates that fall he was placed with Jefferson and a number of prominent men from both the conservative and radical Whigs on the highly contentious committee on religion.

It was in the daily work on this committee, which was besieged with petitions for the repeal of the laws infringing on religious liberty, that Jefferson first recognized the younger man from Montpelier as an intellectual kinsman. Just launched on the career of statesmanship which would culminate in *The Federalist Papers* and in his collaboration in the federal Constitution, he became Jefferson's ablest assistant in the contest which began with that first session of the assembly, to establish the commonwealth on a pattern they considered "truly republican."

A great many different questions had to be handled simultaneously. The struggle for disestablishment, in which Madison was particularly useful because he had been educated in the Presbyterian atmosphere of Princeton and had personal experience with the persecution of dissenters in his own Orange County, developed in the committee on religion into what Jefferson referred to as "the severest contests in which I have ever been engaged."

At the same time Jefferson was at work on a series of bills to start up the machinery of the law courts, stalled since Dunmore's flight to the man-of-war *Fowey* in 1775. A strange listlessness fell over the assembly, however, at the notion of reopening the courts. All the delegates could think of was that the minute the courts were opened the Glasgow and London merchant would come swarming over to sue them for debts they had no way of paying. Only one of Jefferson's judiciary bills passed that session. That was the bill to establish a court of admiralty which could condemn and sell prizes captured from the enemy.

By the time the session of a scant eight weeks ended in the middle of December, Jefferson had become the prime mover in legislation which would establish a self-governing commonwealth of landowners, based on the theory he had frankly put forward in a letter to the more conservative Pendleton that summer. "You have lived longer than I have & perhaps have formed a different judgment on better grounds," he'd written him from Philadelphia in August, "but my observations do not enable me to say I think integrity the characteristic of wealth. In general I believe the decisions of the people, in a body, will be more honest & more disinterested than those of wealthy men: and I can never doubt an attachment to his country in any man who has his family and peculium in it."

Looking back to these early days when he sat writing his autobiography at the end of his life, it seemed to him that the laws abolishing primogeniture, disestablishing the Church and asserting complete freedom of religion, along with the measure he drafted, which was unfortunately never adopted, to set up a modest but thoroughgoing system of free public schools, were the most important accomplishments for which the foundations were laid in that great session.

Of course Jefferson wasn't alone. He was surrounded by a group of men who were determined to incorporate Whig principles into the law of the land. "In giving this account of the laws of which I was myself the mover & draftsman," he wrote, "I by no means mean to claim for myself the merit of obtaining their passage. I had many occasional and strenuous coadjutors in debate, and one most steadfast able & zealous, who was himself a host. This was George Mason, a man of the first order of wisdom among those who acted on the theatre of the revolution, of expansive mind, profound judgment, cogent in argument, learned in the lore of our former constitution, & earnest for the republican change on democratic principles."

MEANWHILE THE PRACTICAL PROBLEMS of nation building had to be met. The commonwealth of Virginia represented a huge area extending from the old settled regions of tidewater across the mountains into the bluegrass country and the rich plains beyond the Ohio and the Mississippi. As the capital for such an empire Williamsburg was an anachronism. Its location was inconvenient for the up-country delegates. Without any of the advantages of a seaport, it was too near the coast to be safe from attack by the British fleet. To bring the vague sentiment for relocating the seat of government to a head, Jefferson, always ready with his pen, drafted a bill. The architect in him came to the surface for a moment when he sketched out a provision for public buildings: "Said houses shall be built in a handsome manner with walls of Brick, & Porticos, where the same may be convenient or ornamental."

While so many of his great projects failed of execution, this one at least succeeded. When Richmond at the falls of the James was chosen for the capital it was Jefferson, not many years later, who was responsible for the design of the statehouse.

Already the western settlers were petitioning for the establishment of new counties beyond the mountains. The center of population was shifting, and the westerners were demanding fair representation. A complicated parliamentary battle took up most of October between the representatives of the tidewater families who wanted the vague and enormous Fincastle County divided into two counties; and the up-country men, under Jefferson's leadership, who wanted it divided into three. In this form the issue became straight politics, because three counties naturally would give the westerners more representation than two. The Jefferson party won and Fincastle became Washington, Montgomery and Kentucky counties.

Parallel to the tussle in the state legislatures was the pulling and hauling in Congress where the question of state lands to the westward was to be crucial for many years to come. A number of people of influence wanted to use the western lands to pay off the war debt. Jefferson was opposing that view both in Williamsburg and in Philadelphia.

In time, after settling many problems, that tremendous session of the first Virginia assembly came to a close. By then Jefferson as if he had not already taken on enough work to kill a mule had accepted a place on a committee which was set no less an aim than that of modernizing and clarifying the entire code of English law in use in Virginia. The committee members promptly elected Jefferson chairman and decided to meet in January at Fredericksburg to take up their task.

THEY MET JANUARY 13, 1777, in the quiet little wintry town in a moment of mighty hopes. The day after Christmas Washington had brought his retreat across the Jerseys to a brilliant close by surprising the Hessians at Trenton and by checking the main British force at Princeton a few days later. It began to look as if the Continental Army could really hold its own against British regulars and the hired German troops.

At home in Virginia, enough of Jefferson's program was started on its way through the legislative mill to make him feel some confidence in his parliamentary ability. Now in the revision of the laws he felt his chance had come to impose these parts of the framework of "a government truly republican" which had failed of adoption in the state constitution.

He was sitting down, away from the pressure of parliamentary detail, far from the distasteful stamping and tramping of the military, with his revered friend and teacher, George Wythe; with George Mason who, like him, took an amateur's pleasure in the machinery of self-government and whose mind like Jefferson's resolutely faced west; with Edmund Pendleton, a conservative whom he liked and thoroughly understood, and with Thomas Ludwell Lee, the oldest surviving of the brilliant sons of old Thomas Lee, an associate of George Mason's in the Ohio Company. Jefferson knew that there were only certain times in the history of nations when fundamental reforms were possible. The iron was glowing and malleable. Now was the time to hammer it out. It was the work for which his Latin, his Anglo-Saxon, his close reading of old Norman French texts, his enthusiasm for the great republicans of the English commonwealth had long been preparing him.

In the end, the most important measures failed to pass. It was ten years later, after Jefferson had virtually retired from the contest, that his young friend and disciple, little James Madison of Montpelier, established on the statute books the ruins of the great reform.

From the beginning the drudgery fell on Jefferson and Pendleton. George Mason, always an indolent man, begged off because he was no lawyer. Thomas L. Lee retired to his home on the same pretext and soon after died. George Wythe remained the sympathetic consultant. In all one hundred and twenty-six bills were presented to the House of Delegates. Jefferson worked on considerably more than half of them. In its inception it was one of the boldest enterprises in the history of laws. As the five men gathered round a table in the wintry quiet to settle to the work the greatness of the task must have made their blood tingle. It was one of those times when everything seems possible.

Chapter 5

IN VIRGINIA THESE WERE THE YEARS when change came easy. In August 1777 Jefferson was writing triumphantly to Benjamin Franklin, already established in Paris: "With respect to the state of Virginia in particular, the people seem to have deposited the monarchical & taken up the republican government with as much ease as would have attended their throwing off an old & putting on a new suit of clothes." Still Jefferson well knew that there was no time to be lost. In the life of a community of men there come only rare moments when the relationships that give a shape to society are fluid enough to permit fundamental reforms. The outlines of the new government would rapidly harden. Vested interests would grow up to resist any change. Let others wrangle in Congress over the daily chore of waging war against the British. It was Jefferson's own function to retire to his hilltop and there to engrave the tablets of the law for his commonwealth.

For once his public duty and his private pleasure coincided. He was always more the man of letters than the man of action. Now he could stay home with a clear conscience, take care of Patty who was pregnant again, start educating his little daughter and his sister Martha Carr's brood; build the columned porches he had planned, and keep an eye on his farming and his gardens. While he dug into the law, he could ride in the mountains and feed his tame deer and keep up his weather charts.

All this did not mean that he ceased performing his local duties. He was still county lieutenant, handling the enlistment of militia and other chores of county government. The republic, he was convinced, began at home. And one of his first public acts on record after he settled down was to put his name, with that of his dull young brother Randolph, to a subscription for the support of the minister at Charlottesville, Charles Clay. The Reverend Clay was switching from the Church of England to a persuasion he described as the Calvinistical Reformed Church. Now that the Church was practically disestablished and they had a patriot for a clergyman, a man who, Jefferson wrote, was "rejecting the tyrant & tyranny of England," it was the business of the parishioners to support him. Naturally Jefferson's had to be the largest subscription.

Among the subscribers to the printed sheet there appears the name of Philip Mazzei. This Mazzei was a mercurial little Tuscan, part philosopher, part promoter, who a few years before had brought over to Virginia a group of Italian wine-growers. Mazzei was going to introduce the growing of grapes and olives and the culture of the silkworm and make his fortune in America. A glib talker, he'd managed to interest such worthies as Governor Dunmore, Peyton Randolph, Robert Carter Nicholas, George Mason, George Washington and John Page. Jefferson himself, who had been studying Italian out of books, jumped at the opportunity to converse with a live Italian. He latched on to Mazzei and induced him to plant his vineyards on an estate adjoining Monticello which they named Colle. Mazzei's gardeners taught Jefferson superior Italian methods of growing vegetables. They helped him plant a vineyard at Monticello. Right away Jefferson began listing the names of vegetables in his garden book in Italian.

Mazzei was a man of many interests. He had a project for a philosophical gazette to be published in Albemarle County and distributed to the philosophers of Europe. Painfully Jefferson translated his articles into English for him. When the wine-growing enterprise began to prove somewhat impractical, Mazzei's imagination spread to new fields, and he induced Jefferson to suggest to John Hancock that Congress should send him back to Italy to negotiate a loan with the Grand Duke of Tuscany. Eventually, somewhat to the relief of the family at Monticello to whom Mazzei's demands were getting to be a headache, Governor Patrick Henry commissioned him to sail for Europe to drum up credit for Virginia.

Meanwhile the fortunes of war were furnishing Jefferson with a set of even more agreeable European connections. When Mazzei left to strut about the courts of Europe, his house at Colle was rented by a genial German baron, General Frederick von Riedesel, who had been taken prisoner with the British army at Saratoga. His wife joined him in his internment in Albemarle County, and turned out to have a lovely singing voice and nice little daughters around the age of Jefferson's daughter Patsy. The general's aides-de-camp played musical instruments. They were fashionably philosophical young men. The household, in the bleak winter of the Virginia hills, glowed with the warm charms of the cultivated Rhineland.

General von Riedesel, under a stuffy English General William Phillips who kept haughty state at the Carters' Blenheim, commanded the four thousand interned troops established in barracks near Charlottesville. When it began to look as if Virginia would soon be in danger of a British attack, there was talk in governing circles of moving the convention troops, as they were known, out of Albemarle. Jefferson wrote Governor Henry urging they be allowed to stay. "Is an enemy so execrable that tho' in captivity his wishes & comforts are to be disregarded & even crossed? I think not. It is for the benefit of mankind to mitigate the horrors of war as much as possible."

He goes on to explain that the officers had gone to considerable expense to rent and fix up houses for themselves and that moving would be a great hardship. He had admired the industry and skill with which these Europeans had built up a little civilization round their cantonments. "They have generally laid in their stocks of grain & other provision . . ." he continues. "They have purchased cows, sheep &c., set in to farming, prepared their gardens and have a prospect of comfort and quiet before them." You can see that Jefferson feels that these thrifty people would make the best possible population for the red hills of his home country. He wishes they would stay there forever. "To turn to the soldiers, the environs of the barracks are delightful. . . . Their poultry, pigeons and other preparations of that kind present to the mind an idea of a company of farmers rather than a camp of soldiers."

The phrase "a company of farmers" expressed Jefferson's hopes for his country. He wanted a republic of medium-sized farms. He felt that only on the independence and integrity of men who farmed their own lands could a government truly republican be founded. As all men who have tried to mold institutions have discovered, from the days of Confucius on down, Jefferson was already discovering that men can be led only a little way before they stick on the old Adam of real or imagined personal interests.

AS IT TURNED OUT, a disproportionate amount of work of revising the legal code had devolved on Jefferson. In the spring of 1777 Edmund Pendleton had had a fall from his horse which dislocated his hip. He was bedridden for months and never again walked without crutches. In the House of Delegates, George Wythe took his place as Speaker, but Wythe's law courses took up a great deal of his time. It was Jefferson who, in John Adams's words, was "the greatest rubber off of dust."

As fast as they were completed the most needed bills were sent down to the legislature. The entire set of a hundred and twenty-six—covering topics which ran the whole gamut of human affairs, from state and county elections to the upkeep of roads and ferries, habeas corpus and the crime of treason— was presented to the legislature in the spring session of 1778. But it was years before the legislature found time to take the bulk of them under advisement. Their minds that spring were preoccupied with more urgent matters than law reform.

For many months an ominous note had been creeping into the letters that found their way up to Jefferson at Monticello. "From the best observations I have been able to make," his old friend Will Fleming wrote him from Congress, "our great concerns wear a very gloomy aspect, owing principally to the rapid and excessive depreciation of our money, which is almost beyond conception, and the misfortune is [that] the mischief is daily increasing, and no man can see where it will stop; and I am persuaded if something effectual is not speedily done, it will in a short time cease being current at all. Should that happen the disbanding our army must inevitably be the consequence. . . ."

Will Fleming's letter expresses pretty clearly the military and political situation at the time. There had been many a victory won but the end was not in sight. Burgoyne's surrender at Saratoga in the fall of 1777 had marked the decline of English offensive power on land, but the English blockade of the seacoast was proving dangerously effective. Now the port of Boston was free, but the British were still in New York, had landed in Savannah, and were gradually invading the southerly states. Their fleet patrolled the seas. More dangerous than the blockade to the Continental cause, many thought, were inflation, speculation and the gradual disintegration of the will to fight.

Even George Washington, who had so resolutely faced the miseries of Valley Forge the winter before, was for once in his life thoroughly discouraged. The intrigue and dissipation he found all about him shook his confidence. This was the winter of some of his gloomiest letters. "It appears to me as clear as the sun ever did in his Meridian brightness," he wrote in a letter to Benjamin Harrison in December, "that America never stood in more eminent need of the wise, patriotic and Spirited exertion of her sons than at this period. . . . It is much to be feared my dear Sir that the States in their separate capacities have a very inadequate idea of the present danger." And in March he wrote to George Mason: "Let this voice, my dear Sir, call upon you, Jefferson and others; do not from a mistaken opinion that we are about to set down under our vine and our own fig tree, let our hitherto noble struggle end in ignominy."

Washington felt that Jefferson ought to be at work in Congress instead of on his hilltop engaging in research on the laws. He was not the only one who felt this. Richard Henry Lee was making discreet digs at Jefferson in his letters from Philadelphia. Edward Rutledge of South Carolina was referring pointedly to a hoped-for period "when you have condescended to come down from above and interest yourselves in human Affairs."

Since Jefferson had been one of the members who drew up the bill making attendance obligatory there was a certain irony in the fact that he attended the fall session of the House of Delegates in 1778 in the custody of the sergeant at arms.

IT WAS CHARACTERISTIC of his cast of mind to be more absorbed in the long-term business of planning a code of laws than in the practical daily problems of war and inflation. But at last the long stint which had so absorbed him was coming to an end. His mind, too, was more at ease about his family. In the summer of 1778, Patty had been successfully delivered of a daughter. They named her Mary. As she grew up to womanhood, Jefferson usually spoke of her as Polly; with Patsy she became the chief pleasure of her father's life. In May 1779 the family stayed at Patty's old home, The Forest, while Jefferson attended the House of Delegates in Williamsburg.

There's nothing in the record to show that the Virginia delegates who assembled in Williamsburg shared the bleak discouragement of their representatives in Congress. There was good news from the West. Virginia's frontiers were expanding. In February George Rogers Clark, one of the redheaded Clarks already famous in Albemarle as pioneers, had captured Vincennes in the Illinois country. The French court was appointing a consul to represent it in Virginia. The assembly was debating what to do with the forfeited estates of Englishmen and Tories. To be sure, the British fleet presented a growing threat off the Virginia capes, and their men had landed almost unopposed at Falmouth, across the river from the ruins of Norfolk, and burned stores and rounded up cattle and horses off farms south of the James. It was under the impulse of this raid that Jefferson's bill to move the seat of government away from the coast finally passed, in spite of the fact that many Virginians looked on the war as virtually won.

When Jefferson's fellow citizens chose him to take up public office again, it was not for Congress, where his talents had shone so brilliantly before. The question of the governorship was now nearer the surface of men's minds than the problems of Congress. Patrick Henry's third term was drawing to a close.

As an executive the great actor-orator had been a disappointment. Claiming poor health, he had spent a good deal of his time at his up-country plantation and left the daily work of administration to whatever members of the council chose to attend meetings. Now to succeed him the delegates nominated for governor three young men who were warm personal friends. They were Thomas Jefferson, John Page of Rosewell and Thomas Nelson, Jr., of Yorktown. On the second ballot Jefferson got a plurality of votes and was elected. He was just thirty-six. St. George Tucker, an admirer of Jefferson who had come from Bermuda to study law under George Wythe, wrote a friend to tell him of the election: "I wish excellency's activity may be equal to the abilities he possesses in so eminent a degree. In that case we may boast of having the greatest man on the continent at the helm. But if he should tread in the footsteps of his predecessor, there is not much to be expected from the brightest talents."

"MY GREAT PAIN IS, lest my poor endeavors should fall short of the kind expectations of my country," answered Jefferson with becoming modesty when he accepted his election as governor. The politely deprecating words may well have echoed bitterly in his ears now and then during the two years of thankless labor that followed. The Virginia governor, according to the constitution of 1776, was very little more than the chairman of the Council of State. And Jefferson, with all his varied accomplishments, lacked, at that time of his life at least, the self-dramatizing gift so necessary to leadership. Furthermore he was convinced that the governor was constitutionally obliged to act only with the advice of the council. When he spoke of the executive he meant the governor and council acting as a board. Conscientiously he tried to make up for his own shortcomings and the shortcomings of his office by passionate attention to detail.

When he moved his family in mid-June 1779 into the old palace at Williamsburg, which must have stirred in him memories of himself as a lanky youth, dining there in the peaceful old days of Fauquier, we find him meticulously checking over the inventory of furnishings Patrick Henry's family had left behind. Before endorsing it, having noted that "vallons top and headpiece" were missing to a set of green bed curtains, he added in his small hasty careful hand: "Things omitted; 2 delft wash basons. 4 blankets."

Immediately he was assailed by multifarious chores. The war had dragged on for four years. The self-sacrificing enthusiasm of the early days was gone. And 1779 was a disastrous crop season. Late frosts had damaged the winter wheat. Finding grain to supply the Continental commissary was becoming a problem. Buyers for the various commissaries under Congress and the state militia could only offer in payment hastily printed paper money which depreciated daily in value. Many preferred to hoard their products rather than to sell them. Not a few planters along the coast were surreptitiously selling produce to the English who paid in hard cash. The king's ships commanded Hampton Roads. Tory privateers dodged in and out of the deep indentations of the coastline, stealing cattle and occasionally burning barns. Speculation and skulduggery flourished.

The practical work of the governorship, meanwhile, was carrying Jefferson further and further afield from the philosophical paths of research and theory where he felt at home. His position turned out to be that of a glorified quartermaster general. It was not work for which he was fitted, but he threw himself into it with boundless patience.

In the stress of war some sort of service of supply had to be improvised. It was a heartbreakingly difficult task. Jefferson's letters are full of coats and shirts and waistcoats for the Virginia regiments. There were never enough shoes. Grain had to be bartered for salt from Bermuda. Manufacturers had to be encouraged to make gunpowder. Lead had to be hauled from the mines. A navy had to be built. The galleys the assembly had invested so much money in were sinking at their slips. The West was always in his mind. Virginia troops along the Ohio had to be strengthened. Nails and broadaxes and mattocks and hoes had to be sent out over the treacherous trails to George Rogers Clark's tiny stations in the Illinois country. Friendly Indians had to be supplied. Wagons for transport had to be found, harness and horses to draw them. Wagoners and drovers, artisans, clerks; everybody had to be paid. Then as the autumn advanced all the stores collected with such arduous pertinacity were jeopardized by the threat of a British invasion.

In April 1780 the seat of government was moved to Richmond, two days' ride farther inland. An effort had been made to improvise public buildings in that village at the falls of the James and to patch up a temporary capitol. But when the assembly convened, the scattered houses of Richmond became horribly overcrowded. The delegates met in a wooden building on a hill shedded round like a barn. They slept where they could. Unpaved streets were lined with tethered horses until the place looked like an Arab village. A German traveler described Formicola's tavern, the Richmond substitute for the handsome old Raleigh, as consisting of two large rooms on the ground floor and two above, "the apartments under the roof furnished with numerous beds standing close together, both rooms and chambers standing open to every person throughout the day . . . Generals, Colonels, Captains, Assembly-men, Judges, Doctors, Clerks and Crowds of Gentlemen of every weight and calibre and every hue of dress, sat all together about the fire drinking smoking singing and talking ribaldry. . . ."

The Jeffersons and their children, at least, were comfortably established in his uncle Thomas Turpin's brick house on a hill. Thomas Mann Randolph, with whom Jefferson had been raised almost as a foster brother, had his family at Tuckahoe nearby. For Jefferson it was a return to the country of his childhood.

When the council moved out of Williamsburg, Jefferson's dear friend John Page resigned, explaining that he felt Richmond was too far from Rosewell to allow him to attend to the business of his plantation. Two other councillors resigned with Page. During this whole period one of the most acute problems of Jefferson's government was keeping a quorum in the council and the assembly. The pay was negligible and inflation had thrown every man's affairs into confusion. The more disturbed the country got the harder it was to get Virginians of any class to leave their isolated plantations. It was not so much the fear of the enemy that kept them away from Richmond. It was the fear of leaving their wives and children and their horses and barns unprotected in the face of a rising of the slaves. For the same reason militiamen called up for service moped and worried about their crops and their families and took the first opportunity to slip off for home.

As soon as Jefferson was settled in his new quarters he sat down to dictate a letter of instructions to George Rogers Clark. This was part of the work he enjoyed. He'd been brought up with his face to the West. Clark's settlement at Louisville had secured the falls of the Ohio. The next step was to secure that river's junction with the Mississippi. He built a fortification there and named it Fort Jefferson.

Clark's reports that summer were encouraging, but the news from the South could hardly have been worse. Congress had detailed a considerable body of Virginia troops to help Governor Rutledge of South Carolina. The last day before they moved out of Williamsburg the governor and council, after poring over a list of clothing for sixty-eight hundred men in the Continental service, added an allowance for sixty officers in service in Charleston: "180 yards of Linen for Shirts, 50 yards of Cambrick for Ruffles, 60 pair of Shoes, 90 handkerchiefs, 270 yards of Jeans for summer Vests and Breeches, 60 Hatts." It's doubtful whether any of these officers ever got to wear their new hats or their summer jeans, because at the end of May General Benjamin Lincoln surrendered the city and all the troops in it to the king's forces.

THE BRITISH GENERAL CORNWALLIS began his northward march. It was obvious that this was the beginning of a pincers movement to crush Virginia. Congress sent Horatio Gates, the hero of Saratoga, off posthaste to try to pull things together in the Carolinas. From Richmond, Jefferson strained every resource in the state to raise and equip a body of militia under General Edward Stevens to reinforce Gates's army. The militia, the wagon trains disappeared into the forest paths. How to keep track of them? He had to have exact news. He had to know which way Cornwallis was heading. While setting up two routes of express riders to Philadelphia, he organized an intelligence service of his own to the southward.

There had come to call on him in Williamsburg a tall sturdy young man of twenty-four named James Monroe. Monroe had been raised in upper Westmoreland County. As his father doesn't seem to have been too well off, an uncle had helped him start his studies at William and Mary. When the war began he'd ridden north to join Washington, had been wounded at Trenton and had lived through the winter at Valley Forge. He was shy and tongue-tied and not too well educated. When he failed of advancement in the Continental Army he made his way back to Williamsburg with the idea of studying law under Wythe while he waited for a commission in one of the new Virginia regiments. Jefferson had taken a fancy to him, lent him books, and advised him on how to prepare himself for the law.

Jefferson's outlines of study courses were already famous in Virginia. There was nothing he liked better than directing the education of industrious young men. Monroe was slow but he was hardworking and methodical. He was husky and responsible. It occurred to Jefferson that he'd be just the fellow to organize a line of expresses to keep Richmond in touch with the war in the Carolinas. In picking Monroe for this task, Jefferson gained a lifetime friend and supporter. "Your kindness and attention to me in this and a variety of other instances has really put me under such obligations to you that I fear I shall hardly ever have it in my power to repay them," Monroe wrote when this particular tour of duty was over.

It wasn't Monroe's fault that most of the news his expresses brought in was bad. Cornwallis gave Gates's hastily improvised army a thorough beating at Camden, South Carolina.

In June Jefferson had been elected governor for a second term without opposition. Now his administration reacted with a good deal of resilience. New supplies were requisitioned. Plans were laid for raising fresh levies of militia. That great old backcountry warrior Daniel Morgan was induced to head a troop of riflemen to reinforce Gates. Maryland and Virginia were at last uniting to patrol Chesapeake Bay.

But the state just didn't have the organization necessary for carrying out a full-scale war. Every day it was the same story. How to find hunting shirts, uniforms, saddles, horses, tents;

there were never enough tents. If the governor found the equipment there were no wagons to haul it in. Every day more money bought less. In the back of his account book Jefferson carefully kept a chart of the inflation.

By late autumn Congress had recalled Gates and replaced him with Nathanael Greene, and sent General Friedrich Wilhelm von Steuben to Richmond to whip the Virginia soldiers into shape. December was spent in a fruitless effort to get him supplies for a small body of troops he was drilling in Petersburg to send south to reinforce Greene. Always the same story: no blankets, no tents, no guns. To a professional soldier brought up, so he claimed, in the rigid school of Frederick of Prussia's staff, the laxity of the Virginians was unbelievable. Almost daily Steuben bombarded the governor with demands. He'd seen disorganization in Philadelphia, but nothing like this. His opinion of the Virginians was unprintable. By the time a militiaman had learned a smattering of soldiering his term had expired and he was off for home. How could an officer drill troops when they didn't have shoes?

At the end of the month a merchant down at Hampton wrote rather casually to Thomas Nelson, Jr., who commanded the militia in the lower counties, that a fleet of twenty-seven sail was making its way up the James. But it was not until the British had anchored quietly off Westover and the traitor Benedict Arnold had landed and been hospitably received by William Byrd's widow there that the government at Richmond really took alarm.

The delegates adjourned and hurried home to call up the militia of their respective counties. The members of the governor's council went off to attend to their private affairs. Jefferson found himself facing the enemy virtually alone. He wore out his horse riding round the county trying to get munitions.

Arnold promptly sent a detachment overland to destroy the foundry at Westham. On the way they ransacked Richmond and burned some houses and barns, wrecked the new printing office and scattered the public documents. Jefferson, who had moved his family to his father's old place at Fine Creek, rode back to watch the redcoats from across the James. The weather turning rainy, they retired to their camp at Westover. With the best will in the world all that the handful of Virginia militia could do was watch them from behind hedgerows and bushes.

January 10 Jefferson was back in Richmond writing Washington: "The loss sustained is not yet adequately known. As far as I have been able to discover it consisted at this place in about 300 musquets, some soldiers' clothing to a small amount some quarter masters' Stores of which 120 sides of Leather was the principal article, part of the artificers tools & 3 waggons, besides which 5 brass four pounders which we had sunk in the river were discovered to them, raised and carried off. At the Foundry we lost the greater part of the papers belonging to the auditors office & the books and papers of the Council office. About 5 or 6 tons as we conjecture of powder was thrown into the canal. . . . Within Less than 48 hours from the time of their landing and 19 from our knowing their destination they had penetrated 33 miles, done the whole injury and retired."

The British said they had used only eight hundred men. It wasn't much of a raid but it laid bare to the enemy the complete helplessness of the Virginia government. Jefferson knew he was no military leader. Determined to resign at the first possible moment he went on, working with tight lips at his traveling desk, doing the best he could, collecting workmen to repair guns, trying to mollify Steuben, presiding politely when the councillors could be induced to attend meetings.

The county lieutenants were instructed to call in new drafts of militia, but in county after county men were sullenly refusing to be drafted. Planters were hiding their horses to keep them from being requisitioned. Merchants were refusing the depreciated currency. Organized administration was just about at an end. As governor, Jefferson was proving as much of a disappointment as his predecessor.

Patrick Henry, smoldering in eclipse at Leatherwood, had been listening with a scornful smile to stories of his successor's deficiencies. He was allowing himself to be coaxed back into politics. He consented to serve as a delegate in the legislature. During the debates he sat aloof and sullen while men occupied the public stage who had been mere stripling boys in the great days when he'd rallied the Virginians to the cause of independence. He dreamed of finding some way of reviving the old acclaim. He did not attack Jefferson's administration directly, but he made his disapproval known with the nods and hints and knowing looks he was such a master of, and he was gathering followers. The rarefied and speculative quality of Jefferson's mind tended to offend the plain ordinary men who constituted Patrick Henry's particular audience. Henry took to playing on the uneducated man's contempt for cogitation.

Jefferson's friends well knew that he was looking for an opportunity to resign. John Page wrote begging him to hold on at least till the end of his term. Richard Henry Lee and others tried to encourage him; but he was already being greeted by Horatio Gates as a fellow member of the club of the discredited.

One last chance remained to save something from the wreck. The French had promised to send ships to the relief of Virginia. If Arnold could be bottled up in Portsmouth, the French fleet might blockade him by sea and starve him into surrender before Cornwallis had time to relieve him from the south. Washington, as his contribution to the plan, detached Lafayette and a body of troops which the theatrical young Frenchman led down to Head of Elk [now Elkton], the northernmost port on the Chesapeake.

Lafayette at twenty-three had already made his reputation. Added to the awe the Americans felt for his wealth and noble birth, and the glamour Washington's affection cast around him, was their admiration for his courage and for his dash and judgment in the field. With his long horseface and high forehead, he looked almost the cartoon of the romantic aristocrat. Everybody knew he had run off to join the Americans to escape imprisonment. There was a high-spirited friendliness about him that charmed high and low. He was tireless. In this war of endless delays the young marquis had a way of arriving before he was expected. His name had hardly been mentioned in the council at Richmond when it was known that he was already reconnoitering the lower James.

With Lafayette's youthful energy added to Steuben's sound military scholarship it seemed hardly possible that the plan

could go wrong. Jefferson threw himself into arming and equipping the men needed as Virginia's contribution. He offered a reward for Arnold's capture. There was private talk of getting some of Clark's reckless Indian fighters to sneak into the town and catch the traitor in his bed.

Early in March Jefferson was writing Lafayette who had already hurried back north to start his troops moving: "The Number of Militia desired by the Baron will be provided though not quite so early as had been proposed. . . . Provisions and Arms for the Troops are in readiness and the Quarter Masters are exerting themselves to get Horses."

The month was spent in a fever of preparation. The last week in March news came that a fleet had been sighted between the capes, but when the men-of-war dropped anchor in Hampton Roads, instead of the lilies of France they showed the colors of King George. Only then did the information trickle in that the expected French squadron had retired to Newport after an engagement off the capes.

After this disappointment Jefferson refused to consent to a plan of Steuben's to lead the two thousand freshly drilled militia south to help Greene intercept Cornwallis. It was too great a risk of the men's lives. Jefferson had little real faith in military solutions. He was trusting to the rough country and the heat. Disease and desertion he said would eventually whittle down Cornwallis's forces.

Even in the moment of direst extremity Jefferson never felt that the demands of the military were paramount over the interests of private citizens. The militia had been called up to defend their own state. It would not be right to risk their lives in a hazardous enterprise elsewhere. As he put it, they had been harassed enough.

One of the worst harassments was the requisitioning of horses.

Lafayette had to have cavalry; Greene was daily calling for more horses. A passionate lover of horseflesh himself, Jefferson fully sympathized with the wrath of his fellow planters when the quartermasters tried to drive off irreplaceable blooded stallions or brood mares. The feeling about horses was so strong that when the assembly met they passed a resolution limiting their requisition. Greene answered tartly from South Carolina "If horses are dearer to the Inhabitants than the lives of Subject or the liberties of the People there will be no Doubt of the Assembly persevering in their late Resolution, otherwise I hope they will reconsider the matter."

While the governor and the few council members who still attended were arguing about the impressment of horses, British ships were sailing up the James and Appomattox rivers. Landing parties scooped up the few small batteries the Virginians had established. The Virginia fleet was scuttled by its own crew in the Chickahominy. All Tidewater lay open to the enemy.

The haughty Phillips, Jefferson's old acquaintance from Blenheim, had been exchanged and had replaced Arnold in command. He was preparing for a knockout blow against Virginia. Only the arrival of Lafayette with his still dismounted dragoons saved Richmond from another British visit. Phillips occupied the south bank of the James but he balked at trying to cross the river at the falls when he saw Lafayette's troops deployed on the heights above. Instead he set up headquarters at Steuben's old drill field at Petersburg and waited for Cornwallis to join him. So when Jefferson first met Lafayette, it was as the gay and graceful savior of his capital.

There was not much left in the capital to save. The place was too near the enemy lines to suit the members of the governor's council. One dreary day in April Jefferson had decided not to attend himself. "The day is so very bad," he'd written to the senior member of the council, "that I hardly expect a council, and there be nothing that I know of very pressing, and Mrs. Jefferson in a situation in which I would not wish to leave her, I shall not attend today." Their baby daughter, Lucy Elizabeth, whom they had managed to nurse through the hustle and exposure of that agitated winter, was dead.

Often when Jefferson rode up heavily to the council house on its hill he found no councillor at all. The assembly was due to meet in early May. A few members straggled into town but since no quorum could be found they decided to meet two weeks later in Charlottesville. What was left of the Virginia government was on the run.

When Lord Cornwallis reached Petersburg the rumor went out that he had a mind to bag as many delegates as he could and was particularly anxious to lay his hands on the governor and the council. The Virginia climate had been too much for General Phillips. He had been taken ill of a fever and died at Petersburg. Arnold had been recalled to other service so Cornwallis had his command to himself.

The councillors made themselves scarce, and since the government had fled to Charlottesville, there was nothing to it but for the governor to follow. By slow stages Jefferson and his family rode home to Monticello.

The assembly and the governor's council had been called to meet in Charlottesville on May 24, but no quorum appeared till May 28. Jefferson had made it clear that he would not serve another term and suggested that the assembly's first business should be to elect a new governor. Meanwhile he wrote Washington explaining the desperate turn affairs were taking and begging him to take command in his home state. At the same time he dotted the last *i* on the agreement between Virginia and Pennsylvania over their disputed western frontier and sent a messenger to ask a Scottish engraver in Fredericksburg to strike a medal to please an Indian chief who had come all the way from the Illinois country to seal a treaty with His Excellency. This Indian chief and his delegation, from Kaskaskia, had brought him buffalo hides with pictures painted on them to symbolize their alliance with the Virginians. It must have been with the agreeable feeling that he was worthily performing his last duty as governor that Jefferson prepared his speech and went out to their campfire to smoke, although he hated tobacco, the peace pipe with their chief.

Monday morning, June 4, the day the assembly had set for the election of a new governor, the delegates were routed out of their beds by young Jack Jouett who had ridden all night from the Cuckoo Tavern to warn them that Sir Banastre Tarleton, Cornwallis's cavalry commander, was on the way from Louisa Courthouse. Tarleton's plan was to surprise and nab the Virginia leaders. The delegates saddled their horses, passed the word they would meet again at Staunton, and galloped off by different roads. The government documents they packed in an iron chest and sent off by wagon. When Jefferson was aroused up at Monticello, he saw off the Speakers of the two Houses and several members who'd been spending the night with him. Then he started his family, but this time fairly inured to running away from the English, off towards Blenheim. When they were safe on their way he rode back to Monticello to see what he could see. When he looked down from his terrace he saw that a detachment of horsemen was already climbing the hill. Jefferson put the spurs to his horse and for fear they would catch up with him on the road plunged into the woods. He dined with his family that afternoon at Blenheim, quiet in the assurance that his political career was over.

"EVERYBODY SCAMPERING" was how Councillor Jacquelin Ambler's young daughter lightheartedly put it in a letter to a friend. In their hideouts and their isolated manors the Virginians fumed over their humiliation at Charlottesville. At Chantilly, his place in Westmoreland, Richard Henry Lee had been fretting for months. June 12 he sat down in a highly disturbed state to write the Virginia delegates in Congress: "I do give it to you gentlemen as my serious opinion that if immediate and powerful interposition does not take place, commensurate to the certain danger, that all the country below the Mountains will be in the power of the enemy in a few months."

Things were not quite so bad as they seemed to Richard Henry Lee on that day. Supplies and troops were gathering. The foundations had been laid for the strategy that culminated at Yorktown. Washington, who was hanging on in the North hoping to spring a trap on the British in New York, had already ordered General Anthony Wayne with Pennsylvania troops to Lafayette's support, and they were on the way. Steuben had made a mess of his part of the show and lost the stores he had been detached to guard at the fork of the James, but Lafayette had handled his army like an old soldier. "When one is twenty three, has an army to command and Lord Cornwallis to oppose," he wrote, "the time that is left is not too long for sleep."

The marquis saved the day. Attracted by his talent, his youth and his charm, volunteers riding their own horses began to join him. Never risking an engagement, he managed, by making brilliant use of the rivers and backcountry trails, to hang on Cornwallis's flanks just out of reach and little by little to turn Cornwallis's stately march down the peninsula between the York and the James into what looked more and more like a retreat. By the time the French fleet finally did arrive he had Cornwallis so cooped up that the American forces were able to carry out the plan he and Jefferson and Steuben had worked out against Arnold the spring before.

The Virginia legislators, however, drawing rein at Staunton, would hardly have been human if they hadn't wanted to pin the blame for Virginia's humiliation on somebody. Steuben, they said, ought to be hanged for his conduct; and Jefferson didn't escape his share of abuse.

On the same day that Richard Henry Lee was writing his letter at Chantilly, fat but nimble Thomas Nelson, Jr., who already commanded the militia under Lafayette, was duly elected constitutional governor with a few added emergency powers. The delegates further voted to present an elegant sword and a pair of pistols to Jack Jouett in gratitude for his warning that Tarleton's cavalry was on the way. Then George Nicholas, the son of Jefferson's old political opponent and admirer, Robert Carter Nicholas, got to his feet, and moved an inquiry into the conduct of the executive. The motion passed.

No political dart ever found its mark in a less protected hide. It was particularly painful that it came from the son of an old friend, and from one of those young men the conduct of whose education, in law and letters, Jefferson so much enjoyed. Yet he knew quite well whom he had to blame: it was not so much George Nicholas as it was Patrick Henry.

Jefferson could not get accustomed to criticism. He'd given

up the best years of his life to the public service. He would never serve again; he would remain a private man.

The news of the action of the House of Delegates had reached him at Poplar Forest. That remote plantation, just beyond the gap through which the James breaks so picturesquely out from the mountains, had been part of Patty's inheritance from her father. All his life it was to be Jefferson's favorite haven of refuge. This time he'd barely settled his family in the house and begun to get accustomed to the bad news that Cornwallis had established his headquarters at Elk Hill down the James when he suffered a further misfortune. Riding over the farm he had a fall from his horse. He was so badly shaken up he kept his bed for several weeks. For a man reputed to be one of the crack riders of Virginia, this accident was hard to take.

As soon as Jefferson could get his long aching frame into the saddle he hurried back to Monticello to ready his papers for an inquiry at the next session of the assembly. From there he wrote George Nicholas asking him to list his charges so that he could prepare his defense. George Nicholas replied rather lamely denying that he was an accuser, and was careful to make it clear, by speaking of the executive in the plural in his letter that his inquiry referred to the governor and council as a board and not to any single individual. But Jefferson persisted in treating the motion as a personal affront.

Jefferson's friends, and the large group of conservatives who distrusted Patrick Henry, prepared to defend him. A special election was arranged in Albemarle so that Jefferson could appear in the House of Delegates in his own defense. When the assembly met in Richmond that fall no charges were brought Jefferson rose in his seat and read off the list of queries George Nicholas had sent him, answered them, point by point, and the assembly hastened to vote him a congratulatory address The agonies of the invasion were being forgotten anyway in jubilation over Cornwallis's surrender. As a mark of their confidence they elected Jefferson their delegate to Congress.

He refused the appointment to Congress as he'd refused earlier in the summer, Congress's appointment as one of the plenipotentiaries to negotiate a peace. As he wrote Lafayette, i wasn't without a pang that he had turned down that chance to travel abroad: "I lose an opportunity, the only one I ever had and perhaps ever shall have of combining public service with private gratification, of seeing countries whose improvements in science, in arts, and in civilization it has been my fortune to admire at a distance but never to see." There were limits, he kept explaining, to the demands the public could make on a citizen. He felt he had earned the right to give his time to his studies, to his philosophical pursuits and to his farm and family.

His farm indeed needed his attention, for though Tarleton's men had behaved like gentlemen at Monticello, Cornwallis's troops had ravaged his wife's properties on the James, burning barns and fields and fences, slaughtering pigs and cattle and commandeering horses. "He carried off also about thirty slaves," Jefferson wrote of Cornwallis a few years later. "Had this been to give them freedom he would have done right; but it was to consign them to inevitable death from the smallpox and the putrid fever, then raging in the camp." In his papers there is a list of the names of the poor creatures who came back to die in the slave quarters. On the James River plantations all the slow hard work of getting a plantation in running order had to be begun again from the beginning.

He'd never thought managing his plantations work enough to keep him busy. He started to practice law again. He had been appointed one of the examiners for the bar, and as a result had a visit from William Short, a rich and charming young man from Spring Garden in Surry County. Under Wythe and the Reverend Madison, Short had graduated with honors from William and Mary just before the British invasion. Jefferson suffered for lack of sons of his own, though he had almost a son in young Peter Carr, his nephew. He liked Short the moment he set eyes on him. Like Monroe, at this confused point in his country's affairs, Short, an ardent and temperamental young man, found himself at loose ends. He became almost immediately another adopted son of Jefferson. Jefferson passed him for the bar, advised him on his reading and course of study; and, when he planned to go to Philadelphia to finish his studies, furnished him with letters to friends.

ALL THROUGH THE EXACTING ROUTINE of his public service he had dreamed of reaching a point where he could give up most of his time to natural philosophy. To his mind the subject included the whole field of science, from the study of the weather through botany, zoology and the philology of Indian language to his private observations of how long it took a slave to dig so many cubic feet of clay out of a ditch. Now there had already lain many months on his desk a series of questions forwarded to him from the secretary of the French ambassador. This Monsieur de Barbé-Marbois was eager to collect exact information about the politics, the economics and the natural history of North America to pass on to his government and to his friends among the Encyclopedists in Paris.

It was just the pretext Jefferson needed. He'd hardly settled in bed after his fall from his horse when he forgot the pain in his ribs and the greater agony of the smart of public criticism in formulating his answers to the Frenchman's questions. By the end of the summer he'd written out an account of the geography of his country clear to the Mississippi which sparkles freshly to this day. In his discussion of various hypotheses on the origin of marine shells found in high mountains, he expressed in a sentence what was to be the motto of scientists in the century to come. "Ignorance is preferable to error; and he is less remote from the truth who believes nothing, than he who believes what is wrong." At the end of the year he happily shipped off his *Notes on Virginia* to the French Embassy.

When the Albemarle electors met to choose their delegate for the House in the spring of 1782, they selected Jefferson and his father's old associate, Dr. Thomas Walker. They acted against Jefferson's expressed wishes because he was determined not to serve. He had been officially exonerated from accusation of wrongdoing as governor, and he considered that his public life was at an end. Even if he hadn't made his decision it would have been hard for him to leave Monticello at that moment Patty was soon to be brought to bed.

In this moment of anxiety and tension, the little society on the hilltop was enlivened by a visit from an agreeable French man. Jefferson had been flattered the summer before by his

ppointment as councillor of the American Philosophical Soci-
ty which had grown up around Benjamin Franklin and David
ittenhouse, the astronomer and mathematical-instrument
aker, in Philadelphia, though he was waiting, so he said, to
e told what his duties were. Now he was able to forget his
oubles for a few days in the congenial conversation of a man
ho hailed from the very inner circle of the Enlightenment.

The chevalier François Jean de Chastellux, who was a pro-
ssional soldier and amateur naturalist, was the author of works
ot only on military supply but on Italian music. He was a
ember of the French Academy. In his account of his visit he
rote that he found Jefferson cold and unsmiling at first but
hat after he'd been with him a couple of hours he felt that he'd
nown him all his life. He was amazed to find in the wilds of
irginia a man who not only kept a good table and knew French
ines and Italian vegetables, but who had built himself a stylish
ouse of great elegance; and who was as well posted as a Parisian
n the latest in literature and the arts.

They took walks together; they talked about art and music
nd politics, and about the animals and the birds that so inter-
ted Chastellux. He went down into a deep ravine near the
ouse to watch Jefferson's tame deer eat corn out of his hand.
Jefferson urged Chastellux and his friends not to miss the
Natural Bridge. When they tore themselves away from the
ttle civilized oasis of Monticello he rode sixteen miles with
em on their trail up into the Blue Ridge. It was only Patty's
pproaching confinement that prevented him from guiding
em all the way himself.

WHEN JEFFERSON RODE HOME, after putting his French friends
n their road, feeling a lingering glow from the wit and polish
f the chevalier's conversation, he must have already been full of
pprehension about Patty's condition. Childbearing for her
as a time of mortal danger. Medicine had no measures to cope
ith these troubles. What treatments the doctors used did
sually more harm than good. Men and women were pathet-
ally helpless before the curse of Eve in those days.

In early May Jefferson wrote the Speaker of the House firmly

declining to serve as a delegate. Two days later, too soo
perhaps, Patty was brought to bed. A little girl was born. Agai
they named her Lucy Elizabeth. At least this time the chil
lived. Patty herself never recovered.

The House refused to accept Jefferson's resignation an
threatened, as had happened once before, to send the sergear
at arms after him. When the news of Mrs. Jefferson's illne
reached Richmond, since his feeling for her was well knowr
the matter was by common consent let drop for a while, eve
though he'd been already appointed to a committee to de
with the pressing matter of the conflict of claims over Virginia
western lands. But his friends would not reconcile themselve
to his retiring permanently. For one thing no one else had s
much knowledge of the history of the western land question.

Jefferson could think of nothing but nursing his wife. Wit
that absolute devotion which was so characteristic of him h
threw himself into the task with meticulous care. Little Pats
who was ten at the time wrote half a century later a recor
of her mother's last illness. "As a Nurse no female ever ha
more tenderness or anxiety; he nursed my poor mother in tur
with Aunt Carr and her own sisters, setting up with her an
administering her medicines and drink to the last. For fou
months that she lingered he was never out of Calling. Whe
not at her bedside he was writing in the small room whic
opened immediately at the head of her bed."

At some time during her illness they must have been read
ing *Tristram Shandy* together. Sterne's fluent narrative, whic
combined bedchamber whimsy and damp-eyed pathos with
peculiar drollness of characterization, was immensely appreci
ated at the time, and Uncle Toby and Dr. Slop and the Widov
Wadman were familiar figures in the conversation of ever
literate Virginian. A taste for Sterne would exactly correspon
to the pungence of something racy and vivid and a little modis
that rises from the scant references to Patty found in Jefferson
letters. Now they'd been reading the inimitable descriptio
of Uncle Toby, marching forth with Corporal Trim to la
siege to the heart of the Widow Wadman.

"Now what can their two noodles be about, cried my fathe

o my mother—by all that's strange they are besieging Mrs. Wadman in form, and are marching round her house to make out the lines of circumvallation.

"I dare say, quoth my mother—But stop, dear Sir—for what my mother dared say upon the occasion of what my father did say upon it—with her replies and rejoinders, shall be read, perused, paraphrased, commented and discanted upon—or to say it all in a word, shall be thumbed over by Posterity in a chapter apart. . . .

"I will not argue the matter. . . ."

Patty knew that she was dying. She must have felt that the words that followed said just what she wanted to say because, sometime possibly when she was left for a moment alone, she copied them down on a piece of paper, painfully, because she was very weak, in her distinctive perpendicular hand:

> Time wastes too fast: every letter
> I trace tells me with what rapidity
> life follows my pen. The days and
> hours of it are flying over our heads
> like clouds of windy day never to
> return—more every thing presses on . . .

Perhaps it was from memory. She left out several words. Perhaps she was too weak to get them all down. Sometime later Jefferson came with his own pen and completed the paragraph

> . . . and every
> time I kiss thy hand to bid adieu, every absence
> which follows it, are preludes to that eternal separation
> which we are shortly to make!

She died September 6. "Mrs. Jefferson has at last shaken off her tormenting pains, by yeilding to them," wrote Edmund Randolph, who was living at nearby Colle, "and left our friend inconsolable."

"The scene that followed I did not witness but the violence of his emotion," wrote Patsy years later trying to piece out her ten-year-old's memories, "of his grief when almost by stealth I entered his room at night to this day I do not trust myself to describe. He kept his room for three weeks and I was never a moment from his side. He walked almost incessantly night and day only lying down occasionally when nature was completely exhausted on a pallet that had been brought in during his long fainting fit. . . . When at last he left his room he rode out and from that time he was incessantly on horseback rambling about the mountain on the least frequented roads and just as often through the woods."

Sometime in October Jefferson himself wrote Patty's sister Elizabeth Eppes, who had gone home to her family: "Patsy rides with me 5. or 6. miles a day and presses for permission to accompany me on horseback to Elk Hill whenever I shall go there. When that may be however I cannot tell; finding myself absolutely unable to attend to anything like business. This miserable kind of existence is really too burthensome to be borne, and were it not for the infidelity of deserting the sacred charge left to me, I could not wish its continuance for a moment. For what could it be wished? All my plans of comfort and happiness reversed by one single event and myself thrown on the world at a time of life when I should be withdrawn," he wrote. Then he crossed out the last few words and added, "and nothing answering in prospect before me but a gloom unbrightened with one chearful expectation."

Thomas Jefferson's grief at his wife's death became a legend in the family: the story was that he had sworn on her deathbed never to remarry. He buried her with his dear sister Jane and his dear friend Dabney Carr amid the pathetic little graves of the infants that had died so soon. On her stone he had engraved in Greek letters Achilles' plaint in the *Iliad* over the body of his comrade Patroclus:

> *Though the dead forget their dead with Hades in the grave*
> *Even there I shall remember my sweet friend.*

Gradually as the chestnuts began to turn russet with autumn and the sumac and the gum to catch fire on the hills he began to feel the blood flowing through his veins again. One channel of his life was stopped forever. The need to continue some kind of existence somehow began to find other courses. He

egan to answer letters which had lain all summer unanswered,
o pick up his law business.

Late in November he took the whole family of children
own to Ampthill, his good friend Archibald Cary's house
n the James, to be inoculated against smallpox. There he sat
own to write George Rogers Clark. As always he enjoyed
orresponding with his friend on the western frontier. For some
ime he'd been pondering stories he'd heard of mammoth bones
iscovered in the salt licks of Kentucky. "Any observations of
our own on the subject of the big bones or their history, will
ome acceptably to me, because I know you see the works of
ature in the great, and not merely in detail."

As he wrote he remembered that Clark too had been criti-
ized. His great services too were being belittled by the swarms
f little men who went around repeating Patrick Henry's slurs.
That you have enemies you must not doubt," Jefferson wrote,
when you reflect that you have made yourself eminent. If you
neant to escape malice you should have confined yourself with-
1 the sleepy line of regular duty." He went on to put Clark
n his guard against his enemy, who was the same as Jefferson's:
man, he wrote, who was "all tongue without head or heart."
Ie concluded defiantly: "That you may long continue a fit
bject for his enmity and for that of every other person of his
omplexion in the state, which I know can be only by contin-
ing to do good to your country and honor to yourself is the
arnest prayer of one who subscribes himself with great truth
: sincerity, Dr. Sir Your friend & servt."

Inside the calm philosopher who was to look on all things
vith an equal eye, desiring only to discover what was true,
nere was appearing the bitter shape of the virulent partisan
:ader. Already Jefferson knew that public life had claimed
im again. Earlier that month Congress had once more sent
im an appointment as plenipotentiary in Paris to negotiate
ne peace. This time he had accepted. "December 19 1782,"
e wrote on one of the blank pages of Dixon and Hunter's
'irginia Almanac for 1778: "Set out from Monticello for Phila-
elphia, France &c." The ampersand is written with a fine
ourish of the pen.

Chapter 6

IT WAS NOT till eighteen months later, after a term in Congress
and a tour of the New England towns, that Jefferson set sail
from Boston on the ship *Ceres*. He took his eleven-year-old
daughter Patsy with him and a Negro servant from Monticello.
He had left the two smaller girls with his sister-in-law, Elizabeth
Eppes, at Eppington on the lower James. The month was July.
It was a beautiful summer crossing with favoring winds.
Jefferson passed the time drinking light wines, reading *Don
Quixote* in Spanish, and drawing out the ship's owner on the
subject of the trade and commerce of the northern ports. As an
ambassador he was determined to represent the entire Confederation. He was an American first now and a Virginian
second. In his account book he noted the miles logged and the
seabirds and sharks and whales sighted. On the twenty-first day
the *Ceres* cast anchor at Cowes.

Jefferson put up at the Crown Inn in Portsmouth. While the
local doctor brought Patsy around from a bout of fever, he
passed his time driving around the countryside through narrow
lanes hemmed by hedges of thorn. As soon as Patsy felt better
they went on board the packet for Le Havre. They had the
usual Channel weather, and poor little Patsy was seasick. Their
cabin was a kind of hutch you had to crawl into on all fours.
The ship creaked and groaned and smelled villainously of pitch
and bilge, but by the first of August they were resting up at the
Aigle d'Or on the soil of France in the gray stone seaport of
Le Havre. Jefferson, who read French fluently, naturally discovered that he couldn't understand a word of the gabble of
porters and beggars that assailed their ears the minute they set
foot on the quai. The porters overcharged ferociously. Without
the help of an agreeable Irishman who spoke the vernacular
they would hardly have reached their hotel.

They drove to Paris in their own phaeton which had traveled

all the way from America with them. The post road led through Rouen and Mantes and Meulan, between the gently swelling cultivated hillsides of the valley of the Seine. It was harvesttime. Jefferson admired the careful cultivation of the fields; at the same time he was horrified by the ragged degradation of the working people. They stopped at Saint-Germain-en-Laye while Jefferson inspected the fourteen waterwheels and the complicated ducts and pumps which lifted the water of the Seine to the reservoirs on top of the hill that supplied the fountains at Versailles. Then next morning they found themselves driving in through the teeming streets of the largest city they had ever seen.

Paris in 1784 was a city of narrow thoroughfares that skirted huddles of medieval dwellings packed around Gothic churches and abbeys and huge fortifications like the Bastille. Here and there the tangled streets had been opened up into formal squares, like the place des Victoires or the place Royale. Driving through one of the crowded thoroughfares that cut through the city, hemmed by blocks of tall houses, the traveler occasionally caught a glimpse of trees in a paved open space, or a fountain set about with market stalls, or the massively ornamented portal of a palace or monastic building. In the vast place Louis Quinze, with its vista up the rue Royale towards the elegant façade of the old church of the Madeleine, the stonework was still creamy and new, and the bridge which continued from there across the Seine was still under construction.

At an hôtel d'Orléans on the rue de Richelieu right in the middle of the city they settled in the unfamiliar-smelling rooms and ate the unfamiliar-tasting food sent in from a nearby restaurant. Through the musty draperies that masked the tall windows they heard the chanting of street vendors and the shouts of carters and the clatter on the paving stones of hoofs of the horses of hackney cabs.

After a tremendous bout with tailors, shoemakers, peruke makers and the like, all very polite and expensive, Jefferson sallied forth dressed in proper Parisian style. Patsy too was transformed into a small model of a lady of fashion. He placed the little girl in a convent, the Abbaye de Panthémont on the rue de Grenelle, where he had received every assurance from the abbess that the good nuns tactfully refrained from trying to convert their Protestant students.

His first call was on Dr. Franklin, as senior of the three com-missioners who were to negotiate treaties with the European powers. The third commissioner, John Adams, had not returned yet from a trip to England to fetch his wife and daughter.

Franklin was living next door to Paris in the pleasant village of Passy. He was feeling his age; he had fits of the gout and was painfully afflicted with a stone in the bladder; but, now that the years of conniving had come to an end with the signing of the preliminaries of peace, he was thoroughly at ease in the world, and his establishment was no longer so enmeshed in painful webs of espionage. He was finding a little leisure for the pleasures of his private printing press; and to follow Mont-golfier's experiments with balloons; and to show up Mesmer's animal magnetism for a fraud; and finding time for one or two elderly flirtations. Without taking the business too seriously he was allowing himself to be crowned with laurels at garden fetes and apostrophized in couplets by young women in tunics, and petted and cuddled by all the sprightly noble ladies.

At this moment he probably was the most influential man in France. He was courted by old and young; his portrait was everywhere; Franklin busts and statuettes, Franklin jugs were on every mantelpiece. His face, so the story went, even appeared painted on the chamber pot. Now that Voltaire was dead Franklin had become the *philosophe par excellence* for the liber-tarian world of the Enlightenment, then ardently preparing the revolution which was to prove its monument and its grave.

Jefferson liked and appreciated Franklin. He became good friends with Franklin's grandson, William Temple, who was the illegitimate son of Franklin's own illegitimate son William and who had recently produced with the help of a young woman of Passy an illegitimate son of his own. Franklin's other grand-son, Ben Bache, sixteen at the time and fresh from a school in Switzerland, was to become Jefferson's devoted adherent. Still in spite of the admiration of the younger generation, and all the congenial contacts with the philosophical world of which that household was the center, Jefferson did not become exactly an intimate of Franklin's at Passy.

It was John Adams's family that furnished the homesick widower, in a foreign country, with the refuge among congenial compatriots he so much needed. In the pretty little village of Auteuil on the edge of the Bois de Boulogne, the Adamses had set up an outpost of New England. They shared with Richard Henry Lee's youngest brother Arthur a certain suspicion of the goings-on at Passy. In Congress the Virginian Lees and the Massachusetts Adamses, both John and Samuel, had consistently opposed the financial operations of Robert Morris, with whom Franklin had commercial ties. Jefferson, particularly on the question of western lands, had opposed them too. At Auteuil he could speak his mind about American politics a great deal more freely than he could at Passy.

John and Abigail Adams were a solidly devoted couple. Their children loved and admired them. Young Abigail and John Quincy, who at seventeen was already portentously learned, were with them at Auteuil. There could hardly have been a more perfect example of the domestic happiness Jefferson's heart so craved. With Adams as with no other man, he could talk deeply of the science of government, and Abigail kept him continually amused by her reports on the follies of the French, as seen through the sturdy spectacles of her New England prejudices.

By the time Jefferson had moved to a house of his own in a new garden quarter growing up near where the Paris Opéra now stands, a small but agreeable American colony had begun to center in him and the Adams family. There was amiable Thomas Barclay, a Philadelphia merchant who had become established at Nantes, and who was now appointed consul general to take the commercial routine off Franklin's aged hands. There was Colonel David Humphreys, the Connecticut poet, who had arrived fresh from Washington's staff, and from the society of the young republic's first literary coterie which evolved at that time around the boomtown of Hartford. Humphreys was a solemn young man in his early thirties, an enthusiastic member of the Society of the Cincinnati, the

patriotic organization which had been formed by officers of
the Continental Army, and a great wearer of the uniform. He
came as secretary to the American mission. In spite of his
military bearing and his taste for pomp and circumstance, he
was an able person with many interests similar to Jefferson's
As soon as he arrived Jefferson asked Humphreys to live with
him, pointing out that another mouth to feed would add little
to his expenses. Soon they were joined by William Short, who
brought all the Virginia news. Short had been elected to the
Council of State but had resigned to follow Jefferson abroad
as private secretary. The three of them kept bachelors' hall that
first winter in Paris, drawn together by the strangeness of this
foreign land and of its inhabitants.

In spite of the pleasant company, the interest in learning the
language and rummaging in bookstores, and the richness of
architecture, sculpture and painting, Jefferson's winter was thoroughly miserable. At first sight the diplomatic circle of the
court of Versailles, in which Franklin had managed so sturdily
to thrive, appeared to him a hopeless morass of bribery, spying
and corruption. Jefferson doubted if he could ever learn to
swim in these foul waters. Then the climate didn't agree with
him. The sun never shone. The air was damp. For six week
that winter he didn't leave his room. "A seasoning," he called
it in a letter to Monroe.

Soon after he settled into his own house, Lafayette brought
him the news that his baby girl, the second Lucy Elizabeth
had died at Eppington of the whooping cough. The whole
family there had been ill. Elizabeth Eppes had lost one of her
own children too. Polly fortunately had recovered. The loss
of the little girl threw him back into the mood of the month
following his wife's death. Out of six children only two survived, and between him and his younger daughter the whole
ocean raged.

Added to the ache of bereavement, and to the frustrations of
trying to learn the intricacies of protocol and diplomacy, was
a continual harassment about money. A diplomat had to keep
up a certain style. As a landed Virginian Jefferson had been a
free spender all his life. Now he found his expenses far out

running his income. It took so many servants to keep a house going. Whenever an envoy made an official call at Versailles, protocol proved a bottomless pit. A sulky had to be hired. Flunkies had to be tipped. Jefferson wrote Monroe to see whether, without insisting too much, he couldn't induce Congress to pay at least the unavoidable expenses of a diplomat's outfit.

Jefferson never learned to like the diplomatic life. At first he smarted a little at finding himself very much out on the fringes as "the lowliest of the diplomatic tribe," but when he did get to know the *corps diplomatique* he found the envoys of the powers of Europe boring when they weren't scoundrelly.

"My duties at Paris were confined to a few objects," he summed up his mission in his autobiography, "the receipts of our whale oils, salted fish & salt meats on favorable terms: the admission of our rice on equal terms with that of Piedmont Egypt & the levant; a mitigation of the monopolies of our tobacco by the Farmers-general, and a free admission of our productions into their islands were the principal commercial objects which required attention."

Opening the French market to American products was an endless slow grind; but there came to him two commissions from his native state which gave him real pleasure to execute. One was to find a sculptor worthy of carving a statue of Washington and the other was to furnish the state of Virginia with plans for a new state capitol.

For the sculptor, he picked Jean Antoine Houdon whose seated figure of Voltaire, now at the Théâtre Français, was already famous. Houdon at forty-four was undoubtedly the best sculptor in Europe. He had won the grand prize at the Beaux-Arts at eighteen and had hurried off to Rome to study. Ten years later he had carved a Diana so thinly draped that she caused great scandal when she was exhibited at the Louvre. Catherine of Russia, patron of the avant-garde arts of the time, carried the lady off to Saint Petersburg. As a result Houdon received orders from all the cultured European courts.

When Jefferson went to see him he nevertheless consented to leave the statues of kings unfinished and to make the hazardous voyage to America to do a head of Washington. Jefferson had brought along a portrait of Washington, but they agreed it was absurd to try to work from a portrait when the original was available at Mount Vernon. Houdon, attracted by the glory of the libertarian general, after considerable haggling, it must be admitted, agreed to do a bust for much less than he charged royalty; but he insisted that his life must be insured at ten thousand livres in case he perished on the Atlantic. For Houdon the professional attraction of the trip was that besides doing the bust he hoped to win the commission for an equestrian statue of Washington which Congress had voted. He and a couple of his workmen sailed on the same ship with Dr. Franklin, who, finally released from his embassy, was being conveyed to Le Havre in a royal litter amid the blessings of all France.

Meanwhile, in the execution of his second commission for the state of Virginia, Jefferson, whose taste was always for the cogent and the fresh, found himself embarked on the full current of the classical revival. Ever since he had drawn up the first bill for the removal of the Virginia capital to Richmond he had been exercised about what sort of buildings would be constructed there. At an early date he had already experimented with a tentative sketch of a plan for a temple-form building with columns. From the moment he first opened a copy of Leoni's translation of Andrea Palladio's *Four Books of Architecture* he must have been taken with Palladio's drawings and measurements of the Maison Quárree (he always followed Palladio's archaic spelling of the French *carrée*) at Nîmes. When he came to think over the need for an architecture which would express the essence of the young republic his mind settled more and more on the Maison Quarrée. Now in Paris he discovered a man who had recently published a set of drawings of the Augustan temple even more carefully measured than Palladio's had been. That man was Charles Louis Clérisseau who was dean of the academy of painting and sculpture which had its seat in a set of apartments in the Louvre.

When Jefferson went around to Clérisseau's studio, soon after he'd settled in Paris, the elegance and balanced strength of the Greek temple form burst on him anew. Immediately he bought

Clérisseau's book on Nîmes, and volumes by Englishmen under similar inspiration.

At Clérisseau's too for the first time, Jefferson found himself with the resources of a proper architect's drafting room. Here were modelers and draftsmen ready to put his amateur's sketches into a form where they could be used by a contractor. It was here that he learned to work with a hard pencil. Henceforth his architectural drawings had a professional air. He bought enough coordinated paper in Paris to last him most of his life.

In choosing the temple at Nîmes as his model he was choosing Roman architecture at the moment when it was nearest to Greek. Since Fiske Kimball made his careful study of the drawings in the Coolidge collection there has been no doubt that the basic plan for the Richmond capitol was Jefferson's. For simplicity, or perhaps because he despaired of getting Corinthian capitals properly executed in America, he changed the order of the porch to Ionic and thereby helped give the whole school of architecture which was to follow in the United States its distinctively Ionic flavor. He designed the interior chambers for the House and Senate and the conference room between. The arrangement of the windows was Jefferson's, and it was he who insisted, against the Frenchman's advice, on following exactly the proportions indicated by Clérisseau's own measurements of the actual temple at Nîmes. It is likely that Clérisseau furnished a good deal of the decorative detail. His draftsmen executed Jefferson's sketches and made a scale model in plaster, which is still preserved in the now very much transformed state capitol in Richmond.

The drawings and the model were finally shipped off to Monroe in Virginia. He was urged to make sure they were accepted even if it meant tearing down some of the work already done. Meanwhile Jefferson was writing Madison: "Do my dear friend exert yourself to get the plan begun on set aside & that adopted which was drawn here. It was taken from a model which has been the admiration of sixteen centuries."

As the building progressed, a good deal of Jefferson's original plan was changed by the commissioners. The pitch of the roof was altered, a bastard type of Ionic capital was used on the porch and three ugly windows were put in the pediment to give light to the attic. Even so, in its essence the transformed temple remains to this day as Jefferson planned it. From Latrobe's watercolor of Richmond in 1796 you can get an inkling of how cogently the capitol with its high white porch stood guard on its hill over the clapboard houses and the log huts of the raw little town at the falls of the James, its Ionic style admirably expressing the civic dignity of the republican frontier.

WHILE CLÉRISSEAU'S CRAFTSMEN were putting the finishing touches on the model of the Virginia capitol in March and April of 1786, Jefferson made an unexpected trip to England. When Franklin retired Congress had split up the European mission. Jefferson was accredited as sole minister to Versailles and John Adams was sent to the Court of St. James's. Their business was to keep up American credit with the bankers, to negotiate treaties of amity and commerce, particularly, if possible, with England; and to do something about putting an end to the attacks of Barbary corsairs on American shipping in the Mediterranean. Now that Lafayette was back in Paris and could prepare the way for him, Jefferson was beginning to find it easier to open doors at Versailles. "I was powerfully aided," wrote Jefferson, "by all the influence & the energies of the Marquis de la Fayette who proved himself equally zealous for the friendship & welfare of both nations."

Meanwhile John Adams in London had been taken with a fit of optimism. For a rebel he had not been too badly treated in England. He'd been received several times by His Majesty. The Prince of Wales had eaten supper with the Adams family on Grosvenor Square. There was just enough of John Bull about John Adams's pompous manner to make him personally likable to the men in the circle of government. Perhaps King George hoped, by playing on the vanity that stood out like a lace ruffle from Adams's shirtfront, to make him into a British agent; he had done it with other Americans.

Anyway Adams was allowed to believe that the prospects of a commercial treaty with England were improving. Then there was a treaty with Portugal ready to be signed, and Adams had all at once found himself on cozy terms with one Abdrahaman, the envoy from Tripoli. Adams had smoked with him and drunk Turkish coffee and conversed in a mixture of French, Italian and lingua franca on such friendly terms that Abdrahaman had sworn by his beard that he was for peace, and his secretary had cried out, "in extasy," so young Abigail reported: "Monsieur vous êtes un véritable Turk." At this juncture Adams, who may have suspected that a certain amount of wool was being pulled over his eyes, felt he needed Jefferson's cool head, so he packed off his secretary, young Abby's fiancé, Colonel William Smith of New York, to Paris to fetch him over.

Jefferson arrived early in March and was settled in lodgings in one of the handsome new dwellings on Golden Square. A few days later he was presented at court. King George took a look at Jefferson's tall frame and cold eyes and at the unyielding lines of his slender countenance and deliberately turned his back on him. There was no question in the king's mind as to which of the men had worded the Declaration of Independence. "It was impossible for anything to be more ungracious," wrote Jefferson in his autobiography. "I saw at once that the ulcerations in the narrow mind of that mulish being left nothing to be expected on the subject of my attendance."

The Portuguese ambassador immediately took sick, and Abdrahaman, when pinned down to chapter and verse, fingered his conversation beads and began to talk about money, much more money than the Americans had been authorized to offer as the price of a treaty.

There was nothing to it but to wait around and see the sights while hoping that the Portuguese diplomat would see fit to recover his health. Two days after he arrived Jefferson had already been to Drury Lane to see Mrs. Sarah Siddons. He took in the opera and a concert at the Pantheon. He drove out to Windsor Castle. He sat for his portrait to Mather Brown. The shops he found superb. He bought himself a set of china, a new harness for his carriage, some newly patented whale-oil lamps for his friends, and some bolts of muslin for his sister; and of course he acquired a great many books. He had a suit of clothes made and started a cabinetmaker to work on a copying press of his own designing. Since the royal snub, every English official door was closed, but he did accompany the Adams family in full regalia to a gaudy evening at the embassy of France's Most Christian King, Louis XVI.

Before going to the ball the party gathered for dinner at the Paradises' on Charles Street. The Paradises' dinners were famous. One of the landed Ludwell girls had married a most extraordinary character; John Paradise was an Oxford man, the son of a factor for the Levant Company who had made a stack of money in the Levant and settled in the West End of London to enjoy it. His mother was half Greek. He was a man of great personal attractiveness, extremely learned, a spendthrift, an occasional drunkard, and a devoted libertarian. His wife, Lucy Paradise, was the prototype of all charming, maddening southern belles. She was handsome, talkative, a nimble dancer and a good hostess; but she had a most disproportionate idea of her own importance. The Paradises couldn't get on together for a moment and they didn't care who knew it. The minute Lucy Paradise caught sight of Jefferson she fell in love with him, as "the First Character of our State." She never could understand why he did not share her passion.

Jefferson and John Paradise became good friends immediately. As a member of the Royal Society, Paradise knew everybody worth talking to in London. Right away he promised to teach Jefferson modern Greek, and to put him in touch with Dr. Charles Burney, the leading musical amateur of the time, for advice as to where to buy a harpsichord. He won Jefferson's heart by announcing his intention of setting sail immediately for Virginia to see to the management of his wife's estate—he'd already squandered his own—and to take up his duties as a citizen of the young republic. Jefferson wrote him a letter of introduction to George Wythe, which he took with him when he left for America. From then on Jefferson was the family friend. To the crushing volume of his correspondence was added a ceaseless flow of letters from the Paradises in Virginia begging for help and advice in their personal and financial difficulties, which didn't cease until John Paradise died a ruined inebriate and Lucy Paradise, still convinced that she ought to be married to Jefferson and first lady of the land, was shut up in Bishop Madison's fine new insane asylum at Williamsburg.

That afternoon on Charles Street the Paradises, though their debts were already enormous, still rode high. The food was good, the wines delicious, the company carefully chosen. Outside of the Adamses and their ever faithful Colonel Smith, there were the Russian ambassador, his attaché and his chaplain, the Venetian minister and the ever present Dr. Edward Bancroft, one of the king's American agents, who undoubtedly reported to the king next day everything that was said.

Dinner lasted three or four hours. Then the company scattered to their houses to dress, and met again to proceed in a body to the French Embassy. Mrs. Adams wore a full-dress court cap and two black and blue feathers which, she confided to her niece Miss Cranch in Braintree, cost her half a guinea apiece. Of the embassy ballroom she wrote, "It is most elegantly decorated, hung with a gold tissue, ornamented with twelve brilliant cut lustres, each containing twenty-four candles."

Two days later, Jefferson and Adams ventured forth in a hired chaise to get out from London and to see something of the English countryside. Both men needed a breath of air. Jefferson particularly, with his acute sensitivity to personal antagonism, was suffering from the snubs and slights the English inflicted on them in the course of official business. Now he and Adams, full of anticipation of green landscapes after the mud and soot of London, and of friendly talk unreported by prying ears, set out through the West End. The postilion cracked his whip. The harness jingled. It was the first of April and the hawthorn hedges were dewy with showers and sunshine.

Their first stop was at Chiswick where, early in the century, an Earl of Burlington had built a miniature version of the Villa Rotunda which had come to be considered the prime exemplar of the strict Palladian style in Great Britain. It had set the fashion for the Palladian craze in England, in spite of the raillery of the London wits, who went around saying that Chiswick House was too small to live in but too large to hang on a watch. To judge from his notes, Jefferson didn't think much of Chiswick

House either: "The octagonal dome has an ill effect both within & without; the garden shows too much of art." Still, even in its present shabby state one can see, in that very octagonal dome and in the scale of the columns of the pedimented porch, a hint of Jefferson's own second plan for Monticello.

They continued the excursion out through Buckinghamshire, winding through country lanes past villages of thatched stone cottages, stopping at the gatehouses of great estates to be escorted by flunkies, for a fee, over rolling lawns and along gravel paths. At Stowe, which in the great days of the Whig oligarchy had been the center of the political connivings of all England, Jefferson discovered that it took the work of fifteen men and eighteen boys to keep the enormous pleasure grounds weeded and trimmed. However, considerable portions of the lawns were used for pasture, he noted approvingly.

THE CURSE OF INEQUALITY had been impressed on Jefferson's mind by everything he saw in Europe. The division of mankind into master and servant continually irked him and dampened his delight in the architecture and the music. In the late fall of 1785, several months before his trip to England, he had sat down one evening in his lodgings at Fontainebleau to pour out his feelings to his old schoolmate, the Reverend Madison at the college at Williamsburg.

"Seven o'clock & retired to my fireside, I have determined to enter into conversation with you," he began. He explained that as a member of the diplomatic corps he had been forced to put in an appearance at Fontainebleau during the period of the royal hunts. The royal hunts, one of the more absurd of the gorgeous mummeries of the *ancien régime*, must have offended Jefferson both as a democrat and as a woodsman. "Courts," he wrote when jotting down advice to young Americans traveling in Europe, "to be seen as you would see the tower of London or menagerie of Versailles with their lions, tigers, hyenas & other beasts of prey."

"I set out yesterday morning," he told Madison of his first visit to Fontainebleau, "to take a view of the place. For this purpose I shaped my course towards one of the highest of the

mountains in sight, to the top of which was about a league...."
The forest of Fontainebleau, with its silvery brown beeches
and yellow poplars and shivering silver birches standing up out
of the russet bracken round gray outcroppings of rock, would
have had a special muted misty beauty in late October. The
air would have been full of the pungence of dry fern and
rotting leaves.

"As soon as I had got clear of the town I fell in with a poor
woman walking at the same rate with myself & going the same
course. Wishing to know the condition of the laboring poor I
entered into conversation with her, which I began by enquiries
for the path which would lead me into the mountain: & thence
proceeded to inquiries into her vocation condition & circumstances. She told me she was a day laborer at 8 sous or 4d. the
day: that she had two children to maintain, & to pay a rent
of 30 livres for her house (which would consume the hire of
75. days), that often she could get no employment & of course
was without bread. As we had walked together near a mile &
she had so far served me as a guide, I gave her on parting 24. sous.
She burst into tears of a gratitude I could see was unfeigned
because she was unable to utter a word. She had probably never
before received so great an aid. This little attendrissement with
the solitude of my walk, led me into a train of reflections on
that unequal division of property which occasions the num-
berless instances of wretchedness which I had observed in this
country & which is to be observed all over Europe...."
After some explanation he came to his conclusion: "I am
conscious that an equal division of property is impracticable,
but, the consequences of this enormous inequality producing
so much misery to the bulk of mankind, legislators cannot
invent too many devices for subdividing property, only taking
care to let their subdivisions go hand in hand with the natural
affections of the human mind, the descent of property of every
kind therefore to all the children, or to all the brothers and
sisters, or other relations in equal degree, is a politic measure &
a practicable one." He's justifying of course the necessity for
his own laws of inheritance for the state of Virginia, which he
already knew were earning him, every year in greater degree,

the dislike and suspicion of the large landowners. "Another means of silently lessening the inequality of property is to exempt all from taxation below a certain point, & to tax the higher portions of property in geometrical progression as they rise. Whenever there are in any country uncultivated lands & unemployed poor, it is clear that the laws of property have been so far extended as to violate natural right. The earth is given as a common stock for man to labor & live on."

Part of the stimulus of travel in foreign countries lies in the fact that it makes clearer to you the picture of your own country you hold in your mind's eye. As Jefferson grew older and found no one to replace his dead wife he was becoming hedged in with a peculiar private solitude, in spite of his love for his daughters and his good friendships. In that solitude the driving passion that kept him trudging ahead through the drudgery of public life was love of country. In Europe, America was always in the back of his mind as a standard of reference. Everything he saw and learned he judged accordingly as he thought it harmful or beneficial to the people of his young republic.

THE SUMMER AFTER HIS TRIP to England, Parisian society, where Jefferson had found himself lonely notwithstanding the universal politeness he so appreciated in the French, suddenly opened up vistas in every direction. This was partly due to the devotion of Lafayette, who had come back to France more American than ever, bringing with him two young Indian attendants in deerskins and feathers; he was ready to exert himself to the utmost to serve the American cause.

Lafayette admired Jefferson for the rigor of his mind and his complete dedication to human freedom. Now that Franklin had gone home no one else exemplified so completely the republican virtues. Lafayette, theatrical, and rich and wellborn enough to scorn money and care only for fame, was full of disinterested enthusiasm for noble causes. His wit and high spirits were irresistible. His faults, his appetite for popularity and his pathetic ignorance of men's ordinary motives that came from being brought up in a rank of society too remote from the petty toils of everyday life, were to show up later. Fresh arrived from triumphs in America he seemed to the French reformers to be the chivalrous young marshal of every tendency which could lead France to a better future. Already the reformers among the nobles and in the law courts were becoming known as *les américains*. Lafayette was the *américain par excellence*. The fact that he was feared and hated by the reactionaries merely added to his charm. An introduction by Lafayette into the stylish salons brought the bright eyes of the ladies, brimful of love, to bear on the tall rusty-haired Virginian.

Jefferson was a little more at home with the language by now. Parisian manners were no longer strange to him. He had moved to the charming hôtel de Langeac, a town house decorated in the delicate style then in fashion, out near the end of the Champs Elysées. He had met a number of attractive women.

There was Madame de Tessé, a lady-in-waiting to the queen and one of Lafayette's favorites. She lived amid great gardens at Chaville not far from Versailles. She shared Jefferson's passion for horticulture and his taste for the classical revival, and became his lifelong friend. There was the salon at the hôtel des Monnaies of the brilliant young wife of the mathematician the Marquis de Condorcet. Frail Madame de Corny, the wife of another French veteran of the American war, was always ready to pour Jefferson a cup of tea at their house on the chaussée d'Antin. There was the drawing room of nervous Madame Necker, wife of the Swiss banker, and their daughter who was to be one of the renowned women of Europe under the name of Madame de Staël. They all loved to talk politics, they dabbled in painting, they reveled in the antique.

Jefferson had a gift for friendship with women: his most self-revealing letters are always to the wives of his friends. His faculty of really paying attention to what women had to say, combined with just a trace of gallantry, endeared him to the well-read ladies who were the pivots round which French society revolved. That summer was full of petticoats and tender messages. As the liberal tide rose in France, it was enough to be an American. As American minister Jefferson found himself very much à la mode.

The de la Rochefoucaulds, great friends of Jefferson's old

acquaintance Chastellux, who had visited Monticello, kept continuous open house at their town house on the rue de Seine or at their rural mansion; they were the center of a whole society of enthusiasts for the American republic. It was amid the splendor and the hospitality and the libertarian talk of this household that young Short, Jefferson's secretary, fell desperately and visibly in love with the pretty wife of one of the dukes, who, twenty years younger than her husband, was known affectionately to her friends as Rosalie.

The liaison worried Jefferson. No doubt he was pleased that the ladies found the graceful young man, whom he considered virtually his adopted son, attractive; but he feared, and with justification so it turned out, that a love affair of this sort would interfere with the wholesome American career he was planning for him. He wanted Short, after he'd absorbed all the European information that could be useful to a Virginia gentleman, to go home and settle down to the stable pleasures he himself so craved. He had great hopes of Short's abilities but he felt the young man would become a more useful citizen of the commonwealth if he were happily married to a devoted wife, raising a family of children and managing a good-sized farm.

In his guarded way he lectured Short on the subject. It must have amused young Short, and possibly alarmed him in turn for his preceptor's happiness, to discover before the summer was out that Jefferson himself was deep in an amourette of the most fashionable sort.

It all began with a trip to Les Halles. Jefferson, who was ruminating a plan for a new market for Richmond, was interested in the novel lighting of the dome being erected over one of the Parisian market buildings. He asked John Trumbull, the Connecticut painter, who was staying with him at the time, to drive downtown with him to take a look at it. In London, Trumbull had made friends with Richard Cosway, a painter of miniatures much the rage, who was now in Paris getting the likenesses of the Duchesse d'Orléans and her children. Though Cosway was a dandified monkey-faced little man, he was asked everywhere in London painting and literary circles, for the simple reason that Cosway had an attractive wife. Trumbull, perhaps himself not unmoved by the young lady's charms, asked the Cosways to join the party.

Maria Cosway had been brought up in Florence. She was the daughter of an English couple who had kept a boardinghouse there. A painter of some talent in her own right, she had been taken up by Angelica Kauffmann, the young Swiss painter who had become Sir Joshua Reynolds's "Miss Angel" when she went to England. Sir Joshua had been very kind to Miss Angel's protégée. Everybody admired her fluffy hair and her tender landscapes. When she let Cosway, whose miniatures were highly profitable, marry her, the pair took a house in Pall Mall and entertained there in noble style. A pretty wife could be an asset to a fashionable portrait painter; Cosway knew just when to look the other way while Maria was receiving the attentions of a prospective sitter. Maria enjoyed playing Beauty to his Beast. She was indeed pretty, as the surviving portraits bear witness. Her hair had a golden glint. Her eyes were very blue and her skin very fair. She had a cute little pout and used little Italianate shrugs and gestures and spoke English with a trace of an accent. Jefferson found her irresistible.

He disguised the story a little under the philosophical whimsy of the dialogue between his head and his heart which he sent her later after her husband had snatched her away to London. "My visit to Legrand & Molinos had public utility for its object," he had his head say. "A market is to be built in Richmond. What a commodious plan is that of Legrand and Molinos; especially if we put on it the noble dome of the Halle aux Bleds. If such a bridge as they showed us can be thrown across the Schuylkill at Philadelphia, the floating bridges taken up & the navigation of that river opened, what a copious provision will be added, of wood & provisions, to warm and feed the poor of that city. While I," his head tells his heart, "was occupied with these objects, you were dilating with your new acquaintances & contriving how to prevent a separation from them. Every soul of you had an engagement for the day. Yet all these were to be sacrificed that you might dine together, lying messengers were to be despatched into every quarter of the city, with apologies for your breach of engagement. You particularly had the effrontery to send word to the Dutchess Danville"—he meant the Duchesse d'Anville, a sarcastic and strong-minded old lady—"that, on the moment we were setting out to dine with her, despatches came to hand which required immediate attention . . . well, after dinner to St. Cloud, from St. Cloud to Ruggieri's . . ."

Ruggieri's was a public garden where the belles and the beaux walked in the evening through illuminated perspectives of trees and watched fireworks, while among the cadences of the orchestra they overheard the whispers of gallantries around them. Even after the rockets and set pieces Jefferson and Maria Cosway felt that the magical evening must be stretched out longer. "& if the day had been as long as a Lapland summer day, you still would have contrived means among you to have filled it." Even then it was hard to part.

It was early September, when a little russet appears on the horse-chestnut trees and the greens in the gardens of the valley of the Seine are at their darkest and densest, and at the end of every vista the river glistens under a blue haze. Every day the American minister's phaeton appeared at the Cosways' lodgings to take Maria on a fresh excursion. She was full of charming little caprices. She took in the buildings and the gardens with a painter's eye. Jefferson neglected his dispatches, forgot responsibilities, let himself go on a series of days of pure pleasure as he never had before. After Trumbull left Paris, Jefferson managed to take Maria tête-a-tête to every garden and building he loved best in the environs of Paris.

"How well I remember them all," he had his heart say in one of his letters after her return to London, "& that when I came home at night & looked back to the morning, it seemed to have been a month agone. . . . Paint to me the day we went out to

St. Germains. How beautiful was every object! The Pont de Neuilly, the hills along the Seine, the rainbows of the machine of Marly, the terrace of St. Germains, the chateaux, the gardens ... the wheels of time moved on with a rapidity of which those of our carriage gave but a faint idea. And yet in the evening when one took a retrospect of the day, what a mass of happiness had we travelled over."

Of course Jefferson began to dream of getting the Cosways, and particularly Maria, over to America. "I see nothing impossible," he had his heart write, "in that proposition. And I see things wonderfully contrived sometimes to make us happy. Where could they find such subjects as in America for the exercise of their enchanting art? Especially the lady, who paints landscapes so inimitably. She wants only subjects worthy of immortality to render her pencil immortal. The Falling Spring, the Cascade of Niagara, the Passage of the Potowmac through the Blue Mountains, the Natural Bridge ... and our own dear Monticello, where has nature spread so rich a mantle under the eye? Mountains, forests, rocks, rivers. With what majesty do we there ride above the storms! ...

"If your letters are long as the bible," he added after a mock apology for boring her with the long sermon of his dialogue, "they will appear short to me. Only let them be brimful of affection."

Her letters turned out to be short indeed. Maria Cosway was very much taken up with her own affairs. She and her husband had their careers to make. Americans were the vogue that season. Nothing could have been more in fashion than a few weeks' flirtation with the long-limbed minister plenipotentiary from the wilds of Virginia; but all the really important customers were in England. Her answers to his letters gradually revealed a spoiled, self-centered, and not too interesting young woman. Even before the Cosways left Paris the rosy interlude had been brusquely interrupted.

Her curly golden hair under the broad hats, the scent of her ruffles, the sweet intimacies while the phaeton whirled through the lanes of early autumn: the idyll had gone to Jefferson's head. He felt like a boy again. Under circumstances that are far from clear, the minister plenipotentiary had tried to jump a fence while out walking in some public garden near his house, failed to clear it, and had dislocated his wrist in falling. The pain was atrocious. He hurried back to his house and called in a brace of surgeons. The wrist was to trouble him for the rest of his life.

Pretty little Maria, instead of hurrying to her lover's side when she heard of the accident, had hurried with her husband out to Saint-Cloud to dine with the Duchess of Kingston.

Chapter 7

JEFFERSON USED HIS BROKEN WRIST as a pretext to learn to write with his left hand. He was soon writing as clearly with it as with his right. He put the best face he could to his bruised feelings by setting the little liaison in a playful literary light in the famous *Dialogue*. He and Maria continued writing each other letters which were mutually unsatisfactory. Hers were full of complaints. There was a painful episode the following summer when she returned to Paris queening it over a fashionable crew. She had invited Jefferson to eat an English breakfast with her the morning before she left for London. When he went to her lodgings she had already gone. She sent back a flutter of awkward little notes of apology as she fled.

His accident, a sudden spate of official business, and perhaps his preoccupation with the lovely Maria, caused him to put off a drive south he'd been planning in the fall of 1786 down into the Midi. He wanted to study the workings of the canal de Languedoc, which linked the Loire River and the French ports on the Bay of Biscay with the Mediterranean. And he wanted to be sure to see Nîmes where stood the Maison Quarrée which he had studied with such affection.

Finally in February 1787 he was able to break off his official duties for long enough to climb into a hired chaise and rumble out of Paris for his tour. He had been determined to go alone. 'I think one travels more usefully alone because he reflects more," he had told a friend. Having a servant, he wrote back to Short whom he'd left in charge, would "only serve to insulate me from the people among whom I am." On this one excursion he was bound he would act according to the advice he gave other American travelers: "Take every possible occasion for entering the houses of the laborers, & especially at the moments of their repast; see what they eat, how they are clothed, whether they are obliged to work too hard; whether the government or their landlord takes from them an unjust proportion of their labor; on what footing stands the property they call their own, their personal liberty &c &c."

His letters from the road are brimful of delight. From Lyons he writes Short that in spite of the rain, hail and snow that had followed him down from Paris, he had thoroughly investigated the wine country. French wines were getting to be one of his specialties, but he was even more interested in the people who tended the vineyards. "I . . . rambled through their most celebrated vineyards, going into the houses of the laborers, cellars of the Vignerons & mixing & conversing with them as much as I could.

"Architecture," he went on, "painting, sculpture"—from the giddy sight-seeing days with Maria Cosway he'd learned to be more than ever aware of the pleasures of the trained eye— "antiquities, agriculture & the condition of the laboring poor fill all my moments. . . ."

Somewhere below Lyons in the deep valley of the Rhône he came out into the sunshine. The almonds were in bloom. There was a pale yellow green on the willows. "I am now in the land of corn, vine, oil & sunshine," he wrote Short. "What more can a man ask of heaven? If I should happen to die in Paris I should beg you to send me here, and have me exposed to the sun. I am sure it will bring me to life again." This was from Aix-en-Provence, a little red-tiled white-walled resort town where the doctors had instructed him to bathe his wrist in the warm springs.

He was delighted with the town and the white sunshine that shimmered among the pollarded planes of its shady walks. He lightheartedly wrote Short that the cleanliness of its streets was the result of the poverty of the soil which made manure such a rarity it was brushed up into a basket as soon as it fell. He spoke of the thyme and lavender growing on the waste grounds. He found out what the peasants ate: "Their bread is half wheat, half rye, made once in three or four weeks to prevent too great consumption. In the morning they eat bread with an anchovy or an onion. Their dinner in the middle of the day is bread, soup and vegetables. Their supper the same. With their vegetables they always have oil & vinegar. The oil costs about eight sous the pound. . . ."

After four days he got tired of sitting with his wrist in the warm water and hurried on. Wherever he went, he was "nourished with the remains of Roman grandeur." Already at Lyons he'd seen "some feeble Roman remains." At Vienne there was a palace; at Orange an amphitheater and an arch of Marius; and at Nîmes he finally found the long waited for exquisite morsel of architecture, the square house he'd studied with so much care, the Maison Quarrée. There he gazed up at the gold-tinted fluting of the columns crowned with acanthus "like a lover at his mistress," for so long that in later life he used to tell people he'd spent a whole ten days there doing nothing else.

Marseille came next. He enjoyed Marseille. He inquired about the drying of figs, the culture of capers, the harvesting of pistachio nuts, the planting of vineyards. He wrote enthusiastically to Mazzei that a friend of Mazzei's there had promised to introduce him to a well-informed gardener. "From men of that class I have derived the most satisfactory information in the course of my journey & have sought their acquaintance with as much industry as I have avoided that of others who would have made me waste my time in good society."

As he drove along the dry flowering hillsides looking out over the briny azure of the Mediterranean, however, he thought not only of the scenery, of agriculture and of architecture; his mind also kept dwelling on the Assembly of Notables which had come to Versailles to advise the king on reforms governmental and financial. He had been present at the opening sessions a few days before he left Paris. This was a moment when the reform-minded French might be expected to listen to a sugges-

tion from the author of the Declaration of Independence. He was no man to try to impose his ideas directly, but he knew that the salon of his dear friend Madame de Tessé, so near Versailles, would become the center of all the progressive circle. So he had included in a letter to her on the beauties of Nîmes a detailed plan for reform of the French government. It was the same plan he had sketched for Lafayette in a hasty note before he had left Paris. Jefferson's great hope at that time was in Lafayette, who he felt was thoroughly enough steeped in American institutions to lead his people to liberty.

In Marseille he made the decision to push on into Italy. One of the aims of his journey had been to find out why Piedmont rice brought a better price on the market than Carolina rice. He wanted to study its cultivation at first hand.

, engraving of a
e harvest in eighteenth-
ury France. Inset, a
iature of Jefferson's
;hter Patsy, painted in
; by Joseph Boze
n she was seventeen
s old. Bottom, the
;on Carrée in Nîmes,
:h inspired Jefferson's
plans for the new
:ol in Richmond.

As his little mule train zigzagged up the mountains beyond Nice, the road rose above the fragrance of the blossoming orange. Then it left the olives below and crossed bare flanks of mountains thick with aromatic herbs. There was still snow among the pines on the upper slopes. A thousand mules, he noted, passed every week between Nice and Turin. He was impressed by the sight of olive trees growing out of mere masses of rock in the mountains. Immediately he guessed the immense importance of the olive in the economy of the Mediterranean peoples, and began to wonder whether it could be of use in America.

He was a week out of Nice before he could ride out over the embankments round the rice fields of the Lombard plain. He carefully noted every detail of the construction of the machine that beat the husks off the rice, decided that the Lombard rice was a special variety and arranged to have a bag of the seed smuggled back to Nice for him by a stout muleskinner named Poggio.

In Milan, Jefferson was struck with the scenes painted on the outside walls of the houses. He took up his part of minister plenipotentiary long enough to try to induce the merchants there to import American whale oil. The cathedral, he told his friends, was "a worthy object of philosophical contemplation; to be placed among the rarest instances of the misuse of money," which is as good a description as you can find of that particularly mistaken pile of bombastic masonry.

In the dry grounds of Pavia he found them planting Indian corn. With a pang of homesickness he watched the peasants cover the yellow grains with a pointed hoe. He was as far from the cornfields of Albemarle as he'd ever be in his life again. Before he left the rice fields he stuffed the pockets of his great-coat with the famous seed rice which he later sent over for trial to the Agricultural Association in Charleston.

In Genoa he ate strawberries, visited the marble workers with an eye to the mantels at Monticello, and noted an economical type of scaffolding used by masons building houses. From there he took passage on a tartan; but after two seasick days, possibly bucking a mistral, the ship put into Noli. Meanwhile he had been distracting himself from his discomfort by cogitating on how the reflection of the sky changed the color of seawater. From the little fishing port he continued by the coastal path. The trip, he wrote Patsy, was fatiguing: two days "clambering the cliffs of the Appenines, sometimes on a mule, sometimes on foot, according as the path was more or less difficult,—& two others travelling through the night as well as the day without sleep." Still he was delighted with the sheltered valleys, the shingly beaches, the tiny harbors, the continually changing combinations of steep green land with blue sea of the Italian Riviera. "If any person wished to retire from his acquaintance to live absolutely unknown, & yet in the midst of physical enjoyments, it should be in some of the little villages of this coast where air, water and earth concur to offer what each has most precious Here are nightingales, pheasants, partridges, quails. . . . The earth furnishes wine, oil, figs, oranges, & . . . the sea yields lobsters, crabs, oysters, thunny. . . ."

May 1 he was in Nice again. His next objective was to see

he Languedoc canal; canals were needed in America. Heading
or Cette, where Louis XIV's great work began, he stole a few
minutes on the way to visit a gristmill where the water that
urned the mill wheels was pumped up by steam. There he
alked with the engineer, an Abbé Arnal who held a royal
atent to apply steam to the propulsion of boats. While Jefferson
lways disclaimed any expert knowledge of steam engines,
alking about machinery gave him as much pleasure as gazing
t a well-modulated building or a lovely landscape.

Driving on, at Cette he at last gave himself a rest from the
hafing of saddles on mules and the jouncing of the carriage
ver stony roads.

"I dismounted my carriage from its wheels, placed it on the
eck of a light bark & was thus towed on the canal instead of
ie post road," he wrote Short. "Of all the methods of travel
have ever tried, this is the pleasantest. I walk the greater part
f the way along the banks of the canal, level and lined with a
ouble row of trees which furnish shade. When fatigued I take
at in my carriage, where, as much at ease as in my study I
ad, write and observe. My carriage being of glass all round
lmits a full view of all the varying scenes through which
am shifted, olives, figs, mulberries, wines, corn & pasture,
illages & farms . . . [even] a double row of nightingales along
ie banks of the canal in full song. . . . What a bird the night-
igale would be in the climates of America! We must colonize
im thither."

As he glided along the canal on a bark drawn by a single
orse, he ruminated on the lives of the people. It offended him to
:e women working the locks and handling the heavy sweeps.
[e also disliked the notion of country people huddling in vil-
ges. "Certain it is that they are less happy & virtuous in villages
ian they would be insulated with their families on the grounds
iey cultivate." The people were poor. Everything had a down-
odden look. The more he saw of European governments the
ore he felt that their chief function was to beat the people
irther down into misery.

He continued jotting down his notes as his barge slid gently
irough the early summer landscape. In the distance the Pyre-

nees were still snowy to the left. "The canal yeilds abundanc
of carp and eel." He drifted through Marseillette and Car
cassonne. At Naurouze he studied the locks. As soon as h
reached Paris his notes on their construction were to be for
warded to Washington to use in planning the Ohio canal.

From Toulouse he set out in his carriage for Bordeaux. The
he took a sweep through part of Brittany. "The villages an
nounce a general poverty, as does every other appearance.
At last he drove back to Paris. At the hôtel de Langeac he wa
embraced by the welcoming arms of young Short, and wa
greeted by a circle of countenances beaming and bowing
Petit, his maître d'hôtel, and Espagnol, his valet; and the flash
ing teeth of the slaves from Monticello, and the porter and th
cook and the gardener and the footmen and perhaps the mys
terious "poor old woman" who bobs up from time to time a
the recipient of gratuities in his account book. When he an
Short retired upstairs to the study to take up official busines
the minister plenipotentiary found himself confronted b
staggering great packages of mail, piled high on the delicat
Louis XVI tables.

THE LOOSE ENDS OF ALL THE TASKS Jefferson had set himself a
minimum accomplishments when he first arrived in Paris wer
still dangling from his desk to plague him. First was the probler
of the Barbary States. As the Mediterranean trade in America
bottoms increased, the pirate galleys of the Moors and th
Algerines were increasingly seizing American ships and holdin
their crews for ransom. Congress was slow in transmitting th
funds needed to buy the poor devils out. When Jefferson fir
arrived in France it had seemed to him reasonable to hope tha
he might induce a few European governments to combine i
an expedition against these raiders. Lafayette in his grandios
manner had offered himself to head an international punitiv
force, but not even Lafayette could rouse in the chancellerie
any interest in the plan. Jefferson was to learn from experienc
that European governments could not be induced to work to
gether for any reasonable purpose whatsoever.

Then there was his daily struggle, in which again Lafayette

help proved unavailing, to shake loose the tobacco trade, so important to Virginia, from the French monopoly of the farmers-general. Here he was hindered by the fact that Robert Morris, the wizard of congressional finances, had made his own arrangements from Philadelphia with the farmers-general in the hope of setting up a similar monopoly for his own benefit at the American end of the trade. Impediments of the same sort lay in the way of the importation of fish oils and New England products. Though all the more intelligent officials at Versailles readily admitted that the monopolies of the farmers-general strangled the French economy and were one of the main causes of popular discontent, every time a definite effort was made to mitigate them, hidden forces of privilege quietly blocked the move. There was also the need to negotiate with France for the regulation of the consular service, and the nagging knowledge that the arrears in interest on the American war debt complicated every other problem.

The fact that a solution seemed logical never meant that it would be adopted. There were always vested powers behind the scenes which had to be satisfied first. Jefferson never could get over his surprise at what seemed to him the obvious wrongheadedness of European statesmen. "I never yet found any other general rule for foretelling what they will do," he confided to John Adams, "but that of examining what they ought not to do."

As he pondered the political landscape of Europe, he was beginning to see signs of the stresses and strains which presaged the French revolution. It was a time of buzzing tongues; everybody talked reform. The disciples of the philosophers wore out the presses with pamphlets and broadsides advocating reform; the courtiers at Versailles discussed economics, but the deficit piled up. Government obligations sold at new lows.

In spite of universal frustration everybody was still respectful to poor befuddled King Louis. At first Jefferson had accepted the stories of what a nice man the king was, but now he had discovered the truth. "The king goes for nothing," he reported to John Jay. "He hunts half the day, is drunk the other & signs whatever he is bid."

Distracted by internal struggles, the court of Versailles, which was still the leader of whatever forces could be described as liberal on the international stage, was losing ground in the pulling and hauling which followed the death of Frederick of Prussia. And the proud republic of Holland, whose institutions Jefferson and Adams had studied with such sympathy, had come to an end. The Dutch government, under a monarchy modeled on England's, became a puppet of the British. The Patriots, as the Dutch republican party called itself, poured out of their tulip gardens to take refuge in Brussels and Paris. The French, instead of going to war for their Dutch allies, acquiesced. So much for monarchy as a defender of popular liberties.

The upset in the Netherlands made the question of the American war debt in Europe a little more pressing. The greater part was owed to the French government but perhaps a fourth was held by private Dutch bankers. Now that they were under English domination Jefferson was wondering how friendly they would be to further American loans. He had already sketched out a plan to get the Dutch bankers to buy out the French court, which was in daily need of cash, at a discount, and to pay off the private claimants; but he had much more confidence in John Adams's ability to bargain with bankers than in his own. When he heard that Adams, that stickler for etiquette, was going to take pompous leave of the Dutch authorities before returning home to America, he got ready at once to join him in the Netherlands.

Together they managed to patch up an arrangement with the Dutch bankers. "I am happy to inform you that we were able to set the loan going again & that the evil is at least postponed . . ." Jefferson explained to George Washington. "Much conversation with the bankers, brokers & money holders, gave me insight into the state of national credit there, which I had never before been able satisfactorily to get. . . . They consider us the surest nation on earth for the repayment of the capital: but as the punctual payment of interest is of absolute necessity in their arrangements, we cannot borrow but with difficulty & disadvantage. The moneyed men however look to our new government with a great degree of partiality." If the United States he concluded, adopted the British policy of promptly paying interest, they would never lack credit.

When Adams left for England, Jefferson set off in his carriage for Paris. Their success with the bankers had taken the load of that mountain of figures off his mind. The Connecticut painter Trumbull had been sending him enthusiastic reports of the Rhineland. These had stirred his memories of the congenial German officers he'd known when they were prisoners of war in Albemarle; ever since, he'd had a hankering to take a look at their country. He wanted to complete his study of the European wine industry by examining the vineyards of the Rhine and Moselle. He wrote Short he would drive up the river as far as he could find roads before turning back into France.

He was curious to see how the Germans lived. He remarked in his notes on the transition from ease and opulence to extreme poverty he noticed on passing from Holland into Germany: "The fear also of slaves is visible in the faces of the Prussian subjects. . . . No chateaux nor houses that bespeak the existance even of a middle class. Universal & equal poverty overspreads the whole."

Frankfort reminded him of Philadelphia; and he called the neighborhood of Frankfort "a second mother country. It is from the Palatinate on this part of the Rhine," he wrote to Short, "that those swarms of Germans have gone who, next to the descendants of the English, form the greatest body of our people. I have been continually amused in seeing here the origin of whatever is not English among us. I have fancied myself often in the upper parts of Maryland or Pennsylvania."

At Mainz he crossed the Rhine on a long bridge carried on forty-seven boats. He described the way the draw worked to let vessels through. To a Virginian bridges and ferries were always cogent; they were so much needed at home. Sailing downriver in "a dull sort of batteau" to visit the famous vineyards at Rüdesheim, he saw floating mills worked by the current. Finally he drove back through the French border provinces to Nancy, eating early asparagus on the way. "The most forest I have seen in France, principally of beech, pretty large. . . . The women here as in Germany do all sorts of work." It was on this part of the drive that he began to put his mind on the problem of a proper moldboard for a plow. One reason for the miseries he saw in Europe was that people had to work too hard for their bread. "The awkward figure of their mouldboard leads one to consider what should be its form," he noted after watching the peasants and their oxen dragging shapeless knobs of wood through the heavy loam. A diagram for a moldboard was already taking form in his head as he drove back to Paris.

JEFFERSON SETTLED INTO THE ROUTINE of his mission with a feeling of refreshed confidence. The news of the success of the Philadelphia convention in establishing a new constitution for the Confederacy was heightening American prestige in France. American political ideas were more the vogue than ever. Chastellux's book on his American travels with its panegyrics of Jefferson and of Lafayette was being eagerly read. Bookshops teemed with pamphlets on American subjects.

For France itself the summer of 1788 turned out to be a period of stalemate. The three main parties which had appeared in the struggle for reform seemed about equally matched. The court wanted money; and a considerable faction at Versailles was willing to join with the commercial classes, the third estate to squeeze the money out of the nobility and the Church. The nobles wanted a restoration of their ancient powers. The third estate wanted free trade, freedom of action and speech, freedom to climb the ladders of power. "The king and the parliament are quarreling for the oyster," was how Jefferson explained it to a friend; "the shell will be left as heretofore to the people."

He was weary of living in a foreign land. It was time he went home for a few months. Watching the French struggle with the problem of government was instructive, but events in America were what really mattered to him; and, he was convinced, to mankind as a whole. For the second time he'd been left out of the affairs of his own country in a crucial moment of state building. He needed to see and to hear. No letters could give him the political feel of Virginia, where he dreaded the influence of Patrick Henry, who was now opposing the constitution. His personal reasons were even more urgent.

He'd finally managed to unite his family in Paris the summer before, when Polly had arrived a very confused and tearful little girl, after having been handed from one kind friend to another clear across the Atlantic. But now it was essential to get both girls back to America. When the time came he wanted them to marry decent Virginia landowners. Much as he liked the French, he found their private lives barren and empty. Patsy was growing to womanhood and the last thing he wanted was for her to marry in France. More distressing still, she had threatened to become a nun. Both Henry Randall and Sara N. Randolph, who wrote while the word-of-mouth traditions of the Jefferson family were still alive, tell of a letter the sixteen-year-old girl wrote to her father and how he jumped into his carriage and drove to the rue de Grenelle and fetched the girls home from the convent forthwith. As the story went neither father nor daughter ever mentioned the matter again.

Every year in France he'd lived beyond his income. He had to spend a few months at Monticello to see what could be done to turn up some cash. His estates were still weighed down by obligations which dated back to the days of his father-in-law, John Wayles. While urging his friends in the new government in every letter home that they arrange a leave of absence for him, he settled down to one last negotiation. Late in the fall he finally signed the new consular convention with France which became for the young State Department the model for similar agreements with other countries.

That winter was so cold that the Seine froze; and the extreme cold of that year and the famine that went with it were the beginning of a train of events in France which not only brought down the old regime, but wrecked the chances of that revolution without bloodshed which Jefferson and his French friends were still sanguinely expecting. The disciples of the philosophers were promising a return to the golden ages but the common people were finding themselves without bread to eat or fire to warm themselves. The nobles and the middle and upper bourgeoisie had achieved already a certain liberty of speech and action and publication. *Les américains* were busy with their plans and their arguments and their speeches. In spite of virtual gov-

ernment bankruptcy the commercial classes were making
money. The economic condition even of the working people
had improved. It had improved just enough to make them want
more. In the city slums and the sordid hunched-up villages
peasants and artisans and manufacturing hands were beginning to
think that they too had a right to liberty. All through that winter
of freezing and deprivation in the Faubourg Saint-Antoine
the laborers' quarter of Paris, heads seethed with that thought.

A riot exploded suddenly in April of 1789 in the Faubourg
Saint-Antoine. The daily proliferation of newspapers, brochure
and pamphlets was making highly profitable every busines
connected with paper, ink and the printing press. At a rumor
of a wage cut in a paper factory a mob appeared armed with
staves and scythes and butcher knives. The manufacturer'
house and factory were torn to the ground. When troops arrived
to clear the streets the mob refused to give ground. The soldier
fired. The blood on the paving stones of Paris that day was the
first ripple of the great wave that would engulf France.

Time was running out. A few little riots in the provinces
now a great riot in Paris. It was becoming clear that the people
would not sit starving patiently in their hovels while their
betters argued as to whether the masses were sufficiently informed
to sit on juries and enjoy the benefits of habeas corpus. The
pent-up energy of the nation was struggling to find an outlet.

Jefferson's diplomatic business was completed. The girls were
beginning to pack their trunks. While he waited for his leave
of absence to come from America he could give his whole
attention to the daily pageant of political change. At the same
time he had leisure to mature his thinking about the constitution
his dear friend Madison of Montpelier had taken such a large
part in establishing in those long-drawn-out closed meetings
at the statehouse in Philadelphia. At first he'd been uneasy. He
feared the too great power of the presidency. He was shocked
by the lack of a bill of rights. But now by contrast with the
anguished struggle his French friends were having to reconcile
the blind and bitter self-interest of the various orders of society
the proceedings at Philadelphia seemed the work of an assembly
of demigods. "The operations which have taken place in

America lately fill me with pleasure," he'd written David Humphreys. "In the first place they realize the confidence I had that whenever our affairs go obviously wrong the good sense of the people will interpose & set them to rights."

On the fifth day of May out in the Salle des Menus Plaisirs at Versailles the States-General convened. It was the first convocation of this venerable institution since 1614. Jefferson was there. From now on he was to drive out almost daily over the road crowded with coaches and carriages and couriers on horseback, to Versailles. "The states General was opened the day before yesterday," he wrote William Carmichael, the American chargé d'affaires in Madrid. "Viewing it as an opera it was imposing. As a scene of business, the King's speech was exactly what it should have been & well delivered: not a word of the Chancellor's was heard by anybody so that as yet I have never heard a single guess as to what it was about."

As he listened to the set speeches and to the reports his friends brought him from the lobbies, Jefferson soon understood that the meeting would turn into a tug of war between the nobles who wanted their old privileges restored and the commercial classes who wanted all privileges abolished. Where would that leave Lafayette?

Jefferson had real affection for the effervescent marquis, and as a statesman he felt that Lafayette was the only Frenchman who could bridge the gap between the old and the new. But now that the moment had come, in spite of all his ardor for reform, Lafayette was hesitating at the Rubicon. "I am in great pain for the Marquis of Lafayette," Jefferson wrote Washington who he knew loved Lafayette as a son; "his principles you know are clearly with the people. But having been elected for the Noblesse of Auvergne, they have laid him under express instructions to vote for the decision by orders & not persons. This would ruin him with the tiers état [the third estate or the common people] & it is not possible he could continue to give satisfaction long to the noblesse."

"You will in the end," he wrote to Lafayette, "go over wholly to the tiers état because it will be impossible for you to live in a constant sacrifice of your own sentiments to the prejudices of the noblesse. But you would be received by the tiers état at any future day coldly & without confidence. This appears to me the moment to take at once that honest & manly stand with them which your own principles dictate. This will win their hearts forever, be approved by the world, & will be an eternal consolation to yourself."

Had Lafayette taken Jefferson's advice wholeheartedly, he might have become, as he dreamed of being, the George Washington of France, and the history of that revolution might have been very different. As it was he delayed so long the choice, which he eventually had to make, between his family connection and the reformers that bolder men took over the leadership of the assembly and Lafayette became the patriot general on horseback whom the crowds always cheered but whom nobody obeyed. Meanwhile throughout France the bastions of the *ancien régime* crumbled. The question soon would be not who would lead, but who would ride the avalanche.

THE FOURTH OF JULY Jefferson entertained the American colony for dinner at the hôtel de Langeac. Lafayette and his wife were there; and John Paradise over from London; and Mazzei, now riding high as an authority on every American subject; and Gouverneur Morris, who was keeping his magnificent diary of the events of that summer in the intervals of pegging about the streets of Paris on his wooden leg, on his devious mission of trying to straighten out for Robert Morris [not a relative of Philadelphia, whose agent he was, the affairs of his tobacco monopoly—wheels within wheels into which Jefferson, the enemy of monopolies, continued to stick what spokes he could.

After dinner and many a toast to independence and the new Constitution, the guests drafted a testimonial to their minister thanking him for his kindness and attention "to every American" and praising his "comprehensive views & minute attentions to every interest of every part of the country." Though the rest of them put their names to it Gouverneur Morris somehow managed to avoid signing his.

Morris was miffed because Jefferson, on the pretext that he would find the dignitaries boring, had evaded introducing him to the officials at Versailles. He and Jefferson were somewhat less than congenial. As a New York patroon Morris suspected humbug in the Virginia landowner's advocacy of popular government. Morris was a devoted friend of Washington. He had copied out the final draft of the Constitution in his own hand. Though an enthusiastic American patriot he was instinctively on the aristocratic side. A gay dog with the ladies, with a gift for bawdy epigrams, he found the exalted tone of Jefferson's friends distasteful. He cultivated a worldly skepticism in conversation. The outpourings at dinner of learned idealists like John Paradise undoubtedly nauseated him. In spite of all his, he couldn't help betraying a reluctant admiration for the American minister.

"I feel it a Duty also to mention that he commands very much Respect in this Country," Gouverneur Morris reported to Robert Morris, "and which is merited by good Sense and good intentions. The french who pique themselves on possessing the Graces, very readily excuse in others the Want of them; and to be an *Etranger* (like Charity) covers a Multitude of Sins. On the whole therefore I incline to think an American Minister at this Court gains more than he loses by preserving his Originality. For the Rest, Mr. Jefferson lives well, keeps a good Table and excellent Wines which he distributes freely and by his Hospitality to his Countrymen here possesses very much their good Will."

During the wild acceleration of events in the weeks that followed, Jefferson and Morris saw each other almost every day, and to Jefferson, who liked to keep his high-flying hopes hitched to realities, there may well have been something tonic, during those dizzy weeks, in Morris's disenchanted comments.

"It is very hard to navigate on such a whirling," Lafayette had written in a hasty note to Jefferson around July 1. A whirling it was. At Marly-le-Roi, a château near Versailles, the princes of the blood were taking fright at the rights of man. The king, always ready to agree with the last man he'd talked to, began to listen to his relatives. In the queen's boudoir they planned a coup d'etat on July 11.

On Sunday, July 12, Gouverneur Morris had gone to call

on Madame de Flahaut, the mistress of Talleyrand, then known as Bishop of Autun. Morris had just begun to fall in love with this imaginative and charming lady, whose heart was to prove big enough to accommodate not only her husband and the subtle bishop but the peg-legged American from Morrisania. At her home he heard the news and set off for the hôtel de Langeac to hear what Jefferson had to say.

The streets were already full of clamor. "In riding along the Boulevards," Morris noted, "all at once the Carriages, Horse and Foot Passengers turn about and pass rapidly. Presently after we meet a Body of Cavalry with their Sabres drawn, and coming Half Speed. . . .When we come to the Place Louis Quinze observe the People, to the Number of perhaps an hundred picking up Stones, and on looking back find that the Cavalry are returning. Stop at the Angle to see the Fray, if any. The People take Post among the Stone which lies scattered about the whole Place, being there hewn for the Bridge now building. The officer at the Head of his Party is saluted by a Stone and immediately turns his Horse in a menacing Manner towards the Assailant. . . . The pace is soon increased to a Gallop amid a Shower of Stones, One of the Soldiers is either knocked from his Horse or his Horse falls under him. He is taken Prisoner and ill-treated." Since they couldn't reach the people among the piles of stones, the cavalry rode off.

At the hôtel de Langeac Morris found that Jefferson had seen the same affray and that the news was that, emboldened by the defeat of the cavalry, the people of Paris were pouring out into the streets. When he left Jefferson to drive to the Palais Royal to see what people had to say at his Club de Valois, Morris observed a new commotion: "The People are employed in breaking open the Armorer's Shops, and presently a large Body of the Gardes Françaises appear with Bayonnets fixed, in the Garden, mingled with the Mob, some of whom are also armed. These poor Fellows have passed the Rubicon with a Witness. Success or a Halter must now be their Motto."

Two days later they stormed the Bastille. After dinner on July 14 Morris was sitting at his banker's talking business when "a Person comes in and announces the taking of the Bastille

394

he Governor of which is beheaded and the Provost des March-
nds is killed and also beheaded: they are carrying the Heads in
Triumph through the City."

The great moment of the appeal to the rights of man had
come. All the tyrannies of Europe were shaken. Not even the
skeptical Morris could restrain his enthusiasm. At supper that
night with two deputies of the *noblesse*, he proposed a toast
in the best claret, so he noted, he'd yet tasted in France): "I gave
them as a toast the Liberty of the French Nation, and then the
City of Paris, which are drunk with very good Will."

On the seventeenth the king, in the midst of a procession led
by Lafayette on a white horse, was induced to manifest his
repentance by showing himself to his loving subjects of the
Ville de Paris. Meanwhile the Constituent Assembly, when the
members weren't wearing themselves out marching in parades,
was busy arguing the outlines of a liberal constitution. Time
was pressing.

Only a constitution could avert civil war. Who could be
better consulted by the committee appointed to draft a constitution than the American minister? July 19 Jefferson answered
his learned old philosopher friend the Abbé Arnoud, who had
been asking him for information about trial by jury:

"The annexed is a catalogue of all the books I can collect on
the subject of juries. With respect to the value of this institution
I must make a general observation. We think in America it is
necessary to introduce the people into every department of
government, as far as they are capable of exercising it: and
that this is the only way to insure a long-continued & honest
administration of its powers."

When the Archbishop of Bordeaux, however, wrote Jefferson
next day asking him to join in the deliberations at Versailles
of this same constitutional committee, over which he was then
presiding, the American minister begged off in his roundabout
French. Since he was accredited to the king it surely would not
be right for him to join with a public body which had been
appointed to shear His Most Christian Majesty of his powers.

Meanwhile the princes of the blood and the courtiers impli-
cated in the attempted coup d'etat were fleeing the country. All

the reactionary ministers had fled. Jefferson declared it was a mighty good riddance.

By late in August he was writing John Jay: "There is still such a leaven of fermentation remaining in the body of the people, that acts of violence are always possible & are quite unpunishable. . . . For several days past a considerable proportion of the people have been without bread altogether; for though the new harvest has begun there is neither wind nor water to grind the grain. For some days since the people have beseiged the doors of the bakers, scrambled with one another for bread, collected in squads all over the city & need only some slight incident to lead them to excesses which may end in nobody can tell what."

THE TIME OF LEAVE-TAKING came at last. The minister plenipotentiary went through the routine of farewell visits. Then at the end of September he set out with his daughters in his phaeton for Le Havre. His chariot followed with the faithful Petit and the blacks. Forty or fifty packing cases of baggage had been sent on ahead by boat down the Seine.

There were delays on the road; a cracked axletree, a broken tire. There was need for haste. As they bowled along the road they looked out through the autumnal hedgerows at the russet trees and the green hills, and the stone villages and the pointed churches. They took in the last limpid pictures of France with the dispassionate eyes of travelers already committed to the ocean and new sights beyond the seas.

Already terror nestled in the ivied towers of hilltop castles. Behind the high glazed windows of the manors fear looked out with a white face. Tenants were storming and burning their landlords' châteaux. Aristocrats were hurrying their wives and children into the towns. It was the beginning of the time known as *la grande peur*.

It was a relief when Jefferson was finally able to hand his daughters out of their carriage in the shelter of the courtyard of l'Aigle d'Or at Le Havre. They were to catch the first packet to meet at Cowes the ship *Clermont*, sailing for Norfolk Virginia, direct. When Jefferson walked down towards the briny-smelling stone quays of the harbor, a gale lashed in his face. Rain poured from the gutters. A fishy reek of salt spume drove in from the sea. The storm was to last nine days.

Meanwhile in Paris the first phase of the revolution was reaching its shuddering climax. Young Short, left as chargé d'affaires at the hôtel de Langeac, wrote on October 5 describing the final and absolute collapse of royal authority. Neither Lafayette nor the Constituent Assembly had any magic to take its place. "The scarcity of bread continuing on sunday evening the 4th inst. crowds assembled as on former occasions in the Palais Royale. . . . On monday morning a number of women assembled at the place de Grève & took possession by surprize of the hôtel de ville [town hall]—there they found some old arms &c—the Marquis de la fayette, informed of this circumstance, went to the hôtel de ville, recovered possession of it & endeavored though in vain, to recover also the place de Grève—the women to the number of 5 or 6 thousand marched off to Versailles. . . . The people & soldiers joined in insisting that the Mrqs. de la fayette should march with them to Versailles—he resisted as long as possible but was forced to yeild & about half after five set off at the head of his troops— the women had arrived at Versailles crying du pain, du pain [bread, bread]. . . . The night was employed in preventing dis- orders. . . . The next morning began by the gardes de corps being pursued and fired at everywhere by the people. . . . The large court under the king's apartments before 9 became full of people—the king showed himself to them—they insisted on his coming to Paris—he assented and added he wd. bring the queen & his children—they accepted and between 12 & 1 the march began."

Two days later Jefferson sat down at his traveling desk in his room at the inn to write Short:

"I was yesterday roving through the neighborhood of this place to try to get a pair of shepherd dogs. We walked 10 miles, clambering the cliffs in search of the shepherds, during the most furious tempest of wind & rain I was ever in. The journey was fruitless. On our return we came on the body of a man who had that moment shot himself. His pistol had dropped at his feet & himself fallen backward without ever moving. The shot had completely separated his whole face from his forehead to the chin and so torn it to atoms. The center of the head was entirely laid bare. This is the only kind of news I have for you."

The same day somebody brought around to the inn a "chienne bergère big with pup" which Jefferson accepted in lieu of a pair of dogs. When late that night the wind suddenly moderated he bundled his daughters and the blacks and the newly acquired sheepdog onto the packet *Anna*. Next morning the coast of stormy France was out of sight, and after twenty-six hours of "boistrous navigation and mortal seasickness," they arrived at Cowes, where they were to meet the *Clermont*.

Chapter 8

"AFTER GETTING CLEAR of the eternal fogs of Europe, which required 5. or 6. days sailing, the sun broke out upon us," wrote Jefferson to Short once the *Clermont* was safe at anchor in Lynn-haven Bay. Two days later he was landing, with the girls and the servants and the pregnant sheepdog and the cases of diplomatic records and the boxes of plants and the forty or fifty articles of baggage, amid the piled brick and the stacked lumber and the sawing and the hammering of the rebuilding city of Norfolk. In the first newspaper that was handed him he found the news that President Washington had appointed him Secretary of State in the new government now seated in New York, and that the appointment had been confirmed by the Senate.

Immediately the official addresses of welcome began; and moist-eyed meetings with old friends, with George Wythe and the Reverend Madison in Williamsburg, with Thomas Mann Randolph at Tuckahoe, who had recently lost his wife, and with his tall stringy son of the same name, and with the dear Eppes family at Eppington.

From Eppington Jefferson wrote Short more at length

listing the marriages and deaths among the younger man's friends. William Short's brother Peyton had married the daughter of a gentleman who had made great purchases of lands through Congress, and was moving the family to Kentucky. Wherever he went Jefferson found the young men packing up and moving west. North Carolina had accepted the Constitution; Rhode Island was still holding out. The ten amendments which were to constitute a bill of rights had passed the Virginia House of Delegates but were stalled in the Senate. "Antifederalism is not yet dead in this country. The Gentlemen who opposed the new constitution retain a good deal of malevolence towards the new Government: Henry is it's avowed foe."

So pleasant was the Virginia hospitality the Jeffersons encountered on the way that they reached Monticello barely in time for Christmas. Immediately after, Madison of Montpelier, who was serving in the new House of Representatives, rode over from Orange to spend a couple of days on the hilltop.

In the five years since Jefferson had seen him, his salty little friend had developed a fresh skill in the clear presentation of his thoughts. Through their constant correspondence Jefferson had collaborated in the growth of his theory of politics, but he was probably surprised to discover how Madison's mind had matured during those closed debates in Philadelphia which built, out of a pile of discordant opinions, the tight structure of the Constitution.

Now, walking up and down in Jefferson's library, these winter days in Monticello, Madison was uneasy. He had been profoundly alarmed by the authoritarian trend he had noted in the "court" of General Washington at New York. Alexander Hamilton, Washington's Secretary of the Treasury, was taking the bit in his teeth. Madison felt that the moneyed interests were reaching for more power than was their due. Moreover his sense of justice was outraged by the funding plan sponsored by Hamilton. As a landed Virginian he was suspicious of the speculators and the moneylenders who would benefit by the financial system the gaudy young man was seeking to establish. He felt that this sudden access of financial power to a small group, many of them returned Tories and English and Scottish merchants whose only thought was to make money, would dangerously disturb the careful balance between interests which it had been one of the purposes of the Constitution to establish. Enlivening the conversation over the wine after dinner with the saucy stories and the sly digs at personalities he was becoming famous for, Madison was able to convince Jefferson that his duty lay in New York.

After "three months of parleying," as he put it, and a couple of tactfully insistent letters from the President, Jefferson accepted the office of Secretary of State. He answered Washington's urgent plea for haste with: "Your desire that I should come on as quickly as possible is a sufficient reason for me to postpone every matter of business however pressing. . . ." Still there was one matter of business that could not be postponed. Patsy had told him she wanted to marry young Thomas Mann Randolph. He couldn't leave Monticello without seeing them wed.

This was for Jefferson a very tender moment. Since her mother's death, his older daughter had been closer to him than anyone on earth. Patsy had grown up to be a tall redheaded sturdy girl with features like her father's, and was showing every sign of having inherited some of his brains. The match was the most Virginian conceivable. The young people were cousins. Jefferson and old "Tuckahoe Tom" had been raised together; Jefferson spoke of him as "my bosom friend." When the son went abroad to study at Edinburgh he had not failed to consult Jefferson, like so many other young Virginians, about his courses and his choice of a career. It wasn't like bringing a stranger into the house.

The young Randolphs eventually settled at Monticello where they furnished Jefferson with a mob of grandchildren and with the close-knit family group he so craved. For the rest of his life, Patsy and her children made his home a nest of refuge to him from the stings and galls of political conflict.

THE NEW SECRETARY OF STATE arrived at the temporary capital on March 21, 1790, a Sunday, after a slow journey over roads so deep in snow and mud that he had to leave his carriage in

Alexandria, Virginia, and to undergo the discomfort of the public stages. The reward of riding the stages was, as he put it, that it plunged him into "the aggregate mass" of the "mixed characters" of his fellow citizens. After five years he was finding people changed. The inns were full of recent immigrants from Europe: Englishmen, Scots, Frenchmen, Irish. Everybody talked about money. Everybody was speculating in land or government paper. Everybody was on the move.

New York had changed more than anywhere else. In the quarter of a century since Jefferson's first visit the city had lost its Dutch look. Now he found the narrow island rebuilding after the great fires that had gutted many streets during the British occupation. There were new wharves and great ships in the slips. New York merchants were making big profits on the triangular run: round the Horn and north for sea otters; then to China with the pelts and back to New York with spices and tea. The city had almost doubled in population. Jefferson had difficulty in finding himself a house.

Immediately paper work swallowed him up. "Much business," he wrote his son-in-law, "had been put by for my arrival, so that I found myself all at once involved under an accumulation of it." The function of his office, as he saw it, was simply that of a secretary carrying out the President's policies. He consulted Washington on every detail. To help him, in the two rooms the State Department occupied, Jefferson found a chief clerk, a couple of underclerks, a doorkeeper and a messenger boy. In addition to correspondence with American envoys abroad, he was charged with the custody of the great seal, with the publication of the laws and their distribution to the state governments, with the management of the mint, with instructions to federal marshals and attorneys, correspondence with federal judges, the preparation of the President's commissions, and with the taking of the census. A few days after he arrived Congress added the granting of patents and copyrights.

"Behold me, my dear friend, elected Secretary of State," he wrote Lafayette. ". . . I have been here then ten days harnessed in new geer. . . . The opposition to our new constitution has almost totally disappeared. . . . If the President can be preserved a few years till habits of authority & obedience can be established generally, we have nothing to fear."

Jefferson arrived in New York determined to sacrifice every consideration to the establishment of these habits of authority and obedience which he felt were needed to weld the Confederacy into a nation. Immediately he found that the trend of Washington's administration was at variance with his most passionately held beliefs. The conflict that ensued between his determination to bolster the federal government and his fundamental political instincts would have destroyed a man made of less sinewy stuff. As it was it led him into some of the most painful inconsistencies of his career.

"Here certainly," he later wrote in his preface to his book called *The Anas*, "I found a state of things which, of all I had ever contemplated, I least expected. I had left France in the first year of its revolution, in the fervor of natural rights and zeal for reformation. My conscientious devotion to these rights could not be heightened, but it had been aroused and excited by daily exercise. The President received me cordially, and my Colleagues & the circle of principal citizens, apparently with welcome. The courtesy of dinner parties given me as a stranger newly arrived among them, placed me at once in their familiar society. But I cannot describe the wonder and mortification with which the table conversations filled me. Politics were the chief topic, and a preference of kingly, over republican, government, was evidently the favorite sentiment."

Jefferson was using the phrase "kingly government" to describe society based on the preponderance of the "rich and wellborn." What he was being confronted with, though he had found no name for it yet, was the quick burgeoning of the moneyed interest. In his five years' absence the profiteering mania had reigned unchecked in America. Business was good. Everybody was speculating in everything. New men surging up out of the manufacturing and commercial interests were avid for political power. Their way was made easy by the inevitable slipping back into old authoritarian habits of aging leaders like Washington and Adams, in whom the emotional urge of the revolution had subsided, and who looked with alarm at the eruption of the mob, nameless and uncontrollable, into the streets of the cities of Europe.

Jefferson was slow in admitting, even to himself, the need to check the authoritarian trend. Newly arrived from abroad, he at first lagged behind many of his friends more in touch with opinion. The moment he arrived in New York, however, he discovered an important fact. John Adams was a mere wax-work: the real leader of the party of the rich and well born was Alexander Hamilton.

From his letters of the time you get the impression that at first Jefferson, who always admired a good mind wherever he found it, went along with Hamilton's schemes. Though Jefferson's political aims were the most far-reaching conceivable, his methods never were radical. His early experience in the Virginia assembly had taught him "that the ground of liberty is gained by inches." Part of Hamilton's impatience with him was based on the fact that Hamilton was a man of radical and aggressive methods who could see only hypocrisy in Jefferson's gradualism. He wrote scornfully that the Virginian was "crafty and per-severing in his objects . . . a contemptible hypocrite"; then he added with the paradoxical honesty which was one of his most attractive traits, "he is too much in earnest in his democracy."

When Jefferson arrived Hamilton was cock of the walk. After Washington, whom Hamilton had slated in his own mind to wield the scepter of constitutional monarch, no one in the administration could compare with him in energy and ability. And Washington, who was a great administrator himself, couldn't help looking with admiration on the developing administrative skill of his early protégé. Except in name Hamilton was his prime minister.

A man without a country, Hamilton had been born on the English West Indian island of Nevis and shunted in his childhood to the Danish island of Saint Croix; his only roots in the American soil were through his father-in-law's great estates. He was a true New Yorker, perhaps the first of the breed. New York's coffeehouses were full of men talking money. His early experience with practical affairs had been as a merchant. It was inevitable that when he looked around for the materials out of which to build himself a political machine he should light on the money interest. Washington, who distrusted special interests, had called in Jefferson as a counterweight. From the first moment the tall drab-coated Virginian appeared in the general's study, wavy-haired little Hamilton, bustling about in his frills and his buckles, felt a check to his career.

Hamilton was all ambition. Though far from being the "bastard brat of a Scotch peddler," as Gouverneur Morris insisted on calling him, the fact that his mother's first husband wouldn't recognize her divorce and that his father was more or less of a deadbeat had let him in for a mixed-up childhood and launched him precociously on a career of self-advancement. After his mother's early death he had gone to work at the age of twelve for a relative in a general store on Saint Croix. At fourteen he had amazed the islands with a description of a hurricane in the local newspaper. Meanwhile he had been studying with a Presbyterian minister of some learning. At fifteen his aunts sent him to New York to complete his education at King's College. He astonished everybody there by his brilliantly logical mind and his capacity for hard work.

When the split came with the mother country young Alexander got himself a commission in an artillery company of the Continental line and, after saving single-handed his college president, who was a Tory, from a mob, he found himself, not yet turned twenty, an aide of the commanding general. Washington, recognizing a bright young man, made Hamilton his personal secretary. As an officer Hamilton proved courageous, egotistical and a glutton for work. He was a little rosy-cheeked bantam of a man, a flashy dresser; with the ladies he had a soft-voiced manner they found irresistible. Before the war was over he had married a pretty daughter of rich General Schuyler of New York. In spite of his infidelities Elizabeth Schuyler loved Hamilton to the end, and he seems to have loved her.

Hamilton's political reputation even more than Madison's resulted from the immense success of *The Federalist Papers*. His writing was always clear and energetic; he was probably the most brilliant of the argumentative journalists of the day.

Supported as he was by the powerful Schuyler interest in New York, he seemed to everyone the logical choice when Washington appointed him his Secretary of the Treasury.

Hamilton was a man who could never find enough work to do. He devoted to the office all his great organizing skill. Outside of his haphazard philandering and a little sociable drinking after dinner, there was very little in his life but business. Power was his delight. It was inevitable that his organization should impinge on the other departments.

"Hamilton's financial system . . ." wrote Jefferson in the preface to *The Anas*, "had two objects. 1st as a puzzle to exclude popular understanding & inquiry. 2nd, as a machine for the corruption of the legislature; for he avowed the opinion that man can be governed by one of two motives only, force or interest: force he observed in this country was out of the question; and the interests therefore of the members must be laid hold of, to keep the legislature in unison with the Executive. And with grief and shame it must be acknoledged that his machine was not without effect. That even in this, the birth of our government, some members were found sordid enough to bend their duty to their interest and to look after personal rather than public good. It is well known that during the war, the greatest difficulty we encountered was the want of money or means to pay our soldiers who fought, or our farmers, manufacturers, merchants who furnished the necessary supplies of food and clothing for them. After the expedient of paper money had exhausted itself, certificates of debt were given to the individual creditors, with assurance of payment, as soon as the U. S. should be able. But the distresses of these people often obliged them to part with these for the half, the fifth and even the tenth of their value, and Speculators had made a trade of cozening them from the holders. . . . When the trial of strength on these several efforts had indicated the form in which the bill would finally pass . . . the base scramble began. Couriers & relay horses by land, and swift sailing pilot boats by sea, were flying in all directions. . . . Immense sums were filched from the poor & ignorant, and fortunes accumulated by those who had been poor enough before. Men thus enriched by the dex-

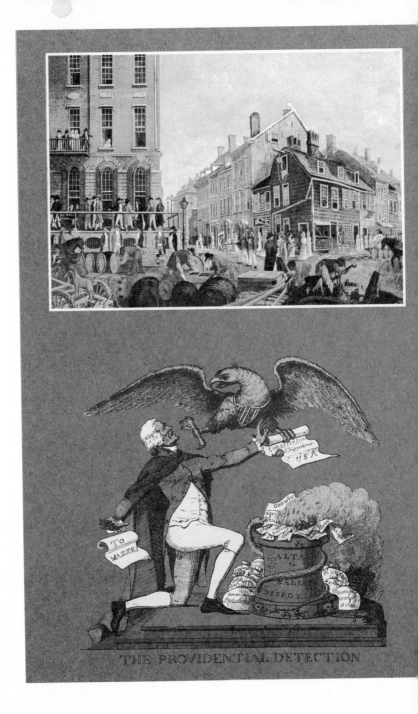

THE PROVIDENTIAL DETECTION

erity of a leader, would follow of course the chief who was leading them to fortune, and become the zealous instruments of all his enterprizes."

During Jefferson's first month in New York, a cold and snowy April, Hamilton's financial measures were still being held up by Madison in the House and by fervent adherents of the farmers' interests like William Maclay of Pennsylvania in the Senate. "So high were the feuds excited by this subject," Jefferson wrote, "that on it's rejection business was suspended . . . the parties being too much out of temper to do business together."

Maclay hated Hamilton's bills because, besides being unjust to the soldiers and farmers, he felt they would lead, as Hamilton wanted, to federal powers great enough to destroy the state governments.

the Tontine Coffee
?e at the corner of
and Water streets in
York, about 1797.
?m, Jefferson, who
?d enemies for his love
?ance and the common
?le, is caricatured
?ing before the "Altar
?llic Despotism" and
?; menaced for his folly
?e American eagle.

ALL THIS TIME Jefferson was going through one of those periods of misery and ill health that tended to come over him when he was faced by difficult situations. On May 27 he wrote Short that he had been tortured for a month by one of his headaches. He'd not yet been able to move into comfortable quarters. He hated the unseasonable weather. He was of divided mind as to whether as Washington's Secretary of State he should take sides in the contest which was tearing Congress apart.

Three days before, at a committee meeting, he had come for the first time under Maclay's searching eye. "When I came into the Hall," wrote the senator from Pennsylvania, "Jefferson and the rest of the committee were there. Jefferson is a slender man; has rather the air of stiffness in his manner; his clothes seem too small for him; he sits in a lounging manner, on one hip commonly, and with one of his shoulders elevated much above the other; his face has a sunny aspect; his whole figure has a loose shackling air."

407

Maclay was an extraordinarily sharp observer. He went on, without knowing it, to give a brilliant clinical description of a man trying to shake off the agony of a migraine headache enough to get some business done: "He had a rambling, vacant look, and nothing of that firm collected deportment which I expected would dignify the presence of a secretary or minister. I looked for gravity but a laxity of manner seemed shed about him. He spoke almost without ceasing. But even his discourse partook of his personal demeanor. It was loose and rambling, yet he scattered information wherever he went, and some even brilliant sentiments sparked from him. The information he gave us respecting foreign ministers etc. was all high-spiced."

Jefferson had probably been amusing the committeemen with sarcastic stories about the private lives of European diplomats. Maclay hated what he considered lax talk about women. He'd been disgusted by the bawdy stories at dinner of his own Pennsylvania congressmen. Of Jefferson he added, "He has been long enough abroad to catch the tone of European folly."

It must have been during those days when the laggard spring was turning into early summer that Jefferson had the meetings with Hamilton which he described in the preface to *The Anas* and in the following undated note which most historians agree was written while he was still Secretary of State:

"Going to the President's house one day I met Hamilton as I approached the door, his look was sombre, haggard and dejected beyond description, even his dress uncouth & neglected, he asked to speak to me, we stood in the street near the door, he opened the subject of the assumption of the State debts, the necessity of it in the general fiscal arrangement & it's indispensible necessity towards a preservation of the union. . . . That as to his own part, if he had not credit enough to carry such a measure as that he could be of no use & was determined to resign, he observed at the same time, that tho' our particular business laid in separate departments, yet the Administration & it's success was a common concern, and that we should make common cause in supporting one another. . . . I thought the first step towards some conciliation of views would be to bring Mr. Madison and Colo. Hamilton to a friendly discussion of the subject. I immediately wrote to each to come and dine with me next day. . . . They came."

For years Jefferson had been working to have the federal city established on the Potomac. Here was a chance to save some good out of what he had come to consider an inevitable evil.

"I opened the subject [of Hamilton's measure] to them, acknowledged that my situation had not permitted me to understand it sufficiently," he added in that slyly self-deprecatory tone that maddened his enemies and sometimes even embarrassed his friends, "but encouraged them to consider the thing together. They did so, it ended in Mr. Madison's acquiescence in a proposition that the question should be again brought before the House by way of amendmt. from the Senate, that tho' he would not vote for it, nor entirely withdraw his opposition, yet he should not be strenuous but leave it to it's fate. It was observed, I forget by which of them, that as the pill would be a bitter one to the Southern States, something should be done to soothe them, that the removal of the seat of Government to the Patowmac was a just measure."

Later Jefferson felt he'd made a bad bargain, and tried to explain it away, but the bargain itself was of the essence of his political behavior. It was because such bargains could be made that the republicans of America were able to cope with the Federalist reaction without destroying the fabric of government. Not even after his retirement did Jefferson quite admit to himself the virtues of his own inconsistencies while he was serving in Washington's cabinet. Under the cool exterior he was a man of violent passions that occasionally degenerated into a shrewish vindictiveness. He never could forgive himself for having let Hamilton inveigle him into "holding the candle for his game." When in that famous preface to *The Anas* he tried to put down for posterity his recollections of the beginnings of his struggle against Hamilton's consolidation of a government of the money interests, he left a false impression. His memory was so warped by the emotional strain of the partisan battles which followed that he forgot what excellent reasons he'd had for going along with Hamilton in the first place.

As soon as the bargain was made Jefferson put his inimitable powers of persuasion to work. Daniel Carroll of Maryland, who owned land in what was to be the District of Columbia, changed his vote on Hamilton's measure and so did two of the Potomac members from Virginia, Alexander White and Richard Bland Lee, "the former," so Jefferson put it, "with a revulsion of stomach almost convulsive." To give time to erect buildings for a national capital and to mollify the money interests of Pennsylvania, the government was established in Philadelphia for the next ten years.

Once Congress passed funding and assumption the administration was all Hamilton's. When he set up his national bank, modeled on the Bank of England, most of the leaders of his party in Congress turned out to be directors.

In Philadelphia plausible Robert Morris, the son of a Liverpool tobacco factor in Maryland, who had arrived in Philadelphia a penniless boy to take a job as a clerk, and who, through his handling of continental finance, had built himself an empire of speculation piled on speculation so intricate that to this day historians haven't been able to make up their minds whether he financed the Revolution or the Revolution financed him, was setting the tone for a light-headed parvenu capitalism. His strongboxes bulged with government securities. He held title to hundreds of square miles of western lands. He sat in the Senate. His finger was in every pie. With Robert Morris an intimate of every department of the government and Hamilton the gay young leader in the Treasury, the merchants and the bankers and the brokers and the speculators found themselves for the first time at the top of the social heap. From that giddy pinnacle they could look forward to the soaring splendors of the money interests in the nineteenth century.

IN AN EFFORT TO EXPLAIN the apparent subservience of his own ideas to those of Washington's administration Jefferson wrote Monroe that there had to be "some give and take in a government such as ours." During most of his tour of duty as Secretary of State it was all give and no take. The other side of the medal of Hamilton's admirable administrative skill was his knack for bureaucratic aggrandizement. The Secretary of the Treasury vas everywhere. Through his intimacy with George Hammond, he shrewd young Yorkshireman who was finally accredited s the British minister to Washington's court, he kept inter-ering even in Jefferson's conduct of foreign affairs. He couldn't elp trying to discredit his rival in any way he could.

In one enterprise alone Jefferson was able to work whole-eartedly with the President. Hamilton and his moneymen had ery little to do with the planning of Washington City. Here vas Jefferson's justification for the bargain he had made in New 'ork. He and the President were both Virginians. Always appiest when they looked to the west, they both believed the 'otomac valley was the natural route to the Mississippi. Wash-igton, one of the most successful dealers in western lands of the ime, was deeply involved in the Potomac and Ohio canal. efferson's vocation as an architect, his local patriotism, and is conviction that, if the eastern and western states were to emain united, a cheap and easy passage through the Appala-hians must be opened up at once, combined to involve all he great enthusiasms of his life in the project.

When Congress adjourned in August 1790 to meet in Phila-elphia late in the fall, Jefferson and Madison, who was still a achelor, traveled home together. These jaunts in Jefferson's haeton were getting to be increasingly important to both men s their intimacy increased. They could talk as they drove. They udied the flora and fauna. They examined the buildings. On iis particular journey they stopped off at Georgetown to look t the site of the federal city-to-be. Congressman Carroll, one f the gentlemen who had been induced to change his vote, ook them riding, with a cavalcade of local landowners, over ie tract of farmland and meadow that lay between Rock reek and muddy little Goose Creek. After dinner they rowed 1 a boat up to the Little Falls and admired the romantic beauty f the river. When they drove on to Mount Vernon the next ay, Jefferson and Madison were well primed with the lay of ie land. The plan of the city was the chief subject of their onversation with Washington.

Washington, as he'd shown in his rebuilding of Mount 'ernon, had a taste for architecture himself and gloried in the spacious laying out of grounds. Planning a city suited him t a T. Next month he himself rode round the edges of the marshe and up the hills between Rock Creek and the Eastern Branc to establish definitely where the limits of the city should be Showing more foresight than later administrations that aban doned the Virginia territory, he chose for the federal distric a region ten miles square on both sides of the Potomac. Th southern point of the square would include Alexandria an its wharves as far south as Hunting Creek. He hoped to fin a way of taking in Bladensburg to the northward.

Both Washington and Jefferson felt there was a danger tha Congress in a flighty mood might change its mind. Losing n time, as soon as Jefferson settled into his office in Philadelphia, h drew up for the President's attention a document which stretche Congress's rather vague enactment to the point where it coul be put to some practical use. He spoke of conversations he ha held with local landowners, and he suggested various methoc for paying owners for land turned to public use without need less expenditure of public funds by playing on their hopes c rising values once the city was a going concern.

Meanwhile the President was appointing a board of com missioners to superintend the work and a surveyor was bein found to lay out boundaries. As early as February 2 of th following year Jefferson wrote Andrew Ellicott, one of th ablest surveyors of the time, instructing him in how to mak his preliminary rough survey along the lines President Wash ington had decided on.

A few days later, in spite of the wintry weather, Ellicott wa writing back that he would soon submit a plan "which will believe embrace every object of advantage which can be in cluded within the ten miles square."

Ellicott's assistant on this work was a neighbor of his, Ben jamin Banneker, a self-educated colored man who was receivin considerable notice in the newspapers of the time as a livin refutation of the doubts about the abilities of the Negro rac Jefferson had expressed in his *Notes on Virginia*. There has com down a touching letter from Banneker to Jefferson urging hir to apply his theories of equality to black as well as white, an to urge his friends who loved liberty themselves to put, in the words of Job, "your souls in their souls' stead."

Jefferson, in his own particular way, made honorable amends. "Nobody wishes more than I do," he wrote back, thanking Banneker for the almanac he had sent with the letter, "to see such proofs as you exhibit, that nature has given to our black brethren talents equal to those of the other colors of men and that the appearance of a want of them is owing merely to the degraded conditions of their existence both in Africa & America. I can add with truth that nobody wishes more ardently to see a good system commenced for raising the condition both of their body and mind to what it ought to be, as fast as the imbecility of their present existence, and other circumstances which cannot be neglected, will admit."

He sent the almanac on to his old friend Condorcet in France. Condorcet was secretary of the Academy of Sciences in Paris and a prime mover in a society for the liberation of Negroes from slavery. "I am happy to be able to inform you," he wrote, "that we have now in the United States a negro . . . who is a very respectable mathematician . . . [and] a very worthy & respectable member of society. He is a free man."

Ellicott and Banneker had hardly started to carry their lines across the wooded hills by the Potomac when Washington and Jefferson, in a fever to get sod turned for the foundations of the capital, sent frothy Major L'Enfant after them to draw a city plan.

Pierre Charles L'Enfant had arrived in America at his own expense as a volunteer to fight the British. The son of a court painter, he had been brought up at Versailles, and had been trained as an artist. In America he'd served with credit in the artillery, and had been discharged with the rank of major. Washington thought highly of him. In the Federal Hall in New York he had made the first essay towards a distinctive American style. In decoration he was a brilliant innovator, but he doesn't seem to have had the necessary training as an architect to execute his grand ideas. He was in his element in the enthusiastic atmosphere of the founding of the federal city.

L'Enfant took with him Jefferson's modest sketch with its suggestion of an open mall between the President's house at

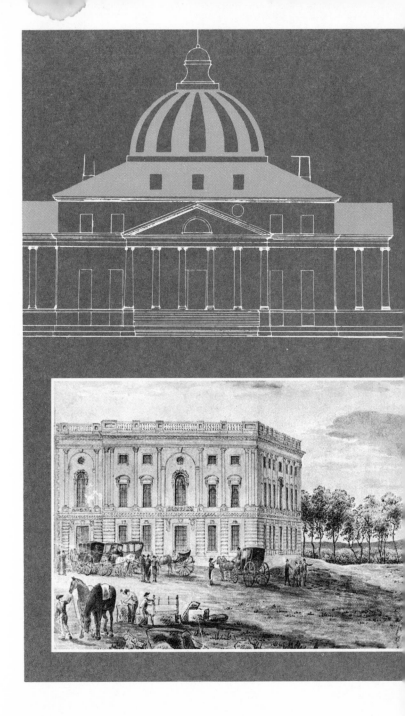

one end and the house for Congress at the other. As soon as he saw Jenkins' Hill far to the east, he seized on that as a site for the capitol, and placed the President's house about on the spot Jefferson had indicated. He immediately tripled the scale of Jefferson's sketch. Jefferson had furnished him with maps of a number of European cities, but freshest in L'Enfant's mind was the plan of Versailles, where he had spent his youth. So he took Jefferson's gridiron and imposed on it an arrangement of broad avenues branching out from round points.

L'Enfant was so impressed by the grandeur of the work of founding a city that he quite lost his head. He wouldn't co-operate with the commissioners. He wouldn't explain his plans. He suddenly and without warning ordered his men to tear down a house one of the Carrolls had started to build in what L'Enfant decided was the middle of one of his favorite avenues.

Before long, to the horror of Jefferson and Washington who wanted to have the city an accomplished fact before there was too much talk about it, he had managed to flush every local vested interest so that the Georgetown people and the speculators were all at sixes and sevens. There appeared a L'Enfant faction and an anti-L'Enfant faction. He became so embroiled that he could not find time to prepare plans for the federal buildings. He had them in his head, he told Jefferson. "I rest satisfied the President will consider," he wrote in a breathless letter that has come down in fragmentary form, "that erecting houses for the accommodation of Government is not the only object, nay not so important a one, as the encouragement to prepare buildings at those principle points, on the speedy settlement of which depends the rapid increase of the city."

Houses for the accommodation of government, however, Jefferson and Washington were determined to have. The foun-

the famous drawing
Jefferson submitted in
architectural competition
the President's house
92. He signed it
in order to keep
authorship secret.
m, a watercolor by
m Birch of the Senate
of the Capitol in
ington City as of
ar 1800.

dations must be laid before some faction reared up in Congress and squelched the whole scheme. After some further urging that L'Enfant present the plans he kept talking about, they decided to hold a competition. In March 1792 Jefferson drew up an announcement that the commissioners would offer five hundred dollars for a suitable plan for the President's house.

When few architects appeared to take part in the competition Jefferson submitted a drawing of his own, in which he set a skylighted dome, similar to the dome which had so intrigued him on the Paris grain market the day he first met Maria Cosway, on a version of his favorite Villa Rotunda. He signed it with the initials AZ and kept the secret of his authorship so close that for years the sketch was attributed to an Alexandria builder named Abraham Faws.

The prize was awarded to James Hoban, a young Irish immigrant who had designed the first South Carolina statehouse. The drawing he presented was eminently practical and had a pleasing modesty which immediately attracted Washington and Jefferson too, who was not the man to push his own project. It was part of his code that a gentleman didn't claim authorship of designs for a building any more than he wrote in the newspapers or published books. But neither was he a man to neglect to make his influence felt. So it turned out, by no accident, that the architectural character of the White House as it stands today depends on those later additions such as the terraces and the curved south portico which Jefferson either designed or had built under his direction.

When the time came to open the competition for the capitol Jefferson wrote the commissioners, as usual putting his own ideas in another man's mouth, that the President felt that instead of facing the buildings with stone of different colors as had been suggested, he would prefer them faced with brick, possibly above a stone water table and using stone for ornament and trim. "The remains of antiquity in Europe," he added, "prove brick more durable than stone." The program he drafted called for a brick building, gave dimensions for a Senate chamber and a House chamber to hold three hundred men and left about everything else to the ingenuity of the architect.

By this time news of the competition had spread through the states. The projects submitted for the capitol showed an unexpectedly high order of invention. Samuel Dobie, who'd helped to construct Jefferson's Virginia statehouse, sent in a monumental Villa Rotunda. Samuel McIntire, already busy ornamenting sea captains' houses at Salem and Newburyport, worked out a highly accomplished design in the full tradition of the late eighteenth century in England, which some architects still consider his best work. A man named Diamond, probably a practical contractor with a feeling for brick construction, presented a square building set about a court that harked back even further in English taste, but struck an up-to-date note by indicating locations for water closets. There were some enlarged versions of the Annapolis statehouse. There were some intriguing experiments with oval rooms. A recently arrived Frenchman named Stephen Hallet drafted a dome over a pediment supported by Ionic columns. He had been talking to Jefferson, who wanted a domed building and who had made a vigorous little sketch of his recollections of a particular domed church in Paris to show what he meant.

Jefferson and the board of commissioners favored Hallet's plan, but the President found only one drawing which satisfied his sense of pomp and his desire for great scale. This had been submitted by a Dr. William Thornton, who boasted of being a rank amateur. Thornton claimed that he'd never thought of architecture till he'd seen an advertisement in a Philadelphia newspaper of a competition for a library. He'd bought himself some books, fudged a set of plans and carried off the prize. Now President Washington could think of nothing but his elevation of the façade for the national capitol. Jefferson immediately concurred. Thornton had put the antique forms to modern use. The center of Thornton's plan was a bold Roman Pantheon set up on a sturdy set of rusticated arches. It had the New World flavor.

The prize was no sooner awarded to Dr. Thornton, however, than it became apparent that it would be impossible to erect the building as planned. The columns of the portico were too far apart, there was no way indicated to support the floor of the central peristyle, there was no headroom on the stairways, and important parts of the interior totally lacked light and air. It was up to Jefferson to get the plan into practical shape.

Hallet had been awarded second prize. Jefferson, who recognized the Frenchman as a competent technician, promptly engaged him to work on Thornton's drawings. He called in Dr. Thornton, Stephen Hallet, James Hoban and a contractor named Carstairs to a conference on ways and means. Dr. Thornton brought along a certain Colonel Williams, an architect who had a notion all difficulties could be handled by the use of "secret arches of brick" for support. Jefferson abhorred the notion, but he kept his feelings to himself. He managed to keep all these gentlemen happy and pulling together, and by August 19 he had a set of workable drawings ready to send on to Washington City. Somehow, in spite of all the burnings and reconstructions and the thousandfold modifications of the original plan, the Capitol, as it at present stands, has, in the relationship of the dome to the general mass and balance of the wings, more affinity to Jefferson's tiny sketch which he made for Hallet than to Thornton's original plan.

Meanwhile, though many loved him and all admired his talent, nobody could work with L'Enfant. His disregard for money was epic. He was too grand to study ways and means. Jefferson wrote tactful letters. Washington sent one of his personal secretaries with soothing explanations to try to induce the major to cooperate with the commissioners. The secretary was rebuffed. Washington took the rebuff as a personal slight, closed his thin lips over his uncomfortable dentures, set his great jaw and retired into his implacable dignity.

For years L'Enfant, with his mighty imaginings unrealized, haunted the unfinished city, the first of a long train of injured men waiting for redress. Then Ellicott resigned in a huff as surveyor. In the end Thornton too joined the ranks of the disappointed. The federal city seemed to devour men of talent.

As Jefferson's collaboration with Washington's administration became more and more uneasy, his personal influence diminished at the federal city. Flocks of speculators rode in, bought lots on borrowed money, took fright in the panic that

ollowed the inflation of the stock in Hamilton's Bank of the
Jnited States, sold at a loss and were ruined. The streets were
 morass. At high tides the creeks backed up into the low-lying
ots. Clumps of unfinished buildings moldered in the scrubby
nderbrush. There was never enough money to pay the work-
1en. There were never enough workmen to do the work. When
vorkmen arrived they found no houses to live in.

Washington and Jefferson were both stubborn men. Each in
is own way pushed the work on the government buildings
n through inconceivable disappointments. But not until 1800
vould the survival of Washington City be assured.

Then, when Jefferson himself became President, backed by
1e western settlers and the farmers and mechanics and trades-
1en who made up the Republican Party, in the fresh air of the
ew century he was able to take full charge of the work in
rogress. He appointed Benjamin Latrobe, a really great archi-
ct, as surveyor of public buildings; and together he and
atrobe were able, by pulling down the bad workmanship and
10ring up the good, to complete the White House and the
'apitol's two wings and to set the print of their fresh republican
yle on the government buildings so that the national capital
ecame the radiating center of the first great period in Ameri-
1n architecture.

Chapter 9

N THE SPRING OF 1793 Jefferson moved out from the house he'd
een renting in downtown Philadelphia to a cottage on the
ank of the Schuylkill. He could stand no more of the life he'd
een forced to lead as a member of Washington's cabinet among
eople who could barely disguise their detestation of him. As
e wrote to Madison of Montpelier, even those moments he
ways looked forward to, of conviviality and unguarded talk
ver the wine after the cloth had been removed at dinner, were
oisoned by the knowledge that most of the men at the table

hated him for his opinions. "Party animosities here," he' written a friend in England the autumn before, "have raised wall of separation between those who differ in political senti ments." Then he wrote a line and crossed it out, "The oldes friends will cross the street to avoid meeting each other."

As he walked out from the new cottage and under the tree beside the green river he could draw a breath. He intended t resign at the end of the year and this was a first step on the roa to Monticello. The contest with Hamilton, even more than th daily drudgery of the work of his office, had cooped him o from everything he enjoyed in life. Philadelphia had become to small to contain both men. For more than a year now they ha been waging a surreptitious war. They dined and drank togethe at friends' tables, addressing each other courteously when the met; they called at each other's houses and had rational cor versations on subjects connected with foreign affairs. They ha reached a sort of intimacy in disagreement. Even in their mo violent moments of antagonism, there was in each of them a odd streak of respect for the other.

With the President, a fiction was kept up that there were n factions in the administration, that nobody wrote for the news papers. Yet about every time Jefferson opened a gazette he foun a lead column flaying him to the quick. John Fenno's *Gazet of the United States*, which was the closest to the Secretary of the Treasury, was the worst offender.

It was Madison who had insisted that the opposition to th Treasury policies must have a press. He had arranged with printer named Childs who ran a Hamiltonian paper in Ne York to back Philip Freneau, Madison's old college mate a Princeton, in a paper in Philadelphia. It was understood th Freneau would be free to express his own opinions. Freneau wa a seafaring man, a poet of spirit and a good hater. He was fu of republican ardor. He was familiar with foreign language Jefferson gave him a job as translator for the State Departmer and furnished him with his file of the *Leyden Gazette* from whic to clip out foreign news. "And I can safely declare," he wrot Washington, in answer to Hamilton's charge that he was en gineering attacks on the administration, "that my expectatior ooked only to the chastisement of the aristocratic & monarchical writers & not to any criticisms of the proceedings of government."

The appearance of an opposition paper had stimulated Hamilton's flowing pen to a fresh flood of furious communications signed An American, Catullus, Metellus, Scourge and other high-sounding pseudonyms. Jefferson hadn't answered them himself. He never could shake off his old-fashioned notion that he shouldn't meddle with the press. On the other hand, he was becoming increasingly eager to have his younger friends write in his behalf; in fact he had taken great pleasure in Madison's series entitled "A Vindication of Mr. Jefferson," which had appeared in *Dunlap's American Daily Advertiser*. Meanwhile in doggerel and prose, Freneau, who loved a fight, was gaily bombarding Hamilton's bank and his financial system, and the monocrats and the Anglomen. Some of his shots went so far beyond their mark as to wound the President himself.

Though Jefferson was immured in the administration, Madison and Monroe had been experimenting with the beginnings of a political party. The clerk of the House of Representatives, John Beckley, was a Virginian. He was proving to be one of those busy modest anonymous men so essential to political organization. The son of a titled Englishman, he'd been educated at Eton, and combined great knowledge of the world with a passionate devotion to Jefferson's republicanism. He knew everybody who'd ever held federal office, and he kept his mouth shut and his ears open. He brought all his news to Jefferson or Madison. After traveling about the country, talking with local leaders, letting drop here and there damaging scraps of remarks about his friends' political enemies, he would hurry back to Congress with an itemized tally of men's attitudes. There Madison, always clear and humorously cool, furnished the strategy, while Monroe, the bluff partisan who tended to see things either black or white, stood firm as a rock for his friends.

Jefferson sincerely believed he was going to retire and refused to think of himself as a party leader, but he couldn't restrain his impulse to set younger men on the proper path. He couldn't help putting forth his views in conversation and in letters so plausibly that people found them in their own mouths before they knew it. He had a fellow feeling for the "aggregate mass of my fellow citizens," which he declared were "the most useful school we can enter into," that none of the other men had.

As he wrote Paine, who had sent him his latest pamphlet, "Our people, my good friend, are firm and unanimous in their principles of republicanism & there is no better proof of it than that they love what you write and read it with delight." Paine and Jefferson, of all the leaders of the age, were drawn together by their common respect for the average literate citizen. In spite of his insulation from everyday life by public office, and of his bookishness and his philosopher's oddities, the "aggregate mass" of the people didn't need to be told that Jefferson was "in earnest in his democracy."

It was the violence of the attacks of the politicians of the money interests who had usurped the name of Federalists that forced Jefferson into the Republican leadership. While the party was forming he had no other notion than that once the balance was restored against Hamilton he would go home to Monticello for the rest of his life.

"I acknowledge," he wrote Madison from the banks of the Schuylkill in June of 1793, trying to explain that he would not be running away in the face of the enemy, "that a tour of duty, in whatever line he can be most useful, is due from every individual. . . . I have now been in the public service four & twenty years; one half of which has been spent in total occupation with their affairs, & absence from my own. I have served my tour then." It was an old notion of his that the citizen's duty to the commonwealth was strictly limited by his rights as a man entitled to the pursuit of his own happiness.

Living in the city had always galled him. Now, with the river at his back and the air sweet and the birds singing, he was ready to do his best in a last set-to with the foreign problems of Washington's administration. His younger daughter Mary—for whom his nickname used to be Polly but whom, since she was almost grown, he now called Maria—was finishing her schooling in Philadelphia. She could spend two or three days a week with him on the Schuylkill, and this pleased him greatly

He was to need, it turned out, all the solace he could get. In Europe '93 was the year of wrath. Every packet arriving from overseas brought bloody news. The courts of Europe, lashed to fury by the remnants of the ancient regime at Versailles, streaming out of France in every conceivable disguise, had formed a military coalition. France answered the threat to her frontiers with the triumph at the polls of the extremest party of republicans. Armed mobs patrolled the towns. Aristocrats were arrested without regard to their opinions or behavior. Lafayette, still trying to head an army against the Austrians, was impeached in the assembly. Impeachment meant conviction. To save his head he rode with his staff into the enemy lines, was promptly arrested and interned at Olmütz in a castle.

The assembly dissolved itself to make way for the National Convention. The convention, made up of new men elected by universal suffrage who had come to the top tormented by the envies and hatreds of a hundred years of oppression, wiped the slate clean and declared the Year One. Aristocrats and monarchists were herded into the prisons, where the men of the mob could butcher them at their leisure. The French republic was at war with the world.

Meanwhile from England came news of violent reaction. British envoys had been intriguing with the coalition. A few days after the guillotine lopped off King Louis's head, the convention had declared war on Great Britain. Mobs rose in England too, and a period of repression set in.

The news from Europe was a tonic to the discouraged Hamiltonians. What better proof that your people is a great beast than the massacres in France? Now they could dream of an alliance with England, repudiation of the debt to France, sedition laws, censorship of the press, suspension of awkward old habeas corpus. Immediately the skirmishing between parties in Philadelphia became part of the worldwide war between revolution and the privileged orders.

Washington, however, was determined to steer a middle course between England and France. He believed neutrality to be a duty of necessity for Americans.

The Republicans as well as the Federalists were gleefully

sniffing the smoke of battle. Jefferson had long felt that a wa between France and England, if the United States could keep out of it, would do his country no harm. But like Washington he hoped for what he called "a fair neutrality."

A fair neutrality was easier to hope for than to attain. The British were trying to cut off shipment of food to France while the French were trying to use the American coast as a base for raiding British shipping. Edmund Charles Genêt, the new French minister, had arrived in Charleston with three hundred blank letters of marque in his traveling bag to license privateers. He had been greeted everywhere by cheers and toasts and salvos of musketry. His reception went to his head. He was a beaked blustering redheaded man whose sister had been one of Marie Antoinette's maids. Representing the French republic in the land of liberty in the Year One he overplayed his role to such an extent that he did the Republican Party a great deal of harm.

Genêt seemed convinced that Americans ought to be willing to play the role of subservient allies to the leadership of revolutionary France. Every time the administration demurred on one of his high-pitched demands, he threatened, in the style of the Paris convention, to appeal to the people. The people, so Jefferson and his friends were discovering with dismay, did not take at all kindly to the notion. The tirades Genêt stirred up in the Republican press, where writers full of libertarian zeal were coming out in the open with personal attacks on the President stirred up the plain people to support their beloved general just as they inclined Washington himself, whose wife's tea table was already shuddering with pity for the butchered aristocrats to side with the English.

Jefferson could see that the "satellites and sycophants" who surrounded Washington were using all this to undermine his influence with the President. Without Washington's approval he was helpless in his effort to pick his difficult path between France and England. Being sure that there was nothing but hostility towards the American people at Westminster, he hoped that by giving the Paris convention the benefit of every doubt he could serve the principles of revolution and the rights of man at the same time as he defended the true interests of the

United States. There was never any doubt in his mind that the interests of the United States should come first. His hatred of Hamilton's party was based on his fear that they would go to any length for an alliance with England. His position in Washington's cabinet had become impossible.

Late in August the political war was suddenly stilled. The yellow fever broke out in Philadelphia. The city was full of refugees from France. When in Santo Domingo the black slaves took the rights of man at their face value and rose against their French masters, shipload after shipload of escaping planters arrived at every southerly Atlantic port. In Philadelphia the taverns and the coffeehouses resounded with their horrifying reports of the slave insurrections. Along with the contagion of the hatred born of fear of the white masters against their black slaves, there came a contagion carried by a wan little low-flying mosquito that nobody at that time imagined carried death in its feeble sting.

"A malignant fever," Jefferson wrote Madison, who was happily home in Montpelier, on September 1, "has been generated in the filth of Water street which gives great alarm. About 70. people died of it two days ago, & as many more were ill of it. It has now got into most parts of the city & is considerably infectious. . . . It comes on with a pain in the head, sick stomach, then a little chill, black vomiting and stools, and death from the 2nd to the 8th day. Everybody who can is flying from the city. . . . I have withdrawn my daughter from the city but am obliged to go there every day myself."

"The president goes off the day after tomorrow as he had always intended," he wrote Madison a week later, making sure that nobody would take him to mean that George Washington had been scared out of Philadelphia by a few cases of yellow fever. "Hamilton is ill of the fever, as it is said. . . . I would really go away," he added, "because I think there is a rational danger, but that I had before announced that I should not go till the beginning of October, & I do not like to exhibit the appearance of panic. Besides that I think there might serious ls proceed from there not being a single member of the administration in place. Poor Hutcheson dined with me on Friday

. . . was taken that night on his return home & died day befor
yesterday."

Every hot September day Jefferson rode into town, leavin
little Maria—she was the prettier of the girls; she is said to hav
been small and lively like her mother—at the house by th
river, not knowing whether when he rode home for dinner i
the afternoon he would find her taken with the deadly symp
toms. When he arrived at his office on High Street he was m
with ever more alarming recitals of how this man and th
man had complained of a headache, gone home, been seize
with the black vomit and died. The fever took Federalist an
Republican alike. Nobody dared visit the sick. When a ma
didn't appear at his business it was taken for granted that h
was gone. The doctors were dying or had fled. Bodies wer
left to rot in the streets. At night carts moved from house t
house collecting the dead.

Meanwhile Jefferson, with despair in his heart, worked a
his copying desk, with meticulous application drafting his lon
careful letters to the French and English ministers and t
Gouverneur Morris in France, trying to explain the neutr
course over which he was trying to steer Washington's admi
istration between the presumptions of the French ministe
Genêt and the intrigues of Hamilton and the English ministe
Hammond. The French consuls were assuming extraterritori
rights, setting up admiralty courts of their own to condem
the prizes their privateers brought into American ports. Th
British were stopping and searching American ships, seizin
contraband and impressing their crews. No use complainin
anymore of the acts of Monsieur Dupont, the French consu
in Philadelphia. He was already dead.

The evening of September 10 Jefferson sat down to write a
answer long overdue to a letter from his old friend of the earl
days of the American Revolution, St. George Tucker, a con
genial Bermudian who had come to Williamsburg as a youn
man to study law and had settled in Virginia. He mentione
the "load of business" which was preventing his answerin
personal letters. He lamented the torture which an unname
young woman, a mutual friend whom they both esteeme

426

had suffered from the calumny of spiteful tongues. He remarked with feeling on "the proneness of the world to sow and spread slander." In the middle of it he suddenly broke off with the exclamation: "What an ocean is life!" He was thinking of himself. Already the spiteful tongues were busy distorting to his discredit every incident of his life.

The danger of death makes memory clear. He was thinking most likely of what a different destiny had been his from that he had planned as a young man, when he had looked forward to a life of farming and study, of pleasant talk among friends, a little practice of the law perhaps, a great deal of architecture and music. His life was not as he'd planned it. There was the gulf within that Patty's death had left. People told him that Maria looked like her mother. Now she too was in danger.

The danger of death makes thought lucid. There was no longer any doubt that to defeat the Federalists who, gathered under Washington's long shadow, were tightening their hold on the country's destinies, he would have to throw everything he had into the struggle, arguing, scheming, defaming, passing his days among men embittered by calumny and reprisal. Others could enunciate the strategy and manage the political organizations, but no man but Jefferson had the fellow feeling with the farmers, the planters struggling with the brutalities of slave labor, the mechanics and artisans in the towns, the settlers on the wide western rivers. He must be the leader.

Even while with the facile optimism that furnished his spirit with a sort of protective sheath in the bitterest moments of conflict his pen was tracing out words: "One of the greatest comforts of the retirement to which I shall soon withdraw will be it's rejoining me to my earliest and best friends,"—even while he wrote, he must have known it was not to be. Political differences had already separated him from many of his earliest and best friends. How many more friendships were changing to hatred and spite? "What an ocean is life," he wrote, "and how our barks get separated in beating through it!"

When at last he made up his mind not to risk Maria's life and his own by staying on any longer in Philadelphia, he discovered that, as it happened so often, he was clean out of cash.

427

"All the world is flying," he wrote the cashier of the Bank of the United States, asking for an advance of a hundred dollars on some payment due him in a few weeks. "I think to fly too in two or three days, but I am *money-bound*."

September 15 he wrote Madison telling of more deaths and the spread of the disease. Hamilton and his wife were recovering. "I have some expectations to set out tomorrow and shall make it eight days to your house, but it is possible I may yet be detained here two or three days."

The same day he wrote Washington, who was already on his way to the health and quiet of Mount Vernon: "Having found on my going to town, the day you left it, that I had but one clerk left, and that business could not be carried on, I determined to set out for Virginia as soon as I could clear my letter files. I have now got through it," he added with the satisfaction of having conquered the paper work, "so as to leave not a single letter unanswered, or anything undone, which is in a state to be done." He was leaving the administration to lead the opposition to its policies.

Three days later he was handing Maria into the phaeton and cracking the whip over the horses and driving away from Philadelphia.

THE
LIFE OF
CHARLOTTE
BRONTË

THE LIFE OF CHARLOTTE BRONTË

by

ELIZABETH GASKELL

ILLUSTRATIONS BY
DONALD M. HEDIN

The dour parsonage of Haworth, on the edge of the moors in the North of England, sheltered early in the nineteenth century a family of doomed children touched with genius. There were Charlotte, who wrote *Jane Eyre;* Emily, who wrote *Wuthering Heights;* their sister, Anne, also a published writer; and, in the background of all their lives, the brooding and wastrel brother, Branwell, who might have become a great painter. The tragic story of the Brontës has been told many times by different writers; yet nowhere has it been told so well as in this unusual biography written shortly after Charlotte's death by her talented contemporary and friend, Elizabeth Gaskell.

Mrs. Gaskell, herself a writer highly popular in her own day, had come to know Charlotte intimately in the last years of her life and was devoted to her. Her memoir of her friend and the Brontë family has become a classic, acclaimed by generations of critics as masterly, and as one of the most vivid and fascinating biographies in the English language.

CHAPTER I

THE LEEDS AND BRADFORD RAILWAY runs along a deep valley of the Aire. Keighley station is on this line of railway, about a quarter of a mile from the town of the same name. The importance of Keighley has very greatly increased during the last twenty years, owing to the rapidly growing market for worsted, which is manufactured in this part of Yorkshire. Thus Keighley is in process of transformation from a populous, old-fashioned village into a still more populous and flourishing town, where nearly every dwelling seems devoted to some branch of commerce, and where gray stone buildings abound.

The town of Keighley never quite melts into country on the road to Haworth, although the houses become more sparse as the traveler journeys westwards and upwards towards gray round hills. The distance to Haworth is about four miles. For two miles the road is tolerably level, with a small stream flowing through meadows on the right, furnishing waterpower to the factories built on its banks. The air is dim and lightless with smoke from all the habitations and places of business. As the road ascends, the vegetation becomes poorer; and, instead of trees, there are only bushes and shrubs about the dwellings.

Right before the traveler on this road rises Haworth village; he can see it for two miles before he arrives, for it is situated on the side of a steep hill, with a background of dun and purple moors rising and sweeping away yet higher than the church, which is built at the very summit of the long narrow street. All round the horizon there is this same line of sinuous, wavelike hills crowned with wild, bleak moors. For a short distance the road appears to turn away from Haworth, as it winds round the base of a hill. Then it crosses a bridge over the stream, and the ascent through the village begins. The flagstones with which the street is paved are placed endways, in order to give a better hold to the horses' feet; and, even with this help, they seem to be in constant danger of slipping backwards. Going past old stone houses, the street makes an abrupt turn before reaching more level ground at the head of the village. Here the church lies a little off the main road on the left; a hundred yards or so and the driver relaxes his care, and the horse breathes more easily, as they pass into the quiet little bystreet that leads to Haworth Parsonage.

The churchyard is on one side of this lane, the schoolhouse and the sexton's dwelling on the other. The parsonage stands at right angles to the road, facing down upon the church; so that, in fact, parsonage, church, and belfried schoolhouse form three sides of an irregular oblong, of which the fourth is open to the fields and moors that lie beyond. The area of this oblong is filled up by a crowded churchyard and a small garden in front of the clergyman's house. Within the stone wall, which keeps out the surrounding churchyard, are bushes of elder and lilac. The house is of gray stone, two stories high, heavily roofed with flags. There are windows on the right of the front door, and two on the left. Everything about the place tells of the most dainty order, the most exquisite cleanliness. The doorsteps are spotless; the small old-fashioned windowpanes glitter like looking glass.

The little church lies above most of the houses of the village, and the graveyard rises above the church. The church claims great antiquity; inside, the character of the pillars shows that they were constructed before the reign of Henry VII. The pews are of black oak, with high divisions, and the names of those to whom they belong are painted in white letters on the doors.

There are neither brasses nor altar tombs nor monuments, but there is a mural tablet on the right-hand side of the communion table, bearing the following inscription:

HERE

LIE THE REMAINS OF

MARIA BRONTË, WIFE

OF THE

REV. P. BRONTË, A.B., MINISTER OF HAWORTH.

HER SOUL

DEPARTED TO THE SAVIOUR, SEPT. 15TH, 1821,

IN THE 39TH YEAR OF HER AGE.

"Be ye also ready; for in such an hour as ye think not the Son of Man cometh."—Matthew xxiv. 44.

ALSO HERE LIE THE REMAINS OF

MARIA BRONTË, DAUGHTER OF THE AFORESAID;

SHE DIED ON THE

6TH OF MAY, 1825, IN THE 12TH YEAR OF HER AGE,

AND OF

ELIZABETH BRONTË, HER SISTER,

WHO DIED JUNE 15TH, 1825, IN THE 11TH YEAR OF HER AGE.

"Verily I say unto you, Except ye be converted, and become as little children, ye shall not enter into the kingdom of heaven." —Matthew xviii. 3.

HERE ALSO LIE THE REMAINS OF

PATRICK BRANWELL BRONTË,

WHO DIED SEPT. 24TH, 1848, AGED 30 YEARS.

AND OF

EMILY JANE BRONTË,

WHO DIED DEC. 19TH, 1848, AGED 29 YEARS,

SON AND DAUGHTER OF THE

REV. P. BRONTË, INCUMBENT

THIS STONE IS ALSO DEDICATED TO THE

MEMORY OF ANNE BRONTË,

YOUNGEST DAUGHTER OF THE REV. P. BRONTË, A.B.

SHE DIED, AGED 27 YEARS, MAY 28TH, 1849,

AND WAS BURIED AT THE OLD CHURCH, SCARBORO'.

At the upper part of this tablet ample space is allowed between the lines of the inscription; but as one member of the household follows another fast to the grave, the lines are pressed together and the letters become small and cramped. After the record of Anne's death, there is room for no other.

But one more of that generation—the last of that nursery of six little motherless children—was yet to follow, before the survivor, the childless and widowed father, found his rest. On another tablet, below the first, the following record has been added to that mournful list:

ADJOINING LIE THE REMAINS OF
CHARLOTTE, WIFE
OF THE
REV. ARTHUR BELL NICHOLLS, A.B.,
AND DAUGHTER OF THE REV. P. BRONTË, A.B., INCUMBENT.
SHE DIED MARCH 31ST, 1855, IN THE 39TH
YEAR OF HER AGE.

FOR A RIGHT UNDERSTANDING of the life of my dear friend, Charlotte Brontë, the reader should be made acquainted with the forms of population and society amidst which her earliest years were passed.

Yorkshiremen display a peculiar force of character. This makes them interesting as a race; while at the same time, as individuals, the remarkable degree of self-sufficiency they possess gives them an air of independence rather apt to repel a stranger. The practical qualities of a man are held in great respect. The affections are strong and their foundations lie deep: but they are not wide-spreading, nor do they show themselves on the surface. Indeed, there is little display of any of the amenities of life among this wild, rough population. Their greeting is curt; their accent and tone of speech blunt and harsh. Something of this may probably be attributed to the isolated hillside life. They have a quick perception of character and a keen sense of humor; the dwellers among them must be prepared for uncomplimentary, though likely true, observations, pithily expressed.

Yorkshiremen are not easily made into either friends or enemies; but once lovers or haters, it is difficult to change their feeling. I remember Miss Brontë once telling me that it was a saying round about Haworth, "Keep a stone in thy pocket seven year; turn it, and keep it seven year longer, that it may be ever ready to thine hand when thine enemy draws near."

The people of Haworth were not less strong and full of character than their neighbors. About the middle of the last century, their village became famous in the religious world as the scene of the ministrations of the Reverend William Grimshaw, curate of Haworth for twenty years. It seems that he had not been in any way remarkable for religious zeal until a certain Sunday in September, 1744. On that day, as he was reading the second lesson, he fell down, and on his partial recovery had to be led from the church. As he went out, he told the congregation not to disperse. When he returned presently, the first words he uttered were, "I have had a glorious vision from the third heaven," and he began the service again, at two in the afternoon, and went on until seven.

From this time he devoted himself, with the fervor of a Wesley, to calling out a religious life among his parishioners. By various means he wrought a great change in his parish. In his services, if he perceived anyone inattentive to his prayers, he would stop and rebuke the offender, and not go on till he saw everyone on their knees. He would not even allow his parishioners to walk in the fields between services. He sometimes gave out a very long Psalm, and while it was being sung, he left the reading desk, and taking a horsewhip went into the public houses and flogged the loiterers into church. They were swift who could escape by sneaking out the back way.

After his time, however, I fear there was a falling back in Haworth into the wild rough heathen ways from which he had pulled them up. Revenge was handed down from father to son as a hereditary duty; and a great capability for drinking was considered one of the manly virtues. Games of football on Sundays, discontinued while Mr. Grimshaw was alive, were resumed, bringing in an influx of riotous strangers to fill the public houses. As few "shirked their liquor," there were very frequently "up-and-down-fights" before the close of the day.

Into the midst of this lawless yet not unkindly population, Mr. Brontë brought his wife and six little children, in February 1820. There are those yet alive who remember seven heavily laden carts lumbering slowly up the long stone street, bearing the "new parson's" household goods to his future abode. One wonders how the bleak aspect of her new home struck on the gentle, delicate wife, whose health even then was failing.

THE REVEREND PATRICK BRONTË is a native of the County Down in Ireland. His father, Hugh Brontë, was left an orphan at an early age. He settled near Loughbrickland, made an early marriage, and reared ten children on the proceeds of a few acres of farmland. This large family were remarkable for great physical strength and much personal beauty. Even in his old age, Mr. Brontë is a striking-looking man, above the common height, with a nobly shaped head and erect carriage.

Born on Saint Patrick's day, 1777, Patrick Brontë early gave tokens of extraordinary quickness and intelligence. He had also his share of ambition; and, knowing that his father could afford him no pecuniary aid, he opened a public school at the early age of sixteen; and this mode of living he continued to follow for five or six years. He then became a tutor in the family of the rector of Drumgooland parish. Thence he proceeded to St. John's College, Cambridge, where he was entered in July 1802, being at the time five-and-twenty years of age. After four years he obtained his B.A. degree and was ordained to a curacy in Essex, whence he removed into Yorkshire.

We take him up now in 1811, settled as a curate at Hartshead, in Yorkshire—a very small village lying east of Huddersfield. Those were the days of the Luddite riots, when workers were resisting the introduction of machinery into factories. Mr. Brontë was for the peremptory interference of the law, at a time when no magistrate could be found to act, and all the property of the West Riding was in danger. He became unpopular among the mill workers, and so he then began the habit of invariably carrying a loaded pistol about with him.

While the incumbent of Hartshead, Mr. Brontë wooed and married Maria Branwell. She was the third daughter of Mr. Thomas Branwell, merchant, of Penzance. Mr. Branwell and his wife died within a year of each other, when their daughter Maria was twenty-five or twenty-six years of age.

In the summer of 1812, when she would be twenty-nine, she came to visit her uncle, the Reverend John Fennel, living near Leeds. Mr. Brontë had the reputation of being a very handsome fellow, full of Irish enthusiasm, and with something of an Irishman's capability of falling easily in love. Miss Branwell was extremely small in person, not pretty, but very elegant. Mr. Brontë was soon captivated by the little, gentle creature, and this time declared that it was for life. In her first letter to him, dated August 26, she seems almost surprised to find herself engaged and alludes to the short time which she has known him. There was no family opposition to her engagement.

The journey from Penzance to Leeds in those days was long and expensive, the lovers had not much money, and, as Miss Branwell had neither father nor mother living, it appeared a seemly arrangement that the marriage should take place from her uncle's house in Yorkshire. So, on the twenty-ninth of December, 1812, the lovers were married.

They remained for five years at Hartshead. There their first two children, Maria and Elizabeth, were born. At the expiration of that period, Mr. Brontë had the living of Thornton, in Bradford parish, and it was here that Charlotte Brontë was born, on the twenty-first of April, 1816. Fast on her heels followed Patrick Branwell, Emily Jane, and Anne. After the birth of this last daughter, Mrs. Brontë's health began to decline. It is hard work to provide for the little tender wants of many young children where the means are but limited. Maria Brontë, the eldest of six, could only have been a few months more than six years old when Mr. Brontë removed to Haworth, on February 25, 1820. Those who knew Maria then describe her as grave, thoughtful, and quiet, to a degree far beyond her years. She must have been her mother's companion and helpmate in many a household and nursery experience, for Mr. Brontë was much engaged in his study; and besides, he was not naturally fond of children, and felt their frequent appearance on the scene as a drag on his wife's strength and as an interruption to the comfort of the household.

Haworth Parsonage is an oblong stone house. It consists of four rooms on each floor, and is two stories high. When the

Brontës took possession, they made the larger parlor, to the left of the entrance, the family sitting room, while that on the right was appropriated to Mr. Brontë as a study. Behind this was the kitchen; behind the sitting room, a storeroom. Upstairs were four bedchambers, with the addition of a small apartment over the "lobby," as we call it in the North. This little extra upstairs room was appropriated to the children.

Maria Branwell as a young girl of sixteen. Thirteen years later, at the age of twenty-nine, she married the Reverend Patrick Brontë. The portrait at right shows him as he looked in 1825—five years after he and Maria arrived at Haworth.

The servants—two rough, warmhearted sisters, who cannot now speak of the family without tears—called the room the children's study. The age of the eldest student was perhaps by this time seven.

The people in Haworth were none of them very poor. Many of them were employed in the neighboring worsted mills; a few were millowners; there were also shopkeepers for the humbler everyday wants; but for medical advice, for books, dress, or dainties, the inhabitants had to go to Keighley. There were several Sunday schools in the village, and also Methodist and Baptist chapels. Mr. Brontë was ever on friendly terms with each denomination as a body; but from individuals in the village the family stood aloof. "They kept themselves very close," is the account given by those who remember Mr. and Mrs. Brontë's coming amongst them. Mr. Brontë was faithful in visiting the sick and those who sent for him; but, valuing privacy themselves, the Brontës were perhaps overdelicate in not intruding upon the privacy of others.

Mrs. Brontë's illness—an internal cancer—gathered upon her not many months after her arrival at Haworth. A good old woman who came to nurse her tells me that at that time the six little children used to walk out, hand in hand, towards the glorious wild moors, which in afterdays they loved so passionately, the elder ones taking thoughtful care for the toddling wee things.

They were grave and silent beyond their years, subdued by the presence of serious illness in the house; for at this time Mrs. Brontë was confined to the bedroom from which she never came forth alive. She was very ill, suffering great pain but seldom if ever complaining; devotedly fond of her husband, who warmly repaid her affection and suffered no one else to take the night nursing. But the mother was not very anxious to see much of her children, probably because the sight of them, knowing how soon they were to be left motherless, would have agitated her too much. So the little things clung quietly together, for their father was busy in his study and in his parish, or with their mother, and they took their meals alone; sat reading, or whispering low, in the children's study, or wandered out on the hillside. "You would not have known there was a child in the house, they were such still, noiseless, good little creatures," my informant said. "There never were such good children. I used to think them spiritless, they were so different to any children I had ever seen. Emily was the prettiest."

Mr. Brontë wished to make his children hardy, and indifferent to the pleasures of eating and dress, and he went at his object with unsparing earnestness. Mrs. Brontë's nurse told me that one day when the children had been out, and rain had come on, she thought their feet would be wet, and she rummaged out some colored boots which had been given to them by a friend. These little pairs she ranged round the kitchen fire to warm; but when the children came back, only a very strong odor of burnt leather was perceived. Mr. Brontë had seen the boots; they were too gay and luxurious, and would foster a love of dress, so he had put them into the fire.

He spared nothing that offended his antique simplicity. Long before this, someone had given Mrs. Brontë a silk gown which

442

did not accord to his notions of propriety, and Mrs. Brontë in consequence never wore it. But she kept it treasured up in a locked drawer. One day, however, while in the kitchen, she remembered that she had left the key in her drawer, and, hearing Mr. Brontë upstairs, she augured some ill to her dress, and, running up, she found it cut into shreds.

His strong, passionate Irish nature was, in general, compressed down with stoicism. He did not speak when he was annoyed, but worked off his wrath by firing pistols out of the back door in rapid succession. Mrs. Brontë, in bed, would hear the explosions and know that something had gone wrong. He fearlessly took whatever side in local or national politics appeared to him right. His opinions might be often wild and erroneous, but not one opinion that he held could be stirred or modified by any worldly motive.

Mrs. Brontë died in September 1821, and the lives of those quiet children must have become quieter and lonelier still. Charlotte tried hard, in afteryears, to recall the remembrance of her mother, but the recollections of four or five years old are of a very fragmentary character.

Owing to some illness of the digestive organs, Mr. Brontë was obliged to be careful about his diet; and, in order to avoid temptation, and possibly to have the quiet necessary for digestion, he had begun before his wife's death to take his dinner alone—a habit which he always retained. He did not require companionship. The quiet regularity of his hours was broken in upon only by visitors on parochial business, and sometimes by a neighboring clergyman, who came across the moors to spend an evening at the parsonage. But, owing to Mrs. Brontë's death so soon after her husband had removed into the district, and also to the distances, the wives of these clerical friends did not accompany their husbands; and the daughters grew up bereft of all such society as would have been natural to their age and station.

But the children did not want society. They were all in all to each other. I do not suppose that there ever was a family more tenderly bound to each other. Maria read the newspapers, and reported intelligence to her younger sisters. But I suspect that they had no "children's books," and that their eager minds "browsed undisturbed among the wholesome pasturage of English literature," as Charles Lamb expresses it. The servants of the household appear to have been much impressed with the little Brontës' cleverness. In a letter which I had from him on this subject, their father writes: "The servants often said that they had never seen such a clever little child" (as Charlotte).

A photograph of Haworth Parsonage as it looked when the Brontës lived there. The dark figure silhouetted against the side of the building is thought to be that of Charlotte. Today the early Georgian structure houses the Brontë museum.

These servants speak of her unvarying kindness from the "time when she was ever such a little child!" Once she would not rest till she had got the old disused cradle sent from the parsonage to the house where the parents of one of them lived, to serve for a little infant sister. They tell of one long series of kind and thoughtful actions from this early period to the last weeks of Charlotte Brontë's life. There might not be many to regard the Brontës with affection, but those who once loved them, loved them long and well.

I return to the father's letter. He says:

When mere children, as soon as they could read and write, Charlotte and her brother and sisters used to invent and act little plays . . . in which the Duke of Wellington, my daughter Charlotte's hero, was sure to come off conqueror; when a dispute would not unfrequently arise amongst them regarding the comparative merits of him, Buonaparte, Hannibal, and Caesar. When the argument got warm, I had sometimes to come in as arbitrator and settle the dispute. I frequently thought that I discovered signs of rising talent, which I had never before seen in any of their age. . . . A circumstance now occurs to my mind which I may as well mention. When my children were very young, the oldest was about ten, and the youngest about four, thinking that they knew more than I had yet discovered, in order to make them speak with less timidity, I deemed that if they were put under a sort of cover I might gain my end; and

ld Haworth Church,
here the Brontës
orshipped. Originally
ilt before 1500, it was,
ith the exception of the
d tower, completely
built in 1879.

happening to have a mask in the house, I told them all to stand and speak boldly from under cover of the mask.

I began with the youngest (Anne), and asked what a child like her most wanted; she answered, "Age and experience." I asked the next (Emily), what I had best to do with her brother Branwell, who was sometimes a naughty boy; she answered, "Reason with him, and when he won't listen to reason, whip him." I asked Branwell what was the best way of knowing the difference between the intellects of men and women; he answered, "By considering the difference between them as to their bodies." I then asked Charlotte what was the best book in the world; she answered, "The Bible." And the next best; she answered, "The Book of Nature." I then asked the next [Elizabeth] what was the best mode of education for a woman; she answered, "That which would make her rule her house well." Lastly, I asked the oldest [Maria] what was the best mode of spending time; she answered, "By laying it out in preparation for a happy eternity." I may not have given precisely their words, but I have nearly done so, as they made a deep impression on my memory. . . .

445

The quaint simplicity of the mode taken by the father t ascertain the hidden characters of his children, and the tone an character of these questions and answers, show the curiou education which was made by the circumstances surroundin the Brontës. They knew no other children. They knew n other modes of thought than what were suggested to them b the fragments of clerical conversation which they overheard i the parlor, or the subjects of local interest which they hear discussed in the kitchen, or the politics which they found dis cussed in the newspapers. Each had their own strong character istic flavor.

CHAPTER II

ABOUT A YEAR after Mrs. Brontë's death, one of her elde sisters came from Penzance to superintend her brother-in-law' household. Miss Branwell was a kindly and conscientiou woman but with somewhat narrow ideas, and she soon took distaste to Yorkshire. From Penzance, where the climate is sof and warm and where plants grow in profusion, it was a grea change for a lady considerably past forty to take up her abod in a place where neither flowers nor vegetables would flourish where the snow lay long and late on the moors, and where often on winter nights, the four winds of heaven seemed to meet an rage together around the house as if they were wild beast striving to find an entrance. She missed the small round o cheerful social visiting perpetually going on in a country town and she missed her friends. In the later years of her life, Mis Branwell passed nearly all her time in her bedroom, from he dread of catching cold.

The children respected Miss Branwell, but I do not thin they ever freely loved her. I do not know whether she taugh her nieces anything besides sewing and the household arts Their regular lessons were said to their father; and they wer always in the habit of picking up an immense amount o miscellaneous information for themselves. But a year or s before this time, a school had been begun in the North o

gland for the daughters of clergymen. The place was Cowan
idge, a small hamlet on the coach road between Leeds and
ndal, and thus easy of access from Haworth. The yearly
pense for each pupil was £14, half to be paid in advance. The
stem of education comprehended history, geography, the use
the globes, grammar, writing and arithmetic, needlework,
d the nicer kinds of household work.

*e parlor at Haworth
rsonage today. This
m was used mostly
the children, but the
verend Brontë would
asionally take meals
e while the children
in the kitchen.*

The entrance rules state the clothing and toilette articles
hich a girl is expected to bring with her: "The pupils all
pear in the same dress. They wear plain straw bonnets, in
mmer white frocks on Sundays, and nankeen on other days;
winter, purple stuff frocks, and purple cloth cloaks. For the
ke of uniformity, therefore, they are required to bring £3 in
u of frocks, pelisse, bonnet, tippet, and frills." There is nothing
markable in any of the other regulations, a copy of which was
ubtless in Mr. Brontë's hands when he formed the deter-
ination to send his daughters to Cowan Bridge school; and he
cordingly took Maria and Elizabeth thither in July 1824.
harlotte and Emily followed in September.

Miss Brontë more than once said to me that she should
ot have written what she did of Lowood, the school which
pears in *Jane Eyre*, if she had thought the place would have
en so immediately identified with Cowan Bridge, although
ere was not a word in her account of the institution but what
as true at the time when she knew it. I believe she herself would

have been glad of an opportunity to correct the overstro
impression which was made upon the public mind by her viv
picture, though she suffered her whole life long, both in hea
and body, from the consequences of what happened there.

A wealthy clergyman, living near Kirkby Lonsdale, t
Reverend William Carus Wilson, was the prime mover in t
establishment of the school. Cowan Bridge is a cluster of s

*The Cowan Bridg
school, on the bord
of Lancashire and
Westmorland, whe
the Brontë girls
received their early
schooling. Charlot
later immortalized
as Lowood, the sch
in "Jane Eyre."*

or seven cottages, gathered at both ends of a bridge, over whic
the highroad from Leeds to Kendal crosses a little stream, calli
the Leck. The stream is shallow, sparkling, and vigorous; ai
by its course alders and willows and hazel bushes grow. I ca
hardly understand how the school there came to be so u
healthy, the air all round about was so sweet and thyme
scented when I visited it last summer.

A house that formed part of the school is still remainin
It is a long, low bow-windowed cottage facing the Lec
Running from this building, at right angles, there was former
a bobbin mill connected with the stream. Mr. Wilson adapte
this mill; there were schoolrooms on the lower floor and dorm
tories on the upper. The present cottage was occupied by t
teachers' rooms, the dining room, and kitchens. It has the lo
ceilings and stone floors of a hundred years ago; the window
do not open freely; altogether, smells would linger about th
house and damp cling to it. But sanitary matters were littl
understood in the 1820's, and numbers of ill-paid clergyme

448

hailed the educational scheme with joy; they eagerly put down the names of their children as pupils, and Mr. Wilson opened the school with, as far as I can make out, from seventy to eighty students.

He felt, most probably, that the responsibility of the whole plan rested upon him. The payment made by the parents was barely enough for food and lodging, and great economy was necessary in all arrangements. He determined to enforce this by frequent personal inspection; and his love of authority seems to have led to a great deal of unnecessary meddling with little matters. Yet, although there was economy, there does not appear to have been any parsimony. The meat, flour, milk, etc., were of fair quality; and the dietary was not unwholesome. Oatmeal porridge for breakfast; a piece of oatcake for those who required luncheon; baked and boiled beef, and mutton, potato pie, and plain puddings for dinner. At five o'clock, bread and milk for the younger ones, and one piece of bread (this was the only time at which the food was limited) for the elder pupils, who sat up till a later meal of the same description.

Mr. Wilson himself ordered in the food and was anxious that it should be of good quality. But the cook, who had much of his confidence, was careless and dirty. To some children oatmeal porridge is distasteful even when properly made; at Cowan Bridge school it was too often sent up, not merely burned, but with offensive fragments of other substances in it. The beef had often become tainted from neglect; the rice pudding was often made of rice boiled in water from the rain tub, and was strongly impregnated with dust that had trickled down from the roof; the milk, too, was often "bingy," to use a country expression for a kind of taint that is far worse than sourness and is caused by want of cleanliness about the milk pans. On Saturdays, a kind of pie, or mixture of potatoes and meat, was served up, which was made of all the fragments accumulated during the week.

One may fancy how repulsive such fare would be to children whose appetites were small, and who had been accustomed to food far simpler, perhaps, but wholesome. Many a meal the little Brontës went without food, although craving with hunger. They were not strong when they came, having only just recovered from a complication of measles and whooping cough; indeed, there was some consultation on the part of the school authorities whether Maria and Elizabeth should be received or not.

There was another trial of health common to all the girls. The path from Cowan Bridge to Tunstall Church, where Mr Wilson preached and where they all attended on Sunday, is more than two miles in length, through unsheltered country. It was a bitter cold walk in winter. The church was not warmed and the damp mists must have crept in at the windows.

The arrangements for this day were peculiarly trying to delicate children, particularly to those who were spiritless and longing for home, as poor Maria Brontë must have been. For her ill health was increasing. She was far superior in mind to any of her companions; and yet she had faults so annoying that she was in constant disgrace with her teachers, and an object of merciless dislike to one of them, who is depicted as Miss Scatcherd in *Jane Eyre* and whose real name I will be merciful enough not to disclose. I need hardly say that Helen Burns in *Jane Eyre* is as exact a transcript of Maria Brontë as Charlotte's wonderful power of reproducing character could give.

One of the fellow pupils of Charlotte and Maria Brontë's gives me the following statement: The dormitory in which Maria slept was a long room, at the end of which was a small bed chamber used by Miss Scatcherd. Maria's bed stood nearest to the door of this room. One morning, after she had become so seriously unwell as to have had a blister applied to her side, when the getting-up bell was heard, poor Maria moaned out that she was so very ill, she wished she might stop in bed; and some of the girls urged her to do so, and said they would explain it all to Miss Temple, the superintendent. But Miss Scatcherd was close at hand, and her anger would have to be faced before Miss Temple's kindness could interfere; so the sick child began to dress, shivering with cold, as, without leaving her bed, she slowly put on her black worsted stockings. Just then Miss Scatcherd issued from her room and took her by the arm, on the side to which the blister had been applied, and whirled her out into the middle of the floor, abusing her all the time for dirty and untidy habits. There she left her. In slow, trembling movements, with many a pause, Maria went downstairs at last—and was punished for being late.

Anyone may fancy how such an event would rankle in Charlotte's mind.

In the spring of 1825 that low fever—or typhus—broke out

Tunstall Church, attended by Cowan Bridge students, and the Reverend Wilson, the Mr. Brocklehurst of "Jane Eyre."

which is spoken of in *Jane Eyre*. Mr. Wilson was extremely alarmed at the first symptoms of this, and he went to a kind motherly woman who had had some connection with the school—as laundress, I believe—and asked her to come and tell him what was the matter. When she entered the schoolroom, she saw twelve or fifteen girls lying about; some resting their aching heads on the table, all heavy-eyed and flushed. Some peculiar odor, she says, made her recognize that they were sickening for "the fever"; and she told Mr. Wilson so, and that she could not stay for fear of conveying the infection to her own children; but he half commanded, half entreated her to remain and nurse them, and finally mounted his gig and drove away.

When she was left in this unceremonious manner, she determined to make the best of it, and a most efficient nurse she proved. Mr. Wilson supplied everything ordered by the doctors; he even sent for additional advice, in the person of his brother-in-law, a clever medical man in Kirkby; and it was this doctor who tasted and condemned the daily food of the girls by the expressive action of spitting out the portion which he had taken. About forty of the girls suffered from this fever, though none of the Brontës had it. The principal cause was the food. The cook was blamed for this; she was dismissed, and the woman who had been forced to serve as nurse took the place of housekeeper; and henceforward the food was so well prepared that no one could reasonably complain of it.

Of course it cannot be expected that a new institution should work quite smoothly at the beginning. But Mr. Wilson seems to have had the unlucky gift of irritating even those to whom he meant kindly. He had, too, so little knowledge of human nature as to imagine that, by constantly reminding the girls of the fact that they were receiving their education from the charity of others, he could make them lowly and humble. Painful impressions sink deep into the hearts of delicate and sickly children. The pictures, ideas, and conceptions of character received into the mind of the child of eight years old were destined to be reproduced in fiery words a quarter of a century afterwards. She saw only one side, and that the unfavorable side of Mr. Wilson.

The recollections left of the four Brontë sisters at this period of their lives on the minds of those who associated with them are not very distinct. The only glimpse we get of Elizabeth, through the few years of her short life, is contained in a letter which I have received from "Miss Temple."

> The second, Elizabeth, is the only one of the family of whom I have a vivid recollection, from her meeting with an alarming accident . . . I had her for some days and nights in my bed-room, that I might watch over her. Her head was severely cut, but she bore all her suffering with exemplary patience, and by it won much upon my esteem. Of the two younger ones I have very slight recollections, save that one, a darling child, under five years of age, was quite the pet nursling of the school.

This last would be Emily. Charlotte was considered the most talkative of the sisters—a "bright, clever little child."

In this spring of 1825, Maria, who was suffering from con

umption, became so rapidly worse that Mr. Brontë was sent
or. He had not been aware of her illness, and the condition in
which he found her was a terrible shock to him. He took her
ome, and she died a very few days later.

Perhaps the news of her death made those who remained at
Cowan Bridge look with more anxiety on Elizabeth's symp-
oms, which also turned out to be consumptive. She was sent
ome; and she, too, died in the early summer of that year.
Charlotte and Emily also returned to Haworth, and Charlotte
was thus suddenly called into the responsibilities of eldest sister in
motherless family. She remembered how anxiously her dear
ster Maria had striven to be a tender helper and a counselor to
hem all, and the duties that now fell upon her seemed almost
ke a legacy from the gentle little sufferer so lately dead.

CHAPTER III

THE LITTLE GIRLS had been sent home in the summer of 1825,
when Charlotte was nine years old. About this time, an elderly
woman of the village came to live as servant at the parsonage.
he remained there, as a member of the household, for thirty
ears, and the attachment and respect which she inspired is
eserving of mention.

Tabby was a thorough specimen of a Yorkshire woman. She
bounded in strong practical sense and shrewdness. Her words
vere far from flattery, but she would spare no deeds in the
ause of those whom she kindly regarded. She ruled the children
retty sharply; and yet never grudged a little extra trouble to
rovide them with small treats. In return, she claimed to be
ooked upon as a humble friend.

Tabby had lived in Haworth in the days when the packhorses
vent through once a week, with their tinkling bells and gay
vorsted adornment. No doubt she had many a tale to tell the
hildren of bygone days in the countryside, of old ways of
ving, former inhabitants, family tragedies, and dark super-
itious dooms; and in telling these things would give at full
ength, unsoftened, the bare and simple details.

453

Miss Branwell instructed the children at regular hours in a she could teach, making her bedchamber into their schoolroom Their father was in the habit of relating to them any public new in which he felt an interest, and from the opinions of his in dependent mind they would gather much food for thought Charlotte's thoughtful spirit appears to have felt almost pain fully the responsibility which rested upon her with reference t her remaining sisters. She was only eighteen months older tha Emily; but Emily and Anne were simply companions and play mates, while Charlotte was motherly friend and guardian t both, and this assumption of duties beyond her years made he feel considerably older than she was.

Patrick Branwell, their only brother, was a boy of remarkabl promise, and, in some ways, of extraordinary precocity o talent. Mr. Brontë's friends advised him to send his son t school, but he believed that Patrick was better at home and tha he himself could teach him well. So Patrick, or, as his famil called him, Branwell, remained at Haworth, working for som hours a day with his father; but, when the time of the latter wa taken up with his parochial duties, the boy was thrown int chance companionship with the lads of the village—for yout will to youth, and boys will be boys.

Still, he was associated in many of his sisters' plays and amuse ments. These were mostly of an intellectual nature. I have ha a curious packet confided to me, containing an immense amoun of manuscript in an inconceivably small space: tales, drama poems, written principally by Charlotte, in a hand which it i almost impossible to decipher without a magnifying glass.

Among these papers there is a list of her works, part of whic I copy as a curious proof how early the rage for literary compo sition had seized upon her:

CATALOGUE OF MY BOOKS, UP TO AUGUST 3RD, 1830

Two romantic tales in one volume; viz., The Twelve Adventurers and the Adventures in Ireland, April 2nd, 1829.
The Search after Happiness, a Tale, Aug. 1st, 1829.
Leisure Hours, a Tale, and two Fragments, July 6th, 1829.
The Adventures of Edward de Crack, a Tale, Feb. 2nd, 1830.

The Adventures of Ernest Alembert, a Tale, May 26th, 1830.

Tales of the Islanders, in four volumes . . . ; completed July 30th, 1830.

The Poetaster, a Drama, in 2 volumes, July 12th, 1830.

A Book of Rhymes, finished December 17th, 1829; Contents: 1. The Beauty of Nature; 2. A Short Poem; 3. Meditations while Journeying in a Canadian Forest; 4. A Song of an Exile; 5. On Seeing the Ruins of the Tower of Babel.

Altogether there were twenty-two volumes. As each volume contains from sixty to a hundred pages, the amount of the whole seems very great if we remember that it was all written in about fifteen months. So much for the quantity; the quality strikes me as of singular merit for a girl of thirteen or fourteen. Both as a specimen of her prose style at this time, and also as revealing something of the quiet domestic life led by these children, I take an extract from the introduction to *Tales of the Islanders*, the title of one of their *Little Magazines:*

June the 31st, 1829.

The play of the *Islanders* was formed in December, 1827, in the following manner. One night, about the time when the cold sleet and stormy fogs of November are succeeded by the snow-storms, and high piercing night-winds of confirmed winter, we were all sitting round the warm blazing kitchen fire, having just concluded a quarrel with Tabby concerning the propriety of lighting a candle, from which she came off victorious, no candle having been produced. A long pause succeeded, which was at last broken by Branwell saying, in a lazy manner, "I don't know what to do." This was echoed by Emily and Anne.

Tabby. "Wha ya may go t' bed."

Branwell. "I'd rather do anything than that."

Charlotte. "Why are you so glum to-night, Tabby? Oh! suppose we had each an island of our own."

Branwell. "If we had I would choose the Island of Man."

Charlotte. "And I would choose the Isle of Wight."

Emily. "The Isle of Arran for me."

Anne. "And mine should be Guernsey."

We then chose who should be chief men in our islands. Branwell chose John Bull, Astley Cooper, and Leigh Hunt; Emily, Walter Scott, Mr. Lockhart, Johnny Lockhart; Anne, Michael

Sadler, Lord Bentinck, Sir Henry Halford. I chose the Duke of Wellington and two sons, Christopher North and Co., and Mr. Abernethy. Here our conversation was interrupted by the, to us, dismal sound of the clock striking seven, and we were summoned off to bed.

Two or three things strike me much in this fragment; one is the graphic vividness with which the time of the year, the hour of the evening, the feeling of cold and darkness outside is contrasted with the glow and brightness of the kitchen where these remarkable children are grouped. Tabby moves about in her quaint country dress, prone to find fault, yet allowing no one else to blame her children, we may feel sure. Another noticeable fact is the intelligent partisanship with which they choose their great men, who are almost all staunch Tories of the time. Little Anne, aged scarcely eight, picks out the politicians of the day.

There is another scrap of paper written about this time which gives some idea of the sources of their opinions.

THE HISTORY OF THE YEAR 1829

Once Papa lent my sister Maria a book. It was an old geography book; she wrote on its blank leaf, "Papa lent me this book." This book is a hundred and twenty years old; it is at this moment lying before me. While I write this I am in the kitchen of the Parsonage, Haworth; Tabby, the servant, is washing up the breakfast-things, and Anne, my youngest sister, is kneeling on a chair, looking at some cakes which Tabby had been baking for us. Emily is in the parlour, brushing the carpet. Papa and Branwell are gone to Keighley . . . for the newspaper, the *Leeds Intelligencer*, a most excellent Tory newspaper. . . . We take the *Leeds Intelligencer*, Tory, and the *Leeds Mercury*, Whig. We see the *John Bull;* it is a high Tory, very violent. Mr. Driver lends us it, as likewise *Blackwood's Magazine*, the most able periodical there is. . . .

Our plays were established; *Young Men*, June, 1826; *Our Fellows*, July, 1827; *Islanders*, December, 1827. These are our three great plays, that are not kept secret. Emily's and my bed plays were established the 1st of December, 1827; the others March, 1828. Bed plays mean secret plays; they are very nice ones. All our plays are very strange ones. . . . The *Young Men's* play took its rise from some wooden soldiers Branwell had; *Our Fellows* from *Aesop's Fables;* and the *Islanders* from several events which happened. . . . Papa bought Branwell some wooden soldiers at Leeds; next morning Branwell came to our door with [the] soldiers. Emily and I jumped out of bed, and I snatched up one and exclaimed, "This is the Duke of Wellington! This shall be the

At the age of fourteen Charlotte wrote a lengthy treatise entitled "The History of the Young Men." This is a double page from the work written in Charlotte's own hand.

Duke!" When I had said this Emily likewise took one up and said it should be hers; when Anne came down, she said one should be hers. Mine was the prettiest of the whole, and the tallest. Emily's was a grave-looking fellow, and we called him "Gravey." Anne's was a queer little thing, much like herself, and we called him "Waiting-boy." Branwell chose his, and called him "Buonaparte."

The little Brontës' desire for knowledge must have been excited in many directions, for I find a "list of painters whose works I wish to see," drawn up by Charlotte Brontë when she was scarcely thirteen. The list includes Titian, Raphael, Michelangelo, Coreggio, Vandyke, Rubens, and others. Here is this little girl, in a remote Yorkshire parsonage, who has probably never seen anything worthy of the name of a painting in her life, studying the names and characteristics of the great old masters!

Politics were evidently their grand interest; the Duke of Wellington their demigod. Did Charlotte want a knight errant or a devoted lover, one of the Duke's sons, the Marquis of Douro or Lord Charles Wellesley, came ready to her hand. There is hardly one of her prose writings at this time in which they are not the principal personages, and in which their "august father" does not appear as a deus ex machina.

THIS IS PERHAPS A FITTING TIME to give some personal description of Miss Brontë. In 1831 she was a quiet, thoughtful girl, nearly fifteen years of age, very small and slight in figure, with soft, thick, brown hair, and peculiar eyes, of which I find it difficult to give a description as they appeared to me in her later life. They were large and well shaped, their color a reddish brown. The usual expression was of quiet, listening intelligence, but now and then a light would shine out, as if some spiritual lamp had been kindled, which glowed behind those expressive orbs. I never saw the like in any other human creature. As for the rest of her features, they were plain, large, and ill set; but you were hardly aware of the fact, for the eyes and power of the countenance overbalanced every physical defect; the crooked mouth and the large nose were forgotten, and the whole face arrested the attention. She was remarkably neat in her whole personal attire. Her hands and feet were the smallest I ever saw; when one of her hands was placed in mine it was like the soft touch of a bird in my palm. The delicate long fingers had a peculiar fineness of sensation, which was one reason why all her handiwork, of whatever kind—writing, sewing, knitting—was so clear in its minuteness.

In that year we must think of her as a little, set, old-fashioned-seeming girl, very quiet in manners and very quaint in dress; for her aunt, who dressed her, had never been in society since she left Penzance eight or nine years before, and the Penzance fashions of that day were still dear to her heart.

This time, when Charlotte was sent to school again, in January 1831, she went as a pupil to Miss Wooler, who lived at Roe Head, a cheerful roomy country house, standing a little apart in a field, on the road from Leeds to Huddersfield.

Although Roe Head and Haworth are not twenty miles apart, the aspect of the country is totally dissimilar. The soft curving and heaving landscape around Roe Head gives a stranger the idea of cheerful airiness on the heights, and of sunny warmth in the broad green valleys below. Ancient halls are still to be seen in every direction—picturesque, many-gabled, with heavy stone carvings of coats of arms—belonging to decayed families from

Roe Head, Miss Wooler's school, was a spacious, cheerful eighteenth-century house situated on a rising slope. The drawing of it shown here was done by Anne Brontë.

whose lands field after field has been shorn away. Oakwell Hall, for instance, stands in a pasture field about a quarter of a mile from the highroad. You enter a short byroad called the Bloody Lane—a walk haunted by the ghost of a certain Captain Batt, the reprobate proprietor of an old hall close by, in the days of the Stuarts. From the Bloody Lane, overshadowed by trees, you come into the rough-looking field in which Oakwell Hall is situated. It is known in the neighborhood to be the place described as Field Head, Shirley's residence in Charlotte Brontë's novel *Shirley*. The enclosure in front, half court, half garden; the paneled hall with the gallery running round; the grassy lawns and terraces, where the soft-hued pigeons still strut in the sun, are all described in *Shirley*. The scenery of that fiction lies close around the real events which suggested it took place in the immediate neighborhood.

The number of pupils at Roe Head ranged from seven to ten during the two years Miss Brontë was there. The kind motherly nature of Miss Margaret Wooler, the headmistress, and the small number of the girls made the establishment more like a private family than a school. Moreover, Miss Wooler was a native of the district immediately surrounding Roe Head, as were the majority of her pupils. Most likely Charlotte Brontë came the greatest distance of all. Ellen Nussey, who was to become Charlotte's dearest friend, lived five miles away; two other dear friends, Mary and Martha Taylor (the Rose and Jessie Yorke of *Shirley*), lived still nearer.

I shall now quote from a valuable letter which I have received from Mary Taylor, a cherished associate of Charlotte Brontë's. The time referred to is Charlotte's first appearance at Roe Head, on January 19, 1831.

> I first saw her coming out of a covered cart, in very old-fashioned clothes, and looking very cold and miserable. . . . When she appeared in the schoolroom . . . she looked a little old woman, so short-sighted that she always appeared to be seeking something, and moving her head from side to side to catch a sight of it. She was very shy and nervous, and spoke with a strong Irish accent. When a book was given her, she dropped her head over it till her nose nearly touched it, and when she was told to hold her head up, up went the book after it, still close to her nose, so that it was not possible to help laughing.

This was the first impression she made upon one of those whose dear and valued friend she was to become in afterlife. Another of the girls—Ellen—recalls her first sight of Charlotte on the day she came, standing by the schoolroom window looking out on the snowy landscape and crying. Ellen was younger than Charlotte, and her tender heart was touched by the apparently desolate condition in which she found the oddly dressed little girl as "sick for home she stood in tears" in a new strange place. Any overdemonstrative kindness would have scared the wild little maiden from Haworth, but Ellen managed to win confidence and was allowed to give sympathy.

To quote again from Mary's letter:

> We thought her very ignorant, for she had never learnt grammar at all, and very little geography.

This account of her partial ignorance is confirmed by her other schoolfellows. But Miss Wooler was a lady of remarkable intelligence and sympathy. She gave a proof of this in her first treatment of Charlotte. The little girl was well read but not well grounded. Miss Wooler told her she was afraid that she must place her in the second class till she could overtake the girls of her own age in grammar, etc.; but poor Charlotte received

The friendship of Charlotte Brontë and Ellen Nussey began at Roe Head, where both were students, and continued throughout the course of Charlotte's life. It was Ellen's home, Rydings, that became the model for Thornfield, Mr. Rochester's seat in "Jane Eyre." This drawing of Ellen was done by Charlotte.

this announcement by so sad a fit of crying that Miss Wooler's heart was softened, and she wisely perceived that with such a girl it would be better to place her in the first class and allow her to make up her deficiencies by private study.

Mary continues:

> She would confound us by knowing things that were out of our range altogether. She was acquainted with most of the short pieces of poetry that we had to learn by heart; would tell us the authors, the poems they were taken from, and sometimes repeat a page or two, and tell us the plot. . . .
>
> In our play hours she sate, or stood still, with a book. Some of us once urged her to be on our side in a game at ball. She said she had never played, and could not play. We made her try, but soon found that she could not see the ball, so we put her out. . . . She used to go and stand under the trees in the play-ground, and say it was pleasanter. . . . She always showed physical feebleness in everything. . . . It was about this time I told her she was very ugly. Some years afterwards, I told her I thought I had been very

impertinent. She replied, "You did me a great deal of good, so don't repent of it." She used to draw much better, and more quickly, than anything we had seen before, and knew much about celebrated pictures and painters. Whenever an opportunity offered of examining a picture, she went over it piecemeal, with her eyes close to the paper, looking so long that we used to ask her "what she saw in it." She could always see plenty, and explained it very well. She made poetry and drawing, at least exceedingly interesting to me; and then I got the habit, which I have yet, of referring mentally to her opinion on all matters of that kind, resolving to describe such and such things to her, until I start at the recollection that I never shall.

To feel the full force of this last sentence I must mention that the writer of this letter, dated January 18, 1856, in which she thus speaks of constantly referring to Charlotte's opinion, has not seen her for eleven years, nearly all of which have been passed in a new continent, at the antipodes.

We used to be furious politicians, as one could hardly help being in 1832. She knew the names of the two ministries. She worshipped the Duke of Wellington, but said that Sir Robert Peel was not to be trusted. I, being of the furious radical party, told her "how could any of them trust one another; they were all of them rascals!" . . . She said she had taken interest in politics ever since she was five years old. . . .

She used to speak of her two elder sisters, Maria and Elizabeth, who died. . . . She told me, early one morning, that she had just been dreaming; she had been told that she was wanted in the drawing-room, and it was Maria and Elizabeth. I was eager for her to go on, and when she said there was no more, I said, "but go on! *Make it out!* I know you can." She said she would not. . . .

This habit of "making out" [pretending or imagining] interests for themselves, that most children get who have none in actual life, was very strong in her. The whole family used to "make out" histories, and invent characters and events.

What I have heard of her school days from other sources confirms the accuracy of the details in this remarkable letter. Charlotte was an indefatigable student, constantly reading and learning. She was also a great favorite with her schoolfellows and always ready to try and do what they wished, though not sorry when they left her out of their sports. Then, at night, she was an invaluable storyteller, frightening them almost out of their wits as they lay in bed.

Her craving for knowledge tempted Miss Wooler on into setting her longer and longer tasks of reading, and towards the end of her two years at Roe Head she received her first bad mark for an imperfect lesson. Charlotte cried bitterly. But her schoolfellows were more than sorry—they were indignant. They declared that the infliction of ever so slight a punishment on Charlotte Brontë was unjust. Miss Wooler, who was only too willing to pass over her good pupil's first fault, withdrew the bad mark.

Miss Wooler had a remarkable knack of making the girls feel interested in whatever they had to learn. Charlotte Brontë was happy in the choice made for her of this second school. There was a robust freedom in the out-of-doors life of her companions. They played at merry games in the fields round the house; on Saturday half-holidays they went for long scrambling walks.

Fearless—because the local people were quite familiar to all of them—lived and walked the gentle Miss Wooler's eight or nine pupils. The girls talked of the little world around them as if it were the only world that was; and had their opinions and their parties, and their fierce discussions like their elders. And among them—beloved and respected by all, laughed at occasionally by a few, but always to her face—lived, for two years, the plain, shortsighted, oddly dressed, studious little girl they called Charlotte Brontë.

CHAPTER IV

Miss Brontë left Roe Head in 1832, having won the affectionate regard both of her teacher and her schoolfellows, and having formed there two fast friendships which lasted her whole life; the one with Mary Taylor, who has not kept her letters; the other with Ellen Nussey, also called Nell, who has kindly entrusted me with as much of her correspondence as she has preserved. In looking over the earlier portion, I am struck afresh by the absence of hope, which formed such a strong characteristic in Charlotte. At an age when girls, in general, look forward to the eternal duration of friendship, she is surprised that Ellen keeps her promise to write. In afterlife, I was painfully impressed with the fact that Miss Brontë never dared allow herself to look forward with hope; and I thought, when I heard of the sorrowful years she had passed through, that it had been this grief which had rushed all buoyancy of expectation out of her. But it appears from the letters that it must have been, so to speak, constitutional—or, perhaps, due to the deep early pang of losing her two elder sisters.

After her return home, she employed herself in teaching her sisters, over whom she had had superior advantages. She writes thus, July 21, 1832, of her course of life at the parsonage:

> An account of one day is an account of all. In the morning, from nine till half-past twelve, I instruct my sisters, and draw; then we walk till dinner-time. After dinner I sew till tea-time, and after tea I write, read, or do fancy work, or draw, as I please. Thus, in one delightful, though monotonous course, my life is passed. I have been only out twice to tea since I came home.

It was about this time that Mr. Brontë provided his children with a teacher in drawing; he was Mr. William Robinson, a Leeds artist. Although they never attained to anything like proficiency, they took great interest in acquiring this art. Charlotte told me that, at this period of her life, drawing and walking out with her sisters formed the two great pleasures of her day.

The three girls used to walk upwards towards the "purple-black" moors; they seldom went downwards through the village. They were shy of meeting even familiar faces, and were scrupulous about entering the house of the very poorest uninvited. They were steady teachers at the Sunday school but they never faced their kind voluntarily, and always preferred the solitude of the moors.

In the September of this year, Charlotte went to pay her first visit to her friend Ellen. After this visit, she and her friend seem to have agreed to correspond in French, for the sake of improvement in the language.

There were no events to chronicle in the Haworth letters. Quiet days did not present much to write about, and Charlotte was naturally driven to criticize books. Mr. Brontë encouraged a taste for reading in his girls; and though Miss Branwell kept it in due bounds by assigning household occupations, they were allowed to get books from the circulating library at Keighley; and many a happy walk, up those long four miles, must they have had, burdened with some new book.

What was formal and set in Charlotte's way of writing to Ellen diminished as their personal acquaintance increased, and as each came to know the home of the other. In the summer of 1833, Charlotte wrote to invite her friend to come and pay her a visit. The first impression made on the visitor by the sisters of her school friend was that Emily was a tall, long-armed girl, more fully grown than her elder sister, extremely reserved in manner. I distinguish reserve from shyness, because I imagine shyness would please, if it knew how; whereas reserve is indifferent whether it pleases or not. Anne, like Charlotte, was shy; Emily was reserved.

Branwell was rather a handsome boy, with "tawny" hair, to use Miss Brontë's word for its color. All were very clever, original, and utterly different from any people or family Ellen had ever seen before. But, on the whole, it was a happy visit for all parties. Charlotte says, in writing to Ellen just after her return home, "Were I to tell you of the impression you have made on every one here, you would accuse me of flattery. Papa and aunt are continually adducing you as an example for me to shape my actions by. Emily and Anne say 'they never saw any one they liked so well as you.'"

Haworth is built with an utter disregard of all sanitary conditions: the great old churchyard lies above all the houses, and it is terrible to think how the very water springs of the pumps below must be poisoned. But this winter of 1833–34 was particularly rainy, and there were an unusual number of deaths in the village. A dreary season it was to the family in the parsonage: their usual walks obstructed by the spongy state of the moors, and the funeral bells frequently tolling, filling the heavy air with their mournful sound.

About the beginning of 1834, Ellen went to London for the first time. The idea of her friend's visit seems to have stirred Charlotte strangely. Her own imagination seems to have been deeply moved by the ideas of what great wonders are to be seen in that vast and famous city. "Did you not feel awed while gazing at St. Paul's and Westminster Abbey?" she wrote. "Had you no feeling of ardent interest, when in St. James's you saw the palace where so many of England's kings have held their courts? Have you yet seen anything of the great personages whom the sitting of Parliament now detains in London—the Duke of Wellington, Sir Robert Peel, Earl Grey . . . ?"

Although the distance between Haworth and Birstall, where Ellen lived, was but seventeen miles, it was difficult to go straight from the one to the other without hiring a vehicle of some kind for the journey. Hence a visit from Charlotte required a good deal of prearrangement. The Brontës also had all an ample share of that sensitive pride which led them to dread incurring obligations and to fear "outstaying their welcome" on any visit. Charlotte was always fearful of loving too much, of wearying the objects of her affection; and thus she often tried to restrain her warm feelings, and was ever chary of that presence so invariably welcome to her true friends. According to this mode of acting, when she was invited for a month she stayed but a fortnight amidst Ellen's family, to whom every visit only endeared her the more.

In the middle of the summer of 1835, a great family plan was mooted at the parsonage. The question was, to what trade or profession should Branwell be brought up? He was now nearly eighteen, and he was very clever, perhaps the greatest genius in this rare family. The sisters hardly recognized their own or each other's powers, but they knew *his*. Branwell's talents were readily brought out for the entertainment of others; popular admiration was sweet to him. This led to his presence being sought at all village gatherings; and it likewise procured him the undesirable distinction of having his company recommended by the landlord of the Black Bull to any chance traveler who might

466

happen to feel solitary over his liquor. "Do you want someone to help you with your bottle, sir? If you do, I'll send up for Patrick" (so the villagers called him). And while the messenger went, the landlord entertained his guest with accounts of the wonderful talents of the boy, whose precocious cleverness and great conversational powers were the pride of the village. The necessity for Mr. Brontë to take his dinner alone, combined

Two portraits of Brontës painted by Brontës. Charlotte's portrait of Anne, painted in 1834, and, far right, Branwell's haunting study of Emily, c. 1835.

with attention to his parochial duties, made him partially ignorant of how his son employed himself out of lesson time.

It is singular how strong a yearning the whole family had towards the art of drawing. But they all thought there could be no doubt about Branwell's talent. I have seen an oil painting of his, done probably about this time. It was a group of his sisters, life-size, three-quarters' length; not much better than sign painting as to manipulation, but the likenesses were admirable.

The best way of preparing him to become a painter appeared to be to send him as a pupil to the Royal Academy. I daresay he longed to follow this path, principally because it would lead him to that mysterious London which seems to have filled the imaginations of all the younger members of this family. Poor fellow! this craving to know London and that stronger craving after fame were never to be satisfied. He was to die at the end of a short and blighted life. But in this year of 1835, all his home kindred were thinking how they could best forward his views. What their plans were, let Charlotte explain—for I

am convinced that where Charlotte Brontë's own words can
be used to tell her story, no others ought to take their place.
This is to Ellen:

Haworth, July 6th, 1835.

I had hoped to have had the extreme pleasure of seeing you at
Haworth this summer, but human affairs are mutable, and
human resolutions must bend to the course of events. We are
all about to divide, break up, separate. Emily is going to school,
Branwell is going to London, and I am going to be a governess.
This last determination I formed myself . . . knowing well that
papa would have enough to do with his limited income, should
Branwell be placed at the Royal Academy, and Emily at Roe
Head. Where am I going to reside? you will ask. Within four
miles of you, at a place neither of us are unacquainted with, Roe
Head. Yes! I am going to teach in the very school where I was
myself taught. Miss Wooler made me the offer. . . . I am sad—
very sad—at the thoughts of leaving home; but duty—necessity
—these are stern mistresses, who will not be disobeyed. . . . If
anything would cheer me, it is the idea of being so near you.
Surely, you and Mary will come and see me. Emily and I leave
home on the 27th of this month; the idea of being together
consoles us both somewhat, and, truth, since I must enter a
situation, "My lines have fallen in pleasant places." I both love
and respect Miss Wooler.

CHAPTER V

ON THE TWENTY-NINTH OF JULY, 1835, Charlotte, now little
more than nineteen years old, went as teacher to Miss Wooler's.
Emily accompanied her, as a pupil; but she became literally ill
from homesickness, and after passing only three months at Roe
Head, returned to the parsonage and the beloved moors. Her
younger sister Anne was sent to Miss Wooler's in her place.

Charlotte wrote as follows about Emily's leaving school:

My sister Emily loved the moors. . . . She found in the bleak
solitude many and dear delights; and not the least and best-
loved was—liberty. Liberty was the breath of Emily's nostrils;
without it she perished. The change from her own home to a

school, and . . . life of disciplined routine (though under the kindest auspices), was what she failed in enduring. Nobody knew what ailed her but me. I knew only too well. In this struggle her health was quickly broken, and I felt in my heart she would die, if she did not go home.

This physical suffering on Emily's part when absent from Haworth, after recurring several times under similar circumstances, became at length as much an acknowledged fact that, whichever was obliged to leave home, the sisters decided that Emily must remain there. When at home, she took the principal part of the cooking upon herself, and anyone passing by the kitchen door might have seen her studying German out of a book propped up before her, as she kneaded the dough.

Charlotte's life at Miss Wooler's was a happy one, until her health failed. She sincerely loved and respected her former schoolmistress, to whom she was now become both companion and friend. Though the duties of the day might be monotonous, there were always two or three happy hours of quiet pleasant conversations with Miss Wooler to look forward to in the evening.

It was about this time that an event happened in the neighborhood of Leeds which excited a good deal of interest. A young lady, who was governess in a very respectable family, had been wooed and married by a gentleman holding some position in the commercial firm to which the young lady's employer belonged. A year after her marriage, during which time she had given birth to a child, it was discovered that he whom she called husband had another wife. Report now says that this first wife was deranged. But at any rate, the condition of the wife who was no wife excited deep commiseration, and the case was spoken of far and wide. We know from *Jane Eyre* that it must have made a deep impression on Charlotte's mind.

Miss Wooler was always anxious to persuade Miss Brontë to avail herself of the invitations which came, urging her to spend Saturday and Sunday with Ellen and Mary in their respective homes, that lay within the distance of a walk. But Miss Brontë was too apt to refuse herself the necessary change from some-

hing of an overascetic spirit, betokening a loss of healthy balance
n either body or mind. Indeed, it is clear that such was the
ase, from an extract taken out of the letter I have before
eferred to, from Mary.

> I heard that she had gone as teacher to Miss Wooler's. I went
> to see her, and asked how she could give so much for so little
> money. She owned that, after clothing herself and Anne, there
> was nothing left. . . . She seemed to have no interest or pleasure
> beyond the feeling of duty, and, when she could, used to sit
> alone, and "make out." She told me afterwards, that one evening
> she had sat in the dressing-room until it was quite dark, and then
> observing it all at once, had taken sudden fright.

No doubt Charlotte remembered this well when she described a similar terror getting hold upon Jane Eyre.

"From that time," Mary adds, "her imaginations became
gloomy or frightful; she could not sleep at night, nor attend in
he day."

In the midsummer holidays of 1836 her friend Ellen had come
o stay with her at Haworth, so there was one happy time
ecured. Here follows a series of excerpts from letters, not dated,
ut belonging to the latter portion of this year.

> My *dear dear* Ellen—I am at this moment trembling all over
> with excitement, after reading your note; it is the unrestrained
> pouring out of a warm, gentle, generous heart. . . . I thank you
> with energy for this kindness. I will no longer shrink from an-
> swering your questions. I *do* wish to be better than I am. I pray
> fervently to be made so. . . . May the Almighty hear me! and I
> humbly hope he will, for you will strengthen my polluted peti-
> tions with your own pure requests. All is bustle and confusion
> round me, the ladies pressing with their sums and their les-
> sons. . . . If you love me, *do, do, do* come on Friday: if you disap-
> point me I shall weep.

> Weary with a day's hard work . . . I am sitting down to write
> a few lines to my dear Ellen. Excuse me if I say nothing but non-
> sense, for my mind is exhausted and dispirited. It is a stormy
> evening, and the wind is uttering a continual moaning sound.
> At such times—in such moods as these—it is my nature to seek

repose in some calm tranquil idea, and I have now summoned up your image to give me rest. There you sit, upright and still, in your black dress, and white scarf, and pale marble-like face— just like reality. I wish you would speak to me. . . . I have some qualities that make me very miserable, that few people in the world can at all understand. I strive to conceal and suppress them as much as I can; but they burst out sometimes, and then I hate myself for days afterwards.

About this time both Ellen and Mary used to call upon Charlotte on Saturday afternoons, and often endeavored to persuade her to return with them, and be the guest of one till Monday morning; but this was comparatively seldom. Mary says, "She visited us twice or thrice when she was at Miss Wooler's. We used to dispute about politics and religion. She, a Tory and clergyman's daughter, was always in a minority of one in our house of violent Dissent and Radicalism." Into the lively Taylor family circle, twenty years ago, the little, quiet, resolute clergyman's daughter was received, and by them she was truly loved and honored.

CHRISTMASTIME CAME; and this Christmas Ellen promised to visit Haworth, where she was always eagerly welcomed by Charlotte. But her coming had to be delayed on account of a little domestic accident about which Charlotte wrote:

> I am sure you will have thought me very remiss, in not sending my promised letter long before now; but I have a very melancholy excuse in an accident that befell our old faithful Tabby, a few days after my return home. She was gone out on some errand, when, as she was descending the steep street, her foot slipped on the ice, and she fell. She completely shattered and dislocated one leg . . . and she now lies at our house in a very doubtful and dangerous state. Of course we are all exceedingly distressed, for she is like one of our own family.
>
> Since the event the whole work of the house, as well as the duty of nursing Tabby, falls on ourselves. Under these circumstances I dare not press your visit here; it would be too selfish of me, but I [am] most bitterly reluctant to give up all the pleasure I had anticipated so long.

Tabby had now lived with the family for ten or twelve years, and she was past the age for any very active service, being nearer seventy than sixty. Still, at the insistence of the girls she was to be allowed to remain in the household, a helpless invalid, entirely dependent upon them. Meanwhile, during these Christmas holidays at home, the sisters talked over their lives, and the prospect which they afforded of occupation and remuneration.

They felt that it was a duty to relieve their father of the burden of their support, at least that of one or two. They knew that they were never likely to inherit much money. What could they do? Charlotte was trying teaching, but her salary was too small for her to save out of it.

It was the household custom among these girls to sew till nine o'clock at night. At that hour Miss Branwell went to bed, and her nieces put away their work and began to pace the room up and down—often with the candles extinguished, for economy's sake—their figures glancing into the firelight and out into the shadow, perpetually. At this time they talked over past troubles; they planned for the future. In afteryears, this was the time for discussing together the plots of their novels.

Christmas of 1836 was not without its hopes and aspirations. They had tried their hands at story writing long ago; they all of them "made out" perpetually. They had likewise attempted to write poetry, and had a modest confidence that they had achieved a tolerable success. But they knew that sisters' judgments of each other's productions were likely to be partial. So Charlotte, as the eldest, resolved to write to Robert Southey, the poet laureate, sending him some of her poems.

On December 29 her letter to Southey was dispatched, with an excitement not unnatural in a girl who has worked herself up to the pitch of writing to a poet laureate. But morning after morning of the holidays slipped away, and there was no answer; Charlotte had to leave home without knowing even whether her letter had reached its destination.

January and February of 1837 had passed away, and still there was no reply from Southey. Probably she had almost lost hope when at length, in the beginning of March, she received his letter.

After accounting for his delay in replying to hers by the fact of a long absence from home, and also "because in truth it is not an easy task to answer such a letter, nor a pleasant one to cast a damp over the high spirits and the generous desires of youth," he goes on to say:

It is not my advice that you have asked as to the direction of your talents, but my opinion of them, and yet the opinion may be worth little, and the advice much. You evidently possess, and in no inconsiderable degree, what Wordsworth calls the "faculty of verse." I am not depreciating it when I say that in these times it is not rare. Many volumes of poems are now published every year without attracting public attention, any one of which, if it had appeared half a century ago, would have obtained a high reputation for its author. Whoever, therefore, is ambitious of distinction in this way ought to be prepared for disappointment.

But it is not with a view of distinction that you should cultivate this talent, if you consult your own happiness. I, who have made literature my profession, and have never repented of the choice, think myself, nevertheless, bound in duty to caution every young man who applies as an aspirant to me for encouragement and advice, against taking so perilous a course. You will say that a woman has no need of caution; there can be no peril in it for her. In a certain sense this is true; but there is a danger of which I would, with all kindness, warn you. The day dreams in which you habitually indulge are likely to induce a distempered state of mind; and in proportion as all the ordinary uses of the world seem to you flat and unprofitable, you will be unfitted for them without becoming fitted for anything else. Literature cannot be the business of a woman's life, and it ought not to be. The more she is engaged in her proper duties, the less leisure will she have for it. To those duties you have not yet been called, and when you are you will be less eager for celebrity. . . .

But do not suppose that I disparage the gift which you possess; nor that I would discourage you from exercising it. I only exhort you to write poetry for its own sake; not with a view to celebrity. . . . So written, it is wholesome both for the heart and soul. You may embody in it your best thoughts and your wisest feelings, and in so doing discipline and strengthen them.

Farewell, madam. It is not because I have forgotten that I was once young myself, that I write to you in this strain; but because

I remember it. . . . Though I may be but an ungracious adviser, you will allow me to subscribe myself, with the best wishes for your happiness, your true friend,

ROBERT SOUTHEY.

I was with Miss Brontë when, in later life, she received a note ~~from~~ Mr. Cuthbert Southey, requesting her permission to insert ~~the~~ foregoing letter in his book on his father's life. She said to

~~P~~atrick Brontë's study— ~~a~~n inner sanctum where ~~th~~e Brontë children ~~se~~ldom strayed. Here he ~~sp~~ent many hours ~~re~~ading, reflecting, and ~~c~~omposing the sermons ~~h~~e was to deliver before ~~h~~is congregation.

~~m~~e, "Mr. Southey's letter was kind and admirable; a little ~~st~~ringent, but it did me good." At the time, she sent Mr. ~~S~~outhey the following reply:

March 16th.

Sir—I cannot rest till I have answered your letter, even though by addressing you a second time I should appear intrusive; but I must thank you for the kind and wise advice you have given me. . . . At the first perusal of your letter, I felt only shame and regret that I had ever ventured to trouble you; but, after I had thought a little and read it again and again, the prospect seemed to clear. You do not forbid me to write. You only warn me against the folly of neglecting real duties, for the sake of imaginative pleasures; of writing for the love of fame. . . . I am afraid, sir, you think me very foolish. I am not altogether the idle dreaming being [my first letter] would seem to denote. My father is a clergyman of limited income, and I am the eldest of his children. I thought it therefore my duty, when I left school, to become a governess. In that capacity I find enough to occupy my thoughts

475

all day without having a moment's time for one dream of the imagination. . . . Sometimes when I'm teaching or sewing I would rather be reading or writing; but I try to deny myself.

Once more allow me to thank you with sincere gratitude. I trust I shall never more feel ambitious to see my name in print; if the wish should rise I'll look at Southey's letter, and suppress it. It is honour enough for me that I have written to him, and received an answer. That letter is consecrated. . . . If I live to be an old woman, I shall remember it thirty years hence as a bright dream. . . . Again I sign myself,

C. BRONTË.

His "stringent" letter made her put aside, for a time, all idea of literary enterprise, and she bent her whole energy towards the fulfillment of the duties in hand. Her health and spirits, however, were to suffer even more after the midsummer holidays of 1837. At that time Miss Wooler removed her school from the open, breezy situation of Roe Head to Dewsbury Moor, two or three miles distant. Her new residence was a much lower site, and the air much less pure and exhilarating. Charlotte felt the change extremely, and regretted it not merely on her own account but for the sake of her sister Anne.

This autumn Emily had gone as teacher to a school at Halifax, where there were nearly forty pupils. "I have had one letter from her since her departure," wrote Charlotte; "it gives an appalling account of her duties; hard labour from six in the morning to eleven at night, with only one half-hour of exercise between. This is slavery. I fear she can never stand it."

Dewsbury Moor did not agree with her, though she herself was hardly aware how much her life there was affecting her health. But Anne began to suffer just before the Christmas holidays, and Charlotte watched over her younger sister with jealous vigilance. Anne had a slight cough, a pain at her side, a difficulty of breathing. Miss Wooler considered it little more than a common cold; but Charlotte felt every indication of incipient consumption as a stab at her heart, remembering Maria and Elizabeth.

Stung by anxiety for this little sister, she upbraided Miss Wooler for her fancied indifference to Anne's state of health.

Miss Wooler felt these reproaches keenly, and wrote to Mr. Brontë about them. He immediately sent for his children. Meanwhile, Charlotte had resolved that Anne should never return as a pupil, nor she herself as a governess. But, just before he left, Miss Wooler sought for the opportunity of an explanation, and the issue proved that "the falling out of faithful friends, renewing is of love."

And so Charlotte and Anne returned to the parsonage and to that happy home circle in which alone their natures expanded. Emily had given up her position in the Halifax school on account of her health, which could only be reestablished by the bracing moorland air and free life of home, and now she and Anne were bound up in their lives and interests like twins. Emily's love was poured out on Anne, as Charlotte's was on her. But the affection among all the three was stronger than either death or life.

Miss Wooler had entreated Charlotte to return after the holidays, and she had consented. I doubt whether Branwell was maintaining himself at this time. For some unexplained reason, he had given up the idea of becoming a student at the Royal Academy, and his prospects in life were still uncertain. So Charlotte had quietly to take up her burden of teaching again. Brave heart, ready to die in harness! She went back to her work, hoping to subdue the weakness that was gaining ground upon her. About this time, she would turn sick and trembling at any sudden noise, and could hardly repress her screams when startled. This showed a fearful degree of physical weakness in one who was generally so self-controlled; and the medical man, whom at length she consulted, insisted on her return home. The soft summer air, he said, the sweet company of those she loved, the release, the freedom of life in her own family, were needed to save either reason or life. So she returned to Haworth.

Charlotte grew much stronger in this quiet, happy period at home. She paid occasional visits to her two great friends, and they in return came to Haworth. At one of their houses she met Henry Nussey, to whom the following letter refers; someone having a slight resemblance to the character of St. John Rivers in *Jane Eyre* and, like him, in holy orders.

March 12, 1839.

I had a kindly leaning towards him, because he is an amiable and well-disposed man. Yet I had not, and could not have, that intense attachment which would make me willing to die for him; and if ever I marry, it must be in that light of adoration that I will regard my husband. Ten to one I shall never have the chance again; but *n'importe*. Moreover, I was aware that he knew so little of me he could hardly be conscious to whom he was writing. Why! it would startle him to see me in my natural home character; he would think I was a wild, romantic enthusiast.

So that—her first proposal of marriage—was quietly declined. Matrimony did not enter into the scheme of her life. Earnest labor did; the question, however, was as yet undecided in what direction she should employ her forces. She had been discouraged in literature; her eyes now failed her in the minute kind of drawing which she practiced; teaching seemed the only way of earning an independent livelihood. But neither she nor her sisters were naturally fond of children. Consequently, teaching very young children was anything but a "delightful task" to the three Brontë sisters. But their education did not as yet qualify them to undertake the charge of advanced pupils. They knew but little French, and were not proficient in music. But they were all strong again, and, at any rate, Charlotte and Anne must put their shoulders to the wheel. One daughter was needed at home, and Emily, who suffered most when away from Haworth, was the one appointed to remain. Anne was the first to meet with a situation.

April 15th, 1839.

I could not write to you in the week you requested, as about that time we were very busy in preparing for Anne's departure. Poor child! she left us last Monday. . . . We have had one letter from her. She expresses herself well satisfied, and says that Mrs. Ingham is extremely kind. . . . For my own part, I am as yet "wanting a situation," like a housemaid out of place.

Not many weeks after this letter to Ellen was written Charlotte also became engaged as a governess in a temporary position. The family was, I believe, that of a wealthy Yorkshir manufacturer. There are some people still living, respecting whom I may have to tell unpleasant truths; but it is necessary that the difficulties which Charlotte encountered in her life should be made known.

She told me that none but those who had been in the position of a governess could ever realize the dark side of "respectable" human nature, daily giving way to selfishness and ill temper, till its conduct sometimes amounts to a tyranny. She said that once she had been entrusted with the care of a little boy, three or four years old, during the absence of his parents on a day's excursion, and particularly enjoined to keep him out of the stable yard. His elder brother, a lad of eight or nine, and not a pupil of Miss Brontë's, tempted the little fellow into the forbidden place. She tried to induce him to come away; but, instigated by his brother, he began throwing stones at her, and one of them hit her so severe a blow on the temple that the lads were alarmed into obedience. The next day, in full family conclave, the mother asked Miss Brontë what occasioned the mark on her forehead. She simply replied, "An accident, ma'am," and no further inquiry was made; but the children honored her for not telling tales." From that time, she began to gain influence over all, and gained their affection. But one day, at the children's dinner, the small truant of the stable yard, in a little demonstrative gush, said, putting his hand in hers, "I love 'ou, Miss Brontë." Whereupon, the mother exclaimed, before all the children, "Love the *governess*, my dear!"

The following extracts from Charlotte's correspondence at this time show how painfully the restraint of her new mode of life pressed upon her. The first is from a letter to Emily.

June 8th, 1839.

I have striven hard to be pleased with my new situation. The country, the house and the grounds are, as I have said, divine; but, alack-a-day, there is such a thing as seeing all beautiful around you and not having a free moment left to enjoy [it]. The children are constantly with me. As for correcting them, I quickly found that was out of the question; they are to do as they like. A complaint to the mother only brings black looks. I said in my last letter that Mrs. Sidgwick did not know me. I now

479

begin to find she does not intend to know me; that she cares nothing about me, except to contrive how the greatest possible quantity of labour may be got out of me; and to that end she overwhelms me with oceans of needlework. . . . I see more clearly than I have ever done before, that a private governess has no existence, is not considered as a rational being, except as connected with the wearisome duties she has to fulfil.

She writes in pencil to Ellen in July 1839:

I cannot procure ink, without going into the drawing-room, where I do not wish to go. . . . I should have written to you long since, and told you every detail of the utterly new scene into which I have lately been cast. I must not bother you too much with my sorrows. If you were near me, perhaps I might be tempted to pour out the long history of a private governess's trials and crosses in her first situation. As it is, I will only ask you to imagine the miseries of a reserved wretch like me, thrown at once into the midst of a large family . . . a set of pampered, spoilt, turbulent children, whom I was expected constantly to amuse, as well as to instruct. I soon found that the constant demand on my stock of animal spirits reduced them to the lowest state of exhaustion; at times I felt depressed. To my astonishment, I was taken to task on the subject by Mrs. Sidgwick, with a harshness of language scarcely credible; like a fool, I cried most bitterly. And to be treated in that way, merely because I was shy and sometimes melancholy, was too bad. At first I was for giving all up and going home. But, after a little reflection, I determined to summon what energy I had, and to weather the storm. . . . Mrs. Sidgwick behaves more civilly to me now. . . . I have no wish to be pitied, except by yourself; if I were talking to you I could tell you much more.

Her temporary engagement in this uncongenial family ende in July of this year; not before the constant strain upon her spir and strength had again affected her health.

After she had been at home about a week, a proposal w made to her to accompany her friend in some little excursic She caught at the idea most eagerly at first; but her hope sto still, waned, and had almost disappeared before, after ma delays, it was realized.

About this time Mr. Brontë found it necessary, either from failing health or from the increased populousness of the parish, to engage the assistance of a curate—the first of a succession who henceforward revolved round the parsonage. The Haworth curate brought his clerical friends, and the incursions of these, near the parsonage teatime, varied the quietness of the life there, sometimes pleasantly, sometimes disagreeably. The little adventure recorded at the end of the following letter is unusual in the lot of most women, and is a testimony to the power of attraction which Charlotte possessed, when she let herself go in the happiness and freedom of home.

August 4th, 1839.

I have got leave to accompany you for a week—at the utmost a fortnight. . . . Where do you wish to go? When do you set off? Arrange all these things according to your convenience. The idea of seeing the *sea*—of being near it—watching its changes by sunrise, sunset . . . perhaps in storm—fills and satisfies my mind. I shall be discontented at nothing. . . .

I have an odd circumstance to relate to you: prepare for a hearty laugh! The other day, Mr. ——, a vicar, came to spend the day with us, bringing with him his curate. The latter gentleman, by name Mr. B., is a young clergyman fresh from Dublin University. . . . His character quickly appeared; witty, lively, ardent; but deficient in dignity and discretion. At home, you know, I talk with ease, and am never shy—never weighed down by that miserable *mauvaise honte* which torments me elsewhere. So I conversed with this Irishman, and laughed at his jests. I cooled a little towards the latter part of the evening, because he began to season his conversation with something of Hibernian flattery, which I did not quite relish. However, they went away, and no more was thought about them. A few days after I got a letter, which . . . proved to be a declaration of attachment and proposal of matrimony [from] the young Irishman! I hope you are laughing heartily. This is not like one of my adventures, is it? . . . Well! thought I, I have heard of love at first sight, but this beats all! I leave you to guess my answer.

A little more delay, and she was at last able to enjoy the pleasure she had wished for so much. In September she and her friend went to Easton for a fortnight. It was here she received her first impressions of the sea, which so enchanted her that she and Ellen spent the last week of their holiday in Bridlington. Some weeks after her return she wrote to Ellen:

Oct. 24th.

Have you forgotten the sea by this time, Ellen? Is it grown dim in your mind? Or you can still see it, dark, blue, and green, and foam-white, and hear it roaring roughly when the wind is high, or rushing softly when it is calm. . . . I am as well as need be, and very fat. I think of Easton very often, and of our pleasant walks, our merry evenings, etc. If we both live, this period of our lives will long be a theme for pleasant recollection.

But, as the vivid remembrance of this pleasure died away, an accident occurred to make the actual duties of life press somewhat heavily for a time.

December 21st, 1839.

We are at present rather busy, as we have been without a servant. Poor Tabby became so lame that she was at length obliged to leave us. She is residing with her sister. . . . Emily and I are busy, as you may suppose: I manage the ironing, and keep the rooms clean; Emily attends to the kitchen. . . . We do not despair of Tabby's return, and she shall not be supplanted by a stranger in her absence. . . . I intend to force myself to take another situation when I can get one, though I *hate* and *abhor* the very thoughts of governess-ship. But I must do it.

CHAPTER VI

I AM NOT AWARE for what reason the plan of sending Branwell to study at the Royal Academy was relinquished; his talents were certainly very brilliant, and he fervently desired, by their use, either in writing or drawing, to make himself a name.

At this time, the young man was full of noble impulses, as well as of extraordinary gifts; not accustomed to resist temptation, but showing so much power of attachment to all about him that they took pleasure in believing that after a time he would "right imself." There are always peculiar trials in the life of an only oy in a family of girls. In this particular family, while the rest vere almost ascetic in their habits, Branwell was allowed to row up self-indulgent. Of course, he was careful enough not to veal anything before his father and sisters of the pleasures he idulged in; but his tone of thought and conversation became radually coarser, and, for a time, his sisters tried to persuade

Charlotte's love for the sea was inspired by the village of Bridlington on the East Yorkshire coast. It was here he came with Ellen Nussey in vacations. This painting depicts people bathing on the shore at Bridlington.

hemselves that such coarseness was a part of manliness. At resent, though he had, they were aware, fallen into some errors, ill he was their hope and their darling; their pride, who should ometime bring great glory to the name of Brontë.

He and his sister Charlotte were both slight and small of tature, while the other two were of taller and larger make. I ave seen Branwell's profile; it is what would be generally steemed very handsome; the forehead is massive, the eye well et, the nose is good; but there are coarse lines about the mouth, nd the lips are loose and thick. His hair and complexion were andy. He had enough of Irish blood in him to make his manners rank and genial. In a fragment of one of his manuscripts which have read, the beginning of a tale, there is a justness and felicity f expression which is very striking. He had a stronger desire or literary fame burning in his heart than even that which ccasionally flashed up in his sisters'. He wrote and sent poems o Wordsworth and to Hartley Coleridge, the son of the poet, nd he frequently contributed verses to the *Leeds Mercury*.

In 1840, he was residing at home, employing himself i
occasional composition of various kinds and waiting till som
employment, for which he might be fitted without any cours
of preliminary education, should turn up; waiting, not impa
tiently; for he saw society of one kind at the Black Bull; and a
home he was as yet the cherished favorite.

Miss Branwell was unaware of the fermentation of unoccu
pied talent going on around her; but their father, from whor
they derived not a little of their adventurous spirit, was silentl
cognizant of much of which Miss Branwell took no note
Notwithstanding that Miss Branwell might be occasionally ur
reasonable, in general she and her nieces went on smoothl
enough; she still inspired the girls with sincere respect an
affection. They were, moreover, grateful to her for many habir
she had enforced upon them: order, neatness in everything,
perfect knowledge of household work, and punctuality, of whic
no one but themselves could tell the value in afterlife.

People in Haworth have assured me that according to th
hour of day could they have told what the inhabitants of the par
sonage were about. At certain times the girls would be sewin
in their aunt's bedroom; from six to eight, Miss Branwell rea
aloud to Mr. Brontë; at eight, the household assembled t
evening prayers; and by nine Mr. Brontë, Miss Branwell, an
Tabby were all in bed—the girls free to pace up and down (lik
restless animals) in the parlor, talking over plans for the future

At the time of which I write, the favorite idea was that c
keeping a school. They thought that, by a little contrivance,
small number of pupils might be accommodated in the par
sonage. As teaching seemed the only profession open to them
and as it appeared that Emily at least could not live away fror
home, this plan of schoolkeeping presented itself as most de
sirable. But it involved some outlay; and to this their aunt wa
averse. Yet there was no one to whom they could apply for
loan except Miss Branwell. Still, in the evenings of the winte
of 1839–40, this plan formed the principal subject of thei
conversation.

During this winter, Charlotte employed her leisure hours i
writing a story. Some fragments of the manuscript yet remair

but she herself condemned it, saying that in this story she had got over such taste as she might once have had for the "ornamental and redundant."

To fill up the account of this outwardly eventless year, I may add extracts from the letters entrusted to me. The letter below was written when Ellen was trying to decide whether to accept the proposal of marriage of a Mr. Vincent:

Elizabeth Branwell, sister of Mrs. Brontë, and her teapot.

May 15th, 1840.

Do not be over-persuaded to marry a man you can never respect—I do not say *love;* because, I think, if you can respect a person before marriage, moderate love at least will come after; and as to intense *passion,* I am convinced that that is no desirable feeling. . . . I am tolerably well convinced that I shall never marry at all. Reason tells me so, and I am not so utterly the slave of feeling but that I can *occasionally hear* her voice.

August 20th, 1840.

Have you seen anything of Miss H. lately? I wish they, or somebody else, would get me a situation. I have answered advertisements without number, but my applications have met with no success.

I have got another bale of French books containing upwards of forty volumes. I have read about half. They are clever, wicked, sophistical, and immoral. The best of it is, they give one a thorough idea of France and Paris, and are the best substitute for French conversation that I have met with.

After that, Miss Brontë set to advertising and inquiring with fresh vigor, and early in March 1841 she obtained her second and last situation as a governess, at the home of Mr. and Mrs. White. This time she esteemed herself fortunate in becoming a member of a kindhearted and friendly household. The master of it she especially regarded as a valuable friend, whose advice helped to guide her in one very important step of her life. But as her definite acquirements were few, she had to eke them out by employing her leisure time in needlework; and altogether her position was that of "bonne" or nursery governess, liable to never-ending calls upon her time.

This was peculiarly trying to one whose life at home had been full of abundant leisure, which made it possible for her to go through long and deep histories of feeling and imagination. The habit of "making out," which had grown with her growth, had become a part of her nature. Yet all exercise of her strongest and most characteristic faculties was now out of the question. She could not even feel, amidst the occupations of the day, that when evening came, she might employ herself in more congenial ways.

Moreover, the little Brontës had been brought up motherless; and from knowing nothing of the gaiety and the sportiveness of childhood, they were ignorant of the very nature of infancy. Years afterwards, when Miss Brontë came to stay with us, she watched our little girls perpetually; and I could not persuade her that they were only average specimens of well-brought-up children. She was surprised and touched by any sign of thoughtfulness for others, of kindness to animals, or of unselfishness on their part. All this must be borne in mind while reading the following letter.

March 3, 1841.

I told you some time since, that I meant to get a situation. I have at length succeeded, and am fairly established in my new place. . . . The house is not very large, but exceedingly comfortable; the grounds are fine and extensive. I have made a large sacrifice in the way of salary, in the hope of securing comfort—by which word I do not mean good eating, or warm fire, or a soft bed, but the society of cheerful faces, and minds and hearts not dug out of a lead-mine. My pupils are a girl of eight, and a boy of six. . . . Both Mr. and Mrs. White seem to me good sort of people. I have as yet had no cause to complain of want of considerateness or civility. My pupils are wild and unbroken, but apparently well-disposed. . . . If I can but feel that I am giving satisfaction, and if at the same time I can keep my health, I shall, I hope, be moderately happy.

Miss Brontë had not been many weeks in her new situation before she had a proof of the kindness of her employers. Mr. White wrote to her father and urgently invited him to make acquaintance with his daughter's new home; and Mrs. White expressed great regret when one of Miss Brontë's friends came to leave a letter or parcel, without entering. So she found that her friends and her father might freely visit her.

June, 1841.
You can hardly fancy it possible, I dare say, that I cannot find a quarter of an hour to scribble a note in; but so it is. Mr. and Mrs. White have been gone a week. . . . No time is fixed for their return, but I hope it will not be delayed long, or I shall miss the chance of seeing Anne this vacation. She came home last Wednesday, and is only to be allowed three weeks' vacation, because the family she is with are going to Scarborough. *I should like to see her*, to judge for myself of the state of her health.

Soon after this was written, Mr. and Mrs. White returned, in time to allow Charlotte to go and look after Anne's health, which, as she found to her intense anxiety, was far from strong. Apprehension about her brought up once more the idea of keeping a school. If, by this means, they three could live together and maintain themselves, all might go well. They would have some time of their own in which to try again that literary career, which was never quite set aside as an ultimate object. Thus she wrote during those midsummer holidays.

Haworth, July 19th, 1841.
We waited long and anxiously for you, on Thursday. I quite wearied my eyes with watching from the window. You are not to blame. But a hundred things I had to say to you will now be

forgotten, and never said. There is a project hatching in this house, which both Emily and I anxiously wished to discuss with you. The project is yet in its infancy, hardly peeping from its shell. . . .

To come to the point: papa and aunt talk, by fits and starts, of our commencing a school! I never could conceive where the capital was to come from for making such a speculation. I was aware, indeed, that aunt had money, but I always considered that she was the last person who would offer a loan. A loan, however, she intimates that she perhaps *will* offer, in case pupils can be secured, an eligible situation obtained, etc. . . . I do not expect that aunt will sink more than £150 in such a venture; and would it be possible to establish a respectable school with a capital of only that amount? . . . Write as soon as you can. I shall not leave my present situation till my future prospects assume a more fixed aspect.

She inquired in every direction she could, as to the chance which a new school might have of success. But in all there seemed more establishments like the one which the sisters wished to set up than could be supported. Superior advantages must be offered. But how? Of French they knew something; but hardly enough to teach it in competition with natives, or professional masters. Emily and Anne had some knowledge of music; but here again it was doubtful whether they could engage to give lessons in it.

Just about this time, Miss Wooler was thinking of relinquishing her school at Dewsbury Moor, and offered to give it up in favor of the Brontës. But the number of pupils had diminished and, if the Brontës undertook it, they would have to try and work it up to its former prosperity. With the forced calm of a suppressed eagerness, that sends a glow of desire through every word of the following letter, Charlotte wrote to her aunt from the house in which she was governess.

Sept. 29th, 1841.

Dear Aunt—I have heard nothing of Miss Wooler yet since I wrote to her, intimating that I would accept her offer. . . . Meantime, a plan has been suggested by Mr. and Mrs. White and others, which I wish now to impart to you. My friends recommend me, if I desire to secure permanent success, to delay commencing the school for six months, and to contrive, by hook or by crook, to spend the intervening time in some school on the continent. They say schools in England are so numerous, competition so great, that without some such step towards attaining superiority, we shall probably have a very hard struggle, and may fail. They say that, if the speculation is intended to be a successful one, half the sum, at least, ought to be laid out in the manner I have mentioned, thereby insuring a more speedy repayment both of interest and principal.

I would not go to France. I would go to Brussels, in Belgium. The cost of the journey there would be £5; living is there little more than half as dear as it is in England, and the facilities for education are equal or superior to any place in Europe. In half a year, I could acquire a thorough familiarity with French. I could improve greatly in Italian, and even get a dash of German. Mary [Taylor] is now staying at Brussels; if I wrote to her, she, with the assistance of Mrs. Jenkins, the wife of the British Chaplain, would be able to secure me a cheap decent residence and respectable protection. . . .

These are advantages which would turn to real account, when we actually commenced a school; and, if Emily could share them with me, we could take a footing in the world afterwards which we can never do now. I say Emily instead of Anne; for Anne might take her turn at some future period. I feel certain, while I am writing, that you will see the propriety of what I say. You always like to use your money to the best advantage; . . . and, depend upon it, £50 or £100 thus laid out, would be well employed. . . . I feel an absolute conviction that, if this advantage were allowed us, it would be the making of us for life.

It was some little time before an answer came to this letter. Much had to be talked over between the father and aunt in Haworth. At last consent was given.

At Christmas she left her situation, after a parting with her employers, which seems to have touched her greatly. "They only made too much of me," was her remark after leaving them; "I did not deserve it."

All four children hoped to meet together at their father's

house this December. Branwell expected to have a short leave of absence from his employment as a clerk on the Leeds and Manchester Railway, in which he had been engaged for five months. Anne arrived before Christmas Day. She had announced her resolution to leave her situation, partly on account of the harsh treatment she had received, and partly because her stay at home, during her sisters' absence in Belgium, seemed desirable.

After some correspondence and much talking over plans at home, it was arranged at the end of January that Charlotte and Emily were to set off in three weeks.

CHAPTER VII

BRUSSELS HAD HAD from the first a strong attraction for Charlotte; and Mrs. Jenkins had indeed made much inquiry, and at length, after some discouragement, had heard of a school which seemed desirable. This was the pensionnat of Mme Heger. It was decided that, if the terms suited, Charlotte and Emily should proceed thither.

M. Heger, a kindly, wise, good, and religious man, whose acquaintance I am glad to have made, assisted his wife in the work of instruction. He informs me that, on receipt of a letter from Charlotte, making particular inquiries as to the amount of "extras," he and his wife were so much struck by the earnest tone of the letter that they said to each other: "These are the daughters of an English pastor, anxious to learn with a view of instructing others, and to whom additional expense is of great consequence. Let us name a specific sum, within which all expenses shall be included."

This was accordingly done; the agreement was concluded, and in February 1842 the Brontës prepared to leave their native country for the first time. Mr. Brontë determined to accompany his daughters. Mary Taylor and her brother, Joe, who were experienced in foreign traveling, were also of the party.

Charlotte first saw London in the day or two they now stopped there. They all, I believe, stayed at the Chapter Coffee

House, Paternoster Row—an old-fashioned tavern known to Mr. Brontë. Mr. Brontë then took his daughters to the rue d'Isabelle, Brussels; remained one night at Mr. Jenkins'; and straight returned to his wild Yorkshire village.

What a contrast to that must the Belgian capital have presented to those two young women thus left behind! Suffering acutely from every strange and unaccustomed contact—far

In 1842 Charlotte and Emily journeyed to Brussels, where they became boarders at a school for young ladies kept by Mme. Heger, shown in this painting with her family. It is now known that Charlotte fell hopelessly in love with M. Heger, a one-sided passion that Mrs. Gaskell, writing so soon after Charlotte's death, felt it prudent to ignore.

away from their beloved home, and the dear moors beyond—their indomitable will was their great support.

They wanted learning. They came for learning. But they were miserably shy. Mrs. Jenkins told me that she used to ask them to spend Sundays with her, until she found that they felt more pain than pleasure from such visits. Emily hardly ever uttered more than a monosyllable. Charlotte was sometimes excited sufficiently to speak eloquently and well; but she had a habit of gradually wheeling round on her chair, so as almost to conceal her face from the person to whom she was speaking.

And yet there was much in Brussels to strike a responsive chord in her powerful imagination. At length she was seeing somewhat of that grand old world of which she had dreamed. Every spot told a historic tale. The great solemn Cathedral of St. Gudule, the religious paintings, the striking ceremonies of the Roman Catholic Church—all made a deep impression on the girls. And then in their stout Protestant hearts they would become indignant with themselves for having been susceptible.

The very building they occupied as pupils, in Mme. Heger's pensionnat, had its own ghostly train of splendid associations. In the sixteenth century, the Infanta Isabella had caused a "great mansion" to be built for the accommodation of the aristocratic guild of crossbowmen. In that mansion were held all the splendid feasts of the guild. The salon is now a schoolroom for Belgian girls; the "great mansion" is the pensionnat of Mme. Heger in the rue d'Isabelle.

There were from fifty to sixty pupils in the pensionnat when Charlotte and Emily Brontë entered in February 1842. The two sisters clung together, and kept apart from the herd of happy, boisterous Belgian girls, who, in their turn, thought the new English pupils wild and scared-looking, with strange, insular ideas about dress; for Emily persisted in wearing the ugly gigot sleeves long after they were "gone out." Her petticoats, too, had not a curve or a wave in them, but hung down straight, clinging to her lank figure. The sisters spoke to no one but from necessity. They were too full of earnest thought, and of the exile's sick yearning, to be ready for careless conversation, or merry game.

M. Heger soon observed that they knew very little of French. But he perceived that with their unusual characters, and extraordinary talents, a different mode must be adopted from that in which he generally taught French to English girls. He seems to have rated Emily's genius as something even higher than Charlotte's; but she appeared egotistical and exacting compared to Charlotte, who was always unselfish, and allowed the younger sister to exercise a kind of unconscious tyranny over her.

After consulting with his wife, M. Heger told them that he meant to dispense with the old method of grounding in grammar, vocabulary, etc., and to proceed on a new plan. He proposed to read to them some of the masterpieces of French authors and, after having thus impressed the whole, to analyze the parts with them. He also believed that he had to do with pupils capable of catching the echo of a style, and reproducing their own thoughts in a similar manner, and he wanted them to try this. After explaining his plan to them, he awaited their reply. Emily said that she saw no good to be derived from it; and that, by adopting it, they should lose all originality of expression. Charlotte also doubted the success of the plan; but she said she would follow out M. Heger's advice, because she was bound to obey him while she was his pupil.

An extract from one of her letters shows some of her first impressions of her new life.

Brussels, 1842 [*May ?*]

I was twenty-six years old a week or two since; and at this ripe time of life I am a school-girl, and, on the whole, very happy in that capacity. It felt very strange at first to submit to authority instead of exercising it—to obey orders instead of giving them; but I like that state of things. . . . It is natural to me to submit, and very unnatural to command.

This is a large school, in which there are about forty externes, or day pupils, and twelve boarders. Madame Héger, the head, is a lady of precisely the same cast of mind, degree of cultivation, and quality of intellect as Miss Catherine Wooler. . . .

There is one individual of whom I have not yet spoken— M. Héger—the husband of Madame. He is professor of rhetoric, a man of power as to mind, but very choleric and irritable in temperament. He is very angry with me just at present, because I have written a translation which he chose to stigmatise as *"peu correct."* He did not tell me so, but wrote the word on the margin of my book, and asked, in brief stern phrase, how it happened that my compositions were always better than my translations? . . . Emily and he don't draw well together at all. Emily works like a horse, and she has had great difficulties. Indeed, those who come to a French school for instruction ought previously to have acquired a considerable knowledge of French. . . .

You will abuse this letter for being short and dreary, and there are a hundred things which I want to tell you, but I have not time. Brussels is a beautiful city. The Belgians hate the English. Their external morality is more rigid than ours. To lace the stays without a handkerchief on the neck is considered a disgusting piece of indelicacy.

When they had made further progress, M. Heger took up a more advanced plan, that of synthetical teaching. He would read to them various accounts of the same person or event, and make

493

them notice the points of agreement and disagreement. Where they were different, he would make them seek the origin of that difference by examining the character and position of each separate writer. This kind of exercise delighted Charlotte. It called into play her powers of analysis, which were extraordinary, and she very soon excelled in it.

Wherever the Brontës could be national they were so, with great tenacity of attachment, and they were Protestant to the backbone. Something of Charlotte's feeling, too, appears in the following letter:

Brussels, 1842 [*July*]

I consider it doubtful that I shall come home in September. Madame Héger has made a proposal for both me and Emily to stay another half year, offering to take me as English teacher; also to employ Emily part of each day in teaching music. For these services we are to be allowed to continue our studies in French and German, and to have board; no salaries, however, are offered. The proposal is kind, and . . . I am inclined to accept it. What think you? I don't deny I sometimes wish to be in England, or that I have attacks of home-sickness; but, on the whole, I have been happy in Brussels, because I have always been fully occupied with employments that I like.

When the Brontës first went to Brussels, it was with the intention of remaining there for six months, but Mme. Heger's proposal altered their plans. Besides, they were happy in the feeling that they were making progress in the knowledge they had so long been yearning to acquire. They were happy, too, in possessing friends nearby congenial to them; Mary and her sister, the bright, dancing, laughing Martha, were parlor boarders in an establishment at Koekelberg, just beyond the barriers of Brussels. Again, cousins of these friends, the Dixons, were resident in the town; and at their house Charlotte and Emily were always welcome, despite their overpowering shyness. They spent their weekly holiday with the Dixons for many months; and at this house the Taylors and the Brontës could look forward to meeting each other frequently.

There was another English family where Charlotte soon became a welcome guest and where, I suspect, she felt herself more at her ease than at the friends' whom I have first mentioned. An English physician, Dr. Wheelwright, with a large family of daughters, came to reside at Brussels, and Dr. Wheelwright placed his daughters at Mme. Heger's school in July 1842. The scholastic year recommenced in October and the regular school life continued as it had before the *grandes vacances*.

The school was divided into three classes. The first and second classes occupied a long room, divided by a wooden partition; and in the last row of desks, in the quietest corner of the second class, sat Charlotte and Emily, side by side. The school hours were from nine to twelve, when the boarders went to the *refectoire* to partake of bread and fruit. From one to two, there was fancywork—a pupil reading aloud some light literature in each room; from two to four, lessons again. Then the boarders dined in the *refectoire*, M. and Mme. Heger presiding. From five to six there was recreation; from six to seven preparation for lessons; and, after that, the *lecture pieuse*—Charlotte's nightmare. At eight there was a slight meal of water and *pistolets* (the delicious little Brussels rolls), which was followed by prayers, and then to bed.

The principal bedroom was over the long *classe*, or schoolroom. There were six or eight narrow beds on each side of the apartment, every one enveloped in its white draping curtain. The beds of the two Miss Brontës were at the extreme end of the room, almost as private as if they had been in a separate apartment.

During the hours of recreation in the garden they invariably walked together, and generally kept silence. Charlotte would always reply to any remark addressed to both; Emily rarely spoke. Charlotte's quiet, gentle manner never changed. She was never seen out of temper; and occasionally, when she herself had assumed the post of English teacher, and the impertinence of her pupils was most irritating, a slight increase of color, a momentary sparkling of the eye, were the only outward tokens she gave of annoyance.

The first break in this life of regular duties came heavily and sadly. Martha—pretty, winning, mischievous Martha—was taken ill suddenly at the Château de Koekelberg in October. Her sister Mary tended her with devoted love, but in a few days she died.

Charlotte's own short account of this event is as follows:

> Martha Taylor's illness was unknown to me till the day before she died. I hastened to Kokleberg the next morning—unconscious that she was in great danger—and was told that she had died in the night. Mary was taken away to Bruxelles. I have seen Mary frequently since. . . . She appears calm and serious now. I have seen Martha's grave—the place where her ashes lie in a foreign country.

Charlotte was still in the midst of her deep sympathy with Mary, when on November 2 word came from home that her aunt, Miss Branwell, was very ill. Emily and Charlotte hastily packed up for England, doubtful whether they should ever return to Brussels or not. Just as they were on the very point of starting came a second letter, telling them of their aunt's death. They sailed from Antwerp and got home on a Tuesday morning. The funeral was over, and Mr. Brontë, Branwell, and Anne were sitting together in quiet grief.

When the first shock was over, the three sisters began to enjoy the relish of meeting again, after the longest separation they had had in their lives. They had much to tell of the past, and much to settle for the future. For another year or so they were again to be all three apart; and, after that, the happy vision of being together and opening a school was to be realized. The small property which their aunt had accumulated, by dint of personal frugality, was bequeathed to the three of them. The sum which they therefore now independently possessed would enable them to effect such alterations in the house at Haworth as would adapt it to the reception of pupils.

Anne had been for some little time in a situation with Mr. and Mrs. Robinson at Thorp Green, to which she was to return after the holidays. Branwell was to join her there as tutor. Emily quickly decided to be the daughter to remain at home. About Charlotte there was much deliberation.

Even in all the haste of their departure from Brussels, M.

Heger had found time to write a letter of sympathy to Mr. Brontë; a letter which also contained a graceful appreciation of the daughters' characters, and a kind suggestion that they should return to continue for a further year. There was so much kindness in his offer—and it was obvious that a second year of instruction would be so far more valuable than the first—that it was decided that Charlotte should return to Brussels.

Meanwhile, they enjoyed their Christmas together inexpressibly. Branwell was with them; that was always a pleasure; and although he had been sacked from the railway the previous winter his sisters yet held him up as their family hope. Charlotte's friend Ellen came over to see her, and she returned the visit. Winter though it was, the sisters took walks on the snow-covered moors; or went often to Keighley for library books. Charlotte's Brussels life must have seemed like a dream, so completely, in this short space of time, did she fall back into the old household ways.

CHAPTER VIII

TOWARDS THE END OF JANUARY, the time came for Charlotte to return to Brussels. Her journey thither was rather disastrous. She went alone; and the train from Leeds to London was delayed and did not get in till ten at night. She took a cab straight to the London Bridge Wharf, and desired a waterman to row her to the Ostend packet, which was to sail the next morning.

She described to me her sense of loneliness, and yet her strange pleasure in the excitement of the situation, as in the dead of that winter's night she went swiftly over the dark river to the black hull's side. At first she was refused leave to ascend to the deck. "No passengers might sleep on board," they said. Standing up in the rocking boat, she asked to speak to someone in authority. He came, and her quiet statement so impressed him that he allowed her to come on board and take a berth. Next morning she sailed; and at seven the following evening she reached the rue d'Isabelle once more.

This time she was being paid a salary of £16 a year; but out of it she had to pay ten francs a month for her German lesson. She ruled over a new schoolroom, which had just been built for the first class; and henceforward she was called *Mademoiselle* Charlotte, by M. Heger's orders. She continued her own studies, principally attending to German and to literature; and every Sunday she went alone to the German and English chapels. Her walks too were solitary. This solitude was a perilous luxury to one of her temperament, so liable as she was to morbid and acute mental suffering.

On March 6, 1843, she writes thus:

I am settled by this time, of course. I am not too much over-loaded with occupation; and besides teaching English, I have time to improve myself in German. I ought to consider myself well off, and to be thankful. I hope I am thankful; and if I could always keep up my spirits, and never feel lonely, or long for companionship, I should do very well. As I told you before, M. and Madame Héger are the only two persons in the house for whom I really experience regard and esteem, and, of course, I cannot be always with them. They told me, when I first returned, that I was to consider their sitting-room my sitting-room also. However . . . in the evening, I will not, and ought not to intrude on M. and Madame Héger and their children. Thus I am a good deal by myself, out of school-hours. I now regularly give English lessons to M. Héger and his brother-in-law. They get on with wonderful rapidity; especially the first. . . . If you could see and hear the efforts I make to teach them to pronounce like Englishmen, and their unavailing attempts to imitate, you would laugh to all eternity. . . .

I have had two letters from Mary. She does not complain; but her letters are not the letters of a [happy] person. She has nobody to be as good to her as M. Héger is to me; to lend her books; to converse with her sometimes, etc.

Good-bye. When I say so, it seems to me that you will hardly hear me; all the waves of the Channel heaving and roaring between must deaden the sound.

From the tone of this letter it may easily be perceived that the Brussels of 1843 was a different place from that of 1842. Then she had had Emily for a companion, and she had had the frequent happiness of seeing Mary and Martha. Now Emily was far away in Haworth—where she, or any other loved one, might die, before Charlotte could reach them. Mary was gone off on her own independent course to study in Germany. The weather, too, had been piercingly cold; her feeble constitution was always painfully sensitive to an inclement season; and her depression of spirits, when she was not well, was pitiful.

The Hegers have discovered, since the publication of *Villette*, that, at this beginning of Charlotte's career as English teacher in their school, the conduct of her pupils was often impertinent and mutinous in the highest degree. But of this they were unaware at the time. Though, from their testimony, her patience and firmness at length obtained their just reward, yet, with one so weak in health and spirits as she was, the reaction after such struggles as she frequently had with her pupils must have been very painful.

Charlotte now felt that she had made great progress towards obtaining proficiency in the French language. But a knowledge of German now had also become her object; and she resolved to compel herself to remain in Brussels till that was gained.

Brussels, August 1st, 1843.

If I complain in this letter, have mercy and don't blame me, for, I forewarn you, I am low in spirits. In a few days our vacation will begin; everybody is joyous at the prospect, because everybody is to go home. I know that I am to stay here during the five weeks that the holidays last, and that I shall be much alone, and consequently get downcast. Alas! I can hardly write, I have such a dreary weight at my heart.

The *grandes vacances* began soon after the date of this letter, when she was left in the great deserted pensionnat. A low nervous fever was gaining upon her. She had never been a good sleeper, but now she could not sleep at all. In the dead of the night, lying awake in the deserted dormitory, every fear respecting those whom she loved became a terrible reality, oppressing her and choking up the very life-blood in her heart. Those nights were times of sick, dreary, wakeful misery; precursors of many such in afteryears.

In the daytime, driven abroad by the weak restlessness of

fever, she tried to walk herself into such a state of bodily fatigue as would induce sleep. So with weary steps, for hours together, she would traverse the boulevards and the streets. The shades of evening made her retrace her footsteps, fatigued, yet restless still, and doomed to another weary night of sleeplessness. At last she was compelled to keep her bed for some days, and this compulsory rest did her good. She was weak, but less depressed in spirits than she had been, when the school reopened and her positive practical duties recommenced.

She wrote thus to Emily:

This is Sunday morning. They are at their idolatrous "messe," and I am in the Refectoire. I should like uncommonly to be in the dining-room at home, or in the kitchen. I should like even to be cutting up the hash, and you standing by, watching that I put enough flour, not too much pepper, and, above all, that I save the best pieces of the leg of mutton for Tiger and Keeper [Emily's bulldog], the first of which personages would be jumping about the dish and carving-knife, and the latter standing like a devouring flame on the kitchen-floor. To complete the picture, Tabby blowing the fire, in order to boil the potatoes! How divine are these recollections to me at this moment! . . . Is papa well? Are you well? and Tabby? You ask about Queen Victoria's visit to Brussels. I saw her for an instant flashing through the Rue Royale in a carriage and six. She was laughing and talking very gaily. She looked a little stout, vivacious lady, very plainly dressed. The Belgians liked her very well on the whole.

About this time, Charlotte was made painfully conscious of a silent estrangement between herself and Mme. Heger.

One of the reasons for this estrangement is to be found in the fact that the English Protestant's dislike of Romanism increased with her knowledge of it; and when occasion called for an expression of opinion from Charlotte Brontë, she was uncompromising truth. Mme. Heger considered any slight thrown upon her church as blasphemy against the Holy Truth; and her increasing coolness of behavior showed how much her most cherished opinions had been wounded.

As autumn drew on, Charlotte wrote thus to Ellen:

October 13, 1843.

Brussels is indeed desolate to me now. Since the Dixons left, I have had no friend. The family of Dr. Wheelwright too left in August, and I am completely alone. I cannot count the Belgians anything. . . . Sometimes the solitude oppresses me to an excess. One day, lately, I felt as if I could bear it no longer, and I went to Madame Héger, and gave her notice. If it had depended on her, I should certainly have soon been at liberty; but M. Héger sent for me the day after, and pronounced with vehemence his decision, that I should not leave; so I promised to stay a while longer. How long that will be, I do not know. I should not like to return to England to do nothing. I am too old for that now; but if I could hear of a favourable opportunity for commencing a school, I think I should embrace it.

Towards the end of the year, however, various reasons at last conspired to make Charlotte feel that her presence was imperatively required at home. There were causes for anxiety in the news concerning Branwell; and at this time her father's eyesight began to fail. In consequence of this state of things, she again announced to Mme. Heger her intention of returning to England. This time both M. and Mme. Heger agreed that it would be for the best, when they learned about Mr. Brontë's increasing blindness.

But as the inevitable moment of separation from people and places, among which she had spent so many happy hours, drew near, Charlotte's spirits gave way; she had the natural presentiment that she saw them all for the last time, and she received but a dead kind of comfort from being reminded that access from Brussels to Haworth was not so difficult as her tears would seem to predicate; nay, there was some talk of one of Mme. Heger's daughters being sent to her as a pupil if she fulfilled her intention of beginning a school. To facilitate her success in this plan, should she ever engage in it, M. Heger gave her a kind of diploma, certifying that she was perfectly capable of teaching the French language, having well studied the grammar and composition thereof, and the best methods of instruction. This certificate is dated December 29, 1843, and on the second of January, 1844, she arrived at Haworth.

CHAPTER IX

On the twenty-third of January Charlotte writes as follows:

Every one asks me what I am going to do, now that I am re-turned home, and every one seems to expect that I should imme-diately commence a school. In truth it is what I should wish to do. I have sufficient money for the undertaking, and I hope now sufficient qualifications; yet I cannot yet permit myself to touch the object which I have been so long straining to attain. You will ask me why? It is on papa's account; he is now, as you know, getting old, and it grieves me to tell you that he is losing his sight. I feel that it would be too selfish to leave him (at least, as long as Branwell and Anne are absent), in order to pursue interests of my own. With the help of God, I will try to deny myself in this matter, and to wait.

I suffered much before I left Brussels. I think, however long I live, I shall not forget what the parting with M. Héger cost me. It grieved me so much to grieve him who has been so true, kind, and disinterested a friend. . . .

Haworth seems such a lonely spot, buried away from the world. I no longer regard myself as young—indeed, I shall soon be twenty-eight; and it seems as if I ought to be working and braving the rough realities of the world, as other people do. It is, however, my duty to restrain this feeling at present, and I will endeavour to do so.

Of course her absent sister and brother obtained a holiday to welcome Charlotte home, and in March she was spared to pay a visit to her friend Ellen. But she was far from well or strong, and the short journey of fourteen miles seems to have fatigued her greatly.

Soon after she came back to Haworth, in a letter to one of the household in which she had been staying, there occurs this passage: "Our poor little cat has been ill two days, and is just dead. It is piteous to see even an animal lying lifeless. Emily is sorry." These few words relate to points in the characters of the two sisters. Charlotte was more than commonly tender and gentle in her treatment of all dumb creatures. The helplessness of an animal was its passport to Charlotte's heart; the fierce, wild intractability of its nature was what often recommended it to Emily. Her rough, tawny bulldog, Keeper, who was devoted to her, was well known for his ferocity.

Meanwhile the moors were a great resource this spring of 1844; Emily and Charlotte walked out on them perpetually. The old plan of schoolkeeping was often discussed in these rambles; at last they came to a determination.

I have seriously entered into the enterprise of keeping a school —or rather, taking a limited number of pupils at home. That is, I have begun in good earnest to seek for pupils. I wrote to Mrs. White [the lady with whom she had lived as governess just before going to Brussels] informing her of my intention. I received an answer from Mr. White expressive of, I believe, sincere regret that I had not informed them a month sooner, in which case, he said, they would gladly have sent me their own daughter, and also Colonel Stott's, but that now both were promised to Miss Cockhill. I derived quite an impulse of encouragement. . . . I own, I had misgivings that nobody would be willing to send a child for education to Haworth. These misgivings are partly done away with. I have written also to Mrs. Busfield and have enclosed the diploma M. Héger gave me. I have not yet received her answer, but I wait for it with some anxiety. . . . As soon as I can get an assurance of only *one* pupil, I will have cards of terms printed, and will commence the repairs necessary in the house.

Charlotte wrote to M. Heger, informing him of her plans and at the same time confiding in him a particular fear. For secretly by now she had begun to dread a loss of sight, similar to that which afflicted her father. Her long-continued ill health, her too close application to minute drawing and writing in her early years, her now habitual sleeplessness at night, were all telling on her eyes. Her letter says:

There is nothing I fear so much as idleness, the want of occupation, inactivity, the lethargy of the faculties: when the body is idle the spirit suffers painfully. I should not know this lethargy if I could write. Formerly I passed whole days and weeks and months in writing, not wholly without result; but now my sight is too weak to write. Were I to write much I should become blind. This weakness of sight is a terrible hindrance to me. Otherwise, do you know what I should do, Monsieur? I should write a book and I should dedicate it to my *maitre de litterature*—to the only master I ever had—to you, Monsieur! I have often told you in French how much I respect you—how much I am indebted to your goodness, to your advice; I should like to say it once in English. But that cannot be—it is not to be thought of. The career of letters is closed to me. . . . Please convey to Madame the assurance of my esteem. I fear that Marie, Louise and Claire have already forgotten me. . . . I shall see you again one day: as soon as I have earned enough money to go to Brussels, I shall go there.

In the meantime August and September passed away; then October came and still no pupils were to be heard of. Day after day, there was a little hope felt by the sisters until the post came in. But Haworth village was wild and lonely, and the Brontës but little known. Charlotte writes to Ellen on the subject, in the early winter months:

I, Emily, and Anne, are truly obliged to you for the efforts you have made in our behalf. Every one wishes us well; but there are no pupils to be had. We have no present intention, however, of breaking our hearts on the subject, still less of feeling mortified at defeat.

There were, probably, growing up in each sister's heart, secret feelings of relief that their cherished project had been tried and had failed. For that house, which was to be regarded as an occasional home for their brother, could hardly be a fitting residence for the children of strangers. They were by now, in all likelihood, becoming silently aware that Branwell's habits were such as to render his society at times most undesirable. Possibly they had heard distressing rumors concerning the cause of that remorse and agony of mind, which at times made him restless and unnaturally merry, at times moody and irritable.

Early in 1845, Charlotte went to Hunsworth to bid good-by to her dear friend Mary. Mary had returned from Germany; she

had made a great decision to emigrate to New Zealand and she was now leaving for the other side of the world. When Charlotte returned home from visiting Mary she wrote to Ellen:

Feb. 20, 1845.

I spent a week at Hunsworth, not very pleasantly; headache, sickliness, and flatness of spirits, made me a poor companion, a sad drag on the gaiety of all the other inmates of the house. . . . I am sure all, with the exception perhaps of Mary, were very glad when I took my departure. I begin to perceive that I have too little life in me, now-a-days, to be fit company for any except very quiet people. Is it age, or what else, that changes me so?

Alas! how could she be otherwise than "flat-spirited," "a poor companion," and a "sad drag" on the gaiety of those who were lighthearted and happy! Her honest plan for earning her own livelihood had crumbled to ashes. Her poor father, nearly sightless, depended upon her cares. Branwell's mysterious, wayward conduct continued. Then how could she be cheerful, when she was losing her dear and noble Mary?

A few weeks after she parted from Mary, she gives this account of her days at Haworth.

March 24, 1845.

I can hardly tell you how time gets on at Haworth. . . . One day resembles another; and all have heavy, lifeless physiognomies. . . . Meantime, life wears away. I shall soon be thirty; and I have done nothing yet. . . . I feel as if we were all buried here.

One of Charlotte's daily employments was to read to her father, and this required a little gentle diplomacy on her part for it reminded him painfully of the deprivation under which he was suffering. What eyesight she had to spare she reserved for his use. She now did but little plain sewing; not more writing than could be avoided; and employed herself principally in knitting. She writes to Ellen on June 13:

I feel reluctant to leave papa for a single day. His sight diminishes weekly; and can it be wondered at that his spirits sometimes sink? He has now the greatest difficulty in reading; and then he dreads the state of dependence to which blindness will inevitably reduce him. . . . Still he is never peevish, never impatient; only anxious and dejected.

For the reason just given, Charlotte declined an invitation to visit Ellen. Then Anne came home, and Charlotte, feeling more at liberty, went to Ellen's after all. On her return from her short visit to her friend, she traveled with a gentleman in the railway carriage, whose features and bearing betrayed him as a Frenchman. And so her journey back to Haworth was pleasantly beguiled by conversation with the French gentleman; and she arrived at home refreshed and happy. What to find there?

It was ten o'clock when she reached the parsonage. Branwell was there, unexpectedly, very ill. He had come home a day or two before, apparently for a holiday; in reality, I imagine, because some discovery had been made which rendered his absence imperatively desirable. The day of Charlotte's return, Branwell had received a letter from Mr. Robinson sternly dismissing him, intimating that his proceedings were discovered, characterizing them as bad beyond expression, and charging him, on pain of exposure, to break off immediately, and forever, all communication with every member of the family.

All the disgraceful details came out. Branwell, I have mentioned, had obtained a situation as a private tutor with Mr. and Mrs. Robinson, where Anne had been employed as governess. Full of talent, a brilliant talker, and with a not unhandsome person, he took the fancy of his employer's wife, who was nearly twenty years older than himself. It is no excuse for him to say that she was so bold and hardened, that she began the first advances, and "made love" to him. He was so beguiled by this mature and wicked woman that he went home for his holidays reluctantly, stayed there as short a time as possible, perplexing and distressing his family by all his extraordinary conduct—at one time being in the highest spirits, at another in the deepest depression—and altogether evincing an irritability of disposition bordering on insanity.

Now all the variations of spirits and of temper—the reckless gaiety, the moping gloom—were explained. Branwell was in no state to conceal his agony of remorse, or his agony of guilt love, from any dread of shame. He gave passionate way to hi feelings; he shocked and distressed his sisters inexpressibly; th blind father sat stunned.

There was now a reason deeper than any mere indulgence c appetite, to account for Branwell's intemperance; he began hi career as a habitual drunkard. The pitiable part was the yearnin love he still bore to the woman who had got so strong a hol upon him. Charlotte wrote to Ellen:

> *July 31, 1845.*
> We have had sad work with Branwell. He thought of nothing but stunning or drowning his agony of mind. No one in this house could have rest; and, at last, we have been obliged to send him from home for a week, with some one to look after him. He has written to me this morning, expressing some sense of contrition . . . but as long as he remains at home, I scarce dare hope for peace in the house.

> *August 18th, 1845.*
> I have delayed writing, because I have no good news to communicate. My hopes ebb low indeed about Branwell. . . . It is only absolute want of means that acts as any check to him.

> *Nov. 4th, 1845.*
> I hoped to be able to ask you to come to Haworth. It almost seemed as if Branwell had a chance of getting employment. But the place [a secretaryship to a railway committee] is given to another person. Branwell remains at home; and while *he* is here, *you* shall not come. . . . I wish I could say one word to you in his favour, but I cannot.

> *Dec. 31, 1845.*
> You say well that no sufferings are so awful as those brought on by dissipation; alas! I see the truth of this observation daily proved. . . . It seems grievous, indeed, that those who have not sinned should suffer so largely.

Thus ended the year 1845.

I may as well complete here the narrative of the outwar events of Branwell Brontë's life. A few months later, th

valid husband of the woman with whom he had intrigued
ed. Branwell had been looking forward to this event with
uilty hope. The young man still loved her passionately, and
ow he imagined the time was come when they might look
rward to being married. She had offered to elope with him,
d had sent him money—twenty pounds at a time. He thought
deed she must love him; he little knew how bad a depraved

Branwell Brontë's
mous "gun" portrait
his sisters and himself.
nne and Charlotte
e at the left; Emily is
the right.

oman can be. Her husband had made a will, in which what
operty he left to her was bequeathed on the condition that she
ould never see Branwell Brontë again. She dispatched a servant
hot haste to Haworth. He stopped at the Black Bull, and
anwell came down to the inn, and was shut up with the man
r some time.

At last the groom came out, mounted his horse, and was off.
anwell remained in the room alone. More than an hour
apsed before sign or sound was heard; then, those outside
ard a noise like the bleating of a calf, and, on opening the door,
was found in a kind of fit, succeeding to the stupor of grief
hich he had fallen into on hearing that he was forbidden by
s paramour ever to see her again.

For the last three years of Branwell's life, he took opium
bitually; he drank, moreover, whenever he could get the
portunity. He took opium because it made him forget for a
ne more effectually than drink. In procuring it he would steal
t while the family were at church and manage to cajole the

509

village druggist out of a lump; or, it might be, the carrier ha
unsuspiciously brought him some in a packet.

For some time before his death he had attacks of deliriu
tremens of the most frightful character; he slept in his father
room, and he would sometimes declare that either he or l
father should be dead before morning. The trembling sister
sick with fright, would implore their father not to expose him
self to this danger; but Mr. Brontë is no timid man, and perha
he felt that he could influence his son to self-restraint, more l
showing trust in him than by showing fear. The sisters ofte
listened for the report of a pistol in the night, till watchful e
and hearkening ear grew heavy and dull with the perpetu
strain upon their nerves.

All that is to be said more about Branwell Brontë shall l
said in time by Charlotte herself, not by me.

CHAPTER X

IN THE COURSE of this sad autumn of 1845, a new interest can
up; faint, indeed, and often lost sight of in the pain of anxie
respecting their brother. In a biographical notice which s
later wrote about her sisters, Charlotte describes it as follow

One day in the autumn of 1845, I accidentally lighted on a
MS. volume of verse, in my sister Emily's hand-writing. I looked
it over, and something more than surprise seized me—a deep
conviction that these were not common effusions. I thought
them condensed and terse, vigorous and genuine. To my ear
they had also a peculiar music, wild, melancholy, and elevating.
My sister Emily was not a person of demonstrative character,
nor one, on the recesses of whose mind and feelings, even those
nearest and dearest to her could, with impunity, intrude unli-
censed: it took hours to reconcile her to the discovery I had
made, and days to persuade her that such poems merited publication. . . . Meantime, my younger sister quietly produced
some of her own compositions, intimating that I might like to
look at hers. I could not but be a partial judge, yet I thought
that these verses too had a sweet sincere pathos of their own. We

had very early cherished the dream of one day being authors. . . . We agreed to arrange a small selection of our poems, and, if possible, get them printed. Averse to personal publicity, we veiled our names under those of Currer, Ellis, and Acton Bell; the ambiguous choice being dictated by a sort of scruple at assuming names, positively masculine, while we did not like to declare ourselves women. . . . The bringing out of our little book was hard work. As was to be expected, neither we nor our poems were at all wanted. The great puzzle lay in the difficulty of getting answers from the publishers to whom we applied. I ventured to apply to the Messrs. Chambers, of Edinburgh, for advice; *they* may have forgotten the circumstance, but *I* have not, for from them I received a civil and sensible reply, on which we acted, and at last made way.

The publishers to whom she finally made a successful application for the production of "Currer, Ellis, and Acton Bell's Poems" were Messrs. Aylott and Jones, Paternoster Row. Mr. Aylott has kindly placed the letters which she wrote to him on the subject at my disposal. The first is dated January 28, 1846, and in it she inquires if they will publish one volume octavo of poems; if not at their own risk, on the author's account. It is signed "C. Brontë." They must have replied speedily, for on January 31 she writes again:

Gentlemen—Since you agree to undertake the publication of the work respecting which I applied to you, I should wish now to know, as soon as possible, the cost of paper and printing. I should like [the work] to be printed in one octavo volume, of the same quality of paper and size of type as Moxon's last edition of Wordsworth. The poems will occupy, I should think, from 200 to 250 pages.

During the whole time that the volume of poems was in the course of preparation, no word was written telling anyone, out of the household circle, what was in progress. Nevertheless, an old school friend suspected that the sisters wrote for magazines; and in this idea she was confirmed when, on one of her visits to Haworth, she saw Anne with a number of *Chambers's Journal*, and a smile of pleasure stealing over her face as she read.

"Why do you smile?" asked the friend.

"Only because I see they have inserted one of my poems," was the quiet reply; and not a word more was said on the subject.

To this friend Charlotte addressed the following letter:

March 31, 1846.

I reached home a little after two o'clock yesterday; I found papa well; his sight much the same. . . . I went into the room where Branwell was, to speak to him. I might have spared myself the trouble, as he took no notice, and made no reply; he was stupefied. I hear that he got a sovereign while I have been away, under pretence of paying a debt; he went immediately to a public-house, and has employed it as was to be expected. In his present state it is scarcely possible to stay in the room where he is. What the future has in store I do not know.

Meanwhile the printing of the volume of poems was quietly proceeding. The sisters had determined to correct the proofs themselves. Up to March 28 the publishers had addressed the correspondent as C. Brontë, Esq., but at this time some "little mistake occurred," and she desired Messrs. Aylott and Co. in future to direct to "*Miss* Brontë." She had evidently implied that she was not acting on her own behalf, but as agent for the real author, as in a note, dated April 6, she makes a proposal on behalf of "C. E. and A. Bell."

This proposal states that they are preparing for the press a work of fiction, consisting of three distinct and unconnected tales, which may be published either together, as a work of three volumes, or separately, as single volumes. She states that it is not their intention to publish these tales on their own account; but that the authors direct her to ask Messrs. Aylott and Co. whether they would be disposed to undertake the work after having, of course, inspected the MS. To this letter of inquiry the publishers replied speedily, and the tenor of the answer may be gathered from Charlotte's, dated April 11.

I beg to thank you, in the name of C. E. and A. Bell, for your obliging offer of advice. I will avail myself of it, to request information on two or three points. It is evident that unknown authors have great difficulties to contend with, before they can succeed in bringing their works before the public. Can you give me any hint as to the way in which these difficulties are best met? For instance, in the present case, would a publisher be most likely to accept the MS.? Whether offered as a work of three vols., or as [separate] tales? What publishers would be most likely to receive favourably a proposal of this nature? Would it suffice to *write* to a publisher on the subject, or would it be necessary to have recourse to a personal interview?

I suppose the little volume of poems was published some time bout the end of May 1846. It stole into life; some weeks passed without the mighty murmuring public discovering that three more voices were uttering their speech. Then in the *Athenaeum* f July 4 came a short review. The reviewer assigns to Ellis the ighest rank of the three "brothers," as he supposes them to be; e calls Ellis "a fine, quaint spirit"; and speaks of an "origiality" and of "an evident power of wing that may reach eights not here attempted." Currer Bell is placed midway etween Ellis and Acton. We can fancy with what interest the eview was read at Haworth Parsonage, and how the sisters would endeavor to find out hints for the future guidance of heir talents. Still, I fear, but few copies were sold.

All this time, notwithstanding their anxieties over Branwell nd their father—notwithstanding the ill success of their poems —the three sisters were trying that other literary venture, to which Charlotte made allusion in one of her letters to the Messrs. Aylott. Each of them had written a prose tale, hoping hat the three might be published together. *Wuthering Heights*, y Emily, and *Agnes Grey*, by Anne, are before the world. The hird—Charlotte's contribution, *The Professor*—will be published shortly after the appearance of this memoir.

The three tales tried their fate in vain together, at length they vere sent forth separately, and for many months with stillontinued ill success. Meanwhile, during this summer of 1846, while their literary hopes were waning, an anxiety of another ind was increasing. Old Mr. Brontë was nearly blind. His yesight had become seriously impaired by a cataract. He could rope his way about; he continued to preach; and under his great sorrow he was always patient. But he was driven inwards and must have dwelt much on what was painful and distressing in regard to his only son.

For some time before this autumn, his daughters had been collecting all the information they could respecting the probable success of operations for cataract. About the end of July, Emily and Charlotte made a journey to Manchester, and there they heard of the fame of the oculist Mr. Wilson. They went to him but he could not tell, from description, whether the eyes were ready to be operated upon. Towards the end of August, therefore, Charlotte took her father to him. Mr. Wilson determined at once to undertake the operation, and recommended them to comfortable lodgings, kept by an old servant of his. From thence the following letter is dated, on August 21, 1846:

> Papa and I came here on Wednesday; we saw Mr. Wilson, the oculist; he pronounced papa's eyes ready for an operation, and has fixed Monday for the performance of it. Think of us on that day! . . . There will be a nurse coming in a day or two. . . . Mr. Wilson says we shall have to stay here for a month at least. I wonder how Emily and Anne will get on at home with Branwell. . . . What would I not give to have you here! One is forced, step by step, to get experience in the world; but the learning is so disagreeable. One cheerful feature in the business is, that Mr. Wilson thinks most favourably of the case.

> *August 26th, 1846.*
> The operation is over; it took place yesterday. . . . Mr. Wilson says, he considers it quite successful; but papa cannot yet see anything. The affair lasted precisely a quarter of an hour. . . . Papa is now confined to his bed in a dark room, and is not to be stirred for four days.

A few days later, she writes thus:

> Papa is still lying in bed, in a dark room, with his eyes bandaged. . . . He was allowed to try his sight for the first time yesterday. He could see dimly. Mr. Wilson seemed perfectly satisfied. I have had bad nights from the toothache since I came to Manchester.

Among the dispiriting circumstances connected with her anxious visit to Manchester, Charlotte told me that her tale, *The Professor*, came back upon her hands, curtly rejected by some publisher, on the very day when her father was to submit to his operation. But she had the heart of Robert Bruce within her, and failure upon failure daunted her no more than him. Not only did *The Professor* return again to try his chance among the London publishers, but there and then, in this time of care and depressing inquietude, did the brave genius begin *Jane Eyre*. She herself says, "Currer Bell's book found acceptance nowhere, nor any acknowledgement of merit, so that something like the chill of despair began to invade his heart."

I have already mentioned that some of her surviving friends consider that an incident which she heard, when teaching at Miss Wooler's, was the germ of the story of *Jane Eyre*. But of this nothing can be known, except by conjecture. I remember, however, many little particulars which Miss Brontë gave me, respecting her mode of composition. She said that it was not every day that she could write. Sometimes weeks or even months elapsed before she felt that she had anything to add to that portion of her story which was already written. Then, some morning, she would wake up, and the progress of her tale lay clear and bright before her. When this was the case, all her care was to discharge her household and filial duties, so as to obtain leisure to sit down and write out the incidents and thoughts, which were more present to her mind at such times than her actual life itself.

Anyone who has studied her writings—whether in print or in her letters; anyone who has enjoyed the rare privilege of listening to her talk, must have noticed her singular felicity in the choice of words. She herself, in writing her books, was solicitous on this point. One set of words was the truthful mirror of her thoughts; no others, however apparently identical in meaning, would do. She wrote on scraps of paper in a minute hand, holding each against a piece of board for a desk. This plan was necessary for one so shortsighted as she was; and, besides, it enabled her to use pencil and paper, as she sat near the fire in the twilight, or if she was wakeful for hours in the night. Her finished manuscripts were copied from these pencil scraps, in clear, delicate writing, almost as easy to read as print.

The sisters retained the old habit of putting away their work at nine o'clock, and pacing up and down the sitting room. At this time, they talked over the stories they were engaged upon. Once or twice a week, each read to the others what she had written, and heard what they had to say about it. Charlotte told me that the remarks made had seldom any effect in inducing her to alter her work. But the readings were of great and stirring interest to all, taking them out of the pressure of daily cares.

It was on one of these occasions that Charlotte determined to make the heroine of *Jane Eyre* plain, small, and unattractive, in defiance of the accepted canon. The writer of the beautiful obituary article on "the death of Currer Bell" most likely learned from Miss Brontë herself what is there stated: "She once told her sisters that they were wrong—even morally wrong—in making their heroines beautiful as a matter of course. They replied that it was impossible to make a heroine interesting on any other terms. Her answer was, 'I will prove you wrong; I will show you a heroine as plain and small as myself, who shall be as interesting as any of yours.' Hence *Jane Eyre*, said she in telling the anecdote; 'but she is not myself, any further than that.'"

This wonderful book was, however, only at its commencement when Miss Brontë returned with her father to Haworth after their expedition to Manchester. They arrived home about the end of September. Mr. Brontë was daily gaining strength, but he was still forbidden to exercise his sight much. Things had gone on comfortably while she was away.

Soon after this a proposal was again mooted for Miss Brontë opening a school at some place distant from Haworth. It elicited the following reply: "Leave home! Whenever I consult my conscience, it affirms that I am doing right in staying at home."

This next extract gives us a glimpse into the cares of that home. It is from a letter dated December 15.

I hope you are not frozen up; the cold here is dreadful. . . . England might really have taken a slide up into the Arctic Zone; the sky looks like ice; the earth is frozen; the wind is as keen as a two-edged blade. We have all had severe colds and coughs. Poor Anne has suffered greatly from asthma. . . . You say I am to "tell you plenty." What would you have me say? Nothing happens at Haworth; nothing, at least, of a pleasant kind. One little incident occurred about a week ago, to sting us to life. It was the arrival of a Sheriff's officer on a visit to Branwell, inviting him either to pay his debts or take a trip to York. Of course his debts had to be paid. It is not agreeable to lose money, time after time, in this way; but where is the use of dwelling on such subjects? It will make him no better.

So ended the year 1846.

CHAPTER XI

THE NEXT YEAR opened with a spell of cold dreary weather, which told severely on a constitution already tried by anxiety and care. Miss Brontë describes herself as having utterly lost her appetite, and as looking "grey, old, worn and sunk." The cold brought on severe toothache, which caused restless nights; and long wakefulness told acutely upon her nerves. "I shall be thirty-one next birthday," she wrote in March. "My youth is gone like a dream; and very little use have I ever made of it. What have I done these last thirty years? Precious little."

The quiet, sad year stole on. The sisters were contemplating the terrible effects of talents misused and faculties abused in the person of that brother, once their darling and dearest pride. They had to cheer the poor old father. They had to order the frugal household with increasing care, and they visited the parish schools duly.

In the intervals of such a life as this, *Jane Eyre* was making progress. *The Professor* was passing slowly from publisher to publisher. *Wuthering Heights* and *Agnes Grey* had been accepted by a publisher, "on terms somewhat impoverishing to the two authors."

Meanwhile, *The Professor* had met with many refusals from different publishers; some not overcourteously worded, and none alleging any reasons for its rejection. "Currer Bell" writes,

"As a forlorn hope, we tried one publishing house more." Th
was Messrs. Smith, Elder and Co. Some time elapsed before a
answer was returned. Then, as "Currer Bell" continues, "the
came a letter, which he opened in the dreary anticipation
finding two hard hopeless lines, intimating that 'Messrs. Smit
and Elder were not disposed to publish the MS.,' and, instea
he took out of the envelope a letter of two pages. He read
trembling. It declined, indeed, to publish that tale, for busine
reasons, but it discussed its merits and demerits, so courteousl
so considerately, that this very refusal cheered the author bett
than a vulgarly-expressed acceptance would have done. It w
added, that a work in three volumes would meet with caref
attention."

On August 6 Miss Brontë writes in reply:

> Your objection to the want of varied interest in the tale is, I
> am aware, not without grounds; yet it appears to me that it
> might be published without serious risk, if its appearance were
> speedily followed up by another work from the same pen, of a
> more striking and exciting character.... I have a second narrative
> in three volumes, nearly completed, to which I have endeavoured
> to impart a more vivid interest than belongs to *The Professor*. In
> about a month I hope to finish it, so that if a publisher were
> found for *The Professor*, the second narrative might follow as
> soon as was deemed advisable. Will you be kind enough to
> favour me with your judgment on this plan?

While the minds of the three sisters were in this state of su
pense, their friend Ellen came to pay a promised visit. She w
with them at the beginning of the glowing August of that yea
They were out on the moors for the greater part of the da
basking in the golden sunshine. The royal ground on whi
they stood would expand into long swells of amethyst-tint
hills, melting away into aerial tints; and the fresh and fragra
scent of the heather, and the "murmuring of innumerable bees
would lend a poignancy to the relish with which they welcom
their friend to their own true home on the wild and open hil
There, too, they could escape from the shadow in the hou
below.

Throughout this time—during all these confidences—not a word was uttered to their friend of the three tales in London; nor did she hear of that other story "nearly completed," lying in manuscript in the old parsonage down below. She might have had her suspicions that they all wrote with an intention of publication sometime; but she knew the bounds they set in their communications; nor could she, nor can anyone else, wonder at their reticence, when remembering how scheme after scheme had failed, just as it seemed close upon accomplishment.

Mr. Brontë, too, had suspicions of something going on; but, never being spoken to, he did not speak on the subject, and consequently his ideas were only just prophetic enough to keep him from being actually stunned when, later on, he heard of the success of *Jane Eyre;* to the progress of which we must now return. Charlotte wrote to Messrs. Smith and Elder on August 24:

> I now send you per rail a MS. entitled *Jane Eyre*, a novel in three volumes, by Currer Bell. I find I cannot prepay the carriage of the parcel, as money for that purpose is not received at the small station-house [here]. If, when you acknowledge the receipt of the MS., you would mention the amount charged on delivery, I will immediately transmit it in postage stamps. It is better in future to address Mr. Currer Bell, under cover to Miss Brontë, Haworth, Bradford, Yorkshire, as there is a risk of letters otherwise directed not reaching me. To save trouble, I enclose an envelope.

When the manuscript of *Jane Eyre* had been received by the future publishers of that remarkable novel, it fell to the share of a gentleman (Mr. W. S. Williams) connected with the firm to read it first. He was so powerfully struck by the tale, that he reported his impression in very strong terms to Mr. Smith, who appears to have been much amused by the admiration excited. "You seem to have been so enchanted, that I do not know how to believe you," he said. But when a second reader, a clearheaded Scotchman not given to enthusiasm, took the manuscript home in the evening, and became so deeply interested as to sit up half the night to finish it, Mr. Smith's curiosity was excited; he read it for himself; and great as were the praises which had been bestowed upon it, he found that they had not exceeded the truth. *Jane Eyre* was accepted, printed, and published by October 16.

ON ITS PUBLICATION, copies of *Jane Eyre* were presented to a few literary friends of the publishers. Among them was Thackeray, the great writer of fiction for whom Miss Brontë felt so strong an admiration; he immediately appreciated and, in a note to the publishers, acknowledged its extraordinary merits.

The reviews were more tardy, or more cautious. The *Athenaeum* and the *Spectator* gave short notices, containing qualified admissions of the power of the author. The *Literary Gazette* was uncertain as to whether it was safe to praise an unknown author. The *Examiner* came forward to the rescue, as far as the opinions of professional critics were concerned. Its notice of *Jane Eyre* was full of hearty, yet discriminating praise. Otherwise, the press in general did little to promote the sale of the novel; the demand for it among librarians had begun before the appearance of the *Examiner* review; the power of fascination of the tale itself made its merits known to the public; and, early in December, the rush began for copies.

I will insert two of Miss Brontë's letters to her publishers, in order to show how timidly the idea of success was received by one so unaccustomed to adopt a sanguine view.

Oct. 19th, 1847.

Gentlemen—The six copies of *Jane Eyre* reached me this morning. You have given the work every advantage which good paper, clear type, and a seemly outside can supply; if it fails, the fault will lie with the author—you are exempt.

Dec. 10th, 1847.

Gentlemen—I beg to acknowledge the receipt of your letter inclosing a bank post bill, for which I thank you. Having already expressed my sense of your kind and upright conduct, I can now only say that I trust you will always have reason to be as well content with me as I am with you. If the result of any future exertions I may be able to make should prove agreeable and advantageous to you, I shall be well satisfied.

There is little record remaining of the manner in which the first news of the book's wonderful success reached and affected the three sisters. I once asked Charlotte whether the popularity to which the novel attained had taken her by surprise. She hesitated and then said, "I believed that what had impressed me so forcibly when I wrote it must make a strong impression on anyone who read it. I was not surprised at those who read *Jane Eyre* being deeply interested in it; but I hardly expected that a book by an unknown author could find readers."

Anne Brontë had been more than usually delicate all the summer, and now that *Jane Eyre* gave such indications of success, Charlotte began to plan schemes of relaxation from care for this darling younger sister. Anne led far too sedentary a life, continually stooping either over her book, or work, or at her desk. "It is with difficulty," writes Charlotte, "that we can prevail upon her to take a walk, or induce her to converse. I look forward to next summer with the intention that she shall, if possible, make at least a brief sojourn at the sea-side."

The sisters had kept the knowledge of their literary ventures from their father, fearing to increase their own anxieties and disappointment by witnessing his; for he took an acute interest in all that befell his children, and his own tendency had been towards literature in the days when he was young and hopeful. He says now that he suspected it all along, but all he was certain of was that his children were perpetually writing—and not writing letters. We have seen how the communications from their publishers were received "under cover to Miss Brontë." Once, Charlotte told me, they overheard the postman meeting Mr. Brontë, as the latter was leaving the house, and inquiring from the parson where one Currer Bell could be living, to which Mr. Brontë replied that there was no such person in the parish.

Now, however, when the demand for the work had assured success to *Jane Eyre*, her sisters urged Charlotte to tell their father of its publication. She accordingly went into his study one afternoon, carrying with her a copy of the book, and one or two reviews. Something like the following conversation then took place.

"Papa, I've been writing a book."

"Have you, my dear?"

"Yes, and I want you to read it."

"I am afraid it will try my eyes too much."

"But it is not in manuscript; it is printed."

"My dear! you've never thought of the expense it will be! It will be almost sure to be a loss, for how can you get a book sold? No one knows your name."

"But, papa, I don't think it will be a loss; no more will you, if you will just let me read you a review or two, and tell you more about it."

So she sat down and read some of the reviews to her father; and then, giving him the copy of *Jane Eyre* that she intended for him, she left him to read it. When he came in to tea, he said, "Girls, do you know Charlotte has been writing a book, and it is much better than likely?"

But while the existence of Currer Bell was like a piece of a dream to the quiet inhabitants of Haworth Parsonage, who went on with their uniform household life, the whole reading world of England was in a ferment to discover the unknown author. No one they knew had genius enough to have written *Jane Eyre*. Even the book's publishers were ignorant whether Currer Bell was a real or an assumed name—whether it belonged to a man or a woman. Every little incident mentioned in the book was turned this way and that to answer, if possible, the much-vexed question of sex. All in vain.

CHAPTER XII

IN DECEMBER 1847 *Wuthering Heights* and *Agnes Grey* appeared. The first named of these stories has revolted many readers by the power with which wicked and exceptional characters are depicted. Others, again, have felt the attraction of remarkable genius, even when displayed on grim and terrible criminals. Emily's powerful imagination, as Charlotte later wrote, "was a spirit more sombre than sunny."

But whether justly or unjustly, the productions of the two

younger Miss Brontës were not received with much favor at the time of their publication.

"Critics failed to do them justice," Charlotte later wrote. "The immature, but very real, powers revealed in *Wuthering Heights*, were scarcely recognised; the identity of its author was misrepresented: it was said that this was an earlier and ruder attempt of the same pen which had produced *Jane Eyre*. . . . Unjust and grievous error! We laughed at it at first, but I deeply lament it now."

Henceforward Charlotte Brontë's existence becomes divided into two parallel currents—her life as Currer Bell, the author; her life as Charlotte Brontë, the woman. There were separate duties belonging to each character—not opposing each other but difficult to be reconciled.

Meanwhile, the year 1848 opened. The second edition of *Jane Eyre* appeared in January 1848, with the dedication to Mr. Thackeray, and people looked at each other and wondered afresh as to the authorship. But Currer Bell knew no more of William Makepeace Thackeray—of his life or circumstances— than that he had placed his name as author upon the title page of *Vanity Fair*. She was thankful for the opportunity of expressing her high admiration of a writer whom, as she says, she regarded "as the social regenerator of his day."

But even while *Jane Eyre* was bringing Charlotte fame and success, the year 1848 also opened with sad domestic distress. Not from the imagination—not from internal conception—but from hard cruel facts, pressed down by external life upon their very senses for months and years together, did the Brontës write out in their tales what they saw.

Jan. 11th, 1848.

We have not been very comfortable here at home lately, Branwell has, by some means, contrived to get more money from the old quarter, and has led us a sad life. . . . Papa is harassed day and night; we have little peace; he is always sick; has two or three times fallen down in fits; what will be the ultimate end, God knows. But who is without their scourge, their skeleton behind the curtain? It remains only to do one's best, and endure with patience what God sends.

The winter in Haworth had been a sickly season. Influenza had prevailed amongst the villagers, and where there was a real need for the presence of the clergyman's daughters they were never found wanting, though they themselves had suffered from the epidemic.

There is no doubt that the proximity of the crowded church-yard rendered the parsonage unhealthy, and occasioned much illness to its inmates. Mr. Brontë represented the unsanitary state of Haworth pretty forcibly to the Board of Health; and obtained a recommendation that all future interments in the churchyard should be forbidden, and means set on foot for obtaining a water supply to each house. But he was baffled by the taxpayers; as, in many a similar instance, quantity carried it against quality, numbers against intelligence. And thus we find that illness often assumed a low typhoid form in Haworth, and fevers visited the place with sad frequency.

Charlotte's birthday came round. She wrote to Ellen, whose birthday was within a week of hers; and we perceive the difference between her thoughts and what they were a year or two ago, when she had said, "I have done nothing." There must have been a modest consciousness of having "done something" present in her mind, as she wrote this year:

> I am now thirty-two. Youth is gone—gone—and will never come back; can't help it. . . . It seems to me, that sorrow must come some time to everybody, and those who scarcely taste it in their youth, often have a more brimming cup to drain in after life; whereas, those who exhaust the dregs early, who drink the lees before the wine, may reasonably hope for more palatable draughts to succeed.

The authorship of *Jane Eyre* was as yet a close secret in the Brontë family; not even Ellen, who was all but a sister, knew more about it than the rest of the world. She might conjecture, it is true; but she knew nothing, and wisely said nothing, until she heard a report from others that Charlotte Brontë was an author—had published a novel! Then she wrote to her; and received the following letter; confirmatory enough, as it seems to me now, in its very vehemence of intended denial.

All I can say to you about a certain matter is this: the report—if report there be—must have had its origin in some absurd misunderstanding. I have given *no one* a right either to affirm, or to hint, that I was "publishing"—(humbug!) Though twenty books were ascribed to me, I should own none. I scout the idea utterly.

The reason why Miss Brontë was so anxious to preserve her secret was, I am told, that she had pledged her word to her sisters that it should not be revealed through her.

The dilemmas attendant on the publication of the sisters' novels, under assumed names, were increasing upon them. Many critics insisted on believing that all the fictions published as by three Bells were the works of one author, but written at different periods of his development and maturity.

Ever since the completion of Anne Brontë's tale of *Agnes Grey*, she had been laboring at a second, *The Tenant of Wildfell Hall*. The subject—the deterioration of a character, whose profligacy and ruin took their rise in habits of intemperance—was painfully discordant to one who would fain have sheltered herself from all but peaceful and religious ideas. "She had," says her sister of that gentle "little one," "in the course of her life, been called on to contemplate near at hand the terrible effects of talents misused and faculties abused; hers was naturally a sensitive nature; what she saw sunk very deeply into her mind. She brooded over it till she believed it to be a duty to reproduce every detail (of course, with fictitious characters, incidents, and situations), as a warning to others."

In June of this year, *The Tenant of Wildfell Hall* was sufficiently near its completion to be submitted to the person who had previously published for Ellis and Acton Bell.

In consequence of his mode of doing business, considerable annoyance was occasioned both to Miss Brontë and to them. The circumstances, as detailed in a letter of Charlotte's to her friend Mary Taylor in New Zealand, were these: One morning, at the beginning of July, a communication was received at the parsonage from Messrs. Smith and Elder, which disturbed its quiet inmates not a little. *Jane Eyre* had had a great run in

America, and a publisher there had consequently bid high for the next work by "Currer Bell." This Messrs. Smith and Elder had promised to let him have. The American publisher was therefore greatly astonished, and not well pleased, to learn that a similar agreement had been entered into with another American house, and that the new tale was shortly to appear.

It turned out, upon inquiry, that the mistake had originated in Acton and Ellis Bell's publisher having assured this American house that, to the best of his belief, *Jane Eyre*, *Wuthering Heights*, and *The Tenant of Wildfell Hall* were all written by the same author.

Though Messrs. Smith and Elder distinctly stated in their letter that they did not share in such "belief," the sisters were impatient till they had shown its utter groundlessness. With rapid decision, they resolved that Charlotte and Anne should start for London that very day, in order to prove their separate identities to Messrs. Smith and Elder.

Having arrived at this determination, the two sisters each packed up a change of dress and set off in some excitement after early tea to walk to Keighley station. A great storm overtook them on their way that summer evening to the station; but they had no time to seek shelter. They only just caught the train at Keighley, arrived at Leeds, and were whirled up by the night train to London.

About eight o'clock on the Saturday morning they arrived at the Chapter Coffee House, Paternoster Row. They had some breakfast and then set forth to walk to Cornhill, quite forgetting, in their "queer state of inward excitement," that they might have hired a cab.

The crowded streets and impeded crossings so dismayed them that they stood still repeatedly, in complete despair of making progress, and were nearly an hour in walking the half mile they had to go. Neither Mr. Smith nor Mr. Williams knew that they were coming; they were entirely unknown to the publishers of *Jane Eyre*, who were not, in fact, aware whether the "Bells" were men or women.

On reaching Mr. Smith's, Charlotte put his own letter into his hands, the same letter which had excited so much disturbance at Haworth Parsonage twenty-four hours before. "Where did you get this?" said he—as if he could not believe that the two diminutive young ladies dressed in black, looking pleased yet agitated, could be the embodied Currer and Acton Bell, for whom curiosity had been hunting so eagerly.

An explanation ensued, and Mr. Smith at once began to form plans for their stay in London. He urged them to meet a few

The railway station at Keighley as it looked in the 1840's. Roughly four miles from Haworth, it was the gateway through which travelers to and from the parsonage would have to pass.

literary friends at his house; and this was a strong temptation to Charlotte; but her resolution to remain unknown induced her to put it firmly aside. The sisters were equally persevering in declining Mr. Smith's invitation to stay at his house. They refused to leave their quarters, saying they were not prepared for a long stay.

When they returned to their inn, poor Charlotte paid for the excitement and agitation of the last twenty-four hours by a racking headache and sickness. Towards evening, as she expected some of the ladies of Mr. Smith's family to call, she took a strong dose of sal volatile, which roused her a little, but still, as she says, she was "in grievous bodily case" when their visitors were announced, in full evening costume.

The sisters had not understood that it had been settled that they were to go to the opera, and they had no elegant dresses either with them or in the world. But Miss Brontë resolved to raise no objections in the acceptance of kindness. She says in a letter to Mary Taylor:

Fine ladies and gentlemen glanced at us with a slight, graceful superciliousness, quite warranted by the circumstances. Still I felt pleasurably excited in spite of headache, sickness, and conscious clownishness. The performance was Rossini's "Barber of Seville" —very brilliant, though I fancy there are things I should like better. We got home after one o'clock. We had never been in bed the night before; had been in constant excitement for twenty-four hours; you may imagine we were tired. The next day, Sunday, Mr. Williams came early to take us to church; and in the afternoon Mr. Smith and his mother fetched us in a carriage, and took us to his house to dine.

On Monday we went to the Exhibition of the Royal Academy, the National Gallery, dined again at Mr. Smith's, and then went home to tea with Mr. Williams at his house.

On Tuesday morning, we left London, laden with books Mr. Smith had given us, and got safely home. A more jaded wretch than I looked, it would be difficult to conceive.

The impression Miss Brontë made upon those with whom she first became acquainted during this visit to London, was of a person with clear judgment and fine sense; and though reserved, possessing unconsciously the power of drawing out others in conversation. All conversation with her was genuine and stimulating; and when she launched forth in praise or reprobation of books, or deeds, or works of art, her eloquence was burning. She was thorough in all that she said or did, yet so open and fair, that instead of rousing resentment she convinced her hearers of her earnest zeal for the truth and right.

Mr. Williams tells me that on the night when he accompanied the party to the opera, as Charlotte ascended the grand flight of stairs to the first tier of boxes, she was so much struck with the architectural effect of the splendid decorations that involuntarily she slightly pressed his arm, and whispered, "You know I am not accustomed to this sort of thing." Indeed, it must have formed a vivid contrast to what they had been doing the night before, when they had trudged along, with beating hearts, on the road between Haworth and Keighley. It was no wonder that they returned to Haworth utterly worn out, after the fatigue and excitement of this visit.

THE NEXT NOTICE I find of Charlotte's life at this time is of a different character to anything telling of enjoyment.

July 28th.

Branwell is the same in conduct as ever. His constitution seems much shattered. Papa, and sometimes all of us, have sad nights with him. He sleeps most of the day, and consequently will lie awake at night. But has not every house its trial?

The dark cloud was hanging over that doomed household, and gathering blackness every hour. On September 24, Branwell died. On October 9, she thus writes:

The past three weeks have been a dark interval in our humble home. Branwell's constitution had been failing fast all the summer; but still, neither the doctors nor himself thought him so near his end as he was. He was confined to his bed but for one day, and was in the village two days before his death. He died, after twenty minutes' struggle, on Sunday morning, September 24th. He was perfectly conscious till the last agony came on. His mind had undergone the peculiar change which frequently precedes death, two days previously; the calm of better feelings filled it; a return of natural affection marked his last moments. . . . A deep conviction that he rests at last—rests well, after his brief, erring, suffering, feverish life—fills and quiets my mind now. . . . Papa was acutely distressed at first, but, on the whole, has borne the event well. Emily and Anne are pretty well, though Anne is always delicate, and Emily has a cold and cough at present. It was my fate to sink at the crisis. . . . Headache and sickness came on; internal pain attacked me. . . . I was confined to bed a week. But, thank God! health seems now returning.

When Branwell's fatal attack came on, his pockets were found filled with old letters from the woman to whom he was attached. I turn from her forever.

Let us look once more into the parsonage at Haworth.

Oct. 29th, 1848.

I think I have now nearly got over my late illness, and am almost restored to my normal health. . . . I feel much more uneasy about my sister than myself. Emily's cold and cough are very obstinate. I fear she has pain in her chest, and I sometimes catch a shortness in her breathing. . . . She looks very thin and pale. Her reserved nature occasions me great uneasiness of mind. It is useless to question her; you get no answers. It is still more useless to recommend remedies; they are never adopted. Nor can I shut my eyes to Anne's great delicacy of constitution. The late sad event has, I feel, made me more apprehensive than common. I cannot help feeling much depressed sometimes. I try to leave all in God's hands; but faith and resignation are difficult to practise under some circumstances. The weather has been most unfavourable for invalids of late; sudden changes of temperature, and cold penetrating winds have been frequent here. . . . Papa has so far stood it better than any of us.

I go on now with Charlotte's own affecting words in the biographical notice which she wrote about her sisters.

But a great change approached. Affliction came in that shape which to anticipate is dread; to look back on grief. . . . My sister Emily first declined. . . . Never in all her life had she lingered over any task that lay before her, and she did not linger now. She sank rapidly. She made haste to leave us. . . . Day by day, when I saw with what a front she met suffering, I looked on her with an anguish of wonder and love. I have seen nothing like it; but, indeed, I have never seen her parallel in anything. Stronger than a man, simpler than a child, her nature stood alone. The awful point was that, while full of ruth for others, on herself she had no pity; from the trembling hands, the unnerved limbs, the fading eyes, the same service was exacted as they had rendered in health. To stand by and witness this, and not dare to remonstrate, was a pain no words can render.

In fact, Emily never went out of doors after the Sunday succeeding Branwell's death. She made no complaint; she rejected sympathy and help. Many a time did Charlotte and Anne drop their sewing, or cease from their writing, to listen with wrung hearts to the failing step, the labored breathing with which their sister climbed the short staircase; yet they dared not notice in words what they observed, with pangs of suffering even deeper than hers; they could only sit, still and silent.

Nov. 23rd, 1848.

I told you Emily was ill, in my last letter. She has not rallied yet. She is *very* ill. A more hollow, wasted, pallid aspect I have not beheld. The deep tight cough continues. . . . In this state she resolutely refuses to see a doctor. God only knows how all this is to terminate. . . . But nature shrinks from such thoughts. I think Emily seems the nearest thing to my heart in the world.

When a doctor had been sent for, and was in the very house, Emily refused to see him. Her sisters could only describe to him what symptoms they had observed; and the medicines which he sent she would not take, denying that she was ill. She was, in fact, growing rapidly worse. Yet, to the last, she adhered tenaciously to her habits of independence. She would suffer no one to assist her. One Tuesday morning in December, she arose and dressed herself as usual, making many a pause, but doing everything for herself, and even endeavoring to take up her employment of sewing; the servants looked on, and knew what the catching, rattling breath and the glazing of the eye too surely foretold; but she kept at her work; and Charlotte and Anne, though full of unspeakable dread, had still the faintest spark of hope. So the morning drew on to noon. Emily was worse: she could only whisper in gasps. Now, when it was too late, she said to Charlotte, "If you will send for a doctor, I will see him now." About two o'clock she died.

Dec. 21st, 1848.

Emily suffers no more from pain or weakness now. She is gone, after a hard, short conflict. She died on *Tuesday.* . . . Yesterday we put her poor, wasted, mortal frame quietly under the church pavement. We are very calm at present. Why should we be otherwise? The anguish of seeing her suffer is over. We feel she is at peace. . . . She died in a time of promise. We saw her taken from life in its prime. But it is God's will.

As the old, bereaved father and his two surviving children followed the coffin to the grave, they were joined by Keeper, Emily's fierce, faithful bulldog. He walked alongside of the mourners and into the church, and stayed quietly there all the time that the burial service was being read. When he came home, he lay down at Emily's chamber door and howled pitifully for many days. Anne Brontë drooped and sickened more rapidly from that time; and so ended the year 1848.

CHAPTER XIII

Jan. 10th, 1849.

Anne had a very tolerable day yesterday, and a pretty quiet night last night, though she did not sleep much. Mr. Wheelhouse ordered the blister to be put on again. She bore it without sickness. . . . She has had one dose of the cod-liver oil; it smells and tastes like train oil. I am trying to hope, but the day is cloudy and stormy. My spirits fall at intervals very low; then I look where you counsel me to look, beyond earthly tempests and sorrows. I seem to get strength, if not consolation. . . . Dear Ellen, I see few lights through the darkness of the present time; but amongst them the constancy of [your] kind heart is one of the most cheering and serene.

Anne had been delicate all her life; a fact which perhaps made them less aware of the true nature of those fatal first symptoms. Yet they seem to have lost but little time before they sent for expert medical advice. She was examined with the stethoscope, and the dreadful fact was announced that tubercular consumption had already made considerable progress. A system of treatment was prescribed. For a short time they hoped that the disease was arrested. One comfort was that Anne was the patientest, gentlest invalid that could be. Still, there were hours, days, weeks of inexpressible anguish to be borne; under the pressure of which Charlotte could only pray.

Ellen's family proposed that Anne should come to them, in order to try what change of air could do towards restoring her health. In answer to this proposal Charlotte writes on March 24.

I read your kind note to Anne, and she wishes me to thank you sincerely for your friendly proposal. She feels, of course, that it would not do to take advantage of it; but she intimates there is another way in which you might serve her. Should it, a month or two hence, be deemed advisable that she should go to the seaside, or to some inland watering-place—and should I be obliged to remain at home—she asks, could you be her companion? . . . This, dear Ellen, is Anne's proposal; for my own part, I must add that I see serious objections to your accepting it—objections I cannot name to her. . . . Write such an answer to this note as I can show Anne. You can write any additional remarks to me on a separate piece of paper.

I take Charlotte's own words as the best record of her thoughts and feelings during all this terrible time.

April 12th.

I read Anne's letter to you; . . . I am glad your friends object to your going with Anne: it would never do. . . . If, a month hence, she continues to wish for a change, I shall (D.V.) go with her myself. Mr. T—— recommends Scarborough, which was Anne's own choice. I trust affairs may be so ordered, that you may be able to be with us at least part of the time.

May came, and brought the milder weather longed for; Ellen agreed to accompany them on the trip, and Miss Brontë wrote to engage the lodgings at Scarborough. They took a good-sized sitting room and an airy double-bedded room, both commanding a sea view. On May 16, Charlotte wrote to Ellen:

It is with a heavy heart I prepare; and earnestly do I wish the fatigue of the journey were well over. . . . I fear you will be shocked when you see Anne; but be on your guard, dear Ellen, not to express your feelings; indeed, I can trust your self-possession and your kindness. You ask how I have arranged about leaving Papa. I could make no special arrangement. He wishes me to go with Anne; so I do what I believe is for the best, and leave the result to Providence.

They had made an appointment with Ellen to meet them at the Leeds station on Thursday, May 24, in order that they might all proceed together. But on Wednesday morning Anne was so ill that it was impossible for the sisters to set out; yet they had no means of letting Ellen know of this, and she consequently arrived at Leeds station and sat waiting there for several hours.

The next day she could bear suspense no longer, and set out for Haworth, reaching there just in time to carry the feeble, fainting invalid into the chaise which stood at the gate to take them to Keighley. The servant who stood at the parsonage gates saw death written on her face, and spoke of it. Charlotte saw it

Suffering from fatal consumption, Anne Brontë expressed a wish to visit the seaside resort of Scarborough. Here she died and was subsequently buried. This lithograph shows the Spa and bay as they looked when Charlotte and Ellen Nussey took Anne to visit there.

and did not speak of it; if this last darling yearned for the change to Scarborough, go she should, however Charlotte's heart might be wrung by fear. Charlotte's beloved friend has kindly written out for me the following account of the journey—and of the end.

She left her home May 24th, 1849—died May 28th. Her life was calm, quiet, spiritual: *such* was her end. Through the trials and fatigues of the journey, she evinced the pious courage and fortitude of a martyr. . . . Her weakness of body was great, but her gratitude for every mercy was greater.

On the 25th we arrived at Scarborough; our dear invalid having, during the journey, directed our attention to every prospect worthy of notice.

On the 26th she drove on the sands for an hour; and lest the poor donkey should be urged by its driver to a greater speed than her tender heart thought right, she took the reins herself.

On Sunday, the 27th, she wished to go to church, [but] we thought it prudent to dissuade her from the attempt. She walked a little in the afternoon, and . . . the evening closed in with the most glorious sunset ever witnessed. The castle on the cliff stood in proud glory gilded by the rays of the declining sun. The distant ships glittered like burnished gold. The view was grand beyond description. Anne was drawn in her easy chair to the window, to enjoy the scene with us. Her face became illumined almost as much as the glorious scene she gazed upon. Little was said, for it was plain that her thoughts were driven by the view before her to penetrate forwards to the regions of unfading glory. . . . On returning to her place near the fire, she conversed with her sister upon the propriety of returning to their home. She was fearing others might suffer more if her decease occurred where she was. She probably thought the task of accompanying her lifeless remains on a long journey was more than her sister could bear.

The night was passed without any apparent accession of illness. She rose at seven o'clock, and performed most of her toilet herself, by her expressed wish. . . . About 11 a.m. she spoke of feeling a change. "She believed she had not long to live. Could she reach home alive, if we [departed] immediately?" A physician was sent for. She begged him to say "How long he thought she might live; not to fear speaking the truth, for she was not afraid to die." The doctor reluctantly admitted that life was ebbing fast. She thanked him for his truthfulness. She still occupied her easy chair, looking serene, reliant. She clasped her hands, and reverently invoked a blessing from on high; first upon her sister, then upon her friend, to whom she said, "Be a sister in my stead. Give Charlotte as much of your company as you can." . . . Shortly after this, seeing that her sister could hardly restrain her grief, she said, "Take courage, Charlotte; take courage." Her faith never failed, and her eye never dimmed till about two o'clock, when she calmly and without a sigh passed from the temporal to the eternal.

Anne died on a Monday. On Tuesday Charlotte wrote to her father; knowing that his presence was required for some annual church solemnity at Haworth, she informed him that she had made all necessary arrangements for the interment, and that the funeral would take place so soon that he could hardly arrive in time for it.

Mr. Brontë wrote back to urge Charlotte's longer stay at the seaside. Her health and spirits were sorely shaken; and much as he naturally longed to see her, he felt it right to persuade her to take, with Ellen, a few more weeks' change of scene. Late in June the friends returned homewards, parting rather suddenly from each other when their paths diverged.

July, 1849.

I intended to have written a line to you to-day, if I had not received yours. I got here a little before eight o'clock. All was clean and bright waiting for me. Papa and the servants were well; and all received me with an affection which should have consoled. The dogs seemed in strange ecstasy. I am certain they regarded me as the harbinger of others. The dumb creatures thought that as I was returned, those who had been so long absent were not far behind.

I left Papa soon, and went into the dining-room: I shut the door—I tried to be glad that I was come home. I have always been glad before—except once—even then I was cheered. But this time joy was not to be the sensation. I felt that the house was all silent—the rooms were all empty. I remembered where the three were laid—in what narrow dark dwellings—never more to reappear on earth. So the sense of desolation and bitterness took possession of me . . . to-day I am better.

I do not know how life will pass, but I certainly do feel confidence in Him who has upheld me hitherto. . . . The great trial is when evening closes and night approaches. At that hour, we used to assemble in the dining-room—we used to talk. Now I sit by myself—necessarily I am silent.

CHAPTER XIV

THE TALE OF *Shirley* had been begun soon after the publication of *Jane Eyre*. The stories and anecdotes of the Luddite riots that Charlotte had heard at Roe Head as a schoolgirl came up in her mind when, as a woman, she sought a subject for her next work; and she sent to Leeds for a file of the *Mercurys* of 1812, 1813 and 1814, in order to understand the spirit of those eventful times.

In *Shirley* she took the idea of most of her characters from life, although the incidents and situations were, of course, fictitious. Thus she thought she might draw from the real without detection, but in this she was mistaken; her studies were too closely accurate. People recognized themselves, or were recognized by others, in her graphic descriptions.

The character of Shirley herself is Charlotte's representation of her sister Emily, as what Emily would have been had she been placed in health and prosperity. As for the family of the Yorkes, they were, I have been assured, almost daguerreotypes of the family of her friend Mary Taylor.

Down into the very midst of her writing came the bolts of death. She had nearly finished the second volume of her tale when Branwell died, after him Emily, after her Anne; the pen, laid down when there were three sisters living, was taken up when one alone remained.

Once back at work, she went on with it steadily. It was dreary to write without anyone to listen to the progress of her tale, to find fault or to sympathize. But she wrote on, even though she again felt ill and was struggling against "continually recurring feelings of slight cold; slight soreness in the throat and chest, of which I cannot get rid."

In August there arose a new cause for anxiety, happily but temporary.

Aug. 23rd, 1849.

Papa has had another attack of bronchitis. After what has happened, one trembles at any appearance of sickness; and I feel too keenly that he is the *last*—the only near and dear relative I have in the world. To-day he has seemed better, for which I am truly thankful.

After Emily's death, there was no longer any need for Charlotte to keep her writing secret from her friend Ellen, and on September 10 she writes:

My piece of work is at last finished, and despatched to its destination. You must now tell me when there is a chance of your being able to come here. I fear it will now be difficult to arrange, as it is so near [your sister's] marriage-day. . . . But when it is *convenient*, I shall be truly glad to see you. . . . Papa, I am thankful to

537

say, is better. My cold is much less troublesome. A few days since, I had a severe bilious attack; but it is gone now. It is the first from which I have suffered since my return from the sea-side. I had them every month before.

Ellen's sister was about to be married, and this prevented Ellen from visiting Haworth at this time. It was perhaps just as well, for within a week or two both Tabby and Martha, the young servant whom they had to assist her, were ill in bed; and, with the exception of occasional aid, Miss Brontë had all the household work to perform, as well as to nurse the two invalids.

But there was one day when the strung nerves gave way—when, as Charlotte says, "I fairly broke down for ten minutes; sat and cried like a fool. Tabby could neither stand nor walk. Papa had just been declaring that Martha was in imminent danger. I was myself depressed with headache and sickness. That day I hardly knew where to turn. Thank God! Martha is now convalescent: Tabby, I trust, will be better soon. Papa is pretty well. I have the satisfaction of knowing that my publishers are delighted with what I sent them. This supports me. But life is a battle. May we all be enabled to fight it well!"

Towards the close of October in this year, Charlotte went to pay a visit to her friend; but her enjoyment in the holiday was deadened by a continual feeling of ill health. Moreover, she was anxious about the impression which her second work would produce on the public.

Shirley was published on October 26. When the earliest reviews were published, and asserted that the mysterious writer must be a woman, Miss Brontë was much disappointed. She had been as anxious as ever to preserve her incognito; she had even fancied that there were fewer traces of a female pen in *Shirley* than in *Jane Eyre;* and she especially disliked the lowering of the standard by which to judge a work of fiction, if it proceeded from a feminine pen.

But the secret, so jealously preserved, was oozing out at last; and a visit to London, which Miss Brontë paid towards the end of the year 1849, made it distinctly known.

The visit was made because of the feelings of illness from

which she was now so seldom free. She constantly suffered from headaches and indigestion, and the slightest exposure to cold added sensations of hoarseness and soreness at the chest. In consequence of this, she determined to take the evil in time, and go up to London and consult some physician there. She had been all along on most happy terms with her publishers; their friendly urgency prevailed, and it was decided that she would

William Makepeace Thackeray, the celebrated author of "Vanity Fair," very much admired "Jane Eyre," and it was to him that Charlotte dedicated the second edition of her famous novel.

be the guest of Mr. Smith. Thus at the end of November she went up to London, and was immediately plunged into what appeared to her a whirl.

She had stipulated that she should not be expected to see many people. Still, she longed to have an idea of the personal appearance and manners of some of those whose writings had interested her. Mr. Thackeray was accordingly invited to meet her; so in time were others. "Thackeray is a Titan of the mind," she wrote later in a letter; "I was fearfully stupid with him." Her hosts also took pleasure in showing her the sights of London, and she renewed her friendship with the Wheelwright family, whom she had known in Brussels.

She soon acquiesced in the recognition of herself as the authoress of *Jane Eyre*, because she perceived that there were some advantages to be derived from dropping her pseudonym. One result was an acquaintance with Harriet Martineau, the author and social reformer. On behalf of Miss Martineau, some friend who lived in Mr. Smith's neighborhood invited the unknown Currer Bell to tea. They were ignorant of whether the name was that of a man or a woman; then "Miss Brontë" was announced; and in came a young-looking lady, almost childlike in stature, "in a deep mourning dress, neat as a Quaker's, with her beautiful hair smooth and brown, her fine eyes blazing with meaning, and her sensible face indicating a habit of self-control." She hesitated at finding four or five people assembled, then went straight to Miss Martineau, and soon became as one of the family round the tea table; by the time she had left, a foundation had been laid for her intimacy with Miss Martineau.

After some discussion on the subject, some gentlemen were invited by Mr. Smith to meet her at dinner the evening before she left town. Respecting this dinner party she thus wrote to Laetitia Wheelwright, a former Brussels schoolfellow:

> The evening after I left you passed better than I expected. Thanks to my substantial lunch, I was able to wait the eight o'clock dinner with complete resignation, and to endure its length quite courageously. . . . There were only seven gentlemen at dinner besides Mr. Smith, but of these five were critics— men more dreaded in the world of letters than you can conceive. I did not know how much their presence and conversation had excited me till they were gone, and the reaction commenced. When I had retired for the night, I wished to sleep—the effort to do so was vain. I could not close my eyes. Night passed; morning came, and I rose without having known a moment's slumber. So utterly worn out was I when I got to Derby [on the way to Haworth], that I was obliged to stay there all night.

So she returned to her quiet home, and her noiseless daily duties. The winter of this year in the North was hard and cold it affected Miss Brontë's health less than usual, however, probably because the change and the medical advice she had taken in London had done her good. But she could scarcely help feeling much depressed in spirits as the anniversary of her sister Emily's death came round. At this time, as at others, I find her alluding in her letters to the solace she found in the books sent her from her publishers; for they had adopted the habit of sending her boxfuls of books from time to time.

What, I sometimes ask, could I do without them? I have re-course to them as to friends; they shorten and cheer many an hour that would be too long and too desolate otherwise. I am still very rich, for my stock is far from exhausted. Some other friends have sent me books lately. The perusal of Harriet Martineau's *Eastern Life* has afforded me great pleasure.

By this time, all in the area knew the place of residence of Currer Bell. Far and wide in the West Riding had spread the intelligence that the eminent author was no other than a daughter of the venerable clergyman of Haworth.

Miss Brontë was extremely touched in her heart by the way in which those who had known her from her childhood were proud and glad of her success. All round about the news had spread; strangers came to see her, as she went into church; and the sexton "gained many a half-crown" for pointing her out.

Her health was again suffering at this time. Even in persons of naturally robust health, the nerves and appetite will give way in solitude. How much more must it have been so with Miss Brontë, delicate and frail in constitution, tried by such anxiety and sorrow!

Owing to Mr. Brontë's long-formed habits of solitary occupation when in the house, his daughter was left to herself for the greater part of the day. The hours of retiring for the night had always been early in the parsonage. But Charlotte could not have slept if she had gone to bed. She stayed up late and later, striving to beguile the lonely night with some employment, till her weak eyes failed to read or to sew, and could only weep in solitude.

No one on earth can even imagine what those hours were to her. All the grim superstitions of the North, implanted in her by servants during her childhood, recurred to her now—with such an intense longing once more to stand face-to-face with the souls of her sisters. On windy nights, sobs and wailings seemed to go round the house, as of the dearly beloved striving to force their way to her. Someone conversing with her once objected, in my presence, to that part of *Jane Eyre* in which she hears Rochester's voice crying out to her in a great crisis of her

541

fe, he being many, many miles distant at the time. I do not now what incident was in Miss Brontë's recollection when she ?plied, in a low voice, drawing in her breath, "But it is a true ing; it really happened."

It was no bad thing for her that about this time various people egan to go over to Haworth, curious to see and to meet the riter. Among this number were Sir James and Lady Kay-huttleworth. Their house lies over the moors at about a dozen iles from Haworth as the crow flies.

According to the meaning of the word in that uninhabited istrict, they were neighbors, and Sir James and his wife drove ver one morning, at the beginning of March, to call upon 1iss Brontë and her father. Before taking leave, they pressed ?r to visit them at Gawthorpe Hall. After some hesitation, and : the urgency of her father, she consented to go.

On the whole, she enjoyed her visit very much, in spite of her 1yness. She later wrote to Mr. Williams that she took great leasure in the "quiet drives to old ruins and old halls; the ialogues by the old fireside in the oak-paneled drawing-room id not too much exhaust me. The house, too, is much to my ᵻste; near three centuries old, grey, stately, and picturesque. . . . 'he worst of it is, that there is now some menace hanging over 1y head of an invitation to go to them in London during the ᵻason. This, which would be a great enjoyment to some people, a perfect terror to me."

CHAPTER XV

ᴰURING THE EARLIER MONTHS of this spring of 1850, Haworth ᵛas extremely unhealthy. The weather was damp, low fever ᵛas prevalent, and the household at the parsonage suffered along ᵛith its neighbors. Charlotte says, "I have felt it [the fever] in ᵛequent thirst and infrequent appetite; Papa too, and even 1artha, have complained." This depression of health produced ᵉpression of spirits, and she grew more and more to dread the ᵗoposed journey to London with Sir James and Lady Kay-huttleworth. In the end this journey was put off, and on

May 22 she wrote the following letter to Mr. James Taylor, th
manager of Smith, Elder and Co., who by now had become
much valued friend:

> I had thought to bring the *Leader* and the *Athenaeum* myself
> this time, and not to have to send them by post, but my journey
> to London is again postponed, and this time indefinitely. Sir
> James Kay Shuttleworth's state of health is the cause. . . . Once
> more, then, I settle myself down in the quietude of Haworth
> Parsonage, with books for my companions, and an occasional
> letter for a visitor. . . .
>
> I have just received yours of this morning; thank you for the
> enclosed note. The longings for liberty and leisure which May
> sunshine wakens in you, stir my sympathy. It is a pity to think
> of you all [at Cornhill] toiling at your desks in such genial
> weather as this. For my part, I am free to walk on the moors;
> but when I go out there alone, everything reminds me of the
> times when others were with me, and then the moors seem a
> wilderness, featureless, solitary, saddening. My sister Emily had
> a particular love for them, and there is not a knoll of heather, not
> a branch of fern, not a young bilberry leaf, not a fluttering lark
> or linnet, but reminds me of her. The distant prospects were
> Anne's delight, and when I look round, she is in the blue tints,
> the pale mists, the waves and shadows of the horizon. In the
> hill-country silence, their poetry comes by lines and stanzas into
> my mind: once I loved it; now I dare not read it, and am driven
> often to wish I could taste one draught of oblivion, and forget
> much that, while mind remains, I never shall forget. Many
> people seem to recall their departed relatives with a sort of mel-
> ancholy complacency, but I think these have not watched them
> through lingering sickness, nor witnessed their last moments:
> it is these reminiscences that stand by your bedside at night, and
> rise at your pillow in the morning. At the end of all, however,
> exists the Great Hope. Eternal Life is theirs now.

It became requisite, however, before long, that Charlott
should go to London on business. She went up to town at th
beginning of June, and much enjoyed her stay, seeing very fe
persons this time, and thus suffering much less from exhaustio
When she left London she went to stay with her friend Elle

it her visit was a short one, for, in accordance with a plan made before leaving London, she went on to Edinburgh to join the Smiths for a few days. She was delighted with Edinburgh, calling London a "dreary place" in comparison. As she wrote some weeks later to Laetitia Wheelwright, "Edinburgh, compared to London, is like a vivid page of history compared to a large dull treatise on political economy."

Edinburgh as it looked around the time of Charlotte's visit there. She was delighted with the city, calling it a "vivid page of history."

On her return from Scotland, she again spent a few days with Ellen's family. Her friend mentioned in a letter to Mr. Brontë that Charlotte was suffering from a bad cold, and he could not rest till he dispatched a messenger to see her.

It may easily be conceived that two people living together as Mr. Brontë and his daughter did would have their moments of keen anxiety respecting each other's health. There is not one letter of hers which I have read that does not contain some mention of her father's state in this respect. He, in his turn, noted every indisposition of his one remaining child's, and sometimes worked himself up into a miserable state of anxiety.

While Miss Brontë had been in London, she had been induced to sit for her portrait to Richmond. It is a crayon drawing; in my judgment an admirable likeness. Mr. Brontë thought that it looked older than Charlotte; but that the expression was wonderfully good and lifelike. To Mr. Smith, the donor, she sent the following amusing account of the arrival of a portrait of the Duke of Wellington that came with the one of herself:

545

The little box for me came at the same time as the large one for Papa. When you first told me that you had had the Duke's picture framed, and had given it to me, I felt half provoked with you, but now I cannot but acknowledge that, in so doing, you were felicitously inspired. It is his very image, and I esteem it a treasure. . . . Papa seems much pleased with the portrait [of me], as do the few other persons who have seen it, with one notable exception; viz., our old servant, who tenaciously maintains that it is not like—that it is too old-looking. . . . Requesting always to be very kindly remembered to your mother and sisters, I am, yours very thanklessly (according to desire),

C. BRONTË.

SIR JAMES KAY-SHUTTLEWORTH had taken a house in the neighbo hood of Bowness. In August, Charlotte was invited to go the for a week, and she says, "I consented to go, with reluctanc chiefly to please Papa; but I dislike to leave him." It was durin this visit at Briery Close—Lady Kay-Shuttleworth havin kindly invited me to meet her there—that I first made acquain ance with Miss Brontë. I copy out part of a letter, which I wro soon after this to a friend, Catherine Winkworth.

Dark when I got to Windermere station; a drive along the level road to Low-wood; then a stoppage at a pretty house, and then a pretty drawing-room, in which were Sir James and Lady Kay Shuttleworth, and a little lady in a black-silk gown, whom I could not see at first for the dazzle in the room; she came up and shook hands with me at once. I went up to unbonnet, etc.; came down to tea; the little lady hardly spoke, but I had time for a good look at her. She is (as she calls herself) *undeveloped*, thin, and more than half a head shorter than I; soft brown hair; eyes (very good and expressive, looking straight and open at you) of the same colour; a large mouth; the forehead square, broad, and rather overhanging. She has a very sweet voice; rather hesitates in choosing her expressions, but when chosen they seem without an effort admirable, and just befitting the occasion; there is nothing overstrained, but perfectly simple. . . .

We were only three days together; the greater part of which was spent in driving about, in order to show Miss Brontë the Westmoreland scenery. We were both included in an invitation to drink tea quietly at Fox How; and I saw how severely her nerves were taxed by the effort of going amongst strangers. . . .

Briery Close commanded an extensive view. I was struck by Miss Brontë's careful examination of the shape of the clouds and the signs of the heavens, in which she read what the coming weather would be. I told her I saw she must have a view equal in extent at her own home. She said that I was right, but that the

The famous crayon drawing of Charlotte by the fashionable portraitist George Richmond. Originally a gift of George Smith, Charlotte's publisher, to Mr. Brontë, it was later bequeathed to Charlotte's husband, Arthur Nicholls. Today it is the property of the National Portrait Gallery, London.

character of the prospect from Haworth was very different; that I had no idea what a companion the sky became to any one living in solitude—more than any inanimate object on earth—more than the moors themselves.

I must now quote from the first letter I had the privilege of receiving from Miss Brontë. It is dated August 27.

Papa and I have just had tea; he is sitting quietly in his room, and I in mine; "storms of rain" are sweeping over the garden and churchyard: as to the moors, they are hidden in thick fog. Though alone, I am not unhappy; I have a thousand things to be thankful for, and, amongst the rest, that this morning I received a letter from you, and that this evening I have the privilege of answering it. . . .

I have read Tennyson's *In Memoriam*, or rather part of it; I closed the book when I had got about half way. It is beautiful; it is mournful; it is monotonous. . . . I promised to send you Wordsworth's *Prelude*, and, accordingly, despatch it by this post; the other little volume shall follow in a day or two. I shall be glad to hear from you whenever you have time to write to me, *but you are never, on any account, to do this except when inclination prompts*. I should never thank you for a letter which you had felt it a task to write.

The "other little volume" was the book of Currer, Ellis, and Acton Bell's poems.

CHAPTER XVI

IT WAS THOUGHT DESIRABLE, about this time, to republish *Wuthering Heights* and *Agnes Grey*, and Charlotte undertook the task of editing them. Early in October she wrote to Ellen respecting the painfulness of her task:

> There is nothing wrong, and I am writing you a line as you desire, merely to say that I *am* busy just now. Mr. Smith wishes to reprint some of Emily's and Annie's works, with a few little additions from the papers they have left; and I have been closely engaged in revising, transcribing, preparing a preface, etc. . . . I found the task at first exquisitely painful and depressing; but regarding it in the light of a *sacred duty*, I went on, and now can bear it better. . . . I am both angry and surprised at myself for not being in better spirits; for not growing at least resigned to the solitude of my lot. But the reading over of papers brought back the pang of bereavement, and occasioned a depression of spirits well nigh intolerable. For one or two nights, I scarcely knew how to get on till morning. I tell you these things, because it is absolutely necessary to me to have some relief.

The revision of her sisters' works, and writing a short memoir of them, was Charlotte's painful employment every day during the dreary autumn of 1850. Wearied by the vividness of her sorrowful recollections, she sought relief in long walks on the moors. The dark, bleak season of the year brought back the long evenings, which tried Charlotte severely. For her father's sake, as well as for her own, she found it necessary to make some exertion to ward off depression of spirits. She accordingly ccepted an invitation to spend a week or ten days with Miss Martineau at Ambleside. She also proposed to come to Manchester and see me, on her way to Westmorland. But, unfortunately, I was from home, and unable to receive her.

On the tenth of December, the second edition of *Wuthering Heights* was published. Immediately after the republication of her sister's book Charlotte went to Miss Martineau's.

Charlotte was greatly drawn to the social reformer and novelist Harriet Martineau, with whom she carried on a warm and lively friendship. This is Miss Martineau as she appeared in 1834.

I can write to you now, dear Ellen, for I am away from home, and relieved, temporarily, at least, by change of scene, from the heavy burden of depression which, I confess, has for nearly three months been sinking me to the earth. . . . I am at Miss Martineau's for a week. Her house is very pleasant, both within and without. . . . Her visitors enjoy the most perfect liberty. I rise at my own hour, breakfast alone (she is up at five, takes a cold bath, and a walk by starlight, and has finished breakfast and got to her work by seven o'clock). I pass the morning in the drawing-room—she, in her study. At two o'clock we meet—work, talk, and walk together till five, her dinner-hour, spend the evening together, when she converses fluently, and with the most complete frankness. I go to my own room soon after ten—she sits up writing letters till twelve. She appears exhaustless in strength and spirits, and indefatigable in the faculty of labour. She is a great and a good woman; of course not without peculiarities, but I have seen none as yet that annoy me. . . . I thought I should like to spend two or three days with you before going home; so, if it is not inconvenient to you, I will (D.V.) come on Monday and stay till Thursday.

Miss Brontë paid the visit she here proposes to her friend; she then returned home, and immediately began to suffer from her old enemy, sickly and depressing headache. Still, this visit to Ambleside did her much good, and gave her a stock of pleasant recollections, and fresh interests.

So began the year of 1851. She was employing herself by now upon a new novel, *Villette;* but she was frequently unable to write, and was both grieved and angry with herself for her inability. In February, she writes as follows to Mr. Smith:

> Something you say about going to London; but the words are dreamy. London and summer are many months away: our moors are all white with snow just now. One can lay no plans three or four months beforehand. Besides, I don't deserve to go to London; nobody merits a change or a treat less. I secretly think, on the contrary, I ought to be put in prison, and kept on bread and water in solitary confinement—without even a letter from Cornhill—till I had written a book.

As spring drew on, depression of spirits began to grasp her again, and "to crush her with a day- and night-mare." She became afraid of sinking as low as she had done in the autumn, and to avoid this, she prevailed on her old friend and school-fellow to come and stay with her in March; she found great benefit from this companionship.

I shall now make an extract from one of her letters to Ellen which relates to a third offer of marriage she received round this time:

> Could I ever feel enough for [James Taylor] to accept of him as a husband? Friendship—gratitude—esteem—I have; but each moment he came near me my veins ran ice. Now that he is away, I feel far more gently towards him; it is only close by that I grow rigid with a strange mixture of apprehension and anger. I did not want to be proud, but I was forced to be so.

I have now named all the offers of marriage she ever received until that was made which she finally accepted.

Before Ellen took her departure, Mr. Brontë caught cold

d continued for some weeks much out of health, with an
tack of bronchitis. When he grew better, Charlotte resolved
 avail herself of an invitation which she had received some
ne before, to pay a visit in London. This year, 1851, was, as
eryone remembers, the time of the great exhibition; but she
d not intend to stay there long; and, as usual, she made an
reement with the Smiths that her sojourn at their house was
 be as quiet as ever.

From London she wrote to Ellen on June 2:

I came here on Wednesday, being summoned a day sooner
than I expected, in order to be in time for Thackeray's second
lecture. This, as you may suppose, was a genuine treat to me. . . .
I had a long talk with him, and I think he knows me now a
little better than he did. He is a great and strange man. There
is quite a furor for his lectures, [which are] a sort of essays, char-
acterised by his own peculiar originality and power. . . .

On Friday, I went to the Crystal Palace; it is a marvellous,
stirring, bewildering sight—a mixture of a genii palace, and a
mighty bazaar, but it is not much in my way; I liked the lecture
better. On Saturday I saw the Exhibition at Somerset House;
about half a dozen of the pictures are good and interesting. Sunday—yesterday—I went to hear D'Aubigné, the great Protestant
French preacher; it was pleasant—half sweet, half sad—and
strangely suggestive to hear the French language once more.
For health, I have so far got on very fairly, considering that I
came here far from well.

Mrs. Smith, who accompanied Miss Brontë to Thackeray's
:ture, says that she was aware that Thackeray was pointing out
r companion to several of his friends, but she hoped that
iss Brontë herself would not perceive it. After some time,
wever, during which many heads had been turned and many
asses put up, in order to look at the author of *Jane Eyre*, Miss
·ontë said, "I am afraid Mr. Thackeray has been playing me
rick." Then, as they were preparing to leave the room, Mrs.
nith saw with dismay that many of the audience were forming
emselves into lines, on each side of the aisle down which they
d to pass. Mrs. Smith took Miss Brontë's arm in hers, and
ey went along the avenue of admiring faces. During this

passage through the "cream of society," Miss Brontë's ha
trembled to such a degree that her companion feared lest s
should turn faint and be unable to proceed.

On June 18 Charlotte wrote to Ellen, "I cannot boast tl
London has agreed with me well this time; the oppression
frequent headache, sickness, and low spirits, has poisoned ma
moments which might otherwise have been pleasant." (
June 24 she wrote:

> People are very kind, but it is often a little trying at the
> time. . . . On Friday I dined at the ——'s, and met Mr. Moncktor
> Milnes. On Saturday I went to hear and see Rachel [the great
> French actress]; a wonderful sight. She made me shudder tc
> the marrow of my bones. She is not a woman; she is a snake
> On Sunday I went to the Spanish Ambassador's Chapel, where
> Cardinal Wiseman held a confirmation. The whole scene wa?
> impiously theatrical. Yesterday (Monday) I was sent for at ten
> to breakfast with Mr. Rogers, the patriarch-poet. After break-
> fast, Sir David Brewster came to take us to the Crystal Palace. . .
> After two hours spent at the Exhibition, where, as you may
> suppose, I was *very* tired, we had to go to Lord Westminster's
> and spend two hours more in looking at the pictures in hi
> splendid gallery.

Miss Brontë returned from London by Manchester, and pa
us a visit of a couple of days at the end of June. The weather v
so intensely hot, and she herself so much fatigued with l
London sight-seeing, that we did little but sit indoors, w
open windows, and talk. The only thing she made a point
exerting herself to procure was a present for Tabby. It was
be a shawl, and Miss Brontë took great pains in seeking out c
which she thought would please the old woman. While she v
with us she also became very friendly with my youngest lit
girl, Julia. The child would steal her little hand into M
Brontë's, and each took pleasure in this apparently unobserv
caress. Yet once when I told Julia to show her the way to so!
room in the house, Miss Brontë shrank back: "Do not *bid* l
do anything for me," she said; "it has been so sweet hitherto
have her rendering her little kindnesses *spontaneously*."

On her arrival at home, she addressed the following letter to the friend with whom she had been staying in London:

Haworth, July 1st, 1851.

My dear Mrs. Smith—Once more I am at home, where, I am thankful to say, I found my father very well. . . . The visit to Mrs. Gaskell formed a cheering break in the journey. Haworth Parsonage is rather a contrast, yet even Haworth Parsonage does not look gloomy in this bright summer weather; with the windows open I can hear a bird or two singing on certain thorn-trees in the garden. My father and the servants think me looking better than when I left home, and I certainly feel better myself for the change.

But summer passed, and the effects of her visit dwindled. "You charge me to write about myself," she wrote to me on September 20. "What can I say on that topic? My health is pretty good. My spirits are not always alike. Nothing happens to me. I hope and expect little in this world, and am thankful that I do not despond and suffer more. Thank you for inquiring after our old servant; she is pretty well. Papa likewise, I am glad to say, is pretty well."

Before the autumn was far advanced, the usual effects of her solitary life, and of the unhealthy situation of Haworth Parsonage, began to appear in the form of sick headaches and miserable, wakeful nights. She does not dwell on this in her letters; but there is an absence of all cheerfulness of tone. There was illness all through the parsonage household, and all domestic exertion fell for a time upon her shoulders.

Increasing indisposition subdued her at last, in spite of all her efforts of reason and will. She tried to forget it in writing. Her publishers were importunate for a new book from her pen. *Villette* was begun, but she lacked power to continue it. A little event which occurred about this time did not tend to cheer her. It was the death of poor old Keeper, Emily's dog. "He went gently to sleep," she wrote. "We laid his old faithful head in the garden. Flossy [the 'fat curly-haired dog'] is dull, and misses him. There was something very sad in losing the old dog."

When Miss Brontë wrote this, on December 8, she was suffering from a bad cold, and pain in her side. Her illness increased, and on December 17 she—so patient, so afraid of taxing others— had to call to her friend for help:

> I cannot at present go to see you, but I would be grateful if you could come and see me, even were it only for a few days. To speak truth, I have put on but a poor time of it during this month past. I was at last obliged to have recourse to a medical man. . . . [He] speaks encouragingly, but as yet I get no better. I am not confined to bed, and I know a little cheerful society would do me more good than gallons of medicine.

Of course, her friend went; and Miss Brontë derived a certain amount of benefit from her society. But the evil was now too deep-rooted to be more than palliated for a time by the "little cheerful society." A relapse came on before long. She was very ill of a liver ailment, and Mr. Brontë was miserably anxious about her, for she was reduced to the last degree of weakness, unable to swallow food for above a week.

When she was recovering, her spirits needed support, and then she yielded to her friend's entreaty that she would visit her. Happily for all parties, Mr. Brontë was wonderfully well this winter; and Charlotte could leave him for a week without any great anxiety. She benefitted greatly by the kind attentions and cheerful society of the family with whom she went to stay. To them, who had first known her as a little motherless schoolgirl, her invalid weakness was only a fresh claim upon their tender regard.

Miss Brontë's health continued such, that she could not apply herself to writing as she wished, for many weeks after this attack. Again and again, her friends urged her to leave home; nor were various invitations wanting to enable her to do this. But she would not allow herself any such indulgence. As far as she could see, her life was ordained to be lonely, and she must subdue her nature to her life. When she could employ herself in fiction, all was comparatively well; her characters were her companions in the quiet hours. But too frequently she could not write, could not see her people, nor hear them speak; a great mist of headache had blotted them out.

This was the case all through the present spring; and anxious as her publishers were for its completion, *Villette* stood still.

"It is not at all likely [she says in a letter to Mr. Williams dated March 4] that my book will be ready at the time you mention. If my health is spared, I shall get on with it as fast as is consistent with its being done. *Not one whit faster*. When the mood leaves me (it has left me now) I put by the MS. and wait till it comes back again. Meantime, if I might make a request to you. . . . Please to say nothing about my book till it is written, and in your hands. You may not like it. I am not myself elated with it as far as it is gone. Even if it should turn out reasonably well, still I regard it as ruin to an ephemeral book like a novel, to be much talked of beforehand, as if it were something great."

The "mood" here spoken of did not go off; it had a physical origin in indigestion, nausea, and sleeplessness. But as the milder weather came on, her health improved and her power of writing increased. She set herself with redoubled vigor to the work before her; and denied herself pleasure for the purpose of steady labor. Hence she writes to her friend on May 11:

Dear Ellen—I must adhere to my resolution of neither visiting nor being visited at present. Stay you quietly at B., till you go to S., as I shall stay at Haworth. . . . Thank you for Mary's letter. She *does* seem most happy. I think so much of it is in herself, and her own serene, pure, trusting, religious nature.

I wish you, dear Ellen, all health and enjoyment in your visit.

AT THIS TIME, however, she did make one trip. The reader will remember that Anne Brontë had been interred at Scarborough. Charlotte had left directions for a tombstone to be placed over her; but many a time during the past winter, her sad, anxious thoughts had revisited the scene of that last great sorrow, and she resolved to see for herself whether the stone and inscription were in a satisfactory state.

Cliffe House, Filey, June 6th, 1852.

Dear Ellen—I am at Filey utterly alone. Do not be angry, the step is right. Change of air was necessary; there were reasons why I should come here. On Friday I went to Scarborough, visited the churchyard and stone. It must be refaced and relettered; I gave the necessary directions. *That* duty, then, is done; long has it lain heavy on my mind; and that was a pilgrimage I felt I could only make alone.

Soon after her return from Filey, she was alarmed by a very sharp attack of illness with which Mr. Brontë was seized. There

The Reverend Patrick Brontë as he looked at the age of fifty-six. It was his custom to wear at his throat a high white cravat, around which he wound several layers of white silk.

was some fear, for a few days, that his sight was permanently lost, and his spirits sank painfully under this dread.

Before the end of August, however, his convalescence became quite established, and he was anxious to resume his duties for some time before his careful daughter would permit him.

Haworth was in an unhealthy state, as usual; and Miss Brontë suffered severely from the prevailing epidemics. She was too ill to write; and with illness came on the old heaviness of heart. At last in October she was well enough to "fall to business," and write away, almost incessantly, at her story of *Villette*, now drawing to a conclusion. The following letter, to Mr. Smith, seems to have accompanied the first part of the MS.

Oct. 30th, 1852.

My dear Sir—You must notify honestly what you think of *Villette* when you have read it. I can hardly tell you how I hunger to hear some opinion besides my own, and how I have sometimes desponded, and almost despaired, because there was no one to whom to read a line, or of whom to ask a counsel. . . . As to the anonymous publication, I have this to say: If the withholding of the author's name should tend materially to injure the publisher's interest, I would not press the point; but I should be most thankful for the sheltering shadow of an incognito. I seem to dread the advertisements—the large-lettered "Currer Bell's New Novel," or "New Work, by the Author of Jane Eyre."

On a Saturday in November, Miss Brontë completed *Villette* and sent it off to her publishers. "I said my prayers when I had done it," she wrote to Ellen. "Whether it is well or ill done, I don't know; D.V., I will now try and wait the issue quietly. The book, I think, will not be considered pretentious; nor is it of a character to excite hostility."

CHAPTER XVII

THE DIFFICULTY that presented itself to me, when I first had the honor of being requested to write this biography, was how I could show what a noble, true, and tender woman Charlotte Brontë really was, without mingling up with her life too much of the personal history of her nearest and most intimate friends.

One of the deepest interests of her life centers naturally round her marriage, and the preceding circumstances; but, more than all other events, her marriage requires delicate handling on my part, lest I intrude too roughly on what is most sacred to memory. Yet I have two good reasons for giving some particulars of the course of events which led to her few months of wedded life—that short spell of exceeding happiness. The first reason is my desire to call attention to the fact that Mr. Nicholls was one who had seen her almost daily for years; seen her as a daughter, a sister, and a friend. He was not a man to be attracted by any kind of literary fame. He was a grave, reserved, conscientious man, with a deep sense of religion, and of his duties as one of its ministers.

In silence he had watched her, and loved her long. The love of such a man—a daily spectator of her manner of life for years—is a great testimony to her character as a woman.

How deep his affection was I scarcely dare to tell, even if I could in words. She did not know—she had hardly begun to suspect—that she was the object of any peculiar regard on his part, when, in this very December, he came one evening to tea. After tea, she returned to her own sitting room, leaving her father and his curate together. Presently she heard the study door open, and expected to hear the succeeding clash of the front door. Instead, came a tap; and, "like lightning, it flashed upon me what was coming. He entered. He stood before me. What his words were you can imagine; his manner you can hardly realise, nor can I forget it. He made me, for the first time, feel what it costs a man to declare affection when he doubts response. . . . The spectacle of one, ordinarily so statue-like, thus trembling, stirred, and overcome, gave me a strange shock. I could only entreat him to leave me then, and promise a reply on the morrow. I asked if he had spoken to Papa. He said he dared not. I think I half led, half put him out of the room."

So deep, so fervent, was the affection Miss Brontë had inspired in the heart of this good man! And now I pass to my second reason for dwelling on a subject which may possibly be considered by some of too private a nature for publication.

When Mr. Nicholls had left her, Charlotte went immediately to her father and told him all. He instantly and strongly disapproved of the marriage; he could not bear the idea of this attachment of Mr. Nicholls to his daughter. Fearing the consequences of agitation to one so recently an invalid, she made haste to give her father a promise that, on the morrow, Mr. Nicholls should have a distinct refusal. Thus quietly and modestly did she receive this vehement, passionate declaration of love—thus unselfishly for herself put aside all consideration of how she should reply, excepting as her father wished!

The immediate result of Mr. Nicholls' declaration of attachment was that he sent in his resignation of the curacy of Haworth; and that Miss Brontë held herself simply passive, as far as words and actions went, while she suffered acute pain from the strong expressions which her father used in speaking of Mr. Nicholls, and from the too evident distress and failure of health on the part of the latter. Under these circumstances she more gladly than ever, availed herself of Mrs. Smith's proposal that she should again visit them in London; and thither she accordingly went in the first week of the year 1853.

This visit at Mrs. Smith's was passed more quietly than any previous one. Charlotte saw things rather than persons; and being allowed to have her choice of sights, she selected the "*real*" in preference to the *decorative*." She went over two prisons,

The Reverend Arthur Bell Nicholls became the curate of Haworth in 1845 and in that year first set eyes on Charlotte Brontë. She drew him as Mr. Macarthy, the curate in her novel "Shirley." Their marriage took place June 29, 1854.

Newgate and Pentonville; over two hospitals, the Foundling and Bethlehem, and she went to see several of the great City sights— the Bank, the Exchange, Rothschild's, etc. She received the utmost kindness from her hosts, whom she saw for what was to be the last time on a Wednesday morning in February. She met her friend Ellen at Keighley on her return, and the two proceeded to Haworth together.

Villette—which, if less interesting as a mere story than *Jane Eyre*, displays yet more of the extraordinary genius of the author—was received with one burst of acclamation. "The import of all the notices is such as to make my heart swell with thankfulness to Him," she wrote on February 15. Still she suffered one sizable disappointment, which arose from her great susceptibility to an opinion she valued much—that of Miss Martineau, who, both in an article on *Villette* in the *Daily News* and in a private letter to Miss Brontë, wounded her to the quick by expressions of censure. Charlotte writhed under what she felt to be injustice.

It was the cause of bitter regret to her; her woman's nature had been touched, as she thought, with insulting misconception, and she had dearly loved the person who had thus unconsciously wounded her.

I turn to a pleasanter subject. While she was in London, Miss Brontë had seen Lawrence's portrait of Mr. Thackeray, and admired it extremely. The likeness was by this time engraved, and Mr. Smith sent her a copy of it.

Haworth, Feb. 26th, 1853.

My dear Sir—At a late hour yesterday evening, I had the honour of receiving, at Haworth Parsonage, a distinguished guest, none other than W. M. Thackeray, Esq. Mindful of the rites of hospitality, I hung him up in state this morning. He looks superb in his beautiful, tasteful gilded gibbet. For companion he has the Duke of Wellington, (do you remember giving me that picture?) and for contrast Richmond's portrait of an unworthy individual, who, in such society, must be nameless. Thackeray looks away from the latter character with a grand scorn. I wonder if the giver of these gifts will ever see them on the walls where they now hang; it pleases me to fancy that one day he may.

Miss Brontë was in much better health during this winter of 1852–53 than she had been the year before. "For my part," she wrote to me in February, "I have thus far borne the cold weather well. I have taken long walks on the crackling snow, and felt the frosty air bracing. This winter has, for me, not been like last winter. Thank God for the change and the repose! My father too has borne the season well; and my book, and its reception thus far, have pleased and cheered him."

IN MARCH the quiet parsonage had the honor of receiving a visit from the then Bishop of Ripon. He remained one night. Some of the neighboring clergy were invited to meet him at tea and supper; and during the latter meal some of the "curates" began merrily to upbraid Miss Brontë with "putting them into a book"; and she, shrinking from thus having her character as authoress thrust upon her in the presence of a stranger, pleasantly appealed to the bishop as to whether it was fair thus to drive her into a corner. His lordship, I have been told, was agreeably impressed with the gentle unassuming manners of his hostess, and with the perfect propriety of the arrangements in the modest household.

By this time, some of the reviews had begun to find fault with *Villette*. Miss Brontë made her old request to Mr. W. S. Williams of Smith, Elder and Co.:

> My dear Sir—Were a review to appear, inspired with treble their animus, *pray* do not withhold it from me. I like to see the satisfactory notices; but I *must* see such as are *un*satisfactory and hostile; these are for my own especial edification—it is in these I best read public feeling and opinion.

When Easter was over and gone, she came, at the close of April, to visit us in Manchester. We had a friend, a young lady, staying with us. Miss Brontë had expected to find us alone; and although our friend was gentle and sensible after Miss Brontë's own heart, yet her presence was enough to create a nervous tremor; I saw a little shiver run from time to time over Miss Brontë's frame. The next day Miss Brontë told me how the unexpected sight of a strange face had affected her, and that she labored under severe headache.

I had several opportunities of perceiving how this nervousness was ingrained in her constitution, and how acutely she suffered in striving to overcome it. One evening we had, among other guests, two sisters who sang Scottish ballads exquisitely. Miss Brontë had been sitting quiet and constrained till they began "The Bonnie House of Airlie," but the effect of that and "Carlisle Yetts," which followed, was as irresistible as the playing of the Piper of Hamelin. The beautiful clear light came into her eyes; her lips quivered with emotion; she forgot herself and crossed to the piano, where she asked eagerly for song after song. The sisters begged her to come and see them the next morning, when they would sing as long as ever she liked, and she promised gladly. But on reaching their house her courage failed. We walked some time up and down the street, she trying not to dwell on the thought of a third sister to be faced if we went in.

Dreading lest this struggle with herself might bring on one of her headaches, I entered at last and made the best apology I could for her nonappearance.

Much of this nervous dread of encountering strangers I ascribed to the idea of her personal ugliness, which had been strongly impressed on her imagination early in life, and which she exaggerated to herself in a remarkable manner. "I notice," said she, "that after a stranger has once looked at my face, he is careful not to let his eyes wander to that part of the room again!" A more untrue idea never entered into anyone's head. Two gentlemen who saw her during this visit, without knowing at the time who she was, were singularly attracted by her appearance; and this feeling of attraction towards a pleasant countenance, sweet voice, and gentle timid manners was so strong in one as to conquer a dislike he had previously entertained to her works.

One day we asked two gentlemen to meet her at dinner, expecting that she and they would have a mutual pleasure in making each other's acquaintance. To our disappointment, she drew back with timid reserve from all their advances, till at last they gave up in despair and talked to each other and my husband. Presently Thackeray's Lectures were spoken of, and that on Fielding dwelt upon. One gentleman objected to it strongly, as calculated to do moral harm. The other took the opposite view. This roused Miss Brontë, who threw herself warmly into the discussion; the ice of her reserve was broken, and from that time she contributed her share to the conversation.

AFTER HER VISIT to Manchester, she had to return to a reopening of the painful circumstances of the previous winter, as the time drew near for Mr. Nicholls' departure from Haworth. A testimonial of respect from the parishioners was presented, at a public meeting, to one who had faithfully served them for eight years; and he left the place, and she saw no chance of hearing a word about him in the future, unless it was some secondhand scrap of intelligence dropped out accidentally by one of the neighboring clergymen.

I had promised to pay her a visit on my return from London

in June; but, after the day was fixed, a letter came from Mr. Brontë, saying that she was suffering from influenza and that he must request me to defer my visit. While sorry for the cause, I did not regret that my going would be delayed till the season when the moors would be all glorious with the purple bloom of the heather. In September I made the visit. Though I risk repeating things which I have previously said, I will copy out parts of a letter which I wrote at the time.

It was a dull, drizzly Indian-inky day, all the way on the railroad to Keighley. I left Keighley in a car for Haworth, four miles off—four steep, scrambling miles, the road winding between the wave-like hills. The day was lead-coloured; the road had stone factories alongside of it, stone cottages, and poor, hungry-looking fields. Haworth is a long, straggling village: one steep narrow street—we (the man, horse, car, and I) clambered up this street, and turned off into a lane to the Parsonage. I went round the house to the front door, looking to the church—moors everywhere beyond and above. The crowded grave-yard surrounds the house.

I don't know that I ever saw a spot more exquisitely clean. To be sure, the life is like clock-work. No one comes to the house; nothing disturbs the repose; hardly a voice is heard; you catch the ticking of the clock in the kitchen, or the buzzing of a fly in the parlour, all over the house. Miss Brontë sits alone in her parlour, breakfasting with her father in his study at nine o'clock. She helps in the housework: for one of their servants, Tabby, is nearly ninety, and the other only a girl. I accompanied her in her walks on the sweeping moors: the heather-bloom had been blighted by a thunder-storm a day or two before, and was all of a livid brown colour, instead of the blaze of purple glory it ought to have been. Oh! those high, wild, desolate moors, up above the whole world, and the very realms of silence!

Home to dinner at two. Mr. Brontë has his dinner sent into him. All the small table arrangements had the same dainty simplicity about them. Then we talked over the clear, bright fire; it is a cold country, and the fires were a pretty warm dancing light all over the house. The parlour had been evidently refurnished within the last few years, since Miss Brontë's success has enabled her to have a little more money to spend. Everything is in harmony with the idea of a country parsonage, possessed by people of very moderate means. The prevailing colour of the room is crimson, to make a warm setting for the cold grey landscape without. There is her likeness by Richmond, and an engraving from Lawrence's picture of Thackeray; and two recesses, on each side of the high, narrow, old-fashioned mantel-piece, filled with books. . . .

But now to return to our quiet hour of rest after dinner. I soon observed that her habits of order were such that she could not go on with the conversation, if a chair was out of its place; everything was arranged with delicate regularity. We talked over the old times of her childhood; of her elder sister's (Maria's) death—just like that of Helen Burns in *Jane Eyre;* of those strange, starved days at school; of the desire (almost amounting to illness) of expressing herself in some way—writing or drawing; of her being a governess; of her going to Brussels. . . . One day Miss Brontë brought down a rough, common-looking oil-painting, done by her brother, of herself—a little, rather prim-looking girl of eighteen—and the two other sisters, girls of sixteen and fourteen, with cropped hair, and sad, dreamy-looking eyes. . . . We have generally had another walk before tea, which is at six; at half-past eight, prayers; and by nine, all the household are in bed, except ourselves. We sit up together till ten, or past; and after I go, I hear Miss Brontë come down and walk up and down the room for an hour or so.

Copying this letter has brought the days of that pleasant visit very clear before me—very sad in their clearness. We were so happy together; we were so full of interest in each other's subjects. I understood her life the better for seeing the place where it had been spent—where she had loved and suffered. Mr. Brontë was a most courteous host; he had a sort of grand and stately way of describing past times. He never seemed quite to have lost the feeling that Charlotte was a child to be guided and ruled, when she was present; and she herself submitted to this with quiet docility. But when she had to leave the room, then all his pride in her genius and fame came out. He eagerly listened to everything I could tell him of the high admiration I had at any time heard expressed for her works.

We went to see various poor people in our distant walks. In all these cottages her quiet presence was known. At three miles from her home, the chair was dusted for her, with a kindly "Sit ye down, Miss Brontë"; and she knew what absent or ailing members of the family to inquire after. Her quiet, gentle words were evidently pleasing to those Yorkshire ears. Their welcome to her was sincere and hearty.

During one of the conversations which she and I held in the evenings, I asked her whether she had ever taken opium, as the description given of its effects in *Villette* was so exactly like what I had experienced—vivid and exaggerated presence of objects, of which the outlines were indistinct, or lost in golden mist. She replied that she had never, to her knowledge, taken a grain of it, but that when she had to describe anything which she had not experienced she had thought intently on it for many a night before falling to sleep—wondering what it was like—till at length she wakened up in the morning with all clear before her, as if she had in reality gone through the experience, and then could describe it as it had happened.

We talked about the different courses through which life ran. She said that she believed some were appointed beforehand to sorrow and much disappointment; that it was well for those who had rougher paths to perceive that such was God's will concerning them, and try to moderate their expectations. I took a different view: I thought that human lots were more equal than she imagined. She smiled and shook her head, and said she was trying to school herself against ever anticipating any pleasure; that it was better to be brave and submit faithfully.

We parted with many intentions on both sides of renewing very frequently the pleasure we had in being together. I was aware that she had a great anxiety on her mind at this time; and, being acquainted with its nature, I could not but deeply admire the patient docility which she displayed in her conduct towards her father.

SOON AFTER I LEFT HAWORTH, she went on a visit to Miss Wooler, who was then staying at Hornsea. The time passed quietly and happily with this friend, whose society was endeared to her by every year.

Of course, as I draw nearer to the years so recently closed, it becomes impossible for me to write with the same fullness of detail as I have hitherto not felt it wrong to use. Miss Brontë passed the winter of 1853–54 in a solitary and anxious manner. But the great conqueror Time was slowly achieving his victory over prejudice. By degrees Mr. Brontë became reconciled to the idea of his daughter's marriage.

Soon we lose all thought of the authoress in the timid and conscientious woman about to become a wife, and in the too short, almost perfect happiness of her nine months of wedded life.

By April 12 she was able to communicate the fact of her engagement to Miss Wooler.

My dear Miss Wooler —The truly kind interest which you have always taken in my affairs makes me feel that it is due to you to transmit an early communication on a subject respecting which I have already consulted you more than once. I must tell you then, that since I wrote last, papa's mind has come round to a view very different to that which he once took; and that after some correspondence, and as the result of a visit Mr. Nicholls paid here about a week ago, it was agreed that he was to resume the curacy of Haworth, as soon as papa's present assistant is provided with a situation, and in due course of time he is to be received as an inmate into this house.

It gives me unspeakable content to see that now my father has once admitted this new view of the case, he dwells on it very complacently. Mr. Nicholls seems deeply to feel the wish to comfort and sustain his declining years. . . . The destiny which Providence in His goodness and wisdom seems to offer me will not, I am aware, be generally regarded as brilliant, but I trust I see in it some germs of real happiness. . . .

It is Mr. Nicholls' wish that the marriage should take place this summer; he urges July. . . . I have [therefore] now decidedly declined the visit to London; the ensuing three months will bring me abundance of occupation. Papa has just got a letter from the dear bishop, which has touched us much; it expresses so cordial an approbation of Mr. Nicholls' return to Haworth, and such kind gratification at the domestic arrangements which are to ensue. It seems his penetration discovered the state of things when he was here in June 1853.

She felt what most thoughtful women do who marry when the first flush of careless youth is over, that in making announcements of an engagement, cares and fears come mingled inextricably with hopes. One great relief to her mind at this time was derived from the conviction that her father took a positive pleasure in all the preparations for her wedding.

At the beginning of May, Miss Brontë left home to pay several visits before her marriage. The first was to us. She only remained three days, as she had to go to Leeds, there to make such purchases as were required for her marriage. Her preparations, as she said, could be neither expensive nor extensive; consisting chiefly in a modest replenishing of her wardrobe, some repapering and repainting in the parsonage; and, above all, converting the small flagged passage room behind her sitting room into a study for her husband. On this idea, and plans for his comfort, as well as her father's, her mind dwelt a good deal; and we talked over these plans with the same unwearying happiness which, I suppose, all women feel in such discussions.

Haworth, May 22nd.

Since I came home I have been very busy stitching; the little new room is got into order, and the green and white curtains are up; they exactly suit the papering, and look neat and clean. Mr. Nicholls comes to-morrow. I feel anxious about him. It seems he has again been suffering from his rheumatic affection. I hear this not from himself, but from another quarter. He uttered no complaint to me; dropped no hint on the subject. Alas! . . . For unselfish reasons he did so earnestly wish this complaint might not become chronic. Well! come what may, God help and strengthen both him and me! I look forward to to-morrow with a mixture of impatience and anxiety.

Mr. Brontë had a slight illness which alarmed her. Besides, all the weight of care involved in the household preparations pressed on the bride in this case. She was too busy to unpack her wedding dresses for several days after they arrived from Halifax; yet not too busy to think of arrangements by which Miss Wooler's journey to be present at the marriage could be facilitated.

I write to Miss Wooler to-day. Would it not be better, dear, if you and she could arrange to come to Haworth on the same day, arrive at Keighley by the same train; then I could order the cab to meet you at the station, and bring you on with your luggage? . . . Be sure and give me timely information, that I may write to the Devonshire Arms about the cab.

Mr. Nicholls is a kind, considerate fellow. With all his masculine faults, he enters into my wishes about having the thing done quietly, in a way that makes me grateful; he will manage it so that not a soul in Haworth shall be aware of the day. . . . Precisely at eight in the morning [he and the minister] will be in the church, and there we are to meet them. Mr. and Mrs. Grant are asked to the breakfast, not to the ceremony.

It was fixed that the marriage was to take place on the twenty ninth of June. Miss Wooler and her friend Ellen arrived a Haworth Parsonage the day before; and the afternoon and evening were spent by Charlotte in thoughtful arrangement for the morrow, and for her father's comfort during her absence from home. When all was finished—the trunk packed, break fast arranged, the wedding dress laid out—just at bedtime, Mr Brontë announced his intention of stopping at home while the others went to the church. What was to be done? Who was to give the bride away? There were only to be the officiating clergyman, the bride and bridegroom, the bridesmaid, and Mis Wooler present. The Prayer Book was referred to; and it wa seen that the minister shall receive "the woman from her father's or *friend's* hand." So Miss Wooler, ever kind in emer gency, volunteered to give her old pupil away.

The news of the wedding had slipped abroad before the little party came out of church, and many old and humble friend were there, seeing her look "like a snow-drop" in her dress o white embroidered muslin, with a lace mantle, and white bonnet trimmed with green leaves.

Mr. Nicholls and she went to visit his friends and relations in Ireland; and made a tour by Killarney, Glengariff, Tarbert Tralee, and Cork, seeing scenery of which she says, "some part exceeded all I had ever imagined. . . . I must say I like my new relations. My dear husband, too, appears in a new light in hi own country. More than once I have had deep pleasure in hearing his praises on all sides. Some of the old servants and followers of the family tell me I am a most fortunate person; for I have got one of the best gentlemen in the country. . . . I feel thankful to God for having enabled me to make what seems a right choice; and I pray to be enabled to repay as I ought the affectionate devotion of a truthful, honourable man."

Henceforward the sacred doors of home are closed upon her married life. We, her loving friends, standing outside, caught occasional glimpses of brightness, and pleasant peaceful murmurs of sound, telling of the gladness within; and we looked at each other and said, "After a hard and long struggle—after many cares and sorrows—she is tasting happiness now!"

Here are some of the low murmurs of happiness we, who listened, heard:

I really seem to have had scarcely a spare moment since that dim quiet June morning, when you, Ellen, and myself all walked down to Haworth Church. My time is not my own now; somebody else wants a good portion of it, and says, "we must do so and so." We *do* so and so, accordingly; and it generally seems the right thing. . . . We have had many callers from a distance, and latterly [were occupied] in preparing for a small village entertainment. Both Mr. Nicholls and myself wished much to make some response for the hearty welcome shown by the parishioners on his return; accordingly, scholars, teachers, church-ringers, singers, etc., to the number of five hundred, were asked to tea and supper in the School-room. They seemed to enjoy it much, and it was very pleasant to see their happiness. One, in proposing my husband's health, described him as a *"consistent Christian and a kind gentleman."* I own the words touched me deeply, and I thought that to merit and win such a character was better than to earn either wealth, or fame, or power.

September 19th.
Yes! I am thankful to say my husband is in improved health and spirits. It makes me content and grateful to hear him from time to time avow his happiness in the brief, plain phrase of sincerity. My own life is more occupied than it used to be: I have

not so much time for thinking: I am obliged to be more practical, for my dear Arthur is a very practical, as well as a very punctual and methodical man. Every morning he is in school by nine; he gives the children religious instruction till half-past ten. Almost every afternoon he pays visits amongst poor parishioners. Of course, he often finds a little work for his wife to do, and she is not sorry to help him. I believe it is not bad for me that his bent should be so wholly towards matters of life and active usefulness; so little inclined to the literary and contemplative. As to his continued affection and kind attentions, it does not become me to say much of them; but they neither change nor diminish.

Her friend and bridesmaid came to pay them a visit in October. I was to have gone also, but I allowed some little obstacle to intervene, to my lasting regret.

You kindly inquire after Papa; he is better. We are all indeed pretty well; and it is long since I have known such comparative immunity from headache, etc., as during the last three months. My life is different from what it used to be. May God make me thankful for it! I have a good, kind, attached husband; and every day my own attachment to him grows stronger.

About this time, Mr. Nicholls was offered a living of much greater value than his curacy at Haworth; but he felt himself bound to Haworth as long as Mr. Brontë lived. Still, this offer gave his wife great pleasure, as a proof of the respect in which her husband was held.

Nov. 29.

I intended to have written a line yesterday, but just as I was sitting down for the purpose, Arthur called to me to take a walk. We set off, not intending to go far; but, when we had got about half a mile on the moors, Arthur suggested the idea of the water-fall; after the melted snow, he said, it would be fine. I had often wished to see it in its winter power—so we walked on. It was fine indeed; a perfect torrent racing over the rocks, white and beautiful! It began to rain while we were watching it, and we returned home under a streaming sky. However, I enjoyed the walk inexpressibly, and would not have missed the spectacle on any account.

She did not achieve this walk of seven or eight miles, in such weather, with impunity. She began to shiver soon after her return home, in spite of every precaution, and had a bad lingering sore throat and cold, which hung about her, and made her thin and weak.

Then early in the new year of 1855, she and her husband went to visit Sir James Kay-Shuttleworth at Gawthorpe. They only remained two or three days, but it so fell out that Charlotte increased her lingering cold by a long walk over damp ground in thin shoes.

Soon after her return, she was attacked by new sensations of nausea and faintness, and after a time she yielded to Mr. Nicholls' wish that a doctor should be sent for. He came, and assigned a natural cause for her miserable indisposition; a little patience and all would go right. She, who was ever patient in illness, tried hard to bear up. But the dreadful sickness increased, till the very sight of food occasioned nausea.

Tabby's health had suddenly and utterly given way, and she died in this time of distress and anxiety.

Martha tenderly waited on her mistress, and from time to time tried to cheer her with the thought of the baby that was coming. "I daresay I shall be glad sometime," she would say; "but I am so ill—so weary—" Then she took to her bed, too weak to sit up. From that last couch she wrote two notes—in pencil. The first, which has no date, is addressed to her own "Dear Ellen."

> I must write one line out of my dreary bed. I am not going to talk of my sufferings—it would be useless and painful. I want to give you an assurance, which I know will comfort you—and that is, that I find in my husband the tenderest nurse, the kindest support, the best earthly comfort that ever woman had. His patience never fails, and it is tried by sad days and broken nights. Papa—thank God!—is better. Our poor old Tabby is *dead* and *buried*. Give my kind love to Miss Wooler. May God comfort and help you.
>
> C. B. Nicholls.

The other—also in faint, faint pencil marks—was to her Brussels schoolfellow, Laetitia Wheelwright.

Feb. 15th.

A few lines of acknowledgement your letter *shall* have, whether well or ill. At present I am confined to my bed with illness, and have been so for three weeks. Up to this period, since my marriage, I have had excellent health. My husband and I live at home with my father; of course, I could not leave *him*. No kinder, better husband than mine, it seems to me, there can be in the world. I do not want now for kind companionship in health and the tenderest nursing in sickness. . . . I cannot write more now; for I am much reduced and very weak. God bless you all. Yours affectionately,

C. B. NICHOLLS.

I do not think she ever wrote a line again. Long days and longer nights went by, with still the same relentless nausea and faintness. About the third week in March there was a change; a low wandering delirium came on, and in it she begged constantly for food and even for stimulants. She swallowed eagerly now; but it was too late. Wakening for an instant from this stupor of intelligence, she saw her husband's woe-worn face, and caught the sound of some murmured words of prayer that God would spare her. "Oh!" she whispered forth. "I am not going to die, am I? He will not separate us, we have been so happy."

Early on Saturday morning, March 31, the solemn tolling of Haworth church bell spoke forth the fact of her death to the villagers who had known her from a child, and whose hearts shivered within them as they thought of the two sitting desolate and alone in the old gray house.

FEW BEYOND THAT CIRCLE of hills knew that she, whom the nations praised far off, lay dead that Easter morning. The two mourners, stunned with their great grief, desired not the sympathy of strangers. One member out of most of the families in the parish was bidden to the funeral; and it became an act of self-denial in many a poor household to give up to another the privilege of paying their last homage to her; and those who were excluded from the formal train of mourners thronged the churchyard, to see carried forth, and laid beside her own people, her whom not many months ago they had looked at as a pale white bride, entering on a new life with trembling happy hope.

I have little more to say. I cannot measure or judge of such a character as hers. I cannot map out vices, and virtues, and debatable land. One who knew her long and well—her old friend Mary Taylor—writes thus of her:

> She thought much of her duty, and had loftier and clearer notions of it than most people, and held fast to them with more success. It was done, it seems to me, with much more difficulty than people have of stronger nerves, and better fortunes. All her life was but labour and pain; and she never threw down the burden for the sake of present pleasure. I don't know what use you can make of all I have said. I have written it with the strong desire to obtain appreciation for her. Yet, what does it matter? She herself appealed to the world's judgment for her use of some of the faculties she had—not the best—but still the only ones she could turn to strangers' benefit. They heartily, greedily enjoyed the fruits of her labours, and then found out she was much to be blamed for possessing such faculties. Why ask for a judgment on her from such a world?

But I turn from the critical, unsympathetic public—inclined to judge harshly because they have only seen superficially and not thought deeply. I appeal to that larger and more solemn public, who know how to look with tender humility at faults and errors; how to admire generously extraordinary genius, and how to reverence with warm, full hearts all noble virtue. To that public I commit the memory of Charlotte Brontë.

ACKNOWLEDGMENTS

The condensations in this volume have been created by The Reader's Digest Association, Inc., and are used by permission of and special arrangement with the publishers and the holders of the respective copyrights.
CHRISTOPHER COLUMBUS, MARINER, copyright © 1942, 1955, by Samuel Eliot Morison, renewed © 1983 by Emily Morison Beck, is reprinted by permission of Little, Brown and Company, Inc.
MARIE ANTOINETTE, first published in 1933. Latest edition copyright © 1988 by Atrium Press Ltd., is reprinted by permission of Cassell PLC and Atrium Press Ltd.
THE HEAD AND HEART OF THOMAS JEFFERSON, copyright © 1954 by John Dos Passos, is reprinted by permission of Doubleday.

ILLUSTRATION CREDITS